About the Author

LEN DEIGHTON is the author of more
than thirty books of fiction and non-
fiction, including his classic novels *The
Ipcress File* and *Funeral in Berlin,* and
his internationally acclaimed histories
of World War II. Born in London, he
served in the RAF before graduating
from the Royal College of Art, which
has elected him a Senior Fellow.

Also by Len Deighton

Nonfiction

Fighter: The True Story of the Battle of Britain
Blitzkrieg: From the Rise of Hitler to the Fall of Dunkirk
Airshipwreck

ABC of French Food
Basic French Cookery Course
The Battle of Britain (*with Max Hastings*)

Fiction

Violent Ward
The Ipcress File
Horse Under Water
Funeral in Berlin
Billion-Dollar Brain
An Expensive Place to Die
Only When I Larf
Bomber
Declarations of War
Close-Up
Spy Story
Yesterday's Spy
Twinkle, Twinkle, Little Spy
SS-GB
XPD
Goodbye Mickey Mouse
Mamista
City of Gold

The Samson Stories

Berlin Game
Mexico Set
London Match
Game, Set and Match (*presentation set*)
Winter
Spy Hook
Spy Line
Spy Sinker

Len Deighton

BLOOD, TEARS, AND FOLLY

An Objective Look at World War II

With maps and drawings
by Denis Bishop

Harper

An Imprint of HarperCollins*Publishers*

First HarperPerennial edition published 1994.
First Harper paperback published 2005.

Library of Congress Cataloging-in-Publication Data has been applied for.

ISBN-10: 0-06-092557-4
ISBN-13: 978-0-06-092557-4

05 06 07 08 09 RRD 10 9 8 7 6 5 4 3 2 1

Contents

Part Four: The War in the Air

Part Five: Barbarossa: The Attack on Russia

Part Six: Japan Goes to War

Illustrations

Permission to reproduce the photographs is acknowledged with thanks to the following sources: Bibliothek für Zeitgeschichte, Stuttgart (no. 20), Bildarchiv Preussischer Kulturbesitz, Berlin (no. 13), Bilderdienst Süddeutscher Verlag, Munich (nos. 2, 3 and 6), E.C.P. Armées, France (no. 5), Hulton Deutsch Collection (nos. 1, 14 and 15), Robert Hunt Library (no. 18), Imperial War Museum, London (nos. 8, 9, 10, 11, 16, 17 and 19), and Ullstein Bilderdienst, Berlin (nos. 4, 7 and 12). The maps and drawings are by Denis Bishop.

To your children, and ours

Acknowledgements

I HAVE TAKEN the time, picked the brains and raided the archives of a great number of people while writing this book – so many that I would need another book to give them all proper credit. It is more appropriate to ask forgiveness of all those generous helpers in museums, archives, bookshops, air shows, trains, planes and cafés who have provided me with ideas, books, photocopies and references galore and now don't have their names mentioned.

This book, like *Fighter* and *Blitzkrieg* before it, would never have seen publication without the late A.J.P. Taylor, who told me that an amateur historian is an historian nevertheless.

But first and foremost I must thank Tony Colwell at Jonathan Cape, my publisher, who has contributed an immense amount of good advice and has nursed the book along for over a decade, as he nursed *Fighter* and *Blitzkrieg* and many of my novels. Steve Cox, my editor, has made contributions far beyond editing and research. Thanks too to David Godwin at Jonathan Cape, and to Kate Fitch, who double-checked so many facts when I was far away, and my warm appreciation to my friends at Harper Collins New York – George Craig, Bill Shinker and Buz Wyeth – who have been extremely patient and supportive over many years.

Thanks too to Jonathan Clowes, my agent, Anton Felton and Brie Burkeman, ace co-ordinator, and to John Ellis, who was kind enough to read the typescript.

The mistakes I made all on my own.

*'Death and sorrow will be the companions of our journey;
hardship our garment; constancy and valour our only shield.'*

**Winston Churchill, addressing the House of Commons,
8 October 1940**

Introduction

IT IS A NATIONAL characteristic beloved of the British to see themselves as a small cultured island race of peaceful intentions, only roused when faced with bullies, and with a God-given mission to disarm cheats. Rather than subjugating and exploiting poorer people overseas, they prefer the image of emancipating them. English school history books invite us to rally with Henry V to defeat the overwhelming French army at Agincourt, or to join Drake in a leisurely game of bowls before he boards his ship to rout the mighty Armada and thwart its malevolent Roman Catholic king. The British also cherish their heroes when they are losers. The charge of the Light Brigade is seen as an honourable sacrifice rather than a crushing defeat for brave soldiers at the hands of their incompetent commanders. Disdaining technology, Captain Scott arrived second at the South Pole and perished miserably. Such legendary exploits were ingrained in the collective British mind when in 1939, indigent and unprepared, the country went to war and soon was hailing the chaotic Dunkirk evacuation as a triumph.

Delusions are usually rooted in history and all the harder to get rid of when they are institutionalized and seldom subjected to review. But delusions from the past do not beset the British mind alone. The Germans, the Russians, the Japanese and the Americans all have their myths and try to live up to them, often with tragic consequences. Yet Japan and Germany, with educational systems superior to most others in the world, and a generally high regard for science and engineering design, lost the war. Defeat always brings a cold shock of reality, and here was defeat with cold and hunger and a well clothed and well fed occupying army as a daily reminder that you must do better. The conquerors sat down and wrote their memoirs and bathed in the warm and rosy glow that only self-satisfaction provides.

Half-finished wartime projects, such as the United Nations, fluid and unsatisfactory frontiers and enforced allegiances suddenly froze as the war ended with the explosion of two atomic bombs. The ever-present threat of widespread nuclear destruction sent the great powers into a sort of hibernation that we called the Cold War. The division of the world into two camps was decided more by the building of walls, secret police and prison camps than by ideology. Expensively educated men and women betrayed their countrymen and, in the name of freedom, gave Stalin an atomic bomb and any other secrets they could lay their hands on. Only after the ice cracked half a century later could the world resume its difficult history.

But not everyone was in hibernation. With the former leaders of Germany, Italy and Japan disposed of as criminals, more criminal leaders came to power in countries far and wide. The Cold War that seemed to hold Europe's violence in suspense actually exported it to places out of Western sight. The existence of Stalin's prison camps was denied by those who needed Lenin and Marx as heroes. The massacre of Communists in Indonesia raised fewer headlines than Pol Pot's year zero in Cambodia, but they were out on the periphery. Newspapers and television did little to counteract the artful management of news at which crooks and tyrants have become adept. Orthodontics and the hair-dryer have become vital to the achievement of political power.

The postwar world saw real threats to the democratic Western ideals for which so many had died. Is the European Community – so rigorously opposed to letting newsmen or public see its working and decision-making – about to become that faceless bureaucratic machine that Hitler started to build? Is the Pacific already Japan's co-prosperity sphere? Hasn't the Muslim world already taken control of a major part of the world's oil resources, and with the untold and unceasing wealth it brings created something we haven't seen since the Middle Ages – a confident union of State and Religion?

Britain's long tradition of greatly over-estimating its own strength and skills leads it to under-estimate foreign powers. Our Victorian heyday still dominates our national imagination and our island geography has often enabled us to avoid the consequences of grave miscalculations by our leaders. Such good fortune cannot continue indefinitely, and perhaps a more realistic look at recent history can point a way to the future that is not just 'muddling through'.

In Germany in 1923 runaway inflation produced the chaos in which the Nazis flourished. Today the United States is very close to the position where even the total revenue from income tax will not pay the *interest* on its National Debt.[1] While the Japanese enjoy one of the world's highest saving rates, Americans are notoriously reluctant to put money into the bank. Furthermore Japan, with a population less than half that of the USA, employs 70,000 more scientists and engineers, uses seven times more industrial robots, and spends over 50 per cent more per capita on non-military research and development.[2]

Hans Schmitt, who grew up in Nazi Germany, returned to his homeland as an officer of the American army and become professor of history at the University of Virginia, wrote in his memoirs: 'Germany had taught me that an uncritical view of the national past generated an equally subservient acceptance of the present.'[3] It is difficult to understand what happened in the Second World War without taking into account the assumptions and ambitions of its protagonists, and the background from which they emerge. So in each part of this book I shall take the narrative far enough back in time to deal with some of the misconceptions that cloud both our preferred version of the war, and our present-day view of a world that always seems to misunderstand us.

One good reason for looking again at the Second World War is to remind ourselves how badly the world's leaders performed and how bravely they were supported by their suffering populations. Half a century has passed, and the time has come to sweep away the myths and reveal the no less inspiring gleam of that complex and frightening time in which evil was in the ascendant, goodness diffident, and the British – impetuous, foolish and brave beyond measure – the world's only hope.

Part One

THE BATTLE OF
THE ATLANTIC

1 BRITANNIA RULES THE WAVES

For the bread that you eat and the biscuits you nibble,
The sweets that you suck and the joints that you carve,
They are brought to you daily by all us Big Steamers
And if any one hinders our coming you'll starve!

Rudyard Kipling, 'Big Steamers'

IT IS NOT in human nature to enshrine a poor view of our own performance, to court unnecessary trouble or to wish for poverty. Myths are therefore created to bolster our confidence and well-being in a hostile world. They also conceal impending danger. Having temporized in the face of the aggressions of the European dictators, Britain went to war in 1939 without recognizing its declining status and pretending that, with the Empire still intact, the price of freedom would not be bankruptcy.

In 1939 the British saw themselves as a seafaring nation and a great maritime power, but the two do not always go hand in hand. In order to understand the Royal Navy's difficult role in the Atlantic in the Second World War, it is necessary to return to the past and separate reality from a tangled skein of myth. Later in the book similar brief excursions will give historical perspective on the performance of the army and the air force, both in Britain and in the other main wartime powers.

After the Renaissance it was Portuguese and Spanish sailors who led the great explorations over the far horizons, while the English concentrated upon defending the coastline that had insulated them from the rest of Europe for centuries. By the middle of the sixteenth century Spain and Portugal had established outposts in America, Asia and Africa, and their ships carried warriors, administrators and freight around the globe in 2,000-ton ships made in India from teak and in Cuba from Brazilian hardwoods. But when England's shores were threatened, small and less mighty vessels made from English oak and imported timber, sailed by skilful, intrepid and often lawless Englishmen, came out to fight. Using fireships, and helped by storms and by the hunger and sickness on the Spanish vessels,

Francis Drake and his the men decimated the mighty Armada.

Such dazzling victories have prevented a proper appreciation of the maritime achievements of our rivals. While English privateers were receiving royal commendations for preying upon the Spanish galleons from the New World, the Dutch and the Portuguese were fighting on the high seas for rule of the places from which the gold, spices and other riches came.

The Dutch were an authentic seafaring race. They had always dominated the North Sea herring fishing, right on England's doorstep, and traded in the Baltic. Their merchant ships carried cargoes for the whole world. By the early 1600s one estimate said that of Europe's 25,000 seagoing ships at least 14,000 were Dutch. The English sailor Sir Walter Raleigh noted that a Dutch ship of 200 tons could carry freight more cheaply than an English ship 'by reason he hath but nine or ten mariners and we nearer thirty'.

In 1688 the Dutch King William of Orange was invited to take the English throne. Dutch power at sea was subordinated to English admirals. At this time England had 100 ships of the line, the Dutch 66 and France 120. England's maritime struggles with the Netherlands ended, and France – England's greatest rival and potential enemy – was outnumbered at sea. The French were not a seafaring race, they were a land power. Their overseas colonies and trade were not vital to France's existence. Neither were exports vital to England, where until the 1780s the economy depended almost entirely upon agriculture, with exports bringing only about 10 per cent of national income.

The Dutch king's ascent to the English throne was the sort of luck that foreigners saw as cunning. It came at exactly the right moment for England. From this time onwards the French seldom deployed more than half of the Royal Navy's first-line strength. Soon the industrial revolution was producing wealth enough for Britain to do whatever it pleased. But that wealth depended upon the sea lanes, and the Royal Navy had to change from a strategy of harassing and plundering to escorting and protecting merchant shipping. It was not easy to adapt to the shepherd's role. The Royal Navy was by tradition wolflike; its speciality had always been making sudden raids upon the unprepared. 'It could be fairly said,' wrote the naval historian Jacques Mordal, 'that with the exception of Trafalgar, the greatest successes of the British navy were against ships at their moorings.'[1] Damme, Sluys, La Hougue, the Nile, Copenhagen, Navarino and Vigo Bay were all such encounters. So were the actions against the French navy in 1940.

It was Napoleon's defeat at Waterloo that gave the Royal Navy mastery of the seas. France, Holland and Spain, weakened by years of war, conceded primacy to the Royal Navy. Britain became the first world power in history as the machines of the industrial revolution processed raw materials from distant parts of the world and sent them back as manufactured goods. Machinery and cheap cotton goods were the source of great profits; so were shipping, banking, insurance, investment and all the commercial services that followed Britain's naval dominance. The British invested abroad while Britain's own industrial base became old, underfinanced, neglected and badly managed, so that by the mid-nineteenth century the quality of more and more British exports was overtaken by her rivals. Manufacturing shrank, and well before the end of the century service industries became Britain's most important source of income. The progeny of the invincible iron masters dwindled into investment bankers and insurance men.

To cement the nineteenth century's Pax Britannica Britain handed to France and the Netherlands possessions in the Caribbean, removed protective tariffs and preached a policy of free trade, even in the face of prohibitive tariffs against British goods and produce. The Royal Navy fought pirates and slave traders, and most of the world's great powers were content to allow Britain to become the international policeman, especially in a century in which restless civil populations repeatedly threatened revolution against the existing order at home.

The British fleet showed the flag to the peoples of the Empire in five continents and was a symbol of peace and stability. Well-behaved children of the middle classes and workers too were regularly dressed in sailor costumes like those the British ratings wore.[2] But appearances were deceptive. The Royal Navy was unprepared for battle against a modern enemy.

As the nineteenth century ended the importance of the Royal Navy was diminishing. Population growth, and efficient railway networks, meant that armies were becoming more important than navies. The new-found strength that industrialization, much of it financed by Britain, had given to other nations ended their willingness to let Britain play policeman. Although in 1883 more than half of the world's battleships belonged to the Royal Navy, by 1897 only two of every five were British[3] and countries such as Argentina, Chile, Japan and the United States had navies which challenged the Royal Navy's local strength.

Since the time of Nelson the cost of the Royal Navy had increased to a point where it tested Britain's resources. Nelson's ships were cheap to build and simple to repair. Needing no fuel, sailing ships had virtually unlimited range, and by buying food locally cruises could be extended for months and even years. But the coming of steam engines, screw propellers and turbines, together with the improving technology of guns, meant supplying overseas bases with coal, ammunition and all the tools and spares needed for emergencies. Full repairs and maintenance could only be done in well equipped shipyards. A more pressing problem was the steeply increasing cost of the more complex armoured warships. In 1895 the battleship HMS *Majestic* cost a million pounds sterling but HMS *King George* in 1910 cost almost double that.

The time had come for Britain's world role, its methods and its ships, to be totally revised. An alliance with Japan, and the recognition that cultural ties made war with the USA unthinkable, released ships from the Pacific stations. An alliance with France released ships from the Mediterranean so that the Royal Navy could concentrate virtually its entire sea-power in home waters facing the Germans. Germany had been identified as the most potent threat, and anxiety produced a climate in which talk of war was in the air.

The German navy

Germany dominated Europe. Prussia, where in 1870 nearly 45 per cent of the population was under twenty years of age, dominated Germany. Otto von Bismarck (nominally chancellor but virtually dictator) had remained good friends with Russia while winning for his sovereign quick military victories over Denmark and Austria-Hungary. Then to the surprise of all the world he inflicted a terrible defeat upon France. Reparations – money the French had to pay for losing the war of 1870 – made Germany rich, universal conscription made her armies large, and Krupp's incomparable guns made them mighty. After the victory over the French, the German king became an emperor and, to ensure France's total humiliation, he was crowned in the Hall of Mirrors in Versailles. Bismarck now had everything he wanted. He looked for stability and was ready to concede the seas to Britain.

But in 1888 a vain and excitable young emperor inherited the German throne. Wilhelm II of Hohenzollern had very different ideas. 'There is only one master in the country, and I am he.' He sacked Bismarck, favoured friendship with Austria-Hungary instead of Russia, gave artillery and encouragement to the Boers who were fighting the British army in southern Africa (a conflict that has been called Britain's Vietnam), spoke of a sinister-sounding *Weltpolitik* and, in an atmosphere of vociferous anti-British feeling, began to build his *Kaiserliche Marine*.

Despite Britain's small population[4] and declining economic performance, the strategic use of sea-power had given the British the most extensive empire the world had ever seen. Yet although a large proportion of the world lived under the union flag, Britain had nothing like the wealth and military power to hold on to the vast areas coloured red on the maps. Tiny garrisons and a few administrators convinced millions of natives to abide by the rules of a faraway monarch. The army's strategic value was in guarding the naval bases where the Royal Navy's world-ranging ships were victualled, coaled or oiled. Luckily for Britain, its military power was not seriously challenged for many years. Only when the Boers in South Africa erupted was Britain's tenuous grip on its territories clearly demonstrated.

The German army on the other hand had shown its might and skills again and again, and having seen their army march into Paris in 1870 the German navy itched to test itself against the British. With almost unlimited funds at his disposal Rear-Admiral Alfred Tirpitz was to build for the Kaiser the sort of fleet that would be needed to challenge the Royal Navy. In anticipation of this moment, German naval officers more and more frequently held up their glasses and toasted 'Der Tag!' – the day of reckoning.

Admiral Tirpitz claimed to be unaware that his preparations were aimed at war with Britain. 'Politics are your affair,' he told the Foreign Ministry, 'I build ships.'[5] And as if to prove his point he sent his daughters to study at the Cheltenham Ladies' College in England.

The British were alarmed by the prospect of an enlarged German navy. Still more worrying for them was the rise in German trade, which went from £365 million in 1894 to £610 million in 1904, with a consequent increase in German merchant ship tonnage of 234 per cent. In fact Britain's foreign markets were suffering more from American exporters than from German ones but – still smarting from Germany's pro-Boer stance – the British resented the Germans, while Anglo-American relations on personal and diplomatic levels remained very good.

In December 1904 Britain's new first sea lord, Admiral Fisher, started planning his new all-big-gun battleships. Although naval architects in Italy, America and Japan had all predicted the coming of a super-warship, this one was so revolutionary in design that it gave its name to a new category of battleship.

The big hull had spent only one hundred days on the stocks when King Edward VII launched HMS *Dreadnought* on a chilly February day in 1906. He wore the full dress uniform of an admiral of the fleet, which Britain's monarchs favoured for such ceremonials, when he swung the bottle of Australian wine against her hull. The bottle bounced and failed to break and he needed a second attempt before the wine flowed, and the great warship went creaking and groaning down the slipway into the water.

She was completed in record time: one year and a day. The use of the rotary turbine, instead of big upright pistons, made her profile more compact and thus better armoured. According to one admiral the bowels of previous battleships were uncomfortable:

> When steaming at full speed in a man of war fitted with re-
> ciprocating engines, the engine room was always a glorified
> snipe marsh; water lay on the floor plates and was splashed
> about everywhere; the officers often were clad in oilskins to
> avoid being wetted to the skin. The water was necessary to keep
> the bearings cool. Further the noise was deafening; so much so
> that telephones were useless and even voice pipes of doubtful
> value ... In the *Dreadnought*, when steaming at full speed, it
> was only possible to tell that the engines were working, and not
> stopped, by looking at certain gauges. The whole engine room
> was as clean and dry as if the ship was lying at anchor, and not
> the faintest hum could be heard.[6]

Figure 1:
HMS *Dreadnought*

Gunnery was also changed. Ships armed with many short-range guns – exemplified by the 100-gun *Victory* – were no match for ships which could fire salvos of very heavy shells at long range. The big gun had proved itself. For the Americans sinking the Spanish ships at Santiago and Manila Bay, for the Japanese destroying the Russian fleet at Tsushima, the big gun had proved the decisive weapon. 'Dreadnoughts' – as all the new type of capital ships were now to be called – would have speed enough to force or decline a naval action. Furthermore the long-range gun would offset the threat of the torpedo; a sophisticated weapon that, wielded by dashing little vessels, threatened the future of the expensive warships.

The introduction of the Dreadnought design was a denial of Britain's decline. It signalled that Britain had started to build its navy afresh, and that its sea-power could be equalled only by those who kept pace with the building programme. Almost overnight Admiral Tirpitz found his 15-battleship fleet completely outclassed. The Kaiser responded at once. SMS *Nassau*, the first of Germany's Dreadnoughts, was ready for action by March 1908. On paper the German ships seemed inferior in design to the Dreadnoughts of the Royal Navy – for instance *Nassau* employed reciprocating engines and had 11-inch guns compared with HMS *Dreadnought's* 12-inch ones. But the *Nassau's* guns had a high muzzle-velocity, which gave a flat trajectory for better aim and penetration. The ship's interior was very cramped, but top-quality steel was used as armour. Her small 'honeycomb-cell' watertight compartments made her extremely difficult to sink; a feature of most German warships.

The big new German ships provided the Berlin planners with an additional problem. The 61-mile-long Kiel Canal was essential to German naval strategy, for it eliminated a long and hazardous journey around Denmark, and the need for a separate Baltic Fleet to face the threat of Russian sea-power. But the Kiel locks had been built for smaller warships; there was no way that the Germans could squeeze a ship the size of a *Dreadnought* through the Canal.

Churchill – first lord of the Admiralty

In 1911, when the 36-year-old Winston Churchill was appointed first lord of the Admiralty (the minister responsible for the Royal Navy), he was appalled to find his Whitehall offices deserted, and ordered that there be always officers on duty. On the wall behind his desk he put a case, with folding doors which opened to reveal a map on which the positions of the German fleet were constantly updated. Churchill started each day with a study of that map.

Churchill revolutionized the navy. His principal adviser was the controversial Sir John Arbuthnot Fisher, who predicted with astounding accuracy that war against Germany would begin on 21 October 1914 (when widening of the Kiel Canal for the new German battleships was due to be completed). The Royal Navy did not welcome Churchill's ideas. When he wanted to create a naval war staff, they told him they did not want a special class of officer professing to be more brainy than the rest. One naval historian summed up the attitude of the admirals: 'cleverness was middle class or Bohemian, and engines were for the lower orders.'[7]

Churchill forced his reforms upon the navy. He created the Royal Naval Air Service. Even more importantly, he changed the navy's filthy coal-burning ships, with their time-consuming bunkering procedures, to the quick convenience of oil-burning vessels with 40 per cent more fuel endurance. As industry in Britain was built upon coal but had no access to oil, this entailed creating an oil company – British Petroleum – and extensive storage facilities for the imported oil. He ordered five 25-knot oil-burning battleships – *Queen Elizabeth*, *Warspite*, *Barham*, *Valiant* and *Malaya* – and equipped them with the world's first 15-inch guns. Normally a prototype for such a gun would have been built and tested, but rather than waste a year or more, Churchill put the guns straight into production so that the ships could be ready as soon as possible.

Britain's need for naval alliances had dragged her into making an agreement with France that should war come Britain would send an army to help defend her. This was a dramatic change in Britain's centuries-old policy of staying out of mainland Europe. Cautious voices pointed out that no matter what such an expeditionary force might achieve in France, Britain remained vulnerable to foreign fleets. It was a small offshore island dependent upon imported food, seaborne trade and now oil from faraway countries instead of home-produced coal. The extensive British Empire was still largely controlled by bureaucrats in London. Defeated at sea, Britain would be severed from its Empire, impoverished and starved into submission.

The First World War

To what extent Emperor Kaiser Wilhelm was set upon war with England in 1914 is still difficult to assess. If there was one man who, by every sort of lie, deceit and stupidity, deliberately pushed the world into this tragic war, that man was Count Leopold 'Poldi' Berchtold, Austrian foreign minister. But the German Kaiser stood firmly behind him and showed no reluctance to start fighting.

Bringing recollections of Fisher's warning, elements of the Royal Navy were at Kiel, celebrating the opening of the newly widened canal, when news came of the assassination at Sarajevo. A few weeks later Europe was at war. It was also significant that Britain's widely distributed warships were told 'Commence hostilities against Germany' by means of the new device of wireless.

Germany had 13 Dreadnoughts (with ten more being built); Britain had 24 (with 13 more under construction, five of which were of the new improved *Queen Elizabeth* class). However this superiority has be seen against Britain's worldwide commitments and Germany's more limited ones.

Britain's Admiral Fisher had gloated that the Germans would never be able to match the Royal Navy because of the untold millions it would cost to widen the Kiel Canal and deepen all the German harbours and approaches. The Germans had willingly completed this mammoth task. The British on the other hand had refused to build new docks and so could not build a ship with a beam greater than 90 feet. Sir Eustace Tennyson-d'Eyncourt (Britain's director of naval construction) was later to say that with wider beam, 'designs on the same length and draught could have embodied more fighting qualities, such as armour, armament, greater stability in case of damage, and improved underwater protection.'

The Germans built docks to suit the ships, rather than ships to fit the docks. With greater beam, the German ships also had thicker armour. Furthermore the German decision to build a short-range navy meant that less space was required for fuel and crews. More watertight compartments could be provided, which made German warships difficult to sink. This could not be said of ships of the Royal Navy.

The Royal Navy's planners would not listen to the specialists and experts and continuously rejected innovations for the big ships. While British optical instrument companies were building precise range-finders (with up to 30 feet between lenses) for foreign customers, the Admiralty was content with 9 feet separation. When Parsons, the company founded by the inventor and manufacturer of turbine engines, suggested changing over to the small-tube boilers that worked so well in German ships, the Admiralty turned them down. The triple gun-turrets that had proved excellent on Russian and Italian ships were resisted until the 1920s.

The German navy welcomed innovation. After a serious fire in the *Seydlitz* during the Dogger Bank engagement of 1915 they designed anti-flash doors so that flash from a shell hitting a turret could not ignite the magazine. On Royal Navy ships cordite charges in the lift between magazine and turret were left exposed, as was the cordite handling room at the bottom of the lift, and the magazine remained open during action. This weakness was aggravated by the way that British warships were vulnerable to 'plunging fire' that brought shells down upon the decks and turrets. Typically turrets would have 9-inch-thick side armour and 3-inch-thick tops. This deficiency would continue to plague the Royal Navy in the Second World War.

Churchill's gamble with his 15-inch guns paid off, but the smaller German guns had the advantage of high muzzle-velocity. The Royal Navy knew that its armour-piercing shells broke up on oblique impact with armour but had not solved this problem by the time the First World War began. Only eight Royal Navy ships had director firing (as against gunners choosing and aiming at their own targets), while it was standard in the German navy. The superior light-transmission of German optics gave them better range-finders, and German mines and torpedoes were more sophisticated and more reliable. The Royal Navy neglected these weapons, regarding them as a last resort for inferior navies. It was a view open to drastic revision when HMS *Audacious*, a new Dreadnought, sank after collision with a single German mine soon after hostilities began.

As warfare became more dependent upon technology German superiority in chemistry, metallurgy and engineering became more apparent. The German educational system was ahead of Britain. In 1863 England and Wales had 11,000 pupils in secondary education: Prussia with a smaller population had 63,000. And Prussia provided not only *Gymnasien* for the study of 'humanities' but *Realschulen* to provide equally good secondary education in science and 'modern studies'.[8] The French scholar and historian Joseph Ernest Renan provided an epilogue to the Franco-Prussian War by saying it was a victory of the German schoolmaster. The education of both officers and ratings, coupled to the strong German predilection for detailed planning and testing, produced a formidable navy. Its signalling techniques and night-fighting equipment were superior to those of the British and this superiority was to continue throughout the war. Churchill warned in 1914 that it would be highly dangerous to consider that British ships were superior or even equal as fighting machines to those of Germany.

For many years the American Rear-Admiral A. T. Mahan's book *The Influence of Sea Power upon History* had specified the way in which all sea wars must be fought: by big ships battling to contest sea lanes. But the British would not play this game. Surprising many theorists, the Royal Navy of 1914 refused battle and instead set up a blockade of German ports. The geographical position of the British Isles, and a plentiful supply of ships, persuaded the Admiralty to create barriers across the open water by means of mines and patrols. The Germans responded by a less ambitious blockade of Britain. German warships prowled the sea routes to sink the merchant ships bringing supplies to the British Isles.

Given this strategy, German engineering and the development of the torpedo, it was inevitable that the German navy became interested in submarines. Although they were the last of the major powers to adopt that weapon, the Germans had watched with interest the designs and experiments of other nations. The first German-built submarines were supplied to overseas customers. The *Forel*, built and tested at Kiel, was supplied to Russia and went by railway to Vladivostok.

The Germans rejected ideas about using submarines for coastal defence, or as escorts for their fleet. They wanted an offensive weapon. This meant longer-range, more seaworthy vessels. Because they considered the petrol engines used by the Royal Navy as too hazardous, their early U-boats used a kerosene (liquid paraffin) engine, but it was the development of the diesel engine that made the submarine a practical proposition. The first production diesel was made in the M.A.N. factory in Augsburg in 1897, and a much improved version was tested in a U-boat in Krupp's Germania Works in Kiel in 1913. At that time the U-boat was still a primitive device. During the First World War the submarine tracked, attacked and escaped on the surface, its low silhouette making it difficult to spot. It could only hide briefly below the surface but (in a world without asdic, sonar or radar) hiding was enough. The British had more or less ignored the dangers of commerce raiding by submarines because the Hague Convention denied any warship the right to sink an unescorted merchant ship without first sending over a boarding party to decide if its cargo was contraband.

Whatever the rights and wrongs of commerce raiding, any last doubts about the value of torpedo-equipped submarines vanished in 1914, less than two months after the outbreak of war, when Germany's *U-9*, commanded by a 32-year-old on his first tour of duty, hit HMS *Aboukir* with a torpedo and she sank before the lifeboats could be lowered. HMS *Cressy* lowered her boats to pick up men in the water, but while so doing was hit by a second torpedo. A third torpedo hit HMS *Hogue*, which also sank immediately. More than 1,600 sailors died. About three weeks later the same rather primitive type of submarine sank the cruiser HMS *Hawke*.

The development of wireless was changing naval warfare, as it was changing everything else. The admirals seized upon it, for it gave the men behind desks the means of controlling the units at sea. Intelligence officers saw that enemy ships transmitting wireless signals could be located by direction-finding apparatus. Better still, such radio traffic could be intercepted, the codes broken, and messages read.

Intercepted wireless signals played a part in the battle of Jutland in 1916, when Britain's Grand Fleet and the German High Seas fleet clashed in the only modern battleship action fought in European waters. Lack of flash doors caused HMS *Queen Mary* to disappear in an explosion, HMS *Indefatigable* blew up and sank leaving only two survivors, and HMS *Lion* was only saved because a mortally wounded turret commander ordered the closing of the magazine doors. The loss of the Royal Navy's three battle cruisers and three armoured cruisers could all be ascribed to their inadequate upper protection.

There were many ways to evaluate the battle of Jutland, and both sides celebrated a victory with all the medals and congratulatory exchanges that victory brings for the higher ranks. In tonnage and human lives lost the British suffered far more than the Germans, but the Royal Navy was more resilient. The British were seafarers by tradition, and regular long-service sailors who fought the battle accepted its horrors in a way that conscripted German sailors did not. Britain's Grand Fleet took its sinkings philosophically. Within a few hours of returning to Scapa Flow and Rosyth, the fleet reported itself ready to steam at four hours' notice.

There can be no doubt however that Britain's technological shortcomings were startlingly evident at Jutland. Once the envy of all the world, Britain's steel output had now sunk to third place after the United States and Germany, and German steels were of higher quality. Anyone studying the battle had to conclude that German ships were better designed and better made, that German guns were more accurate and German shells penetrated British armour while many of the Royal Navy's hits caused little damage.

Radio had also played a part in the battle. Helped by codebooks the Russians salvaged from a sunk German cruiser, the men in Room 40 at the Admiralty ended the war able to read all three German naval codes. After the war the work in Room 40 was kept completely secret so that even the official history made only passing mention of it.

By the end of 1916, despite patrols by planes, dirigibles and thousands of ships, U-boats had sunk 1,360 ships. The German U-boat service, which grew to 100 submarines, had lost only four of them to enemy action. The Admiralty stubbornly refused to inaugurate a convoy system, and produced rather bogus figures to 'prove' that convoys would block up the ports and harbours. Convoys might never have been started but for the French government insisting that their cross-Channel colliers sailed in convoy. The result was dramatic but the Admiralty remained unconvinced. Perhaps the Admiralty officials thought that escorting dirty old merchant ships was not a fitting task for gallant young naval officers. Whatever their reasons, it took an ultimatum from the prime minister to make them change their minds. (Although later the admirals petulantly said they were about to do it anyway.) When convoys began in May 1917, only ships that could do better than 7 knots, and could not attain 12 knots, were allowed to join them. Losses fell about 90 per cent. The British had come close to losing the war, and before the effect of the convoy system became evident the nerve of the first sea lord, Admiral Jellicoe, broke. On 20 June he told a high-level conference that, owing to the U-boats, Great Britain would not be able to continue the war into 1918. He proved wrong and, thanks to the convoys, the crisis abated.

German U-boats continued sinking passenger ships even after negotiations for peace began on 3 October 1918. The following day *Hiramo Maru* was sunk off the Irish coast, killing 292 out of the 320 aboard. The following week the Irish mail boat *Leinster* was torpedoed without warning and torpedoed again while it was sinking: 527 drowned. 'Brutes they were, and brutes they remain,' said Britain's foreign secretary. President Wilson warned that America wouldn't consider an armistice so long as Germany continued its 'illegal and inhuman practices'. The U-boat's Parthian shots had not helped to create a climate suited to negotiations for a lasting peace.

By the time the First World War ended, about 200 U-boats had been sunk, but the submarine menace had been countered only by means of escorted convoys and the use of about 5,000 ships, hundreds of miles of steel nets and a million depth charges, mines, bombs and shells. Yet for those who wanted to find it, the most important lesson of the 1914–18 war in the Atlantic lay in the statistics. In the whole conflict only five ships were sunk by submarines when both surface escort and air patrol was provided, and this despite the fact that no airborne anti-submarine weapon had been developed.

2 DAYS OF WINE AND ROSES

The man who with undaunted toils
Sails unknown seas to unknown soils
With various wonders feasts his sight:
What stranger wonders does he write!

John Gay, 'The Elephant and The Bookseller'

B Y THE END of the First World War Britain was exhausted, financially bankrupt and in debt to the USA. The Empire, having made a selfless and spontaneous commitment to the war, no longer wanted to be ruled by men of Whitehall. British leaders, both civilian and military, had proved inept in conducting a war which, had the United States not entered it, Germany might well have won.

In 1922, Britain formally acknowledged her declining power. Since Nelson's day Britain's declared policy was to have a navy as strong as any two navies that could possibly be used against her. Even into the 1890s Britain was spending twice as much on her fleet as any other' nation. With the Washington treaty of 1922 such days were gone. The politicians agreed that the navies of Britain, USA and Japan should be in the ratio of 5:5:3. Britain also accepted limitations upon the specifications of its battleships, and promised not to develop Hong Kong as a naval base and to withdraw altogether from Wei-hai-wei, China. In conforming to the treaty, the Royal Navy scrapped 657 ships including 26 battleships and battle-cruisers. One history of the British Empire comments: 'So ended Britain's absolute command of the seas, the mainstay and in some sense the raison d'être of her Empire.'[1]

After the First World War, the surrendered German fleet sailed to Scapa Flow, between Orkney and the Scottish mainland. There, in a gesture of defiance, they scuttled all their ships. This provided Germany with a chance to start again with hand-picked personnel and modern well designed ships, while the victorious nations were patching up their old ships to save money.

The treaty of Versailles stipulated that Germany's navy must be kept very small but in June 1935, acting without reference to friends or enemies, the British government signed an Anglo-German naval agreement permiting Hitler to build a substantial navy, up to 35 per cent as strong as the Royal Navy, and include battleships, virtually unlimited submarines and eventually cruisers and aircraft-carriers.[2]

This notable concession to Hitler's belligerence encouraged him to ever more reckless moves and deeply offended Britain's closest ally France. It went against all Britain's international undertakings and, in grossly breaching the peace treaty, nullified it. The first lord of the Admiralty said: 'the naval staff were satisfied and had been anxious to bring about an agreement'. Stabilization of Anglo-German naval competition would release RN ships to distant waters. Perhaps the British politicians – and the men in the Admiralty who advised them – believed that showing good will towards the Nazis would bring lasting peace. One suspects that it revealed some calculation in the minds of Britain's leaders that a more powerful Fascist Germany would keep Communist Russia contained.

Significantly perhaps, the Reichsmarine was renamed Kriegsmarine and the Germans began building immediately. Germany's four biggest battleships, *Scharnhorst*, *Gneisenau*, *Bismarck* and *Tirpitz*, which were later to give the Royal Navy so many sleepless nights, were laid down as an immediate result of this treaty. The following year Germany agreed – in the London Submarine Protocol of 3 September 1936 – that it would adhere strictly to the international prize law, which provided for the safety of merchant ship passengers and crews in time of war.

In 1937 came a supplement to the 1935 treaty. A German naval historian, Edward P. von der Porten, has described it as 'a German attempt to convince the British of sincerity'. The Germans affirmed that they would build no battleships bigger than 35,000 tons. The *Bismarck* and *Tirpitz*, then in production, were 41,700 and 42,900 tons respectively. The extra tonnage, explained U-boat C-in-C Karl Dönitz after the war, was for 'added defensive features'. In fact the extra size was due to Hitler specifying 15-inch guns instead of the previous 11-inch ones.

While German shipyards were producing these impressive warships Britain's shipbuilding industry was antiquated and inefficient. It had suffered from the strikes and slumps that other British industry knew well. Yet while Britain's merchant navy, although still large, was in decline, no such decline befell the bureaucrats of Whitehall. In 1914, with 62 capital ships in commission, the Admiralty employed 2,000 officials. By 1928 – with only 20 capital ships in commission, and the Royal Navy officers and men reduced from 146,000 to 100,000 – there were 3,569 Admiralty employees. Although the Washington naval treaty prevented any increase in Britain's naval forces, there were by 1935 no less than 8,118 Admiralty staff on the payroll.[3]

Germany had ended the war without ships or shipbuilding facilities but the creation of a strong navy and a merchant fleet had been decided upon long before Hitler came to power. In the summer of 1929 these plans bore fruit as the ocean liner *Bremen* snatched the Atlantic Blue Ribbon from the elderly British liner *Mauretania*. The following year *Bremen*'s sister ship *Europa* took the record. Both German liners displaced about 50,000 tons, with top speeds of about 27 knots. These products of German shipyards were given energetic publicity by the Nazi propaganda machine. Germany had staked its claim to the Atlantic sea routes and intended to remain there.

Equipping for war

On Sunday 3 September 1939 Britain declared war on Germany. Although there were no treaty obligations between Britain and the Dominions, Australia and New Zealand also declared war at once. The Canadians declared war on Germany after Britain (but were later to declare war on Japan before Britain). South Africa followed after some fierce parliamentary debate, and the Viceroy took a similar decision for India seemingly without reference to anyone. Virtually the whole of the Empire and Commonwealth, from Ascension Island to the Falklands, joined the mother country. A newly independent Ireland remained neutral and was represented in Berlin throughout the war by an ambassador accredited in the name of King George.

In the course of time, 5 million fighting troops were raised from these overseas countries, with India contributing the largest volunteer army that history had ever recorded.[4] But warships were in scarce supply. The navy was still regarded as the factor which both bound the countries of the Empire and protected their sea routes. So, for Britain's Royal Navy, the war was a global one right from the first hour of hostilities.

Britain went to war with a Royal Navy that was highly skilled and totally professional, although its officers and men were poorly educated when compared with men of the other industrialized nations. Most of its 109,000 sailors had joined as boys aged sixteen, and most of its 10,000 officers as thirteen-year-old cadets. Steeped in tradition, its ratings wearing curious old uniforms which could not be put on without help, the navy provided a tot of rum each day for every man, and the fleet retained corporal punishment long after the other services had abolished it.

When wartime's compulsory military service first sent civilians to sea, they regarded this narrow-minded, time-warped community with awe. They took it over, and changed it for ever. Soon the regular sailors with their distinctive rank badges were outnumbered by HO (Hostilities Only) ratings and RNVR (Volunteer Reserve) officers with 'wavy-navy' rings on their cuffs. By the middle of 1944 the wartime navy totalled 863,500 personnel of whom 73,500 were WRNS (Women's Royal Naval Service). The sailors who fought and won the Atlantic battle were in the main civilians.

When war started the Admiralty was calm and confident. With fifteen battleships, of which thirteen had been built before 1918 (and ten of these were designed before 1914), and six aircraft carriers of which only HMS *Ark Royal* was not converted from other ships' hulls, it knew exactly what sort of war it was going to fight. Unfortunately Germany's naval staff, the Seekriegsleitung (SKL), had a different rule book.

A less parsimonious British government or a more realistic Royal Navy might have expected the Germans to break their agreements, but the interwar years had been noted for self-delusion, and the admirals did not readily learn lessons. The Royal Navy seemed indifferent to the threat of air attack. Its multiple pom-pom antiaircraft guns had proved completely ineffective, but only when war was imminent were Swedish Bofors and Swiss Oerlikon guns put into production.

A closed eye had been turned to the potential of the submarine. With lofty disdain, most Royal Navy officers regarded the submarine service as a refuge for officers of low ability. Submarines participating in fleet exercises were always ordered to withdraw during the hours of darkness. Anyone who suggested that in a future war the enemy might not be willing to withdraw during the hours of darkness was told that the miracle apparatus asdic could counter submarines.

Asdic (later named sonar) was a crude device first introduced at the end of the First World War, although never used operationally in that war. Mounted under a ship's hull, it emitted sound waves and picked up their reflections to detect submarines. Always demonstrated in perfect weather by well rehearsed crews, it enabled a confident Admiralty to declare the U-boat to be a weapon of the past. By 1937 the Naval Staff said that 'the submarine would never again be able to present us with the problem we were faced with in 1917.' Even if the Admiralty's assessment of asdic had been right, there were only 220 warships equipped with it, while the British merchant service had 3,000 oceangoing ships and 1,000 large coasters to be protected.

The range of the asdic was a mile at best. It could not pierce the layers of differing temperature and salinity that are commonly found in large bodies of water. Nor could it be used by a ship steaming at more than 20 knots, or in rough weather. It was useless in locating a surfaced submarine and did not reveal the depth of a submerged one. All of these shortcomings could benefit a skilful U-boat commander, and it might have been remembered that by the end of the First World War attacks by surfaced U-boats had become the favoured tactic.

Admirals everywhere prefer big ships. The United States navy lined them up in Pearl Harbor and, even in the middle of the war, German admirals were still telling each other that the battleship was the most important naval weapon and pressing for a programme to build more and more of them. So the British navy, like the United States navy, began the war with plenty of expensive battleships for which there was little or no need and a grave shortage of small escort vessels.

Canada wanted to make a contribution to the war without having its soldiers decimated at the commands of British generals on some new 'western front'. It elected to concentrate on ships, which could be kept under its own control. The Canadian navy started a construction programme exclusively devoted to escort vessels – corvettes and frigates – to protect the Atlantic traffic. The corvettes were slow and seaworthy, although the way in which they rolled and wallowed from wave top to wave top made crewing them one of the war's most queasy assignments. Nevertheless by May 1942 Canada had 300 ships – a magnificent achievement.

The U-boat

Since the First World War, submarine design had improved only marginally, and then chiefly in greater hull strength. This enabled them to dive far deeper, and provided escape for many U-boats under attack. (Due largely to inter-departmental squabbles, it took some time before British depth charges were designed for deep water use.) Although more efficient electric batteries enabled submarines to stay submerged longer, they still spent almost all their time on the surface, submerging only to escape attacks from the air or avoid very rough seas.

A submarine of this period consisted of a cylindrical pressure hull like a gigantic steel sewer pipe. To this pipe, a stern and bow were welded and the whole vessel was clad in external casing to give it some 'sea-keeping capability', although submarines could never be manoeuvred like ships with regular hulls. A casing deck and a conning tower – what the Germans called an 'attack centre' – was added to the structure. Directly below the conning tower was the 'control room' where the captain manned the periscope. The tower was given outer cladding to provide some weather protection to men standing there, as well as some measure of streamlining when the boat went underwater. An electric motor room and an engine room with supercharged diesels of about 3,000 bhp were positioned well aft for the sake of sea-keeping and to cut diving time. The great bulk of a submarine was below the water-line, and visitors going below are always surprised to discover how big they are, compared with the portion visible above water. For instance, the long-range Type IXC U-boat that displaced 1,178 tons submerged would still displace 1,051 tons when on the surface.

There were two basic types of German U-boat used operationally in the Atlantic campaign, the big long-range Type IX and the smaller Type VII, which was the standard German U-boat of the

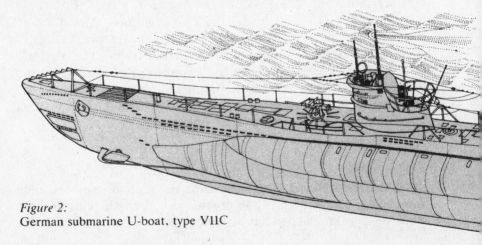

Figure 2:
German submarine U-boat, type VIIC

Second World War.[5] The VII typically had a displacement of 626 tons, a crew of four officers and forty-four ratings (enlisted men), and carried about fourteen 21-inch torpedoes. Four tubes faced forward and one aft. All the tubes were kept loaded and when they had been fired, the awkward business of reloading had to be done. On the surface the diesel engines gave a range of 7,900 nautical miles at 10 knots. If they pushed the speed up to 12 knots it would reduce their range to 6,500 nautical miles. In an emergency the diesels could give 17 knots for short periods. With a fully trained crew a Type VII dived in thirty seconds and when submerged used electric motors. The rechargeable batteries could go for about 80 nautical miles at 4 knots. Maximum speed underwater was reckoned to be 7.5 knots, depending upon gun platforms which obstructed the water flow. Most reference books give manufacturer's specification speeds which are faster than this.

The whole purpose of the submarines was to fire torpedoes. These big G7 – seven metres long – devices were no less complicated than the submarine itself, and in some respects exactly like them. They were treated with extraordinary care. Each torpedo arrived complete with a certificate to show that its delicate mechanisms had been tested by firing over a range. It had been transported in a specially designed railway wagon to avoid risk of it being jolted or shaken. One by one, with infinite concern, the 'eels' were loaded into the U-boat, which was usually moored inside a massive concrete pen. From then onwards, all through the voyage, each and every eel would be hung up in slings every few days, so that the specialists could check its battery charge, pistols, propellers, bearings, hydroplanes, rudders, lubrication points and guidance system.

To make an attack it was necessary to estimate the bearing and track of the target. Usually the submarine was surfaced, and the captain used the UZO (*U-Boot-Zieloptik*) which was attached to its

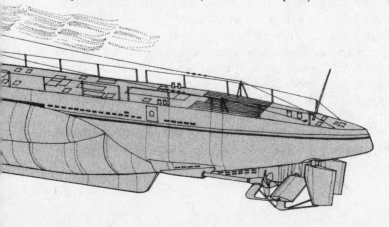

steel mounting on the conning tower. This large binocular device had excellent light-transmission capability, even in semi-darkness, and from it the bearing, range and angle of the target vessel was sent down to the *Vorhaltrechner*. This calculator sent the target details to the torpedo launch device, *Schuss-Empfänger*, and right into the torpedoes, continuing to adjust the settings automatically as the U-boat moved its relative position. By means of these instruments the U-boat did not have to be heading for its target at the moment of launching its torpedo. The torpedo's gyro mechanism would correct its heading after exiting the tube. Thus a 'fan' of shots, each on a slightly different bearing, could be fired without turning the boat. This device was coveted by British submarine skippers who aimed their torpedoes by heading their submarines towards the target.

By using 'wakeless' electric G7e torpedoes – and suppressing the water swell – a submarine could fire without betraying its position. Smaller targets were sunk by means of the deck gun, which was usually an 8.8-cm artillery piece. To fire it in anything but calm water without going overboard demanded the agility of an acrobat. Hitting anything other than a large target was very difficult. When war began there was also a single 2-cm Flak gun (short for *Flugab-wehrkanone*, anti-aircraft gun) but this proved of little use against aircraft and bigger and better ones were fitted as the war continued.

Life aboard a submarine was rigorous. The hull's interior was the size and shape of a passenger train but the 'train' was crammed with machinery into which the men were artfully fitted. There was no privacy whatever for anyone. Even the captain had no more than a curtained desk, past which everyone pushed to get to their stations. This is how an official German navy war correspondent saw it:

> My bunk is in the petty officers' quarters, the U-room, the most uncomfortable on board: it has the most through traffic. Anyone who wants to get to the galley, or to the diesels or the E-motors has to come through here. At every change of watch the men from the engine room squeeze through from astern, and the new watch comes through from the control room. That means six men each time. And the stewards have to work their way past with their full dishes and pots. In fact, the whole place is nothing more than a narrow corridor with four bunks on the right and four on the left. In the middle of the passage, screwed to the floor, there's a table with folding leaves. The space on

both sides is so narrow that at mealtimes the men have to sit on the lower bunks with their heads bent. There is far too little space for stools. And there is mess and confusion whenever someone has to get from the engines to the control room or vice versa during a meal.[6]

There were no bathing facilities, and only one lavatory which could not be used when the submarine dived. When under attack the lavatory might well be out of action for 24 hours. No one shaved and most didn't change even one article of clothing for the entire voyage. The stink of human bodies was mixed with those of oil and fuel. There was also the pervading smell of mould, for in the damp air everything, from bread to log books, went mouldy. The men – mostly young, for only young men could endure the hardships and the stress – were apt to douse themselves in eau de cologne to exchange one smell for another.

The Commander is astride the periscope saddle in the narrow space between the periscope shaft and the tower wall, his face pressed against the rubber shell, his thighs spread wide to grip the huge shaft. His feet are on the pedals that enable him to spin the great column and his saddle through 360 degrees without making a sound; his right hand rests on the lever that raises and lowers it. The periscope motor hums. He's lowering it a little, keeping its head as close to the surface of the water as he possibly can.

The Chief is standing immobile behind the two men of the bridge watch who are now operating the hydroplanes. His eyes are glued to the Papenberg and its slowly rising and falling column of water. Each change in it means that the boat is doing the same.

Not a word from anyone. The humming of the periscope motor sounds as if it's coming through a fine filter; the motor starts, stops, starts again, and the humming resumes. The Commander ups periscope for fractions of a second and immediately lets it sink below the surface again. The destroyer must be very close.[7]

Most of the time was spent on the surface. In the Atlantic this meant endless rolling and pitching. Boats on the surface needed lookouts who got very cold and wet. In the northern waters lookouts grew accustomed to icy water breaking over them with such force that they required leather harness to secure them to the bridge brackets. Reminders about wearing such restraints sometimes included the names of U-boat men who had recently been washed overboard. The men on watch wore protective clothing of leather, or sometimes of rubber, under their oilskins, with towels around their necks. Even so they usually became soaked to the skin in anything but calm weather. Almost every submariner complained of rheumatic pains. Below decks the crew were permitted to wear any clothing they wished. 'Lucky' sweaters, knitted by loved ones, were popular, so were British army khaki battledress jackets, thousands of which had come from captured dumps in France. Some captains would distribute a measure of schnapps at times of great joy or great suffering; other boats were completely dry.

> The men of the preceding watch come down the ladder stiffly. They are soaking wet. The navigator has turned up his collar and drawn his sou'wester down over his face. The faces of the others are whipped red by spray. All of them hang their binoculars over hooks and undress as silently as the new watch dressed, peeling themselves awkwardly and heavily out of their rubber jackets. Then they help one another off with their rubber pants. The youngest member of the watch loads himself with the whole mass of wet oil-skin trousers, jackets, and sou'westers, and carries it aft. The spaces between the two electric motors and on both sides of the stern torpedo tube are the best for drying. The men who have come off duty gulp down a mouthful of hot coffee, polish their binoculars, and stow them away.[8]

When in May 1941 a young British officer led a boarding party to search a U-boat captured at sea, he was impressed by its fine construction, the fittings and the way in which the ward room had varnished woodwork and numbered cupboards with keys to fit them. He remarked upon the magnificent galley and the cleanliness of the boat throughout. During his search he found other evidence of the high living standards the Germans enjoyed; cameras and even a movie camera were among the crews' personal effects. He said the sextants were of far better quality than the Admiralty issue and the binoculars the best he'd ever seen. He kept a pair for himself.[9]

In the war at sea, as well as on land and in the air, radio brought changes in tactics. Better longer-range radios enabled the submarines to be sent to find victims in distant waters or concentrated against a choice target. Admiral Karl Dönitz was the German navy's single-minded submarine expert. He thought primarily, if not solely, in terms of war against Britain. He had long since decided that a future submarine war would be an all-weather one, and that (with asdic unable to detect small surface targets) he would coordinate night attacks by surfaced submarines. This line of thinking was published in his prewar book. It was to prove one of the most effective tactics of the war.

The Royal Navy liked to believe that U-boats could be countered by means of 'hunting groups' of warships. Such warfare had the name, colour, speed and drama that suited the navy's image of itself. But this idea had been tried and found useless in the First World War. Experience proved that in the vastness of the seas the submarine could remain undetected without difficulty. It was one of these hunting groups – an aircraft carrier with a destroyer escort – which was attacked at night by *U-29* just two weeks after the declaration of war. The carrier HMS *Courageous* sank with heavy loss of life.

The way in which *Courageous* was exposed to danger was proof that the Admiralty truly believed that asdic and depth charges provided adequate protection against the U-boat. But now there were second thoughts about 'hunting groups' which had depleted the number of escorts available for the merchant convoys. The way to kill U-boats was to guard the merchantmen. Then the submarines would have to come and find you.

3 EXCHANGES OF SECRETS

We shall not cease from exploration
And the end of all our exploring
Will be to arrive where we started
And know the place for the first time.

T. S. Eliot, *Little Gidding*

A FTER THE WAR Churchill admitted that the U-boat successes had been the only thing that frightened him, and it has been widely assumed that Hitler went to war understanding the submarine's potential value. The truth is that the German navy was completely unprepared for war. At its outbreak, Germany had built 56 U-boats,[1] of which some were short-range Type IIs seldom used beyond the North Sea. The building programme was providing two or three submarines a month (in some months only one), and it was taking about a year to build and test each boat. After the war Admiral Dönitz said: 'A realistic policy would have given Germany a thousand U-boats at the beginning.' We can but agree and shudder.

One of the war's most eminent naval historians, S. E. Morison, said Hitler was *landsinnig* (land-minded) and believed, like Napoleon, that possession of the European 'heartland' would bring England to heel. Winston Churchill, like President Roosevelt, knew that Britain's survival depended upon sea-lanes, for without supply by sea there could be no continuation of the war.

Dönitz and Raeder: the German commanders

Hitler had only one sailor among his high commanders, the 63-year-old Grand Admiral Erich Raeder, who was commander in chief (Oberbefehlshaber) of the navy. He was old-fashioned and aloof, as photos of him in his frock-coat, sword and high stiff collar confirm. Although Raeder looked like a prim and proper officer of the Kaiserliche Marine, his speech in 1939 declared his full support for 'the clear and relentless fight against Bolshevism and International Jewry whose nation-destroying deeds we have fully experienced.'

At the Nuremberg trial he was found guilty of having issued orders to kill prisoners. His memoirs, published a decade after the war ended, reiterated his belief in Hitler.

The man conducting the submarine battles, Karl Dönitz, was a quite different personality. The son of an engineer working for Zeiss in Berlin, he had never had staff college training. As a U-boat commander in the First World War, he had survived a sinking to become a prisoner of war. Despite other jobs in signals, and command of a cruiser, his primary interest was with undersea warfare. The rebuilding of Germany's submarine fleet gave him status. He was a dedicated Nazi and his speeches usually included lavish praise for Hitler: 'Heaven has sent us the leadership of the Führer.' Anything but aloof, he delighted in mixing socially with his officers, who referred to him as 'the lion'. Luncheons and dinners with him were remembered for their 'tone of light-hearted banter and camaraderie'. Dönitz was 47 years old at the start of the war. Morison (the author of the official US navy histories) was moved to describe him as 'one of the most able, daring and versatile flag officers on either side of the entire war'. Eventually, in January 1943, Dönitz was to become C-in-C of the navy, succeeding Raeder, and in the final days of the war it was Dönitz whom Hitler chose to take his place as Führer of the collapsing Third Reich.

Widespread misunderstandings persist as to Dönitz's role in the war at sea. The submarine arm was not controlled by him; it was run from Berlin by the Seekriegsleitung, which was both a staff and an organ of command. In May 1940 Dönitz was not even among the thirty most senior naval officers. He was not consulted on such matters as crew training, submarine design, or construction schedules, nor on technical matters about weaponry such as mines and torpedoes. His chief, Admiral Raeder, emphasized this to him in a memo dated November 1940: 'The Commander-in-Chief for U-boats is to devote his time to conducting battles at sea and he is not to occupy himself with technical matters.' It is also an revealing sidelight on the cumbersome way in which dictatorships distort the chain of command that, when there came a shortage of torpedoes, Dönitz went to Raeder and asked him to persuade Hitler to order increased production.

In the opening weeks of the war the opposing navies were discovering each other's weaknesses as well as their own. Dismayed at first by the severe limitations of asdic, the Royal Navy found that skilled and experienced operators could overcome some of its faults. The German navy, like other navies, was discovering that under active service conditions the torpedo was a temperamental piece of machinery.

All torpedoes normally have two pistols which can be selected quickly and easily immediately before use. A hit with the cruder contact pistol will usually result in a hole in the ship's hull, which can often be sealed off and the ship saved. A magnetic pistol is activated by the magnetism in a ship's metal hull and explodes the charge *under* the ship, which is likely to break its back. The German magnetic pistols gave so much trouble that crews switched to contact pistols and found that they were faulty too. The trigger prongs were too short: a torpedo sometimes hit a ship and was deflected without the prongs being touched. The torpedoes of the submarine fleets were also affected by a design problem in the detonators. Constant pressure variations inside the U-boats affected the torpedoes' depth-keeping mechanisms.

Although the official explanation for some of the failures was that magnetic triggers could be affected by changes in the earth's magnetic field, due to latitude or to iron ore or volcanic rock in the sea bed, to me it seems extremely likely that the degaussing of British ships – to protect them against magnetic mines – protected them against magnetic pistols too. Whatever the causes, these troubles continued all through the war, and the faults were not finally diagnosed until after hostilities were over.[2]

Understandably Dönitz complained bitterly to the Torpedo Directorate. He said pointedly that he remembered the same trouble in 1914 but in the first war the Torpedo Inspectorate knew how primitive mechanisms worked! The torpedo experts – their experimental firing ranges frozen in the first winter of war – responded to most criticism by blaming the U-boat crews. Postwar research suggested a failure rate of almost 30 per cent overall. On one war cruise the *U-32* fired 50 per cent duds. An inquiry showed that the contact pistols had only been tested twice before the war, and had failed both times. It became clear that torpedo failures had been experienced and reported since December 1936 but nothing had been done about them. When the war made it impossible to ignore the faults any longer, Raeder demanded action. A rear-admiral was court-martialled and found guilty, a vice-admiral dismissed. The scandal shook the navy and affected the morale of the U-boat service, as well as providing a glimpse of the sort of bureaucratic bungling that was a well established feature of Hitler's Third Reich, when Nazi loyalty tended to outrank competence.

Unrestricted submarine warfare

Article 22 of the 1930 London naval treaty, which Germany signed, held that merchant vessels might not be sunk until the passengers, crew and ships papers were in a place of safety, adding that the ship's boats were not regarded as a place of safety unless land or another vessel was nearby in safe sea and weather conditions. Anyone who hoped that the Germans might observe their treaty obligations had only twelve hours to wait after the declaration of war. The *U-30*, commanded by Kapitänleutnant Fritz-Julius Lemp, sighted the unescorted passenger ship *Athenia* while it was 200 miles off the coast of Donegal. It had left Liverpool at 4 o'clock on the afternoon before war began. Its passenger accommodation was fully booked and included 316 Americans heading home before war engulfed them.

Lemp saw the 16-year-old liner at 7.30 pm. It was getting dark and he made little or no attempt to distinguish whether she was a passenger ship or an auxiliary cruiser which would have been a legitimate target. He fired a salvo of torpedoes, one of which wrecked the bulkhead between the boiler rooms. In the words of one ship's passenger:

> I was standing on the upper deck when suddenly there was a terrific explosion. I reckon I must be a very lucky woman because when I recovered from the shock I saw several men lying dead on the deck.[3]

The passengers in the tourist and third class dining rooms were trapped when the explosion wrecked the stairways. *Athenia* listed and settled down. About half an hour later Lemp's submarine surfaced and fired at his victim with the deck gun. Now it must have been clear that she was a passenger liner, the torpedoing of which was explicitly forbidden by the prize laws of the Hague Convention. Without making contact, or offering directions or assistance of any kind, Lemp submerged and went away.

The *Athenia* sank: 112 people died, including many women and children. The German Admiralty instantly denied the sinking and ordered Lemp to remove the page from his boat's war diary and substitute false entries.[4] Those officers and men of the German navy who knew the truth were sworn to secrecy and the Reich propaganda ministry issued a statement that a bomb had been placed aboard the *Athenia* on the instructions of Winston Churchill.

The *Athenia* sinking came just as President Roosevelt asked Congress to pass Neutrality Act amendments, allowing Britain and France to buy war material. Seeing that the unlawful sinking of *Athenia* would persuade Congress to say yes, the German propaganda machine employed its formidable resources. An American survivor was persuaded to say that the ship was carrying coastal defence guns, destined for Canada. The allegation that Churchill put a bomb aboard the liner, in order to drag America into his war, was repeated time and time again in radio broadcasts, newspaper items and in letters mailed to prominent Americans. The German navy in Berlin issued a series of warnings about Churchill's bombs on other American ships. This bombardment of lies scored many hits. A Gallup poll revealed that 40 per cent of Americans believed the Germans. The Senate voting reflected a similar feeling when Roosevelt's amendments passed by 63 votes to 31. The House of Representatives also voted in favour of the French and British, by a majority of 61.

By Christmas 1939 Berlin's orders decreed that all ships except fully lit ones identified as Italian, Japanese, Russian, Spanish or Portuguese (United States shipping was excluded from the 'war zone' by American neutrality laws) must be sunk without warning. U-boat captains were told to falsify their logs and describe unlit target ships as warships or auxiliary cruisers.

Just in case there was any misunderstanding, Dönitz's Standing Order No. 154 told his commanders: 'Rescue no one and take no one aboard. Do not concern yourselves with the ship's boats. Weather conditions and the proximity of land are of no account.'

However there was another more heroic aspect of the U-boat war. On 14 October 1939 there came a dashing action that was planned and briefed by Dönitz himself. Kapitänleutnant Günther Prien, commander of the *U-47*, is said by one historian to have been to Scapa Flow and studied the Royal Navy anchorage as a tourist before war began. Whether this is true or not, Prien showed amazing skill as he threaded his boat through the defences and into the British main fleet anchorage there. Two of his torpedoes hit HMS *Royal Oak*. There were explosions and the battleship turned over. Kirk Sound, through which Prien navigated, was 170 metres wide and only seven metres deep. It was such a notable achievement that even after an Admiralty inquiry had identified fragments of the German torpedoes, many people in Britain insisted that the sinking was due to sabotage. Another, completely unfounded, story told of a German spy who shone lights to guide the U-boat through Kirk Sound. In fact the sinking of the *Royal Oak* was one more indication of the Royal Navy's failure to prepare for war.

Britain's loss was an ancient battleship, but at this time unrestricted U-boat warfare was being criticized, and the German propaganda ministry saw its opportunity. The *U-47* crew were heroes and gained headlines across the world. In Berlin they were congratulated by Adolf Hitler. Prien was awarded the Knight's Cross[5] and Dönitz was promoted to admiral and appointed BdU, Befehlshaber der Unterseeboote (C-in-C of U-boats). The whole German U-boat arm rightly rejoiced in this proof that the Royal Navy were unable to protect their battleships even in their fleet anchorage.

Benefiting from their First World War experience, the British started convoys as soon as war began. It paid off: between September 1939 and the following May, 229 ships were sunk by U-boats but only twelve of these were sailing in convoy. The organization of the convoys was managed, despite the difficulties of making the civilian ships' captains do things the Royal Navy way, and there were fast and slow convoys to accommodate ships of varying performance. The layman usually supposes that it was the protection given by escort vessels that made it safer to go in convoy, but this was not so. Churchill provided the true reason:

> The size of the sea is so vast that the difference between the size of a convoy and the size of a single ship shrinks in comparison almost to insignificance. There was in fact very nearly as good a chance of a convoy of forty ships in close order slipping unperceived between the patrolling U-boats as there was for a single ship; and each time this happened, forty ships escaped instead of one.[6]

The basic Dönitz tactic was to have surfaced submarines patrol across known shipping routes until one of the lookouts spotted a convoy. The radio monitoring service in Germany, with its ability to read the secret British merchant ship code, helped Dönitz to position his 'rake' of boats. The first submarine to sight a convoy sent high-frequency radio signals to a master control room ashore, and made medium-frequency signals to nearby submarines to bring them to the convoy.

At night on the surface the U-boats engaged the merchant ships independently, and often at point-blank range. Before daylight came, they ran ahead to concentrate for another attack on the following night, the submarine's surface speed being faster than its speed underwater.

The Admiral Graf Spee *action*

Submarines were not the only threat to Britain's sea lanes. *Admiral Graf Spee* and *Deutschland* had put to sea a few days before war began. Construction of these cruisers had been started before Hitler came to power, when the peace treaty restricted Germany to ships of less than 10,000 tons. Perhaps in reaction to the way in which the Royal Navy had lost three cruisers at Jutland by single well placed shots, these Panzerschiffe ('armour ships') were given thick armour and big guns. Newspaper writers called them 'pocket battleships' but they were designed to prey upon merchant shipping. Their innovations included electrically welded hulls. Welding requires metal to be heated to an even temperature; for that reason the welding of thick steels is vastly more difficult than welding light aircraft alloys. The new ships had very shallow draught, and their honeycombed hulls reduced the danger from torpedoes. Heavy top-side armour protected them from air attack and their 11-inch guns had a range of 20 miles. They were powered by diesel engines – which until that time had only been used as auxiliary engines in such vessels – and could steam at 26 knots, an unimpressive speed for a cruiser but suitable for a raider. Each warship had a tanker at its disposal.

The *Deutschland* was assigned to raid the routes of the North Atlantic. She sank two merchant ships and captured a third (the *City of Flint* sailing under a US flag) and then returned to Germany, skilfully using the long November nights to elude the Royal Navy blockade. Her two-month voyage had destroyed 7,000 tons of small shipping; it was a disappointing debut for the 'pocket battleship'. Soon she was renamed *Lützow* because Hitler feared the propaganda effect of a mishap to a ship named *Deutschland*.

Admiral Graf Spee was sent to the sea lanes of the South Atlantic and the Indian Ocean. By 7 December 1939, in a voyage that included the South African coast and South America, she had sunk nine merchant ships. The captain, Hans Langsdorff, a handsome fifty-year-old, had strict ideas about the rules of war. His targets were sunk without loss of life, his prisoners were all treated well and German morale was high. His only setback was a cracked engine block in the battleship's spotter plane and no spare to replace it.

When *Graf Spee* sank the *Trevanion* in the South Atlantic on 2 October 1939, the men in the Admiralty had looked at their charts and guessed that the raider would head for the shipping lanes of South America. They stationed HMS *Ajax* off the River Plate, the

Figure 3: HMS *Ajax*

New Zealand warship *Achilles* off Rio de Janeiro, and HMS *Exeter* off Port Stanley in the Falklands. But the next signal was an RRR – 'raider sighted' – from the tanker *Africa Shell* off the East African coast. Had *Graf Spee*'s captain immediately sent a signal to inform Berlin of his success things might have ended quite differently for him; there would have been no way of guessing whether he was bound for the Indian Ocean or back into the South Atlantic. But Langsdorff waited ten hours, and when his signal was transmitted, three British Direction Finding Stations took a bearing on the signal. These bearings were sent to London on priority channels but even the Hydrographic Section at the Admiralty had no charts large enough to plot them.

Fortunately Merlin Minshall, a young officer of the Volunteer Reserve, had bought a globe four feet in diameter. It was, he calculated, 'equivalent to a flat chart nearly twelve feet from top to bottom . . . Within seconds I had placed three thin loops of rubber round my newly acquired globe. Their intersection clearly showed that the *Graf Spee* was heading not north up into the Indian Ocean but south back into the Atlantic.'[7] It was 4 o'clock in the morning. Rear Admiral 'Tom Thumb' Phillips, the vice-chief of naval staff, arrived dressed in a scruffy kimono to see the globe which was too big to be moved. 'Good idea using the globe,' he said. (Admiral Dönitz had come to the same idea as Lieutenant Minshall and was using a similar globe in his situation room.)

Figure 4:
HMS *Exeter*

More sinkings confirmed this route. *Graf Spee* was in the southern hemisphere and the 13 December 1939 was an idyllic calm summer's day. Visibility was perfect and at 0614 hours *Graf Spee*'s spotters saw the heavy cruiser HMS *Exeter* (8-inch guns) and turned towards her. The *Graf Spee* had six 11-inch guns and Langsdorff assumed that the two vessels with *Exeter* were destroyers escorting a merchant shipping convoy of the sort that *Graf Spee* was seeking as prey, but without the use of his spotting aircraft he was unable to confirm this.

In fact Langsdorff was heading towards one of the many 'hunting groups' that were looking for him. *Exeter* had seen *Graf Spee*'s smoke and had turned towards it. And the destroyers Langsdorff had spotted were actually light cruisers: HMS *Ajax* and the New Zealand navy's *Achilles* (each with eight 6-inch guns). He was probably misled by the fact that both ships were of unusual profile, having single funnels serving boilers sited together so as to economize on weight.

These three ships provide three different answers to the question that had plagued the world's navies for half a century: what should a cruiser be? Should it be a light vessel, fast at 32 knots with small 6-inch guns like the *Ajax* and *Achilles*; should it be of medium weight like the *Exeter*, with 8-inch guns; or should it be a heavy ship with massive 11-inch guns that make it so formidable that it is called a pocket-battleship but unable to exceed 26 knots? No wonder the camouflage experts had painted a huge white wave curling from the *Graf Spee*'s bow. It would never make such a wave in real life – and now it could not speed away.

Ajax – the group's flagship – catapulted a Seafox aircraft into the air. The difficulties of launching and recovery made this the only time such a warship used aircraft in a surface action.[8] On most Royal Navy ships, space designed for aircraft, catapults and hangars was soon to be occupied by radar and AA guns. With the reconnaissance plane in the air searching for her, *Graf Spee* turned away and made smoke. The encounter presented tactical problems for both sides. The *Graf Spee*'s guns far outranged her adversaries, but with enemy ships to both port and starboard the German captain hesitated before choosing his target.

Eventually *Graf Spee* opened fire at maximum range. At first one turret was firing to port and the other to starboard but then all six big guns were concentrated on the *Exeter*, whose 8-inch guns were the most dangerous threat. While the British force had no radar, the German Seetakt radar provided hits on *Exeter*'s turret and then on her main steering. Had it not been for the fact that some of the German shells failed to explode, she would have been sunk. After an unsuccessful riposte with torpedoes, the badly damaged *Exeter* withdrew, listing to starboard and taking in water forward. There were serious fires below decks and a near miss had put enough water through the shell holes in her side to short-circuit the electricity to her last remaining turret. Telephones and radio links were also lost. There was a real chance that *Exeter* would sink.[9]

Langsdorff might have closed and finished off the stricken vessel had the two 6-inch-gun ships not dashed in close and forced the *Graf Spee* to switch her attention to them, moving fast enough to avoid mortal hits by the big German guns, which could not change elevation and bearing fast enough.

After one and a half hours, during which the British warships got close enough to use even secondary armament, all four ships had suffered damage. Having taken hits from two 11-inch shells, the *Ajax* lost two of her four turrets, while the hoist failed in a third turret. The main top mast was chopped off by one of *Graf Spee*'s last salvoes. Three of her guns were still operating but she had used up 80 per cent of her ammunition. *Achilles* had suffered the least damage but she had no radio gunnery control in operation. *Graf Spee* had been hit many times but all her armament was still in operation.

The action was broken off by the British commander, who put up a smokescreen. There is no doubt that Langsdorff would have done better to have pressed home his attack on the battered trio but he did not, and afterwards it was said he had suffered flesh wounds and been knocked unconscious during the encounter. This might have been enough to affect his decision to head for a neutral port.

According to one account the *Exeter* had suffered more than one hundred serious hits. Five of her six big guns were out of action and there was so much smoke and flame that the Germans expected her to blow up and sink at any moment. With 61 dead, and many wounded, she made for the Falkland Islands while the two light cruisers trailed *Graf Spee* to the neutral South American port of Montevideo in Uruguay.

Had the Germans gained access to the sort of port facilities that the British had provided for themselves at strategic spots throughout the world, *Graf Spee* could have been replenished with ammunition and her minor battle damage – which might have proved dangerous in heavy seas – quickly repaired. But Germany was unable to provide for such needs in distant seas. With a more audacious captain the *Graf Spee* might have turned north and braved the northern seas in winter despite the battle damage and her 36 dead and 59 wounded. It was not to be.

When the *Graf Spee* docked in Montevideo, many local people, many of them expatriates, warmly welcomed the Germans but diplomats began arguing fiercely about the rights of belligerent warships in neutral ports. The Uruguayan government gave Langsdorff permission to remain in port for no more than 72 hours, the minimum permitted by international law. It was not enough time for repairs to be effected. Langsdorff tried, and failed, to charter a plane from which to see any Royal Navy ships that might be waiting for him.

To deter Langsdorff from fighting his way past them, the British were keen to give the impression that a large naval force was waiting for *Graf Spee*. A deception plan included the BBC radio bulletins and the British naval attaché who, knowing that the phones were tapped, called the ambassador in Buenos Aires and told him the Admiralty wanted 2,000 tons of fuel oil to be made available for two capital ships that evening at the Argentine naval base of Mar del Plata. It was enough to get the story circulated. There can be little doubt that Langsdorff believed that a sizeable naval force was ready to pounce on him.

On the evening of 17 December the *Graf Spee* moved out of harbour watched by the world's Press and newsreel cameras. At sunset the great ship came to a standstill and, to the astonishment of most of the spectators, blew up. Torpedo heads had been suspended above open ammunition hatches which led to the main magazines. Petrol was ignited to burn through the ropes. The explosion in the forward part of the ship went as planned but seawater came in and doused the aft fires. *Graf Spee* lurched forward and settled fo'c'sle down. Langsdorff shot himself. The German crew were interned but many of them escaped and got back to Germany to fight again.

Those ship designers who said the German pocket battleships were misconceived had been proved right. A commerce raider did not need 11-inch guns to sink merchant ships. With smaller guns the specifications would have been lighter and considerably faster. Raiders which fight and run away live to fight another day.

Still today little is said of the contribution that German gun-laying radar made to this or any other sea battle. Frequently throughout the war, German naval gunners seemed to enjoy 'lucky shots' for which we might read accurate gun-laying. In London the Admiralty was sufficiently impressed by *Graf Spee*'s performance to offer the government of Uruguay £14,000 for the *Graf Spee*'s smoking hulk, whose decks remained above water. British radar experts rowed out and boarded her to examine, sketch and dismantle the Seetakt radar. HMS *Exeter* and *Ajax* were eventually fitted with British Type 79, an air defence radar that could be used for gun-laying and gave a performance not unlike the German Seetakt.

While Raeder, the German naval chief, said the *Graf Spee* should have run rather than fight, Hitler found the loss of his battleship intolerable, but neither man was deterred by the sinking. During the winter of 1940–41 the *Scheer*, the *Gneisenau* and the *Hipper* left their ports to raid Atlantic shipping. The men in the Admiralty had cause to worry, for the German naval Enigma code[10] remained unbroken and the spectre of the German surface raider was given new substance by the trouble that *Graf Spee* had given them. Precious warships – including battleships, cruisers and carriers – were to spend the next few years chasing phantom German commerce raiders 'seen' by nervous merchant seamen on distant horizons.

The changing map of Europe

At the start of the war the only fully updated operational maps in Whitehall were to be found in the Admiralty's Upper War Room. This 300-year-old library had been made into a map room which was manned round the clock. The maps were coloured in pastel shades (because Churchill said primary colours gave him headaches) and pins showed the position of every British and Allied warship and convoy as well as the position of every German vessel reported by intelligence. The U-boat war, complete with a day-by-day account of shipping sunk and the import figures, was the room's most important concern.

The map room became a regular treat for guests after Churchill's Tuesday evening dinner parties. He was first lord of the Admiralty[11] at this time, slept nearby, and would appear suddenly in his multi-coloured dressing-gown inquiring about the latest news. Last thing at night and first in the morning he was briefed. When in May 1940 he became prime minister he no longer had this map room close at hand but the same officers provided a similar early morning briefing to him throughout the war.

In September 1939 Germany went to war with only minimal need for ocean trading. Agriculture, which the Nazis had encouraged, supplied enough food; and German mines enough coal and iron-ore. When and if some special top-grade ores were needed by the armaments industry Sweden was very close and willing to sell. Other imports came from Switzerland and Italy. Rubber and oil were the most vital necessities but German scientists were already able to provide adequate synthetic versions of both, and the Romanian oilfields were on the doorstep. Furthermore Germany had a new friend and trading partner – the USSR – which had oil to spare. Poland had been invaded by both countries, split down the middle and shared between them. Direct cross-border trade began. The Germans could now reach the whole of Asia without worrying about the Royal Navy's blockade.

All this was evident from a map, but there was little sign that many members of the British government looked at a map. In March 1940 Prime Minister Chamberlain was calling blockade 'the main weapon'. Britain's Ministry of Economic Warfare said, and believed, that the German economy was on the point of break-down. On 27 May 1940 Britain's chiefs of staff predicted that Germany's economic collapse would take place by the end of 1941. By September 1940 – with Hitler controlling Europe from Norway to the Spanish border, and the Battle of Britain still undecided – the chiefs of staff had not changed their mind. The prevailing opinion was that Germany's inevitable collapse would now be speeded by the rebellious people of the occupied countries. The role of the British army in 1942, they cheerfully predicted, would merely be to keep order in that chaotic Europe left by the German disintegration! We must not be too hard on those wishful thinkers: such fantasies kept Britain and her Dominions fighting in a situation that more realistic minds would have pronounced hopeless.

The division of Poland, between Germany and the Soviet Union, and the trade between them was not the only bad news that the admirals had to swallow in that 1940 summer. The Admiralty had always assumed that in the event of war it would enjoy port facilities in Ireland. From fuelling bases at Queenstown (Cobh) and Berehaven and the naval base at Lough Swilly on the west coast, anti-submarine flotillas would have ranged far out into the Atlantic. Without them every escort vessel would add 400 miles to its patrol. The use of the bases in wartime had been confirmed in a conversation between the Irish patriot Michael Collins, Admiral Beatty and

Winston Churchill as long ago as 1922, when Churchill, as colonial and dominions secretary, was concerned with the Irish Settlement.

The story behind this change has still to be told to everyone's satisfaction. In April 1938 the Chamberlain government renounced the right to use the ports which it had been granted under the 1922 Irish treaty. Churchill was appalled and said that it would be hard to imagine a more feckless act at such a time. In the House of Commons he spoke against what he called a 'gratuitous surrender' and a 'lamentable and amazing episode'. He found himself unsupported. Virtually the whole Conservative party, and the Labour (Socialist) and Liberal opposition, sided with Chamberlain. But when war came, the Irish Republic remained neutral and Churchill's warnings proved exactly true. Ireland's government resisted Britain's requests to use the ports, although some of the material brought in the convoys was destined for neutral Ireland.

The convoys, channelled into the narrow waters around Ireland, provided rich pickings near home for bold U-boat captains. The Admiralty was still coming to terms with these difficulties when, in the summer of 1940, an even worse change came to the operational maps. The Germans conquered Denmark, so providing a gate to the Baltic, and Norway, with its bases and access to the North Atlantic. The only alleviation of this gloom was that the Norwegian merchant fleet – one of the world's largest – sailed to England to evade the Germans. This enormous addition to the shipping tonnage was to become the margin by which Britain survived in the dark days to come.

When in the summer of 1940 France was conquered by the Germans its fleet did not sail to British ports to continue the fight. In the Atlantic and Mediterranean the Royal Navy took on the whole load the French navy had shared. France's Atlantic coast also provided magnificent submarine bases, well away from RAF bomber airfields. From these ports the U-boats could sail directly into the world's oceans.

When Admiralty radio interceptions and bearings indicated that U-boats were using French ports the Foreign Office insisted that it was impossible; the French would not permit it. Lt Minshall RNVR, the same young officer who had provided the globe for the Admiralty, volunteered to investigate. One of the Royal Navy's submarines took him to the French coast, where he spotted and commandeered a French boat which he sailed into the mouth of the Gironde. He stayed there for six days, noting the U-boat movements and enough details to convince even the men of the Foreign Office that the ports were being used.[12] He got back to England in the sailing boat and was awarded a 'mention in dispatches'.[13]

Britain's armed forces had gone to war expecting to fight in the way they had fought in 1914. The British Expeditionary Force would go to France and hold a small section of the Western Front while the Royal Navy – aided by the French fleet – protected the sea routes and waited to re-fight the battle of Jutland. Now everything was changed. Britain was isolated and the Germans held most of Europe, including the Channel coast just twenty-one miles away. With Italy fighting alongside Hitler the Mediterranean sea routes were fiercely contested and Britain's army in Egypt was under constant threat. By the summer of 1940 no one could continue to believe that this war would much resemble the previous conflict.

Cracking the naval codes: Enigma

In 1920 the organization known in the First World War as I.D. 25, and usually referred to as Room 40, changed its name to the Government Code and Cypher School (GC&CS). This name served to hide its true purpose, which was to protect British official communications and intercept foreign ones. It was a part of the Secret Intelligence Service, and in 1925 it was moved from a building behind Charing Cross railway station to the SIS headquarters at 54 Broadway, London, near St James's Park underground station, a site conveniently close to the Foreign Office. A few days before the outbreak of war its name was again changed – to Government Communications Headquarters – and it moved to an endearingly ugly but conveniently secluded Tudor-Gothic Victorian house at Bletchley Park, about fifty miles north of London. Its principal task was to read German radio messages encoded on Enigma machines.

The Enigma started its career as a commercial enciphering machine, a sort of typewriter that scrambled text using notched wheels or rotors. The message could be unscrambled by a recipient using an identical Enigma with its rotors adjusted to the same settings, known only to the sender and the receiver. When the Germans bought some Enigma machines they adapted them to make them more difficult to counter. The improved machine had plugs, varying the circuits, which the operators changed every twenty-four hours according to a dated instruction book of 'keys'. This gave an astronomical number of alternatives for each letter.

The story of the breaking of the Enigma can be said to start in October 1931, at the Grand Hotel, Verviers, a town in Belgium not far from the German border. Hans-Thilo Schmidt, a highly placed official in the German Defence Ministry, made contact with Rodolphe Lemoine, an agent of the Deuxième Bureau, the French military intelligence service. Lemoine, a widely travelled linguist, had been born in Berlin, the son of a jeweller. A naturalized French citizen, he had taken his French wife's name and, despite being a successful businessman, he went to work as a secret agent. Lemoine got along well with his fellow Berliner. Schmidt's father was a professor and his mother a baroness, but this highly intelligent and well educated veteran of the First World War found it difficult to manage on the salary he earned as a clerk distributing cipher material. He offered to sell the operator's instruction manual for the Enigma machine and some other notes and manuals. He also offered to continue to supply information about the updating of the machine and its codes as well as details of the workings of the German High Command (where Schmidt's elder brother was now a lieutenant-colonel and chief of staff of the signal corps). At one time Rudolf had been the head of the cipher section – Chiffrierstelle – where Hans-Thilo now worked, and it had been Rudolf's decision to purchase the Enigma machines that his brother was offering to compromise.

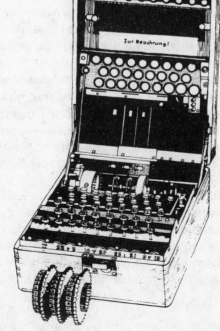

Figure 5:
German Enigma
coding machine

It was Lemoine's stated belief that every man had his price, and at their first meeting he offered Hans-Thilo Schmidt payments equal to three times what he was getting in salary. The Service de Renseignement in Paris approved the deal and gave Schmidt the codename HE, which spoken in French eventually gave way to the German word *Asche*, ash. Although the material from Hans-Thilo enabled the French to read a few messages, the complex wiring inside the machine made it a daunting challenge. Paris, deciding that cracking such a machine was beyond their resources, offered to share the task with the British, but the Secret Intelligence Service in London was not interested. The French decided to give everything they had collected to the Poles.

The successes of French and British linguistic cryptanalysts, working on methods perfected during the First World War, persuaded their masters to ignore the problems of mathematical cryptanalysis. This was why the Enigma machine defeated them. The Poles had superior mathematicians, more men familiar with the German language, and the will to succeed at a task no one else believed possible.

By 1933 the Poles had rigged up a reproduction of the Enigma. They kept the French informed about their progress and the French faithfully passed to Warsaw the new codes and whatever mechanical changes to the machine Hans-Thilo could discover. However over a period of five years few of these messages got to the codebreakers. The Polish high command wanted its men to crack the German codes without outside help, and it doled out the material from Hans-Thilo only in small amounts when the codecrackers were stuck.

The Germans improved their coding machines while the Poles improved their codecracking ones, constructing what they called a bombe, a computer consisting of six linked Enigma machines. In September 1938 the fears of the Polish intelligence chiefs came true. Hans-Thilo was transferred to Göring's Forschungsamt and the supply of codes ended. But by now the codecrackers had learned to manage without his help.[14]

On 24 July 1939, with war only a week away, the Poles invited the French and the British to Warsaw to show them in great detail the work they were doing breaking the German codes. They showed them the bombe, a method of using overlaid perforated sheets, and calculations about wiring. Mathematical talent was at the heart of the Polish work. Some of the most notable breakthroughs had been made by Marian Rejewski, a young mathematician who has been described as one of the greatest cryptanalysts of all time.[15]

As a going-away present both French and British representatives were given a 'replica' Enigma machine. Although as the Germans got nearer to war they changed the codes, and added an extra rotor to their Enigmas to make the machine codes more complex, this gift was beyond price. Gustave Bertrand, a senior French intelligence officer, described how he brought the machine to the chief of Britain's Secret Intelligence Service.

> On 16 August 1939 I was on my way to London accompanied by Uncle Tom – the diplomatic courier of the British Embassy in Paris – who was carrying a diplomatic bag with the Enigma machine. At Victoria Station Colonel Menzies, head of the [S] IS wearing the rosette of the Legion of Honour in the button-hole of his dinner-jacket (he was going to a soirée) was waiting for us: triumphal welcome! Which occasioned him to say one day [that the French intelligence service] had done him a 'considerable service on the eve of the war'.[16]

Considering how little accurate information his SIS was able to supply about even peacetime Nazi Germany, the ill-judged rejection of the French offer of the Enigma secrets and a total lack of any preparations for war, Colonel Menzies did not exaggerate.

Poland was invaded, but keeping ahead of the Germans the Polish codecrackers moved to France. Then France fell too. The French team escaped the German invaders, set up shop near Uzès in the unoccupied sector of France, and continued their work, sending their solutions to London (enciphered in Enigma!). Many Polish and French cryptologists ended up as captives of the Germans, but all managed to convince their interrogators that Enigma was beyond their abilities. The Germans believed them; such is the power of self-deception.

In 1943 some Polish members of the original team reached England after harrowing experiences. According to one notable historian of the Enigma story: 'The Poles reaped the customary reward of the innovator whose efforts have benefited others: exclusion. The British kept Rejewski and the others from any work on Enigma, assigning them instead to a signals company of the Polish forces in exile, where they solved low-level ciphers. It was not one of Britain's finest hours.'[17]

Bletchley Park was sited halfway between Oxford and Cambridge universities, and with more and more big wooden huts built in the grounds, GC&CS were able to recruit and accommodate academics including the junior dean and mathematical tutor of Sidney Sussex College who arrived on the first day of war. Hurrying back from an International Chess Olympiad in Buenos Aires came Britain's chess team. More such men and women followed.

No one in the world had ever attempted to break machine-enciphered messages on a regular basis with all the urgency that war brings to such a task. The resulting intelligence – eventually to be called Ultra – came solely from radio transmissions in Morse code. No teleprinter message or telephone conversation was included, and since most of the vital messages were sent by those means, the greater proportion of secret enemy communications were never intercepted. Sometimes a radio message in Enigma was answered by telephone or teleprinter, or vice versa, so that only one side of a dialogue was available. Radio reception was often subject to interference, and errors were commonly included, making the job even more perplexing.

The British took up where the Poles left off. The first breakthroughs came from analysis of the uncoded message prefixes that told the recipient the key settings for the Enigma machine. Analysing the electrical wiring in rotors and plug boards, mathematicians and 'probability specialists' soon 'reduced the odds against us by a factor of 200 trillion'.[18] However there was still about a million to one against the men trying to conquer the Enigma messages. Wheel order and ring settings, the two most vital secrets, were sometimes guessed at by 'sheet stacking', a technique the Poles had pioneered. Holes – one per letter – punched in large sheets of paper allowed light through to reveal the pattern of the day's key.

The repetitive phrases used in much of the traffic also helped: especially the formal way in which people and organizations were addressed in full. Often the codebreakers were waiting for the Germans to describe something that had already happened, such as a bombing attack or a weather report. Sometimes the same message was sent in a low-grade code – already cracked – and in Enigma too. In that case the two messages could be compared.

From time to time a rotor or two was retrieved from the pocket of a rescued U-boat crewman. By summer 1941 much-improved bombes came into use at Bletchley Park. These were 10-feet-high electro-mechanical machines like calculators. Using rotors like those inside the Enigma machines, the bombe searched rapidly through, not every possibility but the limited number chosen by the operator. The clickety-clickety sound came to a sudden stop when the bombe found a letter substitute for which the operator was looking. This would provide a setting that could be tried on a British encoding machine that had been adapted to perform like an Enigma. The printer started and produced a long strip of text. If it was 'a good stop' it might mean a batch of messages could be broken.[19]

If it was a navy message it would then go to the Royal Navy section in one of the huts, where a dozen or more men juggled with the German military jargon to make an intelligible message in English. This done, English and German versions might be sent by teleprinter to the Submarine Tracking Room in the OIC Operational Intelligence Centre in the Admiralty's Citadel near Trafalgar Square in London.

The 'key', the settings of the rotors and the plugs, changed daily, or sometimes every two days. It was the most difficult problem, but even after the settings were discovered, the deciphered messages still had to be translated and made intelligible. Many messages were long, and included codenames and complicated service references that would be baffling to any civilian. There were technical aspects of stores, requisitions, meteorology, aviation or maritime matters. There were newly minted technical words and acronyms. A great deal of the intercepted material was banal and of little or no possible use as intelligence. And of course everything was in German. For some messages a result in two or three days was too late, and this was usually the case with the constantly moving war at sea.

The military wisely gave way to the boffins in the matter of getting useful results quickly. The first stage was a job for mathematicians; the second stage for men who spoke German. One of the Bletchley Park team remarked:

> The rise to prominence of the translators – their pivotal position was already an accomplished fact by the winter of 1940-41 – inaugurated a revolution which gave primacy to the end over the beginning.[20]

A navy, army or air expert assessed and annotated the translation to underline its significance. He would add, for instance, references to a unit, a place or person mentioned, bringing into use the big card-reference system that each service maintained. The next stage was the drafting of a signal to the field commander who could make use of the intelligence. The syntax of the message was changed, or 'sanitized', so that if the Germans encountered it they would not be able to identify the original message and guess how it had been obtained.

The British army monitors at Chatham, on the Thames estuary, and later other stations too, listened to all German short-wave radio traffic. According to the weather, reflections from the upper atmosphere would sometimes enable transmissions from U-boat to U-boat in the farthest reaches of the Atlantic to be heard.

The Enigma coding machine was a remarkable invention. The most surprising aspect of the story is that the experts agree that a few simple changes to the original design could have made it foolproof in use, and its output totally invulnerable. Messages were usually broken because of German carelessness and lax procedures. The Luftwaffe provided most opportunities; the navy was far more careful, so the German navy's Enigma codes were not broken on anything like a regular basis. A founder member of the Bletchley Park team commented: 'At any time during the war, enforcement of a few minor security measures could have defeated us completely.'[21]

In any case it wasn't necessary to understand what a message said to benefit from knowing where your enemy was. High Frequency Direction Finding (HF/DF or what the Royal Navy called 'Huff Duff') could estimate the position of U-boats (or enemy surface ships) by getting a compass bearing on the transmissions. BP staff also made valuable assessments of German preparations and operations by studying the volume, character and point of origin of signals traffic.

Oscilloscope patterns (which depict voltage or current fluctuations on a cathode ray tube) were also photographed and filed to provide a 'fingerprint' that could positively identify a radio transmitter, and this in effect was enough to identify a ship or U-boat. Such fingerprinting was another of Lt Merlin Minshall's ideas. It was in this way that the *Bismarck* was positively identified.[22]

Britain's Secret Intelligence Service retained control of their GC&CS, and so deciphered material went to their Broadway HQ for distribution to whoever 'C' – Colonel Stewart Menzies, the organization's chief – thought deserving. The Royal Navy did not trust SIS with this task, and right from the beginning the navy kept its facilities at Bletchley Park entirely separate from those of the army and the RAF. The admirals had not been satisfied with SIS since November 1939 when Menzies, an army man, was appointed to be 'C'. The navy said that previous SIS chiefs – Captain Smith-Cumming and Admiral Sinclair – had established a tradition that 'C' would always be a job for a sailor.

So all naval material was handled independently and went to the OIC (Operational Intelligence Centre) in Whitehall. In early 1941 the OIC moved to the Citadel (a lumpy brown granite building between Admiralty Arch and Horse Guards; it is still there, mercifully hidden under ivy).

The navy's system worked reasonably well. By the end of July 1941 – due largely to the capture of some Enigma machine rotors and dated settings in February, March and May – there was regular interception of Enigma signals. These were being added to all the other signals intelligence, collectively known as SIGINT, which included data from diplomats, foreign newspapers and secret agents, as well as from interrogating, bugging and planting stool-pigeons among captured U-boat crewmen. It was all analysed and put together, and with these sources the Admiralty's Submarine Tracking Room tried to predict the intention of the U-boat captains.

Radio transmissions from U-boats were few and far between. Getting one solitary fix on a U-boat simply put a coloured pin into a big plotting table. From that there was no telling which way the submarine was heading. Was it outward-bound, with a full complement of torpedoes, or was it limping home with engine troubles? Or was. it part of a 'rake' of other U-boats across the expected route of a convoy? The Submarine Tracking Room – using all its resources – tried to answer such questions, often guessing right and telling transatlantic convoys to change route and avoid the places where the U-boat packs were waiting. This rerouting of convoys was to become the most effective counter to the U-boats, and – since signals avoided all references to German movements – it was unlikely to reveal British successes with Enigma.

By 1941 the German armed forces had thousands of Enigma machines in use. One of the disadvantages to such machines was that they could be lost or stolen, and so could the keys, the settings for rotors and plug boards. Ever since the remarkable luck of finding some Enigma settings in the patrol boat *VP2623*, captured off Norway long before in April 1940, the codebreakers had been crying out for more.

On 23 February 1941 during a commando raid on the Lofoten Islands, northern Norway, the destroyer HMS *Somali* fought off a suicidal attack by a tiny German trawler, *Krebs*, which was left holed and beached. The *Somali*'s signals officer volunteered to search the little ship. From it he got some spare rotors and the Enigma 'keys' for the month of February. It was a splendid haul, more important to the war than the destruction of ships and factories and oil that had been the purpose of the commando raid.

It wasn't the rotors found on *Krebs* that pleased the men at BP – they already had them. The keys however were very valuable; with them current messages could be read without any delay. Even outdated keys were useful, enabling older messages to be examined. Such keys were always printed in water-soluble ink, and a dousing in seawater was enough to render them illegible. Ian Fleming, later to gain fame as the creator of James Bond, was at this time in naval intelligence and he came up with a hare-brained scheme to get some more of these keys. A captured airworthy German plane would be crash-landed in the sea and (it was hoped) found by a German ship. The rescued airmen would thereupon seize control of the ship and grab its codes. It says a lot about the desperate need for settings that this idea was taken seriously and a captured Heinkel made ready. Fortunately one of the boffins came up with a more practical adventure. The bounty of the February intercepts revealed that German weather-ships out in the Atlantic used Enigma. It also disclosed their movements. Why not capture one of those? The weather-ships were on station for months, so they might have longer lists of keys.

The destroyer *Somali* was used also in this engagement, which depended upon closing on the little weather-ships as quickly as possible in the hope that not everything would be tossed overboard. In the case of the weather-ship *München* the seizure and boarding went according to plan, and among the bundles of paperwork seized there were German Enigma keys for June. This would not enable the Bletchley Park men to read the whole of German naval traffic, for the navy had many different keys. But now the important 'home waters' radio traffic would be available. A second weather-ship, the *Lauenberg*, was intercepted on 28 June, just as the next month's settings were due to come into use. Now traffic up to the end of July could be read.

By this time there had been another dramatic success in the story of Enigma. It was early morning on Friday 9 May 1941 and the outward bound convoy OB 318 was seven days out of Liverpool. There was reason for the British sailors to feel that the most hazardous part of the voyage was done; no U-boat had made a kill this far west. But trailing the convoy came *U-110*, one of the big long-range Type IX submarines. It was commanded by Kapitänleutnant Lemp, the man who sank the passenger liner *Athenia* in the first hours of the war. He now wore the Knight's Cross – or 'tin tie' – at his collar. With him to the *U-110* he had brought his cousin, who was regarded as a Jonah by the crew, after having two previous boats sunk under him.

In daylight, submerged, Lemp fired three torpedoes. Two merchant ships were hit. One ship's stern tipped up so steeply that crates on her deck rolled into the ocean like 'a child pouring toys out of a box'.[23] One of the convoy's escorts spotted the racing white wake of his periscope, sped towards it and dropped a pattern of depth charges. But Lemp escaped and without delay came back up to periscope depth just in time to see the destroyer coming at him. The second scatter of depth charges was close. The underwater explosions stopped the electric motors, started leaks in the oil bunkers and sent the U-boat plunging downwards. Lemp ordered the tanks blown. This not only stopped the descent but brought *U-110* back up to the surface with a boiling of water that got the immediate attention of the deck crews of all three destroyers. Flustered, Lemp failed to have the pressure valve released, so that when the hatch opened a great cloud of dust came pouring out of the submarine. So did the crew, who jumped into the sea with their captain.

The captain of HMS *Bulldog* was shouting for a boarding party almost as soon as the mortally damaged *U-110* surfaced. Ignoring the probability that the Germans had set explosives before abandoning ship, a 20-year-old sub-lieutenant, rowed out by five sailors, clambered aboard the slippery hull of the wallowing boat and went down into the dark interior followed by his men. They formed a human chain to pass back the codebooks, charts and, having unscrewed it from its mounting, the Enigma machine itself. With great thoroughness and an iron nerve the sub-lieutenant scoured through everything on the U-boat from charts to 'art studies'. He searched through discarded clothes to find anything of value to intelligence from the contents of wallets to recreational reading matter. It took three or four hours to get everything valuable aboard *Bulldog*.

From the water Lemp watched the British go aboard his command. Realizing that his detonators had failed and knowing that he was responsible for the destruction of the Enigma machine and all the secret material, he seems to have deliberately allowed himself to drown. (Ex-U-boat men – and at least one account[24] – say that Lemp swam back to the U-boat to sink her and was shot by the British boarding party as he climbed on to the deck, but I find no evidence to support this allegation.)

HMS *Bulldog*'s captain tried to tow the U-boat back to port but failed. He showed masterly restraint and impeccable good sense in keeping his extraordinary success secret, so that no news of it could leak back to German intelligence, but he little knew what a tremendous coup he had brought off. The men from BP had never had such a wonderful collection of data: a new machine, spare rotors and a list of the prescribed rotor settings for the length of the U-boat's cruise – three months – and a mountain of helpful material that enabled them to read most Enigma machine messages in the code Hydra for the rest of the war. It also helped with the big warship code Neptun and the Mediterranean codes Sud and Medusa.

The ups and downs of the Enigma struggle meant that messages were sometimes read almost immediately and at other times there were long delays. Most messages were never read. The naval Enigma was the most difficult to crack and many successes came from captured current German keys. Without such helpful clues the German naval secrets could seldom be tapped. And yet it was only because Bletchley Park had been set up with its Enigma machines and bombes that the captured keys could be used.

But Enigma was only one part of the Atlantic battle. Nothing was more decisive than the rate at which merchantmen and escorts could be constructed in British and North American shipyards. The construction of U-boats was equally telling, and so were the global demands that took warships and U-boats to other parts of the world. The weather played a part, and so did the successes of the German B-Dienst, the service which intercepted British signals. The availability of Allied air cover and of long-range aircraft, and the extent of Luftwaffe reconnaissance and anti-shipping operations, influenced the monthly figures, as did the operations of German surface raiders. The rationing of food and petrol was vital to the struggle, as was the improving technology of anti-submarine weapons – such as the hedgehog depth-charge thrower – and the use of better explosive charges. Just as deadly in effect were airborne and shipborne radar and, perhaps most important of all, 'Huff Duff', which provided ever better 'fixes'.

The Germans never suspected that the British might be reading their Enigma traffic on a regular basis. The chief of the German

Navy's Signals, and the head of the Naval Intelligence Service, assured Dönitz that it was not possible to crack such machine codes. After the war Dönitz still believed them. To some extent of course this was true.

By 23 June 1941 British penetration of the Hydra traffic had given the OIC (Operational Intelligence Centre, of which the Submarine Tracking Room was a part) a great deal of supplementary data, including details of all German inshore traffic and thus minelaying operations, as well as the routine messages that marked the beginning and end of a U-boat's cruise.

Enigma intercepts also revealed the positions of five tankers, two supply ships and a scouting ship positioned for the commerce-raiding cruise by *Bismarck* and *Prinz Eugen*. When plans were made to attack these auxiliary vessels, the navy decided to leave two of them – the tanker *Gedania* and the scout *Gonzenheim* – unmolested. To attack them all might prompt the Germans to guess their Enigma had been penetrated. By chance the Royal Navy happened upon those ships too, and so the whole lot was sunk. As feared, this massacre – five of the sinkings occurring over a three-day period – made the Germans investigate the possibility that Enigma was insecure. They decided that the spate of sinkings was probably a coincidence, but additional security measures were introduced just to be on the safe side.

One of the planned measures was a fourth rotor for the navy's Enigma machines. A shiny new Enigma machine had been recovered from *U-570*, which in August 1941 surfaced near Iceland and fell victim to an RAF plane. The Enigma machine had been built with an extra window, all ready for the extra rotor when it was issued. The sight of it sent a shudder through the personnel at BP, for the mathematicians calculated that it would multiply their already Herculean task by a factor of 26! They were right: 1942 brought the four-rotor machine and a year of darkness for the men peering into the German navy Enigma. Sinkings went from 600,000 tons in the second half of 1941 to 2,600,000 tons in the second half of 1942.[25]

A last word about Bletchley Park is a cautionary one. Considerable opportunities for intelligence gathering were neglected because the pre-war SIS took no interest in foreign radio transmissions other than messages. It wasn't until 1940 that there was any attempt to intercept or analyse radar or radio navigation signals. GC&CS was responsible not only for cryptography and communications intelligence but also for safeguarding British communications. Whatever its glittering, and much trumpeted, successes at the former, its role as guardian was a chronic and dismal failure.

The Submarine Tracking Room

The Submarine Tracking Room used a wide range of incoming data. Anything that could possibly help was funnelled here. For the admirals perhaps the most disconcerting thing about this place, where Britain's most vital battle was being fought and from which came the operational decisions that sent orders to the warships, was that by 1941 no regular naval officer was anywhere to be seen.

The room was run by Rodger Winn, a 30-year-old lawyer with degrees from Cambridge and Harvard. He had drifted into this job as a civilian, after volunteering to interrogate enemy prisoners. Winn would never have passed a Royal Navy physical examination: childhood polio had left him a hump-backed cripple who walked with a limp. Neither would he have found favour in the peacetime navy, for he had limited respect for authority. Like many barristers he was a talented story-teller with a sharp tongue. The security of having a well paid profession waiting for him encouraged him to stand firm against authority. When a decision of Winn's was challenged by an admiral, Winn put a vast heap of reports, sightings, charts and intercepts on to the admiral's desk and politely asked him for his solution.

When Winn joined the Tracking Room staff, the emphasis was on plotting the present state of the Atlantic battle, rather than predicting the future. But such was Winn's talent for reading the minds of the U-boat men, that in January 1941 his boss was moved out of the Tracking Room and Winn was given sole command of it and made a commander in the Royal Navy Volunteer Reserve. And when in January 1942 he chose an assistant, it was another 'civilian', a bespectacled insurance broker from Lloyd's.

Most of the Tracking Room's floor space was occupied by a seven-foot-square plotting table depicting the North Atlantic. It was covered with sheets of white paper and brightly lit from above, like a billiards table. Pins showed the progress of the convoys on their two-week voyages across the ocean, while others showed the U-boats on their month-long sorties. All the evidence of U-boat activity – radio fixes, sightings, signals and sinkings – was written in pencil on to the paper table cover. The coloured pins revealed the source: red-topped pins for a fix, white for a sighting, blue for Enigma intercepts. Red lines showed the extreme limits of air cover. A cluster of pins showed where a convoy was at that moment under attack by a wolf pack.

Another large table was covered by a captured map to show the German navy grid. There was also a map showing the Huff Duff stations that took bearings on U-boat radio messages. Strings could be stretched across the map to intersect. A 'good fix' was within 40 or 50 miles, a 'very good fix' meant within 10 to 15 miles. On one notable occasion a U-boat was found within three miles of its fix in the Baltic, and sunk by a Coastal Command plane, all within 30 minutes of the U-boat's tell-tale radio transmission.[26]

The walls of the Tracking Room were covered in charts and graphs showing such things as U-boat sinkings and estimated production. There were pictures too, including a photograph of Dönitz. Winn tried to make this room as he imagined Admiral Dönitz had his operations room.

Each day at noon the information from the table was translated into a situation report. The most vital parts of the plot were used each day to update Churchill's map in the War Room. Once a week, during the night, staff renewed all the white paper sheets on the plotting table, carefully transferring all the current data to them. The Submarine Tracking Room became a favourite place to take VIPs. For extra security the plotting table used coded references so that visitors would not get an accurate or complete view of what was happening.

Around the Tracking Room there were offices for the watch-keepers. Winn's office had a glass front so that he could see the civilian watchkeepers plotting the convoys while RNVR officers (wearing mufti) plotted the enemy movements. Civilian day-workers kept the records and card indexes. A nearby office held telex machines connected by direct line to Bletchley Park. Arriving Enigma messages were brought into the Tracking Room by a Wren (Woman's Royal Naval Service) who was called 'the secret lady'.[27] One of the tasks of the Tracking Room staff was to compile an account of each new U-boat. Such a record might start with the low-grade radio traffic sent while the new boat was working-up in the Baltic. From that time onwards every possible detail of boat and crew would be filed for reference. Names, sinkings, medals and commendations, damage and refits were all noted.

Because the Royal Navy gave most of its officers sea duties

between spells at a desk, the plotting table often showed the hazards of friends who had recently worked here. One officer, Commander Boyle, was well known to the men in the Tracking Room and was married to a secretary who worked there. He was escort commander for a convoy of eleven tankers and his friends watched the plot day after day as its ships were picked off one at a time. Finally only one ship survived but Boyle was saved.[28]

By using his background material, and watching all the movements on the plotting table, Winn made decisions about re-routing convoys or even detaching precious warships if the situation required it. Each morning he phoned to the Western Approaches Command in Liverpool and spoke with RAF Coastal Command too. When Enigma material was available, it made Winn's job incomparably easier. Often he phoned directly to those other civilian boffins at Bletchley Park and asked them to keep a lookout for messages with some known component.

B-Dienst

The German navy's Observation and Cryptanalytic Service, Beobachtungs und Entzifferungs Dienst, was housed at 72 Tirpitzufer, Berlin. In the first two years of war there is no doubt that the German navy gained more advantage from the intelligence provided to them by their Beobachter-Dienst than did the Royal Navy from the Enigma work at Bletchley Park. The men of the German navy's B-Dienst (modelled after the Royal Navy's Room 40) had been listening to British fleet signals long before war began, and they broke the British convoy code (BAMS: British and Allied Merchant Ship Code) without difficulty. The Germans could read a great deal of the Royal Navy traffic too, and Dönitz planned his Atlantic operations upon the wealth of material he got from B-Dienst.

The British Admiralty had resisted the idea of having coding machines. The Typex, resembling the Enigma, had been offered to them but was turned down. One would have thought that a sample of what a potential enemy was using might have been recognized as a worthwhile investment. Lord Louis Mountbatten, when still a Lieutenant-Commander, had drawn attention to the weakness of the whole system of Royal Navy codes and was ordered 'to mind his own business'.[29]

The Royal Navy's refusal to use ciphering machines made it easier for the Germans. Even the convoy designations gave vital information: ONS was a slow outward-bound convoy to North America (Nova Scotia); HX homeward bound from Halifax. From such tags it was possible to guess the routes, and merchantmen were listed by name with a short description of their cargo: war material, eight aircraft on deck, locomotives on deck, chemicals, machine parts. Thus Britain's most critical supply convoys were exposed to attack and continued to be so until the codes were changed in the summer of 1943.

All the same the U-boat commander's task was not an easy one. The convoys maintained radio silence most of the voyage. On a clear day, an alert lookout on a submarine conning-tower might spot a convoy's smoke (against clear sky or cloud) at 50 miles. In calm seas, and at the right depth, a submarine's hydrophones might pick up the sound of a convoy at the same distance. Yet endless chivvying by the convoy commodores discouraged smoke, and the North Atlantic's clear days, and calm days, are not numerous. Lookouts, even German lookouts, are not always alert. We can therefore think in terms of a 25-mile visibility or less.

Always we must remember the speeds at which the opposing units could travel. It has been nicely depicted by a historian who suggested that we think of the Atlantic in terms of European distances: a U-boat in Vienna is told to attack a convoy in London. On the surface he can move at the speed of a pedal cycle, submerged he will go at approximately walking pace. Then we understand why convoys sometimes escaped intact, despite the men of B-Dienst.

4   SCIENCE GOES TO SEA

*Do you really believe that the sciences would
ever have originated and grown if the way had not been
prepared by magicians, alchemists,
astrologers and witches . . .*

Friedrich Wilhelm Nietzsche

I N THE OPENING DAYS of the war, the German magnetic mine gave
the Royal Navy one of its first big shocks. It was a simple weapon,
but the method of its activation demonstrated some of the curiosities
of the natural world. The mines sat on the seabed and came to the
surface to explode against the hulls of ships that passed over them.
Inside each mine there was a 'dip needle' which was pushed down by
the 'downwards north pole' of the ship passing over it. Such mines
were activated only by ships built in the northern hemisphere. Ships
built south of the equator had a 'downwards south pole' which pulled
the contacts further apart, so they could pass quite safely over magnetic mines.

In fact it was more complex than that: the magnetism of a ship's
hull was not simply north or south. Each ship was different. The hulls
varied according to the direction, relative to magnetic north, in which
the ship's keel had been laid down when built. Even more surprisingly, it was discovered that ships sailing to the southern hemisphere
and back again changed their 'magnetic signature'. Prefabricated
ships were sometimes assembled from two halves made in different
places; the halves then had different magnetic properties. Once a
ship's signature was known, it could be demagnetized by means of
a fluxmeter. When the threat of the magnetic mine was suddenly
understood, Britain's only manufacturer of fluxmeters was asked to
supply 500 on a rush order; before that only a dozen had been made
since 1898.

By their nature these 'influence mines' were restricted to use in
shallow water, the type TMB in 15 fathoms and the TMC no deeper
than 20 fathoms. Smaller mines could be laid through the U-boat's
torpedo tubes; three of them together were about the length of a

torpedo. Laid by U-boats or parachuted from low-flying aircraft into harbours, estuaries and coastal sea routes, the German mines caused consternation. The battleship HMS *Nelson* and the cruiser HMS *Belfast* were seriously damaged by mines, three destroyers were sunk and so were 129 merchant ships. The Thames Estuary became so littered with German mines that there was talk of closing down the Port of London.

It seemed at first as if it was a problem easily solved, since the Royal Navy had used magnetic mines in 1917. In the interwar years Admiralty scientists had experimented with the magnetic properties of ships' hulls, but the emphasis was upon counter-measures to the magnetic torpedo. This meant a powerful magnetism that would prematurely explode a torpedo as it approached. But scientists and technicians were few in number and their work was overruled by officials at the Admiralty who thought that mines, like submarines, were weapons for inferior naval powers. Dusting off their old research, the navy tried it out. But they found that magnetic sweeps that countered British magnetic mines exploded German ones. The sweeping devices were often destroyed and sometimes mine-sweepers were badly damaged.

The night of 22/23 November 1939[1] was dark and moonless. Between 9 and 10 pm a Heinkel He 111, following the Thames Estuary, flew very low over the tip of Southend pier. It was a good landmark: probably Luftwaffe crews were briefed to use the pier as a navigating fix. A machine-gun team at the pier's far end opened fire and saw two parachutes fall from the plane. Startled by the unexpected gunfire, the Germans had dropped two mines into the shallow tidal water. Its load lightened, the Heinkel sped away.

The report that men had jumped out of the aircraft was discounted. Before midnight, Churchill was told that there was probably going to be a chance to examine the new weapon. By 1.30 am on that same night two experts briefed by Churchill, and the first sea lord, were on their way by car to Shoeburyness, where the mines were exposed by the outgoing tide. By 4 am – with rain falling heavily – the investigating team was out on the exposed mud-flats. Using a powerful portable signal lamp, they were looking at a black aluminium cylinder, seven feet in length and about two feet in diameter. Before anything much could be done, beyond securing the mines, the incoming tide had swallowed them out of reach until the following afternoon.[2]

Next day steel-nerved technicians from HMS *Vernon* (the RN's mine school) defused the weapon. By a stroke of fortune, a mechanical device to keep the mine safe until it had settled on the seabed had jammed. It was actuated by the technicians rolling the mine over but by that time the mechanism had been rendered safe. Stripped of its detonators and priming charges the mine was taken for examination to a 'non-magnetic laboratory'. In a matter of hours the new weapon was understood: it operated on a vertical magnetic field and required about 50 milligauss to fire it. The threat remained.

When, on Saturday morning, Rear-Admiral W. F. Wake Walker told government scientist Frederick Brundett about the capture of the mine and that he would need twelve engineers by Monday morning, Brundett drove to the south coast to seek out individually men with special engineering skills and sign them up on the spot. One whom he considered essential was already being paid £2,000 a year. 'As it happened the Director of Scientific Research at the time was only getting about £1,700 a year, and I was subsequently told by the Treasury that I couldn't do it. I pointed out that I'd already done it and that he was in fact already working for us.'[3]

Some anti-mine experiments were performed by sailors who towed toy ships backwards and forwards over cables in 'canoe lake', a children's boating pool in Southsea, near to HMS *Vernon*. Various counter-measures were devised and put into operation immediately. These included 'de-gaussing', which neutralized the vertical magnetism of a ship. The mines could be swept by floating electrical cables (through which a current pulsed) behind a de-gaussed ship. Large coils were also installed in low-flying aircraft as a quick way to neutralize minefields.

Such measures were not enough to solve the problem completely. Channels swept by aircraft were narrow and unmarked. The German aviators were bold: one minelaying seaplane landed in Harwich harbour, carefully placed its mines, and then took off again. It was the minelaying operations of low-flying aircraft that led to the construction of new radar stations with apparatus designed for low-level detection. When the Battle of Britain began, these stations were to play a vitally important part in detecting low-flying formations that would otherwise have got in under the radar screen.

The de-gaussing that all British warships were given at this time probably saved some of them from attack by magnetic torpedoes, notably during the Norwegian campaign. At the time these failures were considered to be due to faults in German torpedoes, and no one can be sure of what exactly happened inside the warheads.

The Germans hit upon the idea of sowing mixed minefields with both magnetic and moored mines. These required tricky sweeping techniques. They reversed polarity to catch ships that had been 'over-de-gaussed'. Delayed-action fuses kept the mines inactive for a period; thus sweeping would be without result.

Then came acoustic mines, which had to be swept with noisy 'hammer boxes'. There were double fuses that would work only when two triggers were activated, such as noise and polarity. But by the summer of 1940 the magnetic mine had ceased to be a real danger.

On 7 May 1940 a new threat arose. A modified version of the BM 1000, intended as a sea mine in the Clyde, overshot and landed on the Clydeside hills near Dumbarton. These ingenious dual-purpose 'bomb mines' were fitted with Rheinmetall inertia fuses when used against land targets. Falling into water at least 24 feet deep they functioned as a magnetic mine; on soft mud or in shallow water they would self-destruct. They would also self-destruct (by means of a hydrostatic valve) when the water pressure lessened, as it would when they were lifted to the surface. It was an example of German thoroughness that, despite all the foregoing precautions, the BM 1000 also incorporated one of the most cunning booby traps ever built. A set of photo-electric cells connected to a detonator would explode the bomb if light got inside it. This was a way of killing any bomb team who got to see the workings. By amazing luck, the bomb found at Dumbarton had suffered a circuit failure.[4]

A few months later this sort of bomb-mine was extensively used during the night bombing of London. They parachuted down and caused widespread destruction without forming a crater. Londoners found it easy to recognize the results and called them 'land mines'.

The menace of the magnetic mine had been overcome by the scientists, and this was the important fact. Before the war the admirals and generals in Whitehall had showed little interest in science and technology, but success with the magnetic mine changed that attitude. According to Dr C. F. Goodeve, who was a physicist and RNVR officer: 'it was the first technical battle in which we won a decisive victory over the enemy; but more important still, it was one which brought science fully into the war in the very early days.'[5]

In Germany the Nazis had broken with the nineteenth- and early twentieth-century tradition of political encouragement and social respect for science and its practitioners, and there was little or no collaboration between the scientists and the military until the end of 1943, when German scientists were invited to help with the Battle of the Atlantic. Even then they were simply asked to identify Allied radio and radar transmissions.

But Nazi distrust of science and top-level obstruction of research did not change the way in which German industry employed men who knew how to apply science and engineering to design and production. The magnetic mine provides a good example of the excellence of German design. The only reason for the mine's failure to cripple British shipping was that Germany went to war with only 1,500 of them in stock. After the first sequence of minelaying operations, the Germans had to wait until March 1940 for more to be manufactured.[6] It was this respite that saved Britain's defences from being overwhelmed, and provided an interval during which the menace could be countered.

Admiral Dönitz at his command post

From its creation, the German U-boat arm had its most important bases at Kiel and Wilhelmshaven, in that flat and lonely part of Germany that has long belonged to the German navy. To get to the Atlantic shipping, U-boats had to negotiate the narrow sea lane between Scotland and Norway. Worse, German coastal regions were shallow and could be mined. So, as soon as France was defeated, Admiral Dönitz moved his submarine fleet to its west coast which faced directly to the Atlantic. It was done with remarkable speed and efficiency. On his own initiative, Captain Godt, chief of staff to Dönitz, dispatched workmen from the Germania construction yards at Kiel, and selected men from the flotilla commands. A train loaded with fuel, torpedoes, supplies and paperwork departed from Wilhelmshaven on the day following the French armistice. Less than three weeks later, the *U-30*, commanded by Kapitän-leutnant Lemp, was in Lorient, loading torpedoes. One account records that:

> The advance guard of the flotilla staff had moved into the French Naval Préfecture at Lorient. They had plenty of booty – uniforms, footwear, equipment – some of it bearing the names of British and American firms and the date 1918: there were piles of tropical kits, arms, ammunition, food, and a thousand and one items which the enemy had had no time to destroy . . . And now the flotilla depot was there, with everything one's heart could desire – transport, fuel, money; only the sanitary

arrangements left something to be desired, but that was soon rectified.[7]

After a brief spell in Boulevard Suchet, Paris, Dönitz set up his headquarters in Kernéval, near Lorient, on 1 September 1940. His commandeered villa near the sea at Lamorplage had belonged to a sardine merchant. Sheltered by trees, it had a view towards Port Louis and the old fort at the harbour entrance. From here Dönitz could watch his U-boats as they came into the harbour and tied up at the wooden prison ship *Isère* which had once been used to transport French convicts to Devil's Island in French Guiana. Now it was the first and last mooring for each U-boat that went on an operational trip. Comrades, female naval telegraphers and other well-wishers would gather on the *Isère*; sometimes a military band played patriotic songs and marches. U-boats departing had their crews paraded on deck; those arriving would often be flying the home-made pennants that denoted the tonnage of their victims.[8]

One room in the Dönitz mansion was called 'the museum'. Here, by means of charts, diagrams and the graphs he liked so much, he could see, or show others, the progress of the submarine war measured by such things as the Allied tonnage sunk per operational U-boat day at sea. Here were the turn-round times and the changing enemy tactics and routes. The next room – his 'situation room' – had a big plotting table and walls covered with maps and charts. Pins showed the positions of the U-boats and of convoys and RN units, and even – thanks to the men of B-Dienst – the places where the British believed the U-boats to be! There were air-reconnaissance photos and, from secret agents, reports of the sailing of individual ships or convoys. On the map could be seen the way in which long-range Sunderland aircraft were being sighted further and further west. Dönitz described the room in which he spent so many hours:

> The maps were supplemented by a number of diagrams showing the differences between our local time and that in the various areas of operations, charts showing tides and currents and ice and fog conditions with special reference to the north-west Atlantic ... A large globe more than three feet in diameter gave a realistic picture of the wide Atlantic as it really is and was of great assistance in determining distances which could be worked out only approximately on ordinary charts, which, where great distances are concerned, make no allowance for the curvature of the earth's surface.[9]

On that first day of September 1940 his charts showed that his
U-boat losses to date – 28 – exactly equalled the number of new
boats commissioned in the same period. That still left him fewer
than at the start of the war because of the needs of training, repairs,
trials and shakedowns. Of his 27 operational U-boats only seven
or eight would be at sea on an average day, too few for Dönitz
to operate the sort of 'wolf-pack' tactics he wanted, though sometimes several boats could be brought together to converge on a
target.

The chart recording his successes would have shown an aircraft-
carrier, a battleship, three destroyers, two submarines, five auxiliary cruisers and 440 merchant ships estimated at a total 2,330,000
tons. Dönitz used tonnage sunk per U-boat day at sea as a measure
of the U-boat arm's efficiency. By this measure October 1940 was
the peak of his success, with five and a half ships sunk each month
per U-boat at sea. (The high figures achieved later in the war were
sinkings by larger numbers of boats, and Dönitz remained acutely
aware of his failure to get back to his 1940 peak.)

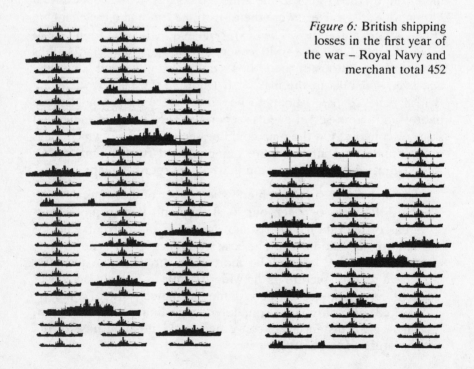

Figure 6: British shipping
losses in the first year of
the war – Royal Navy and
merchant total 452

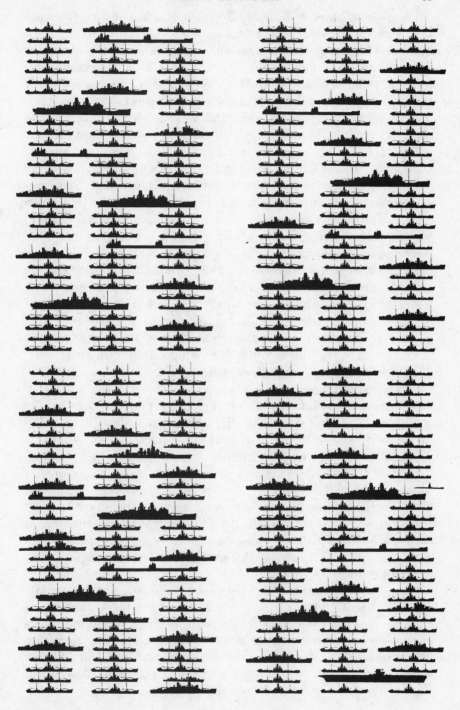

The French bases at Lorient, Brest, St Nazaire and La Rochelle were near deep water and difficult for the British to mine. RAF Bomber Command did not mount an all-out bombing campaign against them until it was too late. For in 1941, at Hitler's command, concrete shelters were constructed over the pens and made so thick and strong that normal RAF bombs had little effect. Virtually indestructible, these pens are still there today. The French show perverse pride in them and permit only their own citizens to look inside.

The Germans also had the benefit of skilled French technicians. Delighting their German masters, the French shipyard workers laboured even harder than their counterparts in Germany. They reduced the turn-around time that U-boats spent in port by no less than 22 per cent. 'Until this time two and a half boats had been in port for every submarine at sea and the French helped to reduce this figure to a ratio of 1.8:1.'[10]

As German armies consolidated their conquest of France and the Low Countries in the summer of 1940, the British kept many destroyers and other craft in base, ready to repel an invasion of their islands. Convoys sailed with few escorts, and for much of the crossing had to manage without protection. Out in the North Atlantic the U-boats were sinking merchant ships at a dismaying rate. U-boat commanders, with their battered hats and white roll-neck sweaters, were coming home from patrol to report the sinking of forty or fifty thousand tons of shipping. These undersea aces got the same sort of film star treatment in Germany that the Spitfire pilots (often with similarly battered hats and similar white roll-neck sweaters) were enjoying in Britain. U-boat crews were cosseted. French resort hotels were converted to rest homes for them, or they could return to Germany on the special U-boat train that went backwards and forwards with supplies, ammunition and spare parts. If they stayed near their bases, their high pay (with double pay for each day in the Atlantic operational zone) ensured their warm welcome in restaurants, nightclubs and brothels despite their reputation for boisterous behaviour.

From the bases in France U-boat men could strike at ships bringing fuel, wheat and war supplies to Britain from the United States and Canada, as well as beef from South America, while the routes of vital ore from South Africa and oil from Nigeria were almost on their doorstep. The African convoys were seeking safety further west and the transatlantic routes were going ever more northwards into icy seas. The U-boats followed them.

Aircraft: the lonely sea and the sky

Until war started, the British had given little thought to the weapons needed if aircraft were to sink submarines. The Blackburn Kangaroo, a twin-engined biplane used against U-boats in the final weeks of the First World War, could carry four 250-lb bombs. The twin-engined Avro Anson, which in 1939 comprised well over half of RAF Coastal Command's aircraft, could carry only four 100-lb bombs. Although these were specially designed anti-submarine bombs their efficiency had never been properly tested. The first chance to measure Coastal Command's anti-submarine bombs came on 5 September 1939, two days into the war, when an Anson of 233 Squadron dropped two 100-lb bombs on a submarine that surfaced off the coast of Scotland. The bombs bounced off the water and exploded in mid-air, causing enough damage to bring the Anson down into St Andrews Bay. The submarine proved to be one of the Royal Navy's fleet.

A few days later, on 14 September, two Blackburn Skua dive-bombers from the aircraft-carrier HMS *Ark Royal* attacked the *U-30* which had surfaced alongside the freighter *Fanad Head* while a German boarding party searched for food (the U-boat rations had gone mouldy) prior to opening its sea valves to sink it. Again the anti-submarine bombs exploded in the air, bringing down both planes. The U-boat crew, commanded by Kapitänleutnant Lemp, rescued two of the aviators and then dived with them as prisoners. The next day another Anson was damaged by its own bombs without causing damage to the target. A year later, on 25 October 1940, three Hudson bombers from 233 Squadron subjected the *U-46* to a concentrated attack in which one 100-lb anti-submarine bomb scored a direct hit. The U-boat's pressure hull remained intact and the vessel managed to get back to port.

It is no surprise to learn that the first U-boat sinking from the air was carried out by Bomber Command using ordinary 250-lb general purpose bombs. A Bristol Blenheim on an armed reconnaissance went dangerously low to deliver a determined attack upon *U-31*, which on that day, 11 March 1940, was undergoing sea trials off Heligoland Bight. One, perhaps two bombs, hit the hull. Everyone aboard, including many dockyard workers, died though the hull was salvaged, refitted and went back into action. At last, a month later, a Fairey Swordfish flying off HMS *Warspite* did manage to score with two 100-lb anti-submarine bombs, sinking the *U-64* at anchor.

In view of the ineffectiveness of the anti-submarine bombs, the airmen decided to throw at the enemy the only other anti-submarine weapon available: the depth charge designed in the First World War. This thin metal drum, packed with explosive, had an adjustable fuse which detonated according to water pressure. A nose and tail were fitted and it was dropped with reasonable success on practice targets, although only large aircraft could carry the depth charge since it weighed 450 lb. Altogether different to the bomb, it was designed to go into the water alongside the target rather than strike it (those that hit a submarine seldom exploded), and since the explosion took place underwater it posed far less danger to the airmen. But such depth charges were not in general supply until the summer of 1941.

In 1939 both sides were acutely short of large long-range aircraft. The Luftwaffe had been forced to use a civil airliner, the Fw 200C Condor, a beautiful machine that in August 1938 had flown non-stop from Berlin to New York and back at an average speed of 205 mph. Pressed into use for long-range maritime reconnaissance, the Condor was not rugged enough for the rigours of military flying.

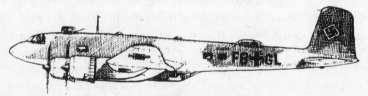

Figure 7: Focke-wulf Fw 200C Condor

The RAF had the equally fine Short Sunderland flying boat, a four-engined machine with a crew of anything up to 13. It came complete with kitchen and beds. Although it looked like the same manufacturer's civil flying boat, this aircraft was built to a military specification and so was much better suited to a military role than the adapted Condor. One Sunderland, forced down on to a very rough Atlantic, with winds gusting up to 100 mph, remained afloat for the nine hours that it took HMAS *Australia* to arrive and rescue its crew.

The Sunderland had won headlines a few days after war began when two of them landed on the sea and rescued the 34-man crew of a torpedoed tramp steamer. Any flying boat – let alone one with a crowd of unscheduled passengers – is difficult to unstick from open water. It was a remarkable feat of airmanship, and seaman-

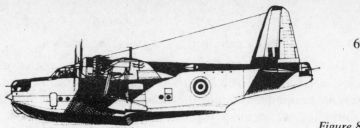

Figure 8:
Short Sunderland flying boat

ship too. With a range of almost 3,000 miles at 134 mph the Sunderlands would no doubt have seriously depleted the U-boat flotillas if suitable bombs or depth charges had been available in the early days of the Atlantic battle.

Since 1936 the United States navy had been using as their patrol plane a reliable two-engined flying boat which the RAF called a 'Catalina' after an island near Consolidated's San Diego plant. The RAF ordered 30 of these aircraft in 1939 and they began arriving in 1941. It was one of these flying boats that sighted the *Bismarck* on 26 May 1941. The pilot who shadowed the German battleship was actually on a check flight with a US navy instructor aboard.[11] They were flying out of Lough Erne in Northern Ireland, which in great secrecy had already been allotted funds and materials for conversion to a US naval air base. The official account of the interception seems to have had some expletives deleted:

> I was in the second pilot's seat when the occupant of the seat beside me, an American, said 'What the devil's that?' I stared ahead and saw a dull black shape through the mist which curled above a very rough sea. 'Looks like a battleship,' he said. I said: 'Better get closer. Go round its stern.' ... two black puffs appeared outside the starboard wing tip. In a moment we were surrounded with black puffs. Stuff began to rattle against the hull. Some of it went through and a lot more made dents in it ... The only casualties occurred in the galley, where one of the crew who was washing up the breakfast things dropped two china RAF plates and broke them.[12]

Figure 9:
Consolidated
Catalina
flying
boat

During the *Bismarck* surveillance a Catalina created a Coastal Command record of 27 hours of continuous reconnaissance. The Cat was remembered by those who flew it for its particularly good auto-pilot, which made it possible to endure long hours at the controls of this heavy machine – patrols regularly lasted 17 hours – and meant there could be an extra pair of eyes watching for U-boats. Later, at the direct instruction of President Roosevelt, these flying boats were joined by another Consolidated aircraft: the B-24J Liberator, a four-engined aircraft with extra fuel tanks fitted. Able to carry antenna, radar sets, bombs, depth charges and even search-lights, the Liberator played a vital part in narrowing that mid-Atlantic 'gap'.

Long-range flying was pioneered during the war by hastily trained young men plucked from civilian jobs. RAF Sunderlands flew a thousand miles out over the Atlantic, and did it day after day. When America entered the war Boeing B-17 Flying Fortress pilots, at the end of their US army air force training, flew their Forts to Britain. It was a Catalina delivered to Australia that made the third air crossing of the Pacific. In normal times these events would have made newspaper headlines.

Maritime patrol aircraft needed a very long range, for they had to reach the convoys far out in the ocean before work could start. Once in place, their chief value arose from the fact that U-boats had to remain below when aircraft were present, or risk being bombed. Even a slow 7-knot convoy would soon outdistance a submerged submarine, and a submerged submarine could be detected on asdic. The start of a convoy's trouble came when one of a rake of submarines spotted smoke, began trailing it at a distance, and then transmitted signals to bring others. A U-boat forced to submerge might well lose contact with the convoy and would have to cease transmitting.[13]

An unforeseen dimension of the encounter between aircraft and submarine was the fact that land-based aircraft could not pick up survivors in the sea. This brought an unexpected outcome in August 1941 when a Lockheed Hudson bombed *U-570* in the open sea to the south of Iceland. The U-boat was one of the large long-range Type IXC vessels that were notorious for the way in which sea water came over the conning tower at above-average speeds or in rough weather. The bombs damaged *U-570* enough for seawater to get to the batteries and create deadly chlorine gas: a constant worry for all submarine crews. The U-boat crew signalled surrender with the captain's white shirt and then found a white board and waved that too. The Hudson circled with guns trained, not realizing that the U-boat could not dive again. While circling the pilot suggested that his co-pilot parachute down as a prize crew, 'but he didn't fancy it' he joked in a BBC broadcast. A Catalina arrived and the Hudson signalled: 'Look after our sub, it has shown the white flag.' Ships sent to rescue the submariners arrived just before nightfall and took the U-boat in tow until eventually it ran aground off Iceland. It was refitted and put into action by the Royal Navy as HMS *Graph*.

Boffins join the navy

During the 1930s scientists in Germany, France, the USA and Britain, working independently and in secret, discovered that a beam of very short pulses, sent and reflected from a target back to a cathode ray tube, would define that object's bearing and range. It was not advanced technology, and it certainly wasn't a British invention. Even the Russian armed forces were equipped with radar by the time war began.

The German battleship *Graf Spee* had excellent gun-laying radar and the *Scharnhorst* and *Gneisenau* both used radar to evade HMS *Naiad* in January 1941. *Naiad*'s Type 279 radar was outranged by the German radar, so that after one brief visual sighting by the British (who never made radar contact) the German ships were able to keep clear of their pursuers. In the Norwegian campaign the same two German ships had surprised HMS *Renown* by using gun-laying radar to hit her while remaining concealed in a snow squall.

The Royal Navy began to equip its ships with Type 79 radar in 1939, although at the outbreak of war only HMS *Rodney* and HMS *Sheffield* had been fitted with it. These sets were intended for the location of enemy aircraft, and were given to the big ships and to anti-aircraft cruisers such as HMS *Curlew*, HMS *Carlisle* and HMS *Caracoa*. In May 1940 two hundred Type 284 (50-centimetre) gun-laying radar sets were ordered. New urgency was given to radar development when, in the Mediterranean in 1941, ships without it were found to be at a grave tactical disadvantage. The US navy had been fitting radar to its ships since 1940, and in the August of that year, long before the United States went to war, the USN and RN began to share their technology.

At the start of hostilities, German radar was more accurate and sophisticated than that of any other nation. The first radar success of the war was on 18 December 1939 when a formation of 22 RAF Vickers Wellington bombers was detected 70 miles off the German coast. Only ten of the bombers returned.

While British designers concentrated on longer-range sets, the Germans wanted accuracy and, where possible, mobility. In the summer of 1940 a German mobile unit on the Cherbourg peninsula fixed the position of an RN destroyer near the British coast and it was sunk by a Luftwaffe attack.

Radar – or Radio Direction Finding as the British called it at that time – was cumbersome, and the use of delicate glass vacuum tubes, known as valves, made it fragile. Such apparatus was regarded as a land-based, or shipborne, anti-aircraft weapon that could also be used against ships. It was probably the British who first tried another idea. A team under Dr Edward Bowen put an early EMI television receiver into an old Handley Page Heyford bomber and was encouraged by getting a flickered reception from a transmitter. From this they went on to design a small high-frequency set to go inside an Avro Anson aircraft. By 3 September 1937 it could detect big ships at about five miles.

The vital factor in the development of British radar was a willingness to improvise. Priority was given to radar – and other scientific ideas – when radar was credited with having saved Britain from defeat in the Battle of Britain. The Nazi creed gave emphasis to rural traditions and old 'Germanic' customs; and the political leaders of the Third Reich were apt to be antagonistic to modern science, sometimes defining it as Jewish. German scientists were not automatically exempted from military service, and civilian scientists assigned to work with the armed forces did not find the welcome that their British counterparts were given. Britain invented the technique of 'operational research', which meant scientists (cheerfully nicknamed 'boffins')[14] advising the armed forces on the most effective way to use existing weapons rather than having to devise new ones.

Operational research boffins demonstrated that you could double the size of a convoy without doubling the length of its perimeter; in fact the perimeter of an 80-ship convoy was only one seventh longer than a convoy of 40 ships. Thus big convoys meant more effective use of escort vessels. Moreover average losses decreased from 2.6 per cent to 1.7 per cent when convoys comprised more than 45 ships. This was partly due to the fact that a wolf pack's activities were limited by the availability of torpedoes, reloading time, stress and fatigue, whatever the size of the convoy.

Operational research also helped decide at what depth a depth charge should be set to explode. The scientists suggested that, given enough time, a U-boat crash-diving usually turned away to escape. Such targets should be abandoned as a lost cause. Depth charges dropped from aircraft should be set to explode near the surface, ensuring the more certain kill of those U-boats attacked early enough. Such ideas brought an immediate and dramatic benefit to British anti-submarine tactics.

When war began, Coastal Command had 12 Lockheed Hudson aircraft fitted with ASV (Air to Surface Vessel) Mark I radar. Better sets – fitted in the larger Armstrong Whitley bombers and Sunderland flying boats – followed. At its best, airborne radar could pick up a U-boat at 25 miles, but these valuable aircraft, with their ineffective anti-submarine bombs, seldom sank U-boats.

The boffins were asked why out of 77 U-boat sightings from aircraft in August and September 1941 only 13 were originated from airborne radar contact. The hastily built equipment was poorly serviced, they said, and operating it was a job assigned to anyone with time to spare. Better training gave aircrews faith in their equipment, and towards the end of 1941 airborne radar became more and more effective. Swordfish biplanes of 812 Squadron Fleet Air Arm showed what it could do by patrolling systematically by day and night against U-boats trying to get through the narrow Strait of Gibraltar in to the Mediterranean. One U-boat was sunk and five damaged so badly that they had to return to base.[15]

In addition, the Royal Navy's big ships were being fitted with its own more sophisticated gun-laying as well as air-warning radar, yet the range of British radar sets was still less than that of an alert lookout on a clear day. The urgent problem was to develop something that could be fitted into an escort vessel, such as a corvette, and detect the conning tower of a surfaced U-boat at night.

Dr S.E.A. Landale was one of the team that set up a short-wave centimetric radar on the cliffs at Swanage and traced a submarine seven miles away. He found practical difficulties when fitting his radar into a ship: 'Corvettes are very wet and in rough weather the discomforts, inconvenience and inflow of water whenever the office door was opened had to be experienced to be believed.'[16] Antenna systems had to be protected against the weather. More problems arose from the rolling and pitching and the effects of engine vibration and of gunfire. Even so, by the end of 1941 the Type 271 radar had been designed, one hundred were built and fifty ships were equipped with it. This was the first operational magnetron-powered centimetric radar in the world. In use it was a revelation: it could even locate the top of a periscope. No longer could a surfaced U-boat sail at night with impunity.

Fragile but lethal: U-boats at work

But in September 1940, long before such sophisticated devices played a part in the Battle, Admiral Dönitz became agitated enough to tell his staff that 'It will not be long before the entire U-boat fleet is lost on our own doorstep.' His distress was due to two factors which still today have scarcely been recognized, says one of the most reliable historians of the U-boat war, J.P.M. Showell. Dönitz was distressed about the number of boats lost to British submarines and mines while crossing the Bay of Biscay. The dangers of the Bay had led U-boat crews to call it Totenallee, or death row.

Leaving aside the efficacy of the mines and submarines, the fears that Dönitz showed were to have an immediate and immense effect upon the U-boat war, for he told his crews to send a radio signal as soon as they had traversed the Bay safely. This signal was transmitted when the U-boat passed the 10 degrees west line (later this was changed to 15 degrees west). The crews looked forward to this stage of the journey, for their daily rate of pay increased. The Admiralty's Submarine Tracking Room personnel also liked it for, using HF/DF, an exact longitude could now be added to an approximate latitude for every U-boat going on patrol. With this 'fix' pinned in to the map it was usually possible to guess which of the convoy routes the U-boat was heading for.

Operating with less than 30 U-boats, Dönitz was fretting for a chance to experiment with his 'wolf pack' tactics. His theories about surface engagements were confirmed. Nearly three-quarters of all successful torpedo attacks were made at night from surfaced U-boats which could not be detected by asdic apparatus. At this stage of the war there were vast areas of ocean where Allied aircraft were never seen, allowing U-boats to function more like torpedo boats than submarines.

Even without the men of B-Dienst the U-boat men could roughly estimate a probable convoy route. Dönitz would assign some his available U-boats to line up across it and wait on the surface, watching for a smudge of smoke on the horizon. When a convoy was sighted, the other U-boats would be called in. Some would be too far away, others would fail to find the rendezvous, but a force would assemble. After dark, without submerging, the U-boats sailed right through the columns of ships. Even on a dark night the sky is faintly visible, and from a conning tower it was usually possible to see the outlines of ships high above. On the other hand U-boats were small, and even in daylight the low silhouette of a conning tower was not easy to spot in the grey Atlantic water.

In October 1940 the experts at B-Dienst provided a map reference for the 35-ship convoy SC 7, a slow convoy out of Sydney, Nova Scotia, made up of five columns of four ships and, in the centre, three columns of five ships.[17] The columns were half a mile apart, each ship 600 yards from the one ahead. This typical broad-fronted rectangle was less likely to straggle and, since U-boats preferred to attack from the flank, it provided a smaller target than a long rectangle.

Thus convoy SC 7 covered an area of about five square miles and was protected by two sloops and a corvette. A gale came and the convoy straggled. Four Great Lakes steamers, not intended for Atlantic rollers, fell back and were lost (U-boats sank three of them). In looking for U-boats, one sloop lost contact and never found the convoy again. U-boats converged. Here was Günther Prien, who had crept into Scapa Flow to sink *Royal Oak*. Here was Joachim Schepke, adding up his score of sunken tonnage. Here was 'Silent Otto' Kretschmer, promptly sinking four ships and finishing the last one off with his 8.8-cm deck gun. The sinkings went on and on until 17 ships were lost and the convoy's passing was marked by survivors in open boats and drowned men floating amid the oil and wreckage. It was October, and in the northerly latitudes the convoys were forced to take the wind was bitterly cold, the seas heavy and the days short. Thirty minutes immersed in the North Atlantic was enough to kill most men. Survivors in an open boat had little chance of reaching land, or of sighting another ship.

The assembled U-boats, feasted and happy, were just in time to encounter the HX 79 (a fast convoy out of Halifax). That night 14 more ships went down. But the slaughter was not finished, for the U-boats found yet another convoy, HX 79A, and on that same night sank seven of them.

Before October was ended, there came another blow to Britain's maritime fortunes. A Focke Wulf Fw 200C Condor, far out over the ocean on a long route from Bordeaux to a base in Stavanger in Norway, spotted the Canadian-Pacific liner *Empress of Britain* about 70 miles from Donegal Bay in the north of Ireland. She was carrying servicemen and their families home to Liverpool. Captain Bernhard Jope of I/KG 40 group was at the controls of his four-engined plane and this was his first sortie. Bombs dropped from very low level set the liner afire and it was finished off by a U-boat's torpedoes. Jope received the Knight's Cross. After the war he became a Lufthansa captain.

The loss of the *Empress of Britain* was not an isolated incident. Aircraft played an important part in the battles of the sea lanes, and by war's end no less than 13 per cent of Allied shipping losses were attributed to air attack. (The U-boat arm accounted for 69 per cent of shipping losses; surface raiders and mines for 7 per cent; navigational hazards and reasons unknown for 4 per cent.)

The bombing of the convoys prompted Churchill to increase the air patrols around northern Ireland but they remained inadequate. A more desperate measure was to shoot a Hawker Hurricane fighter plane from a small platform fitted to a tanker's deck. After combat the pilot was instructed to ditch his plane into the sea near the convoy and be rescued. It was a grim prospect. The first catapult-equipped ship sailed for New York in May 1941 but was the victim of a U-boat. The first kill by such a 'Hurricat' was not until August. Few German planes fell victim to the new device. The MSFU (Merchant Ship Fighter Unit) was a deterrent rather than a weapon, and as the word spread that convoys could produce this spiteful jack-in-the-box, the long-range Condors grew more wary.

Of course not every convoy was attacked from the air or by U-boat. A German historian thinks about nine out of every ten convoys escaped. But there were not many sailors who spent six months at sea without seeing flashes and flames in the night, and a dawn that exposed spaces in their ranks. Only a few sailors took off their shoes – let alone any other articles of clothing – when they went to sleep.

The battle at its peak

After a slow start in 1941 the U-boat building programme began to bear fruit. By the end of the year Dönitz had 247 boats to command. His losses were going up slowly: 9 in 1939; 26 in 1940; 38 in 1941. His building rate was 64, 54, 202.

In the opening months of 1941 the long-range German reconnaissance aircraft showed their teeth. In January aircraft sank 20 ships, while U-boats sank 21. In February the U-boats sank 39 ships while aircraft added 27 and surface raiders brought the total to over one hundred (and over 400,000 tons for the first time since October 1940). More than half the ships lost during this period were stragglers, alone and defenceless.

Dönitz calculated that sinkings (including those by the Luftwaffe) must reach 750,000 tons before Britain could be forced to surrender. The British set the red-line at 600,000 tons. On the charts at his headquarters at Kernéval, the rate of Allied sinkings for early 1941 was shown as 400,000 tons per month. In fact his captains – awarded medals on the basis of tonnage sunk – were giving him outrageous estimates of the size of their victims.[18] But the losses were grave nevertheless, especially when augmented by the depredations of aircraft and surface raiders (see Table 1).

Table 1   *Allied shipping losses May–Nov. 1941 (total gross register tonnage)*

	Claimed	Actually sunk
May	421,440	367,498
June	441,173	328,219
July	227,699	105,320
August	168,734	83,427
September	399,775	207,638
October	601,569	370,345
November	85,811	68,549

In the early part of 1941 RAF Coastal Command was put under the operational control of the navy, and a reconnaissance squadron was sent to be based in Iceland. British air activity, as little as it was, persuaded Dönitz that he too must have air cover for his submarines. He had the experienced bomber group I/KG 40 put at his disposal. After January 1941 Condor aircraft regularly ranged far out into the Atlantic between Bordeaux and Stavanger in Norway. As time went on, Allied ships had enough anti-aircraft weapons to deter bombing attacks. It then became the task of these four-engined planes to scout specific convoy routes, provide Atlantic weather reports and cooperate with the U-boats.

In fact there were too few Condors to make much difference, and despite using radio beacons, few Luftwaffe navigators could pinpoint a position exactly enough to bring a U-boat within sighting distance of a convoy. To add to the confusion, the Luftwaffe map grids did not tally with the navy's charts. At this time, anyone standing at the bar in a U-boat mess could get an easy laugh from any joke about 'air support'. The unseen value of aircraft in the Atlantic battle was the morale boost they gave to their own side and the disturbing sight they made for any enemy seaman.

At first the convoys outward-bound from Britain had been given RN escorts on only the first stage of their journey, about 15 degrees west longitude. Then the escorts stayed as far as 25 degrees west and then – by July 1941 – convoys were given continuous escort. Relays of escorts operated from Britain, from Iceland and from Newfoundland. But warships were scarce, so that even by the end of 1941 the average convoy had no more than two escort ships.

The escort ships were not immune to torpedoes either. I make no apologies for the extra length of this excerpt from one of the most graphic accounts the Atlantic battle provided:

> The sky suddenly turned to flame and the ship gave a violent shudder . . . Looking ahead, I could see something floating and turning over in the water like a giant metallic whale. As I looked it rolled over further still and I could make out our pennant numbers painted on it. I was dumbfounded. It seemed beyond reason. I ran to the after-side of the bridge and looked over. The ship ended just aft of the engine room – everything abaft that had gone. What I had seen ahead of us had really been the ship's own stern. There were small fires all over the upper deck. The First Lieutenant was down there organizing the fire parties. He saw me and called, 'Will you abandon ship, sir?' 'Not bloody likely, Number One . . . We'll not get out till we have to.'

But a ship with its stern blown away does not stay afloat for long:

> The deck began to take on an angle – suddenly – so suddenly. She was almost on her side. I was slithering, grasping all kinds of unlikely things. My world had turned through ninety degrees . . . I jumped for the galley funnel which was now parallel with the water and about two feet clear, and flat-footed it to the end. I paused at the end of my small funnel to look at the faces. They were laughing as if this were part of some gigantic fun fair. The men called to me.

'Come on, sir. The water's lovely.'

'I'm waiting for the Skylark,' I shouted back. But the galley funnel dipped and I was swimming too – madly . . . We swam like hell. I turned once more, but now there were very, very few bobbing heads behind me. I swam on. The destroyer of my old group was passing through us. I could see her men at action stations. They were attacking. They were attacking the wreck of the *Warwick!* I screamed at them in my frenzy. Wherever else the U-boat might have been it could not have been there. The depth charges sailed up in the air. Funny how they wobbled from side to side, I'd never noticed that before. When, I wondered, would they explode? It was like being punched in the chest, not as bad as I had expected. I swam on. Things were a bit hazy. I was not as interested in going places as I had been. I could only see waves and more waves, and I wished they would stop coming. I did not really care any more. Then I felt hands grasp my shoulders and a voice say, 'Christ, it's the skipper. Give me a hand to get the bastard in,' and I was dragged into a Carley-float which was more than crowded to capacity.[19]

To make the most of their pitifully few escorts, the RN had started 'Escort Groups', which usually meant in effect nothing more than RN captains getting together – under one of their number named as escort group commander – to exchange ideas about anti-submarine tactics.

It was the 5th Escort Group which in March 1941 was in the same area as the German navy's three most famous U-boat captains: Günther Prien, Joachim Schepke, the celebrated and colourful captain of *U-100*, and Otto Kretschmer of *U-99*. At their collars these men wore the Ritterkreuz, to which the insignia of the oak leaves had been added to celebrate 200,000 tons of ships sunk. Kretschmer and Schepke were both determined to be the first to sink 300,000 tons of Allied shipping. Kretschmer had left his base at Lorient credited with 282,000 tons (although, as we have seen, such German figures were usually very much inflated).

It was Prien in *U-47* who sighted the outward-bound convoy OB 293 and summoned his colleagues: Kretschmer, Matz in *U-70* and Hans Eckermann in *UA*.[20] Although a primitive seaborne radar set played its part, this encounter marked little change in the methods or technology of either side. But there was a change in the men: the Germans, solidly professional, were at the zenith of over-confidence, while the Royal Navy's landlubbers and weekend yachtsmen had discovered a new determination.

Kretschmer started the sinkings. Firing while surfaced, he hit a tanker which burst into flame and a Norwegian whaling ship *Terje Viken* which remained afloat. Using the same tactics in *U-70*, Matz hit a British freighter and the *Mijdrecht*, a tanker, which with true Dutch resilience steered at him and rammed as *U-70* dived. The *UA* was detected and dived, its course followed by asdic. Depth charges damaged it enough to make the German set course for home.

Matz in *U-70* had submerged. He now came under coordinated attacks from two corvettes. Wallowing and unstable he went to 650 feet: far deeper than the submarine was designed to endure. The damage sustained from the Dutchman which rammed him, together with the depth-charging, started leaks and made the U-boat impossible to control. Despite the crew's efforts the *U-70* surfaced and was fired upon. The crew surrendered as the stricken boat reared, bow in the air, and slid under, taking 20 of the crew with it.

Even the stubborn Kretschmer dived deep and sat 'in the cellar'. He watched the rivets pop and the lights flicker as the explosions came and went. Carefully he withdrew, with half his torpedoes still unused. The convoy sailed on, having lost two ships and had two damaged.

Prien followed the convoy and tried again at dusk, his approach covered in fitful rainstorms. But in a clear patch he was spotted by a lookout on HMS *Wolverine* and his crash dive failed to save him from the depth charges that damaged his propeller shafts. Instead of turning for home, he surfaced after dark for another attack, perhaps not realizing how clearly the damaged propellers could be heard on the asdic. This time *Wolverine*, which had tenaciously waited in the vicinity, made no mistake. As the U-boat crash-dived, an accurately placed depth charge caused the submarine to explode under water, making a strange and awful orange glow. 'The hero of Scapa Flow has made his last patrol,' said the obituary notice personally dictated by Admiral Dönitz when, after 76 days had passed, they finally told the German public of their hero's death. Even then stories about him having survived circulated for months afterwards.

A few days later on 15 March 1941, south of Iceland, Fritz-Julius Lemp, now promoted to Korvettenkapitän, signalled the approach of a convoy. It was an attractive target but the escort was formidable. The escort commander was Captain Macintyre RN, who was to become the war's most successful U-boat hunter. He was in an old First World War destroyer, HMS *Walker*. There were four other old destroyers with him, and two corvettes. The homeward convoy HX 112 consisted of almost 50 ships, in ten columns half a mile apart. They were heavily laden tankers and freighters, and even in this unusually calm sea they could make no more than 10 knots (11.5 mph).

Lemp's sighting signal was intercepted by direction-finding stations in Britain. Such plots could only be approximate, but Captain Macintyre was warned that U-boats were probably converging on HX 112. Without waiting for other U-boats, Lemp's *U-110* surfaced and used darkness to infiltrate the convoy. Two torpedoes from his bow tubes missed, but one from his stern hit *Erodona*, a tanker carrying petrol, and the sea around it became a lake of flames.

The next day other U-boats arrived. The uncertainties of U-boat operations are illustrated by the way in which *U-74* never found the rendezvous and *U-37*, having surfaced in fog, was run down by a tanker and had to return to base for repairs. But Schepke (*U-100*) and Kretschmer (*U-99*) provided enough trouble for the resourceful Captain Macintyre. Having spotted Schepke's boat, the escorts started a systematic search which kept it submerged and allowed the convoy to steam away. At this stage of the war the escorts had not discovered that U-boats impudently infiltrated the convoys to fire at point-blank range. The search for the attackers always took place outside the convoy area. So the chase after Schepke was Kretschmer's opportunity to penetrate the columns of the virtually unprotected convoy, and at 2200 hours there was a loud boom which marked the beginning of an hour during which Kretschmer hit six ships. Five of them sank. The hunt for Schepke's *U-100* was abandoned as the escorts closed upon their charges.

Schepke's *U-100*, damaged by the continuous attacks, soon caught up with the convoy. Although a surfaced submarine was immune to asdic, it was vulnerable to detection by radar, and despite the darkness he'd been detected a mile away by a primitive Type 271 radar set aboard the escort HMS *Vanoc*. A surfaced submarine, if spotted, did not have much time in which to dive to safety. This was Schepke's predicament as *Vanoc* was suddenly seen accelerating to full speed. As she sped past HMS *Walker*, the escort commander ordered a signal made to caution her about speeding. He received the reply 'have rammed and sunk U-boat.' By that time the shriek of the destroyer's bow tearing through the steel U-boat came echoing through the night air. Schepke and the duty watch standing on the tower were all crushed and lost. Someone below gave the order to crash-dive but depth charges ripped the hull open and *U-100* sank with all but seven of its crew.

While *Vanoc* was repairing its damage, and picking up German survivors, HMS *Walker*'s asdic showed another U-boat nearby, and then the set broke down. This brief encounter was with Kretschmer's *U-99*. It was surfaced and heading home under cover of darkness. Kretschmer was below. On the conning tower there was the usual complement of four men: an officer, a petty officer and two ratings. Each man was assigned a quarter of the horizon to watch through his Zeiss 7×50 binoculars. Lighter, smaller and more waterproof than RN binoculars, such glasses were coveted by every Allied sailor who saw them. The officer occasionally swept the entire horizon: it was the routine. Suddenly they came upon the warships that had sunk Schepke's boat. One of them was searching for survivors. One of the German lookouts on *U-99* saw the moonlight reflecting off a gun turret: it was a destroyer about 100 yards away. Had they done nothing they would probably have escaped – standing orders said submarines sighting the enemy at night must stay surfaced – but the submariners were tired. Thinking he'd been seen, and contrary to orders, the officer on watch dived the *U-99*, and it was then that *Walker*'s asdic operator saw it briefly before his screen went blank.

The *Walker*'s depth charge attack had to rely upon skill, instinct and practice. Those first explosions brought Kretschmer's damaged boat to the surface. Both destroyers opened fire. 'With an understandable enthusiasm,' rescued merchant seamen taken on board the *Walker* piled up so much ammunition around the guns as to cause confusion.

Kretschmer was forced back to the surface. All torpedoes expended and his boat crippled, he realized that his career was at an end, but his tonnage claims were foremost in his mind. He ordered his radio operator to send a message claiming 50,000 tons of shipping and telling Dönitz that he was a prisoner of war. When Kretschmer saw *Walker* lowering a boat he took it to be an attempt to capture his submarine. He sent his engineer officer to flood the aft ballast tanks so that the U-boat would sink stern-first. It reared up suddenly and steeply, and slid back into the ocean, leaving the crew swimming. When he climbed aboard the ship that rescued him Kretschmer still had his binoculars round his neck and wore the white-topped hat that had become a captain's prerogative in the U-boat service. All but three of the U-boat's crew were saved, but the engineer officer was one of those lost. Captain Macintyre, the escort commander, used Kretschmer's Zeiss binoculars for the rest of the war.

Kretschmer, a prisoner aboard HMS *Walker*, remarked to George Osborne, her chief engineer, upon the coincidence that both ship and submarine had a horseshoe badge but one was the wrong way up. It was explained to him that in Britain a horseshoe pointing down is considered bad luck. An eyewitness said 'it brought a rueful laugh from our prisoner.'

A destroyer was a cramped place, even without shipwrecked seamen and enemy prisoners aboard, and there was evidence of bad feeling. But the master and chief officer of *J.B.White*, a sunken merchant ship, and Otto Kretschmer an unrepentant Nazi, were persuaded by the chief engineer to join him in a game of contract bridge. Osborne said it was the only decent game he managed to get in the entire war.

Germany had lost her three U-boat aces and the Propaganda Ministry discovered that stardom for fighting men is a two-edged weapon. The loss of three 'experts' made Dönitz suspect that the British must have some new secret weapon. But then he changed his mind and decided it was just bad luck.

Dönitz had been right with his first guess. HMS *Vanoc* had used a primitive radar set, and in this same month, March 1941, a far more sophisticated 10-centimetre set was being tested at sea. It was the cavity magnetron which made such advanced radar possible and put the British work far ahead of the Germans. But in the summer of 1941 the range at which radar gave the first indication of an enemy's presence was not always better than an alert observer could provide on a clear day. In May 1941 the pursuit of the *Bismarck* provided a better example of the contribution radar played in the naval encounters of that period.

5 WAR ON THE CATHODE TUBE

When snatched from all effectual aid,
We perished, each alone:
But I beneath a rougher sea,
And whelmed in deeper gulfs than he.

William Cowper, 'The Castaway'

THE BATTLESHIP *Bismarck* had been launched by the grand-daughter of Germany's great nineteenth-century German chancellor in February 1939. Commissioned in August 1940, it was the most modern and powerful battleship afloat, with eight 15-inch guns in four turrets controlled by the world's best gun-laying radar.

Admiral Raeder's original plan called for *Bismarck* and the heavy cruiser *Prinz Eugen* to sail from the Baltic, while the battleships *Scharnhorst* and *Gneisenau* would sally into the Atlantic from Brest in France. In mid-ocean this powerful force would rendezvous to form a fighting fleet powerful enough to sink convoys, and defeat any escort force they might encounter.[1] This operational plan was code-named Rheinübung, Rhine Exercise, and Raeder saw it as a way of providing a big victory of the sort that 'battleship admirals' still cherished, while continuing the battle of the sea lanes that was obviously the key to victory. He knew that Hitler would invade Russia soon, and Rheinübung had to be staged before the army's needs on the Eastern Front took precedence over everything the navy wanted.

Rheinübung was put under the command of Admiral Günther Lütjens, a bony-faced man with close-cropped hair and a permanent frown. The operation was thwarted when it was found impossible to have the *Scharnhorst*'s high-pressure turbine engines ready in time. Such engines were a notable and chronic failing in German marine engineering. Then, when *Gneisenau* was hit by a desperately brave attack by a Coastal Command torpedo aircraft in Brest Roads, Raeder decided stubbornly to go ahead using only *Bismarck* and *Prinz Eugen*. This plan too was delayed when *Prinz Eugen* was damaged by a British magnetic mine in the Baltic, thus losing the advantage of a month's dark winter nights which would have made it much easier to slip past the Royal Navy.

In May 1941, Hitler was persuaded to make the trip to Gotenhafen (the now renamed Polish port of Gdynia) to inspect his new battleship and address the crew. That evening he dined with his senior officers aboard the *Tirpitz*. Hitler had doubts about the proposed expedition, but Admiral Lütjens reminded him of 'Operation Berlin'. In the first three months of the year Lütjens had taken *Scharnhorst* and *Gneisenau* into the Atlantic, causing the British great anxiety as well as sinking 115,600 tons of shipping. He told Hitler that *Bismarck* was unsinkable. 'Mein Führer, there is virtually nothing that can go wrong with a ship like this. The only danger that I can see is torpedo-aircraft coming at us from aircraft-carriers.' This prophetic caution was due to *Bismarck's* conservative design: its underwater protection had not kept pace with what was now considered essential for British and American ships.

For anyone who believes that the British reading of Enigma traffic provided a constant insight into German intentions, it has to be said that Bletchley Park provided nothing to suggest the *Bismarck* was about to put to sea. And none of the transmissions from *Bismarck* at sea were decrypted until after she was sunk. At that time naval Enigmas were taking anything from three to seven days to crack.

The first tip concerning *Bismarck's* movements was provided by Britain's naval attaché in Stockholm after a cruiser of neutral Sweden spotted 'two large warships' with escorts and air cover steaming through an area cleared of German shipping. Subsequently RAF Spitfires equipped for high-speed photo-reconnaissance scoured likely anchorages and found two German warships in Grimstad Fjord. Photographs revealed the *Bismarck* with an unidentified cruiser. It was alarming news and there were urgent requests for more information. Bad weather grounded RAF aircraft but a particularly daring Fleet Air Arm crew, flying a Martin Maryland that had been used for target-towing and had no navigational instruments or cameras, found an opening in the cloud above Grimstad Fjord at twilight without seeing the big ships. Just to make sure, they flew over Bergen and into a storm of German Flak. Their radio message said: 'Battleship and cruiser have left.'

Anxiously the men in the Admiralty looked at their maps: six homeward and six outward convoys were on the move, including a troop convoy to the Middle East with 20,000 men. Now earlier Luftwaffe Enigma signals, showing Fw 200C Condors on long-range

Figure 10:
The German
battleship
Bismarck

reconnaissance surveying the extent of the pack-ice in the Denmark Strait, began to make sense. RN warships – most of them with radar – were immediately dispatched to patrol the waters round Iceland and in particular the Denmark Strait where, even in May, pack-ice and RN minefields made navigation so restricted that if *Bismarck* went that way it was almost sure to be sighted.

At 1922 hours on 23 May, a lookout on HMS *Suffolk* spotted *Bismarck* and *Prinz Eugen* emerging from a snow-squall at a distance of 11 miles, before the *Suffolk*'s radar made contact. As soon as *Suffolk*'s operator had *Bismarck* on the screen of his Type 284 gun-laying radar she slipped back into the gathering darkness.

The two German ships had obviously seen *Suffolk* on their radar, so they were prepared when a second RN cruiser, HMS *Norfolk*, came close enough for its lookout to sight them (again before making radar contact).[2] *Bismarck* opened fire on her. Unhit, *Norfolk* promptly fell back. The *Bismarck*'s radio room intercepted *Norfolk*'s sighting report and was able to decode the message without difficulty or delay. They kept listening.

For ten hours the two RN cruisers shadowed their prey until powerful naval forces could be brought up from Scapa Flow in the Orkneys. HMS *Hood* and HMS *Prince of Wales*, with destroyer escorts, were ordered to sea from Iceland.

It was a strange twist of fortune that chose HMS *Hood* for this task force, for she was exactly comparable to *Bismarck* in main armament (eight 15-inch guns), secondary armament, speed, thickness of belt and turret armour. In the 1930s *Hood* had been the pride of the Royal Navy, the fastest, most powerful and arguably most beautiful ship afloat. She had spent so much time showing the flag that there never seemed to be an opportunity for the total overhaul and re-furbishing that was so badly needed. Nineteen years older than *Bismarck*, the *Hood*'s 15-inch guns remained unchanged in design since those of 1914, while the big guns of the *Bismarck* provided ex-cellent examples of the way in which gun technology had improved.

Hood was old, but with her was the brand-new *Prince of Wales*, which still had civilian contractors aboard, working on the gun-turret machinery of its ten 14-inch guns. This was a calibre new to the RN. Two of its three turrets had been fitted only four weeks earlier, and one gun was still not in use. The *Prince of Wales* had five of the best radar sets then available, but the warships were ordered to maintain radio and radar silence so that they would not be detected.

It was not easy to keep radar contact with an enemy warship which had excellent radar, eight 15-inch guns and a top speed of over 30 knots: as soon as you were close enough to see your prey on the radar screen, it had not only been watching you for a long time but was all ready to blow you to pieces. In addition the Germans were deciphering and reading all the radio traffic of their pursuers. It was hardly surprising that the two RN cruisers lost contact with both *Bismarck* and *Prinz Eugen*.

As day was breaking at 0530 hours on Saturday 24 May 1941 *Bis-marck* was sighted at 17 miles distance, again by a lookout, not by radar. On German radar the RN ships were clearly visible, and Admiral Lütjens must have been pleased to notice that their angle of approach made it possible for the British to use only forward arma-ment, while the Germans could fire broadsides from all their big guns. This dangerous British tactic can only be explained by the com-mander of the British force wanting to close quickly on the Germans because British deck armour was thin and vulnerable to plunging fire. Close range would ensure that German fire would hit only side armour.

Although *Hood*'s Type 284 radar was no use for ranges beyond 22,000 yards *Hood* opened fire at 26,500 yards. It aimed at the less dangerous *Prinz Eugen*, which had been mistaken for *Bismarck*. Then all the other big ships started firing. The *Prince of Wales*'s first salvo fell 1,000 yards beyond *Bismarck*.

The *Bismarck*'s first salvo was fired at the *Hood*, which was in the lead. Its improved Seetakt 90-cm radar provided the correct range but the shells fell ahead of *Hood* and she steamed into the spray they made. The second salvo from *Prinz Eugen* scored a direct hit on *Hood*. A shell burst on the upper deck, igniting anti-aircraft ammunition stored there in ready-use lockers. The midship section of *Hood* was soon enveloped in flames and giving off dense smoke. *Bismarck*'s third salvo was the high-trajectory fire to which British battleships were so vulnerable. Still today experts disagree on whether an armour-piercing shell penetrated the *Hood*'s thin deck armour to explode in an aft magazine or whether this 42,100-ton battleship was blown in two as a result of fires spreading to a magazine from the earlier hit. The explosion was horrendous. After separated bows and stern had risen high from the water, *Hood* disappeared leaving only a smoky haze over the disturbed water. An officer on a destroyer which went to pick up *Hood*'s survivors wrote:

> But where were the boats, the rafts, the floats? . . . And the men, where were the men? . . . far over to starboard we saw three men – two of them swimming, one on a raft. But on the chilling waters around them was no other sign of life.[3]

Of the crew of 1,419 men, only one midshipman and two ratings survived. The midshipman's survival was especially miraculous. He was in a spotting top, 140 feet above the water. He told his rescuers that 'he didn't know what the hell was happening, save that the compartment was filled mysteriously with water.'

Korvettenkapitän Jaspers, *Prinz Eugen*'s gunnery officer, who was watching the *Hood* said: 'The aft magazine blew up, shooting into the air a molten mass the colour of red lead, which then fell back lazily into the sea – it was one of the rear gun turrets . . . And in the midst of this raging inferno, a yellow tongue of flame shot out just once more: the forward turrets of *Hood* had fired one last salvo.'

Now the *Prince of Wales* became the target for both German ships. The compass platform was hit by a 15-inch shell. It didn't explode but fragments of the binnacle killed or wounded everyone there but the captain and the yeoman of signals. The difficulty of making shells that would penetrate thick steel and then explode was demonstrated now as six more German shells struck home, all of them detonating only partially or not at all. Undeterred, *Prince of Wales* continued on course until it had closed to 14,600 yards. Six salvoes were loosed at *Bismarck* before one of the shells found its mark, flooding the forecastle, rupturing one of the fuel tanks and disconnecting tanks forward of it, so that 1,000 tons of fuel were cut off. Two other shells had hit *Bismarck*: one damaged a dynamo, the other was a dud that glanced off the deck causing only slight damage.

Either ship might have gone on and destroyed its opponent but both had had enough. *Prince of Wales* was badly damaged as well as having trouble with the gun turrets. She turned away under a smoke screen.

In London, as in Berlin, the news that the action had been broken off was not welcomed. Churchill saw the prospect of a rampaging *Bismarck* as a direct challenge to Britain's traditional role, and feared that it would be 'trumpeted round the world to our great detriment and discomfort'. The disengagement was a 'bitter disappointment and grief to me'. Hitler felt the same way and said that *Bismarck* should have immediately dealt with the *Prince of Wales* too, and not run away.

Out in the cold grey ocean, *Prince of Wales* and *Norfolk* were joined by the carrier *Victorious*. So grave was the emergency that the carrier had been detached from escorting Troop Convoy WS 8B to the Middle East. These warships trailed the two Germans using the *Suffolk*'s radar to keep in contact, but again the operators found it difficult to keep radar contact at extreme range. That night the pursuers decided to use the carrier's aircraft in an attempt to slow the *Bismarck*.

With the equipment available at that time, carrier take-offs and landings at night were sometimes permitted in perfect weather. Now the carrier was pitching and rolling in a rising gale and rainstorms from low scudding clouds made visibility zero. The air crews were fresh from training school; some had never made a carrier take-off or landing before. (The desperate shortage of navy pilots had sent these aircrews to *Victorious* to be instructed while the carrier was on convoy duty.) It was 2200 hours (Double Summer Time), and light was changing and deceptive. Dutifully *Victorious* flew off a striking force of Swordfish torpedo-carrying biplanes and Fulmar fighters.

One of the Swordfish was equipped with an ASV MkII radar and its operator 'saw' a ship through cloud. But when the plane descended it was identified as a US coast guard cutter on Atlantic weather patrol. Now that the planes were below the cloud, they spotted *Bismarck* about six miles away, but the element of surprise was lost. It was through heavy gunfire – *Bismarck* had 84 anti-aircraft guns – that they made the slow, low, straight and steady approach that is required for torpedo dropping.

Despite the way in which the aircraft came in from different angles, *Bismarck* was able to swerve violently and avoid seven torpedoes. The eighth one hit the starboard side, near the bridge. This hit shifted one of the heavy side-belt armour plates but its backing of thick teak wood absorbed much of the armour's displacement. The *Bismarck* reported to Naval Group Command West that the torpedo had done no more than 'scratched the paintwork'. It had achieved more than that, but its immediate effect upon *Bismarck*'s performance was negligible.

To find a carrier at night over the ocean is a daunting task, and the *Victorious*'s homing beacon was not working. Upon hearing the planes returning the carrier's captain ordered searchlights on to help them, but they were swiftly doused on the repeated order of the vice-admiral. Despite the admiral's exaggerated caution, and with the help of the flight leader's ASV radar, the 'Stringbags' found their home ship again and landed in the dark. Not all the Fulmar aircraft were so lucky. It was midnight. The crews had had an eventful Saturday night out and a memorable introduction to carrier flying.

Bismarck was not slowed. When the Swordfish aircraft attacked, it had already parted company with *Prinz Eugen*. Now it turned southwest on a direct route for the Bay of Biscay and the French ports. The *Suffolk*, unready for such a move, lost both German ships on the radar, and when daylight came, more flights from the *Victorious* failed to discover any sign of the enemy. Low on fuel, the force – *Prince of Wales*, *Victorious* and *Suffolk* – turned west, still failed to find *Bismarck*, and soon headed for various ports to refuel.

There was no rejoicing aboard *Bismarck*. It was Sunday 25 May 1941 and the 52nd birthday of Admiral Lütjens. He addressed the ship's company, delivering a melancholy message of doing and dying. Gerhard Junack, one of the *Bismarck*'s engineer officers said: 'The admiral wished with these words to rid the crew of their over-exuberance and bring them into a more realistic frame of mind; but in fact he overdid it, and there was a feeling of depression among the crew which spread through all ranks from the highest to the lowest . . . The crew began to brood and neglected their duties.'

Examples of this neglect now played a vital part in the battle. Because *Bismarck*'s electronics specialists were still picking up radar impulses from *Suffolk* they didn't guess that *Suffolk*'s radar could not 'see' *Bismarck*'s pulses. *Bismarck*'s decrypt specialists were neglectful too. They were intercepting *Suffolk*'s regular radio transmissions, and failed to notice that the shadower was no longer sending position reports. And so it was that Admiral Lütjens didn't know that he had given the slip to his pursuers. He betrayed his position by sending a very long signal to the German Naval Command Group West (Paris). They replied telling him that the British cruisers had lost contact with him six and a half hours before.

Lütjens' long message gave the Royal Navy a chance to fix *Bismarck*'s position on the map, but owing to confusion and misunderstandings at the Admiralty – compounded by the fact that the flagship navigator used the wrong charts – the big ship was not found. In the ensuing muddle, signals from other ships were intercepted and plotted and declared to be *Bismarck*. The German navy's radio traffic looked identical as regards letter-grouping, spacing, serial numbers and so on. At 1320 on 25 May, when the search was at its most frantic, a signal from a U-boat was intercepted. The Admiralty intelligence officers decided that this was from the *Bismarck* pretending to be a U-boat, and using the U-boat radio signals and transmitting frequency.

The bungling began to be sorted out when these transmissions were compared with oscilloscope photos of the radio wave of *Bismarck*'s transmitter (taken when it passed Denmark on the outward leg). By that time *Bismarck*'s approximate position had been estimated by someone in signals intelligence who noticed the flurry of German naval signals was no longer coming from Wilhelmshaven; it was coming from Paris. This suggested that *Bismarck* could probably be found somewhere along the line from its last known position to one of the French ports.

Still it was only guesswork; the *Bismarck* might have escaped but for a curious misfortune. The only Enigma signals that the British could read regularly and quickly were those of the Luftwaffe.

In Athens in connection with the Crete invasion, the Luftwaffe's chief of staff, Hans Jeschonnek, worried about his youngest son who was in the crew of the *Bismarck*. Anxiously he called his staff in Berlin to ask what was happening to the ship. His staff in the Berlin Air Ministry found out and transmitted a radio signal (using Luftwaffe Enigma), telling him that his son's ship was heading for the west coast of France. It was a parent's anxiety that provided London with the information that settled the fate of the *Bismarck*.

An RAF flying boat crew of 209 Squadron, Lough Erne, Northern Ireland, and the flyers on the aircraft-carrier *Ark Royal* were briefed on the supposition that *Bismarck* was somewhere on a line drawn from there to Brest. It seems that no one at the Admiralty was aware that the only French port with a dry dock large enough to hold the *Bismarck* was St Nazaire.

It was 31 hours later, on 26 May, that a Catalina flying boat using ASV Mk II radar found *Bismarck*. About 45 minutes later a Sword-fish from the aircraft-carrier *Ark Royal* flew to the spot and confirmed the sighting. HMS *Sheffield*, equipped with an old Type 79 radar designed for air-warning, used it to make contact with the *Bismarck*, and trailed along waiting for *Ark Royal* and the battleship *Renown*.

With the end of the flight deck pitching 60 feet, and a wind over the deck recorder wavering between 45 and 55 knots, the deck crews readied the aircraft aboard *Ark Royal*. No one there had ever tried to fly-off planes in this sort of weather but there was no alternative. One Swordfish pilot gives us this account:

> Ranging the Swordfish that morning called for the strength of Hercules and the patience of Job. Time and time again, as the flight deck tilted at fantastic angles, a plane would slide bodily towards the catwalks, dragging with it forty to fifty ratings who were struggling to man-handle it aft. But somehow by 8.30 am ten planes were ranged and ready to fly off on a broad fronted search to locate *Bismarck*. At 8.35 am the carrier reduced speed and swung into the wind. [Deck officer] Traill choosing his moment carefully, dropped his flag, and aboard both *Ark Royal* and *Renown* ship's companies held their breath as the leading plane gathered way. Would she make it?
>
> As the flight deck tilted down, the take-off degenerated into a frantic, slithering glissade. It looked for one terrible moment as though the aircraft were plunging straight into the maw of an approaching wave. But Traill had timed his signal well. At the last second the deck swung up and the plane was flung off through the spume of a sixty-foot wave as it cascaded over the carrier's bow. And the almost unbelievable thing was this. The miracle was repeated not once, but nine times, until the whole of the searching force was airborne.[4]

The weather was foul, but the Swordfish made good radar contact from above cloud using ASV Mk II radar and launched a low-level attack that failed completely. The torpedoes were set to activate their magnetic pistols but most of them exploded as they hit the water; others dived and disappeared. This was just as well, for the ship they attacked was HMS *Sheffield*! 'Sorry about the kippers,' the attackers signalled the angry men aboard *Sheffield* as they flew back to their carrier. Three of the aircraft crashed on to the pitching deck.

The pilots of the 15-plane second strike were prudently ordered to locate HMS *Sheffield* first and then go to attack the *Bismarck*. And this strike force did not try the magnetic pistols again; its torpedoes were set to 'contact' and they would run at ten feet. It was old technology but more reliable. Three planes attacked just as *Bismarck* went into an evasive turn. One torpedo 'ripped a large hole in the stern structure beneath the steering room gear.' This probably weakened a weld aft of the transverse armoured bulkhead at Frame 10.[5] The immediate effect was damage to the starboard propellers and steering gear and a jammed rudder.

It was dark, late and overcast as the planes returned. All the Swordfish got back safely, although most of them had been damaged by gunfire and many were wrecked on landing. One plane had been hit 175 times. The aircrews claimed no strikes with the torpedoes. The failure of the airstrike was received with mixed feelings. Admiral Tovey in command had never had much faith in the torpedo planes, and the captain of nearby HMS *Rodney* personally took the microphone to tell his crew, over the ship's loudspeakers, that the planes had failed.

But the strike had not failed. The first indication of this was a surprising signal from *Sheffield* that said that *Bismarck* was doing a U-turn and reversing course. Admiral Tovey refused to believe the report and added a sarcastic remark about the *Sheffield*'s seamanship. But the men aboard *Sheffield* were right and *Bismarck* was in a desperate situation. With steering jammed, it could only go round in gigantic circles. An attempt to cut the rudder away with underwater equipment proved impossible in the heavy swell. A suggestion that explosives should be used was rejected because it would inevitably damage the finely balanced propellers.

Now, in his final hours, Admiral Lütjens signalled to Germany 'ship unmanoeuvrable' and to Hitler 'We shall fight to the end trusting in you, mein Führer.' During the night, four destroyers, one of them Polish, attacked *Bismarck* with torpedoes. The German gunnery radar demonstrated its effectiveness in the hours of darkness, and none of the torpedoes scored a hit. No progress was made in mending the ship's rudders.

Afterwards there were those who thought that the melancholy Lütjens had some sort of death wish. At the start of the voyage he had chosen to go through the Kattegat (between Sweden and Den-

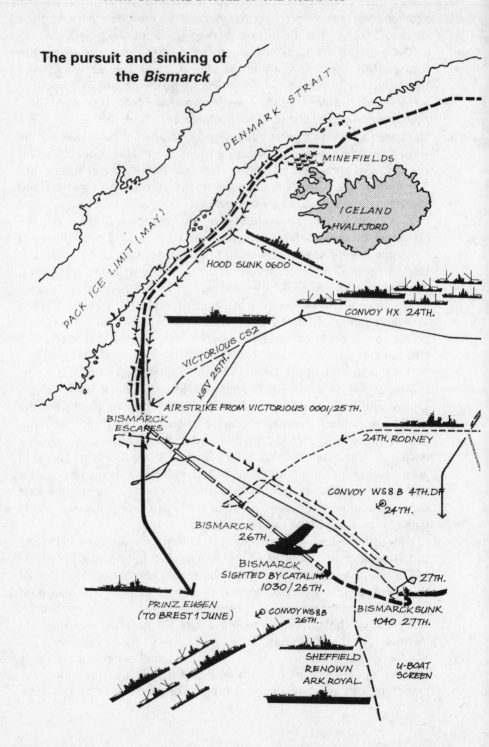

The pursuit and sinking of
the *Bismarck*

DENMARK STRAIT

MINEFIELDS

ICELAND
HVALFJORD

PACK ICE LIMIT (MAY)

HOOD SUNK 0600

CONVOY HX 24TH.

VICTORIOUS CS2

KGV 25TH.

AIR STRIKE FROM VICTORIOUS 0001/25TH.

BISMARCK
ESCAPES

24TH. RODNEY

CONVOY WS 8 B 4TH. DF
24TH.

BISMARCK
26TH.

BISMARCK
SIGHTED BY CATALINA
1030/26TH.

27TH.

BISMARCK SUNK
1040 27TH.

PRINZ EUGEN
(TO BREST 1 JUNE)

CONVOY WS 8 B
26TH.

SHEFFIELD
RENOWN
ARK ROYAL

U-BOAT
SCREEN

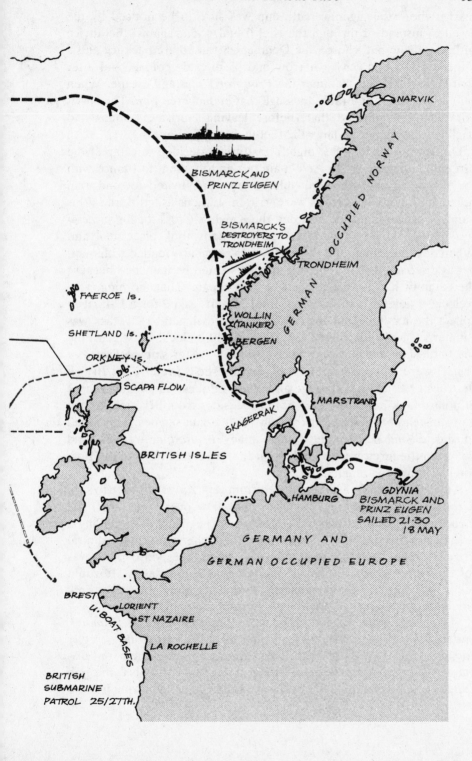

NARVIK

OCCUPIED NORWAY

GERMAN

BISMARCK AND
PRINZ EUGEN

BISMARCK'S
DESTROYERS TO
TRONDHEIM

TRONDHEIM

FAEROE Is.

WOLL IN
(TANKER)

SHETLAND Is.

BERGEN

ORKNEY Is.

MARSTRAND

Scapa Flow

SKAGERRAK

BRITISH ISLES

HAMBURG

GDYNIA
BISMARCK AND
PRINZ EUGEN
SAILED 21·30
18 MAY

GERMANY AND

GERMAN OCCUPIED EUROPE

BREST

LORIENT

ST NAZAIRE

U·BOAT BASES

LA ROCHELLE

BRITISH
SUBMARINE
PATROL 25/27TH.

mark) where the gigantic battleship was sure to be noticed by the Swedes, instead of through the Kiel Canal; then, against the advice of his staff, he had chosen the Denmark Strait where pack-ice and a minefield left him only a narrow and predictable course; and after that he had failed to hammer the *Prince of Wales* and escape. When safe at last, he sent a radio message that endangered him. The survivors also remembered that, before leaving Norway, Lütjens had declined the chance to have the fuel tanks topped up.

On *Bismarck*'s long last night afloat it was decided to catapult the three undamaged Arado Ar 196 aircraft and fly them to France with the ship's log and other valuables. Men were invited to send mail home, and many last letters were written. Lütjens asked Berlin if his gunnery officer could be awarded the Knight's Cross for his successful sinking of HMS *Hood* and the ceremony took place at 4 am. When daylight came, and the first Arado plane was loaded with mail, it was discovered that none of the planes could be launched because the catapult had been damaged beyond repair. That morning, at 7 o'clock, a doleful radio message from Lütjens asked for a U-boat to collect the log-book but the vessel (*U-556*) assigned to this task was submerged and didn't get the order until 10 o'clock, by which time the battleships *Rodney* and *King George V* (sister ship of *Prince of Wales*) were on the scene. One of the first shells fired by the British destroyed the admiral's bridge and killed Lütjens. Shelling *Bismarck* at point-blank range, *Rodney* fired broadsides from her nine 16-inch guns, instead of the more usual four- or five-gun salvoes. This failed to sink *Bismarck*, yet sheared so many of *Rodney*'s rivets, and damaged the foretower so badly, that the vessel had to go to the Boston navy yard for repairs.[6]

At 9.25 am, planes were launched from *Ark Royal* in order to sink *Bismarck* with torpedoes, but when they flew over their target the men in the RN battleships would not pause in their firing, making a low run-in impossible. The airmen sent a signal asking Admiral Tovey to cease fire while they attacked. The only response to this was for *King George V* to fire its anti-aircraft guns at the planes.[7] It would seem that the battleship admirals were determined that *Bismarck* would not be sunk by airmen, even naval airmen.

More ships gathered and more torpedoes were fired at *Bismarck* but she did not sink. At 10.44 a signal from the C-in-C desperately commanded: 'Any ships with torpedoes are to use them on *Bismarck*.' Finally the Germans aboard decided to finish the job themselves. They exploded charges and all became 'a blazing inferno for the bright glow of internal fires could be seen shining through numerous shell and splinter holes in her sides'. Only then did *Bismarck* die. 'As it turned keel up,' said a proud German survivor who was in the water, 'we could see that its hull had not been damaged by torpedoes'. The Germans never lowered their colours. At 11.07 HMS *Dorsetshire* made the signal: 'I torpedoed *Bismarck* both sides before she sank. She had ceased firing but her colours were still flying.' The Swordfish aircraft, which had not been permitted to participate in *Bismarck*'s end, now had to jettison their torpedoes, as it was too dangerous to land carrying them.

Despite the concentration of so many British warships, the *U-74* was determined to get to the scene in order to assist *Bismarck*, or take its log-book back to Germany. But the submarine arrived too late. *Bismarck* had sunk and the water was covered in its fuel oil, its debris and its men. The U-boat periscope was spotted by a lookout on one of the RN ships during the time it had stopped to pick up survivors. Immediately the warning was given, the British ships moved off leaving many Germans to drown. The *U-74* rescued three men, and the RN saved 107. Another German ship, *Sachsenwald*, retrieved two more of the crew. Of a complement of about 2,400 men, all the others perished.

At 1.22 pm German signallers at Naval Group Command West told *Bismarck*: 'Reuters reports *Bismarck* sunk. Report situation immediately.' But by this time *Bismarck* was resting upright on the sea bed 15,317 feet below water.

Prinz Eugen reached Brest safely on 1 June. *Bismarck*'s fate convinced the German navy – and Hitler, who needed far less convincing – that the Atlantic was fast becoming an Anglo-American lake in which submarines might survive but surface raiders could not. In future all German shipbuilding facilities were to give priority to enlarging and repairing the U-boat fleet.

The Royal Navy, ably supported by Britain's Ministry of Information, pronounced the *Bismarck* episode a triumph. Others were not so sure. Churchill thought the Royal Navy had shown a lack of offensive spirit. He persuaded the first sea lord and chief of naval staff that the admiral in HMS *Norfolk*, as well as the captain of *Prince of Wales*, should be court-martialled for failing to engage *Bismarck* during the run south. The C-in-C Home Fleet blocked this[8] and Churchill must have soon realized how damaging such proceedings would be for the British cause.

Hitler became 'melancholy beyond words' at the loss of *Bismarck*.

He was furious that the naval staff had exposed the mightiest warship in the world to such dangers. He had expressed doubts from the beginning and now he was proved right. The Führer complained of 'red tape and wooden-headedness' in the navy and said that the commanders wouldn't tolerate any man with a mind of his own. From that day onwards, Admiral Raeder's ideas were treated with suspicion: eventually command of the navy would be given to Dönitz, whose ideas were more in line with Hitler's.

The 'hunting of the *Bismarck*' certainly provided lessons for those who would learn them. The battleship admirals saw it as proof of the value of the big ship, and the way in which more big ships had to hunt for them. Such people stubbornly persisted with the story that *Bismarck* had been sunk solely by gunfire and denied that the Germans might have opened the sea-cocks. They were wrong: in 1989 the wreck was inspected and the German version of her sinking confirmed.[9]

Hindsight shows that the real lesson was the importance of aircraft. A land-based Catalina had discovered the *Bismarck*; a torpedo-carrying Swordfish had crippled it and thus decided its fate. History provides no evidence that those in authority at the time were converted to this line of thought. The US navy continued to line up the big ships of its Pacific fleet in 'battleship row' Pearl Harbor until the bombers smashed them. Before the year was over the *Prince of Wales*, which had exchanged salvoes with *Bismarck*, would be sent to the bottom by Japanese aircraft. Those tempted by the 'what if?' game asked what might have happened to the two German ships had *Prinz Eugen* been an aircraft-carrier.

On 22 June 1941 Germany invaded Russia, and Churchill immediately declared Britain to be Stalin's ally. Sorely needed Hurricane fighters and other war supplies were loaded and the first North Cape convoy departed for Murmansk in northern Russia in August. These tanks and guns and aircraft were all desperately needed elsewhere, and they would certainly make little difference to the outcome of Barbarossa, the most colossal clash of armed might in the world's history. Perhaps it was a worthwhile gesture in propaganda terms, although Stalin made sure that his people heard little about it. As for the drain upon shipping that would come from sailing heavily escorted convoys so close to German bases in Norway, and mostly in cruel weather, this prospect must have filled the Royal Navy with gloom. It was a time when every ship was badly needed in the Atlantic.

America loses her neutrality

America's neutrality had been defined by Congress and decreed in the Neutrality Act of 1937, but soon after Britain's war began, the Act was modified to permit belligerent powers to buy war materials if they shipped them themselves: so-called 'cash and carry'. This of course benefited Britain and France – whose navies dominated the North Atlantic – while providing no benefit to Germany.

In July 1940 – as France collapsed – Roosevelt signed an act to provide $4 billion to build for America a two-ocean navy. It was an amazing sum of money by any standards. Yet there were many Americans wondering how soon the French fleet, and the British fleet too, would be taken over by the Germans. Meanwhile, in response to an urgent request from Churchill, Roosevelt exchanged 50 old United States destroyers for 99-year leases on naval bases in

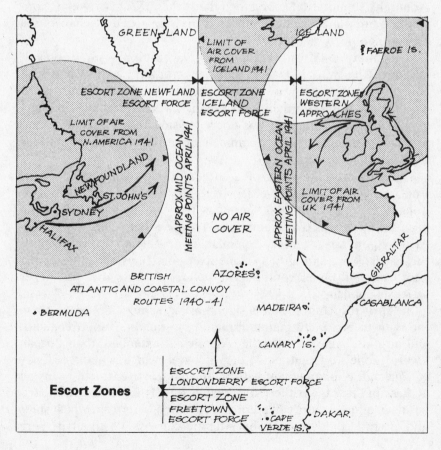

Newfoundland, British Guiana, Bermuda and islands in the West Indies. British sailors were hurried to Halifax and picked up the first of these 'four-stackers' on 6 September 1940. This was essentially a political action; a signal to friends and enemies that Roosevelt, if re-elected in November, would move closer to an endangered Britain. In the latter part of the year, the US navy began to escort its own shipping on 'threatened transatlantic routes'.

Then in December 1940 something happened that would influence the outcome of the Battle of the Atlantic far more than the 99-year leases on naval bases. The American steel magnate Henry Kaiser launched the first 'Liberty Ship'. Its welded hull showed the way to unprecedented production speeds. Welded ships were subject to all sorts of troubles but welded steel – for ships and tanks – was none the less a leap forward in technology. Such welding was strenuously resisted in British yards. It was not until 1943 that the Admiralty supported it. Even then the strikes of angry riveters, confronting timid management, ensured that the speed of change was slower than need be.

By January 1941, with the presidential election won, Roosevelt authorized his military leaders to have secret talks with their British counterparts. Soon it was decided that, should America ever go to war against both Germany and Japan, the conquest of Germany would take precedence. It was not a decision easily arrived at, and for some American military commanders it remained a contentious issue for years to come.

The ever-present threat of a successful German occupation of England, which would have deprived America of a base for operations in Europe, made the 'Germany First' policy logical. Looking back now, it seems that arguments to reverse this policy were bluffs used by American military commanders to get more resources for the Pacific war, and also by American politicians as a threat that kept Churchill under control. The policy, all the same, was never seriously challenged.

In April the United States signed an agreement that gave them the right to build and maintain military installations in Greenland, and in this same month the Americans extended their 'ocean security zone' to longitude 26 degrees west, which is about halfway to England. An agreement with the Icelandic government to install and use military bases there followed in July. It was a vitally important development, for Iceland provided a vital base from which ships and aircraft could protect the Atlantic convoys. Without it there would have always been a mid-Atlantic gap in which the U-boats could operate at will.

Roosevelt and Churchill met in a warship off Newfoundland in August 1941 and pledged themselves to the common goal of destroying Nazi tyranny. It was no empty boast. In a decision no less than breathtaking, America extended $1 billion of credit to a USSR that most observers believed to be near total defeat.

Aboard *Prince of Wales*, returning home from his meeting with the president, Churchill was provided with a chance to see the merchant service at work. On the prime minister's instructions, the battleship went right through a convoy, the escorts taking the outer lanes. The convoy was making a steady 8 knots; the warships doing 22. From the signal halliards *Prince of Wales* flew 'Good luck – Churchill' in international code.

> Those seventy-two ships went mad. Quickly every ship was flying the 'V' flag; some tried a dot-dot-dot-dash salute on their sirens. In the nearest ships men could be seen waving, laughing and – we guessed though we could not hear – cheering. On the bridge the Prime Minister was waving back to them, as was every man on our own decks, cheering with them, two fingers on his right hand making the famous V-sign.
>
> Soon we were through them and well ahead, when to everyone's surprise we did an eight-point turn, and shortly after another. Mr Churchill wanted an encore.[10]

The US navy entered a shooting war in September 1941 when *U-652* was attacked by depth charges and fired two torpedoes at a nearby destroyer. Both missed. The U-boat captain had made two errors: the destroyer was the US navy's *Greer* (a First World War four-funnel profile making it look like those sent to the Royal Navy); and the depth charges had come from an RAF plane. *Greer* retaliated with a pattern of depth charges but did only minor damage to the German boat which crept away. Roosevelt was angry about the 'unprovoked attack' and said that U-boats were the rattlesnakes of the Atlantic. The press echoed his verdict, and reported that the US navy had been ordered to 'shoot on sight' in future. It was a phrase which Roosevelt himself was happy to repeat.[11]

The next month the American destroyer USS *Kearney* was damaged in a convoy battle and eleven American sailors died. At the end of October the American destroyer *Reuben James* – convoying merchant ships between the States and Iceland – was sunk by a U-boat and only 44 of its 120 men were rescued from the ocean. By this time the US navy was fully integrated into the Atlantic battle, to the extent that American orders often went out to Allied warships in the two-thirds of the Atlantic Ocean that was now 'American'.

It was in the final weeks of December 1941 that the Atlantic battle reached a new and ferocious pitch. Dönitz coordinated his U-boats and Condors with skill. The route from Gibraltar to Britain had become especially hazardous. To escort a 32-ship convoy the Royal Navy had sixteen warships, and one of them was a new sort of vessel: the escort carrier. Cheap and hastily prepared, HMS *Audacity* was converted from an ex-German prize, the *Hannover*.

Commanding this escort group there was one of those rare breeds, an RN officer who had specialized in anti-submarine warfare in the prewar years. Commander F.J. 'Johnny' Walker RN had had enough differences of opinion with authority to have damaged his career. Passed over for captain he had spent the first two years of war in 'uninspiring shore appointments'. Now he was about to become the most famous and most successful group commander of the entire Atlantic campaign. His desperate battle with the U-boats lasted six days and nights. Two of the convoy were lost, and so was the escort carrier, but four U-boats were sunk and a Condor shot down. It was a setback for Dönitz and proof that cheap little aircraft-carriers could give convoys air protection far away from land.

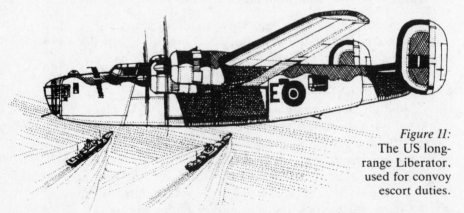

Figure 11:
The US long-range Liberator, used for convoy escort duties.

And on the morning of 22 December 1941, the sixth day of the fight, the weary sailors looked up and saw another new and welcome sight. One of the very long-range Liberators had come 800 miles to perform escort duties. It circled the convoy and dropped depth charges upon some U-boats trailing behind. Dönitz called off his submarines. Air power had begun to turn the tide of the battle.

The ships kept coming

The Atlantic campaign was the longest and most arduous battle of the war, much of it fought in sub-arctic conditions, in gales and heavy seas. When considering the moral questions arising from the RAF 'terror bombing' of cities, consider too the civilians who manned the merchant ships. Casualties of the air raids upon cities usually had immediate succour; the merchant seamen, and ships passengers too, men, women and children, were mutilated, crippled and burned. There was no warning save the crash of a torpedo tearing the hull open. Few men from the engine room got as far as the boat deck. The attacks usually came at night and, on the northerly routes the convoys favoured, it was seldom anything but very cold. Many of the merchantmen's crews were not young. Survivors, many of them bleeding or half-drowned, were abandoned to drift in open boats upon the storm-racked ocean where they went mad or perhaps died slowly and agonizingly of thirst or exposure.

Almost all Britain's oil and petroleum supplies came across the Atlantic by ship.[12] So did about half its food, including most of its meat, cheese, butter and wheat, as well as steel and timber, wool, cotton, zinc, lead and nitrates. British farmers could not have produced home-grown crops without imported fertilizers: neither could farmers in neutral Ireland have survived. 'Ships carried cargoes they were never built for, in seas they were never meant to sail,' said one official publication. During the war I remember that in London scarcely a day passed without someone in my hearing mentioning our debt to the merchant service. Anyone leaving a particle of food uneaten on a plate was risking a reprimand from any waiter or passer-by who saw it. No heroes of the war – not even the fighter pilots – excelled in valour and dogged determination the men of the merchant service and their naval escorts. The public knew it. One merchant navy officer said:

> armed with free railway ticket issued by 'Shipwrecked Mariners Society' to my home in Colchester, Essex, I proceeded on leave. My journey across London via the Underground from Euston to Liverpool Street Station clad in a salt-stained (not to mention vomit!) uniform and still jealously clutching my orange-coloured

life-jacket was more of an ordeal than the whole of the western ocean with the masses of people sheltering from the nightly blitz all wanting to crowd around me to slap my back or shake my hand.[13]

The Battle of the Atlantic continued until Germany surrendered. When that happened, U-boats were ordered to surface, hoist black flags, report position and proceed by fixed routes to designated ports and anchorages. I remember spotting them, one after another, from a Fleet Air Arm plane as they made that final journey up the Channel. It was a heartening sight.

Churchill, in a letter to Roosevelt dated 8 December 1940, declared that the decision for 1941 lay upon the seas. He went on to detail the threat to Britain's lifelines, and his concern was real. 'PM very gloomy on shipping situation,' Sir Alexander Cadogan of the Foreign Office wrote after a meeting of the war cabinet in February 1941. A few days later, on 1 March, the Australian prime minister noted that Churchill called shipping losses the supreme menace of the war. To Mackenzie King, Churchill telegraphed on 24 March: 'The issue of the war will clearly depend on our being able to maintain the traffic across the Atlantic.' Churchill was so concerned that he formed a special Battle of the Atlantic Committee which discussed every aspect of shipping, escorts, imports, repairs and so on. As part of this allotment of resources, 17 squadrons from Bomber Command were assigned to Coastal Command. These heavy aircraft could range out into the ocean where the U-boats were operating so freely. Howls of protest and pain came from Chief of Air Staff Sir Charles Portal and his deputy, Air Vice-Marshal Arthur Harris, who later became known as 'Bomber' Harris.

Harris insisted that patrolling the sea lanes with bombers was a complete waste of time and effort. Citing the records of the Armstrong Whitley bombers used by 502 Squadron over a six-month period, he pointed out that on 144 sorties only six submarines had been spotted: four were attacked and one, perhaps two, sunk. Harris could not resist the observation that this meant 250 flying hours per sighting. In his note to his boss Portal, he scoffed at the Admiralty and the ineffectiveness thus proved. Portal was able to prevent any of the new long-range four-engine Halifax bombers going to Coastal Command. By July 1941 Churchill had been persuaded to switch priority back to the build-up of Bomber Command. Harris and Portal refused to admit the vital difference their planes could have made to closing the 'gap'. They would not see that success in the vital battle for the sea lanes was measured by the number of ships that arrived safely, not by U-boat sinkings.

All the Royal Navy's requests for long-range aircraft to aid in the Atlantic battle were dismissed contemptuously by the RAF. (Three things you should never take on a yacht: a wheelbarrow, an umbrella and an RN officer, advised 'Bomber' Harris in one of his less caustic remarks about the senior service.) Even in 1941, when the April total of lost shipping tonnage went to almost 700,000 and Britain's rations were reduced – 'the moment when Great Britain came nearest to losing the war,' said A.J.P. Taylor[14] – the RAF were vehemently resisting the transfer of any aircraft away from their ineffective bombing campaign.[15]

The battle of the Atlantic was never won in the sense that land battles were. Germany could win the war by cutting the sea traffic to Britain but Britain could not win by conquering the U-boat menace. In fact the submarine was never conquered, which is why the victors all built submarine fleets after the war. Far from being the weapon of minor naval powers, the nuclear submarine became the modern capital ship.

The German navy failed to win the Battle of the Atlantic despite the willingness that Dönitz showed to flout international treaty. In theory it should have worked. Obsessed by the desire to starve Britain, he directed his forces to sink the merchantmen and rewarded his captains according to tonnage sunk. During the entire war his U-boats sank only 34 destroyers and 37 other escort vessels. Strategically it was right and his tactics were sound, but the shipbuilders defeated this effort.[16] And Hitler's Third Reich never put its full strength behind the submarine campaign. Hitler was a soldier and he was determined upon a land victory over the Bolsheviks he detested. Unlike his predecessors, a naval victory over Britain was not something of which he dreamed. Partly for this reason the German navy did not improve their submarines and torpedoes in the fundamental ways that the army's tanks and guns were endlessly modified. Submarine technology did change of course, but the German U-boat fleet did not improve well enough or fast enough. Most of the changes were defensive. By the end of the war German submariners were neither expert nor determined.

Their opponents, on the other hand, learned quickly, and invented tactics and weapons that countered the U-boats, most of which were little different to those in service in 1939. High-frequency direction-finding sets were made small enough to go into ships, and these gave a more exact position for immediate tactical response. Radar improved and it was used more skilfully from ships and from aircraft. Land-based aircraft flew from Newfoundland, Iceland and Britain to provide better and more effective air cover. Escort carriers – their decks built upon merchant ship hulls – brought aircraft to eliminate any last 'gaps' in the ocean.

Technical developments contributed to the Allied success but (senior officers on both sides say) the German U-boat arm liked to declare that Enigma intercepts, radar or HF/DF decided the war because these allowed them an excuse for losing. For many post-war years the British over-emphasized the role that HF/DF had played. This was a way of keeping their Enigma work secret. Once the Enigma secret was out, the contribution of Bletchley Park was in turn exaggerated.

In the final year of war, the U-boat arm became worn out and de-moralized. These men, more than any other Germans, were provided with evidence that Germany could never win. On every operational mission they encountered bigger and better convoys of new ships stacked high with shiny new tanks and planes. They faced tired but highly motivated and ever more expert Allied seamen who knew they were winning. The German sailors, at sea for many weeks, became concerned about what was happening to their friends and families in the cities under Allied air attack by night, and later by day too. As the Russians started their remorseless advance the U-boat men had new worries about what was happening to their families in cities overrun by the vengeful Red Army.

It was German policy to send conscripts (draftees) into the submarines. This was a mistake. The policy in most other navies was to use only tested volunteers in this specialized warfare. And while RN training improved and became more practical as time went on, the U-boat training schools in the Baltic remained out of touch with the latest anti-submarine techniques, and even the sea conditions of the Atlantic. Shortages of men caused U-boat trainees to be posted to operational duties even when instructors had doubts about their ability. Half-trained men made less expert and less resolute adversaries; they also were crippled and killed by the remorseless ocean. Some fell down companionways, others lost their fingers in machinery and still more were swept overboard and never seen again. Towards the end U-boat crews were no longer singing old songs like 'Denn wir fahren gegen Engeland' but cynical ditties about the failings of the mechanisms they operated and about the radar that hunted them. A German historian acknowledges: 'The men knew that they were beaten and that their end was inevitable . . .'[17]

Yet the U-boat as a weapon was certainly not defeated. The *schnorchel* (anglicized as snorkel) enabled the diesel engines to breathe air while the submarine remained just below the surface. Postwar trials showed that 94 per cent of U-boats using the snorkel went undetected by airborne radar. The German Type XXI U-boats could go 300 miles on electric motors while remaining totally submerged. Added to this there were some remarkable target-seeking torpedoes: ones that homed on engine noise and others

Figure 12: Comparative ship sizes

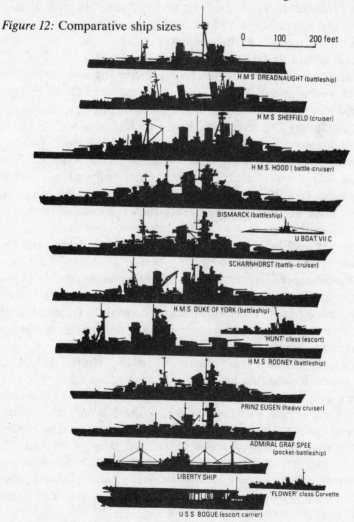

0   100   200 feet

H M S DREADNAUGHT (battleship)

H M S SHEFFIELD (cruiser)

H M S HOOD (battle-cruiser)

BISMARCK (battleship)

U BOAT VII C

SCHARNHORST (battle-cruiser)

H M S DUKE OF YORK (battleship)

'HUNT' class (escort)

H M S RODNEY (battleship)

PRINZ EUGEN (heavy cruiser)

ADMIRAL GRAF SPEE
(pocket-battleship)

LIBERTY SHIP

'FLOWER' class Corvette

U S S BOGUE (escort carrier)

that turned and (programmed for the forward speed of the target) made run after run until they hit something or exhausted their propellant. But such devices were gimmicks rather than innovations.

The Allied sea lanes were kept open because in the long run there were enough ships built, and enough brave men to man them. Britain's merchant service had gone through bad interwar years but during the war seamen were formed into a 'pool' by means of the 'Essential Work Order' of May 1941. This brought permanent engagement and regular pay. Crew accommodation in many ships was squalid, dirty, unhealthy and cramped, and would have horrified any factory-inspector. Yet during the war Britain's Shipping Federation was receiving a hundred letters a day from boys (16 was the minimum recruiting age) asking for a job afloat.

When war began Britain's merchant service included 45,000 men from the Indian sub-continent (including Pakistan) and over 6,000 Chinese, as well as many Arabs. When it ended, the Official History says, 37,651 men had died as a direct result of enemy action, and the true total, including deaths indirectly due to war, was 50,525.

The U-boat war was no doubt difficult and dangerous, and the German navy lost 27,491 men out of approximately 55,000.[18] Perhaps the most important figure – and the most surprising – is that less than 50 per cent of all U-boats built got within torpedo range of a convoy. Of the 870 U-boats that left port on operational trips, 550 of them sank nothing.

The sea has always attracted men from far and wide. On the escorts there were Dutchmen, Free French, Poles, Norwegians, Americans and many Canadians. The Atlantic convoys were not the worst perils the sailors faced: those convoys to Murmansk saw ships labouring under tons of ice and attacked constantly from German bases in Norway. Convoys through the Mediterranean to Malta were equally hazardous.

Ultimately it was the vast resources of the United States of America which decided the outcome. Using the techniques of mass-production, American shipyards proved able to build a freighter in five days! Despite the war in the Pacific, the US spared carriers, escorts and aircraft to supplement British and ever-growing Canadian naval forces in the Atlantic. Soon there would be US armies to be supplied in Europe and North Africa. During a war of unprecedented supply lines and unprecedented amphibious operations, a war in which every front demanded more and more seagoing vessels, the ships kept coming.

Part Two

HITLER CONQUERS
EUROPE

6 GERMANY: UNRECOGNIZED POWER

I have to report that M. Blériot, with his monoplane,
crossed the Channel from Calais this morning.
I issued to him a Quarantine Certificate, thereby treating it
as a yacht and the aviator as Master and owner.

The Collector of Customs at Dover, 25 July 1909[1]

To UNDERSTAND WHY an improvised and inadequate mixture of British military formations were sent to war in 1939 it is necessary to remember that her army had always been quite different in tradition, formation and function to any of the continental armies.

In the late sixteenth and seventeenth centuries, standing armies were established on the Continent, not so much in response to foreign wars as to civil strife and rebellions. From that time onwards continental rulers made sure that every town had its barracks and parade ground. The constant sound of bugles and drums reminded the discontented that 'who draws a sword against a prince must throw away the scabbard.' A centralized and severely regulated life is still the normal one for most Europeans, who remain subject to compulsory military service and are required to carry identity papers that they have to produce for any authorized inquirer.

Apart from a riot here and there Britain did not need such control of its population. England's civil war had ended in a consensus as the English discovered that they hated foreigners more than they hated their own countrymen. Once England was united with Scotland no army was needed to guard the frontiers; keeping invaders at bay was the Royal Navy's job. Britain had no need for a mighty army: its power and wealth came from peace and stability, its wars took place overseas, and agile politicians ensured that England was always allied with the winning side.[2] When the continental powers were evenly balanced, England tipped the scales.[3] The army was simply a refuge for the disinherited rich and the unemployable poor.

The role of Britain's navy was to raid and harass shipping, ports and coastlines to bring the enemy to the negotiating table. Within such a policy, overseas possessions were primarily needed as bases to revictual the fleets. From these, in the course of time, merchants, soldiers and adventurers conquered vast tracts of land. They found that a small armed presence was usually enough to maintain control of even the largest overseas dominions, although much of these was hostile uninhabitable land like the northern part of Canada and the Australian interior. Weapons improved, and in a short time Britain acquired and maintained a vast empire extending far beyond any real power that it could deploy.

Citizen armies

Compulsory military service is not a new device. Press-gangs that kidnapped able-bodied men in seaports and forced them into the slavery of naval service had been keeping the navies manned for many years before Prussia set up a system of compulsory military service in 1733. Prussian regiments, each based in a Kanton or county, kept records of local men and summoned them to military service as needed. But when Napoleon attacked, the Prussian army was mauled and humiliated by the French and the defeat was blamed upon its inefficiency. Two out of three men had been given exemption from military service, so that the Prussian army in the field consisted of mercenaries and peasants in about equal numbers.[4] Now Prussia created a system of service which exempted very few healthy men whatever their social class. They were not simply called in time of war. Each citizen spent a year in uniform and returned to the colours throughout his life.

But compulsory military service as we know it was born, like so many other intolerable devices of the centralized totalitarian state, out of the French Revolution. In 1793 the war minister proposed to the National Assembly that every healthy single Frenchman aged between 18 and 25 should be summoned to the army. Married men of the same age would go into the armoury workshops, and males aged from 26 to 40 would be entered on a reserve list for service in wartime.

Thus Germans and Frenchmen spent their adult lives at the beck and call of the generals. In 1870 the two systems of mobilization could be compared. The Germans attacked France with an army of 1,200,000 men. In that same two weeks of crisis France had mustered only half that number.

By 16 February 1874 Helmuth von Moltke was able to stand up in the Reichstag and claim that the army's prodigious use of civilian manpower had been 'raising the nation for almost sixty years to physical fitness, mental alertness, order and punctuality, loyalty and obedience, love of our country, and manliness.'[5] It had also enabled Prussia to thoroughly thrash her neighbours, including France, into abject submission.

It is difficult to be sure whether the prospect of military service was as unpopular in France and Germany as it was in Britain. But in France and Germany public opinion was disregarded by the government; Britain was different. Dating from Anglo-Saxon times, its army consisted of small companies raised by noblemen under royal commission. Only in dire emergencies were citizens called to serve. Although nineteenth-century Britain was not a democracy – no European state enjoyed democracy – public opinion in Britain was important. This importance did not depend upon the vote. In Britain in 1901 only two-thirds of the men, and no women, had the vote. Government was confined to a small, carefully defined and exclusive class, and these men decided that universal conscription was not politically acceptable.

During the nineteenth century, Britain was protected by its coastline and its unchallenged navy. Half of the army was stationed in India, and most of the other half was winning a succession of small colonial wars in other distant possessions. Only at the century's end was Britain's power tested. In southern Africa, where the world's largest gold deposits had recently been discovered, the Boers, farmers of Dutch descent, besieged garrison towns. Closing their minds to the appalling inefficiency their army had demonstrated in the Crimean War (1854–56), the British decided to exercise their unique resources by dispatching an army to fight six thousand miles away from home. No other country could equal or counter such an expedition. The part that wealth played in such power had long been celebrated in a music hall ditty: 'We don't want to fight but by Jingo if we do, we've got the ships, we've got the men, we've got the money too.'[6]

Britain still had the money but, despite the tied markets provided by her Empire, less and less of it was coming from manufacturing and exporting goods. Financiers, rather than factory owners, were the new elite. Overseas investments in railways, mines and urban expansion were now bringing enough money into London to make up for the drop in exports, but it was another ominous sign that Britain was losing the trade wars to rivals such as Germany and America.

There were also danger signals about the workforce. The British government was reportedly shocked to find that 38 per cent of men volunteering to fight the Boers – a sampling one would expect to be in good health – were not fit enough to serve with the colours. And this despite the way in which the army's height requirement had been brought down to five feet! A subsequent official report stated that about a quarter of the inhabitants of Britain's industrial towns were undernourished because they were poor.

The Boers were fit and strong, hunters and farmers fighting in terrain they knew how to exploit. Moving rapidly on horseback, they fought on foot, using Mauser repeating rifles with deadly accuracy. Lacking discipline, organization, medals and military textbooks, they knew when to sneak away from a lost encounter. There were never more than 40,000 Boers in the field but it took a British army of unprecedented size almost three years to subdue them. Helped by the Dominions, Britain mobilized half a million men.

The controversies, scandals, triumphs and disasters of the war came at a time when rotary presses and improved typesetting machines provided cheap newspapers for a newly literate public. Winston Churchill reported the war for the *Daily Telegraph*, Edgar Wallace, a famous crime novelist, covered it for the *Daily Mail* and Rudyard Kipling worked there on an army newspaper. Arthur Conan Doyle, creator of Sherlock Holmes, was running a field hospital and Mahatma Gandhi was a stretcher-bearer.[7]

The conflict had a profound effect on European politics. The French, the Dutch and the Germans, who had colonized foreign lands with varying degreees of cruelty, objected to the British colonizing European settlers. And Britain's rivals relished the sight of her army suffering humiliating defeats at the hands of a few skilful and tenacious white farmers. When the British started to get the upper hand, their European neighbours became more critical of them and more pro-Boer. Disease-ridden prison camps caused the deaths of many thousand Boers and brought accusations of deliberate murder. The British explained that it was incompetence, but by the time the war was over, Britain's relationship with the rest of Europe was clouded by resentment.

The fighting in South Africa had provided some glimpses of how future wars might be fought. But the machine-gun, which would dominate future battlefields, played little part in the fight against the Boers. It was not a weapon unknown to the British army. Various forms of machine-gun had been used by them since 1871. It had been used in the Ashanti campaign in 1874, the Zulu War, and by General Kitchener in the Sudan. It had killed some 11,000 Dervishes at Omdurman. No wonder Hilaire Belloc's poem, 'The Modern Traveller', confidently claimed that:

> 'Whatever happens, we have got
> The Maxim Gun, and they have not.'

But machine-guns did not defeat the Boers. Some said the British sense of fair play and an antipathy to replacing heroes with machinery made them reluctant to massacre white men with automatic fire.[8] There are other reasons too. The army had given the Maxim, which weighed 40 lb, to artillery-men who put it on a carriage weighing 448 lb, with wheels almost five feet in diameter. Such a large and cumbersome weapon was not so effective against Boers who avoided frontal attacks, used ground and cover with great skill and were masters of the arts of camouflage and sniping. The role of the machine-gun went unremarked in the war, and after it the British army preferred to admire the horsemanship of the foe and concentrated its reforms upon its own horsemen. By 1914 British cavalry were the finest in the world, but there were to be no battles for them to fight.

The decisive components of future warfare were more easily seen in the savage civil war which had torn nineteenth-century America in two. Here was a country where public opinion counted for a great deal. Even in the most desperate days of the war its leaders had stopped short of universal conscription. (The Confederate army was 20 per cent conscript, the Union army 6 per cent.) A cunning combination of cash bounties for volunteers, plus the threat of conscription, had bulldozed enough men into uniform. The inescapable lesson of the civil war was that the industrial might of the North inevitably prevailed. Frequent demonstrations of military prowess by Confederate generals came to nothing because the Union had more soldiers, more miles of railroad, and more factories to produce armaments and all the other resources of war.

Neither the British nor the French seemed to learn much from the American battlefields and the terribly high casualties that were suffered there. After the stunning German victory in 1870, the defeated French generals concluded that it was the nature of the offensive that had been the true secret of Germany's lightning campaign. Assault became the new theory of warfare. France soon paid off the punitive reparations demanded by its conquerors and, inexplicably, regained its reputation as the world's most formidable land power. With Britain's navy considered indomitable, the Anglo-French alliance was not actively challenged.

As the dust of war blew away, it was starkly evident that France would not be content with the European borders that the Germans had imposed upon her. Frenchmen were determined to regain the provinces of Alsace and Lorraine, and redress their humiliating defeat. The thought of Wilhelm posturing in the great Hall of Mirrors in the Palace of Versailles, amid the German princes and the battle-torn standards, while the grand duke of Baden hailed him as emperor had ignited a lasting desire for revenge in every French heart.

A different sort of German ruler might have guided his country through this prevailing French resentment but Wilhelm was a neurotic and enigmatic personality. Despite his seven children, his closest friends were homosexuals. From them he seemed to get the warmth and affection that he needed in order to play the role of a tough and pitiless warlord. When he became ruler of a united and powerful Germany, a war to decide the hegemony of Europe was almost inevitable. Furthermore the unified Germany that came after the victory of 1870 was being transformed. In the following 25 years the national income doubled. Railroads spread across the land. Giant electrical, chemical and industrial enterprises flourished and booming cities absorbed a population which increased 50 per cent. 'German universities and technical schools were the most admired, German methods the most thorough, German philosophers dominant,' said Barbara Tuchman.[9]

Technical advances

Displayed by the Americans at Britain's Great Exhibition of 1851 there were half a dozen mass-produced rifles, every part of them easily and quickly interchangeable. The advantage such precision production brought to an army will be readily understood by those British soldiers who used a hammer and file, and sometimes a hacksaw, when servicing their vehicles and equipment during the Second World War. In the German section of the Exhibition in London, Alfred Krupp displayed a cannon made from cast steel, instead of the usual iron or bronze. He found no buyers.

The nineteenth century transformed warfare, with machine-guns used in conjunction with barbed-wire. Mass-produced weapons and citizen armies were moved by railways. Two inventions were yet to bear fruit: nothing would change the nature of war more than the wireless telegraph and the internal combustion engine.

Britain's industrial revolution had been made possible by the invention of such devices as George Stephenson's steam engine, Richard Arkwright's water-frame, Edmund Cartwright's power loom, Hargreaves' spinning jenny and Samuel Crompton's mule. These inventions were brilliantly simple; the inventors were unsophisticated men. Arkwright was a barber assisted by a watchmaker, Hargreaves a carpenter, Cartwright a clergyman, Crompton a spinner and Stephenson a collier's son who didn't learn to read until he was 17 years old. But the next step in modern progress would delve into such mysteries as chemistry, microbiology, physics and precision engineering. It would require educated people working in well equipped workshops and laboratories.

Inventions were improved at a dazzling speed. A gas engine invented by Dr N. A. Otto in 1876 was developed by Gottlieb Daimler to propel a vehicle. Before the end of the century there was an automobile race covering 744 miles from Paris to Bordeaux and back. By 1903 the Wright brothers were flying their curious contraptions. Six years later Europeans suddenly understood the significance of powered flight when Louis Blériot flew across the English Channel in 31 minutes. The world had been irreversibly transformed and so had the way in which men would fight. War had entered the third dimension.

Wireless was no less important. By 1901 Guglielmo Marconi's development of work by Rudolf Hertz enabled a wireless message to be transmitted 3,000 miles. While the industrial revolution had used crude machines and unskilled labour to produce wealth, this new 'technical revolution' was far more demanding. Nations with leaders who failed to respond to the complexities of this new world ran the risk of rapid decline. In the words of one British major-general who was also an historian:

Mind more than matter, thought more than things, and above all imagination, struggled to gain power. New substances appeared, new sources of energy were tapped and new outlooks on life took form. The world was sloughing its skin – mental, moral and physical – a process destined to transform the industrial revolution into a technical civilization. Divorced from civil progress, soldiers could not see this. They could not see that as civilization became more technical, military power must inevitably follow suit: that the next war would be as much a clash between factories and technicians as between armies and generals. With the steady advance of science warfare could not stand still.[10]

In 1890 Germany's production of iron and steel had been half that of Britain; by 1913 Germany produced twice as much as Britain and half that of the United States. Such advances were matched by progress in manufacturing. German industry – chemical and electric firms in particular – set up research institutes, and worked closely with the universities. By the end of the nineteenth century German technology had left Britain behind. By the time Hitler came to power, Germany had collected one-third of all the Nobel prizes for physics and chemistry.

Since the early nineteenth century, Prussia had given great emphasis to the technical training of the workforce. It had invented such educational refinements as graduate schools, Ph.D. degrees, seminars, research laboratories and institutes, and scholarly and scientific journals. All of these innovations were quickly adopted by American universities. France recognized the importance of education and technology and pioneered colleges for the advanced study of engineering and science. The achievements of such men as J.J. Thomson at the Cavendish laboratory did not allay the fears of the British educational establishment, which, fortified by State and Church, saw science as a dangerous first step towards Godless social reform and resolutely opposed it. Britain's 'public schools' (actually private, fee-paying and exclusive) prepared upper middle-class boys to study in the choice universities where science and engineering were virtually ignored. Association between university and industry was fiercely resisted. As the First World War began, most of Britain's population could expect no education beyond their fourteenth birthdays. Teachers were ill paid and difficult to recruit. Decisions about the nation, its industries and commercial life were made by men who had studied the Classics, Law or Philosophy. Few spoke any modern foreign language fluently.

Britain's contribution to its wars is celebrated by memorable prose and poetry rather than by military successes. The country's subsequent industrial and economic history has been blighted by the way its middle classes have continued to hold any sort of technical accomplishment in low esteem, and prefer their children to study liberal arts in outmoded buildings lacking modern facilities.

Outbreak of the First World War

The assassination that led to the outbreak of war in 1914 took place in the Balkans. The foreign minister of Austria-Hungary was determined to provoke the Serbians into a war. The Serbians, with strong ties to the Slavic nations, were confident and ready to fight. Obligations, both real and imagined, divided Europe into the Central Powers (Germany and Austria-Hungary plus Turkey) on one side and the Allies (France, Russia and Britain) on the other. Britain's commitment to join in the 1914 war was flimsy.[11] So was that of Germany. The war was fought for trade and territory, but men on both sides were moved by romantic ideas rather than practical considerations. The British saw it as a war to resist the German invasion of 'poor little' Belgium. Germans saw it as a war for German *Kultur* against barbaric enemies. In Berlin a Socialist deputy saw the Reichstag vote on war credits and wrote in his diary:

> The memory of the incredible enthusiasm of the other parties, of the government, and of the spectators, as we stood to be counted, will never leave me.[12]

When war was declared there was satisfaction everywhere. In London, Paris and Berlin the crowds cheered the announcement. German artists and intellectuals were foremost among those succumbing to war fever and thousands of students joined the army immediately. At Kiel University, Schleswig-Holstein – following an appeal by the rector – virtually the whole student body enlisted.

What did the cheering men – so many of them doomed to death by the announcements – envisage? Certainly they thought the war would be quick and decisive; in every country there was the stated belief that 'it would be all over by Christmas.'

The thinking of most of the top soldiers was no less carefree. General Ferdinand Foch, who ended the war as commander of the combined French, British and United States armies on the Western Front, thought: 'A battle won is a battle in which one will not confess oneself beaten.'[13] Such folly might have proved less tragic had it not been coupled with Foch's obsession with attacking, and his rationalization that any improvement in armaments could add strength only to the offensive. Such generalship resulted in French *poilus* charging into machine-gun fire dressed in bright red pantaloons. It was only in 1915 that the French army went over to less conspicuous attire, and even that was 'horizon blue'. In an amazing demonstration of the military mind at its most tenacious, Foch ended the war with his views more or less intact.

Because so many of the ideas, events and even the equipment of 1914 clearly foreshadows that of 1939 it is worth while taking a closer look at this 'war to end wars'. It was called 'The Great War' until 1939 brought another and even greater war. Like that second war, the first began with a 'blitzkrieg'. Germany's 'Schlieffen Plan' called for a lightning thrust through (neutral) Belgium, then a massive left wheel across northern France to capture Paris. After that all German resources would be turned upon Russia, which would need more time to mobilize its army and prepare for war.

The man called upon to implement Schlieffen's ambitious plan was Helmuth von Moltke, who said: 'I live entirely in the arts.' He proved it by painting and playing the cello and working on a German translation of Maeterlinck's *Pelléas et Mélisande*. Moltke did not capture Paris; but he got close.

According to plan and aided by a national railway service that was built to a mililtary design, Moltke's armies rolled through Belgium, suffering only a brief delay before flattening its massive fortresses with Krupp's incomparable howitzers. But the Germans failed to capture Paris.

At first it was a war of movement but then weary regiments, slowed by mud and cold and suffering the losses of their best and most experienced soldiers, came to a standstill. Here and there the order to stand fast was best met by digging a trench in which to shelter. Soon, from the North Sea to the Alps the armies were standing in a vast line of muddy trenches garlanded with barbed-wire and traversed by machine-guns. Behind them the cavalry regiments were held in reserve. There they remained, waiting for a gap through which to gallop, until the war ended. Meanwhile the infantry gradually abandoned their fine uniforms as part of the process of adapting to living in wet ditches where artfully positioned machine-guns ensured that any man who climbed out and stood up, almost certainly died. High-ranking officers – who unfortunately never went to the trenches, climbed out and stood up – resolutely refused to recognize the fact that the machine-gun had changed warfare as much as had gunpowder itself.

Lord Kitchener, who had been responsible for the organization and transport of the British Expeditionary Force sent to France, said: 'I don't know what is to be done – this isn't war.' What he really meant was that this was not the short sharp action that so many volunteers had envisaged.

On the Eastern Front, the Germans (and to their south the soldiers of Austria-Hungary) faced the mammoth armies of Russia. Their men were stretched more thinly than in the West, and now and again attacks broke through the front-line defences. But for most of the time the Eastern Front was as static as the Western Front. There the weather was even more cruel.

The British and German armies

Unlike other continental nations, the British had never revered army officers, nor indeed given the army much attention at all. Until 1870 the British army remained a hundred years behind the times. Officers purchased their commissions, men were enlisted for life and flogging was a regular punishment. Reforms were slow and heartily resisted. By the time war came in 1914 the small professional army was made up of poor human material. A prewar study found that British soldiers had a mental age between 10 and 13. Many were illiterate. Troops going on leave were marched to the railway station and put on the trains, because of the problems they had if doing this unaided.

Supporting the regular army there was a part-time defence force called the Territorial Army. In 1914 it had about 250,000 men instead of its establishment of 320,000. Youngsters were not given a medical: 'The men were enlisted only for Home Defence and an inquiry in time of peace as to those willing to serve abroad in event of war disclosed 20,000 ready to take this obligation. The training of the men was limited to an hour's drill at odd times, and an annual training of eight to fifteen days.'[14] The 'Terriers' carried long Lee-Enfield rifles and were armed with converted 15-pounder guns, both weapons which the regular army had discarded.

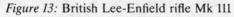

Figure 13: British Lee-Enfield rifle Mk 111

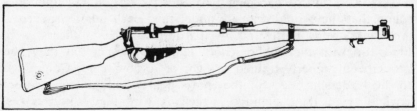

The army may have been unfit for battle but the civilians were in high spirits. When war started in the summer of 1914 great numbers of men volunteered. The nation's health was still poor but medical examinations were cursory. According to the chief recruiting officer for the London District at that time, some doctors examined over 300 men per day while between 20 and 30 per cent of the recruits were given no medical examination at all.[15]

By the middle of 1915 over 3 million British men had volunteered to fight but casualties meant 'the outflow was greater than the intake.'[16] To maintain the field army envisaged for 1916, men would have to be drafted. A Conscription Bill passed through Parliament with overwhelming majorities, and Britain's traditional opposition to citizen armies was overcome with scarcely a ripple of protest.

The drafted men were subjected to no greater scrutiny than had been given to the volunteers. It was only after three years of war that the medical boards were re-organized and improved. Then the doctors were examining about 60 men a day. A very high percentage of these were found unfit for front-line service,[17] but by this time many men unsuited to the physical and mental strains of trench warfare were fighting in France.

All through the war there were shortages of uniforms and equipment and also of instructors. The exceptionally high casualty rate suffered by junior officers might have been met by commissioning experienced NCOs, but this was not considered. The British army believed that officers must be recruited from the middle classes. The normal way to officer rank was through the Officers' Training Corps which were formed in Britain's 'public' schools. The OTC did not provide serious military training. It organized summer camps and training drills, and gave the schoolboys Certificate A, which guaranteed them officer rank.

Young patriotic clerks and manual workers responded well to being commanded by 18-year-old subalterns fresh from school. For the first time 'nicely raised young men from West Country vicarages or South Coast watering places came face to face with forty Durham miners, Yorkshire furnacemen, Clydeside riveters, and the two sides found that they could scarcely understand each other's speech.'[18] All ranks were motivated by patriotism. Their officers were fired also with the public school ethic of service, but they had never been properly trained to fight or to command. Committed to the leadership ideas of the sports field, youthful officers were unyielding in their courage, which is why they suffered disproportionate casualties. A junior officer reporting to his infantry battalion had a 50 per cent chance of being killed or seriously wounded within six months.

War poets have provided an interesting record of the good relationship between British officers and men in the front line. But whatever its virtue and valour, an army based upon improvisation was no match for German professionalism. Neither were the British high commanders.

The commander-in-chief of the British Expeditionary Force in France from December 1915 onwards was Lieutenant-General Sir Douglas Haig. 'A dour hard-working ambitious Scot with little money and few friends, who was not too particular about the methods he used to get to the top of his profession,' said the historian Michael Howard. 'But he was a dedicated professional none the less.'[19] This 53-year-old autocrat distrusted all foreigners, including his French allies, thought that Roman Catholics were likely to be pacifists and detested all politicians, especially Socialists, into which category he was inclined to put anyone with new ideas. These shortcomings were grave, all the more so because Haig proved totally unequipped for the unprecedented military task he had taken upon himself.

In the higher ranks of the British army Haig made sure that important promotions came only to the prewar regulars. Even worse, promotion was decided by the traditional system of age, service and seniority. This ensured that only the grossest incompetents were ever removed, and they almost invariably got a job where they could do even more damage.

The German army was equally reluctant to allow the working class across the great divide into the exalted realm of the commissioned ranks. Officers had always enjoyed a privileged place in German society, and German schools of all kinds prepared youngsters for the military service that followed their schooling. A century of conscription had ensured that German officers, like German other-ranks, were thoroughly trained. Fit 20-year-old men served two years with the army (one year for students). Training was methodical and rigorous; some said it was sadistic. Emphasis was given to specialized skills, such as operating and maintaining engines, artillery and machine-guns. Each man also learned the job of his immediate superior so that every senior NCO was trained to fill an officer's role, should his officer become a casualty.

Until they reached the age of 40, Germans returned to the army for refresher courses that amounted to about eight weeks' training every five years. In this way reservists were taught about new weapons and tactics, and the system provided Germany with a well trained army of over 4 million men in 1914.

The battle of the Somme

Engineers, like scientists of all kinds, were respected in Germany. With the German army reduced to static fighting on the Western Front, engineers built a well designed defence system behind their front line. They dug trenches along contours, taking advantage of every hill and ridge, and where possible the line was linked to shell-racked villages, where machine-gun positions and observation posts were concealed in the rubble.

On the Somme sector, chalk provided a chance to dig deep; 40 feet was not exceptional. Dug-outs were reinforced with cement and steel and had multiple exits. Many underground quarters had electric light and were ventilated by fans. The soldiers had bunk-beds and in some places there was even piped water. No wonder that on 8 August 1916 a British serving soldier's letter in *The Times* said: 'But the German dug-outs! My word, they were things of beauty, art and safety.'

When these defences were ready, the Germans pulled back to them. The British generals moved their men forward to lap against the German line. It was what the Germans wanted them to do, for here the British were constantly observed and under fire. It was this German line that Douglas Haig was to assault on 1 July 1916 in the battle of the Somme, throwing in thirteen British and five French divisions.

Whether Haig's plan was based upon his low opinion of the professional army, or his low opinion of the civilians which now largely manned it, is not clear. The battle plan was detailed and robotic. No opportunity for initiative or independent action was granted to any of the combatants.

The Somme battle opened on a hot July day when 143 battalions attacked and about 50 per cent of the men, and some 75 per cent of the officers, became casualties. Karl Blenk, a German machine-gunner, recalled:

> I could see them everywhere; there were hundreds. The officers were in front. I noticed one of them walked calmly, carrying a walking stick. When we started firing we just had to load and

reload. They went down in their hundreds. You didn't have to aim, we just fired into them.[20]

The German machine-gunners had been ordered to set up their positions at the rear of their trenchline, where they would command a better view and 'In addition, owing to the feeling of safety which this position inspires, the men will work their guns with more coolness and judgement.'

With a thoroughness and dedication that the world usually ascribed to the Prussians, the British infantry had spent many hours preparing for the attack. They practised walking forward in close and exactly prescribed intervals carrying almost 70 lb of equipment.

The Germans were at this time practising carrying their machine-guns from their deep and comfortable dug-outs to position them for firing. They did this as soon as the preliminary artillery barrage lifted for the attack. It took them three minutes.[21]

By the end of the first day, the British attackers had suffered 60,000 casualties, about one-third of them fatal. It was the worst day suffered by any army during the war and the worst in the British army's history.

Haig was not deterred. His futile battle continued for six months, until the Allied casualties numbered 420,000 men.[22] Few of the soldiers engaged in the Somme fighting had been given proper infantry training. Even the British artillery-men were not adequately trained. Afterwards the high command tried to make the artillery's performance an excuse for the disaster.

Between 1914 and 1918 a distinct difference was to be seen in the German and the Anglo-French methods of fighting the war. When France's General Pétain analysed the fighting in Champagne in 1915 he concluded that surprise attacks were useless because of the great depth of defences on both sides. He said artillery bombardment was the only way of preparing for a breakthrough. Britain's General Haig was convinced. Apart from the Neuve Chapelle fighting, in the early summer of 1915, and the Cambrai raid of 1917, Haig studiously avoided surprising the Germans. He said his guiding principle was wearing down the enemy: it was to be a war of attrition. Unfortunately for everyone concerned, Haig's methods wore his own men down more thoroughly than they wore down the enemy.

7 PASSCHENDAELE AND AFTER

The past is a foreign country:
they do things differently there.

L. P. Hartley, *The Go-Between*

D OUGLAS HAIG was not a man to be deterred by failure, or even to learn from it. One year later the Somme battle was staged all over again in the sloppy clay of the north. Men drowned in a quagmire made worse by bombardment. Even artillery pieces were swallowed up into the morass. It was the ultimate nightmare of the war, and many soldiers who were there – such as my father – would not speak of it. Like the Somme fighting of the previous year, it lasted from July until November and secured only a tiny strip of land.

Of this gloomy drama the military historian Liddell Hart said: 'So fruitless in its results, so depressing in its direction was this 1917 offensive, that "Passchendaele" has come to be . . . a synonym for military failure – a name black-bordered in the records of the British Army.'[1]

In the last year of the war the Germans, having knocked Russia out of the war, could turn to the Western Front and stage a 'Somme Battle' of their own design. It was a massive attack, and some of the ideas employed in it were still in evidence in the blitzkrieg of the Second World War.

General Ludendorff – probably the most expert general on either side in the war – in *Notes on Offensive Battles*, published in 1918, drew attention to broad differences in the German approach. The British had based their attacks upon artillery schedules, he said. The 'creeping barrage' – which fell behind the advancing infantry as well as ahead of it – drove the British infantry forward. Men who lingered, and men immobilized by injuries, came under intense shell-fire from their own guns. In such a scheme, said Ludendorff, commanders ceased to have proper control of their men. He condemned such tactics as wasteful and ineffective. Infantry should be used more flexibly, always seeking to get round behind the enemy on the flanks, and thus roll up the enemy and widen the attack.

The Germans did not disdain surprise. It was essential to these new methods. Specially selected men – storm-troops – would lead the assault. They'd use flamethrowers, have large canvas bags crammed full of hand-grenades, and be equipped with a revolutionary development of the machine-gun – the MP 18 machine-pistol. This was a small lightweight automatic, fitted with the barrel and 32-round magazine of the Luger pistol. It sprayed fire at about 400 rounds per minute and by the end of the war the Germans had put into use 35,000 of them.[2]

The opening of the attack was prepared in great secrecy. The storm-troops moved to jumping-off positions under cover of darkness. Artillery was not brought up to the place of attack until five days before it began; heavy mortars came two days before the attack. Such secrecy should have ensured surprise, but General Haig's intelligence section described with considerable accuracy the attack that was about to come. Haig made no changes whatever to his dispositions and even confirmed high-level changes of command that came into effect just hours before the attack started.[3] He decreed that the British tanks were spread out to be employed as static strong-points, in other words not tanks at all.

The Kaiser's Battle, as the Germans named it, started on 21 March 1918 and was aided by fog and by Haig's dispositions in depth. With much of his force too far forward, the unexpected penetration of the front caused a large section of his line to give way. By the 5 April he had lost 1,000 square miles of ground and 160,000 men (killed, wounded and taken prisoner) and many thought Haig's army was on the verge of collapse.

And then, in May, 42 German divisions struck the French armies with such force that Foch issued preliminary orders to prepare for a final stand before Paris. In London the cabinet panicked and even discussed the time it would take to pull the British army out of France. This too was a harbinger of the blitzkrieg of 1940, the evacuation from Dunkirk, and the bitterness that followed it.

But the worst did not happen and the fighting stabilized. Haig put the British forces under the French commander Foch, and the German advance slowed. This time it was the British machine-guns that did the killing. One man remembered: 'When I think of all those brave German infantry, walking calmly and with poise, into our murderous machine-gun fire, now, and as then, we had nothing but admiration for them. Unqualified courage! Poor devils.'[4]

Ludendorff had restored mobility to the fighting, but tanks, which might have transformed the chances of success, were in short supply. On the first day he used four German A7 V tanks – clumsy 33-ton machines with 18 men inside – and five captured British Mark IVs. The British Official History says the British line was broken wherever the tanks appeared.[5]

Even Ludendorff could not change the fact that, with machine-guns on the battlefield, attacks were costly. The greater resources of the Allies, with America now included, paid off as the Germans became exhausted by their successes. Front-line German troops were demoralized to find so much food and equipment piled up in the Allied rear areas. The Allied generals soon recovered their valour. They were drafting plans for ever more mighty battles to be fought in 1919 and 1920, when suddenly the Germans asked for an armistice.

There were a thousand explanations for the German collapse. The men and material from the United States, the strangulating effects of the naval blockade upon Germany's food supply, the naval mutineers roaming through the streets of Kiel, the surrender of their Turkish allies, the break-up of Austria-Hungary, and so on. Even today the real reason for the German collapse is not clear and simple. Many Germans believed that they had been tricked. As they saw it, US President Wilson proposed a peace in which Germany kept her colonies and armies intact. Once fighting ceased the Germany army disengaged and could not be sent back to start fighting again. The Allies then dictated terms and divided Germany's colonies between them. Whatever the reasons, the war came to an end, leaving the historians to continue hostilities by other means.

Throughout the war, troops from Canada, Australia and New Zealand proved to be particularly effective fighting soldiers, and Haig used them, like storm-troops, for most of the toughest attacks. The bloody fiasco at Passchendaele proved too much for the prime ministers of New Zealand and Canada, who had watched General Haig feeding their countrymen into his meat grinder. At a meeting of the imperial war cabinet on 13 June 1918, the New Zealand prime minister, William Massey, complained that his men had been sent against barbed-wire and shot down like rabbits. The Canadian prime minister, Sir Robert Borden, became so enraged that he was said to have grabbed the British prime minister – Lloyd

George – by his coat lapels and shaken him vigorously.

Government and bureaucracy conspired to conceal the incompetence of the British commanders. Even three-quarters of a century later, vital documents and statistics of the First World War are still withheld from public scrutiny, and many papers are said to have been lost in the air raids of 1940. 'Scholars have for long been dissatisfied with the patchy nature of the First World War records in the Public Record Office, which were clearly ruthlessly "weeded" before being made available to the public,' said the historian Michael Howard.[6]

The official histories were apt to provide a constructive account of the war. Cyril Falls, who took the chair of Military History at Oxford University, said: 'Our army was the best disciplined and the least effective in the war, though one can't say so in the Official History.'[7] Haig knew what to say, and it was his account of the war that went into the history books. He rewrote his diary to suit his public image, and the British government instructed the official historian to follow his falsified account. Then the original records were burned, which prevented other historians from discovering the truth. So it remained until Denis Winter pieced together a different account of Haig's flawed generalship by using the papers stored in overseas archives.[8]

The public is not so easily fooled. They had seen so many sons go off to war armed with that sense of duty and dedication that is the currency of the young. Wives, sisters and daughters too had scoured the ever-lengthening casualty lists fluttering in the wind outside the town halls. Nearly a million British soldiers never returned home; of these over 700,000 were from Great Britain. About 2.5 million men were wounded. Even if one includes the men serving in the lines of communication, those on home defence in Britain, and British army garrison troops in India and the Far East, it still means that of ten men joining the army, two were destined to be killed and five injured; only three would survive the war intact. Intact? These figures take no account of the psychological effects of the fighting and the long-term damage done by the various types of war gases. Pensions for the widows and the disabled were minuscule, and the cruelly contrived demands of postwar medical boards persuaded some veterans to give up their pensions rather than annoy their employers by frequent absences.[9]

The First World War marked the death of many human values, and if Christianity was not numbered among the fatalities it certainly suffered injuries from which it has not yet recovered. Another faith shattered on the battlefield was the faith that the Empire had in the Motherland. Haig had ordered too many Australians, New Zealanders and Canadians to certain death for their countrymen ever again to trust their regiments to the direct command of Whitehall. The Australian Official History quotes one officer saying his friends were 'murdered' through 'the incompetence, callousness and personal vanity of those in high authority'. Of the Somme another Australian officer is quoted as saying 'a raving lunatic could never imagine the horror of the last thirteen days.'

Mammon too was among the wounded. In July 1917 Britain's chancellor of the exchequer had admitted to the Americans that Britain's financial resources were virtually at an end. The United States began lending the British $180 million per month. By war's end Britain's national debt had risen from £650 millions in 1914 to £7,435 millions (of which £1,365 millions was owed to the USA). This provided an unbearable postwar burden for the taxpayer, and in 1931 Britain defaulted on its debt. Congress responded with the Johnson Act of 1934: Britain's purchases would now have to be paid for in cash.[10]

Payments in full

The British liked to ascribe Germany's remarkable fighting record to its robotic, merciless war machine, but it was the British soldiers who had been unceasingly ordered into futile and costly offensives. And, while 345 British soldiers faced firing squads during the war, only 48 German soldiers were executed.[11] Prince Rupprecht of Bavaria wrote in his diary in 21 December 1917 that while he knew of only one death sentence in his army, the British had executed at least 67 men between October 1916 and August 1917.

This disparity was partly due to the reckless way in which the British army had recruited men without consideration of their mental and physical stamina. It was also accounted for by the fact that the British army retained no less than 25 offences for which the penalty was death. Some of these, such as 'imperilling the success of His Majesty's forces', gave the courts wide powers. General Haig, who confirmed every sentence, believed that the firing squads were essential to maintaining discipline, and repeatedly demanded that Australian soldiers be made to face them. But the Australian government resisted Haig's pleas, in the confident knowledge that their infantrymen were widely acknowledged to be the best anywhere on the Western Front.[12]

All information about military executions was concealed from the British public. The government would not even tell the House of Commons how many soldiers were being shot, because publishing such figures was 'contrary to the public interest'. No one, not even next of kin, was permitted to know anything of the court-martial proceedings, and British soldiers had no right of appeal against a death sentence.

The army used firing squads to set an example to soldiers who needed one. Proclaimed throughout the army, executions were often staged before troops of the condemned man's unit. It was thus made clear to his comrades that it wasn't only murderers and rapists who were executed, it was exhausted men who closed their eyes, and men who refused to do the impossible. As the war went on, and ever younger conscripts were sent to the trenches, parents worried about how their sons would endure the ordeal. As stories of executions gained wider currency, the under-secretary for war admitted that there was great public anxiety, and questions by members of parliament, about whether wounded or 'shell-shocked' men were being executed, were met by outright lies. In the debate on 17 April 1918, several members, including serving officers, urged the government to change court-martial procedures so that an officer with some sort of legal training should be available to defend a soldier accused of a serious offence, and to ensure that all presidents of the court had previous experience of evaluating evidence. Even these modest reforms were denied.[13]

In February 1919 the most senior of the official historians spent an evening with Douglas Haig, dining and studying the maps and papers. 'Why did we win the war?' Haig asked him.[14] No one knew. But after the war Haig had demanded, and got, a massive cash hand-out. He was also presented with a mansion overlooking the River Tweed, where he carefully revised his memoirs. No matter what lengths he went to in rewriting history, Haig was never forgiven for what he had done. Nor was it forgotten. There was no wild cheering in public places when war was declared on Sunday 3 September 1939. The 'Great War' and the dead in Flanders were still very much in the minds of the survivors from all nations.

The world after the First World War

Georges Clemenceau, the prime minister of France, said in 1917: 'War is a series of catastrophes which result in a victory.' For

France that was true. As in the war to come, she emerged victorious only because the United States entered the war on the Allied side. Her provinces of Alsace and Lorraine were returned to her, and French troops occupied Germany's Rhineland and Saar. But the victory was a sham. The northern region of France had been the heart of its industrial strength, and after many battles had been fought there, it was devastated. France was bankrupt and deeply in debt. Jules Cambon, a French diplomat, saw the drastic decline in fortunes and wrote: 'France victorious must grow accustomed to being a lesser power than France vanquished.'

Germany had fought and survived the combined forces of Britain, France, the USA, Italy and Russia. The Fatherland was intact, and fighting had not brought destruction to any region of Germany, which even in defeat remained the strongest power in Europe. Germany's population of 70 millions was growing, while France's population of 40 millions was static. Within a decade of the peace treaty there would be twice as many Germans reaching military age each year as Frenchmen. Furthermore Germany's potential enemies were weakened; by internal strife (Russia), by division into smaller units (Austria-Hungary); by impoverishment (Britain and France), or by concern for their own affairs (USA).

The sacrifices they had made persuaded the French people that they alone had won the war, and their government did nothing to correct this false impression. The Canadians buried at Vimy Ridge, the British sailors lost at sea, Australians and New Zealanders who had fallen at Gallipoli, the Indian Corps which had frozen at Armentières in the first winter of the war, Americans killed at Champagne and Argonne, all these were forgotten. Her allies became bitter at what they considered a lack of gratitude, and the Anglo-Saxon nations moved into isolation and away from friendship with France. The French thought the world was being too kind to the Germans, and began to regard themselves as the sole guardians of the Versailles treaty. For this reason the French army was never to be short of men or money.

Versailles – the peace treaty

The treaty the great powers signed in 1919 to end the First World War remains one of the most controversial historic documents of the twentieth century. The American President Wilson arrived in Europe with his own programme for a lasting peace. We will never know if his ideas were sound, for his Allies would have nothing to do with his 'Fourteen Points'. Georges Clemenceau said: 'Mr Wilson bores me with his Fourteen Points; why, God Almighty only had ten.' Some said Wilson's proposals were altruistic. Certainly there was nothing benevolent about the twisted political wrangling of the European politicians, but the treaty that finally emerged was not vindictive compared with Germany's peace with France in 1871 or the terms Germany inflicted upon Lenin's Russia in 1917.

In postwar Germany, politicians made much of the £1,000 million charged to Germany in reparations. Less was said about the £1,500 million loaned to her by Britain and the United States. The peace terms laid down that Germany could have an army no bigger than 100,000 men and must not build or buy tanks, submarines and aircraft. Few Germans recognized that this would aid their economic recovery; rather it was seen as an insulting and unreasonable order that had to be flouted and eventually rectified.

Perhaps the path to true democratic government would have proved more certain had the monarchy been maintained. Certainly a hereditary monarchy makes it more difficult for tyrants like Hitler to become the head of state.[15] As it was, Germany's postwar democratic government – the Weimar Republic – was ridiculed as a puppet regime that implemented the forceful terms of the victors.

The most far-reaching effects of the peace treaty were the frontiers it drew. Austria-Hungary was split into pieces by the victors. The lines scrawled across the map cared nothing about consigning large numbers of Germans to live under foreign governments. Eventually, in Czechoslovakia and Poland, these vociferous expatriate communities were orchestrated and used by Hitler as an excuse for invasion.

Soldiers go home

At the end of the Great War the armies went home, and it was the attitudes and actions of these returning soldiers which created the world that went to war in 1939. Virtually all the men returning from the battlefields were to some extent cynical and embittered as they compared what they and their comrades had suffered with what others, less worthy, had gained. Most of the veterans' associations – from the Croix de feu in France to Oswald Mosley's Blackshirts in Britain – were anti-Communist. Communists had conspicuously associated themselves with pacificism and anti-militarism. Returning soldiers despised the men who had stayed at home preaching against the war.

Despite its new democratic government, a defeated Germany was convulsed in a series of localized revolutions as left-wing and right-wing political groups fought for power. There were violent uprisings in many German cities and for a few days Bavaria had 'a Soviet Republic'. Many German institutions – the army, big business and the labour movement – had survived the war intact; now each threw its weight behind the factions it favoured.

The government of this fragile republic saw its prime tasks as protecting the government from Communist takeover and keeping public order. To do this it came to terms with the highly organized veterans' organizations: most notably the Freikorps, a huge patchwork of small armies, illicitly armed and ready to fight all-comers. Such units were used as an armed frontier guard against Polish incursions and as a secret supplement to the army permitted by the peace treaty. At first Freikorps men wore their old army uniforms. Later they were issued with a consignment of shirts originally intended for German soldiers in East Africa. Dressed in them, these men became the brown-shirted Sturm Abteilung – storm-troops – who eventually allied themselves to Hitler's Nazi party to be its tough uniformed auxiliaries.[16]

Few of the veterans were looking for personal material gain. Life in the front line had shown them a special sort of comradeship, a world in which men literally sacrificed themselves for their fellows. The ex-servicemen were looking for such a new idealistic world in peacetime too. In Russia Lenin had not waited for an end to hostilities before harnessing the energies of the soldiers to his Communist revolution. In Italy Benito Mussolini offered such men a uniformed Fascist state. But it was Adolf Hitler, in Germany, who most skilfully designed a political party that could manipulate the ex-servicemen. The declared aims and intentions of the National Socialist German Workers' party swept away their cynical disillusion with politics and transformed such veterans into ardent Nazis.

Adolf Hitler, ex-soldier

Unlike their counterparts in Italy and Russia the German veterans felt that their leader – Führer – was an archetypal ex-soldier. There has been a mountain of contradictory material written about Adolf Hitler's wartime service. In fact he was a dedicated soldier who respected his officers and showed no cynicism about the war.

During the fighting Hitler was selected to be a 'runner' taking messages from the front line to the staff. It was a dangerous job usually given to intelligent and educated fit young soldiers. He won the coveted Iron Cross 1st Class in August 1918 when advancing German troops came under 'friendly fire' and his officer – Lt Hugo Gutmann – promised the award to anyone who could get a message back to the artillery. Hitler completed this 'suicide mission' and Lt Gutmann kept his promise. By that time Hitler had also won the Iron Cross 2nd Class, the Cross of Military Merit 3rd class with swords, and the regimental diploma. Details of Hitler winning his Iron Cross 1st Class – a notable award for a low-ranking soldier – were not widely publicized, leading to suggestions that it was never awarded at all. Probably Hitler felt his virulent anti-Jewish policies did not go well with receiving a medal from a Jewish officer.

Entering politics, Hitler's coarse regional accent and wartime lowly rank were appealing to thousands of ex-servicemen who heard their thoughts about war-profiteers and self-serving politicians voiced by a man with natural skills as an orator. The Communists kept blaming the soldiers for the war: Hitler's patriotic respect for the army was more to the taste of the veterans, and the relatives of those who had been killed and injured. The Nazis were fiercely xenophobic: Germany's troubles were blamed on foreigners. Socialists and Communists owed their true allegiance to Moscow, the Nazis said. Capitalists were equally unpatriotic, for they used cheap overseas labour for their imported goods and sent their profits to foreign banks overseas. Never mind that it wasn't true; in the harsh postwar climate it was the sort of explanation many Germans wanted to believe.

Hitler's anti-Jewish tirades were well received in Bavaria, the Nazi party's home, where both Lutheranism and the Catholic Church provided soil in which deep-rooted prejudice had flourished over hundreds of years. The Communists proposed a workers' paradise from which all 'privileged' Germans should be excluded; while Hitler's vision of a new Germany was designed to appeal alike to generals and tycoons, schoolteachers and physicians, as well as to workers and beggars.

Hitler and anti-Semitism

Hitler was not the first politician to foment anti-Jewish hatreds for political ends. In 1887 an International Anti-Jewish Congress had been organized in Dresden. More such gatherings had taken place in Kassel and Bochum in 1886 and 1889.[17] By 1895 anti-Semites were virtually a majority in Germany's lower house, while in Vienna, Karl Lueger's anti-Jewish Christian Socialists had 56 seats against 71 Liberals. In France the persecution of Captain Alfred Dreyfus revealed anti-Semitism no less deeply seated.[18] A motion in the Senate that would have banned Jews from public service in France was defeated 268:208.

A native of Austria, Hitler centred his political activities upon Bavaria in southern Germany. Always deliberately vague about his political aims and intentions, he artfully used many local prejudices to win support. Berlin bureaucrats ruled the new unified Germany. He attacked the remoteness of the heartily detested central government. He blamed the generals – conveniently regarded as Prussian Protestants – for losing the war. In Catholic Bavaria, traditionally resentful of Prussian attitudes, these views found warm support.

Hitler's vaguely defined anti-Semitism enabled the small farmer to hate the bank to whom he owed money, the small shopkeeper to hate the department store against which he competed. More intelligent Germans were convinced that these rabble-rousing simplifications were temporary measures. They firmly believed that once the Nazis turned their eyes away from Munich, Bavaria, to focus attention on the real seat of power in Berlin, such vicious anti-Semitism would tone down and fade away.

These hopes that Hitler and his Nazis would become moderate and statesmanlike were illusory. Hatred of Jews was Hitler's whole motivation. His campaign against Jews became more and more murderous and demented right up to the time of his death. He fanned ancient irrational fears of Jewish international conspiracies. This gave him the excuse to put peacetime Germany into a permanent state of emergency. That 'war footing' was what gave the Nazi party such tight control of all aspects of the life of every German.

Albert Speer provides a revealing memory of Adolf Hitler:

> He jumped from one subject to another, frequently repeating words like 'fundamental', 'absolutely', 'unshakeable'. Then too he had a special fondness for phrases and words out of the days of the beer-hall brawls, such as 'club down', 'iron perseverance', 'brute force', or 'beat up', as well as scatological words like 'shithead', 'crapper'. In moments of excitement he also tended

to phrases like: 'I'll finish him off myself'; 'I'll personally put a bullet through his head'; or 'I'll fix him.'[19]

The Maginot Line

While the French generals still regarded attack as the secret of success in war, plans were approved for a mighty series of fortifications along her frontier with Germany. This was not incompatible with the military policy of attack; it would provide time for the reserve to be mobilized and for a naval blockade to be established. Attack, using the best forces, would follow.

The 'Maginot Line', as it came to be known, was born out of the

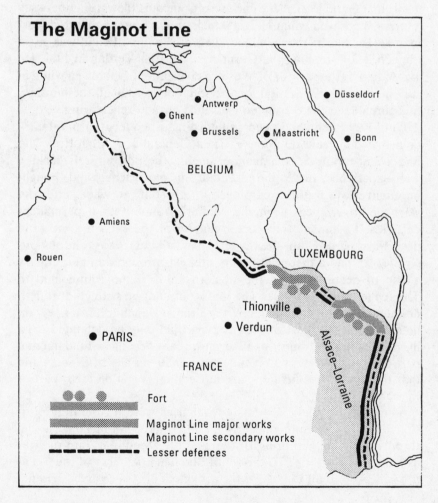

The Maginot Line

Fort

Maginot Line major works

Maginot Line secondary works

Lesser defences

mighty battles that had raged round the French forts at Verdun. These forts had been a part of the defences built after the 1870 defeat. For ten months in 1916 the French and German armies stood toe-to-toe there and countless men died. Almost every French soldier served at Verdun at some time or other. Every family in France had cause to curse its name. After the war it became a shrine and a place of pilgrimage. Still today the echoing footsteps, and whispered words of school parties, can be heard in its monolithic blockhouses which even 42-cm Krupp shells failed to raze.

Liddell Hart's *History of the World War* suggests that it was luck that saved Verdun.[20] All the German 17-inch howitzers were destroyed by French long-range guns and 450,000 ready-fused artillery shells in a German artillery park near Spincourt blew up. Others say Verdun was saved when Haig's attack on the Somme diverted German resources. In France General Henri Philippe Pétain was given the credit for stopping the German advance at Verdun in 1916. He was hailed as the saviour of Western civilization. Doubly so when in 1917 he used his reputation and personal pleas to quell the mutinies that threatened the continued existence of the French army.

Until 1914 Pétain had been an undistinguished lecturer in infantry tactics at the Ecole de Guerre. Then General J. J. C. Joffre, who had been appointed commander-in-chief despite entirely lacking staff experience, remembered Pétain, his old teacher, and thought he might prove useful if employed on his staff. So when, after the war, the government wanted a soldier's opinion about permanent defences, Pétain, now inspector-general of the French army (and designated C-in-C in the event of hostilities), was an obvious choice. He had a theory about 'battlefields prepared in peacetime', a line of defences along the western bank of the Rhine, and to Thionville on the Moselle. The line would not be strongly fortified, neither would it continue along the Franco-Belgium border. Pétain believed that that part of the frontier could only be defended from inside Belgium.[21] From this time onwards it became a fundamental part of French strategy that Belgium remain an ally of France, and that the line of fortifications inside Belgium was a de facto part of French defences.

Some believe that the Maginot defences were deliberately positioned so as to ensure that any German attack would have to go through Belgium and bring Britain and the Dominions into the war as it had done in 1914. To the south, the main defences of the Maginot Line were built to include the provinces of Alsace and Lorraine.

These provinces had been a part of Germany until 1918. The people there had grown up under German rule but the Maginot fortifications told them unequivocally that France would not allow this region to become German again. Thus the siting and building of the Maginot Line took political as well as military ideas into account.

The northern provinces provided special problems. The low lands flooded every winter, as had been discovered by the wretched front-line troops who served in waterlogged trenches there in the First World War. An urban-industrial region straddled the Franco-Belgian frontier and was growing as Europe recovered from the war. It would be difficult to build fortresses amid factories and houses. Any construction along the French side of this border would be a declaration that France would abandon Belgium in the event of war.

For all these reasons, and many more, the Maginot Line was not a continuous series of fortifications. It stopped and started; and in any case it was designed only as a barrier which would enable France to spread second-rate troops thinly behind the forts, and concentrate its best units elsewhere. Many people, including Winston Churchill, agreed that the small population of France, compared with that of Germany, made the construction of the Maginot Line a sensible precaution.

That the Maginot Line 'was an astounding feat of twentieth century engineering'[22] can be seen still today. It was designed however before the use of armoured mobile columns changed the textbooks. When the Maginot Line was being planned, whole armies of tracked and wheeled vehicles were no more than theoreticians' dreams that few soldiers took seriously.

In the long run the Maginot Line had more effect upon the French than it had upon the Germans. It lulled them into a false sense of security. When war began, at a time when the German army was fully occupied in Poland, the French had a wonderful chance to use their fortifications as a base from which to strike against the Rhineland. They did not do it. The 'Maginot mentality' – added to its political confusions and Hitler's fearsome propaganda – had hypnotized France and made it into a victim waiting for an end that many considered inevitable.

Neither did the magic of Maginot totally fade in 1945. At war's end, the French army immediately occupied and reconditioned the Maginot Line. It kept it maintained until 1964. Now its mouldering turrets and weedy entrances are to be found by curious holiday-makers who wander off the highways.[23]

8 FRANCE IN THE PREWAR YEARS

Peace is better than war, because in peace the
sons bury their fathers, but in war the
fathers bury their sons.

Croesus to Cambyses (son of his enemy Cyrus the Great)

IT WAS NOT ONLY the 'Maginot mentality' that rendered France so vulnerable in 1940. Although the generals failed to equip France's army for modern war, the nation itself during those interwar years became ever more demoralized and divided. Political extremists of both left and right had a powerful influence upon French society, as did the widespread corruption that so often procured fat government contracts. The French aircraft industry provided an example of the crippling effect of political theorists. In 1936 all the well established French aircraft manufacturers were nationalized by the Communist air minister Pierre Cot. The effect upon production was devastating, and the resulting chaos was still being sorted out when the Germans attacked in 1940. France's relationships with the rest of the world suffered as a result of its own dissensions. Although the French had remained Britain's close allies since before the First World War, the ties between the two countries had grown more and more uncertain. Even in November 1938 – after the Munich agreement – the British prime minister thought it necessary to ask the French whether they would support Britain if it became the victim of German aggression. In the same cabinet meeting, Prime Minister Neville Chamberlain said he had been assured that France was not proposing to sign a non-aggression pact with Germany that would rule out help to Britain.[1] These were chilly words about Britain's closest neighbours immediately prior to a life-and-death struggle with a well armed and determined enemy.

Hitler's New Order

In the eyes of many people, Adolf Hitler's regime was a success.

Everything seemed to have improved since the waves of economic depression that rolled over Europe in the 1920s. Germans were thankful for the way Hitler's coming to power stopped the vicious and extensive street battles which were a regular ending to all Communist and Nazi political rallies. But the Nazi way of restoring law and order was to execute or imprison without trial all opponents. Equally drastic was the way Hitler reduced unemployment by means of massive public works projects and rearmament. In 1935 conscription was introduced. All German youth was called to serve twelve months in the armed forces following a term of manual work in the RAD, the State Labour Service. In September 1936 Hitler was able to announce to a party congress that the jobless had fallen from 6 million to 1 million. A strictly controlled economy caused living standards to rise sharply, so that Germans soon enjoyed the highest living standards in Europe.

The Nazi propaganda machine brought the arts, theatre, cinema, newspapers and radio under the direct control of the artful Joseph Goebbels. Parades with flaming torches, vast uniformed rallies on monumental stages and stadiums, massed flags and columns of searchlights had made Germany into a political theatre watched by the rest of the world.

As part of the rapid expansion of the German army, during training and exercises it employed motor cars fitted with flimsy wooden superstructures to represent tanks, with other mock-ups for artillery and so on. Such improvised vehicles gave rise to colourful rumours that were repeated everywhere abroad and even got into foreign newspapers. They said the German army was no more than a sham force built for parades, and designed solely to intimidate other nations. A more accurate picture of the expanding war machine was available to motor-racing enthusiasts.

Figure 14: Mercedes and Auto-Union racing cars

During the Thirties the victories of the German motor-racing team shocked and dismayed its competitors. Many, if not most, British racing drivers were competing simply for fun; using the same cars to journey to the circuits, race there and then travel home. The Nazis were quick to see the propaganda benefits of international racing victories. German cars – Mercedes and Auto-Union – were highly specialized designs with engineering that was years ahead of their rivals. The drivers – some of them non-Germans – and fitters were highly trained and dedicated. The team organization was managed with a professional resolution quite unlike anything from other European countries. It could be said that the Germans invented the racing team as we now know it. In every respect those victorious German racing teams of the Thirties provided a glimpse of blitzkrieg to come.

It wasn't only racing cars that Germany was manufacturing: in the period 1930-38 German car production went from 189,000 to 530,000 vehicles. Industrial production soared and unemployment plunged from its 1932 peak.

Hitler's defiant stance, and his violent speeches against the injustices of the peace treaty, gave Germans a new sort of pride. It was the 'stick and carrot' technique. Most Germans turned a blind eye to the persecution of the Jews, and all the other legalized crimes of the Nazis, when the stick might be a spell in a labour camp. Those who objected were arrested; many were never seen again. Article 48 of the Weimar Constitution legalized protective custody and enabled all the fundamental rights of a citizen to be withheld. Using this the Nazis sent thousands of opponents to concentration camps without due process of law. The lawyers found legal reasons to classify such prisoners as citizens assisting in upholding the law.

Here and there a brave German spoke up against the regime. The view that Nazi Germany – whatever its faults – had to be supported because of the 'protection' it provided against the spread of Russian Communism was echoed by the rich and powerful everywhere. It was certainly a view aired in the British cabinet. In Rome the Pope did nothing to stop the anti-Semitic excesses of the 'anti-Bolshevik' state Hitler had created as a bulwark against the Reds.

The German trade unions had been silenced by arrests and threats. The Nazi labour organizations which replaced them gave workers cheap vacations and luxury cruises but deprived them of the right to strike, demonstrate or make any kind of objection to the regime. It succeeded. Working-class Germans – like middle-class ones – offered no serious opposition to the Nazis.

It is difficult to give a balanced picture of the respective strengths of the great powers in that period immediately before the war. But in an attempt to provide some sort of estimate, Table 2 looks at three aspects of each nation. Manpower is a guide to the size of the army that could be put into the field. Annual steel-making capacity estimates the ability to build ships, submarines, tanks and artillery. Annual aircraft production is a guide to the potential production of such items as trucks, cars and infantry weapons, as well as aircraft.

Table 2   Relative strengths of the Great Powers in 1939

	Population (000s)	Steel (000 tons)	Aircraft
Britain	47,961	13,192	7,940
France	41,600	6,221	3,420
Germany	76,000	23,329	8,295
USA	132,122	51,380	5,856
USSR	190,000	18,800	10,382

British population figures do not take account of men in the Dominions. For steel, the figures given are the best for the 1930s, with German figures including Austrian production. Aircraft numbers take no account of size (tending to underrate UK and USA, which were building more large aircraft than the other nations).[2]

The British and their prime minister: Chamberlain

It has become convenient to think of the war as a confrontation between Adolf Hitler and Winston Churchill, but Britain's leader in the years leading up to the war was Neville Chamberlain. Although very much in the minority, there are still those who say that Chamberlain was an astute statesman. They prefer to believe that Chamberlain, by appeasing Hitler and letting him march into Austria and then Czechoslovakia, gained time for Britain to rearm. There is nothing to support this contention.

By 1937 Hitler had provided Germany with formidable fighting forces. His troops had reoccupied the demilitarized Rhineland in open defiance of the peace treaty. In Britain there were no signs of a resolve to confront Germany. According to the foreign minister, Anthony Eden, the elder men of the cabinet were not convinced of the need to rearm.[3] Chamberlain thought armaments were a wasteful form of expenditure and saw no reason to believe that war was bound to come.[4]

In the previous cabinet, Chamberlain had been chancellor of the exchequer. He knew how much a government's popularity depended upon keeping income taxes low. Opposition politicians were certainly not demanding rearmament. Clement Attlee, leader of the Labour (Socialist) party, had said in December 1933: 'We are unalterably opposed to anything in the nature of rearmament.' His party stuck to that line and campaigned against rearmament right up to the outbreak of war. Prominent churchmen and intellectuals said little about the persecution of German Jews, even though refugees brought ever more appalling stories of what was happening. Priests, politicians and writers combined in such pacifist organizations as the Peace Pledge Union, and the influential voices of Aldous Huxley, Siegfried Sassoon and Vera Brittain were heard arguing persuasively against any preparations for war.

Everywhere pacifism was coloured by the fear of what fleets of bombing aircraft might do to large cities. The writings of General J. F. C. Fuller and Bertrand Russell, and the H.G. Wells science-fiction book *Things to Come* (and the frightening Alexander Korda film based upon it), fanned fears of impending devastation and chaos by bomber fleets. It was against this background that Chamberlain made his decisions about rearmament.

Seen in photographs and cartoons, Chamberlain appears a wretched and ridiculous figure with drawn face and craning neck, but an American who met him in 1940 was impressed:

> Mr Chamberlain was seated alone at his place at the Cabinet table when we were both shown in. He was spare, but gave the impression both of physical strength and energy. He appeared to be much younger than his seventy-one years. His hair was dark, except for a white strand across his forehead. His dominating features were a pair of large, very dark, piercing eyes. His voice was low, but incisive.[5]

Chamberlain was concerned with his personal popularity and he spoke of it frequently. The welcoming crowds he saw on his visits to Munich and Rome were reassuring to him. He even remarked that Mussolini did not seem jealous at being welcomed less warmly than Chamberlain and the British party. Chamberlain's ego led him to believe that his personal negotiations with Hitler were a statesman-like contribution to world peace. In fact he did little but give way to

Hitler's bullying, and ratify and assist the aggressions he claimed to be stopping. In addition Chamberlain's well publicized meetings with Hitler encouraged the more extreme Nazis while demoralizing the few influential Germans who opposed Hitler's methods.

The persistent belief that war could be avoided by appeasement made Chamberlain reluctant to form an alliance with Stalin's USSR. He and his colleagues shared a well merited distaste for Stalin's violent and repressive empire, and yet an alliance with Russia – as the British chiefs of staff pointed out – might be the only practical way to stop Hitler. When, in the summer of 1939, General Ironside (inspector-general of Overseas Forces) returned from a trip to Danzig, Chamberlain asked him to confirm that it seemed impossible to come to terms with the Russians. Ironside would not confirm it; he said it was the only thing that Britain could do. Chamberlain was not pleased at this response and retorted: 'The only thing we cannot do.'[6]

Many military men said that the Red Army was worthless, and that an alliance with the USSR would be only an encumbrance. Britain's ambassador in Berlin added to Chamberlain's confusion with a ridiculous warning that a British alliance with Russia would provoke Germany into an immediate war. (To prepare peacetime Germany for a war against Russia would have taken many months.) While Chamberlain vacillated it was Hitler who saw the advantages that a pact with Russia would provide.

Hitler's occupation of the Rhineland and then Austria had been welcomed by virtually the whole population of those German-speaking regions. *Blumenkriege* the German soldiers called these occupations; flower wars in which the soldiers got kisses and posies, not bullets and shells. But the people of Czechoslovakia – apart from the vociferous Volksdeutschen who lived in the border regions – had no love for the Germans.

Czechoslovakia – the Munich crisis

Czechoslovakia had been created in ten minutes at the end of the First World War. The imperial governor of defeated Austria-Hungary telephoned the illegal Czech National Committee and told them to come up to Hradcany Castle and pick up his seals and keys.[7]

Within Czechoslovakia's boundaries remained many of the old Empire's munitions factories. With the newly minted Czech crown unwanted on the international money markets, the Czechs were pleased to find that their armaments could be sold for hard currency.[8] The new government strongly supported the armaments industry – Skoda at Plzen and Zbrojovka at Brno – and the chemical plants too. Within a decade Czech arms salesmen had 10 per cent of the world arms market. In the violent interwar years Czech arms were used by the Japanese and the Chinese, by the Ethiopians and by both sides in the Spanish Civil War. The British army's best light machine-gun was named the Bren because it was evolved by the Czechoslovak factory at Brno and the British factory at Enfield.

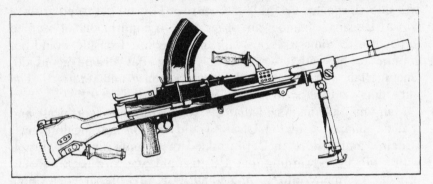

Figure 15: British Bren light machine-gun

The German army greedily eyed the Czech arsenals. Rightly so: tanks and guns of Czech design and manufacture were to serve that army throughout the war. Czechoslovakia's production of aero engines and aircraft components was to prove even more important. Hitler would now add all this to his empire. There was no one in France and Britain with the will and wherewithal to stop him, and yet this was the crisis that eventually signalled the war.

Hitler's claim to Czechoslovakia's Sudetenland was based upon spurious complaints that the German communities resident there were being harshly treated by the government in Prague. It was not true, but German newspapers, manipulated by Goebbels, told the story the way the Nazis wanted it told. The Sudeten Germans lived in the borderlands, an area well fortified against German attack. The Czechs stood firm and mobilized their army. Chamberlain, convinced that Hitler was a rational individual with whom an agreement could be reached, offered to meet him. Old and somewhat frail, he made his first flight in order to meet Hitler at the Führer's mountainside retreat near Berchtesgaden. There were more fruitless meetings and for a time outsiders began to think that war was inevitable. Then at the last moment Chamberlain sent a secret message to Italy's leader, Benito Mussolini, asking him to intercede.[9]

In September 1938 Hitler, Chamberlain, Mussolini and Daladier, the French PM, met in Munich to discuss Hitler's claim. It was a fiasco that might call to mind a Marx Brothers comedy. The room was crammed with all kinds of officials and hangers-on, milling around and eating the buffet food. Hitler, Daladier and Chamberlain had no common language and their interpreters found it difficult to work in such a restless crowd. Mussolini delighted in the fact that he could manage all their languages. He strode about, turning the meeting into a quiz show in which he played question-master. Eventually, at twenty-five minutes past midnight, the Munich Pact was signed.

Chamberlain came back from Munich waving the agreement, and a supplementary joint declaration renouncing war, and saying that it meant peace for our time. The end had always been a foregone conclusion. The meeting was a futile attempt to preserve the dignity of France and Britain, while allowing Hitler to seize the Czech border regions. By occupying the fortified border the Germans rendered the rest of Czechoslovakia defenceless. The only consolation for the Czechs, who were given no say about the dismemberment of their land, was that Britain and France guaranteed the new frontiers against unprovoked aggression. Germany was also asked to do so, but never did.

Winston Churchill, a rebel back-bench member of Parliament with patchy influence, stood up in the House of Commons and said: 'We have sustained a total, unmitigated defeat. We are in the midst of a disaster of the first magnitude . . . And do not suppose that this is the end. It is only the beginning.' He was shouted down by his fellow members of Parliament.

Any last idea that Chamberlain, and his colleagues, were temporizing, permitting Hitler to march into the Sudetenland to give Britain time to rearm, is refuted by Chamberlain himself. When, after the Munich meeting, Lord Swinton (one-time secretary of state for Air) said to Chamberlain: 'I will support you, Prime Minister, provided that you are clear that you have been buying time for rearmament,' Chamberlain would have none of it. He took from his pocket the declaration that Hitler had so cynically signed and said: 'But don't you see, I have brought back peace.'[10]

Most of the cabinet, in fact most of the British public, tried to believe that the joint Anglo-German declaration affirming that the

British and German peoples would 'never go to war with one another again' meant the 'peace for our time' which Chamberlain
promised. But, according to Chamberlain's account of that meeting,
when Hitler went to sign the declaration there was no ink in the ink-
well. A more wary man might have wondered about the sincerity of
German preparations that didn't include filling the inkwells.

The German occupiers of the Sudeten region treated the Czechs
spitefully. Families who had lived in the same house for many generations were expelled without household goods or farm animals.
SS Einsatzkommandos – a newly formed unit which later, in occupied regions of Poland and the USSR, organized mass murders –
were manning the checkpoints to be sure the Czechs took nothing
with them. When Hitler, on a tour of inspection, noticed Czech
refugees being given bread and soup from German field kitchens he
asked General Reichenau: 'Why do we waste good German bread
on those pigs?' In fact the bread was good Czech bread.

Some Germans were shocked at this first sight of the behaviour of
Himmler's SS units. One Abwehr (Army Intelligence) officer wrote
in his diary: 'The SS Standarte Germania has murdered, pillaged
and evicted in a bestial fashion. I saw one unfortunate girl who had
been raped nine times by a gang of these rascals while her father
had been murdered . . . these troops believe all they have read in
the newspapers about Czech atrocities against our brothers.'[11]

Those Sudeten Germans who had encouraged Hitler's claim, by
totally unfounded complaints about the Prague government's treatment of them, gained no lasting advantage. After the war ended, all
the Sudeten Germans were unceremoniously deported back into
Germany at a few hours' notice.

Appeasement

On 9 October 1938, only days after his triumph at Munich, Hitler
made a speech at Saarbrücken in which he attacked the Western
powers and forecast that soon warmongers would take control of
Britain. It was a reference to Churchill and any others who objected
to Chamberlain's appeasement policy.

In those days before worldwide electronic communications, such
as satellite telephones, the role of an ambassador could be vital. It
was unfortunate for all concerned that so many of the ambassadors
involved were men of low calibre. America's man in London was
Joseph Kennedy, father of the future US president. He was rabidly

anti-British and had long since decided (not without some reason) that Britain would not long survive a clash with Germany. The American ambassador in Paris was a man who saw Bolshevik conspiracies everywhere he looked. As their ambassador in Berlin, Britain's cabinet had to depend upon Nevile Henderson, of whom William Shirer – an American journalist and historian who was at the time resident in Berlin – wrote as a footnote in his memoirs:

> I have tried to be as objective as possible about Sir Nevile Henderson, but it has been difficult. From the moment of his arrival in Berlin he struck me as being not only sympathetic to Nazism but to Nazism's aims. The ambassador did not try to hide his personal approval of Hitler's taking Austria and then Czechoslovakia – he seemed to loathe the Czechs as much as Hitler did.
>
> But worse than Henderson's personal prejudices were his personal limitations. Sir L.B. Namier, the British historian, summed them up: 'Conceited, vain, self-opinionated, rigidly adhering to his pre-conceived ideas, he poured out telegrams, dispatches and letters in unbelievable numbers and of formidable length, repeating a hundred times the same ill-founded views and ideas. Obtuse enough to be a menace and not stupid enough to be innocuous, he proved *un homme néfaste* [a very bad fellow].'[12]

By the end of 1938 the threat of war was giving the British government economic worries. In April that year Britain was holding a healthy reserve of £800 million in gold, but appearances were deceptive. The money belonged largely to foreigners seeking a safe haven for their funds. The threat of war and the fact that Britain seemed unready for it[13] caused some £150 million in gold to move out of the country between April and September. Britain's economy was not resilient enough to cope with such swings of fortune. The cost of the First World War was still a burden on the taxpayer, despite the fact that the war debt to the United States was never paid. The Treasury had repeatedly warned that Britain could not afford to fight a major war lasting three years or more. The armed services all needed money and the government's headache was made worse by the ever-growing cost of modern armaments.

The reluctance to spend money was most apparent in cabinet on 2 February 1939 when the secretary of state for war, Leslie Hore-Belisha, sought £81 million to re-equip six divisions of the Regular army and four divisions of the Territorials. Chamberlain was against spending such money, saying that Britain's financial strength would be a decisive factor in any future war. But the French, fearing that the British might be no more than spectators in a future war, had been insisting that the British prepare an army to fight on French soil. In the event, it was decided to re-equip all the twelve Territorial divisions but not the regular army.

Having occupied the Sudetenland, Hitler encouraged Slovakia – a large section of the dismembered country – to demand autonomy. Nazi demands upon the Prague government became more and more outrageous: Czechoslovakia must leave the League of Nations, reduce the size of its army, turn over part of its gold reserves to the Reichsbank, outlaw the Jews in line with the Nuremberg Laws the Nazis had passed. Inevitably, in March 1939, the Germans took over the whole of Czechoslovakia. Bohemia and Moravia were declared a German 'protectorate'. Hitler went to Prague and spent the night in the President's Palace, the castle which was to become the German administrative centre. Soldiers and Nazi party members wearing the red and black ribbon given to those who had 'rendered valuable service' in organizing the occupation of the Sudetenland, now got a 'Prague castle bar' – *Prager Burg Spange* – to put on it. Slovakia became a separate state.

The newly acquired riches made Germany the greatest industrial power in the world after the USA. All the Balkan nations, from Yugoslavia to Turkey, were equipped with Czech weapons. From this time onwards, all foreign powers using Czech armaments would depend upon Hitler's good will for spare parts and replacements. The British could certainly not help such foreign powers by supplying British equipment. British guns, tanks and artillery were in short supply, and they lacked the quality of Czech production. Czech steel was so much better than Britain's that during the Thirties Britain was importing Czech armour plate for building its warships.

In London the news that German troops had driven into Czechoslovakia and occupied Prague came as a shock. Under the terms of the Munich Pact, it was now time for Britain to fight for the Czech borders. The cabinet looked to Lord Halifax, Chamberlain's foreign secretary, for a reaction. He received the news calmly. Halifax was a tall autocratic figure who had taken over as foreign secretary when his predecessor, Anthony Eden, showed opposition to Chamberlain's policy of appeasement. Britain hadn't guaranteed the Czechs against the exercise of moral pressure, explained Halifax. In the circumstances which had arisen, Britain's guarantee had come to an end. Chamberlain agreed and blamed the Slovaks for wanting a separate state: that was what had precipitated the crisis, he said.

Yet despite these self-abasing reactions to it, the German occupation finally persuaded Chamberlain and his cabinet that Hitler might be seeking world domination. Chamberlain aired these thoughts in a speech. Now he began to look for allies who would actively oppose the next act of aggression. Britain's secretary of state for war, Hore-Belisha, pointed out that from the Czechs Hitler had just acquired the complete equipment of 38 infantry divisions and eight mobile divisions. (This might have been an exaggeration, but it was certainly enough for 20 divisions.)

Britain's foreign secretary was hardly the man to put backbone into Chamberlain. An intensely religious former viceroy of India, the first Earl of Halifax was an elitist of the old school, a snob who recoiled at any prospect of true democracy. As more and more was known of his behaviour, he was to emerge as the personification of appeasement. Halifax was prepared to go to extreme lengths to appease Hitler, even to giving Germany some African colonies. It was Halifax who tried to muzzle British newspapers which he thought too critical of the Nazis. It is certainly chilling to consider how near he came (in 1940) to getting the premiership instead of Churchill.

9 AN ANTI-HITLER COALITION?

If it will all be wonderful after the war,
Why didn't we have this old wo-er befo-er?

Wartime ditty by A. P. Herbert

A NY COALITION to resist Hitler would have to include Poland's formidable army and Romania's oil wells. Both countries shared frontiers with Germany and were likely to be attacked, but the Poles and Romanians were not friends and didn't want to be allies. Both felt closer in spirit to Germany than to Soviet Russia. Political creeds made it difficult to put together an agreement that included Russia with such anti-Communist governments as those of Spain, Portugal, Poland and Romania. The recurring problem was that countries with short-term fears of German military actions also had long-term fears about Soviet Communism.

The shape of Poland provided Hitler with an excuse for action. The Poland created after the First World War, with its 'corridor' through Germany to the sea, cut East Prussia away from the rest of Germany. Danzig (present-day Gdansk) was a coastal town on the corridor and the centre of the crisis. Largely German, it had been made a 'free city' under international control in the hope of avoiding such conflicts. In October 1938, even before his troops occupied Prague, Hitler was demanding that Danzig be incorporated into his Third Reich.

In March 1939 the British cabinet was receiving convincing reports that Hitler was planning to attack Poland. One came from America's ambassador in Warsaw and was delivered by the abrasive Joseph Kennedy, the US ambassador in London. Another came via Ian Colvin, Berlin correspondent of the *News Chronicle*, who had just been expelled from Germany because of his continuing contacts with anti-Hitler groups. Colvin's detailed report of German intentions was a mixture of hard secret information, inferences and wild exaggerations. Some of this material originated from General Franz Halder, chief of the army staff.[1] It had been concocted by someone with access to Hitler's 25 March directive to Brauchitsch, the army C-in-C, and was given to Colvin in the hope of provoking resistance to Hitler's aggressive plans.

On 29 March Colvin took his story to the Foreign Office[2] and was immediately asked to recount it first to Lord Halifax and then to Prime Minister Chamberlain, who decided that some sort of undertaking to aid Poland was needed while they continued to seek a coalition of anti-Hitler nations. An 'interim' statement was cobbled together by 31 March. It simply said that in the event of a threat to Poland which that country resisted by force, Britain would go to Poland's support. 'The French Government have authorized me to make plain that they stand in the same position,' Chamberlain added, and a crowded House of Commons echoed with cheers at this more positive news.

Chamberlain looked sick. A mortal illness had begun to take its grip on him, and he seemed not to understand the extent of his momentous undertaking. In a letter dated 2 April, he told his sister: 'And it is we who will judge whether that independence is threatened or not.' Lord Beaverbrook, the newspaper tycoon, writing anonymously in his *Evening Standard*, interpreted Britain's obligations even more loosely. He saw no obligation for Britain to interfere in minor territorial adjustments: a German Autobahn might be constructed through Poland to connect Germany with East Prussia, or Danzig might be handed over to Germany, without any need to rush to Poland's aid.

Such interpretations were not supported by a Foreign Office statement of 3 April which said Britain would not seek to influence the Poles in any way if such pressure arose. Clearly if the Poles asked for help they would get it. It was later discovered that the Polish foreign minister had threatened to cancel his visit to London unless Britain's obligation was clarified. For anyone looking for the moment when war became inevitable then this must be the date. Avoiding the embarrassment that a cancelled visit would bring to the Foreign Office was the trigger.

Less than a week after Chamberlain's momentous statement, news came that Italy – until this time regarded by Chamberlain as an opponent of German expansion – had invaded Albania, a small country that was in any case virtually an Italian mandate. The news sent a ripple of alarm across Europe. In those days European governments were even more secretive than they are today, and rumours mushroomed in the darkness of official silence. Concerted attacks by the German and Italian dictators were expected any minute. The scaremongers said that war would start with bombing raids on London and Paris.

The attacks did not come, but during that winter of 1938–39 the mood in Britain changed. Way ahead of politicians, the British public was starting to believe that war was inevitable. Few people anywhere in the world realized that Britain lacked the financial resources needed for a major war. Everyone assumed that Britain, with the backing of a vast empire, must be strong and rich enough to play policeman to the world. In any case a future war would be fought in France, which possessed the world's most formidable army and the Maginot Line defences. 'Hitler has got to be stopped,' was the prevailing opinion in Britain. Perhaps it was too often said with an air of frightened resignation but it was said nevertheless. There was little excitement. Too many men had vivid memories of the previous war for there to be widespread pleasure at the prospect of doing it all over again. And yet there was a spirit of grim resolve that is peculiarly British. Intellectuals and pacifists who preached peace at any price were finding it more difficult to get a sympathetic hearing.

In line with prevalent fears about the devastating effect of bombing, it was decided that a portion of the anti-aircraft defences should be manned every night. Londoners now saw the night skies crisscrossed by searchlights. Those who knew where to look saw the 3.7-inch guns sitting inside their sandbag emplacements and manned by soldiers in steel helmets. But the bulk of the defences depended upon out-of-date 3-inch guns,[3] and opposition to having guns nearby continued to come from golf club secretaries, farmers, park authorities, residents and the municipal councils. 'In nearly all cases the protests were entirely successful' said the C-in-C of Anti-Aircraft Command bitterly.[4]

On 11 April Lord Gort, chief of the Imperial General Staff, warned the secretary of state for war,[5] Hore-Belisha, that he couldn't keep the air defences at this state of readiness without more men. The government must call up the army reservists by partial mobilization. The only alternative was for Parliament to pass an Act drafting men for peacetime military service. Gort knew that Hore-Belisha was sympathetic to this need, having heard his speech on 31 March saying that conscription might be necessary.

Drafting civilians into the armed services was a painful step for the British. Compulsory military service had been used in the previous war, but it was very distasteful to them. Chamberlain was opposed to the draft because his predecessor had promised the voters that on no account would it come before the next election, and Chamberlain had repeated the promise. He also feared bitter objections from the largely pacifist Socialist opposition and the trade unions. In a last effort to avoid conscription the prime minister proposed an impractical scheme in which Territorials (part-time volunteer soldiers) would man the defences at the end of their day's work as civilians. The army was adamant: the Territorial Anti-Aircraft units were already overworked and finding it difficult to fulfil their civilian and military obligations. Finally, after Lord Halifax was also persuaded of the necessity for compulsory call-up, Chamberlain gave way.

Chamberlain now adopted the idea as his own, although the word conscription was carefully avoided, recruits were called 'militia men', and the draft was described as compulsory military training. The suggestion that the government should declare 'a state of emergency' was abandoned in case it had disastrous effects on the financial markets of the City of London.

In a triumph of party politics over common sense, the (Socialist) Labour party and the Liberals voted against this compulsory military training. The Tory party could muster more than enough votes in the House of Commons to secure the new measures by a large majority: 380 to 143. At least 30 MPs, most national newspapers and some demonstrators aired the view that the time had come for a new government to be formed from men of all parties. Chamberlain was not convinced by them.

By 23 April 1939 cabinet and Treasury approval for some of the army's urgent needs produced some money, but that was not the same as having the equipment to hand. The list of urgently needed items that could not simply be bought off the shelf makes chilling reading now that we can see how close Britain was to war. Tanks were in very short supply: even guns had to be borrowed from the Indian army.

Diplomatic manoeuvres

In response to questions raised by the British ambassador in Moscow the cabinet was astonished to receive on 18 April a long proposal from Maxim Litvinov, Stalin's foreign minister. Litvinov, an urbane and widely travelled Jewish diplomat of long experience, had an English-born wife and was an advocate of stronger Soviet ties with Britain and France. Now he proposed a five- or ten-year military pact with Britain and France, providing for mutual assistance in the case of aggression by Germany. The British cabinet was thrown into disarray by such plain language. The British guarantee to Poland had deliberately not mentioned Germany by name; wouldn't a Russo-British agreement upset Hitler? Surely it would upset all the other east European countries threatened by Hitler. The Poles would scorn a Russo-British pact: they had already made it clear that they would not permit Red Army units to cross their frontier, even to help fight German invaders. What about the Baltic states? What about the United States and the Dominions? An agreement with the Soviets would bring a change to just about every international relationship the British enjoyed.

The French government was ready to explore the Russian proposals, and try to find some form of words that would satisfy London, while Chamberlain was frightened that news of the Russian proposals would leak and become known to the British voters. When he told the leaders of the Labour party, he swore them to secrecy.

The Russian proposals challenged the intelligence and understanding of the men in the British cabinet. They consulted their army, navy and air force chiefs not once but twice. The military chiefs modified their views considerably for the second report but the cabinet ended up as baffled as they ever were. In a private letter Chamberlain said he had 'the most profound distrust of Russia'. As war drew ever closer, Lord Halifax summed up the dismal confusion of these men, to whom the British people looked for wisdom and leadership, with the words: 'we ought to play for time.'

The British got deeper and deeper into a quagmire of words, producing counter-proposals which seemed ever more complex and unsatisfactory to Stalin. The Foreign Office mandarins realized that if they continued to leave Germany unnamed in their agreements Britain could end up guaranteeing everyone in the world against everyone else. The Russians could see that the British were in no hurry and suspected that they were trying to keep the negotiations going ad infinitum. Stalin, who had traitors spying for him in the high levels of virtually every European government, became convinced that Britain and France would never fight anyone until they were directly attacked. He decided that Russia's salvation might after all be a pact with his declared enemy, Nazi Germany.

Whether Hitler or Stalin was first in suggesting a non-aggression pact is still disputed. Before Hitler came to power, Germany had been a major buyer from the Soviet Union and was supplying almost half of all their imports.[6] Hitler's doctrine and his noisy and vituperative propaganda had strangled that trade. Since then Hitler's rearmament programme had drained the German economy so that in January 1939 every director of the Reichsbank had signed a warning memo to Hitler. The German economy was dangerously over-extended and, for reasons both economic and political, it had become more and more difficult for Germany to get foreign credit.

The Soviet Union on the other hand had never ceased to hint that a return to the volume of trade they had enjoyed with pre-Hitler Germany would suit them very well. It was this mutual need to trade that drew the two great powers together. Some accounts, including those by Soviet historians, insist that the German-Soviet Non-Aggression Pact of August 1939 began as Hitler's idea.[7] They cite Hitler's lengthy conversation with the Soviet ambassador at a reception in Berlin in early January 1939.

New Year celebrations had been postponed to 12 January in order to greet the new year in a palatial new Reich Chancellory that Hitler's architect Albert Speer had built on Voss Strasse. It gleamed with marble, mosaics and bronze. Hitler's study, 80 feet long with a 60-feet-high ceiling, was designed to overawe and intimidate visitors as they walked the length of the room to reach the Führer's gigantic marble desk. At the celebration the Papal Nuncio, doyen of the foreign diplomats, gave a formal address wishing Hitler a happy and successful New Year. The brief ceremony over, Hitler watched by everyone present took the Soviet ambassador aside for a talk that lasted 30 minutes or more. Done in the glare of a diplomatic occasion this was a deliberate signal that Hitler wanted to change his foreign policy. In fact it was a response to a meeting of German-Soviet trade experts held in Berlin on 22 December,[8] and Stalin's subsequent approval of a 200 million Reichsmark credit deal.

It is hardly surprising that stories of a forthcoming Russo-German trade pact appeared in newspapers in France and England. In London the *News Chronicle* of 27 January ran a more detailed article saying that a German–Soviet agreement was imminent. The article was written by Vernon Bartlett, who was known to have close contact with Soviet officials, and it was reprinted in the Soviet Press without comment. Perhaps Hitler's calculations concerning the contribution that Austria and Czechoslovakia could make to the German economy lessened his enthusiasm for a pact with Stalin, for it was not until Good Friday 7 April that Joachim von Ribbentrop,

Germany's foreign minister, told Peter Kleist, an expert on his personal staff, to make contact with the Soviet diplomats and push the negotiations along. Ribbentrop was widely regarded as lacking talent, knowledge and experience;[9] his work on the German-Soviet Non-Aggression Pact was to become the high point of his career.

Within a few days Kleist was drinking tea with Georgi Astakhov, the bearded Soviet chargé d'affaires in Berlin, who had the rarely granted power to receive a foreigner and be alone with him. Ten days later the Soviet ambassador in Berlin made his first visit to the Foreign Office. He asked if, in view of the fact that German troops had now seized Czechoslovakia, the arms contract with the Skoda works would still be honoured. It was, admitted the ambassador, a test case to see if Germany was sincerely interested in resuming trade with the Soviet Union.

At the May Day parade in Moscow, Stalin gave his foreign minister a noticeably chilly reception. Ivy Litvinov, the minister's English-born wife said 'Damn that fool Chamberlain!' and others capable of recognizing subtle foretokens of Soviet foreign policy changes guessed that Stalin's eyes were now turned toward Berlin. The delegation of French and British negotiators the Allies sent to Moscow confirmed all Stalin's fears. It lacked the sort of high-ranking figure that the Russians thought appropriate, and instead of travelling by air or fast warship it spent five days aboard an ancient passenger liner, the City of Exeter.

When Astakhov went to the Berlin Foreign Office to get the official answer about the Skoda exports he pointed out that Stalin's new foreign minister, Vyacheslav Molotov, was also prime minister, second in power only to Stalin himself. Unlike his predecessor he was not a Jew, and this too was a signal to the Nazis. In fact he did have a Jewish wife, and this became a closely guarded secret.

Molotov was a man of 'outstanding ability and cold-blooded ruthlessness' Churchill wrote in his war history,[10] adding that Molotov's 'cannon-ball head, black moustache, and comprehending eyes, his slab face, his verbal adroitness and imperturbable demeanour, were appropriate manifestations of his qualities and skill.' Molotov's real name was Scriabin, and, a nephew of the famous composer, he'd studied music before going into politics and becoming a slave to Stalin's ideas and opinions. His appointment was a sign that from now on the Nazis were dealing with Stalin himself.

The next sudden lurch forward in the negotiations came when Ribbentrop told Hitler that the Soviets might be considering a military pact with the British and French. The Nazis had never got beyond discussing trade, and this development caused Ribbentrop to again bypass the usual channels by sending a personal representative to hurry things along. Astakhov and a colleague accepted an invitation for dinner in a private room in a smart little Berlin restaurant called Ewest's, where steak Holstein had been invented and named after a famous diplomat of Bismarck's time.[11] Ribbentrop's envoy and his assistant talked until gone midnight and their discussions were no longer confined to trade but ranged widely and successfully over all manner of political and economic problems.

From now onwards it was the Germans who pushed the talks forward urgently, and the Soviets who met most of their wishes. When Astakhov became suspicious of German motives he was recalled and put into prison, where he remained until he died in 1941. There was good reason for German eagerness. The pact would have to be announced before a German invasion of Poland, and military action there would have to be complete before the winter rains started.

On 20 August Hitler sent a telegram to Stalin asking him to receive Foreign Minister Ribbentrop in Moscow. This direct personal appeal, and the way in which it recognized Stalin as head of state while technically he was only the secretary of the Communist party, arrived at exactly the right time. During that summer, for the second year, fighting had broken out between the Red Army and Japanese troops in the Far East. Stalin, like Hitler, feared a two-front war and to avoid it he was prepared to trust even Hitler.

Warnings about a forthcoming Hitler-Stalin pact, and the way in which the two dictators planned to slice Poland in two and gobble it up, were received in both London and Paris. General Karl Bodenschatz, a wartime comrade of Göring in the old Richthofen squadron and now his liaison officer at Hitler's headquarters, disclosed an outline of the German plans to the French air attaché in Berlin, and to the Foreign Office in London. Dr Karl Goerdeler, one of the most active anti-Nazis, also sent warnings. The Foreign Office ignored them, preferring to believe that these stories were planted to spoil Britain's negotiations with the Russians.[12]

Hitler was confident that Molotov would sign a non-aggression pact with him. Indeed so certain was he that on 22 August, at his mountain home in Berchtesgaden, he briefed his military chiefs about the coming attack on Poland: 'Our opponents [the French and the British] are little worms. I saw them in Munich . . . The victor is not asked afterwards whether or not he has told the truth . . . Close your hearts to pity. Proceed brutally . . . The stronger is in the right.'

On the following day the German-Soviet pact was signed in Moscow. In keeping with the devious and feudal nature of both powers, many of the pact's most important clauses remained closely guarded secrets. Ribbentrop was reassured by the warm welcome he and his team received from the Russians. 'It felt like being with old Party comrades,' he said. There was a great deal of eating and drinking and Stalin toasted Hitler and said he knew how much the German people loved their Führer.

Like Chicago gangsters, Hitler and Stalin had split eastern Europe into two spheres of influence in which each could do more or less as they liked. Stalin's territory included the Baltic states and Finland, while Poland was to be invaded by both armies and divided down the middle.

When the pact was announced *Life* magazine cabled the exiled Leon Trotsky, who had lost to Stalin in the struggle to inherit Lenin's Russia, asking for his views. From Mexico City came a prescient reply: '[Stalin] sees clearly for a short distance, but on a historical scale he is blind. A shrewd tactician, he is not a strategist . . .'

Stalin honoured the German-Soviet pact in a way that Hitler never did. Russian grain and oil soon began moving to Germany. So did iron-ore, manganese and cotton. All over the world, members of the Communist party (many of them secret members) obediently changed their political opinions and switched activities to line up with the new pact. From now onwards Communists would oppose all attempts to bring Hitler to heel. When war began, the Communists in France and Britain would marshal their considerable resources against the war-effort. Allied soldiers were told not to fight in the war against Hitler, for it was a betrayal of the workers.

Hitler attacks Poland

Hitler had arranged everything for action against Poland with uncanny skill. He had become convinced that Britain and France would never fight him, and his demands on the Polish government were based upon that belief. Some historians say that Hitler did not look for concessions from the Poles; what he wanted was a short sharp war that would establish his military skills.

When he heard that a Stalin-Hitler pact was about to be ratified, Chamberlain summoned Parliament back from its summer recess. In a speech on 24 August he told the Commons: 'I do not attempt to conceal from the House that that announcement came to the government as a surprise, and a surprise of a very unpleasant character.' Chamberlain described how an Anglo-French mission had been welcomed in Moscow on 11 August while the Soviets were actually conducting their secret talks with the Nazis. Perhaps Chamberlain's indignation made Stalin smile. Double-dealing was Stalin's regular method of doing business. Perhaps Hitler smiled too. What chance was there now that 'the worms' would be stupid enough to declare war?

The Germans had failed to appreciate that even Chamberlain could not be pushed for ever. The time had come to stand firm and, if need be, to fight. Yet Britain was not prepared enough, strong enough or rich enough to fight; it was an insoluble dilemma. Chamberlain was worried about the way in which events had prompted a drain on the gold reserves; £30 million was withdrawn in one day. Currency exchange control (to prevent anyone converting sterling to other currencies) was discussed, but the government contented itself with doubling the bank rate to 4 per cent and asking businessmen not to purchase foreign exchange or assets, nor move capital out of the country.[13] Despite all his misgivings Chamberlain tried to make his position absolutely clear. To Hitler he wrote:

> apparently the announcement of a German-Soviet Agreement is taken in some quarters in Berlin to indicate that intervention by Great Britain on behalf of Poland is no longer a contingency that need be reckoned with. No greater mistake could be made. Whatever may prove the nature of the German-Soviet Agreement, it cannot alter Great Britain's obligation to Poland, which His Majesty's Government have stated in public repeatedly and plainly and which they are determined to fulfil.
>
> It has been alleged that if His Majesty's Government had made their position more clear in 1914, the great catastrophe would have been avoided. Whether or not there is any force in that allegation, His Majesty's Government are resolved that on this occasion there shall be no such tragic misunderstanding. If the need should arise they are resolved and prepared to employ without delay all the forces at their command, and it is im-

possible to foresee the end of hostilities once engaged . . . I trust that Your Excellency will weigh with the utmost deliberation the considerations that I have put before you.

Even this did not persuade the Germans that Britain was determined to fight. Hitler told Goebbels that Chamberlain would resign. Goebbels, always more devious, wrote in his diary: 'I think it is more likely the Polish government will resign under English pressure. This is England's only chance to get out of this mess halfway safe without a war.'[14] The German army was no less confident. General Halder, the army's chief of staff,[15] wrote in his diary: 'Face must be saved . . . General impression, England soft on the issue of a major war.'

Britain and France go to war

The German army invaded Poland in the early hours of Friday 1 September 1939. All through that day and the next London was pressing Paris to declare war. By Saturday afternoon rumours about more appeasement were being circulated. At 10.30 that evening, members of Parliament sought out Chamberlain as he dined with Halifax. While a thunderstorm raged overhead they demanded action of the prime minister.[16] On Sunday morning Chamberlain broadcast to the nation, telling them that war had begun and that 'It is evil things that we shall be fighting against, brute force, bad faith, injustice, oppression and persecution.' While he was on the air, the air-raid sirens sounded in London. The US ambassador went to his shelter with his wife and two sons. Kennedy was convinced that Britain would not last long against German military power.

The personnel at the German embassy in London were not similarly alarmed by the air-raid sirens. It was during the air-raid alarm that the emergency switchboard at the Foreign Office received an urgent call from the German embassy asking for Lord Halifax. It produced some consternation, for this was only a couple of minutes after the declaration of war. Attempts to contact Halifax at the Cabinet Office failed because he had left there already. The Germans were told this, and asked if the under-secretary would suffice. Yes, said the Embassy official, they simply wanted to be sure that their elderly black dog, which could not be taken back to Germany with them, would be cared for in their absence. When Lord Halifax arrived the problem was put before him and he made the necessary arrangements to have the dog looked after.[17]

Winston Churchill, appointed to be first lord of the Admiralty that Sunday morning, went with his wife to the Westminster apartment of his son-in-law, a stand-up comic named Vic Oliver. They drank champagne and toasted 'victory', after which Churchill took a short nap and then went to the Admiralty to start work.[18]

With conscription as a way of life, France entered the war with an army of 2.7 million men. Most of these were draftees or reservists. Their job was to defend France, and many were being assigned to the subterranean fortresses of the Maginot Line, which were proving an uncomfortable and unhealthy environment. Neither draftees nor reservists were well trained or well equipped, and almost all were unhappy at their plight.

In 1939 the Hotchkiss and Somua tanks used by the French army

Figure 16: British, French and German tanks
in use at the start of the war

were as good as any in the world, and the 4.7-cm gun mounted on the Somua was better than anything the Germans had in use. The French tank force was equal to the Germans in numbers too. But the French generals did not agree on how to use this weapon. In 1939 they were still experimenting, not only with the constituents of the armoured division but also with the methods of its deployment. They spread tanks thinly, assigned them to scouting and reconnaissance duties, or gave them to infantry units. When in 1939 three real armoured divisions were formed there was an overreaction and the high ratio of tanks made these units unwieldy and vulnerable.

To form an effective armoured force it was vital to have the constituents mixed in the right proportions. The German armoured divisions were like very mobile miniature armies, incorporating infantry regiments, combat engineers, anti-tank guns (Pak), artillery and their own Flak.[19] Such wheeled or tracked elements were able to react quickly to the changing situations that battle brings. Germany had ten such divisions ready for action in Poland.[20]

France's professional army was quite different to, and mostly separated from, the mass of its drafted soldiers. The regulars were more likely to be stationed abroad in colonies, such as Africa or Indo-China, where careers were made. The officer corps was a small elite element of the population which did not consider it desirable that the army should distance itself from political ideas and political movements. Few officers thought the Socialist government that ruled France in the Thirties was in any way successful, and monarchist and extreme right-wing organizations had sympathizers in the highest ranks.[21] Many officers thought that eventually the army would be compelled to take a more active part in the nation's political life.

France was a divided nation where Fascists, Communists, Socialists and monarchists were numerous at all levels of society. Since the signing of the German-Soviet pact, in August, Moscow had been instructing Communists not to join the fight against Hitler. These differences of outlook meant that the French began hostilities without the sense of purpose that by this time had unified Britain to a remarkable degree. The French government went to war under pressure from Britain and with considerable misgiving. The National Assembly was not invited to vote on the matter of declaring war. Members were simply asked to vote credits to 'fulfil our treaty obligations' and no debate was permitted. Some leftist members who wanted to speak were silenced. As soon as war was declared, political extremists, and some not very extreme opponents of the war, were taken into custody.

When war began France's agreement with Poland called for substantial French military action in the west. This was an undertaking made by General Maurice Gamelin, the 68-year-old commander-in-chief of the French army, whose influence in shaping his country's foreign policy during the interwar years was disastrous. 'Small, plump, slightly puffy, with his hair tinted, he might, but for the uniform, be an abbé, a fashionable abbé . . .'[22] He had virtually forbidden any discussion of motorization and mechanization of the army, by saying that all lectures and articles dealing with such subjects must be submitted to authority.[23] Although those in contact with him found him lacking in both intelligence and 'guts', the wider world rated him as a high-grade military expert. For this reason perhaps he had decided to manage without the aid of a proper staff.

March 1936, when Hitler occupied the Rhineland in defiance of the Versailles treaty, had been the time to confront the Nazis. Despite the fears expressed by the British government at that time, France's Prime Minister Sarrault and Foreign Minister Flandin had urged Gamelin to eject the Germans, but he would not do so, explaining that Germany had 22 divisions on a war footing. In fact they had three. Afterwards, it was discovered that the Germans had orders to withdraw if they were opposed, and Eden's memoirs said that this was the act of appeasement he most regretted.

Gamelin decided what he wanted to do and invented the reasons afterwards. It was his low opinion of the Czechoslovak army that influenced the Allies to give way to Hitler at Munich.[24] He told his political masters, and the British too, that the 'West Wall' – Germany's concrete fortifications, which the British Press liked to call the 'Siegfried Line' – would possibly halt him and force him to withdraw to his Maginot defences. When asked about the strength of his army he boasted of what it could do, while artfully adding such alarming asides as 'initially [it] will be a modern version of the battle of the Somme.'[25] It was enough to make the politicians sign anything Hitler gave them.

But when the next crisis came Gamelin expressed no such reservations about the Polish army. He thought it was formidable, and this had persuaded him to agree that in the event of war he would attack Germany three days after France's mobilization. Such a two-front war was calculated to divide Germany's effort and give the Poles a chance to defend themselves. And on 7 September 1939, eight divisions of the French army – including two motorized divisions and five tank battalions – moved forward into the region between the Maginot Line and the West Wall. The Germans pulled back, leaving unoccupied some 200 square kilometres of ground and about 50 German villages mined and extensively booby-trapped. Newspaper correspondents exulted, telling of great French victories and deep penetrations into Germany. Photographs and newsreel footage appeared to back up the claims.

As September ended the 'Saar offensive' could be seen for what it really was: a propaganda exercise. The French withdrew having suffered 27 killed and 22 wounded and the loss of a number of aircraft. By the end of October both sides were back in the positions from which they had started. From what we now know of Gamelin's spirit and mentality it seems not impossible that the 'Saar offensive' was staged to prove that the cautions he'd expressed to his government about going to war in aid of Czechoslovakia were correct.

Just one week into the war the British cabinet were told some harsh facts by the chancellor of the exchequer: Britain's financial position was desperate; far worse than it had been in 1914. Her ally France was also far weaker in every respect, and three other allies of that previous war – Russia, Italy and Japan – were now potential enemies. Britain's total resources were about £700 million with little chance of adding to that figure. And, because the government had defaulted on its First World War debts to the United States, purchases there would in future have to be paid for in cash.[26] Surely no one in the cabinet room that day could have missed the implication: America's entry into the war was the Allies' only chance of salvation. And it would have to come very soon.

For two weeks the world watched the Germans smash their way into Poland. Then there came a grotesque finale as the Red Army occupiers came rolling across Poland's eastern frontier. It was clear to anyone who looked at a map that if Germany and Russia were friendly enough to mount a combined attack on Poland, they would be friendly enough for the German army to leave only a token force along that Polish frontier when they regrouped and came clubbing their way westwards.

The German campaign in Poland

For the first time, the new German army was seen in action, using techniques and weapons old and new. The Polish campaign was decided by the fact that the German army went to war by railway. The railheads near the border had to be the jumping-off points for the invaders. The armoured and motorized units that spearheaded the assault constituted only about one-sixth of the invading force; the rest of it was the same plodding horse-drawn German army that had fought in the previous war. Of the whole army only about 10 per cent had been equipped with wheels and tracks.[27] Even this attempt to mechanize the army had been achieved only after 16,000 German civilian vehicles were commandeered in 1939. Germany's auto-industry was big but it never came near to supplying the quantity of vehicles needed. Neither was the quality good enough. Few, if any, German trucks were robust enough for military use. But in 'lightning war' such failures did not matter. By the time the hardware of war fell apart the enemy had surrendered.

The Germans used bases in Czechoslovakia to attack Poland from north and south, as well as from the west. Poland's geography, and the historic threat from both west and east, precluded effective defensive works. Like the French, the Poles would not build any defence lines that relinquished large areas of the country to the enemy, and they tried to hold the Germans along the frontier. It was hoped that this would provide time for the country to mobilize its army and mount a counter-offensive, and for France and Britain to attack Germany from the west.

For the first time, the world saw the sort of opening air attacks that nowadays are the way in which most wars begin. German intelligence – both on the ground and by photo-reconnaissance – had prepared the target lists, and hampered as they were by bad weather, the Luftwaffe managed to destroy much of the Polish air force in the first hours of war. Medium-range bombing attacks on Polish towns disrupted mobilization of the army. At the fighting front Stuka dive-bombers served as efficient artillery, for the Stuka training schools produced men able to get at least 50 per cent of their bombs within 25 metres of the target. (Stuka is an abbreviation of Sturzkampfflugzeug, dive-bomber. The name could be applied to any aircraft used in this role, but was often used to refer specifically to the Junkers Ju 87.)

The Polish army, and its air component, proved a dauntless opponent, but it was not equipped to fight a modern war. The Germans used armoured divisions to pierce the front. Following them, conventional armies converged to surround the Poles in two vast encirclements, one inside the other. It was the seventeenth day of the campaign when the second set of pincers met at Brest-Litovsk in the middle of eastern Poland. On the same day, the Red Army moved across Poland's eastern frontier. The fighting continued but the war was decided.

The Germans, always ready to learn, studied their campaign. The supply of fuel and ammunition to the fast advancing units must be improved. Battalion and regimental commanders were urged to keep closer to the fighting men. Artillery must be pushed forward more quickly. The lighter tanks – the Mark Is and Mark IIs – had suffered 89 per cent and 83 per cent losses, while the heavier ones – Mark IIIs and Mark IVs – had suffered only 26 per cent and 19 per cent casualties.[28] The factories must shift to the production of heavier tanks. Lighter models could be adapted for reconnaissance and command duties; some were converted into self-propelled artillery and anti-tank guns. Every change was designed for striking harder and faster next time. For soldiers who believed that battle was to be revolutionized by mobile forces, the Polish campaign had been too orthodox. They wanted blitzkrieg.

Lord Gort

The 6th Viscount Gort, the hereditary Irish peer appointed to command the British Expeditionary Force, was not unorthodox. He had spent much of the First World War as a staff officer, but when he went to the front line with the Grenadiers he showed himself to be a fearless leader. He ended the war with an amazing array of awards for bravery: a VC, three DSOs, an MC. In 1937 Gort's record as a fighting soldier had played a big part in his becoming Chief of the Imperial General Staff, CIGS, Britain's top soldier. He was the youngest man to get this job and he was jumped a rank to pass many senior officers such as generals Brooke, Dill and Wavell. Gort had been chosen by Leslie Hore-Belisha, the war minister, to revitalize the army. There is little sign that he did this.

In September 1939, Gort relinquished the role of CIGS for the even more coveted job of commanding the BEF. By this time he had made many enemies, including his political chief Hore-Belisha. It was this rift between Hore-Belisha and his most important general that enabled the army's top brass to campaign against the minister. The fact that Hore-Belisha was Jewish gave a specially unpleasant dimension to this squalid intrigue. The end result was that the generals were divided and Gort – whose subordinates, such as the irrepressible Alan Brooke, were less than loyal to him – made no stronger. After Dunkirk, when Gort needed friends in high places, none were to be found.

'Fat Boy' Gort – depicted by the British Press as 'Tiger Gort' – was thought to be directly responsible to his king and government for the British force he led. In fact he was no more than the commander of an army; one of many armies. In Paris, General Maurice Gamelin, the supreme commander, regarded the BEF as a minor element of his western defences but Gort did nothing without first checking with London.[29] This ambivalence was to play a part in the final tragedy of the BEF.

The British Expeditionary Force

In the first hours of war Britain sent RAF units to France and put together the British Expeditionary Force, consisting of all five regular home-based divisions. They were joined in the early months of 1940 by five divisions of Territorials (part-time volunteers now serving full-time). Their restricted prewar training schedule meant that drilling had been neglected in favour of more practical tactical and weapons training. But General Gort was a Guards officer, and the regular soldiers around him were distressed to attend parades alongside soldiers deficient in drill. The 'Terriers' soon found themselves doing quite a lot of marching and parading when they might have been training for combat.[30]

Britain's professional army was prepared to remedy other deficiencies it found in the civilian soldiers who joined up to help fight the Germans:

> The Colonel, the Adjutant told us, had been concerned and shocked on the previous evening – a guest night – to observe that some of the newly joined officers had been in doubt about the correct implements and glasses to employ for the successive courses. If we would be kind enough to pay attention and take notes, he would give us a practical demonstration. Without batting an eyelid this impeccable young man then sat down at the table and an equally solemn mess waiter served him first with token soup, then with token fish, then with token meat, then with token pudding and finally with a token savoury. The wine waiter went through the motions of pouring out sherry, burgundy, port and brandy.

'Somewhere I still possess the valuable notes I made,' added Ralph Arnold, who shortly after this performance at the Infantry Training Centre became an aide with Lord Ironside, now CIGS.[31]

Another three divisions crossed the Channel in April but these were so ill-trained and ill-equipped that they were classified as 'labour' formations. Since the BEF spent more time digging and constructing defence lines than in any form of battle training the distinction made little difference at this stage. Although there were tank formations in the BEF, Britain's one and only armoured division was still not ready for action.[32]

The British force was criticized by the French as being an inadequate contribution. Its size was seen as evidence that the British were relying on the French to fight the war. They had some cause to complain: the British Expeditionary Force was smaller than the Dutch army, and only 40 per cent the size of the Belgian army, while the French fielded 88 divisions from a population smaller than Britain's.

The 150,000 British soldiers put at the disposal of the French were deployed along the frontier of neutral Belgium, where there was not even an enemy to face. It was logical to put the British along this northern part of France's western frontier, for it shortened their lines of supply, which came through Arras from England. There was also the fact that any German attack on France was likely to come this way.

The southern part of the front was defended by the mighty Maginot Line. The sector along the hilly Ardennes forest was almost universally regarded as impassable to armour. Therefore, said the experts, the Germans would have to strike at France by going through Belgium. When this happened, said Gamelin, who made the master plan, the Allied northern armies would swing forward to meet the enemy in Belgium and halt him there. The northern part of this 'door' would have furthest to swing, so the all-mechanized BEF was best equipped to do it.

The British were justifiably proud to field the world's first fully mechanized army. Unlike their contemporaries, the British had relegated the horse to ceremonial duties, while Tommies went to war on wheels and tracks. And yet a closer look reveals that it wasn't all that the War Office Press releases claimed. One division commander, Bernard Montgomery, later wrote:

the British Army was totally unfit to fight a first-class war on the continent of Europe . . . In the years preceding the outbreak of war no large-scale exercises with troops had been held in England for some time. Indeed, the Regular Army was unfit to take part in a realistic exercise. The Field Army had an inadequate signals system, no administrative backing and no organization for high-command; all these had to be improvised on mobilization. The transport was inadequate and was completed on mobilization by vehicles requisitioned from civilian firms. Much of the transport of my division consisted of civilian vans and lorries from the towns of England; they were in bad repair and when my division moved from the ports up to its concentration area near the French frontier, the countryside of France was strewn with broken-down vehicles.[33]

Gort, during his time as CIGS, had done very little to build the modern army that Britain needed to fight the Germans. The armoured division was not ready for war and tank experts had been given no chance to contribute their opinions to the top planners. And Gort had shown little concern about air support for his army. Army Cooperation RAF squadrons were neglected, and the army was permitted no say in the use of the 'Advanced Air Striking Force', the tactical bombing RAF squadrons sent to France to support the land forces.

But France and Britain had a breathing space. While concentrating their efforts on Poland, the Germans remained inactive, apart from a few air reconnaissance sorties, on their Western Front. The Allied politicians, and the soldiers too, breathed a sigh of relief and made sure their German enemies were not provoked. France asked Britain not to bomb Germany lest that brought retaliatory bombing attacks on French factories. Instead the RAF dropped propaganda pamphlets which Churchill sarcastically hoped might rouse the Germans to a higher morality. Only at sea was the phoney war real. Time is on our side, the optimists said.

War production

Had such optimists seen the German production figures they might have been even more complacent. In quantity, if not in quality, the Allies were outstripping the Germans. In the first six months of 1940, Anglo-French factories produced 1,412 tanks compared with German production of 558. The chaos of French aircraft production was being improved and brought Anglo-French aircraft production to 6,794, double that of Germany.[34]

The change of pace resulting from the Munich crisis began to show benefits in the opening months of the war. The organization of Britain's air defences – notably the radar chain – improved every day. The worry was that so many vital items, including Swiss fuses and Dutch and American radio valves used in the radar stations, had to be imported. So did many aircraft components, and as much as 25 per cent of Britain's wartime steel came from overseas.

Britain's steel-making was poor in both quality and quantity. Although German domestic steel production was not large, conquests provided a total of 212 million tons a year by the end of 1940. At this time Britain's annual output was a mere 18 million tons.[35]

Hitler was the most popular leader Germany had ever known.[36] Believing that the naval mutinies had brought Germany's downfall in 1918, and remembering the revolutions that followed, he was determined to avoid discontent at home. He would fight his wars while Germany continued to enjoy many of the luxuries of a peace-time-style economy.

During the prewar years Hitler had built a well equipped army while keeping German living standards as high as any in Europe. To further increase production he would have to do as the British were doing – increase working hours and draft women into the war factories. Hitler was reluctant to do either of these things. (In fact the proportion of women workers was about the same in both countries, but many German women were engaged in such inessential jobs as domestic service. Furthermore the generous allowances paid to the wives of German soldiers gave no immediate incentive for them to do war work.)

As the war continued, the Germans expanded their workforce by using foreign labourers, including those brought by compulsion or coercion, prisoners of war and slaves. Even these drastic measures did little to increase German war production. At no time did the Germans, together with the Austrian and Czech output, reach the level of production they had achieved in the First World War. During the first year of the German assault on Russia, they did not even reach a quarter of their 1918 production. Albert Speer, who became minister of war production in February 1942, had no doubts that bureaucracy – aggravated by the Nazi authoritarian system – was at the heart of the failure. As an example, he pointed out that the Ordnance Office employed ten times as many staff during the Second World War as they had in the First World War.[37]

No accurate estimates of German production were available to the Allied governments because the British intelligence services could not provide regular reliable and informative reports from even one agent in Germany. The Secret Intelligence Service had to depend upon refugees, escapers and what could be gleaned from foreign newspapers.

All the same Germany's victories convinced the world of its overwhelming strength. Even after the war Churchill still believed that, at this time, German munitions manufacture was much more 'fruitful' than that of the Allies.

Norway: the Allies start fighting

The essence of Anglo-French policy in these days of what an American journalist called a Phoney War, and Chamberlain termed Twilight War, was to go and fight somewhere else. The French proposed schemes for fighting in south-east Europe and wanted to bomb Russian oil wells in the Caucasus. Fortunately these crackpot ideas came to nothing. However another lunatic scheme did.

In November 1939 Stalin, quick to utilize his allotted sphere of influence under the pact with Hitler, effectively took control of Latvia, Estonia and Lithuania. Faced with demands for their territory, the Finns refused to fall in with Russia's demands. On 30 November 1939 the Red Army attacked with five armies, against which the Finns put up stout resistance.

Still smarting from the way in which Stalin had done a deal with Hitler, the men in London and Paris impulsively offered aid to the Finns. Without consulting the British, the French Premier Daladier said he'd send 50,000 volunteers and 100 bombers to Finland via northern Norway and Sweden. Britain followed suite and said it would send 50 bombers. Landing at the (iron-ore) port of Narvik, the troops would travel by railway through the mountains to the Swedish iron-ore region, and thus to Finland. Behind these altruistic offers there lurked a cynical plot. On the pretext of aiding the Finns, the Allies planned to seize neutral Sweden's iron-ore fields and prevent them exporting to Germany. It is strange to record that the same Allied leaders who were frightened to attack Germany's Western Front, and were forbidding their air forces to bomb German towns, were planning to send soldiers and bombing planes to fight the Red Army and bring Russia into the war against them.

Before this ill-conceived operation could begin, the Red Army, despite grievous casualties, broke through the Finnish fortified defences. The Finns asked for a cease-fire.

The Allied governments looked again at the map of Scandinavia showing the iron-ore fields. The Royal Navy was ordered to lay a minefield in neutral Norwegian territorial waters. This would block the ice-free route used by the ships carrying ore to German ports. Churchill wrote afterwards:

> As our mining of Norwegian waters might provoke a German retort, it was also agreed that a British brigade and French contingent should be sent to Narvik to clear the port and advance to the Swedish frontier. Other forces should be dispatched to Stavanger, Bergen and Trondheim, in order to deny these bases to the enemy.[38]

It was the same plan as before, but dressed up in new clothes: an Allied force would cross Norway, invade Sweden and seize the iron-ore fields. The plan is noteworthy, not just for its cavalier attitude to the neutral countries but in its revelation of top-level over-confidence and a profound ignorance of what fighting the Germans would entail.

There was an intelligence failure too, for Churchill thought that Swedish iron-ore provided the basis of the German war industry and this has been repeated in most histories of the war. But the idea that Allied seizure of the Swedish ore fields would have slowed the German war machine – let alone brought it to a sudden halt – is difficult to sustain. Germany had no urgent need of the ore. In the first year of war no less than 40 per cent of Germany's steel was still being allocated to civilian needs, and this figure excludes construction work and exports. Germany had immense stockpiles of steel. It was coming from Austria, the Protectorate (as German-occupied Czechoslovakia was now called) and Poland.[39] By the end of 1940 over 200 million tons a year was available to Germany. To what extent, then, was this *casus belli* real? Could it have been Britain's excuse for some other strategy, such as the occupation of Scandinavian naval bases? Or was it intended to provoke the Germans to a Scandinavian campaign that the Allied high commands were confident they could win?

Whatever the true motives, on 8 April 1940 the Royal Navy minelayers began operations. For months Admiral Raeder had been warning Hitler of the consequences of British air and naval bases in

Norway, while telling him too of the door to the outer oceans that Norwegian ports would give German shipping. Other Nazi leaders supported Raeder,[40] although the army thought an invasion of Norway too hazardous to contemplate. Göring's dislike of it came from the need to subordinate Luftwaffe elements to the army's command, but Erhard Milch, Göring's second in command, was happy to cooperate. Actually it was Göring's private intelligence service, blandly named the Research Office, Forschungsamt (FA), that provoked Hitler into action. Göring's men tapped any telephone that might provide useful information. They were helped since 1935 by the Magnetofen, a small recording machine from the laboratories of AEG and IG-Farben.[41] When the recorded voice of a neutral ambassador[42] revealed the British plan to sow mines in Norwegian waters, Hitler gave the invasion forces the go-ahead.

Having dabbled in the Polish campaign, Hitler took personal command of the Norwegian invasion. His plans were drawn up by his small OKW (High Command of the Armed Forces) office. Bypassing the normal channels, orders were funnelled through a corps headquarters where the day-to-day work was done. Much to their consternation, the high commanders of the army, navy and air force had no say in the planning: they were simply told to provide the units as needed for Hitler's campaign. The army's own planners were at this time working on 'Fall Gelb', Plan Yellow: the attack on France and the Low Countries.

The timing of the German invasion of Norway was vital. There were no landing craft: the ships would have to come alongside a jetty and put the troops ashore like passengers getting off a ferry.[43] All the landings would have to be made at exactly the same time because the first landing would warn the Norwegian defences and any delayed landings would attract fierce opposition.

Oslo was still at peace on the evening of Friday 5 April when the German ambassador invited distinguished guests, including members of the Norwegian government, to a film show. *Baptism of Fire* was a stark and horrifying documentary of the war that the Luftwaffe brought upon Poland. Its script and aerial sequences were the work of a former air ace[44] and his airborne camera lingered upon the gutted buildings and smouldering ruins of Warsaw. 'And remember,' said the film narration, 'this is what happens when the German Luftwaffe strikes.' As the film's finale the song 'Bomben auf England', punctuated with trumpets and drum rolls, concluded with the spirited line: 'Bombs! Bombs! Bombs on England!' Just in case anyone in the audience had missed the implication, an end caption said that this outcome was something for which the Poles could thank their British and French friends. It was diplomacy in the true Nazi style: crude and bellicose. When the room lights came on there was no applause; no reaction at all. The audience was stunned.

Hitler chose the same date as the Royal Navy to begin his Norwegian expedition, and for the same reason. It was a dark night of the new moon period and the coincidence almost brought disaster to Hitler's armada. Four days after German supply ships embarked on 3 April the man at Bletchley Park responsible for 'traffic analysis' – interpreting the volume of signals rather than the content – warned the Admiralty's Operation Intelligence Centre of an unprecedented volume of German naval signals activity west of Denmark, and in the exit from the Baltic. It was the German invasion fleet moving to Norway,[45] and the Germans were at their most vulnerable. Yet the warning was dismissed and the British navy continued with its minelaying as planned.

Even when the German shipping movements were confirmed, the navy failed to counter them. Churchill, first lord of the Admiralty, thought the naval movements were German warships heading north to break out into the Atlantic. The Royal Navy's warships were sent too far north to intercept the invasion. The first sign that the RN had been completely outwitted came when the Polish submarine *Orzel* sank a German troopship *Rio de Janeiro* to pitch men and horses into the cold Norwegian coastal water. At 6 am on 9 April, Hitler learned of his success: at Narvik, Trondheim and Bergen U-boats were guarding the port entrances. The bulk of his seaborne invasion force had arrived safely. Two and a half hours later Junkers transport aircraft were landing troops at Oslo's airport.

Figure 17: Junkers Ju 52/3m transport

10 GERMAN ARMS OUTSTRETCHED

*I grieve, not because I have to die for my country,
but because I have not lifted my arm against the
enemy . . . much as I have desired to achieve something.*

Callicrates: dying words when mortally
wounded at Plataea

W HEN GERMANS marched into Denmark, resistance collapsed so
quickly that it became the only occupied nation not to have a
properly constituted government in exile. For a long time the Germans treated the Danes well, and Danish political parties, including
the Communists, continued to function as before.[1]

Norway was not so quickly conquered, but it was a German
triumph nevertheless and one in which the Luftwaffe played a vital
role. At Oslo and Christiansand serious opposition by the Norwegian
coastal defences had been overcome by the Luftwaffe. At Christiansand bombers attacked the harbour forts so that the invaders could
land. Luftwaffe parachute troops captured Oslo airport, permitting
the transport aircraft to come in. The seizure of airports, and the
speed with which Luftwaffe squadrons moved into them, complete
with maintenance and repair units, soon gave the Germans complete
control of the air.

The muddled Allied reaction began at the embarkation port of
Rosyth when the troops were separated from tanks, artillery and
stores. They did not get to Norway until ten days after the German
landings. The French contingent was no better organized: a ship
loaded with vital supplies was found to be too large to enter harbour.
Said General Sir Adrian Carton de Wiart:

> The French Chasseurs Alpins were a fine body of troops and
> would have been ideal for the job in hand, but ironically they
> lacked one or two essentials, which made them completely use-
> less to us. I had wanted to move them forward, but General
> Audet regretted they had no means of transport, as their mules
> had not turned up. Then I suggested that his ski-troops might

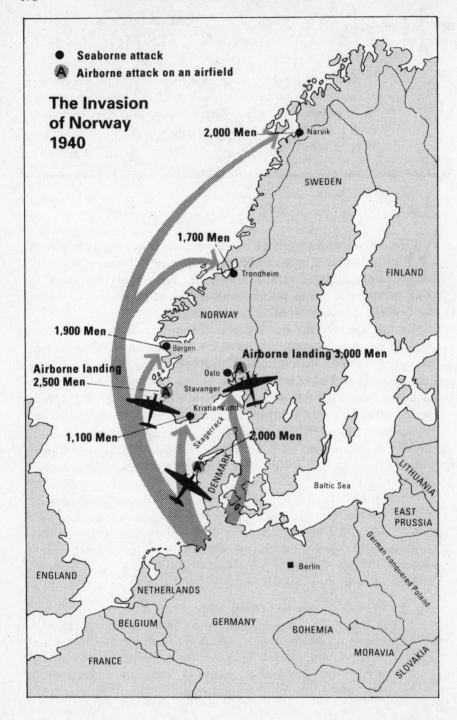

● Seaborne attack
Ⓐ Airborne attack on an airfield

The Invasion of Norway 1940

2,000 Men —— Narvik

SWEDEN

FINLAND

1,700 Men

Trondheim

NORWAY

1,900 Men

Bergen

Airborne landing 3,000 Men

Oslo

Airborne landing 2,500 Men

Stavanger

Kristiansand

1,100 Men

Skagerrack

2,000 Men

DENMARK

Baltic Sea

LITHUANIA

EAST PRUSSIA

Berlin

German conquered Poland

ENGLAND

NETHERLANDS

BELGIUM   GERMANY

BOHEMIA

MORAVIA

FRANCE

SLOVAKIA

move forward, but it was found that they were lacking some essential strap for their skis, without which they were unable to move.[2]

In the north, the landing of British and French troops kept the battle going but there was never any doubt about the outcome. Everywhere the German air force was the decisive factor. It was air cover that permitted the Germans to keep pouring into Oslo the reinforcements that won the campaign. Neither the French nor the British were prepared for the closely coordinated operations of German air and ground forces. Despite grievous errors at the top, units of the Royal Navy fought with distinction and success but the vital damage to the German navy had been done by the Norwegians. And the RN had discovered that its ships could not operate safely in 'narrow seas' – waters within range of land-based enemy bombers. The RN's precious radar-equipped anti-aircraft cruisers (there were only three of them) were severely restricted by high-sided fiords which nullified the radar.

Within six weeks the Germans had Norway. The campaign had called for coordination of air, land and sea forces, and Hitler, having taken control of the invasion, took all the credit for its success. His generals, who had all advised against it, now had to listen to Hitler's humiliating lectures. Only Grossadmiral Raeder, who had pressed for it, was smiled upon.

Like the Polish campaign, it was a victory largely attributable to the efficiency – and sometimes improvisation – of the German supply services. Göring was not thanked for the Luftwaffe's contribution; all credit went to Erhard Milch, who, while retaining his other posts, had gone to Hamburg to take personal command of Luftflotte 5, which carried out the largest air transport movement ever seen up to that time. In over 3,000 sorties by the Junkers Ju 52 transports, almost 3,000 men were moved, together with 2,370 tons of supplies and a quarter of a million gallons of fuel.

The most serious German setback was the German naval losses. All ten destroyers used to ferry the invasion force to Narvik were sunk, along with their tanker refuelling force. The Oslo coastal guns sank the heavy cruiser *Blücher* and, at a time when the navy should have been husbanding all its resources, Raeder recklessly committed his battleships *Gneisenau* and *Scharnhorst* to unnecessary forays in the north where both were seriously damaged and out of commission for many months. So the German navy found itself with only three cruisers and four destroyers fit for sea duty. Admiral Erich Raeder needed all the good will he could get from Hitler. His navy was now quite unfitted to support and protect a seaborne invasion of England.

Winston Churchill

The Anglo-French failure in Norway could not be glossed over. It caused considerable public disquiet, and Chamberlain's Conservative government came under fierce attack even from its own supporters. There was a two-day debate about the débâcle in Norway. Some of Churchill's backers cautiously ensured that their savage attacks upon Chamberlain's conduct of the war did not harm Churchill, but when one of them made excuses for him, he immediately jumped up and told the House: 'I take complete responsibility for everything that has been done at the Admiralty, and I take my full share of the burden.'

The Labour party were afraid to force a division in case a substantial vote of confidence consolidated Chamberlain's power. But some women members of Parliament, having retired to an all-party room of their own, resolved to force a vote, and this made the Labour party chiefs agree to divide the house.[3]

And so, on 8 May, Churchill found himself making the speech winding up the debate for the government. It was probably the most difficult performance of his career. Churchill had spent his life opposing the sort of policies that Chamberlain personified; and now he was making the key speech to defend the man and the policies. But, as first lord of the Admiralty, he was responsible for many of the misjudgements that brought the Norwegian fiasco and caused the widespread rage that was threatening to topple the government. After a two-day recital of German triumphs, and the resulting atmosphere of impending doom, his speech 'amused and dazzled everyone with his virtuosity'.[4] One of his secretariat later wrote:

> He was constantly heckled by the Labour opposition, and he tore into them vehemently and often angrily . . . Churchill knew that he was defending positions which were, in many respects, indefensible. He knew that if the bitterest critics had their way, Chamberlain would resign. He knew that, in that case, he would probably become Prime Minister himself. But throughout the entire political crisis he never spoke or acted except in absolute loyalty to his Prime Minister.[5]

The vote brought the government's majority down from more than 200 to 81. The way in which so many of his own party had either voted against him or abstained was enough to convince even the egoistic Chamberlain that he could not remain as prime minister. The Labour party, which most people now thought should be represented in the wartime government, refused in any circumstances to serve under Neville Chamberlain. Many thought his replacement would have to be Lord Halifax, and yet several people noticed that feeling in the House was veering towards Winston Churchill.[6] Chamberlain, who had been the target of so much of his criticism, had no affection for Churchill. King George VI, who consistently tried to influence political decisions, declared Halifax to be his preference. Fellow Conservatives had no great love for Churchill, who had changed his political allegiance more than once, who had attacked them again and again with uncomfortably accurate warnings of the need for rearmament, and had in the end proved right. The (non-elected) members of the upper House remembered him saying that their chamber was 'filled with doddering peers, cute financial magnates, clever wire-pullers, big brewers with bulbous noses. All the enemies of progress are there.' The Socialists had made him into their bogey man for using troops in the Welsh mining strikes of 1911, and for his role in the General Strike of 1926. Anyone who listened to the debate could see that many of the failures of the Norwegian campaign had been Churchill's fault.

So why did Churchill get his position of ultimate power? His speech had proclaimed him his own man; endearingly loyal to the wretched Chamberlain, fiercely combative with his political opponents, ready to admit mistakes but bending his knee to no one. Certainly a large section of the British public thought that a man who had, during the 1930s, constantly opposed Hitler, and had urged rearmament to stop him, must be the best man now to confront him. But the opinion of the man in the street does not count for much in such a situation. At one time it was widely said that Lord Halifax – who would have had technical problems running the country from the House of Lords – was gentlemanly enough to give way to Churchill on this account.[7] Nowadays more convincing explanations have emerged.

It seems that Chamberlain favoured Churchill as the lesser of two evils. For him to say this openly would have brought the displeasure of his party, so he conspired to get Churchill into the job. Possibly Chamberlain hoped that Churchill's tenure would be short, and he himself would return before long to number ten Downing Street. Some said that the cabinet seat, and the job as party chairman, that Churchill let Chamberlain keep was the offer that tipped the balance. Chamberlain's remarks to his colleagues suggest that he knew that Churchill's elevation to the premiership had been only a matter of time once war began. One recent history says Chamberlain feared that if Lord Halifax gained power he would immediately start armistice negotiations with Hitler.[8]

There is plenty of evidence to support such allegations. Britain's acute financial difficulties meant that continuing the war would involve going to the United States cap in hand. This was not a task that would appeal to Halifax, who had grave doubts about the wisdom of continuing the war in any case.

Winston Churchill never showed any doubts about confronting dictators of the left or of the right. He championed individual freedom to the point of being a maverick. Having an American mother, the daughter of a tycoon, provided Winston with a realistic view of the disposition and power of the United States at a time when most of those around him were patronizing and smugly superior about that nation.

Winston Leonard Spencer-Churchill was born on 30 November 1874 in Blenheim Palace, built and named by Churchill's ancestor the 1st Duke of Marlborough to celebrate the battle he had won. Winston's father was a cynical, irascible and unpredictable politician who spent most of his adult life suffering the agonies of syphilis, from which he eventually died. Churchill's mother was reputed to have had 200 lovers and his brother Jack was probably fathered by one of them.[9] Churchill saw very little of either parent, being attended by a nanny until, still not eight years old, he was sent to boarding school. Lining up in alphabetical order at Harrow, one of England's most exclusive private schools, Winston noticed that he would be nearer to the front if his name began with C. He liked being near the front of everything so he dropped the hyphenated name and became plain Churchill. His performance at school was so lamentable that the housemaster wrote to his mother saying: 'his forgetfulness, carelessness, unpunctuality, and irregularity in every way, have really been so serious, that I write to ask you, when he is at home to speak very gravely to him on the subject.'[10] The decision to send him to Sandhurst Military College was taken as much because of his poor academic performance as because of his interest in things military.

As a cherubic golden-haired lieutenant in the fashionable 4th Hussars, with five months' leave every year, he excelled in polo, steeple-chasing and hunting. Using his father's influence to the full, and subsidized by an allowance from his mother, he chased after wars and made no secret of his determination to win medals. In 1895, on his twenty-first birthday, he came under fire from rebels while visiting Cuba and was awarded a Spanish medal. A sniffy English newspaper said: 'Spending a holiday in fighting other people's battles is rather an extraordinary proceeding even for a Churchill.'[11] He won a coveted 'mention in dispatches' fighting Afghan tribesmen in northern India. At Omdurman on the Nile, he took part in the last great cavalry charge made by the British army.

Churchill supplemented his pay by contributing articles to newspapers and writing books about his adventures. He also showed no reluctance to address political meetings. But a lieutenant who dabbled in politics, and fluently criticized the strategy and tactics of his senior officers, was not universally popular. He left the army and went as a war correspondent to South Africa, where in 1899 he was captured by the Boers. He escaped, and the warrant for his arrest provides this snapshot him: 'Englishman 25 years old, about 5 ft 8 in tall, average build, walks with a slight stoop, speaks through the nose, cannot pronounce the letter S.' It would still do to identify him half a century later. So would the habit of smoking cigars and drinking at all hours of the day.

In 1900 Churchill embarked on the long and restless political career that was to bring him infinite joy and pain. He was elected to Parliament as a Conservative but four years later his beliefs in free trade took him over to the Liberals, who in 1911 made him first lord of the Admiralty (a post which he held again in 1939). His decision to keep the fleet mobilized after exercises in the summer of 1914 was an important one and widely applauded, but he took the blame for what proved a disastrous attempt to seize Turkey's Gallipoli Peninsula in 1915. Some said his ideas had been changed too much for him to be the guilty party. But dejected and almost 40 years old, he resigned from office and went to serve as an infantry colonel on the Western Front. Later he had other important jobs, secretary for war and colonial secretary, before rejoining the Conservative party in 1922. They made him chancellor of the exchequer from 1924 until 1929. But after that his political past caught up with him and he became an obstinate outcast whose career seemed to have ended. All through his life he suffered from the bouts of melancholy that he referred to as 'The Black Dog', but his capacity for reading, writing and working was undiminished.

Churchill's restless political history, and radical ideas, had left him with powerful enemies and few friends. Yet in practical terms he was never an extremist: extremism was more likely to be revealed in his critics. As a Liberal minister in 1909 he'd attacked the gulf between rich and poor, and 'the absence of any established minimum standard of life and comfort among the workers, and at the other end, the swift increase in vulgar, joyless luxury.' In 1918 he demanded lenient terms for the defeated Germans. His official biographer observes: 'A most remarkable feature of Winston Churchill's career is the way in which almost every action of his was interpreted by contemporaries in the worst possible light.'[12] In the interwar years, when lethargy crippled the thought processes of voters and politicians alike, it was Churchill's energy that frightened everyone and excluded him from office. In May 1936 he asked the House: 'Is there no grip, no driving force, no mental energy, no power of decision or design?'

It was an extraordinary coincidence that Chamberlain's enforced decision to step down should come at the same hour that the Germans attacked France and the Low Countries. Churchill, sixty-five years old, came to power at the moment of Britain's direst peril. 'I have nothing to offer,' he told the nation on 13 May, 'but blood, toil, tears and sweat.' He told the House of Commons: 'You ask what is our aim? I can answer in one word: victory, victory at all costs, victory in spite of all terror, victory however long and hard the road may be; for without victory there is no survival.' Then he left the Chamber, eyes brimming with tears, but remarked to an aide: 'That got the sods didn't it?'[13]

In fact these orations cut little ice with his fellow members of the House of Commons. One eyewitness said his speech on the 13 May was not well received, and remarked upon the far warmer welcome given to Chamberlain that day. Although Churchill was popular with a large section of the general public, the cold reception he got from the House provoked journalists to complain (to Chamberlain) that the hostility shown to Churchill was having a bad effect abroad.[14] Only after that did the chief whip persuade backbenchers to rectify their manners. From then onwards Churchill was dutifully cheered and applauded.

The German drive westward

On 10 May 1940, with the battle in Norway still raging, the German armies facing France and the Low Countries moved forward to carry out Plan Yellow. Supported by fierce air attacks, two German Army Groups – A and B – were deployed in a plan devised by General Erich von Manstein. Army Group B, in the north, using largely horse-drawn units, rolled across the frontiers into the Netherlands and northern Belgium. These neutral countries, which had gone to extreme lengths to avoid giving Hitler any excuse to attack them, resisted the invaders. Meanwhile Army Group A was threading its way unseen through the narrow forest roads of the Ardennes. This was a region that the Allies had officially proclaimed to be impassable to tanks. And yet this Army Group included the greater part of Germany's armoured divisions.

Although the Allies were caught completely by surprise, the northern attack was the sort of development that the French and British generals expected. Gamelin's contingency plans were taken out and dusted off while the newspaper photographers provided pictures and platitudes about the sons of Tommy Atkins meeting the daughters of Mademoiselle from Armentières. The British and French armies in the northern section of the front plodded forward to join up with the Belgian and Dutch defenders. They were pleasantly surprised to find how little they were harassed by German air attacks.

In 1940 the kingdom of the Netherlands was, in some ways, the most foreign land in Europe. The Dutch stood apart from other Europeans. Their language was a challenge even for Germans. Their clocks and watches were set to a different time (2 hours and 40 minutes ahead of Germany, 40 minutes behind Belgium, France and Britain, and 20 minutes ahead of Greenwich Mean Time). Their worldwide colonies provided oil and raw materials: Indonesia (at that time the Dutch East Indies of Java and Sumatra) was the 'spice islands' so many early explorers had sought. Neutrality in the First World War had further enriched the Dutch, who had hoped to remain neutral in the Second World War.

They were an easy target. In no way prepared for a European war, their tiny army was trained and equipped only to police a colonial empire. No one seriously considered the possibility that their towns might be bombed and they had not organized the sort of 'air-raid precautions' to be found in France, Germany and Britain.

Their military defence plan consisted of falling back into the part of the Netherlands that the Dutch call 'Holland' and manning trenches with infantry supported by a few light tanks and armoured cars.

The German attack on the Dutch, like others, came without declaration of war. To speed up the crossings of the Dutch waterways, German airborne troops were dropped to seize bridges for the advancing columns. Tricks and deception were used: Dutch Fascists dressed as Dutch military policemen helped to capture key bridges over the Juliana Canal. Many of the nation's vital objectives were taken in the first hours of war.

Belgium was only marginally better prepared for the German onslaught. Like the Dutch, the Belgians had refused to coordinate their defence plans with those of France and Britain lest Hitler use that as an excuse to invade them.

The Belgian border and the Albert Canal's bridges were guarded by the mighty defensive fort of Eben Emael. This huge citadel was soon overcome by German infantry. To everyone's amazement, the soldiers came from gliders towed by Junkers transports. They sailed out of the dawn sky to settle gently on the thick concrete roofs, disgorging specially trained men who were able to subdue the garrison by dropping explosive charges down the air vents.

Bitter charges by the French government immediately after the Belgian capitulation have left in French and British history books the convenient story that the Belgians gave up virtually without a fight. This fiction was given further credence by the self-serving memoirs of General Alan Brooke, one of Gort's corp commanders. The Germans did not share these estimates. 'It was astonishing to see that the Belgians fought with increasing tenacity the nearer the

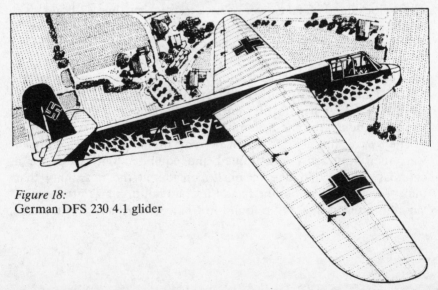

Figure 18:
German DFS 230 4.1 glider

end approached,' said one German officer.[15] The more one delves into the history of this fatal month, the more clearly it emerges that soldiers, sailors and airmen of all nations fought with tenacity when they were properly led. The Belgians were certainly no exception.

Nevertheless within a short time the Dutch and the Belgians found it more difficult to put up a spirited defence when the British and French armies were in retreat. The Germans were nowhere met in full-scale battle nor seriously delayed. Army Group B had followed Manstein's plan and it had worked.

By 13 May it was becoming apparent that the Germans fighting in Belgium and Holland were only one half of the German invading force. Spearheads of Army Group A emerged from the Ardennes forest and were seen along the banks of the River Meuse near Sedan. This unexpected sight did not panic the French, who were well set up in defensive positions on their side of the river. The military textbook said a river would hold the enemy. It said that the Germans would need a long time to bring up their artillery. Then they would subject the French positions to a lengthy bombardment before starting the infantry assault and river-crossing.

The Germans had thrown away that textbook early in the 1914–18 war. Initiative, speed and surprise was the new German technique. Richthofen's Stuka dive-bombers were their artillery. With the defenders taking cover from continuous air attacks, the Germans got their tanks across the Meuse in a matter of hours. Determined and valiant attacks by RAF light bombers did little beyond demonstrating the deadly effectiveness of the Flak with which the Luftwaffe defended the crossing places.

The Germans were not dismayed by tanks in the way that the Allied soldiers were. Rommel, like any good factory manager, liked to be where the hard work was done. He crossed the Meuse in one of the first boats. With a small number of his men on the far bank, he showed what could be achieved by determination and little else:

I then moved up north along a deep gully to the Company Enkefort. As we arrived an alarm came in: 'Enemy tanks in front.' The company had no anti-tank weapons, and I therefore gave orders for small arms fire to be opened on the tanks as quickly as possible, whereupon we saw them pull back into a hollow about a thousand yards north-west of Leffé. Large numbers of French stragglers came through the bushes and slowly laid down their arms.[16]

Maps showing the German movement across the Meuse have to simplify the crossings with a few arrows. In fact the German army filtered across the river man by man, unit by unit. At Leffé, near Dinant, some of Rommel's men captured a footbridge, others paddled across in tiny inflated boats. Elsewhere men dragged motor-cycles along a narrow stone weir to get to the far bank. At Houx they clambered over a lock gate. Light vehicles were ferried across on big rubber boats. At Bouvignes soldiers put their armoured cars on to pontoon rafts. Here and there a bridge was captured, or a damaged bridge repaired. When enough pontoons arrived the engineers fitted them together to make a bridge. Constantly under fire, groups of Germans improvised their crossings to the far bank of the river in increased numbers before they joined up and moved forward.

By nightfall on 15 May a 50-mile gap had been torn into the French defences. Through it came the armour and trucks crammed with infantry, pressing onwards in a long curving route alongside the River Somme, heading for the Channel coast.

And yet this does not tell the whole truth. Many French units

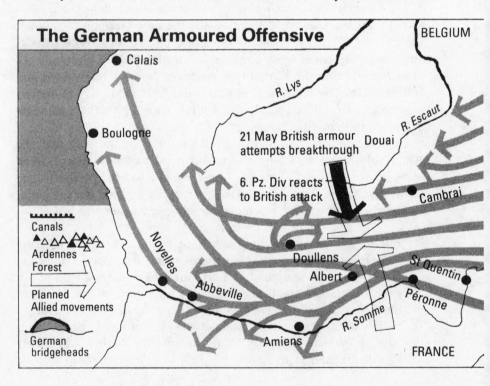

The German Armoured Offensive

BELGIUM

Calais

R. Lys

R. Escaut

Boulogne

21 May British armour attempts breakthrough

Douai

6. Pz. Div reacts to British attack

Cambrai

Canals

Ardennes Forest

Planned Allied movements

German bridgeheads

Noyelles

Doullens

Albert

St Quentin

Abbeville

Péronne

R. Somme

Amiens

FRANCE

contested the advance, fighting bitterly to halt the Germans for a few hours. Follow the routes of the invaders, and you will find the plaques and war memorials where brave Frenchmen died. Read the German diaries to see that many of these tiny actions were fought to bloody conclusions.

'Plan Yellow', the German assault upon France and the Low Countries, was notably different to the attack on Poland. There the Germans had stretched two arms forward before closing them around the enemy in a battle of encirclement. Such envelopments, that embraced the opposing army, were as old as war itself. But Plan Yellow was not that sort of envelopment. Army Group A was a single knife that cut a long sweeping gash – the 'sickle cut'. They didn't need another arm, for the coast provided enclosure enough. Panzer divisions swung away from the southern part of Army Group B to join them and add more steel to the cutting edge. This determined German thrust would quickly separate the Allied armies in the north from their support and supplies. Using good roads the movement was the most perfect example of what blitzkrieg could do.[17]

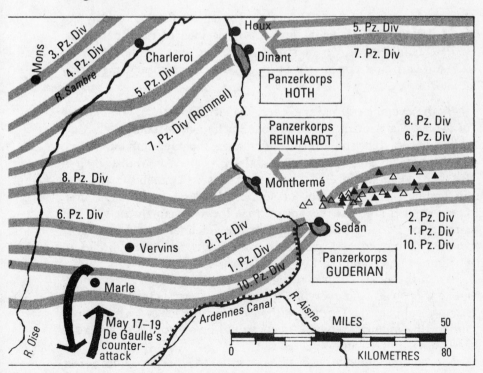

Defensive air cover was continuously provided to the columns. To lessen congestion on the roads men, fuel and spare parts for them were brought forward by Junkers Ju 52 transports. Luftwaffe fighter squadrons kept up with the advance by moving forward into newly captured airfields. Within nine days the Germans had reached Abbeville. So quick and expert had this 'sickle cut' proved that the Allied armies in the north took time to realize that they were now surrounded. The beleaguered armies had to move fast to reorganize themselves and man their defences on all sides.

The Allied reaction

It took many days for anyone on the Allied side to recognize the German attack for what it was. At first it was supposed that the invading columns would not get far. They would hammer away to produce a huge dent in the Western Front, and this great salient would then be contained by the Allied armies and the war would settle into stalemate.

Hitler's Directive of 14 May reported:

> The progress of the offensive to date shows that the enemy has failed to appreciate in time the basic idea of our operations. He continues to throw strong forces against the line Namur-Antwerp and appears to be neglecting the sector facing Army Group A.

By the evening of 15 May General Maurice Gamelin, commander of Allied land forces, realized that he had been completely out-manoeuvred, but still he misunderstood the German intentions. The American ambassador was at the French War Ministry when Edouard Daladier received a phone call from Gamelin to say that he had not a single corps of soldiers between Laon and Paris. Gamelin had still not recognized that the German thrust was not aiming for Paris. It was heading for the Channel and so cut Paris, and its command and supplies, away from the Allied armies in northern France and the Low Countries.

When the sickle cut was recognized for what it was, the counter-move was obvious to everyone. Coordinated thrusts from north and south would cut the German armoured spearheads away from their supporting infantry. The Germans would be sliced up, deprived of essential supplies, and defeated.

No such counter-offensive was launched, because the prime

failure of the French army was not of equipment, manpower, nor even generalship. It was a failure of communications. The French army could not have mounted such a counter-attack in anything less than three weeks. A new commander – Weygand – was called to replace the exhausted Gamelin, but by the time he had travelled from Beirut in the Lebanon, collected his thoughts, and evolved ideas for the counter-attack, the Allied armies in the north were besieged.

The poor communications were reflected in the disposition of the French commanders. General Gamelin, who commanded soldiers as far away as North Africa, was to be found in the gloomy Château de Vincennes, near Paris. He had no general staff. Operational control of the armies in northern France was given to General A. L. Georges (although even his chief of staff was not sure where Gamelin's powers ended and Georges' began). Georges had his headquarters about 35 miles from Gamelin's but spent a great deal of time at his 'personal command post' near his residence and some twelve miles from his HQ. In any case, most of Georges' staff, under General Doumenc, were somewhere entirely different: GHQ Land Forces, a Rothschild mansion at Montry, lay halfway between Gamelin's and Georges' HQ. Together with some of his subordinates, Doumenc habitually spent his mornings at Montry and his afternoons at Georges' HQ, whether his general was there or not. There were no teleprinter connections between these places. At Gamelin's HQ there was not even a radio. Messages were usually sent by motor-cycle, and Gamelin's usual way of communicating with Georges was to visit him by road.

When the German attack came, motor-cycle messengers left Montry HQ every hour. Several of them were killed in traffic accidents said André Beaufre, an officer who was there at the time. He went on:

> Late that night [13–14 May] when I had only just got to sleep I was awakened by a telephone call from General Georges: 'Ask General Doumenc to come here at once.' An hour later we arrived at the Château des Bondons, at La-Ferté-sous-Jouarre, where General Georges and his staff had their command post. In the château, which was rather more a big villa set in a park on a hill, the large salon had been made the map room. Around a long trestle table the staff officers answered the telephone and made notes.

When we arrived at about three o'clock in the morning all was dark except in this room which was barely half-lit. At the telephone Major Navereau was repeating in a low voice the information coming in. Everyone else was silent. General Roton, Chief of Staff, was stretched out in an armchair. The atmosphere was that of a family in which there had just been a death. Georges got up quickly and came to Doumenc. He was terribly pale. 'Our front has been broken at Sedan! There has been a collapse . . .' He flung himself into a chair and burst into tears.

He was the first man I had seen weep in this campaign. Alas there were to be others. It made a terrible impression on me.[18]

French armies on the southern side of the German sickle cut tried to slice through it. On 17 May at Montcornet a collection of armoured elements under the command of Colonel de Gaulle made a determined assault, but German air attacks decided the day. Although de Gaulle tried again, his force of about three battalions was not big enough, or good enough, to have any effect on the German advance. De Gaulle did not give up. He led other attacks and was promoted to the rank of general.

On 19 May General Gort learned from radio intercepts that he was surrounded. The Germans were pressing against his perimeter which was shrinking by the hour. His lines of communication were severed, the railway system was collapsing and all movements had to be made by road. This was particularly hard on the tanks; the endurance of their tracks was limited, and shortened still more by any paved surface. Mechanical problems were common.

Gort moved quickly to form defence lines along the only obstacle available, the Aa Canal, while continuing to fight the main German forces of Army Group B. His ammunition and other supplies were spread thinly. There was little left for any counter-offensive southwards, yet one did take place.

On 21 May a hastily contrived collection of British units – two territorial battalions, a motor-cycle battalion and 74 mixed tanks – was poised for a counter-attack from Vimy in the direction of Arras. They were to advance in conjunction with a larger French force which was still moving into position. The French asked for extra time but the British didn't wait for them. Nevertheless this encounter showed what a well organized, well equipped counter-attack might have achieved. Cutting through the armoured tail of Rommel's 7 Panzer Division they caused consternation akin to panic. Their success was short-lived as the Luftwaffe came into the action and Rommel brought his dual-purpose 8.8-cm guns into use against the thick-skinned Matilda tanks. After 48 hours of combat – as the French were coming up to start fighting – the British force had only two Matildas battleworthy. They began to withdraw. The history of one of the participating regiments said:

> After some initial success the attack broke down under the increasing strength of the enemy. This determined the fate of the BEF. It was clear that an aggressive role was now far beyond its powers and that its extrication from Arras would be of itself a perilous operation.[19]

A coordinated Anglo-French action at this time might have caused the Germans to recoil. As it was, these uncoordinated swipes brought them only to a temporary halt. Valuable time was gained: the Arras attack delayed the Germans by two and half days while Rommel's men paused to rest and refit.

The BEF was not trained, supplied or equipped for full-scale attack. No one properly informed could doubt that any effective counter-offensive would have to come from the larger French resources to the south of the German thrust. But few people were so informed. There were endless discussions, telegrams, orders and instructions between Paris, London and the BEF (which eventually was driven to using public cross-Channel phones to speak to London).

Despite the long period for preparation that the 'phoney war' had provided, the British army, like the French army, was not ready for modern battle. Tank crews were half-trained, tanks lacked radios, sighting telescopes and even armour-piercing ammunition. Reinforcements were hurried to France but even these units were not ready to fight. The 3rd Royal Tank Regiment landed at Calais on 22 May and was ordered to drive straight for St Omer. It was delayed by 'disorderly loading and the loss of much ancillary equipment [which] led to chaos in the French port'.[20] By 26 May this regiment had lost every tank.

While France fielded some excellent tanks, there were few good British designs. In the 1930s works of fiction and non-fiction depicted arms manufacturers as venal and unscrupulous villains, but the truth was that few factories wanted such government contracts. This was especially true of tanks. So British tanks were built by agricultural engineers, locomotive factories and shipyards, at times when those contractors could get no other work. Old techniques, such as riveting, were used even though it had been demonstrated at Woolwich, back in 1934, that welded armour plate was essential for modern tank manufacture. When the test of battle came these failings were evident: their crews deserved better. As a recent official British publication says:

> From this point the histories of all the British cavalry [tank] regiments seem to tell the same story, a repetitive saga of withdrawal from river line to river line, holding on for a while, blowing bridges then falling back. It is a tale of endless duels with German anti-tank guns that sliced clean through thin armour, of suicidal charges to destroy these guns by running over them, and even of scout carriers dashing into action like tanks.[21]

British generalship suffered from conflicting ideas about the role of armour. Heavy tanks were designed to plod alongside the infantry as they had done in 1918. Lighter, thin-skinned models were to gallop about like cavalry. Such specialized roles led to the tanks being spread around, and shared throughout the Allied armies, at a time when the Germans proved that tanks were far more effective if used in armoured divisions. The tactical failing of Allied tank warfare was to send tank against tank; the Germans knew that armour should be used against vulnerable targets, while mobile batteries of high-velocity anti-tank guns dealt with enemy armour. Allied tank experts also knew all this, but tank experts were not consulted by the higher commands. Now Gort had cut back his headquarters to the minimum scale, so that during the fighting in May there was no tank expert at his GHQ and no intelligence staff. It was a severe limitation.

Perhaps intervention by military intelligence could have lessened the hysteria about secret agents which gripped almost all Allied soldiers. Rumours about the successes of German paratroops, and the isolated use of Dutch uniforms, had grown into ever more vivid stories; such as Germans in high-ranking Allied uniforms ordering troops to their deaths. Locals who did not understand English were likely to be categorized as saboteurs; those who did speak English were suspected of being spies. Signals and messages, artfully cut into growing crops, were seen everywhere. The slightest flicker of light, like that through a briefly opened door, was believed to be signalling by German agents. The stories became more and more bizarre. A typical account appears in the otherwise more sober regimental history of the Grenadier Guards:

> One example of this carefully planned [spying] organisation made a great impression on the Battalion. The occupants of the farm where their headquarters was lodged decided to leave the building as the German shelling became more intense. Madame, who had greeted the Grenadiers two days before with warmth and a flood of passable English, now bade farewell to her cows, horses and guests, and left in tears. Two hours later the headquarters was very heavily and accurately shelled. Their suspicions aroused, the Grenadiers searched the immediate neighbourhood and found that arrows, pointing directly towards the house, had been ploughed into all the adjoining fields . . . Germans dressed in British uniforms added to the danger and the strain.[22]

Its regimental history reports that on 20 May this same battalion executed seventeen 'ubiquitous civilian snipers' in one day! There is no evidence that the Germans employed foreign snipers – they needed no help – nor that they had secret agents laboriously ploughing messages in fields. But such summary executions of local people were common, and may well have spread an urge for revenge amongst the friends and relatives of the bereaved. The grave shortage of British soldiers fluent in any foreign language hampered relations with local populations and with Allied units.

In overview it is difficult to refute the criticism made by the French and others that the British were too eager to quit the Continent. Gort had never allowed his army to become an integrated part of the Allied line. His counter-attack at Arras lasted only 48 hours and was the only offensive the British staged. The casualties suffered by the BEF were not severe when compared with the other armies which fought alongside it.[23] The French argued that Gort had pulled back at times when they most needed him to stay put. As they saw it the BEF did nothing but stage an orderly advance, a ragged retreat, and then improvise a sea evacuation to save themselves while the French army defended the evacuation.

11 RETREAT

Berlin. 25 June 1940.
I have the impression that we are rushing for a
common currency for the whole of Europe. That would be
progress, of course, and, one would hope, of lasting
significance.

Letter from Helmuth von Moltke
(military intelligence)[1]

As early as 19 May 1940 the British army had begun to prepare to evacuate its Expeditionary Force from the Continent of Europe. General Lord Gort, its commander, sent an officer to London to discuss pulling out through Dunkirk.[2] At this stage it was only a contingency plan, but on that same day, headquarters troops – not required in battle – were moved to Dunkirk by train. Soon the ships bringing supplies to France took such non-combatants back to England.

On 21 May Gort started pulling his army back to ensure that it occupied a piece of coast from which his force could be lifted off. It was a controversial decision, the more so because of the way the British deliberately kept their Allies in the dark about what they were doing, and what they intended. At Gort's headquarters there was little faith in General Blanchard,[3] who commanded the neighbouring French divisions, while Billotte, commander of the Army Group to which the BEF belonged, had that day been fatally injured in a car crash.

By some bizarre arrangement, Gort's orders had until now been coming from the supreme commander Gamelin, who had just been replaced.[4] Earlier that day, with the Germans racing through France, the newly appointed supreme commander, Weygand, went to judge the situation on the spot. Gort was not summoned to the meeting until the discussion came round to using British troops in a counter-attack. By the time Gort arrived Weygand had departed. The French, who found their flanks exposed by British withdrawals, demanded that Gort stay in position but the BEF kept moving.

By Saturday 25 May there were reports about the Germans capturing the Channel port of Calais, as well as Boulogne. At Dunkirk the bombing had deprived the port of electricity, so that dockside cranes were out of action. Unloading had to be done by small ship's cranes. Time was running out and the section of front held by the Belgian army was vital. They had now become the focus of the German attack and the Luftwaffe was giving them pitiless attention. If they yielded ground, or asked for a cease-fire, Dunkirk, and the British army's only chance of salvation, would be lost.

Sir John Dill arrived in France on a visit. He was the CIGS, Britain's top soldier, and perhaps Gort had hoped to get a direct order from him.[5] Dill was an affable man of courteous disposition, but he brought no news or official instructions for Gort. His only message was that there was 'criticism at home that the BEF, 200,000 fighting men who claimed to be better fighters than the Bosche [*sic*], were not doing enough.'[6] Coming from the genial Dill, this was a slap in the face for Gort.

That evening Gort was sitting alone wondering how long the Belgians could keep fighting. Suddenly he got up and went to the office of his chief of staff. He ordered him to move two British divisions (the 5th and the 50th) to reinforce the line the Belgians were holding. Gort's sudden impulse probably saved the BEF from destruction, but he was using the men General Blanchard had been promised for the much-discussed Allied counter-attack. That night Gort's chief of staff recorded Gort's reasoning in this diary entry about the Belgians:

> If they go from that [line], Dunkirk is taken from the north and we are bust. If the Belgians need help to hold that, only we can give it . . . a beleaguered garrison must first be sure of its perimeter before it can indulge in sorties.[7]

The two divisions travelled all night to move into position facing eastwards on the line of the Ypres-Comines canal. The regimental history of the Royal Scots Fusiliers recorded the crucial outcome of Gort's decision:

> Their arrival was narrowly timed. The Germans attacked after dawn on May 26. The battle raged all day, and so furiously that the three battalions of the 1st Division which had been held in reserve, were drawn in. . . . The Belgians collapsed completely on May 27. Their capitulation was made without previous consultation and at very short notice.[8]

In fact the Belgians had taken the weight of the German attack from the north. For a week King Leopold had been warning the

Allies that his army's capacity to hold out was limited. It was the British who had let their ally down. The Belgians were never informed that the BEF was abandoning them. When the surrender came the French premier Paul Reynaud immediately broadcast a vitriolic diatribe in which he called the Belgian king a traitor. Churchill knew that this abuse was a scandalous untruth because he'd had a special liaison officer at Leopold's headquarters, but he was too anxious about upsetting Reynaud to issue a denial, so King Leopold was widely condemned as a traitor.[9]

For the British everything was happening at great speed. One British artillery officer said after being handed a new map:

> I took mine without paying much attention to it. We were already up in the corner of our last sheet, so I had expected we'd soon get a new issue. Suddenly glancing down at it, I noticed that a great proportion of the new sheet was occupied by the sea. Another look showed me a strip of coast. And the principal name on this strip was Dunkirk. It was the first time the word had struck us with any particular significance.[10]

The BEF was in full retreat. Gort believed the French had been told that he was pulling out of the continental fighting, but when Paul Reynaud went to see Churchill in London on Sunday 26 May, still the news was kept from him. For the British soldiers in France, the planned evacuation was all too evident. Said the same artillery officer:

> Into this pancake of land it seemed as if the whole of the BEF was pouring. Every road scoring the landscape was one thick mass of transport and troops, great long lines of them stretching back far to the eastern horizon, and all the lines converging towards the one focus – Dunkirk. Ambulances, lorries, trucks, Bren-gun carriers, artillery columns – everything except tanks – all crawling along those roads in well-defined lines over the flat featureless country in the late afternoon sunshine, provided an impressive and memorable picture of two modern armies in retreat. Under their greyish camouflage paint they resembled from a distance slow-moving rivers of muddy-coloured lava from some far-off eruption.
>
> It was now that I saw for the first time, regiments in the doleful process of wrecking their equipment. New wireless sets, costing perhaps £20 apiece, were placed in rows in fields, twenty in a

row, sometimes, while a soldier with a pick-axe proceeded up and down knocking them to pieces. Trucks were being dealt with just as dramatically. Radiators and engines were smashed with sledge-hammers; tires slashed and sawn after they had been deflated. Vehicles that were near the canals were finally pushed in. Some of the canals were choked with the wrecks, all piled on top of each other.

To reduce congestion, the British posted military police on the roads to prevent trucks and transport of any kind entering the beach area. This led to angry clashes as the French soldiers objected to leaving behind their ammunition trucks or losing other elements of their fighting force. For the British, Dunkirk was the end of the road; for the French it was one of their towns to be defended with all the means at their disposal.[11]

Perhaps a fierce German assault upon the Dunkirk perimeter would have eliminated the chances of a seaborne evacuation, but it did not come. The armour was halted for a respite and the Germans took their time. Afterwards the 'halt order' became a subject of controversy, but at the time it seemed normal.[12] Paris, and the greater part of France, had still to be conquered by Germany's limited armoured forces. No one, least of all the Germans, thought that the bulk of the British army could be rescued from the beaches by a rag-tag collection of ferry boats, privately owned yachts manned by civilians, and RN warships risked in shallow waters as HM ships have never been before or since. But it was time for the British to pull a rabbit out of the hat. Largely due to the ad hoc skill and foresight of a few naval officers the seemingly impossible was achieved.

Dunkirk

Perhaps the first indication the Germans saw of British determination to continue the war was the fortitude of the RAF fighter pilots covering the Dunkirk evacuation. Men do not readily expend their lives for a cause that is already lost. It was the belief in Winston Churchill that German fliers encountered over Dunkirk. 'The enemy has had air superiority. This is something new for us in this campaign' said the German 4th Army's war diary on 25 May.

The RAF fighter pilots lacked the range to spend much time patrolling over the beaches and there were times when the Germans had the air to themselves. For the most part the RAF tried to

The German Blitzkrieg and evacuation of Dunkirk.

Direction of German Advance — Allied Line

intercept the German bombers before they reached Dunkirk. The Allied soldiers fighting a brave rearguard action in the streets, and the infantry patiently lining up on the mole from which most were rescued, seldom saw the RAF. Neither did the men dug into holes on the beaches, or scrambling across beached ships or over lines of vehicles that had been run into the sea to make piers. They were more apt to remember the enemy bombers that got through time and again, and the German fighters that came roaring out of the haze with their machine-guns blazing. The survivors of Dunkirk did not emerge as admirers of the RAF fliers who had fought to give them air cover. On the contrary, in the English summer of 1940 many men in light blue uniforms were singled out for abuse by angry soldiers with vivid memories of the Luftwaffe's successes.

One RAF Flying Training School commanding officer felt so anxious about the growing hostility that he contacted the nearby army commander in North Wales about the bad effect of BEF troops hissing newsreel pictures of the RAF in local cinemas. He also sent a signal, classified Secret, on the subject to his Group HQ. Churchill was also aware of the problem. Addressing Parliament he gave special emphasis to the contribution the RAF made to the sea evacuation despite the fact that they were above the clouds and out of sight.[13]

In the ports of harbours of southern England yachtsmen and fishermen of all ages were asked to help evacuate the British army from France. Some declined, but many civilians crossed the Channel to help with the rescue. The small boats could not carry many men but they played a vital role in repeatedly ferrying the soldiers out to the larger boats. The *Seasalter*, a smack arriving back from dredging the oyster beds near Burnham-on-Crouch in Essex, was asked to go and help. The skipper said:

> The soldiers were coming off the beach clinging to bits of wood and wreckage and anything that would float. As we got close enough we began to pick them up. We saw a row-boat coming off loaded right down with troops. And with this we went to and fro, bringing as many as it would dare hold, and in the meantime we went round picking up as many as we could. When we got a load we would take them off to one of the ships lying off in the deep water.[14]

All that was good and everything that was bad about men could be found on the Dunkirk beaches. It was a sense of fair play that made men wait their turn, even when it looked as if their turn would never come. But it was a time of cowardice and lies as well as selfless heroism. Allies were deceived, comrades abandoned. Officers trying to organize unruly crowds of weary soldiers sometimes had to draw their pistols. Looting and rape were not unknown. Some men died unheroic deaths. But all in all the Dunkirk evacuation worked because heroism, discipline, self-sacrifice and common sense prevailed. It became the sort of heroic failure that the British cherish, and celebrate for longer than their victories.

Soldiers arrived in England at the same south coast resorts that many of them knew from peacetime holidays. At Dover, Deal, Folkestone, Margate, Sheerness and Ramsgate there was tea and biscuits, apples and oranges, cigarettes and matches, doctors and nurses, coaches and trains. Crowds gathered at the London railway terminals to watch the arrival of subdued, tired and dirty men. A few arrived complete with packs and rifles, some brandished souvenirs, most had only the barest clothes. By 4 June 338,226 had been rescued and of these 123,095 were French. On this day Churchill told the House:

> We shall not flag or fail. We shall go on to the end. We shall fight in France, we shall fight on the seas and oceans, we shall fight with growing confidence and growing strength in the air, we shall defend our island, whatever the cost may be. We shall fight on the beaches, we shall fight on the landing grounds, we shall fight in the fields and in the streets, we shall fight in the hills; we shall never surrender.

Portentously he added: 'in God's good time, the new world, with all its power and might, steps forth to the rescue and liberation of the old.'[15]

The significance of Operation Dynamo cannot be over-emphasized. Although almost all the French rescued went back to fight for a still undefeated France, the British survivors provided the cadre of a new and better army. Had a quarter of a million British men languished in German captivity, it is hard to believe that public opinion would have been in favour of continuing the war.

As the British departed from the Continent, there remained a vast scrapyard of military equipment, the more so since the British Expeditionary Force had been a mechanized army. A German officer[16] wrote home saying:

> Just before La Panne we passed the first collecting point for wrecked vehicles. There were hundreds, possibly thousands, of cars, trucks, armoured vehicles of all sizes. Almost all of them were burnt out, because the British and French had put fire to all the vehicles they had to abandon. In La Panne itself, a harbour which had served for embarkations, there was merely a vast amount of war matériel, all useless. Anti-aircraft guns, machine-guns, motor bicycles, anti-tank guns, etc. From the place where we stopped on the beach we could see a sunken British warship.

Gort was sent to become inspector-general to the forces for training. It was an inappropriate job for a man brimming over with courage who had already demonstrated that training for modern war was not something he understood. One of his subordinates, Alan Brooke, who had not enjoyed being subordinated to Gort in

France, became Commander in Chief Home Forces. His version of the events of May 1940 was that he had shown exemplary skill in covering the withdrawal to Dunkirk while Gort had been found wanting. In December 1941 Brooke's striding energy and sincere ambition gained for him Dill's post of CIGS. Gort, Ironside and Dill had held the job in quick succession, but now it had been given to a man who would never let go. Sir Arthur Bryant, a distinguished writer, used Brooke's war diaries and autobiographical notes to write a history of the war. As proof that the pen can be mightier than the sword, Field Marshal The Viscount Alanbrooke ended up widely regarded as the man who'd won the war almost single-handed. Gort faded into military oblivion.

The end of France

On 5 June the regrouped German armies launched a concerted offensive southwards. Weygand, the new French commander, tried to hold a front to the north of Paris, but by 8 June had begun to re-treat to the River Seine. Two days later the French government fled Paris, and on that same day Italy declared war on Britain and France. 'A great day in the history of the German Army!' said General Franz Halder, chief of the army general staff, on 14 June. 'German troops have been marching into Paris since nine o'clock this morning.'[17]

Now the German drive southwards fanned out both east and west. A week later 32 Italian divisions attacked the six Alpine divisions that manned the French south-east frontier. This was Mussolini's last-minute bid for a seat at the peace conference and a share of the spoils.

Many French units fought hard and well but as Telford Taylor, an American military historian, summed it up: 'The trouble was that those who fought were woefully hampered by those who did not, and fatally handicapped by those who failed to prepare.'[18] Soon the Germans had the French armies pinned against the rear of their Maginot Line, while other spearheads reached the Spanish border.

On 16 June, Marshal Pétain, the 84-year-old hero of Verdun, the war minister whose decisions had played an important part in creating the Maginot Line and the disaster that now befell the French army, came forward to negotiate with the Germans. Hitler simply dictated terms to him, and with a childish and vindictive sense of theatre arranged for the armistice to be signed in the same railway coach in which the Germans had been made to sign the armistice of 1918.[19]

Success always wins friends, and Hitler was not lacking in admirers. Casting aside his feelings about freedom, in the Indian newspaper *Harijan* on 22 June, Mahatma Gandhi wrote: 'Germans of future generations will honour Herr Hitler as a genius, as a brave man, a matchless organizer and much more.' In Moscow Foreign Minister Molotov cast aside his feelings about Fascism and summoned the German ambassador to convey 'the warmest congratulations of the Soviet government on the splendid success of the German armed forces.' The democratically elected government of Denmark, which the Germans had kept in place, allowed gratitude to overcome its respect for democracy and announced: 'The great German victories, which have caused astonishment and admiration all over the world, have brought about a new era in Europe, which will result in a new order in a political and economic sense, under the leadership of Germany.' The Aga Khan cast aside his feelings about alcohol and promised to drink a bottle of champagne 'when the Führer sleeps in Windsor Castle'.[20]

Peace feelers

Hitler and his generals had never anticipated the Dunkirk evacuation, principally because they were men of a continental land power. For them the coast was the end of the road. For the British, with their 'island mentality', the sea was an open door. The poor impression Hitler had formed of Chamberlain made him confident that the British cabinet would come to him seeking peace terms.

Such an opinion was not without foundation. Lord Halifax, who had so nearly become prime minister in May, certainly did not rule out talks with Hitler. As France collapsed, Halifax was hinting to the still neutral Italians that Britain would be interested in the prospect of a conference to decide the fate of Europe.

Britain, like France and many other European countries, was subject to the influence of aristocrats and land-owning gentry who worried about the spread of Communism, and the social upheaval that a major European war would bring. They even feared a British victory: Germany weakened by war would open the floodgates to a tide of Soviet expansion. For such people, appeasement of Hitler had been the only sensible prewar policy. Even after war began, there were a great many men of influence who thought that Britain should admit its error and quickly come to terms with the Nazis. So did those in the Foreign Office and the Treasury who anxiously watched the steady depletion of their country's financial resources.

During the period of the 'phoney war' contacts with prewar personal British friends convinced highly placed Nazis that the British were irresolute. German diplomats and secret agents were alerted to the possibility of making peace with Britain. The armistice sought by Marshal Pétain on 16 June 1940 gave new urgency to British peace feelers, which were now being extended in Spain, Switzerland and Sweden.

There is no known verbatim record of the conversation that took place when on 17 June 1940 R.A.B. Butler (Halifax's deputy) met Björn Prytz, Sweden's minister in London. But long after the war Prytz published the telegram he sent to Stockholm as a result of that meeting.[21] According to Swedish records, Butler told Prytz that 'no opportunity of reaching a compromise peace would be neglected if the possibility were offered on reasonable conditions.'[22] Butler was seeking peace terms on behalf of his boss, and in an unmistakable reference to Churchill and his supporters he added that Lord Halifax specifically promised that 'no diehards would be allowed to stand in the way.'

Churchill was unable to attend a meeting of the war cabinet at 12.30 pm the following day. One item has since been deleted from the official minutes of that cabinet meeting but the diary notes of Alexander Cadogan, head of the Foreign Office, who was present, provide a tantalizing clue to what the closely guarded secret might be. 'Winston not there – writing his speech. No reply from Germans.'[23] It seems that Churchill's authority was flouted by men determined to sue for peace.

Halifax and Butler were not alone in their quest. Lloyd George, who had been prime minister in the First World War, had seen little chance of a British victory in the Second. The Americans would not enter the war, he said, and he made no secret of his readiness to take over his nation in defeat, as Pétain had now taken over France.[24] How many others were of like mind can only be guessed. The Duke of Windsor – who as Edward VIII abdicated from the throne in 1936 – and his wife, the infamous Mrs Wallis Simpson, were outspoken admirers of Hitler and his Third Reich. Bitterly divided from his family on account of his marriage, there are suggestions that Edward hoped to assume the throne of a defeated Britain with Hitler's blessing.

But nothing came of the peace feelers. At 9 pm on 17 June Churchill spoke on the radio for two minutes before the evening's news bulletin. In a hastily prepared response to the French collapse he told the world: 'The news from France is very bad, and I grieve for the gallant French people who have fallen into this terrible misfortune.' He went on: 'We shall defend our island, and, with the British Empire around us, we shall fight on unconquerable until the curse of Hitler is lifted from the brows of men. We are sure that in the end all will be well.'[25]

At 3.45 the following afternoon, while the Germans were still considering how to react to the hints, questions and off-the-record conversations, channelled through their ambassadors in neutral capitals, Churchill stood up in the House of Commons and delivered the speech that he had been writing when he was absent from the cabinet:

> The whole fury and might of the enemy must very soon be turned on us. Hitler knows that he will have to break us in this island or lose the war . . . if we fail, then the whole world, including the United States, and all that we have known and cared for, will sink into the abyss of a new dark age made more sinister, and perhaps more protracted, by the lights of a perverted science.
>
> Let us therefore brace ourselves to our duty and so bear ourselves that if the British Empire and its Commonwealth lasts for a thousand years men will still say 'This was their finest hour.'[26]

It was one of Churchill's finest hours too. At that time there were no recording or broadcast facilities in the House of Commons, and so the prime minister was prevailed upon to deliver the speech again over the radio at 9 pm before that evening's BBC news bulletin. The radio performance did not communicate the Churchill fire that a live audience had produced in the afternoon. Some of his colleagues thought his voice sounded unusual over the air and put it down to emotion, or the imperfections of broadcasting. Less charitably, the publisher Cecil King wondered if he was drunk. Harold Nicolson at the Ministry of Information remarked that a speech that sounded magnificent in the House of Commons 'sounded ghastly on the wireless'.

John Martin, private secretary to the prime minister, said that Churchill's 'halting delivery at the start seems to have struck people and we had a letter from someone saying that evidently something had gone wrong with his heart and he ought to work in the recumbent position. The fact was, I gather, that he spoke with a cigar in his mouth.'[27]

In recent years an elaborate myth has grown up around speculation that maybe the 18 June speech was not broadcast by Churchill at all. The rumours spread when the BBC repertory actor Norman Shelley, who played Winnie the Pooh and Toad of Toad Hall in the BBC Children's Hour, revealed that, with the prime minister's permission, he had recorded Churchill's speeches for American audiences. But there is no real evidence to support the view that Shelley had imitated Churchill's voice on the BBC in June 1940.[28]

In the face of Churchill's fiery rhetoric, the Germans decided that Lord Halifax, Butler and their many peace-seeking friends were no match for him and shelved their hopes of total victory. Hitler's pre-war experience with Chamberlain was no longer a guide to Britain's mood. Winston Churchill had brought a psychological change to Britain that could never have taken place under his predecessor's direction.

A 'successful landing'

The tragedy, comedy and confusion that reigned on both sides is illustrated by what happened to Britain's Channel Islands in this summer of 1940. These small islands, part of Great Britain but not of the United Kingdom, are self-governing communities under the British crown. They are all near to France, and by 19 June 1940 Whitehall had decided that they should be demilitarized and declared 'open towns'. However with that reticence for which bureaucrats are noted, the men in Whitehall did not announce this decision, probably because the humiliation of publicly yielding British territory could not be faced.

To test whether they were being defended the Germans sent aircraft to fly very low across the islands. As one roared across St Peter Port on Guernsey, someone aboard the Southern Railway steamer *Isle of Sark*, sailing from Jersey to Southampton, fired ancient twin-mounted Lewis machine-guns at it. The Germans decided that there was a military force on the islands. As a result Heinkel He 111 bombers bombed and machine-gunned the two principal towns of St Helier in Jersey and St Peter Port, Guernsey, on the evening of 28 June. There were many casualties, and only after this did Whitehall announce that the islands had been demilitarized.

Figure 19:
Heinkel He 111 bomber

The German monitoring service missed the demilitarization announcement put out by the BBC, and it was the United States ambassador in Paris who made sure the Germans knew of it. The commander of the German naval forces in northern France was engaged in a conference on the subject of the Channel Islands when he received the news by telephone. It was decided that occupation would be a propaganda coup. Luftflotte 3 assigned ten Junkers Ju 52 transport planes as well as fighter, bomber and reconnaissance units to the task. Army Group B were to provide soldiers, and naval craft were prepared for the assault on the beaches. Most importantly film camera-men, photographers and writers were sent to Cherbourg and attached to all the participating units.

Meanwhile a Dornier Do 17P – a version of the somewhat outdated 'flying pencil' relegated to reconnaissance duties – landed, apparently on a whim, at Guernsey airport. Locals told the pilot that the islands were undefended. When the Dornier returned to its base, a few Luftwaffe personnel were given rifles and flown across to the island formally to take it over. The next morning another Dornier – piloted by Oberleutnant Richard Kern – flew to Jersey airport. He took over there armed with nothing more than his pistol.

These enterprising men of the Luftwaffe had, of course, completely spoiled the propaganda invasion. To make things even more humiliating for the assembled invasion force, their own start was delayed by fog.

The Channel Islanders' first sight of the rank-and-file German occupation forces was good enough to persuade them that they were specially selected as disciplined, polite and good-looking. In fact these troops were a company of Infantry Regiment 396 (216 Infantry Division) and were simply the nearest available unit.[29]

Men and weapons

In a six-week campaign the Germans had conquered all of western Europe. Their casualties were remarkably few (see Table 3):

Table 3 German and Allied casualties, 1940

	Dead	Wounded	POW/Missing
German	27,074	111,034	18,384
French	90,000	200,000	1,900,000

Other (total) casualties:
BEF (approx. 40 days fighting) 68,111; Belgian (17 days fighting) 23,350; Dutch (5 days fighting) 9,779.

The German army displayed ingenuity and adaptability in the invasion of the Low Countries. In the heart of Rotterdam, Heinkel float planes landed infantry which paddled ashore in inflatable boats. Infantry-carrying gliders had been towed behind transport planes to land on the roof of Belgium's titanic Eben Emael fortress. On the Luxembourg frontier, German soldiers posing as tourists and dressed in civilian clothes went ahead of the main force to disconnect the demolition devices. The invaders used Dutch uniforms and an armoured train to take the bridge at Gennep. Parachute troops came tumbling out of the sky to seize the mile-long undefended bridges at Moerdijk. Three-engined Junkers airliners crammed with infantry were crash-landed on Dutch roads.

Most of this 'exotica' was used against the Netherlands, Luxembourg and Belgium by the Germans of Army Group B. There was not very much of it and its actual contribution was small. These gimmicks were not a portent of wars to come, they were a stage conjuror's trick to hold the attention of the audience while Army Group A brought the rabbit from the Ardennes woodlands.

At the time it was salve for the wounds to believe that the Germans had won by massive force, and revolutionary new weapons. A relative of mine, freshly arrived home after the Dunkirk evacuation, rhetorically asked my father: 'What chance do you have with a bolt-action rifle against a man with a tommy gun?'

Most of the techniques of 1940 could have been seen in the German offensive of March 1918. In that 'Kaiser's Battle' lightly burdened shock-troops had pushed deep into enemy territory spraying rounds from 'machine-pistols' almost identical in size, shape and performance to the MP 38 guns used in 1940.[30] And there was nothing new about the skilled 'combat-engineers' deployed at the very front of the attack. German close-support aircraft had been used in the First World War, as is evidenced by the widespread use of the term 'ground-strafing' at that time. All of these elements could have been anticipated by the Allied generals had they cared to study the previous war.

In 1940 virtually the whole German army was horse-drawn and equipped with the Mauser Kar 98k, a bolt-action rifle, dating, as its

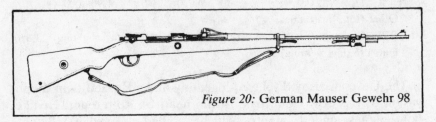

Figure 20: German Mauser Gewehr 98

name implies, from 1898.[31] The British army faced them with an almost identical rifle: the Lee-Enfield introduced at the end of the Boer War (when the Boers had been using the Mauser 98!). Even the German tanks were orthodox developments of the machine the British invented in 1915.

But unlike the Allies, the Germans learned from their defeats and their victories too. After the 1940 fighting they modified their equipment in the light of their experience. Lightweight tanks, armed with only machine-guns, were phased out in favour of heavier models.[32]

The fundamental change in light weapon manufacture that took place in this period is as significant as the one that jet propulsion brought to flight. All the major powers abandoned fine craftsmanship – the blued steel and polished walnut of another age – and turned to truly mass-produced weapons. The MG 34 was the sort of

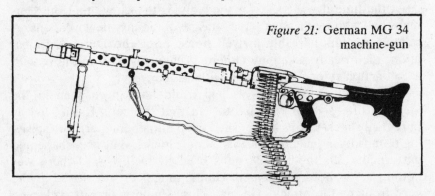

Figure 21: German MG 34 machine-gun

gun a collector cherishes, a Rheinmetall development of a Swiss gun, but its time was past. Mauser produced its replacement, the

MG 42, composed of simple sub-assembled units; its machined parts kept to a minimum. The cost was reduced from 310 Reichmarks for the MG 34 to 250 RM for the MG 42, and even half a century later, the MG 42 is widely used.[33] In 1941 Britain produced the first throw-away machine-gun: the Sten, a lightweight weapon that was accident-prone but suitable and cheap enough to drop in thousands to guerrilla forces.

On the whole, the British army's equipment had proved only marginally inferior. If their trucks succumbed to tough treatment, so did many German ones. European armies depended upon the railway system, and this had ensured that few good heavy-duty trucks were built anywhere except the United States, where customers expected trucks to repeat thousand-mile journeys over poor roads for decades.[34] The British army's Bren light machine-gun proved effective and reliable; it could be fired from the hip and it kept firing even when the barrel glowed red hot. Some British tanks acquitted themselves well enough when deployed skilfully on the battlefield, but after the BEF had abandoned 2,472 guns, 63,879 vehicles and over half a million tons of supplies in France, Britain could not afford the luxury of redesigning, or seriously modifying, the heavy equipment. British factories were put into high gear even when the products coming off the line were obviously inferior.

The production crisis of 1940 helped to ensure that, throughout the war, there never was a well designed British tank.[35] The British forces became more and more dependent upon American equipment sometimes modified to British requirements. When American tanks arrived they were properly packed and weatherproofed and fully equipped. Spare parts fitted without being hammered, filed and bent. They proved reliable[36] and the crews liked them. For many in Britain there came the startling revelation that mass-production methods could be superior to the hand-fashioned low-technology that was called craftsmanship.

The Allied defeats in 1940 were not due to a failure of quality or of quantity. Their air forces were very big and had many well designed aircraft. The French air force had well over two thousand modern fighters, more than twice the number deployed by the Luftwaffe.[37] The French army had excellent tanks and more of them than the Germans and British put together!

Some said it was a victory won by the close coordination of air and ground forces, a triumph for radio communication and ruthless aggression. But the collapse of Britain and France was mostly the outcome of the West's profound failure in political, industrial and military leadership. The men with the authority to write specifications had not done it well enough: and the designers were not skilled enough. Education at all levels of British society was not good enough. Those who had become used to easy profits from outmoded factories failed to meet the nation's needs. There had been no political will to stop Hitler at a time when he would not have dared to go to war. The military leadership, from top to bottom, had been totally outclassed on the battlefield.

The British army's very subjective interview system of officer selection had not stood the test of battle. Young men from esteemed public schools automatically accepted into the regiments of their fathers and grandfathers were not always the best leaders, and the prevailing system discouraged suitable men of other social backgrounds applying for a commission. With up to half the officer candidates failing their wartime training courses, and high levels of psychological breakdown, the Adjutant-General, General Sir Ronald Adam, decided to bring psychologists into the selection process. It became more difficult for commanding officers to commission anyone they thought would prove convivial in the regimental mess. The 'leaderless group test' was one of the new exams. Teams, randomly gathered, were provided with barrels, ropes and planks of wood and given complicated physical tasks to perform, while their actions were evaluated. Examiners looked for the ability to both give and take orders. This method provided a much higher rate of successful officer candidates as well as increasing applications for commissions by 25 per cent.[38] The British army, fast becoming more democratic and more effective than ever before, prepared itself for a return engagement.

In 1940 the European land war ended in stalemate. Germany had expanded its frontiers in all directions and Europe was permanently changed, but Britain was far from defeated. Meanwhile the Germans could celebrate a victory for the German educational system, professionalism, coordinated arms and realistic training. It was also a victory for a malignant dictatorship, and for a people who valued their material standard of living above the personal freedom of themselves and their neighbours.

Britain's spy network

As Britain looked back upon a seemingly endless succession of unpleasant surprises, some taxpayers asked what help had come from the vaunted Secret Intelligence Service. The answer was very little. Until the French and the Poles supplied their work to the British, the cracking of Germany's Enigma coding machine had got nowhere apart from an occasional lucky guess.

In the first weeks of the war the chief of the SIS, Admiral Sir Hugh Sinclair, died unexpectedly in King Edward VII Hospital for Officers, London. His memorial service, held at St Martin-in-the-Fields church in London, was attended by every senior intelligence officer who had ever come in contact with him – 'a very full congregation,' remarked the head of MI5.[39]

Sinclair's death came shortly after the signing of the German-Soviet pact, and the secret protocol by which Stalin would occupy half of Poland. As Chamberlain had admitted to Parliament, the pact came as a grave shock to the British government. This failure of the intelligence service was discussed in an emergency session of Parliament on 24 August, and feelings were running so high that Chamberlain felt bound to offer his resignation.

The death of Sinclair provided an opportunity, as well as a reason, to put the service on a modern and more competent footing. Their personnel might have been drawn from a wider section of the population, and been subject to careful vetting, but Sinclair's successor, Sir Stewart Menzies, was a candidate put forward by Lord Halifax, and he preferred to retain the traditional recruitment methods. Men from good families who had private incomes and had attended expensive private schools seemed to be the most appropriate people to be trusted with secrets, even secrets prised from foreigners. Such men invariably came into the service by personal introduction which seemed sufficient recommendation without inquiries into their previous activities.

Within days of Sinclair's death, the SD (Sicherheitsdienst), the intelligence arm of the Nazi party, showed itself to be far less gentlemanly. Himmler's men put out feelers to London pretending that they were army generals about to stage a coup against Hitler. On 9 November 1939 two top-level executives of Britain's SIS attended a rendezvous at Café Bacchus, an eating place right upon the Dutch frontier at Venlo. One was a flamboyant 55-year-old, Captain Sigismund Best, and the other one Major Richard Stevens, an accomplished linguist but otherwise an inexperienced member of the service who had been appointed 'our man in The Hague'. In broad daylight the two men were seized by a detachment acting under the orders of the German SS officer Walter Schellenberg, who physically resembled Best. He described the arrival of a Buick containing the two British agents and Dirk Klop, a Dutch officer:

> At this moment the SS car came skidding around the corner into the car park. Coppens [Klop], recognising it as the greater danger, turned and fired several shots into the windscreen. I saw the glass shatter and crystalline threads spreading from the bullet holes. [An SS man] had also drawn his pistol and a regular duel developed between him and Coppens. I had no time to move and found myself between them. Both men shot with deliberation, aiming carefully. Then Coppens slowly lowered his gun and sank down on his knees.
>
> I turned and ran round the corner of the house towards my car. Looking back I saw Best and Stevens being hauled out of the Buick like bundles of hay.
>
> . . . I suddenly found myself face to face with a huge SS subaltern whom I had not seen before. He grabbed hold of me and thrust a huge pistol under my nose. It was obvious that he mistook me for Captain Best . . . I pushed him back violently, shouting, 'Don't be stupid. Put that gun away!' . . . whereupon he aimed his gun at me, but in the same second that he pulled the trigger his hand was knocked to one side and the bullet missed my head by about two inches. I owed my life to the second SS leader's alertness. He had noticed what was happening and intervened just in time. I did not wait for further explanations, but got into my car as quickly as I could and drove off, leaving it to the SS detachment to finish the operation.[40]

The Dutch officer died, while Best and Stevens were dragged over the border and taken to Berlin to be interrogated in customary SS fashion. The victims were chosen with commendable skill. Between them they provided a complete description of the personnel and departments at SIS headquarters in London, as well as the names of all the western and central Europe station chiefs, and other information about staff and their sexual activities.[41]

The Germans had a score to settle with Sigismund Best. During the First World War he had secured personal permission from Lloyd George the prime minister to set up as a drug-dealer in Holland, smuggling morphia tablets and cocaine – thirty or forty pounds at a time – to German officers across the border in return for military secrets.

At this time the idea that Germany was on the point of economic collapse was well rooted with the British government and the public at large. The German collapse would bring the overthrow of Hitler and a new government that would sue for peace. There is no evidence that the SIS tried to correct this totally unfounded belief. On the contrary, they clearly were themselves deceived by it, for the 'Venlo incident' had been effected by dangling before the SIS a story about a group of highly placed Germans who were about to overthrow Hitler.

As the German army overran continental Europe the British secret service men – based mostly in British embassies – packed their bags and moved out. The British armed services, more than ever in need of intelligence material, found little of substance coming from the SIS. As winter turned to the spring of 1941, and the possibility of a German invasion increased, the chiefs of staff turned to the SIS for hard facts. Churchill wanted to send reinforcements overseas: were the Germans still intending to invade England or not? All the SIS could come up with was their view that maybe the Germans just wanted to keep the British guessing. The chiefs of staff said they didn't want strategic appreciations, they wanted answers, and they didn't pull their punches: 'the SIS should take every possible step to remedy this extremely unsatisfactory state of affairs.' At a meeting at the Foreign Office on 31 March, Sir Alexander Cadogan, head of the Foreign Office, noted that the armed service intelligence chiefs failed to reach any agreement with Menzies.[42] Cadogan noted in his diary: 'He [Menzies] babbles and wanders, and gives the impression he is putting up a smoke screen of words & trying to put his questioners off the track.'[43]

In fact Menzies and his secret service were remaining in business only by assuming credit for the gradually improving performance of the codebreakers at Bletchley Park. From early 1941 Menzies visited Churchill each day at about 9 am, taking with him as much interesting BP material as he could muster. Often the meetings became cosy chats in which Menzies provided Churchill with Whitehall and clubland gossip and 'indecent jokes'. It was these meetings, said the biographer of Menzies, that enabled SIS to survive rather than be absorbed by its wartime rival organization, Special Operations Executive (SOE). Indeed the relationship helped Menzies to keep control of Bletchley when four of its most important cryptanalysts staged a 'mutiny' against bad management and the chronic staff shortage that was holding up their vital work. Having failed for months to get improvement through the usual channel, they went over the heads of Menzies and his men and got someone to put their letter on the prime minister's desk. The next day, 22 October 1941, Menzies received a caustic message from Churchill:

> ACTION THIS DAY.
> Make sure they have all they want on extreme priority and report to me that this has been done.[44].

The Special Operations Executive had come into being as a result of the collapse of France – not to be primarily an intelligence-gathering operation but to organize movements in enemy-occupied territory. Hugh Dalton, who ran the SOE in its early days, said they had to be comparable to 'the Sinn Fein movement in Ireland, to the Chinese guerrillas now operating against Japan, to the Spanish irregulars who played a notable part in Wellington's campaign or – one might as well admit it – to the organizations which the Nazis themselves have developed.'[45] Churchill simply told them to set Europe ablaze.

Setting Europe ablaze proved a lengthy and difficult business, though they certainly lit a fire under Whitehall. The bureaucrats of the Foreign Office were furious to hear that they were not the only ones to run a spy service. Menzies complained endlessly that the SOE took from him the sort of recruits he wanted. In fact the mixed bag of male and female linguists, foreigners, soldiers and adventurers recruited by SOE were a far cry from the sort of men to be found in Menzies' quiet corridors of power. Perhaps even Menzies came to see that, for he later concentrated his complaints upon the way the SOE was given the use of planes, boats and money.

Summer 1940 – Britain goes bust

With the Swastika fluttering from the Eiffel Tower, and German staff officers investigating the wine cellars at Maxim's, Britain's leaders set aside their hopes of imminent German economic collapse. It was the German army which now had nothing to do while waiting for Britain's collapse. As things stood, it looked as if they would not have long to wait.

Only in Göring's vast Air Ministry building in Berlin was there any real activity, for there were those who felt a need for the Luftwaffe's bombers to fly to England and teach the British one final lesson.

The British prime minister's speech on the 18 June 1940 had already given the forthcoming battle a name. 'The Battle of France is over,' he'd said. 'I expect the Battle of Britain is about to begin . . .'[46] Churchill always had the right words on his tongue. In him the nation had found its leader, its chronicler and its orator. The world's memory of the Second World War is largely formed by Churchill's view of those events. His richly worded speeches provided to the English-speaking world a folk memory: the narration to a horrifying scratchy grey newsreel film where perpetually ships sank, cities burned and bodies were shovelled into mass graves.

Both Churchill and Hitler strove always to get a tighter rein upon the day-to-day conduct of the war. Hitler took control of the Armed Forces Office, the OKW, and from there issued orders to the services. Churchill declared himself minister of defence, carefully not saying what powers that gave him. He took over direction of the Chiefs of Staff Committee when he had a mind to do so and had access to the Joint Planning Staff. Since he was chairman of two defence committees, supply and operations, he had control of the entire nation. But Churchill always had to answer to the war cabinet and to Parliament.

Hitler was a teetotal vegetarian while Churchill was a bon vivant whose consumption of alcohol, according to one witness, 'could be described as unique, for it continued at quite regular intervals through most of his waking hours.'[47] While Hitler was a short-sighted and vindictive 'soldier', who became ever more obsessed with the tactical deployment of smaller and less vital units, Churchill is recorded as a broad-minded and far-sighted 'states-man'. His protracted negotiations for 50 ancient US navy destroyers reveal the clarity of his thinking. Churchill told Roosevelt he wanted them for the Atlantic routes, to release modern escort ships for use against a German invasion fleet. But his true motives were more important ones. He wanted to establish precedents: the release of war equipment by the US armed forces, and the supply of such material without payment. Even when it seemed to be agreed that the destroyers would be swapped for 99-year leases on military bases, Churchill insisted that the wording of the agreement should be changed so that the leases could not be measured in terms of cash. The final deal was said to be part 'gift' and part exchange.

It was not simply a matter of pride. Until the summer of 1940 the United States Treasury had been unyielding in demanding dollars for every item the British received. (A law of 1934 decreed that countries, such as Britain, which had defaulted on their First World War debts could not be given credit.) The British cabinet was faced with the grim outcome of this obligation when on 22 August 1940 the chancellor of the exchequer brought to the meeting his report on the 'Gold & Exchange Resources'. In the first six months of 1940 Britain's total gold and dollar reserves, including US holdings, had fallen from £775 million ($3,100 million) to £156 million ($624 million). Taking into account orders placed by the French government, which the British had now taken over, Britain would have no resources left by Christmas 1940.

At the centre of this crisis were the two schemes put forward by Lord Beaverbrook, a dynamic Press baron who had taken over as minister of aircraft production. One scheme to buy American aircraft would eventually spend £300 million a year, the other £800 million a year. In fact as Kingsley Wood (the chancellor) told the cabinet, 'There is no prospect of our having dollars to pay these sums, nor of our ever paying these amounts, if lent to us by the USA.' He added that it was doubtful if money would be found to pay the £75 million that would be needed by the end of that year.

Beaverbrook urged them to keep ordering war material at such a rate that, when British money ran out, the United States government would be forced to provide aid or else risk a severe jolt to the US economy just as it was feeling the benefit from the war orders.

The cabinet came to no conclusion but, in effect, Beaverbrook's advice was taken, for there was no reduction in the ordering of machine-tools, aircraft, aero-engines and motor vehicles. In all goods worth $3,200 million were ordered over the next twelve months. In addition, steel became the principal Atlantic cargo in the second half of 1940.

Churchill watched the calendar as the time for presidential elections approached, for he was anxious to see Roosevelt reelected. With the American public about to pronounce upon the European conflict, it was becoming more and more evident that propaganda was playing a vital part in the progress of the war. Churchill, believing that the Americans liked nothing so much as a winner, changed his theme from that of 'the English-speaking cousin in mortal peril' to the plucky fighter who, given the tools, will finish the job. Both Germany and Britain were giving ever more facilities, and greater and greater attention, to neutral radio and Press reporters. Fighting men had their photos on the front pages; so did admirals, generals and air marshals. From the smoke and dust of the May fighting in

France and the Low Countries three 'star' personalities emerged: Erwin Rommel, Alan Brooke and Bernard Montgomery. None of them merited the attention given to them. It was a sign of the changing times that all three were somewhat more adept at self-publicity than skilful in the conduct of warfare.[48]

Isolationism and the USA

Perhaps it explains something of Chamberlain's prewar appeasement policy that he believed America could not be depended upon for help in resisting the European dictators. 'It is always best and safest to count on nothing from the Americans but words,' he said. Britain's ambassador in Washington, Lord Lothian, did not do a great deal to improve the transatlantic relationship. One American writer said of him:

> He was an old-school-tie product of the British Foreign Office, with manners fit for the days of dominance. He was six feet nine inches tall and had the bulging eyes, walrus moustache and the austere arrogance of the English clubman. He had little interest in anyone in Washington: a boring and provincial town he thought. He associated with almost no one but the socialites of New York, Newport and Palm Beach.[49]

When Churchill became prime minister a new ambassador was appointed to tackle the difficult task in Washington. In 1939 a poll found that 67 per cent of Americans opted for the United States to remain neutral; only 12 per cent wanted aid sent to the Allies and a mere 2 per cent thought Americans should do battle against the dictators. An organization calling itself 'America First' held rallies and made headlines; its supporters believed that an Axis victory would not menace US security. Some cynics pointed out that the British and the French, who claimed to be fighting a war for democracy, had colonies where millions of people were not permitted to choose their own form of government.

The German victories in Poland and western Europe changed the opinions of some Americans about whether they should fight. Newsreels and newspaper accounts revealed the ruthless methods of the Wehrmacht and the Nazi regime which controlled it. France fell and Britain became the only outpost of democracy in a Nazi Europe. Without Britain, there would be no base from which the United States could ever confront Hitler. And there was the economic effect. The European war brought orders to US factories, and this was welcomed by both capital and labour. Unemployment went down and stayed down; the 1941 jobless percentage was not again reached until 1975.

Yet expressing disapproval of the totalitarian regimes was not the same as wanting to fight them. Isolationists were to be found everywhere; isolationism did not follow social or geographical lines. Neither did it follow party-political lines: Communists and Republicans stood side by side in opposition to Roosevelt's Democratic policies. Roosevelt gave full recognition to this fact when in June 1940 he appointed a Republican as secretary of war and another as secretary of the navy.

The American peacetime army had become a refuge for the unemployed, and a social club for poorly trained officers. Its headquarters was a temporary wooden building dating from the First World War. For the first year of the European conflict, America's secretary of war – who lacked any sort of military background – did nothing to equip or train the US army. He was a dedicated isolationist who opposed any aid to Britain. Roosevelt's replacement for him – Henry L. Stimson – began a long-overdue programme of change. In September 1941, as a dramatic symbol of America's new role in the world, work began on the mammoth Pentagon building. Three hundred architects were at work in an abandoned aircraft hangar trying to keep blueprints coming for 13,000 construction workers working round the clock.

Roosevelt was opposed in the presidential election of 1940 by Wendell Wilkie, who had been a Democrat all his life but was chosen as the Republican candidate. During the lead-up to the election, Roosevelt took care to get Wilkie's support for such warlike actions as transferring the 50 old destroyers to Britain and passing a Selective Service Act that would draft Americans in peacetime. It was difficult to judge the mood of the voters and Roosevelt used his position in the White House to be photographed with the evidence of the expanding economy. Such pictures showed the president with tanks, planes and ships, so enabling Wilkie to warn the voters that Roosevelt would push America into the European war. This campaign strategy backfired. Roosevelt won a third term, with 27 million votes against Wilkie's 22 million.

It was time to look at Britain in a realistic light. Roosevelt found it hard to believe that the mighty British Empire, which seemed to cover most of the globe, could be on the point of bankruptcy, and felt sure that the British must have billions hidden away some-where. For this reason his response to ever more desperate pleas for help from the British was a demand for a complete breakdown of Britain's assets. On 23 December 1940 the president notified London that he had sent the cruiser *Louisville* to Simonstown naval base in South Africa to collect £42 million worth of gold, which was Britain's last negotiable asset. Now British-owned companies in North America were sold at giveaway prices. The Viscose Com-pany, worth $125 million, was liquidated to eventually fetch $87 million. Some businessmen thought such deals disgraceful, but only when they were satisfied that Britain was penniless did the Americans agree to supplying all future war material as gifts.

In January 1941 Roosevelt introduced the Lend-Lease Bill that authorized the president to sell, transfer, exchange, lend, lease, or otherwise dispose of war equipment and other commodities to the government of any country whose defence the president deemed vital to the defence of the United States.

Britain, which had never recovered financially from the First World War, was saved just in time by Roosevelt's Bill. On 1 March, ten days before the Lend-Lease Bill became law, debts of $540 million were due for settlement – some of the money was owed to foreign countries other than the United States. It was double the amount of money Britain possessed, and her gold and dollar re-serves had shrivelled to less than £3 million. Churchill asked the Dutch and Norwegian governments in exile to sell Britain gold for sterling; both said no: Britain was saved from disaster only when the Belgian government in exile lent Britain £60 million from the gold reserves which it had managed to get out when the Germans had overrun the Low Countries.[50]

The Lend-Lease Bill was not unanimously welcomed. Joseph P. Kennedy, former ambassador to Britain, and father of the man who later became president, opposed it. So did the famous aviator Charles A. Lindbergh, as well as Wendell Wilkie. Some feared that Roosevelt would send abroad armaments that America needed for its own defence. Others warned that such a Bill would give the president dangerous powers. The Act became law on 11 March 1941, and Congress authorized him to lend an initial $7 billion worth of war matériel to any nation. On 27 May Roosevelt proclaimed an unlimited national emergency and, three weeks later, suspended diplomatic relations with Germany and Italy and froze all their assets in the United States.

In July the president sent US troops to build and maintain military installations in Iceland.[51] If the Germans were allowed to create military bases there, US sea routes would be threatened. Only two senators protested. American public opinion was changing as the Axis successes could be seen as a threat to even the US mainland, and Washington became involved in Britain's conduct of the war. At first the Atlantic campaign against the U-boats was the prime concern, but more and more US army, and army air force, 'fact-finding observers' were to be seen in London just as British military men were found in Washington DC, where eventually all the big decisions would have to be approved.

The Allied top brass made an Anglo-American Combined Chiefs of Staff Committee dominated by General George C. Marshall, chief of staff of the US Army. His opposite number was General Sir Alan Brooke, newly appointed chief of the Imperial General Staff and thus military adviser to Churchill and the government. Brooke was a prima donna who considered himself above the humdrum tasks of planning and management that Marshall was using to transform the US army. He saw himself as a battle-hardened master of strategy and regarded the Americans as inexperienced newcomers who should be attentive to his teaching. The Americans saw Brooke as the commander of a poorly organized, ill-equipped army that since war began had never beaten the Germans in battle. So it was remarkably good fortune for the Allied cause that Brooke spent so much time in London and George Marshall became friends with General Sir John Dill, an Englishman to whom he could relate. Dill had to heal the wounds that Brooke frequently inflicted upon his allies and doubtless Marshall did the same when Roosevelt got rough. The two men conspired to evade the interference that came from every side. So closely did they cooperate, that each would confide in the other memos and communications that were not even available to their closest colleagues. They regularly lunched before the committee meetings, sometimes with their wives at lunch with them, and by the time the meeting opened the most tricky matters were already agreed.

When, with the war still unfinished, Dill died of anaemia the cortège went along a route lined with thousands of US soldiers. The US Joint Chiefs of Staff acted as honorary pall-bearers and there was a gun carriage drawn by six grey horses. General Sir John Dill was buried with pomp and ceremony in that most sacrosanct ground for American warriors: Arlington National Cemetery.

The development of the atom bomb

Had the United States not gone to war it seems probable that the atomic bomb would never have been made at all. Fiction writers had from time to time scared readers with the idea of an ultimate weapon, and by 1939 most Western nuclear physicists agreed that building such a device was theoretically possible. In the summer of that year leaders of some of the great powers were also told of it.

In August Leo Szilard wrote a letter urging the American president to investigate the use of atomic energy in war. Although Albert Einstein, the most famous scientist in the world, was an ardent pacifist he added his immense authority to the plea by signing the letter. A few weeks earlier, Professor Hentsch of Hamburg had alerted the Berlin War Ministry to the same possibilities and the Reich Ministry of Economics started at once to look for uranium. That summer, Raoul Dautry, the French minister of armaments, also became interested in nuclear research. In Britain, government research was already being done at the universities, and by May 1939 enough was known for Britain's Air Ministry to order one ton of uranium.[52]

At first only Britain and France took the scientists seriously. As the German invaders arrived, in the summer of 1940, French scientists were well advanced. The French secret service had already bought the whole of the world's stock of 'heavy water' for use as a moderator for slowing down neutrons in a controlled chain reaction using uranium. As France fell this work was transferred to Cambridge, England, where work on the isolation of plutonium continued. At the same time two American physicists published an account of their work on the same process. It was becoming clear to all the scientists that further work would be far more demanding; it would require a great deal of money and national backing.

In March 1940 two scientists[53] in England – both refugees from the Nazis – wrote a short description of how a bomb using uranium 235 might be made. They convinced Professor Lindemann that a few more costly experiments would confirm that making an atomic bomb was perfectly feasible. Lindemann, later Lord Cherwell, was an eccentric man who is as well remembered for his bad scientific judgements as for his good ones. But Churchill seemed to believe everything Lindemann told him, and now the atomic project was given all the resources that Britain could spare. In July 1941 those supervising the research (the MAUD Committee: a camouflage title)[54] reported that the bomb definitely could be made and should be hurried forward 'in case the Germans got such a weapon first'. German physicists received no such encouragement, and nuclear research there came to nothing.[55]

In the United States research was proceeding slowly and without much emphasis on the military applications of fission, when E.O. Lawrence, at Berkeley, discussed the conclusions of the MAUD committee with Vannevar Bush, who was close to President Roosevelt.[56] As a result Roosevelt contacted Churchill and suggested that there should be some sort of coordination of efforts, or even a joint atom project. Told by his advisers that Britain could soon have a bomb of its own, Churchill declined the offer.

It was only in July 1942 that Churchill learned that building a nuclear bomb would be so costly that Britain could not possibly do it alone. But by then it was too late to link up with the Americans, who were ahead of the British in theoretical work, in experiment and in production. The English historian R. A. C. Parker wrote:

> [The Americans] thought the help of British scientists, and that of refugees in Britain, might save perhaps a few weeks of valuable time, especially in devising plant for separating uranium-235 by gaseous diffusion.

The Americans considered a few weeks of time too high a price to pay for British interference, and some feared that the British would turn the results of the American work to their own commercial advantage. Roosevelt agreed but added that America must ensure that postwar Britain had nuclear energy as a way of helping an ally with an ailing economy. (President Truman did not honour this pledge.) Only after Churchill had renounced any commercial benefits did the Americans agree to a limited exchange of information, and this was restricted to what the Americans decided was needed to produce a bomb. Postwar Anglo-American cooperation was not helped when, in 1950, it was discovered that Dr Klaus Fuchs – one of the scientists sent by the British to work on the bomb – had all along been spying for the Russians.

By the time it was ready, it had become evident that no nation but the United States had anything like the resources to solve the problems that arose from building the first such bomb. (The bomb was built in the Soviet Union far more cheaply after spies such as Fuchs had turned the results of the American work over to Moscow.)

Part Three

THE
MEDITERRANEAN
WAR

12 THE WAR MOVES SOUTH

I have a tremendous admiration for Caesar.
But . . . I myself belong rather to
the class of Bismarcks.

Mussolini in conversation with Emil Ludwig

THE WAR THAT GERMANY FOUGHT in Northern Europe was grey. Solemn grey-faced civilians, in dark three-piece suits, made the decisions. Hordes of men in Feldgrau flooded the Continent of Europe until they reached the grey waters of the Atlantic, where grey-painted ships fought their grim grey wars.

The war in the Mediterranean was different. It was more varied and complicated than in any other theatre. Mussolini's Italy provided bravura passages for battles fought in the sunshine, with a more vocal scenario. Operatic uniforms and florid speeches sustained a war that was really a series of adventures. A feudal emperor, desert Arabs, a poet soldier, undersea chariots, illustrious noblemen, armies that floated from the sky and landed amid monuments of the classical world. That was the Mediterranean war.

Benito Mussolini: 'Believe! Obey! Fight!'

Despite a certain hypnotic charisma, Adolf Hitler was an embittered man of banal tastes and predictable opinions. Benito Mussolini was a far more complex personality. One of the most intimate portraits of him is to be found in the diaries of his son-in-law, Count Galeazzo Ciano, who became Italy's foreign minister. Ciano promised that his published diary:

> records the mental processes, sudden rages, lechery and sentimentality, flashes of insight, inconceivable stupidities, ingenuousness and shrewdness of the buffoon who for a quarter of a century imposed himself on the Italian people . . . There is the man in all his folly and humanity.[1]

An American sent to speak with him provided a harsher portrait:

> It should never be forgotten that Mussolini remained at heart
> and in instinct an Italian peasant. He was vindictive and would
> never forget an injury or a blow to his personal or national pres-
> tige. He admired nothing except force and power. His own
> obsession was the re-creation of the Roman Empire.[2]

In the years before the First World War, Mussolini was one of the
most respected and well-informed Marxists in Europe. He edited
The Class War, a paper which advocated violent revolution with
such slogans as 'He who has steel has bread'. He saw the coming of
war in 1914 as the event which would bring worldwide Socialist revolution. Lenin, who went some way to proving this theory correct,
wrote enthusiastically of Mussolini in *Pravda*, and the two men saw
eye to eye on most important political matters. Both wanted to be
rid of parliaments and all the inconveniences that multi-party
politics bring to men who wish to wield centralized and permanent
state power.

Italy entered the war in 1915 as an ally of Britain and France in
spite of a treaty binding the country to Germany. The war gave
Italy – a unified nation only since 1870 – an expectation of great-
ness and enlarged its borders. Opportunism paid off and the war
changed Mussolini's ambitions: 'he sniffed the nationalism in the air
and drew down great lungfuls of it. It was intoxicating.'[3]

Mussolini was vain and excitable; he needed the adoration of the
people. Above all he was very human, and his evident love of uniforms and abundant sex life appealed to the Italian crowd. He was
quite unlike the cruel and inhuman Lenin or the narrow-minded
Hitler. Embracing nationalism and the 1914–18 war, Mussolini relished the territorial gains that came from it and eventually came to
despise Lenin for making a separate peace that conceded so much
Russian soil to the Germans.

In March 1919 Mussolini and his friends invented a new political
party, adopting costumes, symbols and ideas for social reform from
many different political groups. Their speeches were angry and
dynamic, if not to say violent in their promises. Black-shirted men,
using the military terminology that all revolutionaries relish, vowed
to take over capitalism rather than destroy it. In passing, they
pledged to seize Church property, give land to the peasants, abolish
the monarchy and give the government absolute control of the
economy. Nowadays it sounds like a recipe for disaster, but at that

time the prospect was new, and the failure of the revised Soviet Russian economy was not yet apparent.

Mussolini was an essential ingredient of the new era. He understood the value of history and how to use its poems, myths and legends. Blood was invoked as an element of Italian heritage and also as something to be spilled in 'the struggle'. Machinery and technology would revitalize Italy.

In Russia and Germany, comparable political ideas had arisen when battle-weary soldiers returned to an angry and bewildered homeland. It can be argued that the Italians were a victorious nation and the Germans a defeated one but it was not easy for the working man to distinguish victor from vanquished. Anyway the Italians had suffered crushing defeats on the Austrian front, and the German army contended that their defeat had come not on the battlefield but at the peace conference table.

The German and Italian experience can be more closely compared, for in both lands soldiers returning from the battlefields were vilified by Communists, Socialists and pacifists. Ex-soldiers, and those who resented the treatment meted out to them, formed the core of the Fascist and Nazi parties. In both countries the middle classes were understandably fearful of the bloody terror that Russia's Communist revolution had demonstrated. Violent clashes between political parties fomented these fears, persuading the middle classes, including ex-soldiers and local police forces, to put their weight behind anti-Communist organizations. As the Fascists and Nazis took power, most people accepted a loss of freedom in exchange for the restoration of law and order.

Italy had joined the Allies in the First World War in the hope of becoming a great power. At the peace conference the Italians were treated with contempt. The permanent under-secretary at Britain's Foreign Office, Sir Charles Hardinge, called them odious colleagues, well known for their 'whining alternated by truculence'. Italian claims to the port of Fiume at the head of the Adriatic Sea were dismissed out of hand.

This treatment unified Italians in a way the war had failed to do. A thousand war veterans, under the poet Gabriele D'Annunzio, marched into Fiume in September 1919 and refused to go away. The victorious Allies were nonplussed by their bellicose stance and did nothing. In 1924 Italian possession of Fiume was ratified. Mussolini, leader of the largest veterans organization, learned the lesson: force pays when words fail.

Fascism (of which Nazism was a later German variant) was Italian in origin. Mussolini organized fasci, or groups of working men, to agitate for social change. A *fascio* is a bundle or a pack. In Ancient Rome *fasces* – a bundle of rods bound together (unity is strength) and containing an axe – had been carried before magistrates as an emblem of official power, and the symbol was adopted in the French Revolution. For Mussolini this classic symbol was perfect, and he used it extensively to promote Italy as a mighty and warlike nation. In 1921 the Fascist party was formed. It wore the all-black uniform of the Arditi, the Italian army's storm-troops.

The word 'totalitarianism' was invented by Mussolini. It decreed (as did the Marxism that Lenin and Stalin inflicted upon Russia) that everyone and every activity came under the direct control of the state. Under both regimes, to be apolitical was a punishable offence.

As he came closer to power Mussolini revised some of his ideas to suit new allies. A thousand deals were done with politicians, businessmen and people of influence who believed that the Fascists would be able to furnish votes enough to win. In October 1922 King Emmanuel III asked Mussolini to form a government, and arriving in Rome in his Fascist uniform he announced dramatically that he had just come from the battlefield. It was to become a well-propagated myth that the Fascists marched on Rome and seized power by force of arms. In fact Mussolini turned up on the overnight train, his wife exclaiming: 'What a character!'

Having forgotten all ideas about ending the monarchy, he abandoned another pledge by eventually coming to terms with the Pope and the Roman Catholic Church. It was an important move, for the Church and the Italian state had been on bad terms for many years. Now Mussolini put a crucifix into every schoolroom and gave his soldiers chaplains. He was, the cynics said, merely displaying the traditional Italian reverence for religion, family and graft.

The black-shirted Fascists chanted *Credere! Ubbidire! Combattere!* (Believe, Obey, Fight) and called Mussolini *Il Duce* (the Leader). The complex uncertainties of democracy were scorned. Death, Violence and Will were among the favoured words as they discovered that the prospect of miracles was easier to sell to the electorate.

Opponents were imprisoned or fled abroad. Newspapers and radio stations were controlled. Local government was made a part of the new movement. 'Our mayor was suddenly wearing a smart

uniform and giving Fascist salutes,' an Italian friend of mine remembered. 'And when we went to the next village their mayor was
also in uniform.'

In the 1920s his Fascist economy flourished: unions were tightly
restricted, the workforce was disciplined and obedient, and industry
cooperated. As Italy slowly recovered from the war Mussolini
promised not the peace and rebuilding that was so obviously
needed, but more war. He told his countrymen that, to stay
healthy, Italy needed a war every 25 years. Perhaps they did not
take him literally (in the same way that Hitler's anti-Jewish diatribes
were not taken literally), or else thought that such 'wars' would be
overseas colonial adventures.

Easy pickings: Abyssinia and Albania

Ever since records were first kept, large numbers of Italians had
been going overseas to live. In many Mediterranean towns – Tunis,
Beirut and Tripoli – they had outnumbered other Europeans, yet
Italian possessions overseas were few. Apart from Tripolitania,
which in 1911–12 the Italians had wrested from the Ottoman Empire
and renamed Libya, they had Eritrea and part of Somaliland. These
two slices of Italian territory in the 'horn of Africa' were separated
by Abyssinia, a primitive kingdom ruled by Emperor Haile Selassie.
Said to have been founded by a son of the Queen of Sheba in the
tenth century BC, it was remembered by the Italians for the town of
Adowa, where in 1896 an invading Italian army had suffered terrible
destruction at the hands of the native defenders.

Mussolini was determined to enlarge his overseas possessions. He
liked to declare his admiration for Julius Caesar and an African
empire smacked of Ancient Rome. Mussolini relished the idea of
erasing the shame of Adowa and teaching the Abyssinians a lesson
by occupying their land. That would unite the two Italian colonies
into one large 'Italian East Africa'.

When in 1934 Mussolini invaded Abyssinia (present-day Ethio-
pia) he was confronted by huge lakes, scorching desert and
formidable mountains. To bring the war to a successful conclusion,
he used bombers – the first town bombed was Adowa – and even
poison gas against barefoot native soldiers armed with nothing more
lethal than spears.

Hitler took advantage of the world's dismay at the Italian atrocities by marching into the demilitarized Rhineland, and so began

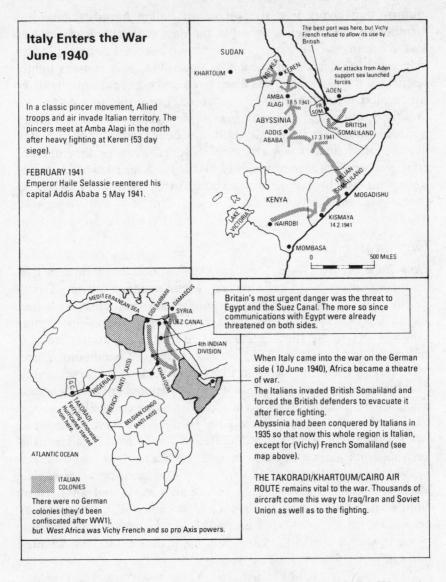

Italy Enters the War
June 1940

In a classic pincer movement, Allied troops and air invade Italian territory. The pincers meet at Amba Alagi in the north after heavy fighting at Keren (53 day siege).

FEBRUARY 1941
Emperor Haile Selassie reentered his capital Addis Ababa 5 May 1941.

The best port was here, but Vichy French refuse to allow its use by British

Air attacks from Aden support sea launched forces.

SUDAN

KHARTOUM ●

KEREN

AMBA ALAGI   18.5.1941

ADEN

ABYSSINIA

ADDIS ABABA   17.3.1941

BRITISH SOMALILAND

FR. SOM.

ITALIAN SOMALILAND

KENYA

MOGADISHU

LAKE VICTORIA

NAIROBI

KISMAYA 14.2.1941

MOMBASA

0   500 MILES

MEDITERRANEAN SEA

SIDI BARRANI

DAMASCUS

SYRIA

SUEZ CANAL

4th INDIAN DIVISION

G.C.

NIGERIA

FRENCH (ANTI AXIS)

KHARTOUM

BELGIAN CONGO (ANTI AXIS)

TAKORADI
Ferrying renovated Hurricanes started from here.

ATLANTIC OCEAN

ITALIAN COLONIES

There were no German colonies (they'd been confiscated after WW1), but West Africa was Vichy French and so pro Axis powers.

Britain's most urgent danger was the threat to Egypt and the Suez Canal. The more so since communications with Egypt were already threatened on both sides.

When Italy came into the war on the German side (10 June 1940), Africa became a theatre of war.
The Italians invaded British Somaliland and forced the British defenders to evacuate it after fierce fighting.
Abyssinia had been conquered by Italians in 1935 so that now this whole region is Italian, except for (Vichy) French Somaliland (see map above).

THE TAKORADI/KHARTOUM/CAIRO AIR ROUTE remains vital to the war. Thousands of aircraft come this way to Iraq/Iran and Soviet Union as well as to the fighting.

the military expansion which led to the Second World War. As Hitler became more and more bellicose the other major powers, which might have restrained the Italians, began vying for Mussolini's friendship. An attempt to cut off Italy's oil was frustrated by the United States, which feared that such a blow to the Italian economy could lead to a Communist revolution there.

The Italian victory in Abyssinia brought Mussolini great popularity with his own people but made him many enemies abroad. A world prepared to support his political experiments in his homeland could not stomach pictures of gassed and bombed native villagers. But international disapproval only served to unite Italians behind Mussolini. The Italian king was acclaimed emperor, and his empress was presented with a golden rose by the Pope.

Mussolini's next adventure was to send troops to assist General Franco's nationalists fighting the civil war in Spain. In Britain and America this bitter struggle was widely portrayed as the extinction of democracy by Franco's entirely evil Fascist forces, although history's verdict on the Spanish Civil War is nowadays less simplistic. Mussolini became isolated and identified with right-wing extremism, yet for him the Spanish fighting was no more than an adventure. He told his son-in-law, Count Ciano, who was also his foreign minister, that it was to mould the character of the Italians. 'When Spain is finished, I will think of something else,' he promised.

Perhaps Mussolini took to reading his own Press releases, an ailment for which even Hollywood has no remedy, and began believing that he commanded a formidable fighting machine. On 30 November 1938 Ciano hinted in the Fascist Chamber at Italy's 'natural aspirations'. It was enough to get the parliamentarians on their feet shouting 'Corsica, Tunis, Nice!' – which did not go down at all well in Paris. It must have reconciled many French voters to the Franco-German Declaration of Friendship which was signed a week afterwards.

As the Romans of the classical world had found, the Mediterranean is an unfriendly lake. Even at the height of Roman power, the Italian mainland was often invaded. Mussolini had not chosen well in conquering Abyssinia, for it was far away, and lay beyond the Suez Canal which Britain jealously controlled. Italy's other great colonial possession, Libya, was on the far side of the Mediterranean, a stretch of water which the Royal Navy and the French fleet could make dangerous for sea traffic.

Bismarck is reputed to have said that Italy had a good appetite but poor teeth. One historian added that Mussolini 'put a lot of effort into national dentistry.'[4] He did, but the teeth Mussolini provided were false ones.

If Mussolini's exhortations had helped to pull Italy into the modern world, it was still far from being a prosperous country, and scarcely even a developed one. It depended upon imported raw materials such as oil, coal and iron ore. Italy's shape, with the mountainous spine that extends its entire length, gives it problems of communications even in peacetime. Italian genius for exquisite design and innovative engineering was there for all to see; its naval architects unsurpassed. But genius and strength do not always go hand in hand. Except for a few showpiece units the Italian army was not mechanized. Its air force consisted largely of out-of-date biplanes. Although the navy was the most impressive of its armed forces, it was by no means adequate to face the combined navies of Britain and France.

In July 1938 5 billion lire were assigned to modernization of the Italian armed forces. Two new battleships were designed and there were to be monoplanes for the airmen. But wars – even small wars – cost money. The fighting in Abyssinia had cost about 13 billion lire and there were still 300,000 Italian troops engaged in occupation duties. The intervention in Spain's civil war had written off many tanks and aircraft, and 50,000 men were still there. As Mussolini's need for money took large bites out of the taxpayer, the population lost some of its enthusiasm for war, although few complained aloud now that the secret police were listening.

Then, as the Spanish Civil War drew to an end in 1939, Mussolini thought of the 'something else'. With little preparation, he sent an invasion force against Albania, a small kingdom that faced the heel of Italy across the Adriatic Sea. The occupation was effortless: Albania had been an Italian protectorate since 1934.

Uneasy Axis

By this time the Western powers had come to see Italy as a close partner of Hitler's Germany, and almost as dangerous. Mussolini thought of the Führer as the only ally who would let him continue his policy of selective aggression. Hitler willingly became Mussolini's accomplice, while keeping his own plans secret until his armies moved. As one crisis followed another, Mussolini became fearful that his partner would involve them in a major war for which Italy was unprepared. It was Mussolini who contrived the Munich Pact to give Hitler what he wanted and avoid war. When the Western powers stood firm against Hitler's demands upon Poland, Mussolini urged caution upon his partner. On 12 August 1939 he sent Ciano to talk to the Führer at the Berghof near Berchtesgaden in Bavaria. Ciano found the atmosphere icy and was shocked to discover that the Germans intended to invade Poland come what may.

> Hitler is very cordial, but he, too, is impassive and implacable in his decision. He speaks in the large drawing room of his house, standing in front of a table on which some maps are spread out. He exhibits a truly profound military knowledge. He speaks with a great deal of calm and becomes excited only when he advises us to give Yugoslavia the *coup de grâce* as soon as possible. I realize immediately that there is no longer anything that can be done. He has decided to strike, and strike he will.[5]

The next day Ciano reported to Mussolini at the Palazzo Venezia:

> And in addition to reporting to him what happened, I also make known my own judgement of the situation, of the men and events involved. I return to Rome completely disgusted with the Germans, with their leader, with their way of doing things. They have betrayed us and lied to us. Now they are dragging us into an adventure we do not want and which may compromise the regime and the country as a whole.

Mussolini was alarmed, and even began to wonder if Britain and France might be better partners for Italy. Meanwhile he sent Hitler a 'shopping list' which detailed all the guns, vehicles and raw materials that Germany would have to supply to make Italy ready to fight a war. It was clearly intended as a way of getting off the hook. Blandly Hitler promised a few of the items but 'he proposes to annihilate Poland and beat France and England without help'.[6] Hitler asked only that Italy should not declare its neutrality in advance, but Ciano immediately told the British ambassador 'we shall never start a war against you and the French.' Secret police reports revealed that the Italian public did not remotely desire a war and didn't like the Germans.

As Ciano realized, the Germans were determined to invade Poland and the British equally determined to oppose them. On 1 September Hitler's attack on Poland began and two days later Britain and France declared war. For months Italy remained neutral while Hitler divided up Poland with his new ally Stalin and then struck at Norway. In May 1940, as German Panzer divisions pushed across France, Italy's position as an ally of Germany was still not established. At that desperate time Churchill wrote Mussolini a letter, expressing the hope that Italy would not join in the war. But it was to no avail: Mussolini wanted a seat next to Hitler at the peace conference, and that meant he must start fighting before the French asked for peace. According to Sumner Welles, the American president's personal representative in Italy: 'One man and one man only, the Dictator Benito Mussolini made the decision.' By 1940 there was no way 'whereby the will of the Italian people could combat the fatal determination of their dictator.'

Ciano was courageous but he quailed before Mussolini, and even the king did not dare oppose him. 'The Italian race is a race of sheep,' said Mussolini '. . . we must keep them disciplined and in uniform from morning until night. Beat them and beat them and beat them . . . This is what I shall do.' He was quite sure that, as soon as France fell, Britain would have to sue for peace, and that promised rich pickings. He made no secret of what he wanted – Malta and Cyprus would become Italian islands, Egypt and the Sudan would be joined to Italian East Africa and Libya to make a vast Italian protectorate. Iraq, with its oil, would become another protectorate and provide the Italian fleet with fuel. Gibraltar would be an international port.

On 10 June 1940 Mussolini sent his troops across the frontier to fight 'against the plutocratic and reactionary democracies'. He was only just in time. France was at her last gasp, but even a mortally wounded France was too much for the Italian army. Five demoralized French divisions found renewed strength and fought back against 32 Italian divisions of the invading army. French Premier Reynaud said: 'What really distinguished, noble and admirable people the Italians are to stab us in the back at this moment.' In far-off Charlottesville, Virginia, President Roosevelt heard the news and, bravely disregarding his Italian voters, said: 'the hand that held the dagger has plunged it into the back of its neighbour.'

Ciano was reported as saying that Italy's chance (to fight an already defeated France) was one that comes only once in five thousand years. Winston Churchill dryly commented that rare chances are not necessarily good ones. In Rome the French ambassador told Ciano: 'The Germans are hard masters. You too will learn this.' Not many Italians needed the reminder: fighting their French neighbours was not a popular task.

When the 84-year-old Marshal Pétain became French president and sued for an armistice, France was split into the occupied north and the unoccupied 'Vichy France' that declared itself neutral. With France out of the war, and Italy a combatant, the balance of force was radically changed. The frontier where the British forces in

Egypt faced the Italians in Libya became a battle front. So did the small enclave where British Somaliland was faced on three sides by Mussolini's Italian East Africa. From here an enemy could menace Khartoum, and even Nairobi to the south in British colonial East Africa. Bereft of French warships, the British naval forces in the Mediterranean suddenly looked very small. There was no sign that French overseas possessions, with their military forces and naval bases, would remain in the war. A French general, Charles de Gaulle, escaped to Britain and become a rallying point for any who wanted to continue to fight. But most Frenchmen felt they owed their duty to the only legitimate government of France, that of Marshal Pétain in Vichy. They were no longer at war with the Germans.

A global war

During 1940 the war changed from being a strictly European conflict to being one of potentially global proportions. The Vichy authorities in French Indo-China (part of which later became Vietnam) passively gave extensive facilities to the Japanese military. These bases were to play a vital part in Japan's manifold attacks at the time of Pearl Harbor. This twelve months, starting with the Battle of Britain in the summer of 1940, was the most complex period of the war. Now began a series of battles and events, each triggering another, leading inevitably to the German-Soviet contest before Moscow in December 1941, and to the Japanese attack on the American fleet at Pearl Harbor.

The Mediterranean was vital to British strategy. It provided the short sea route to India, Australia and the Far East as well as being the door to Egypt and the oil-rich Persian Gulf. Without the aid of French warships the Royal Navy faced a formidable Italian naval presence. The Italians had 6 battleships, 19 cruisers, about 50 destroyers and over 100 submarines. It was partly the threat of Italy's submarines that prompted Churchill to ask Roosevelt if he could spare 30 or 40 reconditioned US navy destroyers. The grim prospect of the sea war was made worse by the nightmare possibility of the Germans taking over the mighty French fleet, either as a part of the peace treaty or simply by force of arms.

The RN fight the French

In the desperate days after the French collapse the British could obtain no information about the terms likely to be agreed for the French surrender, nor of the messages that were being sent to French naval commanders. Churchill and his naval chiefs had not yet fully understood the threat of the U-boat, despite paying lip-service to it. They believed that the surface raider was the real threat to Britain's sea supply lines. The Royal Navy were concerned about France's modern battle-cruisers, *Dunkerque* and *Strasbourg*, and also about two unfinished battleships: *Jean Bart*, which was at Casablanca in French Morocco, and *Richelieu*, at Dakar in French West Africa. The Admiralty thought the *Richelieu* was the most powerful ship afloat.[7]

Churchill ordered that the navy's Force H, based in Gibraltar, be sent to threaten the French at their various North African stations, while French warships in the United Kingdom were taken over by boarding parties. Admiral Andrew Cunningham, the Mediter-ranean commander-in-chief, protested and the whole Royal Navy was horrified by the order. Churchill prevailed, and on 3 July Force H, consisting of the battle-cruiser HMS *Hood*, the aircraft-carrier HMS *Ark Royal* and the old battleships *Valiant* and *Resolution*, stood off shore at Mers-el-Kébir in French Algeria, where most of France's fleet was at anchor. A message from this powerful force demanded that the French should either scuttle or join the British side flying the Free French flag, or else sail to the French West Indies.

Negotiations lasted for many hours, but the French admiral final-ly refused and the British opened fire at point-blank range. The battle-cruiser *Dunkerque* was hit by a salvo of 15-inch shells, the old battleship *Bretagne* was hit in the magazine, capsized and was lost with 977 of her crew. The old battleship *Provence* ran aground, but with exemplary seamanship the battle-cruiser *Strasbourg*, a sea-plane-carrier, *Commandant Teste*, and five destroyers got up steam and escaped past the British force. They reached Toulon in south-ern France. The next day *Ark Royal* sent torpedo bombers to the anchorage to finish off *Dunkerque*. When they hit a lighter laden with depth charges, the resulting explosion killed another 150 sailors.

A couple of days later, French naval units at the Atlantic ports of Dakar and Casablanca refused to comply with the British instruc-tions. They were attacked by motor torpedo boats and torpedo planes. The two unfinished battleships, *Richelieu* and *Jean Bart*, were damaged.

At Alexandria the RN took a more subtle course. Patient negotiations included displaying the offered terms to all ranks by means of placards mounted on small boats. A blind eye was turned to an ill-timed hurry-up message from the Admiralty in London. The good will of the respective admirals – Cunningham and Godfroy – survived even after news came of the Mers-el-Kébir tragedy. The result was an agreed demilitarization of the French ships: the battleship *Lorraine*, four cruisers and some torpedo boats. Fuel stocks were sent ashore and breech blocks and torpedo detonators put into the care of the local French consulate.

The French navy's wartime role at Alexandria was a relaxed one. The French commander, Admiral Godfroy, was permitted to use Vichy French codes and communicate with his masters. His men were paid by the British and, unlike the Free French, were able to send money home to France. They were permitted to take shore leave in Alexandria, and also in Vichy-ruled Syria and Lebanon. The Royal Navy fought a desperate war while these French ships – a battleship, four cruisers and three destroyers – remained unscratched. 'The French ships looked brazenly sleek and shiny compared to the battered British fleet.'[8]

Could the same peaceful agreement have been achieved at Mers-el-Kébir had Churchill shown patience and allowed the local Royal Navy commander more latitude? Certainly all three RN flag officers concerned in these actions thought so, but one of them who expressed that view in a letter to the Admiralty was eventually relieved of his command. Publication of some of the papers of Admiral Cunningham, the Mediterranean C-in-C, revealed the depths of Cunningham's antipathy for Churchill and for this order in particular.[9] Some historians claimed that the record of these exchanges had been deliberately distorted to protect Churchill's reputation.[10]

While Anglo-French relations sank to an all-time low, at least the Royal Navy's shocking action served to show the world that Britain was not just playing for time: Britain was going to continue the war, whatever the cost.

The cost notably and immediately beset the Royal Navy. The central position of Italy, and its shape, provided for the Axis powers naval and air bases that could command the central Mediterranean. Whereas a British convoy sailing from east to west would inevitably come under sustained attack, the short sea crossing from Sicily to Tunisia made it possible to keep open Axis sea lanes to North

Africa. Malta's naval dockyard and well equipped harbour was in the perfect position to harass the Italians, but that meant it was an easy short-range target for Italian bombers, and would be difficult to defend against an invading force. A number of drastic strategies were considered by the British, including the truly desperate one of abandoning the Mediterranean and using all their resources to guard Gibraltar and Suez.

Men, munitions and supplies destined for Egypt and other Middle East countries garrisoned by Britain could no longer pass through the Mediterranean. They were sent all the way round Africa. Only supplies for Malta or urgently needed equipment were put into fast well defended convoys to run the Axis gauntlet in the Mediterranean. The Royal Navy's response to this grim situation was to demonstrate in the Mediterranean the same aggressive spirit that the German army had shown on land. Although its original forces had been depleted by the needs of the Norwegian campaign, the threat of invasion of the British Isles, and the battle of the Atlantic, by May 1940 ships drawn from the East and West Indies, China and Australia had restored the Mediterranean fleet to a considerable fighting force.

Resisting the tentative Admiralty suggestion that perhaps the RN should withdraw from the eastern Mediterranean, Admiral Cunningham took his whole fleet to within sight of the Italian coast, where on 9 July 1940 there was a clash with a strong enemy force of 2 battleships, 16 cruisers and 32 destroyers. But the end result was to be counted more in the morale boost it gave to the Royal Navy than in damage inflicted on either side. On 19 July the Australian-manned light cruiser *Sydney* encountered two Italian light cruisers off Crete and sank one of them. These actions established the aggressive way in which the British would sail the sea, and the Italians would sally out to attack or bomb them.

A plan to abandon Malta to the enemy was changed. It was decided that Malta should be reinforced. The aircraft-carrier HMS *Argus* was sent through the Mediterranean with Hawker Hurricane fighters for the island's defence. It was the beginning of a long hard struggle to keep Malta fed and defended.

Disaster at Dakar

It was General de Gaulle who became convinced that the French colonists of French West Africa, as well as those of North and

Equatorial Africa, were keen to join him. He proposed to send an expedition to Dakar and, just in case his countrymen failed to recognize him as a liberator and friend, it would be an armed expedition.

Dakar was on the extreme tip of the West African coast. A naval presence there would have safeguarded the sea routes around Africa, and a 'Free French' West Africa coloured in as part of Allied power would look good on the map. The British consul-general in Dakar told London that local civil and military leaders were anxious to continue the war on Britain's side. Such unfounded wishful thinking persuaded Churchill to support the idea. After British intelligence told them of German plans to establish a military base in Dakar, the war cabinet agreed. On 31 August 1940 a force of Royal Marines and French and British soldiers was dispatched.

Codenamed 'Menace', the Allied plan of attack was largely dependent upon the state of defences the French had prepared in the First World War remaining unchanged. An-up-to-date French defence scheme had been given to the War Office in June, only to be lost.

The expedition was a failure in every way: politically, because the French colonists certainly did not wish to continue the war as a part of de Gaulle's Free French Forces; in security, as through French sources in London plans of the attack were deliberately leaked to Vichy and to all manner of other parties; through intelligence, because the Germans were not about to establish a base there; in organization, due to the Admiralty not making it clear in Gibraltar whether Vichy French warships should be permitted to pass unopposed; in communication, leading to the landing force not knowing where to land; in naval gunnery, where one hundred 15-inch shells from the RN battleships did not stop the defenders' guns damaging three RN ships; in aviation, where attacks by carrier aircraft were largely ineffective; in anti-submarine tactics, which led to the battleship *Resolution* being torpedoed by a French submarine.

A far from minor benefit to arise from this tragic and absurd fiasco was that his lengthy stay aboard one of the expedition's troopships provided a mature Royal Marine officer named Evelyn Waugh time enough to complete a rough draft of his book *Put Out More Flags*.[11]

13 A TACTICIAN'S PARADISE

'What is happening?' [Hag Latif]
asked one day of his great-grandson.
'It is el Harb – the war.'
'Who makes this war?'
'El nussara – the infidel.'
'Against whom? And why?'
'It is infidel against infidel. Who knows why?'

Paolo Caccia-Dominioni, *An Italian Story*[1]

EARLY IN NOVEMBER 1940 the Royal Navy struck again. Admiral Cunningham took the attack to the Italian anchorage at Taranto. Torpedo-carrying Fairey Swordfish biplanes, flying at night off the carrier *Illustrious*, sank three Italian battleships.

The engagement was historic in its implications, for this was the first time that aircraft had crippled an enemy battle fleet and changed the balance of naval power. The Italian fleet anchorage was a tempting target, and the navy had prepared contingency plans for attacking it as long ago as 1938. However the primary reason for the raid on Taranto was that British intelligence could think of no other place to look for the enemy fleet. Signals intelligence, at any level from Enigma to low-grade ciphers, provided no clues to the movements of the Italian warships.

Martin Maryland aircraft newly arrived from America and based in Malta confirmed that the big ships were at anchor. The air photos, flown to the carrier *Illustrious* from Malta, revealed that a balloon barrage and anti-torpedo nets were now in use, and these demanded last-minute modifications to the plan.

A little Pearl Harbor

Five aircraft from HMS *Eagle* were included in the raid. Two waves of Swordfish aircraft, twenty in all, were divided into a first strike with six torpedo aircraft, four with bombs and two with both bombs and flares. The flares were to illuminate the whole anchorage, the cruisers would be bombed while the torpedo aircraft went in at sea-level to attack the battleships. The 18-inch torpedoes had magnetic pistols which would make them explode under the hulls to do maxi-

mum damage. The usual three-man aircrews were reduced to two in
order to accommodate extra fuel tanks. Flying 170 miles from the
Illustrious to the target, the open cockpits exposed the flyers to
freezing cold.

These Fairey Swordfish biplanes had been first delivered to the
Fleet Air Arm in 1936. The configuration followed the prevailing
policy that carrier aircraft must have low wing-loadings, slow landing speeds and air-cooled engines. Obsolescent when war began, its
replacement, the Fairey Albacore, was even less satisfactory.
Phased out of operational service, the Albacore was relegated to
training, leaving the Swordfish to soldier on. Any word of criticism
or sympathy with its crews is likely to be indignantly answered with
loyal tributes to the nimble flying qualities of the 'Stringbag' and a
claim that Swordfish sank a greater tonnage of shipping than any
other Allied aircraft used in the war.[2]

With its braced wings and fixed landing gear, it could fly as slowly
as 50 mph without risk of stalling. This proved a useful facility that

night when negotiating the almost invisible balloon cables. One pilot remembered asking: 'Where's that bloody balloon barrage?', and his observer answering: 'We've been through it once and are just going through it again.'[3] The slow speed made it possible to spot the defence booms at sea-level. The underwater anti-torpedo nets went down to 25 feet and the torpedoes ran at 30 feet. To run accurately an aerial torpedo must be put into the water gently and from very low altitude. One Swordfish went so low that its wheels touched the water and sent up a great sheet of spray.

A second strike of five torpedo aircraft, two bombers and two flare carriers flew off about thirty minutes later. They left behind a plane which had been slightly damaged in a collision, but the pilot managed to get his plane airworthy and hurried after the others. He arrived fifteen minutes after the second strike had departed and made a solo bombing attack with every gun in Taranto firing at him.

It will come as no surprise that the only two bombs that hit, failed to explode. The torpedoes, however, sank three battleships, one of which never sailed again. For such a small operation, and the loss of only two aircraft, it was a great victory, and early proof that the aircraft-carrier had become the master weapon of naval warfare. Three men survived from the two lost Swordfish, and the Italian navy magnanimously treated their captives with impeccable courtesy. The carrier *Illustrious* turned and sped to rejoin the fleet where, by Cunningham's order, all ships displayed the signal 'Manoeuvre well executed'.

The well executed manoeuvre was not lost on the US navy. Its chief of operations sent a warning to Pearl Harbor telling Admiral Kimmel that the British operation proved aerial torpedoes could be made to run true in shallow water. But no anti-torpedo devices were installed at the American moorings, on the excuse that they would narrow Pearl Harbor's ship channel and cause inconvenience. Admiral Kimmel told Washington that he would make no changes until a light and efficient net was developed.[4]

The Western Desert

The desert is a virtually uninhabited region about the size and shape of India. It stretches from the River Nile to Tunisia about 1,200 miles away to the west, and 1,000 miles south to the place where there is enough light rain to produce scrubland. The western part of Libya was called Tripolitania. Here stands Libya's largest city,

Tripoli, through which most Axis supplies passed. In eastern Libya, which was called Cyrenaica, the port of Tobruk was equally vital for the supply services. The British held Tobruk for most of the war.

Bordering the Mediterranean there is a flat coastal strip from Alexandria in Egypt to Cyrenaica. The seashore, made of limestone sand, is of a memorable whiteness, especially in the summer when the sea is blue. Few and far between, there are towns and villages with miserable palms, bushes and patches of cultivated ground. Many of the names on the map in this region – El Daba, Fuka and Buq Buq – were no more than names: no houses, no people, no drinking water. Here in summer it becomes too hot to fight. In winter there can be a heavy rainfall which turns the dust-like sand into sticky mud. Most of the fighting took place in this northern strip of the desert, which is about 40 miles wide. But the strip was not manned; this was not a war of fixed fronts, rather a war of forts – secured by barbed wire and vast minefields – and moving columns. There were no civilians to get in the way, just rodents and reptiles and dense clouds of flies. 'The Desert,' said General Rommel, 'is a tactician's paradise and a quartermaster's hell.'

The coastal region is higher than the desert behind it. Sooner or later anyone travelling southwards encounters the Great Sand Sea. In some places there is an escarpment which drops away steeply, forming an obstacle that makes movement south difficult for wheeled and even tracked vehicles. This is why the El Alamein region became so vital for the defence of Egypt; for here the Qattara Depression and the sea produce a narrow strip where an army can stand and fight without fear of being outflanked.

At El Agheila the Great Sand Sea comes near enough to the coast to provide another place where an army can rest its flank. Except at these two spots, an army can find long-term security only by means of a fortified perimeter around a water supply, and a port through which supplies can come. So it was that the entire North African campaign was fought for possession of three places: El Alamein in Egypt, El Agheila in Cyrenaica, and the port of Tobruk about halfway between them.

Along the Libyan coast there was a good road; the via Balbia. The section of the road the British built in Egypt was a simple layer of asphalt which could not withstand the continuous weight of heavy vehicles.[5] Alongside their road the British built a very useful railway, but by the end of 1940 it didn't go beyond Mersa Matruh (almost 150 miles short of the Libyan frontier).

Other roads in the desert were just tracks leading over broken stone and pebbles or various sorts of sand. Most of the sand is powdered clay that produces clouds of white dust, making even half a dozen walking men visible for miles. It gets in your eyes and your hair and your clothes and your drinking water. It gets through even the finest dust-filters, and nothing you see or eat is without a coating of it.

Despite the discomfort, most of the soldiers soon got used to the desert. They revelled in the informality that prevailed in this inhospitable place, and it became normal in most units for officers and men to dress as they wished. Sun helmets were soon discarded, along with all the myths about the noonday sun that the Empire's Englishmen had enshrined in dress regulations for a hundred years. It became fashionable for officers to be seen brandishing fly-swatters and dressed in corduroy trousers, coloured scarfs, suede boots or even sandals. In the hot weather many other ranks wore nothing but khaki shorts and boots and, despite the endless tinned food, remained healthy.

Most of the desert could be traversed by motor vehicles, and hard sand made good 'going', although there were always horrifying rumours of parked tanks disappearing into quicksand after a shower of rain. But along the western frontier of Egypt and sprawling westward, unmapped and ever-changing, there stretched the 'Great Sand Sea'. About 600 miles long and 150 miles wide, it is probably the greatest continuous mass of sand dunes in the world, and some of the dunes are 400 feet high. Thus, for all practical purposes, the Libya-Egypt frontier is only about 200 miles long. However the 'sand sea' is not impassable for dedicated travellers. 'To get a heavy truck up 200 or 300 feet of loose sand at a slope of 1 in 3 you have to charge it very fast . . . But it takes a lot of confidence to charge at full speed into what looks like a vertical wall of dazzling yellow,' said Brigadier Bagnold while lecturing at the Royal Geographical Society.[6] To an expert the colour, curvature and ripple marks in sand reveal good going. Soon after war began, a group of soldiers – many of them given ranks overnight – started modifying and equipping Chevrolet trucks for the purpose of exploring and outflanking the Italians in Libya.

This small band of New Zealanders, led by men who had known the open desert for many years, was named the 'Long Range Desert Group' and their strange and dangerous war became something of a legend. They came out of the southern desert at first to observe, and later to attack. By studying the vehicle tracks, they could read the movements of enemy traffic as a Bedouin can estimate the age, breed and condition of every camel that has left a print. In the desert the LRDG found tracks that had been left by Fords of the Light Car Patrols of 1916. And still today the marks of Second World War armies can be seen right across the southern desert.[7]

Their journeys in the south took men far from medical aid or supplies, and required a special sort of nerve. The climate was more extreme than anything known in the coastal strip. There were winds so hot that they could cause collapse. One matter-of-fact report described dead or dying birds in the shade of every rock.

Distances were vast. One patrol went south far enough to make contact with French outposts in Equatorial Africa and found there Frenchmen who wanted to fight Germans. A wounded soldier was taken 700 miles in a truck for treatment at a French post in Tibesti. After that he went 3,000 miles by air to Cairo. Water and fuel were treasured; a truck was towed more than 1,000 miles to get it repaired. By the same measure, patrols would destroy all Italian transport at an outpost and sever it from the world. Sometimes things went wrong. Sharing only two gallons of water and one tin of jam, two Guardsmen and a New Zealander walked across the desert for 10 days, covering 210 miles.

General Wavell

Britain's share of this region was ruled by Lieutenant-General Archibald Percival Wavell, one of the more interesting military personalities of the Second World War. More potentate than army commander, his position as commander-in-chief Middle East gave him control over British forces in Egypt, Sudan, Palestine, Transjordan and Cyprus. When war came his armies fought in East Africa, Syria, Lebanon, Greece and Crete, and the fighting in Iraq brought the Persian Gulf into his field of responsibility. These countries were not Dominions or Empire countries. Egypt, where he had his headquarters in Cairo, remained neutral until the final few days of the war. His soldiers were usually subject to a treaty with, or invitation from, a local ruler. He was not subordinate to British political representatives – ambassadors, high commissioners, governor-generals and so on – but neither were they subordinate to him. These officials reported back to London, some to the Foreign Office and others to the Colonial Office. These Whitehall departments did not coordinate their policies with the army nor with each other. Neither did they try very hard to understand the problems Wavell had fighting the enemy.

No other man was ever given the equal of Wavell's immense territorial responsibility.[8] With scanty resources he often found himself fighting several battles at once. The political, geographical, climatic and military constraints within which he worked called for a diplomat with sharp political sense, a soldier's training and the patience of a saint. Above all he had to please Churchill, whose deep distrust of generals was matched only by Wavell's doubts about politicians. Churchill was ebullient and aggressive, Wavell taciturn and an exponent of mediation. Wavell was by nature hesitant, and his humility encouraged him to think that his enemies would at least be equal to his skills and resource. Churchill's ego persuaded him that an enemy could often be overcome simply by bold action. Churchill's sympathies were Zionist; Wavell was always fearful lest he provoked an armed Arab rebellion.

Wavell has been described as the best-educated soldier of his time. Poetry was 'his strongest and most lasting solace' his biographer wrote. So outstanding was Wavell's prose that, when Churchill talked of sacking him, he was warned about the possible effect of Wavell's postwar memoirs (which in fact were never written). Wavell's lectures at the Staff College are still quoted, yet he attended the Royal Military College, Sandhurst, only briefly and his schooling at Winchester, like most British education, took no account of science, engineering or technology in any form.

Perhaps it would be more accurate to say that Wavell was the most cultured soldier of his time. Even so, we must be cautious, for he shared his time with an immense number of soldiers. He attracted loyalty and affection as few men do. A stocky figure in leather gaiters and with a wrinkled face that almost matched them, he was not a publicist who flaunted the eccentricities of dress and manner that other generals so artfully contrived. Perhaps it was his love of poetry that ensured he wasted no words, although this directness of manner could be disconcerting. A very junior officer seated next to Brigadier Wavell at a regimental dinner in 1931 tried to respond to Wavell's 'good evening'.

'Good evening, sir,' he ventured. 'I think you know Major X, of the Y regiment?'

'Yes,' said Wavell. 'I don't like him.'[9]

His wartime job wore Wavell out. When he left it, on the very day of Hitler's invasion of Russia, he was replaced not by one man but by several. His reputation as a general is legendary, despite Churchill's criticisms, but this is partly due to the way in which he has been given credit for every successful campaign fought under his command and seldom blamed for the avoidable failures. Praise for Wavell has over the years become a method of depicting Churchill as an ignorant, uneducated and dictatorial figure whose understanding of war never progressed beyond his precocious experiences in South Africa. It is difficult to believe that such writings would have given Wavell any pleasure.

Archie Wavell, the son of a general, said he went into the army only to please his father. When the Boer War crisis brought a sudden demand for officers his course at Sandhurst was cut from eighteen months to two terms. By September 1901, Wavell, an eighteen-year-old lieutenant of the Black Watch, was on his way to a war in Africa. In the First World War he served in Egypt and Palestine and returned to Palestine in 1937. Now, back again in Cairo, he was at the height of his career.

General O'Connor almost conquers Libya

The Italian army in Libya had been at war with the British in neighbouring Egypt ever since June 1940, when Mussolini attacked southern France. Here in Africa it was too hot to fight. Cautiously the Italians waited to see if the French forces in Tunisia and Algeria to the west of them were in a mood to fight. They were not. Wavell had already decided that a show of belligerence along the Egyptian frontier wire would be his best form of defence. Three days before Italy declared war Major-General R.N. O'Connor had been called from Palestine, complete with his divisional staff, to command what was called the Western Desert Force.(The misnomer 'Western Desert' had started in the First World War to distinguish it from the Sinai, which was called the Eastern Desert.)

O'Connor was a quiet, modest man, remembered at the staff college for his poor performance as a lecturer. In the First World War he'd fought alongside the Italians and they'd awarded him the Silver Medal for Valour. He was usually shabbily dressed in a very ordinary style, and detested publicity or show of any sort. He was seldom known to smile, and one of his subordinates said he had never seen him laugh. Despite this stern demeanour, O'Connor was a popular general of the old school. For students of warfare he is one of the most successful commanders of his time.

Two days after war began, a patrol of the 11th Hussars, equipped with Rolls-Royce armoured cars dating from the 1920s, crossed the frontier into Libya and captured two Italian officers and 59 other ranks. More such raids followed and the army adapted itself to harassment and hit-and-run patrols:

> It attacked not as a combined force but in small units, swiftly, irregularly and by night. It pounced on Italian outposts, blew up the captured ammunition, and ran away. It stayed an hour, a day, or a week in a position, and then disappeared . . . Fort Maddalena fell, and Capuzzo. Sidi Aziz was invested. British vehicles were suddenly astride the road leading back from Bardia, shooting up convoys.[10]

O'Connor took a personal interest in studying the enemy at close quarters. A patrol of the 11th Hussars, pushing well into enemy-occupied territory, saw a staff car heading from the west but lowered their guns as the car got close enough for them to recognize General O'Connor. 'I did not like this,' said one of the Hussars.

Those who encountered the desert for the first time found the climate alone to be a daunting experience. One young officer newly arrived from England described a khamsin or sandstorm:

> A darkness would come over the land and a hot wind – as if a gigantic oven door had been suddenly opened – would rush in, bringing with it a hot fog of sand. The khamsin was on us. This howling fury, blowing at a steady pace, might keep us occupied for days, filling our eyes and ears with sand, penetrating everywhere . . . and filling the mind with melancholy and foreboding. These depressing sandstorms, we were to learn later, were about the only things that could halt the war.[11]

But for the old soldiers the desert was as familiar as the weapons they used. Little had changed since the First World War. Biplane fighters flew across the barbed-wire, watched by infantrymen equipped with Lee-Enfield rifles. The machine-guns were Vickers and Lewis designs of long ago, and so were the guns: 18-pounders and 6-inch howitzers. When Marshal Italo Balbo – an internationally famous aviator before governing Libya – was killed in an airplane crash, the RAF flew over the Italian lines and, in a scene straight out of Hollywood's *The Dawn Patrol*, dropped a note of condolence.

The Italian armed forces were even more outmoded, with armoured cars dating back to 1909 and tanks that Rommel described as 'totally obsolete'. Marshal Rodolfo Graziani (who took over the Italian forces in Libya and the governorship after the death of Balbo) had gained a considerable reputation fighting in Italy's colonial wars but he had no experience of fighting a modern enemy.

Mussolini ordered Graziani to attack, and in September the Italians advanced about 60 miles, with the British offering only slight resistance. At Sidi Barrani he halted to extend the metalled road and water pipeline, and build a series of fortified camps. The chain of forts, which stretched 50 miles inland, were not built for all-round defence. No two were mutually supporting (with fields of fire that would provide for a neighbour's defence) and there was a gap of 20 miles in the line.

Rome radio proclaimed a victory. 'All is now quiet in Sidi Barrani,' said the announcer. 'The shops are open and the trams running again.'[12] And yet one doesn't have to be a general to see the possibilities offered by a gap in the defences. A force could be marched through the gap and then attack the Italians from the rear. Artillery fire upon the whole camp area would create confusion and panic, while heavily armoured Matilda tanks, almost impervious to light anti-tank gunfire, moved in along Italian vehicle tracks (mapped by means of aerial photographs), thus avoiding minefields and getting right into the compounds. More infantry would follow the tanks in open trucks.

The 'Western Desert Force' was made up of an armoured division and an experienced Indian division which, like most Indian divisions, incorporated British infantry battalions.[13] O'Connor's plan was for a large-scale raid, lasting five days, which would penetrate the enemy line of forts after an approach by night. No-man's-land was about 70 miles wide, so supplies were taken forward and concealed there. In support the RAF was to destroy enemy aircraft on the ground while the Royal Navy bombarded coastal targets.

Security was tight. Troops were not given notice of the offensive, leave was not stopped, the forward dumps were described as precautionary, and even the medical services were not alerted to the possibility of extra casualties. Since O'Connor was planning no more than a five-day raid, he was surprised, shortly beforehand, to know that Wavell had hopes of a big breakthrough. 'It is possible that an opportunity may offer for converting the enemy's defeat into an outstanding victory,' wrote Wavell, adding:

I am not entertaining extravagant hopes of this operation, but I do wish to make certain that if a big opportunity occurs we are prepared morally, mentally and administratively to use it to the fullest.[14]

On the night of 8 December 1940 – in well remembered moonlight and under a starry sky – the attack started. As the artillery fire began, the heavy tanks trundled forward and Cameron Highlanders followed the sound of the bagpipes. The Rajputana Rifles found themselves confronting sleepy and bewildered Italians, some still in pyjamas.

In contrast to the desert fighting portrayed in oil paintings, on this cold night the soldiers wore heavy underwear and woollen sweaters. Many were bundled up in overcoats and laden with three days' rations, lots of grenades and as much ammunition as they could carry.

Many of the Italians fought hard but the plan of attack was a good one. The forts fell and Sidi Barrani was taken. Anyone who'd heard the previous announcements on Rome radio might have looked in vain for its shops and streetcars. Sidi Barrani turned out to be no more than 'a few mud huts and a landing strip'. The British pressed on as the Italians retreated back along the fine coastal road they had built for supplies.

The five-day raid soon turned into a full-scale offensive that captured the coastal strip all the way to Tobruk. By now the 6th Australian Division was in action pressing along the coast, while the 7th Armoured Division struck inland to fight an inconclusive action against a big Italian tank force at Mechili. With considerable skill, the Italians at Mechili withdrew intact into the Jebel Akdar (Green Mountains) during the night of 26 January.

The Jebel was an upland region where some hills were as high as 2,500 feet and where good soil and adequate rain had produced an agricultural area favoured by Italian colonists. In this lush region the Italian colonials rushed out with eggs and gifts for the invading soldiers. They complained that as the Italian army had withdrawn, local Arabs had attacked their farmhouses, looted their possessions and raped their women. The Arabs didn't deny it, but looked to the British for praise and encouragement: the Italians were the enemy of the British, weren't they? 'We could only hope for the best and drive on,' said the war correspondent Alexander Clifford.

While the Italians were retreating along the coastal road, closely followed by the Australians, O'Connor pondered about sending his armoured division on a short-cut. By going across the desert, keeping to the south of the Jebel, they might get to the sea at Beda Fomm ahead of the retreating Italians. The patrol sent to explore the route came back to say that the country was 'impossible'. This report was ignored. O'Connor decided not to wait for new tanks or supplies, and instead transferred armour from other units to make one full-strength brigade. So this much depleted armoured division, followed by every available supply vehicle, set a compass course and headed south-west into a land the maps showed as blank white space. It was not just a matter of getting there intact: the whole operation would be futile unless they reached the coastal road at Beda Fomm before the retreating Italians. Clifford said:

> The advance patrol had not lied . . . For mile after mile they juddered over great slabs of sharp, uneven rock. Then they crossed belts of soft, fine sand which engulfed vehicles up to their axles. Sandstorms blew up, and the trucks had to keep almost touching if they were not to lose one another. Whole convoys lurched off into the gloom and only re-established contact hours later. It was freezing cold, and the latter half of the division had to contend with fierce, icy showers. All kit had been cut to the bone, and there were no extra blankets or greatcoats, and scarcely more than a glass of water per man per day . . . Thus it was that early in the afternoon of February 5 the Seventh Armoured Division cut the road in two places some fifty miles south of Benghasi. And they found they had straddled the entire remaining Italian army, sandwiching it between their two prongs.[15]

'They can't do it,' the Italian commander had said of the short-cut across the desert, 'and even if they do do it we still have two days to spare.' In fact if the Italians had passed through Beda Fomm two hours earlier they would have escaped.

The battle began with the leading Italian trucks being wrecked by gunfire. Now the road was blocked to form a traffic jam that snaked back for miles on the hard land that was flat except for a bitterly contested knoll that the British called the Pimple.

For 36 hours the British fought a battle of constant movement against a superior Italian force by which they were far outgunned. One squadron of British tanks shot its way along the ten miles of fighting, replenished its shells and fuel, and then fought all the way back again. The cooperation between tanks, guns, infantry and engineers was exemplary. When the Italian tanks formed up for a counter-attack, sappers moved forward and laid a minefield in front of them. In another remarkable action, infantry of the Rifle Brigade moved fast to prevent a break-out by means of a track leading down to the coastal road.

All day, with tanks and artillery, the Italians made fierce attempts to break through. Accounts of the battle seldom give sufficient importance to the fact that many Italian civilians were with the retreating army, and this created distressing problems. Their army commander, General Tellera, was mortally wounded. In the early morning of the second day the Italians made one last desperate counter-attack with their armour, but it suffered heavy casualties and that was the end. There were no more tanks and the infantry had been fought to a standstill. At about 9 o'clock in the morning white flags were shown.

O'Connor went to a farmhouse at Soluch where half a dozen Italian generals were held prisoner. There he found senior Italian officers smartly dressed in clean uniforms and polished boots while he appeared in his usual corduroy trousers, leather sleeveless jerkin, tartan scarf and sagging cap.

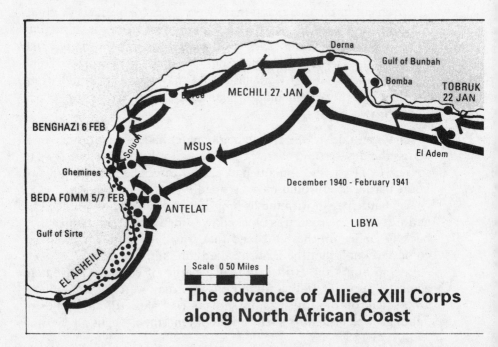

The advance of Allied XIII Corps along North African Coast

'I'm sorry you are so uncomfortable,' said O'Connor. 'We haven't had much time to make proper arrangements.'

'Thank you very much,' said Generale Cona. 'We realize you came here in a very great hurry.'

For years afterwards passers-by saw the wreckage of that day: miles of tanks, guns, lorries, fuel drums and debris in such abundance that even the local Arabs found it too much to carry away.

O'Connor wasted no time. Within hours of the Beda Fomm victory armoured cars of the 11th Hussars were speeding along the road to El Agheila. Apart from a few men surrendering, there was no sign of the enemy. It was February 1941 and Wavell's 'five-day raid' had lasted 62 days. The 4th Indian Division, the heart of the army, had been snatched away to fight in East Africa and the Australians had replaced them. The advance had continued for 500 miles and destroyed Graziani's army. Ten Italian divisions were shattered, 133,295 of their men made prisoner, about 400 tanks and 1,240 guns captured. The British force was exhausted too. Virtually all the transport of the Western Desert Force was either written off or would be when the workshop staff saw it.[16] But its human casualties were few: 500 killed, 1,373 wounded and 55 missing.

Whatever the condition of the Western Desert Force, there was

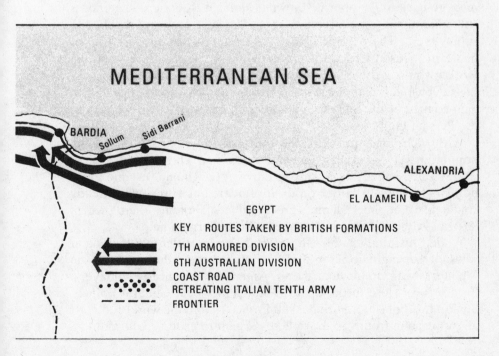

MEDITERRANEAN SEA

BARDIA
Sollum Sidi Barrani

ALEXANDRIA
EL ALAMEIN

EGYPT

KEY   ROUTES TAKEN BY BRITISH FORMATIONS

7TH ARMOURED DIVISION
6TH AUSTRALIAN DIVISION
COAST ROAD
RETREATING ITALIAN TENTH ARMY
FRONTIER

nothing to oppose them. The generals were agreed, the men could smell victory and, while the distances were great, only the soft rear areas remained to be conquered. Supplies and replacements were on their way, the port of Tobruk was in operation and the port of Benghazi, although too shallow for big ships, would soon be an even nearer place for supplying the advance. The navy was fully operational and the RAF would destroy any last remnants of the Italian air force. Everything was ready for the final push that would sweep the Italians out of North Africa.

O'Connor's remarkable campaign was one for the military textbooks, and is to be found there, but it didn't sweep the Italians out of North Africa, for at that crucial moment everything was stopped. Churchill, in what is now almost universally recognized as one of the worst military decisions of the war, halted O'Connor's victorious army and ordered Wavell to detach an armoured brigade and three infantry divisions for shipment to Greece, which the Germans were expected to invade at any moment.

Hitler's great train journey: October 1940

To follow the chain of events that led to the crisis in Greece, we must go back to October 1940, when Marshal Rodolfo Graziani was still building his forts in the desert, and laying a road and pipeline to supply them. There was no hint of O'Connor's offensive and Hitler had every reason to hope that Graziani's promised attack upon the British would carry him through to Cairo. With the Italians occupying Egypt, the Italian fleet would be able to move up to Alexandria, gain control of the Suez Canal and open the way to the oilfields of the Persian Gulf.

With such hopes in mind, the German army had sent a notable armoured warfare expert, General Ritter von Thoma, and a small staff, to assess the Italian army in Libya. Von Thoma was due to report his findings to Hitler on 3 November, but Hitler was already confident 'that the Italians were capable of holding their own in Africa'. Although they might need a little German help.[17]

While Mussolini's armies threatened Egypt, Hitler was looking at ways of seizing Gibraltar and sealing up the other end of the Mediterranean. In his luxury train Amerika, he went to Hendaye, a French town close to the Spanish border, to meet General Franco, Spain's head of state. Hitler asked Franco to join the war, or at least allow German troops to move across Spain to capture Gibraltar.

Franco made no response to Hitler's bountiful inducements of arms and raw materials, some French colonies and Gibraltar too. Even oil was offered, for in French storage depots the invading Germans had found countless tons of it, enough to fuel their Battle of Britain and their first campaign against Moscow. Franco and his advisers had their answers ready. Spain had been torn to pieces by the civil war and Franco was not persuaded that a foreign war would now weld it together. Moreover, his bitter struggle against his own countrymen had been an anti-Communist crusade: how could anyone trust this man who was now the ally of Joseph Stalin? So cold was Franco and his party that eventually Hitler got to his feet and said that there was little point in continuing their talk. Franco made no response. But Hitler was not a man who gave up easily; he talked on and eventually the two dictators retired to the dining car for a meal. Hitler was not used to such indifference and after Franco's train departed to the tune of the Spanish National Anthem at 2.15 am, he ranted about Franco and the 'Jesuit swine' of a Spanish foreign minister who had interrupted him in a way that no German would have dared to do. Hitler had grown used to having his own way. Later he told Mussolini: 'I would rather have three or four teeth extracted than go through that again.'

In June 1940, after France collapsed, many people had expected that Italian troops would march into the French African colonies. Such a vast extension of Italian power would have made Mussolini the powerful statesman that he always wanted to be. The reason why this did not happen is to be discovered in the text of a secret document which Hitler signed while his train was at Montoire, 25 miles north of Tours, the next day.

Here the Führer met Marshal Pétain, the man who now ruled Vichy France. Pétain, a stately old man with large white moustache, arrived wearing the uniform of a general to remind everyone that he was a hero of the First World War. Hitler, who understood such vanities, provided a guard of honour for the old man to inspect. Pétain, equally cunning, ignored the honour guard, knowing full well what the German propaganda service would make of the photographs, and went straight to business – the signing of a secret undertaking with the conqueror.

The Axis Powers and France have an identical interest in seeing the defeat of England accomplished as soon as possible. Consequently the French government will support, within the limits of its ability, the measures which the Axis powers may take to this end.

It sounded good to Hitler, and Pétain's quiet dignified manner impressed him enough to persuade him that it was best to leave the colonies in French hands and allow Pétain to bring them more and more in line with German needs. Hitler had been 'greatly cheered' by the way a few French colonists at Dakar had repulsed the Anglo-French force and the Royal Navy. French colonists handed over to foreigners such as Franco or Mussolini might not be so anti-British. In a directive arising from this meeting, Hitler mentioned 'the urgent duty' of French West and Equatorial Africa to act against Britain and resist the Free French.

Back aboard his private train, Hitler was all ready to return to Berlin to meet Russia's foreign minister when a long coded tele-printer message arrived from Mussolini, warning him that Pétain was secretly conniving with the Free French in London and that the British were about to invade Greece. The latter danger would be forestalled, Mussolini suggested archly, with pre-emptive action by the Italian forces in Albania striking against the Greeks. Both warnings were groundless and self-serving.

Hitler was alarmed enough to change his plans. He requested a meeting with Mussolini, who suggested the following Monday 28 October at Florence. When his train passed through Bologna, Hitler received the news that the Italians based in Albania had invaded Greece that morning. It was of course a demonstration that Mussolini could spring upon his partner the sort of *fait accompli* that he had suffered in the past. Hitler was not pleased, but his objections were not fundamental. He would have preferred the Duce to have waited until after the American presidential elections, which were only one week away. He would have liked to show him the best routes for the invading forces and to have coordinated the move with a German invasion of Crete. Hitler accepted the new situation but it was not easy to look happy when, in Florence, Mussolini came striding up to him calling: '*Führer, wir marschieren!*' and waited to be congratulated.

Hitler liked surprises only when he was springing them. He was furious that not one of the German attachés, or liaison officers attached to Italian units, had warned him of this development. In fact the Italians were not that skilled at keeping secrets: it was German incompetence. Many warnings had been sent about the Italian preparations for the invasion of Greece but none of them had reached Hitler.

While Hitler pondered, the British moved. Only five days after the Italians crossed the frontier the British occupied Crete and the island of Lemnos farther north. On the mainland the Greek army fought fiercely and the Italians retreated. Some rejoiced at the Greek victories but others saw that Italian reverses would draw the Germans into the fighting in Greece. That in turn might bring the British there.

On 15 November, long before the Italian failure was evident, General Thomas Blamey, commander of the Australian forces in the Middle East, wrote an informal letter to his prime minister.[18] The Australians had become a major part of the British resources in North Africa and Blamey said that they must spend all their time and energy in preparation 'if international developments, for example in the Balkan countries, do not force us into the extremely dangerous position of participating piecemeal in land warfare.'

MONTOIRE

Hitler's
train journey

BOLOGNA

FLORENCE

ITALY

HENDAYE

SPAIN
OCTOBER 23, 1940
Hitler meets Franco, asking
him to help seize Gibraltar.
This plus an Italian victory in
Egypt would seal off the
Mediterranean and perhaps
bring the British to the peace
table.

1

MEDITERRANEAN SEA

SICILY
(ITALIAN)

GIBRALTAR

SPANISH

ORAN
MERS EL KEBIR
July 1940 Royal Navy
Bombard French Warships

MALTA
(BRITISH)

TUNISIA

ALGERIA
(VICHY
FRENCH)

MOROCCO

(Vichy
FRENCH)

Tripoli

TRIPOLITANIA

6 14 FEB 1941
The first German troops
arrive in Tripoli

The Mediterranean Theatre 1939 – 40

USSR

APRIL 6, 1941
Germans attack
Yugoslavia

7

HUNGARY

ROMANIA

4

NOVEMBER
Hitler forces
Rumania and
Bulgaria into the
Axis.

YUGOSLAVIA

APRIL 8-21, 1941
Greece attacked

BULGARIA

BLACK SEA

ALBANIA

GREECE

LEMNOS

TURKEY
(NEUTRAL)

2

OCTOBER 28
Without consulting
Hitler, Italy invades
Greece from her
captured territory of
Albania.

3

NOVEMBER 3
British occupy
Lemnos and Crete,
and thus could bomb
Rumanian oil fields.

CRETE

CYPRUS
(BR)

SYRIA
(VICHY FRENCH)

8

MAY 27, 1941
Crete captured by Germans in
first airborne invasion of
history.

MEDITERRANEAN SEA

PALESTINE
(BRITISH)

Tobruk

Benghazi

Alexandria

SUEZ
CANAL

CYRENAICA

5

Dec 9 Sidi Barrani
British inflict crushing
defeat on Italians

EL ALAMEIN

Cairo

EL ARGHEILA

LIBYA
(ITALIAN)

QATTARA
DEPRESSION

GREAT
SAND SEA

THE GREAT SAND SEA

EGYPT
(BRITISH)

**GREAT SAND
SEA LIMITS
MOVE CONSTANTLY**

14 DOUBLE DEFEAT: GREECE AND CYRENAICA

In trouble to be troubled
Is to have your trouble doubled.

Daniel Defoe, *The Further Adventures of Robinson Crusoe*

B RITAIN'S OBLIGATION to Greece was based upon a promise made by the Chamberlain government in April 1939 and was made to discourage Hitler's aggressions. Those circumstances were quite unlike the desperate early days of 1941 with the British fighting for their lives. Now that Greece was at war Churchill told himself, and anyone who would listen, that sending a British expeditionary force to Greece might bring Turkey and Yugoslavia into the war against the Axis and thus create a major new southern front. A better intelligence service might have persuaded Churchill that Turkey had neither the will nor the resources to enter the war on either side, that Germany had 150 divisions and a massive air force all ready to fight, and that his strategic notion was just wishful thinking.

But the British intelligence service was not capable of providing very much useful information apart from the material coming from Bletchley Park, where in early February 1941 they cracked the Reichsbahn (German railways) Enigma. In those days most movement of goods and passengers was made by railways, so BP began to get reliable evidence of German movements, such as those of box-car transports that took Jews to the extermination camps and the flatbed wagons that took Panzer divisions to their assembly areas. A sudden increase in signals indicated the movement of Luftwaffe equipment, supplies and, more significantly, ammunition, to southern Bulgaria where the Germans were busy building airfields. This suggested imminent German invasion of Greece from the eastern side, well away from where the Greeks were fighting the Italians.

Churchill's correct interpretation of those Enigma signals led to the Defence Committee's decision, on 11 February, to order General Wavell to intervene in Greece, and to give this expedition priority over his advance on Tripoli and clearing the Italians out of North Africa. It was one of the most fateful decisions of the war.

Wavell should have refused. He had a sufficiently independent command, and enough authority, to say no to Churchill. The failure of the Allies in France, and the whipping suffered in Norway, showed that control of the air was vital to such operations, and there was no hope of obtaining that with the inadequate RAF squadrons at Wavell's disposal. Wavell didn't say no. He stripped his armies bare to find four divisions to send to Greece. No one seems to have asked where replacements and reinforcements would be found.

After the Germans had conquered Greece, with seemingly effortless skill, many diaries and memories were conveniently changed. The history books leave an impression of Churchill pushing everyone screaming and objecting into a Greek war they did not want.[1] But look at the opinions filed away before the débâcle, and a different picture emerges. Words of caution abound, but it is difficult to find many senior figures steadfastly opposed to the British intervention in Greece. A friend of Wavell's, who was in his headquarters at this time, wrote:

> There were plenty of wiseacres afterwards to say that the intervention in Greece was madness; but in point of fact there was only one responsible staff officer at GHQ who opposed it from the start and consistently, and who can legitimately say: 'I told you so' . . . Both Wavell and Wilson maintained afterwards, and in cold print, that in the light of their then knowledge they would do it again.[2]

This staff officer who was strongly opposed to sending a British army to Greece was Francis de Guingand, on Wavell's Middle East planning staff. In his memoirs he wrote about the Greek campaign:

> As far as I can remember the Planners were not asked to produce a paper giving their views as to the feasibility of the project. We certainly held some very decided ones. The DMI, Brigadier Shearer, did produce a paper drawing attention to the great dangers of this campaign in view of the German resources and methods. I remember this paper coming back from the C-in-C, General Wavell. There was a short note written in his own hand across the top – it said: '"War is an option of difficulties." – Wolfe. A.P.W.' We admired the spirit but questioned – in so far as junior officers are allowed to question – the judgement![3]

Apart from Wavell, there was probably only one man in the Middle East who had enough authority to veto the plan to send men and material to Greece, and that was General Thomas Blamey, commander of the Australians. Blamey was a big jovial 57-year-old who liked to wear a broad-brimmed bush hat and seemed to enjoy his reputation as a ladies' man. He was under orders from his government to prevent any part of his Australian forces being 'detached or employed apart' to serve under British commanders. His government was determined not to allow Australians to be sacrificed in the way they had been in the First World War.

Blamey had already had some confrontations with Wavell. The previous September, when Blamey refused 'Jumbo' Wilson's order to detach an Australian brigade from his force, renewed commands had come from Wavell and then from Churchill, who 'insisted' that the order be obeyed. Blamey stood firm and it was Churchill who backed down. Now on 18 February, having come directly back from his forward headquarters, he listened to Wavell's plans for sending to Greece an expedition consisting largely of Australians and New Zealanders. Blamey's views about the wisdom of such an operation were not sought.

Blamey replied that he would have to refer to his government before the Australians could be committed. Wavell said he had already spoken with Robert Menzies, the Australian prime minister, and in any case the proposal had come from a meeting of the British war cabinet which Menzies had attended. Blamey gave his agreement, feeling that the decision had been made for him, but on 9 March, after another meeting with Wavell, he wired a detailed and despondent report to his government. He told them that he did not relish the prospect of his men facing overwhelming enemy forces completely equipped and trained, and said that the Greek operation was extremely hazardous in view of the disparity between opposing forces in numbers and training.[4]

Menzies and the Australian government read the report and were alarmed. They said they thought that Blamey had been asked about the expedition and approved of it. Without the Dominion troops it would be impossible to mount the operation, but all agreed that it was too late to withdraw now.

Blamey did not want to see his men under British command. 'Past experience has taught me to look with misgiving on a situation where British leaders have control of considerable bodies of first-class Dominion troops,' he said, 'while Dominion commanders are excluded from all responsibility in control, planning and policy.'[5]

Australia and New Zealand would furnish all the fighting troops sent to Greece, apart from an armoured brigade and artillery, but they would not be commanded by Blamey or the New Zealander Sir Bernard Freyberg. Instead command was to be given to a British general, Sir Maitland 'Jumbo' Wilson, who commanded in Egypt and was in effect Wavell's right-hand man. Wilson was not universally popular. He was well remembered for having an acrimonious public shouting match with one of the British army's few armoured warfare experts – Major-General Percy Hobart – and having him sent home in disgrace.

Blamey protested that with so many Dominion troops in the expedition, command of it should be offered to him. Wavell did not deny that he envisaged an Australian and New Zealand component of 42,000 but said that additional supply and 'line of communication' personnel would bring the total force to 126,000 so that Dominion soldiers would be only a third. Blamey backed down on his claim but soon began to suspect that Wavell had deceived him by using a figure for the British troops that was no more than a forecast. 'Some is on its way and some of it is not even in existence,' he wrote. Blamey's suspicions seem well founded: 17,125 Australians and 16,720 New Zealanders were actually sent to Greece, which comprised more than half of the grand total.[6]

If Wavell was being dragged into the fighting in Greece, he was certainly good at hiding his feelings. One of his junior staff officers, de Guingand, was with him in Athens when the British delegation made a definite offer to send a force to help. He wrote:

> When the time came for an expression of opinion on the military prospects, and the chances of success of British intervention, Eden [Britain's foreign secretary] turned to General Wavell and asked him to say his piece. It was a tense moment and you could have heard a pin drop as Wavell climbed to his feet and prepared himself for his reply. I remember almost praying that he would voice some doubt as to the outcome, and when he had completed his exposé I felt a hot wave of anger surge over me, for I failed to understand how it was possible for an experienced soldier to say the things he did say. In a low and subdued voice Wavell told the negotiators that it was his considered view that the assistance being offered held out every chance of permitting the Allies to withstand a German advance into Greece.[7]

It was said by Wavell's supporters that he thought the Greek army much stronger than it really was, and that he thought the mountain landscape of Greece would make it easy to defend. But the final decision made that day, like all strategic decisions, was a political one. It was the foreign secretary, Anthony Eden, who led the delegation to Athens, and led the enthusiasm for getting into the fight in Greece. On the plane to Athens he prepared a long detailed list of guns and tanks and men that he would promise to the Greek government. The Greeks would decline help if they considered the expedition inadequate, and one of Eden's Foreign Office men had the figures 'swelled' upwards. 'I felt that this was . . . bordering upon dishonesty,' de Guingand confided in his memoirs. He went on to describe Eden when the conference ended, and the decision to send troops to Greece was made:

> Eden came in looking buoyant. He strode over to the fire and warmed his hands, and then stood with his back to it dictating signals to his staff. They in turn looked nearly as triumphant as he did, and were positively oozing congratulations. Presumably he had done his job, and accomplished what he had set out to achieve.[8]

That the launching of an impromptu invasion of Europe from the south was even considered is astounding. Leaving aside the lack of air support, which played such a part in the British defeat that the shocked survivors talked of nothing else; discounting, too, the lines of support, supply and communication that stretched right across the Mediterranean; forget that the British Middle East forces were being supplied from the United Kingdom by convoys that had to travel right round Africa to the Suez Canal or through the shooting gallery of the Mediterranean – consider how any British army, let alone four divisions of its 1941 forces, could have been expected to withstand the immense force that Germany held poised to attack Russia.

Wavell acquiesced. Starting on 5 March 1941, convoys from Alexandria to Piraeus in Greece carried an army of 60,000 men, with inadequate weapons and virtually no air cover, to fight a battle already lost. Three weeks earlier O'Connor had been told that continuing his advance in Libya was out of the question. On 12 February the ambitious General Erwin Rommel spent his first night on African soil, having already flown over the front line before going to bed. He was determined to push the British back to Cairo and make his mark on history.

Without the Greek campaign Wavell could have held on to his desert gains, perhaps captured Tripoli and also have held the vitally important island of Crete. The verdict of Correlli Barnett is appropriately severe:

> Thus the Greek episode lengthened the campaign in North Africa by two years – a campaign that sucked in the major ground efforts of the British Commonwealth, and left the Far East almost undefended against the Japanese.[9]

Air and sea

The war was demonstrating the almost insurmountable burdens brought by long supply lines and the vital importance of air superiority on the battlefield. Air superiority had little to do with long-range bombing operations under cover of darkness. It meant commanding the air over the enemy's head, and behind his fighting front, so that he was subjected to relentless bombardment and his supplies and communications seriously impeded. Soon the meaning of the old Roman word 'interdiction' was extended to describe this new dimension of war.

To be successful, interdiction must be relentless and so it needed airstrips – with all the maintenance facilities – near the fighting, permitting relays of aircraft to operate. Such air cover could not be provided at long range, or across a sea.

The regularity of Axis sea traffic between Italian seaports and Tripoli, the only good deep-water port available to them, was a triumph and a tribute to the Axis merchant crews and their naval escort forces. In theory the Royal Navy should have been able to cut off the supplies by sinking the merchant ships, but dark nights and the short sea route enabled the Axis convoys to evade interception. In the second half of 1940 these convoys had moved 690,000 tons of shipping to North Africa with less than 2 per cent losses.

As British shipping to Crete and Greece increased, there was a chance for the Italian fleet to turn the tables by attacking the British troop and supply convoys. The Italian navy was less than ready to oblige. The 1,800,000 tons of fuel oil available at the start of the war had been used at the rate of about 100,000 tons per month, and by March 1941 ship's fuel was carefully rationed.[10] The German promises of oil had never materialized beyond a meagre average

21,166 tons a month. No wonder the Italian chief of staff was moved to say: 'I have two major preoccupations – oil and Malta.'

Any British convoys would undoubtedly be escorted by as many warships as the Royal Navy could spare, and if the Italians intercepted them a naval action would result. The Italian navy had no aircraft-carriers and it was by now becoming clear that ships without air cover were sitting targets. In addition, Mussolini believed that warships, especially big ones, must not be put at risk.

But despite all the objections, the Italian navy was persuaded that it should send out its fleet to attack the British convoys. To help them to this decision the Germans said that the Luftwaffe would provide air support and added that German bombers had, in mid-March, already weakened the Royal Navy by sinking two of its battleships.

Enigma intercepts were at the heart of British counter-plans. Regularly monitored Luftwaffe signals provided information about fighter cover for this operation, and included details of Italian submarine movements. Italy's main naval book ciphers (used by the fleet for important communications) were never broken by the Bletchley Park analysts but on this occasion the Italian navy's Enigma codes, used for only one or two messages a day, provided a vital clue to Italian plans. The mighty *Vittorio Veneto* from Naples, three cruisers from Messina, three cruisers – *Fiume*, *Pola* and *Zara* – from Taranto and two cruisers from Brindisi, with many destroyers, were to coordinate sweeps along the coast of Crete.

In the light of the Enigma messages, all British convoys were directed away from the danger area. This had to be done with discretion in case the Italians realized that their plans were known. Admiral Cunningham went to considerable trouble to conceal his intentions. On the day he sailed, he went to his golf club and arranged overnight accommodation in such a way that the Japanese consul-general (a fellow golfer and well-known Axis collaborator) knew about it. Then Cunningham doubled back to his ship and took his fleet to sea.

Contact with the Italians was made by a light force of four cruisers and four destroyers which tried to lure the Italian ships into range of the main British battlefleet, which included the aircraft-carrier *Formidable*. The Italians didn't take the bait, so the Royal Navy staged air attacks instead. Flying through intense gunfire the naval airmen dropped torpedoes that damaged *Vittorio Veneto* and forced the cruiser *Pola* to stop. *Fiume* and *Zara* were ordered back to protect *Pola* against what the Italian admiral thought to be only light cruisers.

The night was dark and the sky overcast. HMS *Ajax*, the only radar-equipped ship in the light force, found *Pola* on the radar. Cunningham thought this stationary ship must be the *Vittorio Veneto* and closed in with his battleships. Towards midnight HMS *Valiant* made radar contact and began firing. Searchlights probed into the darkness to reveal the Italians, completely unaware of the impending danger, and trying to get the crippled *Pola* in tow. Despite a gallant defending action by Italian destroyers, all three Italian cruisers were sunk. At what came to be called the battle of Cape Matapan the Italians had been beaten by intelligence, air power and radar. In all these aspects of war the British were improving faster than their enemies.

But meanwhile the Royal Navy's campaign in the Mediterranean was proving wearying and costly. As the Germans moved southwards on land, their air force was more and more active over the water. Proof of the Luftwaffe's southwards deployment came on 10 January 1941 when dive-bombers of X Fliegerkorps scored six hits on the carrier *Illustrious* at sea and followed it back to Malta to bomb it again and again until it limped away to Alexandria, and eventually to the United States for major repairs.

The expedition to support Greece would add new dangers and difficulties. The plan called upon the navy to escort convoys, safeguard landings and evacuations, and supply, defend or bombard positions on the coastline, as well as being always prepared for an engagement with the Italian fleet. It was an almost impossible undertaking.

The Balkan campaigns

Having crossed the Adriatic Sea and occupied Albania, Mussolini looked greedily at its neighbour Greece. The Greek dictator General Ioannis Metaxas was a Fascist and pro-Axis in sentiment. Mussolini thought the Greek population, if not Metaxas himself, would welcome Italian occupation. At dawn on 28 October 1940, from bases in Albania, two unsuitably equipped Italian armies crossed the frontier. The Greeks speedily mobilized and within two weeks the invaders were outnumbered and fighting for their lives. Mussolini's choice of season condemned his men to torrential rain and mud, soon followed by temperatures that fell to 20 below zero.

By 3 November the Greeks had gone over to a general offensive along the length of the frontier, and were soon taking thousands of prisoners and pushing the invaders back into Albania. The humiliating defeats forced Marshal Pietro Badoglio, the Italian army's chief of staff, to resign, as did Admiral Domenico Cavagnari, the commander of the navy. In Menton, an Italian-occupied town on the French Riviera, a daring joker printed leaflets saying 'Greeks, this is a French town, stop your advance!'

General Metaxas declined all offers of a British expeditionary force going to the aid of his country, believing that such a force would provoke a German invasion and not be strong enough to resist it. He did however permit the British to occupy the Greek island of Crete, and he accepted the offer of RAF squadrons to help him fight the Italians. By mid-November, aircraft together with 3,400 troops and airfield personnel arrived in Greece.

While the Italians struggled in Greece, and were routed by O'Connor's offensive in North Africa, Hitler demanded that the Balkan states of Hungary, Bulgaria and Romania came into closer alliances with Germany. With varying enthusiasm, they did so.

As the fighting continued through February 1941, the Greek government had a change of men and minds, and said it would accept a British expeditionary force to help fight the Italians, providing it was a large force. Eden assured them it would be large enough. With Mussolini in ever deeper trouble, Hitler saw that he would have to send a German force to join in the war against Greece. To move it and supply it, he would need the roads and railways across Yugoslavia.

Yugoslavia was created at the end of the First World War: an artificial combination of at least six very different nations who were consumed with deep hatred of each other. They were divided by race, religion, culture, history and aspiration. They did not even share the same alphabet. 'Such indeed were the divisions in Yugoslavian society that after 1929 the country had been ruled by a royal dictatorship as the only practical alternative to civil war,' wrote one historian in 1989 shortly before the Communist dictatorship collapsed and a vicious civil war ripped Bosnia, Serbia and Croatia apart.[11]

In 1941 Yugoslavia resisted Hitler's demands. Prince Paul, the regent, had been educated at Oxford and was sympathetic to the British. Married to a Greek, he had no desire to help Hitler conquer Greece. But by March 1941, with German armies threatening them from Hungary, Romania and Bulgaria, the Yugoslavs signed an agreement with Hitler.

On the night of 26-27 March, however, Serbian officers denounced the agreement and took control of the capital Belgrade. This romantic and impulsive act, encouraged by the British secret service, was doomed from the beginning. Hitler could probably have toppled the new regime by peaceful methods, but he had spent months in patient negotiations and now he was in a hurry. 'I have decided to destroy Yugoslavia,' he told Göring, Brauchitsch and Ribbentrop on 26 March. Plans for the campaign had been prepared months before. Yugoslavia, with over 1,000 miles of frontier to defend, was attacked from all sides, with Italian and Hungarian armies coordinating their movements with those of the Germans. The German 12th Army in Bulgaria, with a Bulgarian division attached to it for good measure, invaded northern Greece.

The Yugoslav army was primitive compared to the German armoured columns that advanced down the river valleys, and deep into the heart of the country. The Luftwaffe bombed Belgrade, targeting the city centre, where the government was located, and severing all communications with the field armies. Estimates of the civilian casualties vary from 3,000 to 17,000.[12] (In 1946 the Luftwaffe's Colonel Martin Fiebig was executed as a war criminal for this bombing.)

The German attack revealed the fragmentary nature of the contrived Yugoslavian kingdom. Mostly Serbian, the army put up little resistance. Some of the Croat army units mutinied and went over to the Germans, who in the whole Yugoslavian campaign suffered only 151 dead.

The German victory unleashed a frenzy of slaughter. The widespread cruel and arbitrary killing done by the German and Italian occupying forces has to be compared to the way in which the Fascist Croat militia murdered 250,000 people in three months. The Muslims of Bosnia decimated the Christian population while the Serbs, dividing into Monarchist and Communist guerrilla bands, indulged in the same sort of massacres as the Hungarians did in Vojvodina and the Bulgarians did in Macedonia and Thrace.[13] As the war progressed, torrents of blood were shed while various paramilitary partisan groups fought each other more fiercely than they fought the German occupiers.

Hitler's armies now turned all of their force upon Greece. The Luftwaffe did the same, and it was the assault from the air that most

of the survivors remembered vividly. Against the Italians the RAF
flyers held their own and provided sufficient air cover, but when the
Germans came they were totally overwhelmed.

The RAF had 192 aircraft, of which only about 80 were serviceable on any one day, to combat combined German and Italian air
strength of about 1,000 machines.[14] Obsolete Gladiators, obsolescent Hurricanes and inadequate Blenheims gallantly took off to face
a well equipped and expert enemy which brushed them aside. An
official account describes six Bristol Blenheims which 'took off from
their mountain valley, circled above the olives and the grey cliff
where they used to watch the bears, flew into the north-east and
none returned. For the slow bombers were no match for Messerschmitts in daylight.'[15]

Few RAF airfields had any anti-aircraft guns and there was not
one all-weather airfield anywhere in Greece, while the enemy's
newly built airfields in Albania and Bulgaria were heavily defended
and had the logistic support of home bases that were only a short
flight away. The legacy of the Air Ministry's prewar obsession with
strategic bombing was once again bringing about disaster. An
official historian remarked with uncharacteristic bitterness:

> In 1938 the Chamberlain government had authorized the Air
> Ministry to order virtually all the aircraft the British aircraft in-
> dustry could produce. Large sums had been spent on the
> development of a bomber force which was almost useless for its
> intended purpose of attacking industrial targets in Germany.
> Yet in 1940 the British were painfully short of high-performance
> aircraft with which to support their naval and land forces in the
> Mediterranean and the Middle East.[16]

Once again it became clear that weapons played a large part in
deciding battles. The obsolete tanks the British had taken to Greece
were no match for the Germans or even for the rough terrain. One
British tank regiment lost only one tank to enemy action; its other
51 tanks broke down and had to be abandoned.[17] And without air
cover an army in the field faced inevitable defeat. On 17 April, the
day that Yugoslavia capitulated, Churchill agreed that the British
should begin to evacuate their forces from the Greek mainland.
Defeated in the field, the British had to stage another 'Dunkirk' and
abandon all their precious heavy equipment. Tanks, artillery and
unserviceable aircraft were all lost to an army which needed every
single item. But this was no retreat across 21 miles of English Chan-

nel to a homeland with radar and fighter squadrons. It was a long hard haul to safety, and many failed to make it.

One of the few consolations of the disaster had been the spirit shown by the Greeks. It survived even as the British army was pulling out. A colonel of the 1st Armoured Brigade said:

> No one who passed through the city with Barrowclough's brigade will ever forget it. Nor will we ever think of the Greek people without the warm recollection of that morning – 25 April 1941. Trucks, portées [wheeled guns in trucks] and men showed plainly the marks of twelve hours battle, and the hundred and sixty miles march through the night. We were nearly the last British troops they would see and the Germans might be on our heels; yet cheering, clapping crowds lined the streets and pressed about our cars, so as almost to hold us up. Girls and men leapt on the running boards to kiss or shake hands with the grimy, weary gunners. They threw flowers beside us crying: 'Come back – You must come back again – Goodbye – Good luck.'[18]

As Greece vanished over the skyline it was the British who were shown to have a good appetite but poor teeth. By May the Luftwaffe was ready to show how it should be done. They would swallow the strategically vital island the British had used as a staging post for the movements to Greece.

Crete: 'If yu lei yu uill bi schott'

This is the first sentence printed in a phonetic English phrase book given to German paratroops sent to invade Crete. This machine language seems apt for warriors who would drop from the air under a silken canopy and shoot anyone they thought was lying.

Like so many flawed ideas of the 1930s, it came from Soviet Russia. In 1936 a small British delegation in Moscow was invited to watch the Russian army manoeuvres. The large-scale drop of parachute troops included a military band which picked itself up 'and began to play like men possessed.' One of the delegation was Archie Wavell who, in 1941 on the Mediterranean island of Crete, was to suffer history's only defeat by an unsupported parachute army.

It was awesome to see on artistically shot newsreel films the Red Army's parachute troops descending from the clouds. Schoolboys said they would be shot coming down. Perhaps it was all a propaganda bluff. In the war the Red Army did not use parachute soldiers except in very small numbers for clandestine operations. But the Germans were impressed. The German air force was not like those of other nations. Göring's vast and bureaucratic Luftwaffe also manned most of the anti-aircraft defences and performed many other functions. He made sure that a parachute army was a part of his Luftwaffe, and in this way he expanded his empire.

In 1940 the Germans had used parachute troops to support their invasions of northern Europe. So when, on 26 April 1941, German Reichsbahn Enigma revealed that Germany's only paratroop unit, Fliegerdivision 7, was moving to the Balkans this attracted immediate attention. British intelligence staffs had been trying to guess the next German move. Now a Luftwaffe decrypt of the same date mentioned Crete by name. So Crete was the place; but how much time was left?

Hitler himself chose Crete in preference to Malta. There were not enough resources to hit both. Most high-ranking German officers said Malta was the most desirable target, but General Kurt Student, who would be comanding the airborne attack force, said that Crete was more vulnerable. Student, a First World War fighter pilot, had become a tireless worker on behalf of his airborne army. During the fighting in Rotterdam a Dutch surgeon had prised a sniper's bullet from his brain, but now fully recovered and raring to go, Student explained that Crete, a long island with only one road, would be less well defended than Malta, which had been a British base for many years. German troops were already in nearby Greece. Hitler backed Student. He wanted to avoid coordinating his arrangements with Mussolini, and using bases near Malta would have forced him to do that.

Crete is a mountainous island about 160 miles long and 36 wide. Although it now had three airfields, its ports were fit only for fishing boats, its roads very poor and too narrow for trucks. Much of the island was inaccessible to motor vehicles. Its position on the map, however, made it a desirable base for operations by either side. Waiting for the Germans there were 42,640 men, of whom 10,258 were Greeks.

Karl Student's force consisted of an Air Division (three parachute regiments and a glider regiment) reinforced by parachute engineers, parachute medics and parachute anti-aircraft personnel. Elements of a mountain division were added to make about 25,000 men in all.[19] At his disposal there were 493 three-engine Junkers Ju 52 air-craft, each capable of carrying 14 paratroops or 15 infantrymen, although the weight of machine-guns and mortars meant that some planes carried only one six-man weapons team. Student also had 85 DFS 230 gliders which could hold eight infantrymen or freight. His task was twofold: he had to capture the island and air-supply his fighting men. General Freiherr Wolfram von Richthofen's bombers and fighters were to provide air support, which meant suppressing all action by the RAF and the Royal Navy.

Bletchley Park, always prompt with Luftwaffe Enigma signals, provided a complete German order of battle (strength, position and movement of all the units involved) and the decrypts went directly to Crete. Enigma was unusually precise. It listed exact stages of the German plan, unit by unit and sector by sector. It even gave details of the equipment that would be supplied by sea.

At about 7.30 in the morning on 20 May 1941, in the silence that followed a ferocious air attack, the defenders of Crete heard a faint buzzing in the morning air, like the sounds made by the swarms of flying insects that sometimes infest the island at that time of year. As the sound increased in volume it became possible to see the troop-carrying aircraft quite low against the horizon and heading towards Máleme airport. The island of Crete was being invaded by airborne troops. In the small hours of the morning Student had been warned of the possibility of concentrated anti-aircraft fire from Royal Navy warships placed offshore for that purpose.[20] It had not come; neither did any fighter planes take off to attack the vulner-able troop-carriers. After losing 29 of the 35 fighters it had based on the island, the RAF had withdrawn the six surviving ones the previous day.[21]

The air-raid warning was sounded for the last time: from now on the raids would be unceasing. The gliders arrived first; silent except for the faint hiss of their wings. Then came thousands of para-chutes: green, yellow, red and white. The voices of the Germans calling to each other in mid-air could be heard as they sailed down. 'Beautiful little kicking dolls,' said one who saw them coming. 'Slip-stream and wind carried them indeed like dolls,' said the military historian John Keegan, who added that their American and British contemporaries would have viewed the German equipment 'with horrified incredulity'. They were suspended under their chutes by a single strap to the middle of their back, so that they dangled and twisted. Jump injuries were numerous.[22]

The glider troops were landed close enough to seize specified vital positions – bridges, anti-aircraft batteries and so on. The parachute soldiers were then dropped well away from the defences so that they could form up and go to the support of their comrades. As soon as the invaders gained a foothold on an airfield, transport planes filled with infantry landed on it. Most of them came under fire.

Paratroops were dropped from 400 feet, connected to their planes by 20-feet-long static lines which ripped the covers from their parachutes so that they opened in the air stream. Each paratrooper stretched his arms wide to prevent any chance of his swinging through the lines of a neighbour's parachute. As they floated down, at 16 feet per second, each soldier was about 16 feet below, and 150 feet behind, his successor. Thus 36 men from a three-plane formation arrived in a patch about 120 yards by 500 yards. Each glider was towed to the target zone by a three-engined Ju 52 which would have been specifically loaded for its task with, for instance, a five-man mortar team, two riflemen, ten boxes of bombs and a handcart. A glider might contain combat engineers with special demolition equipment, or only infantry with a good supply of ammunition. The first wave of the German assault had no transport except what it could capture.

The defenders were Greeks, Australians, New Zealanders and British, most of whom had been evacuated from the Greek mainland without their trucks, artillery and anti-aircraft guns. Commanding them was Sir Bernard Freyberg, who was surely one of the most remarkable men to command an army.

Trained as a dentist in New Zealand, he was also a champion swimmer. In 1914 he went to fight under Pancho Villa in the Mexican Revolutionary War. When the First World War began, he deserted Villa and went to London. He became a lieutenant in the Hood Battalion of the Royal Naval Division and served alongside some notable poets, including Rupert Brooke. He fought at Gallipoli, winning the DSO, and then in France. He ended the war with the VC and a bar to his DSO. He had been wounded nine times. By 1919, at the age of thirty, he became one of the youngest generals in the British army.

By the time of Crete Freyberg had been appointed commander of the New Zealand Expeditionary Force. In his biography of his father, Freyberg's son emphasized that Freyberg's prime responsibility was to the government of New Zealand and not to Wavell

(GHQ Middle East), whose handling of Dominion troops was open to criticism.

Freyberg was a fighter, a good choice to command the defence of Crete – he was wounded ten more times! – and his men fought very hard indeed. On the first day the German attack seemed like a failure. Scattered and disorganized, many parachute troops were killed before they could get to the canisters which contained their mortars and machine-guns. Rank offered no immunity. In the first hours of fighting, the Air Division's commanding general was killed when a tow cable broke and his glider crashed into the sea. Another German general was gravely wounded by machine-gun fire soon after landing. The 3rd Parachute Regiment, assigned to capture Rétimo airfield, found itself surrounded by almost a brigade of Australians and was shot to pieces. Most Germans found themselves forced to fight in small groups without their own officers and NCOs. A great number were killed before they touched the ground. One eyewitness recalled how:

> The platoon returned to find the battalion area littered with crumpled parachutes, their gay colours lending an air of macabre festivity to the scene of carnage. On all sides lay the bodies of the dead Germans, most of them still in their harness, the sheets and cords entangling them in death like a strange earth-bound sea-weed.[23]

The same observer – I. McD. G. Stewart, a medical officer of the 1st Welch Regiment – saw how vulnerable the paratroops were to immediate counter-attack. They were equipped only with grenades and a hand-gun, a 9-mm Luger pistol, with two extra 8-round magazines. All their other weapons – machine-pistols, rifles, machine-guns and mortars – were dropped in canisters. Their stubby machine-pistols were originally designed for trench warfare. At close range they were an excellent weapon but at longer distances they were inaccurate and ineffective.

Trained infantry, using old-fashioned rifles, could pick off newly landed troops easily. But overall the defence showed a distinct lack of urgency. Counter-measures were discussed at length. Orders were slow to arrive from battalion, and from company level too. Junior officers were all too often prepared to wait for them. Yet what could be done was demonstrated by 60 soldiers from the Field Punishment Centre near Modhion who, released from imprisonment and told to go after Germans, killed 110 within an hour.

The British, Australians and New Zealanders, proud of their individualism, found it very difficult to believe that the Germans might outdo them in initiative and improvisation. But everywhere there was evidence that the Germans excelled at both. One New Zealand battalion commander soon encountered the hidebound attitude of his commanders. He asked that a mixed collection of RAF and Fleet Air Arm personnel – 339 officers and men – should be officially placed under his command. Some attempt had been made by the New Zealanders to instruct these men in musketry, but they had not wanted to learn, 'They played cards and hoped for the best.' The colonel's urgent request that these men be put under his command was refused by high command. Stewart commented sardonically that 'nothing could be held to justify so revolutionary a liaison of arms'.

On the afternoon of the first day, the same New Zealand colonel, a First World War veteran and winner of the Victoria Cross, came face to face with German resource and determination. His position overlooked Máleme airfield. Two detachments of a German assault regiment, led by a first lieutenant and the regimental surgeon, took Hill 107 using only pistols and hand-grenades. The German medico, who had a reputation for warlike deeds, was awarded the Knight's Cross for this action, although some say he did nothing but occupy ground already vacated.[24] In any case Germans were now holding a position that commanded the airfield.

With their radio out of action, the New Zealanders withdrew to their reserve position, a piece of high ground where the colonel believed he would be reinforced the next day, and so be able to mount an attack that would regain the lost ground. When daylight came the handful of Germans were still on Hill 107. Kurt Student had chosen the airfield at Máleme as his *Schwerpunkt*, main point of attack, and with that determination for which Germans are noted, he now stubbornly continued to land more planes there into what soon became a meatgrinder. It was one of the most reckless battlefield decisions of the entire war. Riddled with shell fragments and bullets of the defenders as they came into their approach run, 40 or so Ju 52s were crash-landed on to the airfield. The Germans scrambled over slumped dead and wounded comrades to get out of the planes and fight. These men were not even trained airborne troops; they were Gebirgsjäger of the 100th Mountain Rifle Regiment. By 5 o'clock that afternoon the town of Máleme and the airport were in German hands. One account says that:

It is not too much to say that this tiny movement [by the New Zealand colonel] lost the Allies the Battle of Crete. By noon on May 21 so many more German paratroops had dropped safely, so many gliders come in, so many Ju-52s had crash-landed on the slowly expanded space, that overwhelming strength had been packed into it. In the afternoon it burst out, and the Fallschirmjäger could follow Student's orders to 'Roll up Crete from the west'.[25]

Crete was not easily conquered. For a week bitter fighting continued. Food, supplies and even ammunition were left behind so that the Junkers could bring more and more combat troops. But by the end of that week the battle was decided. Freyberg was granted permission to start the British evacuation. The Royal Navy played its part to the end. Not only did it cover the withdrawal, taking severe losses in the process, but it prevented the Germans bringing in supplies and reinforcements by sea. Until the end of June all German supplies were brought in by air.

Almost fifty years afterwards, two books took up the issue of the Crete fighting all over again.[26] One said that Freyberg misread the Enigma intercept he was given, and believed that the main German attack would be from the sea. With this in his mind, the writer said, Freyberg saw no reason to squander men in a bitter fight for the airfields.

The other, by Freyberg's son, said that Freyberg was given the complete German battle plan nine days before the attack. It was passed on to every senior commander and staff officer in Crete in an intelligence appreciation dated 12 May 1941. But, added Paul Freyberg, commanders in the field were never allowed to act on information derived solely from Enigma. Wavell was not empowered to vary this order and stopped Freyberg from changing his dispositions at Máleme.

Perhaps it would have made a difference. But the failure to hold Máleme airfield, and indeed the loss of Crete, was largely due to the determination of the elite German paratroops and their willingness to take devastating casualties and go on fighting:

In flexibility of mind, and speed of decision and action, the German battalion and brigade commanders had outdone the officers who had opposed them. The fact is not surprising, nor anything to the dishonour of men leaving their peace-time occupations to make war against opponents whose every thought and ambition for many years had been devoted to nothing else.[27]

However, there were other factors. Little had been done since the army arrived to prepare the island against invasion. Six successive commanders of varying competence and energy had come and gone while Wavell's headquarters had failed to impose any defence plan. Enigma intelligence was not used to the full because so few British commanders knew that it was a flawless glimpse into the enemy's mind. The defenders failed to appreciate that possession of the airfields was the sole decisive factor. Had they understood that, the Germans would probably have been fought to a point where their losses were too severe for the drops to continue.

German commanders were less impressed with the performance of their soldiers. The paratroops suffered very heavy casualties. Of 8,500 men dropped on the first day, 3,764 were killed and 2,494 wounded. Freiherr von der Heydte, commander of the paratroops at Máleme airfield, attributed the high losses to insufficient training and tactical experience, especially among the junior officers. The casualties, and the losses of transport aircraft, helped to ensure that Germany never again used a parachute army for an airborne attack. A plan to follow success in Crete with an immediate airborne invasion of Cyprus – and thoughts of a similar invasion of Malta – were abandoned. Most of the veterans of the Crete battle died fighting as infantry on the Italian or the Russian fronts.

At sea the Royal Navy had attacked convoys bringing seaborne reinforcements, and covered the evacuation too. It was a battle between German bombers and RN warships. The total losses were three cruisers and six destroyers sunk; three battleships, an aircraft-carrier, six cruisers and seven destroyers damaged. Once again it was demonstrated that warships could not operate without effective air cover. Admiral Andrew Cunningham, C-in-C of the Mediterranean fleet, said that three squadrons of fighter planes would have been enough to save Crete (and his warships too, no doubt). But there were no fighters available. The Air Ministry continued to devote the greater part of its energies to strategic bombers. There was no indication that any lessons were learned by the men in London who decided these matters. Little wonder that after the war an official history sardonically quoted Cicero's maxim: 'An army is of little value in the field unless there are wise counsels at home.'

There was a bitter after-taste to the battle. Motivated by a rumour that German prisoners had been mistreated, the victorious paratroops formed firing parties and executed Cretan hostages (200 in one town square alone). The German inquiry that followed said the rumour was groundless. Kurt Student was condemned to five years imprisonment at a postwar war crimes trial for killing British POWs at Máleme but the sentence was not confirmed.

No matter what disillusion with paratroops the Crete battle brought to the German high command, the British and the Americans were thrilled by the idea of parachute armies and began to form and train their own units. Some were used in close support on D-Day. At Arnhem in Holland in 1944 a parachute army was dropped behind the enemy lines. It was not a success.

In strategic terms perhaps the German sacrifice was worthwhile. Crete was a fine prize, as one glance at a map will show. It provided a base from which the Germans could attack the whole eastern Mediterranean – such a good base that some critics of Wavell said that a commander with a better grasp of strategy would have abandoned Greece and used all the available resources to fortify Crete.

The fighting on Crete had revealed the limitations of Enigma and other high-grade decrypts. The Luftwaffe had always been the most vulnerable user of Enigma, largely due to careless mistakes and lack of signals discipline. But a prize-fighter out of training can be told that his opponent weighed in at 250 pounds, and is a great exponent of straight rights, and still get hurt when the punches land. The Enigma interception was passive, just as radar and asdic were passive. These facilities could report the presence of an enemy or reveal his intentions; you still had to find a way to hit him. After Crete, the British were able to reflect upon the German methods while they were full-length on the canvas.

15 TWO SIDE-SHOWS

Diverse paths lead diverse folk
the right way to Rome.

Chaucer, *A Treatise on the Astrolabe*

THE EAST AFRICAN CAMPAIGN has been called a 'side-show' by men who were not there. Perhaps it was. Every confrontation seemed like a side-show to someone, and yet what at the time was called 'The Abyssinian Campaign' has all the ingredients of a great battle, and a unique place in the strategy of the Second World War.

The story begins a few weeks after Italy declared war. On 3 August 1940 three battalions of the Italian army and fourteen battalions of colonial infantry, together with pack-artillery, medium tanks and armoured cars, moved across the border into British Somaliland, in the 'horn of Africa'. It was a small country compared with neighbouring Abyssinia, which the Italians had conquered in 1936, and its defence force consisted of a battalion of the Black Watch, two Indian and two East African battalions and the Somaliland Camel Corps. After two days of heavy fighting the British force was evacuated on 15 August 1940 under a strong rearguard action by the Black Watch.

Churchill was angry. He felt that defeat at the hands of the Italians – for the one and only time on record – would boost the morale of the Italian army in Libya just when 'so much depended on our prestige'. Italy's propaganda service made the most of the British expulsion from its African holding. It was a black mark for General Wavell, and Churchill's black marks were accumulated like trading stamps: when you had a certain number of them, you were traded in for someone else.

To make matters worse for Wavell, he had Abyssinia's Emperor Haile Selassie sitting in Khartoum, waiting for the British to restore his country to him. He had arrived in Egypt by flying boat as long ago as 25 June. The Foreign Office in London had packed him off on one of the last cross-Europe flights before France collapsed, without warning anyone that he was on his way back to Africa. With the British defeat in Somaliland, he had become an even more embarrassing encumbrance with whom all communication was difficult, since the emperor insisted upon speaking Amharic. The only available interpreter of Amharic spoke only Arabic and, on at least one occasion, the Arabic interpreter spoke only French, thus requiring a third interpreter.

The struggle for East Africa

In January 1941, after General O'Connor's victories at Sidi Barrani in the Western Desert, the 4th Indian Division was taken from the fighting and brought 2,000 miles south to East Africa. The 5th Indian Division was brought to Khartoum. West African troops and some South African brigades were moved to Kenya. There were several reasons why Churchill bullied Wavell into a three-pronged assault upon this million-square-mile rectangle of land. Beside his obvious chagrin at having been ejected from British Somaliland by the Italians, and the wish to remove, once and for all, the Italian dream of joining East African possessions to Libya by conquering Egypt, there was a broader strategy behind the move.

Churchill wanted to bring South Africa into a fighting war, and by taking South African army and air force units northwards into areas of greater strategic importance (instead of using them as garrisons, which is all the South African government had promised) there was a chance of blooding them and granting them a victory not too far away from their homeland. Removing the Italians would be a popular action at home in South Africa. The South Africans were not entirely sure about the wisdom of engaging in war against Germany, but Jan Christiaan Smuts – their premier and C-in-C – had won the vote in Parliament by a narrow margin. A victory for the South African fighting men would reinforce pro-British Smuts in his present shaky political position.

Wavell was not privy to Churchill's thinking on the matter. He was no politician and not, in the global sense, a strategist. Wavell did not want to attack Abyssinia; he preferred to wait until the rifles he had supplied to the natives brought about a popular revolt against Italian rule – or at least to wait until the rainy season had ended. Wavell sent a specialist in guerrilla warfare, Captain Orde Wingate, to get a revolt started, but Churchill was not prepared to let large bodies of fighting troops stand idly by, waiting for a revolt to start. He wanted this battle won and the troops – South Africans included – moved north into Egypt to face whatever proved to be the next crisis.

Few campaigns can match this Abyssinian one, either for the fierceness of its fighting or the colourful nature of its combatants. The 5th Indian Division, arriving at Keren, included such units as the 5th Mahratta Light Infantry Regiment, 3/2 Punjab, Skinner's Horse, the Worcesters, motor machine-gun companies of the Sudan Defence Force and the 1st Transvaal Scottish with its own pipe band. On the Italian side there were Blackshirt Legions, the Savoia Grenadiers, and Alpini units.

The landscape was equally exotic. In this land of precipitous mountains, high plateaux, gorges and ravines as well as tropical lowlands, Keren was a road and rail junction and the key to the north. Standing at 4,000 feet above sea-level, the country surrounding Keren was like a lunar landscape. To seal the mighty gorge the Italian engineers exploded charges under 200 feet of cliff and blocked the road. 'Keren,' said one account, describing that moment when the defenders sealed themselves inside, 'was like a great medieval castle whose portcullis has fallen.'

The 4th Indian Division had been chosen because of their experience of mountain warfare.[1] Facing them were crack troops of the Bersaglieri battalion of the Savoia Grenadiers, commanded by a young and energetic colonel. Five days of fighting cost the Italians nearly 5,000 casualties, including 1,135 dead. The Allied casualties were no fewer. The siege of Keren lasted 53 days and the British commander had to pause and bring in another division before finally taking the town.

None of the Allied troops who fought at Keren would dismiss Italian troops as lacking the ability to fight. Some of the most bitter fighting of the whole war was seen in East Africa. The RAF, the South African Air Force and Rhodesian squadrons were using antiquated planes such as Gloster Gladiators, Westland Lysanders, Vickers Wellesleys and Vickers Vincents. Without the air superiority they gained with these machines the Allied forces would never have been able to take Keren. The Italian commander was the Duke of Aosta, who was married to a French princess. He was described by Churchill as 'a chivalrous and cultivated man, partly educated in England'.[2] Churchill may have intended to say 'educated partly in England', but with Churchill you can never be sure.

Other Allied components included a battalion of the French

Foreign Legion and the Highland Light Infantry. Exotic names abounded: a mobile force was called 'Flit'(after a well-known brand of insect repellent) and the commanding general's aircraft was called 'Mrs Clutterbuck'. The official war artist Edward Bawden depicted the campaign in several superb watercolour paintings now to be seen at the Imperial War Museum in London.

One column, 'Gideon Force', was commanded by 'Gideon' Orde Wingate, who said he was given nothing but 'sick camels and the scum of the Cavalry Division'. With them he brought the 'Lion of Judah', otherwise known as Haile Selassie, back to his capital over some of the worst going in the world. The Force included 700 camels, 200 mules and some horses, the emperor and his guard, together with a propaganda unit which had its own printing press, Amharic type-faces and many coloured inks. The emperor's party was said to be able to follow the trail without a compass, using just the smell of the dead camels. Fifty-seven were counted on one day alone. One officer of the Cavalry Division wrote:

> Slowly, at the rate of about two miles an hour, we passed on over desolate ridges where the scrub had been burnt away by the fires of earlier hamlias [camel caravans]. The sun rose hot over a blackened landscape. Dead camels lay stinking in the heat at the foot and top of every khor where the broken ground had proved too much for them. The blood of crippled camels, newly slaughtered, was drying on the rocks. Frightened living camels shied away from the corpses; their drivers sometimes vomited. Hundreds of vultures, gorged with flesh, lurched heavily around.[3]

On 5 May 1941 Haile Selassie was back in his capital at Addis Ababa. It had been a campaign of remarkable chivalry which recorded no rape, murder, plundering or bombing of civilians. In defence of Keren the Italians fought fiercely and their final withdrawal from there was deft and skilful. The final skirmishes of the campaign in East Africa went on for seven months after the fall of Addis Ababa. It would provide time enough to reflect upon the strangely mixed quality of the Italian army. Some units proved brave and efficient while others were either unwilling to fight, or too disorganized to be formidable adversaries. Some said the Italians suffered from a shortage of the sort of officers that a large educated professional middle class could supply.[4] German liaison officers remarked on the low standards of training and the lack of initiative of junior officers. In part it was a matter of weapons. Italy lacked a strong industrial base and had failed to improve weapons which, although good enough in the early 1930s, were outmoded by the 1940s. There was a prevailing feeling amongst all Italian soldiers, except perhaps those in the elite Fascist regiments, that they were fighting on the wrong side; that the English, French and Americans were traditional friends, and the Germans and Austrians Italy's implacable foes.

As the mopping-up continued Churchill's reasoning proved sound. Italian East Africa was Italian no more. It was the first Allied strategic victory of the war, and came at a time when the Allies desperately needed victory of any sort. Here was a clear demonstration of what air superiority over a battlefield could achieve and how unity among disparate forces could win the day. South African, East African, West African, British, Indian, Sudanese and Cypriot troops had taken part and South African soldiers, once committed to serving in only southern Africa, were now a part of the main Allied battle forces. But the campaign had done nothing to ease Churchill's doubts about Wavell. When the two men met for the first time in August 1940 it had been clear to everyone that they were totally incompatible in temperament and outlook. The record suggests that Wavell, taciturn, wary and professional, probably thought Churchill an interfering politician who knew nothing about generalship. Churchill, exuberant, bellicose or laudatory as the mood caught him, certainly found Wavell uncooperative and narrow-minded. The subsequent exchanges betwen them had done nothing to change these first impressions.

The victory brought a vital change, enabling President Roosevelt to declare the Red Sea to be no longer a 'war zone'. This meant that United States shipping was once more permitted, by government and insurance conditions, to sail to Suez. American tanks, guns and planes could now be shipped around the Cape of Good Hope to Egypt.

The war had widened. With cool nerve, the 4th British Indian Division had been pulled south after the battle for Sidi Barrani and used for the assault on the Italians in Keren, where the fiercest fighting took place. Afterwards it was rushed north to fight the Vichy French at Damascus in Syria. With equal facility, the 5th South African Brigade was sent north to Egypt as soon as victory in East Africa was assured. A further indication of the growing scale of the war was the way in which precious Hawker Hurricane fighter planes were being brought to Takoradi in the Gold Coast, some in crates to be assembled ashore, others flown from the decks of air-craft-carriers. From Takoradi the little planes made an astounding journey right across the continent, landing in northern Nigeria, and again in Khartoum in the Sudan before reaching Cairo. They were usually escorted by one twin-engined Bristol Blenheim as an 'insurance policy'.

Habbaniyah and after: Iraq and Syria

For anyone who considers the campaign in Italian East Africa a side-show, the skirmish at RAF Habbaniyah in Iraq must rank as insignificant. But let us suspend judgement for a moment.

Iraq has held a place in the history of the RAF since the First World War, when Australian and New Zealand pilots flew Maurice Farman Longhorn biplanes to cover a British army advancing up the River Tigris to fight the Turks. A postwar mandate put it under British control and Winston Churchill (when secretary of state for the colonies) and Sir Hugh Trenchard (the 'Father' of the RAF) proposed that this huge area of desert, a barren place of stone and sand, could be policed successfully with a few fighter planes and bombers converted to carry soldiers. It would save the British tax-payer the cost of twelve infantry battalions, a cavalry regiment, a pack battery and engineers which it was estimated would otherwise be needed to keep order among the Arabs.

This was the time when Giulio Douhet published his influential book *Command of the Air*;[5] a time when the American flier Billy Mitchell demonstrated that his bombers could sink battleships. So why not make Iraq the first country to be garrisoned from the air? The idea seemed to work. Villages that harboured trouble-making Kurdish tribesmen were bombed. Flyers worked in conjunction with RAF Rolls-Royce armoured-car crews which were supplied from the air. One air force officer, Hugh Dowding, thought that punishment without bloodshed would be equally deterrent. After his commander had gone on leave, Dowding ordered that before a bombing raid all the villagers should be warned by leaflet, in time for them to escape to safety, and this became the standard practice.[6] By the time the mandate ended in 1932, a pro-British monarchy was installed in Baghdad, oil-drilling had started in the north and con-cessions had been granted. The RAF remained behind: a treaty provided them with two bases, defended by locally recruited 'levies', and the right of passage in time of war. The levies were mostly loyal and disciplined Assyrians who hated the Arabs with a deep passion and made a vital contribution to the British presence.

By 1941 this almost landlocked country, with just a tiny strip of coast on the Persian Gulf and a small fertile region watered by the mighty rivers Tigris and Euphrates, was pumping oil through two big pipelines to the Mediterranean. One of these pipelines crossed Vichy French Syria, and its use was denied to the British. The other pipe went through pro-British Jordan, and its outlet at Haifa in Palestine was used to fuel British forces in the Middle East. For some the oil brought great changes and political turbulence as military coups became commonplace. The warring nomadic tribes still fought barbarous skirmishes using Lee-Enfields and Turkish rifles left over from the First World War, while the rich lived quiet lives in fine houses with servants, silk and silver. Successive Iraqi governments always found enough money to keep a small army and air force well equipped with guns and planes.

The Germans had always shown interest in the region. Their archeologists and explorers have written some of the standard works on the desert and its history. Some of its most breath-taking wonders are still to be seen in Berlin's Pergamon museum. But the German interest has been political and military too, and their espionage network was well entrenched in the area and ready to encourage anti-British Arab nationalism. It came as no surprise that Rashid Ali's clique, which seized power in April 1941, was supported by Germany or that the coup should come immediately following Britain's humiliating defeats in Greece and Cyrenaica. Unlike previous coups this one hoped to get rid of the British altogether and May was the month of high floodwater when any British relief force would find its movement impeded.

That Rashid Ali took power from the pro-British regent Emir Abdullah Illah (who ruled in the name of the young King Faisal II) was no great surprise. That it was done without killing him was more a matter of good luck than of good will. The doctors who arrived at the regent's Baghdad home with a death certificate endorsed 'heart failure' were too late. The intended victim had left in the back of the American minister's car and the RAF flew him out of their nearby airfield.

Rashid Ali el Gailani was not the young sleek Arab the name might suggest but a plump bespectacled man of middle age who, while serving as prime minister, had acquired a reputation for duplicity in a region where duplicity was seldom remarked upon. He was known to be a Nazi sympathizer and the British were alarmed by his coup. Britain's proprietorial feelings towards the Suez Canal, about Iraq's oilfields, and communications between Egypt and India, prompted a quick reaction to the Baghdad palace revolution. Garrisoning from the air was temporarily suspended. The 20th Indian Infantry Brigade, waiting in Karachi for embarkation on ships to Singapore, was suddenly given an about-turn and rushed to Basra in southern Iraq. Faced with Iraqi objections, the British blandly denied that the newly arrived men had come to seize control back from the pro-German clique; the Indian Brigade was just passing through Iraq 'en route to Palestine'.

About 60 miles from Baghdad, and close to the River Euphrates, there was a lake used by Britain's 'Empire' flying boats which hopped from water-landing to water-landing all the way to India and beyond. Here too, within a steel fence, were comfortable bungalows with lawns and flower beds, a polo ground and a golf course that the RAF had built in an attempt to forget that just a stroke or two away lay a sandy bunker that stretched to the horizon. This was Habbaniyah: RAF No. 4 Flying Training School. There were no up-to-date fighting planes here – the RAF had none to spare – only 27 Airspeed Oxfords and 32 Hawker Audaxes, as well as some Gloster Gladiators and such remarkable museum pieces as Fairey Gordons and Vickers Valentias.

As one of his first political moves Rashid Ali said he would permit no further landing of troops in Basra. He wanted to limit the number of British troops in Iraq at any one time. Let those passing through pass through, he said, before any more arrive. In London it became known that Rashid Ali had signed a secret treaty with the Germans and the Italians on 25 April. A variety of intelligence material indicated that Rashid Ali was waiting for German armed assistance and that the disembarkation of British troops at Basra had proved an unwelcome impediment to his plans.

In a climate growing ever more tense, it was decided to move British women and children to safety. Some went to the American Legation, some to the British Embassy, and some were to be flown out of the country altogether. On leaving Baghdad, they were held up by Iraqi soldiers, but eventually were allowed to proceed to RAF Habbaniyah, where there were now 1,000 RAF personnel. These were mostly ground crews, administrative staff and flying instructors, as well as 1,200 Iraqi levies – Arabs, Kurds and Assyrian

Christians – employed by the British. In addition 350 infantrymen of the King's Own Royal Regiment had been flown in.

At about this time Rashid Ali's men occupied the oilfields and switched the pipeline controls so that all the oil would flow to (Vichy) Syria and none to (British) Palestine. Red lights flashed: this was a serious threat. The British had persuaded Shell and Anglo-Iranian Oil to build at Haifa a refinery capable of supplying 2 million tons per year. This fuel was required by the Royal Navy's Mediterranean fleet. Additionally the refinery was supplying high-quality oils that were vitally important since the war had cut off Romanian supplies.

Iraqi army units (an infantry brigade accompanied by a brigade of mechanized artillery) soon arrived at Habbaniyah and occupied high ground outside it. The RAF cleaned up and oiled two ancient howitzers, relics of the First World War, which had been used to ornament the lawn outside the depot. In addition there were 18 armoured cars and the infantry's mortars and machine-guns. They fitted some of their Audax biplane trainers, and Oxford twin-engined trainers, with bomb racks, and the theory of bomb-dropping was hastily taught to pupil pilots. It was sobering to remember that the Iraqi air force was equipped with American bombers and Italian fighter planes.

On the morning of 1 May the Iraqis were to be seen siting their pom-pom anti-aircraft guns and bringing their armoured cars as close as possible to the RAF runways. A message from the Iraqi commander dictated that all flying was to cease on pain of aircraft being fired upon. The British replied that the training schedule would continue normally and reprisals would follow any such act of war. An RAF plane did a circuit without incident. The British then sent a note to the Iraqis saying that they must move, as the present disposition of Iraqi troops constituted an act of war. That night, the British decided that if the Iraqis were still there at dawn they would improvise a bombing raid.

The Audaxes and Oxfords were wheeled out under cover of night and took off so as to be in the air by 5 am. They were joined by eight twin-engined Vickers Wellington bombers of 37 Squadron from Shaibah near Basra. These 'Wimpys' were the only modern effective aircraft that took part in the fighting in Iraq. Twisting and turning without any proper formations, and narrowly missing mid-air collisions, the British planes bombed the Iraqi positions. As Iraqi pom-poms shot at the planes, Iraqi artillery bombarded the

RAF station. One Oxford was shot down in flames and a Wellington was hit by shells on landing. The rest got down safely, though many were riddled with bullet holes.

The base was subjected to attacks throughout the day and was bombed by Audaxes of the Royal Iraq Air Force. No vital damage was done before RAF Gladiators chased them away. The artillery fire was a greater threat. 'But though the station church sustained some damage, owing to the powerful attraction invariably exercised by places of worship upon indifferent gunners, the water tower was never hit,' said an Air Ministry account.[7]

Transport aircraft were loaded with women and children and climbed away while RAF Audaxes staged diversionary attacks. When they landed the Audaxes were moved to the polo ground where trees hid them, but take-offs now had to be negotiated through the main gates! Wear and tear on the aircraft was becoming severe, so that only four Oxfords of the original 27 were serviceable, and it was decided that only instructors should fly the remaining aircraft. But the arrival of some Bristol Blenheims persuaded the British to bomb the columns that supplied water, fuel and ammunition to the Iraqi positions. Then they went to make bombing attacks against nearby Iraqi airfields.

Suddenly, and without warning, on the fifth morning of the siege the plateau was empty. The Iraqis had gone. The 'Habbaniyah air force' pursued them, and motor buses which the Iraqis had seized from Baghdad streets to move their infantry were bombed on the road. The announcement that successful operational flights by pupils would mean a remission of further training set the pupil pilots demanding an opportunity to fly, and they were needed.

The British success at Habbaniyah did not deter Rashid Ali. On 12 May he went, together with his ministers and other dignitaries, to Baghdad airport to await the arrival of a German liaison team led by Major Axel von Blomberg (a son of the famous field marshal). Blomberg was to set up a headquarters to direct forthcoming Luftwaffe operations against the British in Iraq. Iraqi police levies on airfield defence duties had not been briefed about the visitors, and when a Heinkel bomber flew into view they opened fire at it. One bullet went through the fuselage, and in a bizarre stroke of fate mortally wounded Blomberg.[8] The following day Baghdad heard the exiled Mufti of Jerusalem broadcast a call for all Islamic countries to join the fight against the British.

More fighting broke out in Basra, where disembarked Indian

troops were somewhat piqued to find themselves subjected to the brutal fire of 2-inch and 3-inch mortars that the British had supplied to the Iraqi army. They were still waiting for theirs, as were most other Indian units. Fighting spread even to the civil population and the British disarmed the police force.

The next day, an RAF Bristol Blenheim at Mosul in northern Iraq was fired upon by a German plane. There were reports that many German aircraft were operating from Mosul and that supplies of arms and ammunition were arriving there on the railway from Syria. Clearly the Vichy French were not only permitting transit facilities but actively supporting German intervention on the side of Rashid Ali.

There were worries about what sort of intervention the Germans might mount. On 20 May the Luftwaffe parachute troops began the assault on the faraway island of Crete. If the Germans were serious about reinforcing Rashid Ali, such airborne forces would be the ones needed. But by 29 May, the Crete fighting ended with Karl Student's Air Division decimated and the wrecks of 151 Junkers transport aircraft scattered across the Cretan landscape. A small collection of transports were scraped together and assigned to support the Iraqi revolt[9] but it had come at the wrong time as far as the German airborne forces were concerned. Rashid Ali and his associates, together with the Italian and German ministers and the ex-Mufti of Jerusalem, fled to Persia. The coup was over and the British reinstalled the regent in Baghdad.

But the story doesn't end there. Before the outcome of the Habbaniyah fighting was settled, some RAF flyers reported back to H 4 (a desolate RAF landing strip on the oil pipeline) in Transjordan after a routine reconnaissance over Syria. (Like those in its neighbour Lebanon, the French in Syria had declined all invitations to join in the war against Germany and Italy.) A big German transport plane was parked on Palmyra airfield. It seemed to be in the process of refuelling for an immediate take-off, its destination undoubtedly Iraq.

The RAF flyers had noticed that the refuelling was being carried out by hand, and pouring from cans of fuel was a slow procedure. One of the pilots suggested to his superior that, given a fighter plane with some incendiary ammunition, he could make sure the German aircraft never took off again.

'Are you two young gentlemen aware that we are not at war with Syria?' asked the man behind the desk.

'Yes, sir,' the flying officer replied, 'I know, sir; but I think it would be a bloody good idea if we were.'

That was in fact how the British went to war with Syria. Permission was granted, and after eating a hasty lunch while an aircraft was prepared they flew off with two supporting Tomahawk fighters to attack the Germans.

In fact London knew well what was happening. Enigma decrypts had revealed that unmarked Heinkel He 111 bombers and twin-engined Messerschmitt fighters were flying to Syria. London judged the German commitment to be strictly limited, but took no chances. A British column set out from Palestine and the troops in Basra were summoned into action.

In the confused and terrible fighting that followed – sometimes in temperatures of 120 degrees (49 C) – Frenchman fought Frenchman and Arab fought Arab in a deeply felt struggle. And, at a time when the British fortunes were very low, Emir Abdullah of Transjordan sent his small but efficient Arab Legion into the battle on the Allied side. Feelings ran even higher when German aircraft bombed (Vichy) Beirut and hit a school and a mosque. Whether this was a navigational error, or a deliberate attempt to have the RAF wrongly blamed for it, has never been established.

On 27 June Luftwaffe Enigma signals revealed that Vichy France was about to send infantry reinforcements to Syria. The troopships were to be escorted by units of the French fleet: one battleship, four cruisers and up to six destroyers. Air cover was to be supplied by the Luftwaffe. It looked as if the war was about to intensify, and France become a full ally of Germany. The Admiralty sent Royal Navy submarines to concentrate against the troopships and the escorting warships. Then, on 2 July, news came that the plan was cancelled. A deep sigh came from those who saw what a catastrophic clash had been so narrowly avoided.

The fighting ended with the British taking control of Syria and Lebanon, but the wounds would never heal. The defeated French servicemen were invited to join de Gaulle's Free French and fight the Germans, but almost all chose to go back to France. De Gaulle, taking seriously his self-declared role as head of state in exile, and pressured by the British (and unofficially by the Americans too), promised the people of the French mandates of Syria and Lebanon their independence.[10] There was uproar. De Gaulle's announcement not only upset the Vichy government, which felt that such decisions were theirs, but also made his Free French soldiers ask why they were fighting and dying for territory in order to give it back when it was taken.

It all ended in farce. In breach of the armistice terms, the Vichy French tried to spirit their prisoners of war back to Germany. This resulted in some senior Vichy officers being put under arrest in their hotel until the POWs were found and handed over. At the signing of the armistice a drunken Australian photographer fell over a cable and put out all the lights. In the darkness and confusion someone stole the gold-decorated képi of a French general.

Afterwards Churchill remarked that: 'Hitler certainly cast away the opportunity of taking a great prize for little cost in the Middle East.' Wavell never saw it in that light. When ordered to send a relief column from Palestine to Iraq, he let it be known that Palestine (with its ruler in league with Rashid Ali, and much anti-British feeling prevalent) could not spare soldiers from its garrison. Showing no sympathy for Britain's problems in Iraq, Wavell irritably replied: 'Your message takes little account of realities. You must face facts . . . a settlement should be negotiated as early as possible'.

Having intercepted an Italian diplomatic message saying that Rashid Ali had used up all his bombs and shells, London (chiefs of staff) replied testily: 'Settlement by negotiation cannot be entertained except on a basis of climb-down by the Iraqis . . . realities of the situation are that Rashid Ali has all along been hand in glove with Axis Powers . . .'[11]

'I am deeply disturbed at General Wavell's attitude,' wrote Churchill, who felt that the essence of war was the rapid movement of forces.[12] He had urged Wavell to exploit the situation and break into Baghdad 'even with quite small forces . . . running the same risks as the Germans are accustomed to run and profit by.'[13]

Only grudgingly had Wavell obeyed the direct order to send a column to Habbaniyah, which he thought was 'a non-vital area'. Even then he pointed out that 'it is not capable of entering Baghdad', and repeated his advice to find a political solution for Iraq. He had always, he said later, 'disliked Iraq, the country, the people and the military commitment'.

Wavell's dislike of Iraq seems to have led him to underestimate its importance. In a telegram dated 25 May, he said that his main task was the defence of Egypt and Palestine and added that this 'would be made more difficult but would not be greatly jeopardized by hostile control of Iraq'. His opinion is difficult to sustain: Palestine and Egypt would have been outflanked by an Axis-controlled Iraq, and Wavell's army, navy and air force depended upon Iraq's oil wells and the pipeline.

Wavell's concern in Syria, Palestine and Iraq, just like his caution in East Africa, came from his belief that all military action, and even cross-country movement, required 'the cooperation of the local population and tribes'. Whatever the morality of this assumption it is not always the case in reality. This was proved when Churchill pressed Wavell into action.

That Churchill took any threat to Iraq very seriously is indicated by the way in which British military intelligence in Palestine sought out the extreme Zionist Irgun Zvai Leumi. They recruited Iraqi Jews to penetrate and spy upon the Rashid Ali organization. One of the volunteers was David Rashiel, Irgun chief of staff, who came from a prosperous Baghdad family and who, in the course of the revolt, was caught and executed by the rebels.[14]

When Wavell was sacked the following month, June 1941, most people put it down to his military failure in North Africa. The reasons for that failure and the injustice of Churchill's decision have been picked over many times, but there can be no doubt that the roots of Churchill's discontent were sunk much deeper.

16 QUARTERMASTER'S NIGHTMARE

Victory is a mirage in the desert
created by a long war.

B. H. Liddell Hart[1]

'CRETE GAVE A GREAT NAME; Africa gave a greater.' The words of the Roman poet Martial describe the rival bids for glory made by Karl Student and the even more ambitious Erwin Rommel, who was appointed to command the Deutsches Afrika Korps on 12 February 1941: 'In the evening the Führer showed me a number of British and American illustrated papers describing General Wavell's advance through Cyrenaica. Of particular interest was the masterly co-ordination these showed between armoured land forces, air force and navy.'[2]

Events moved quickly. A British intelligence summary dated March 1941 said: 'Detachments of a German expeditionary force under an obscure general, Rommel, have landed in North Africa.'

Stripped of much equipment and transport (which had been sent to Greece), tired, depleted and untested units made up much of the British army facing Rommel in North Africa. Wavell and his staff in Cairo were not unduly worried. They comforted themselves with the belief that the Italians in Tripolitania could be disregarded and that German reinforcements would not be sufficient for any attack to be started in the near future.

The codecrackers at Bletchley Park were keeping tabs on Rommel. When Churchill asked what was happening, he was supplied with German OKW, High Command of the Armed Forces, signals showing the approximate arrival dates of components of the Afrika Korps. Although Cairo frequently complained of Bletchley Park's slowness, this time there was no delay in passing on these figures to Wavell.

By early March Wavell's director of intelligence was telling him the Afrika Korps might attack very soon. He showed Wavell the sort of plan he thought might be on Rommel's desk. Wavell dismissed it.

Without disputing the figures from London, his staff – guided by the way the British army did such things – calculated that Rommel could not be ready before May. His supply line was long and he would need considerable time to prepare reserves and dumps before going into action.

In Berlin the German army's C-in-C, Field Marshal von Brauchitsch, came to the same conclusion as Wavell. He told Rommel that there could be no question of staging an offensive in Africa in the near future. The Italian high command took the same view. But Rommel was aggressive and ambitious. He saw that Berlin was hoping that the Western Desert fighting might lull into a stalemate, and he had no intention of letting his command become a backwater. He was determined to make war, and he was in a hurry. When his ships arrived he kept the dockside lights on, and worked all night unloading despite the danger of air raids. The armoured cars that were swinging from the cranes in Tripoli in mid-February were in action ten days later.

The remarkable General O'Connor had been sent away to rest and the fighting army was now commmanded by General Philip Neame, a man of outstanding valour, as his VC indicated, but lacking experience of mechanized desert fighting. Rommel knew from intelligence and air photos that British units were short of transport, which meant uncertain supply lines all the way back to their depots in Egypt. He saw them building defences, and that proved they had no intention of attacking him. In fact Rommel was in a situation exactly like that of General O'Connor when he had faced the Italians a short while before.

Still unconcerned, on 30 March Wavell told Neame that the enemy could not 'make any big effort for at least another month'. At 0944 hours the next day, armoured cars of the Stahnsdorf 3rd Reconnaissance Unit – having already advanced to El Agheila – led the attack. Behind them were the tanks of the 5th Panzer Regiment. The following day Stuka dive-bombers and Rommel's 8.8-cm dual-purpose guns were seen in action. The use of these Flak guns in an artillery role was a great surprise, just as it had been at Arras, before Dunkirk, and in Spain during the civil war. The chronic failure of British military intelligence to record that the 8.8-cm gun was a dual-purpose weapon is in sad accord with a signal Wavell sent to the CIGS in London estimating that Rommel's armoured division was equipped with 400 tanks, when its true strength was 168 tanks and 30 reconnaissance cars.[3]

Desert warfare

The desert was an uninhabited empty space within which 'forts' were held. Capture one of his forts and your displaced enemy flounders and falls back. You outflank him and he tries to find another place to hold fast. This is what happened as Rommel pressed on, sending out the Luftwaffe to see what was happening. The aerial photographs soon showed the British in full retreat.

When Rommel tightened Italian field signals discipline, British listening units, which were not yet taken very seriously, could make nothing of the enemy radio traffic. Rommel on the other hand, gave great importance to his signals intelligence. He used it in combination with air reconnaissance, and armoured car patrols, to follow the movements of the retreating British.

British headquarters now knew the sort of confusion that had earlier hit the Italian staff officers. And exactly as they had done, the British rationalized their failure by larger and larger estimates of the forces ranged against them. On one thing only did the British commanders all agree; what was happening was incredible, if not to say impossible.

The commander of an Australian battalion in full retreat ordered his men to stop for breakfast. Those men who obeyed were known in the prison camp where they spent the next four years as 'the breakfast battalion'.

Still assessing the Germans on his own army's methods and performance, Wavell remained calm. He had personally assured Foreign Secretary Anthony Eden, and told the generals in Whitehall, that the Germans could not attack before mid-May. Now it was April and Wavell's generals reflected his unflustered optimism. They were convinced that Rommel's advance would quickly falter and fail of its own accord: where would he get water? Where would he get fuel? These two vital questions were answered as he captured water, and took fuel forward on trucks. And the Germans had brought excellent containers for water and fuel, made from welded pressed-steel. The British soon named them 'Jerricans' and seized every one they could find. They tossed aside the 4-gallon British cans, aptly known as 'flimsies'. The official history quotes a report dated December 1941 which said that 30 per cent or more of the fuel carried in flimsies to fighting men in the Western Desert was lost by leakage.[4] From an account given by one RASC driver carrying fuel, 30 per cent loss was an understatement:

When we reached [the petrol dump] the 70,000 had been reduced to 30,000 gallons during the desert journey. Much to our surprise, we were told this was a good effort. This wastage was because of the 'flimsy' petrol containers which leaked badly, a state of affairs not eradicated until the introduction of the 'Jerrican' copied from the Germans.[5]

Suddenly Wavell interceded personally in the battle. He countermanded the orders of Neame, his army commander, to cover both the inland and coastal roads. Wavell assumed that Rommel would keep to the via Balbia, the tarmac road along the coast, and so sent all the armour to block it. It was not a good idea to underestimate Rommel. The Germans were just as capable as the British of taking a short-cut across the desert, following the route that General O'Connor's men had proved to be negotiable.

By the end of that day, 3 April, the Germans were moving into Benghasi, where the British had set fire to all their stores. Wavell decided that General Neame had lost control and ordered Major-General O'Connor to go and replace him. O'Connor asked Wavell to reconsider his decision, pointing out that one should not introduce new tactics in the middle of a battle. He said he didn't know the troops and would be better occupied preparing defensive positions to ensure Rommel didn't sweep right into Egypt. Wavell compromised by asking O'Connor to stay at Neame's headquarters for a few days, and offer advice when asked. This was the worst possible decision, and Wavell more or less admitted as much afterwards.

The British army was falling to pieces, and two heads were not better than one. Panicking troops had burned petrol and other stores at Msus long before the Germans got near them. The 3rd Armoured Division ran out of fuel. The 2nd Armoured Division, sent to protect the Australians, disintegrated to a point where it simply relinquished its tanks and joined the retreat. This 'complete disobedience of orders' was, said O'Connor, 'absolutely incomprehensible'.[6] But the problems that came from the shared responsibilities of Neame and O'Connor were soon to be solved. On 6 April, when moving their joint headquarters back a few miles, O'Connor, lacking his own transport, accepted the offer of a ride in Neame's car.

Shortly before dusk it became obvious that they had missed the way and were on one of the northern tracks, but as this seemed anyway a safer route, Neame handed over to his driver and told him to carry on towards Derna. Well after midnight, O'Connor and [Lt-Col.] Combe, who had been asleep in the back of the car, were woken to find the car stationary and voices shouting in front. Combe got out to investigate, quickly realized that the voices were not British and on asking the driver what was happening, received the classic answer: 'I expect it's some of them bloody Cypriot drivers, sir!'[7]

Not quite. The generals had been captured by a motor-cycle reconnaissance unit, those probing patrols that Rommel kept pushing forward. Curiously enough a brigadier in a car ahead of the two British generals reached his destination without a hint of the fate that overtook the men in the car behind. Only early next morning, with his two generals nowhere to be found, was their loss discovered.

Rommel was out-thinking his adversaries at every turn. This was the sort of warfare at which he excelled. He told his air force to concentrate upon destroying the British supply lines. 'Rommel panic' spread. By 7 April the three prongs of Rommel's advance converged on Mechili, where the Indian Motor Brigade had been moved forward to make a stand. Surrounded, the whole brigade surrendered. A more forceful war had now come to the Western Desert.

When all is said, Rommel did little more than repeat O'Connor's methods. In an impudent replay, he had taken O'Connor's 'impossible' desert road south of the Jebel Akdar in order to surprise the British retreating along the coast. But the Germans added a spirit of blitzkrieg to the desert war. One German general ascribed the success of this period to the cooperation and versatility of his units. Batteries of anti-tank guns always accompanied the German tanks and targeted only tanks. Field artillery was there to bombard enemy anti-tank batteries. The general wondered why the British 3.7-inch anti-aircraft gun was not adapted to the anti-tank role. He noted that 'the British regarded the anti-tank gun as a defensive weapon, and they failed to make adequate use of their powerful field artillery, which should have been taught to eliminate our anti-tank guns.'[8] The armour of the heavier German tanks – Panzer III and Panzer IV – was vulnerable not only to 25-pounder field guns but also to the 2-pounder tank and anti-tank guns, providing you got close enough.

General Erwin Rommel

Rommel was not one of the war's great generals. Many Germans express surprise that the British and American public know his name: they think of him as a product of Nazi propaganda. Rommel led from the front and his style suited divisional command. He became a hero for Allied front-line soldiers who seldom – if ever – saw their own top commanders at the front. British generals preferred to have their HQs about 60 miles behind the fighting fronts.[9] Besides, Rommel had for his Afrika Korps exceptional leaders such as Cruewell, Nehring and Bayerlein. But all that said, few other men could have inspired this mixed and demoralized German-Italian desert army in the way that Rommel did. He revelled in popularity and delighted in the sort of informality that the desert provided to both sides. In his paper *Modern Military Leadership* he wrote:

> The commander must try, above all, to establish personal and comradely contact with his men, but without giving away an inch of his authority . . . when an attack is ordered the men must never be allowed to get the feeling that their casualties have been calculated in advance according to the laws of probability.

The deciding factor in Rommel's North African campaign was the shipping and the ports. Even Tripoli was in no way equipped for the massive traffic that such armies demanded. Had the Axis coaxed the French for use of Tunisian facilities and used Tripoli and other less good Libyan ports with impeccable efficiency, and given proper attention to their road transport, they might have mustered the strength to capture Egypt. Then, having captured the port of Alexandria and got it working, they might have fed through it reinforcements enough to occupy Egypt and the Canal Zone. Even then such a strategy would almost certainly have faltered; German factories after the summer of 1941 were to be hard pressed by the demands of the Russian front.

Such a scenario was never a real possibility. Rommel's fatal flaw was his inability to see the importance of logistics. He liked to blame the Italian navy for his shortages, and historians have too readily accepted this judgement. In fact, Italian merchant seamen were nothing less than heroic in their performance. John Ellis reckons that the Axis forces were getting an average 800 tons per division per day, and points out that 'voracious US armoured divisions in North West Europe required only 600 tons of supplies per day, including fuel . . .'[10]

It was Rommel's own land-supply movements that brought him down. In fact his troubles arose from a combination of his own daring and improvisation and a disregard for the terrible problems such impulsive decisions made for his supply staff. He is quoted as saying that he left logistics to his staff officers.[11] It is significant that his supply officer in 1941 had the lowly rank of major.

As an indication of this major's problems, the trucks taking 1,000 gallons of fuel from the docks at Tobruk to Alamein consumed 120 gallons of fuel plus 9.6 gallons of other lubricants. Wastage and spillage in the hot climate would account for at least 10 per cent. Deduct fuel needed for the return journey, and they will have brought no more than 636 gallons to the front. But still more fuel was needed to bring up ammunition and food and all the other supplies. The map reveals that Tobruk, 300 miles from the front, is the key to supplying the desert war. It spent much of the war in British hands, and when in German hands it was a favourite target for the RAF bombers. Tripoli – Rommel's main port – was often 1,500 miles from his front! For their supplies the British used whenever possible the coastal railway out of Alexandria. It was economical and efficient. When Rommel captured 300 miles of it (in 1942) he did little to keep it functioning.

There can be no doubt that much of Rommel's reputation as a general was due to his skilful use of intelligence. Many tactical moves were based upon secrets picked up by his highly efficient Fernmeldeaufklärung. This mobile radio monitoring service listened to everything it could pick up; casual battlefield chat, tank to tank calls, headquarters messages and supply depot reports. Rommel's traffic analysts reaped a rich harvest, for British units in 1941 had not learned of the dangers that poor radio discipline brought. In addition to this tactical intelligence, Rommel was receiving something even better than the British Enigma intercepts: the intercepted messages sent to Washington by the United States military attaché in Cairo.

At this time the British were showing this American everything and anything that he wanted to see. Not only did his messages contain details of British armour strengths and positions, they also reported forthcoming operations such as commando raids. Instead of the spotty information from the Enigma intercepts, Rommel was getting material about air, land and sea operations and getting it with a speed and continuity that BP could never equal. The most knowledgeable historian on this subject remarks:

> And what messages they were! They provided Rommel with undoubtedly the broadest and clearest picture of enemy forces and intentions available to any Axis commander throughout the whole war.[12]

Determined defence of Tobruk by Australian infantry and British artillery denied that port to Rommel even when the remainder of the British army had retreated back to the Egyptian border. Now Rommel came to a stop and concentrated on Tobruk.

Rommel's unexpected advance in April 1941 surprised Berlin and prompted the high command to send a senior observer, Generalleutnant F. Paulus, to find out what this upstart Rommel was doing. Tall and slim, Paulus was one of the army's brightest staff officers and an expert on mobile warfare. His work as chief of staff for the 6th Army during its victorious campaigns in Poland, Belgium and France had resulted in him being selected to be deputy chief of the general staff and told to produce a strategic survey for invading the Soviet Union. Paulus, nicknamed 'the noble lord', was an old-fashioned but meticulous theoretician, who bathed as often as possible and wore gloves to protect himself against dirt. He had been Rommel's company commander in the 1920s and did not care for his cavalier way of waging war. Arriving on his inspection tour on 27 April, Paulus voiced great reservations about Rommel's proposed attack on Tobruk, which had now become a fortress. His scepticism proved well founded after concentrated bombing and shelling made no more than a dent in the Tobruk perimeter and both sides settled into a state of siege punctuated by bloody clashes at night. The Tobruk perimeter consisted mostly of rock-hard ground, so digging trenches or foxholes was not easy. Given the lack of cover, the Australians had to endure baking heat where a careless movement brought accurate sniper fire. On the night of 5-6 May, the defenders were given new hope when for the first time a ship brought supplies into the beleaguered port. From now onwards destroyers would make regular nightly visits, and each week reinforcements would be exchanged for wounded men.

The caustic report resulting from Paulus's inspection tour said that Rommel's supply lines were overstretched, his men exhausted and his reserves inadequate. He was told to forget about reducing

Tobruk and withdraw to Gazala or Mechili and operate within his resources.

The Enigma experts at Bletchley Park sent the intercepted signal to Churchill, who reasoned that if Rommel was weak and over-extended this was the chance to knock him reeling back to Cyrenaica. It was especially urgent since Enigma signals also revealed that 15 Panzer Division would soon be reinforcing Rommel. Ignoring the warnings of everyone around him, Churchill took all the fighter planes and tanks to be spared in Britain and loaded them onto a convoy which, against more advice, he sent through the Axis-dominated Mediterranean. Four of the five freighters got through with 238 tanks and 43 Hawker Hurricane fighter planes and docked in Alexandria in mid-May.

While this newly arrived equipment was distributed and made ready, a limited offensive, codenamed Brevity, was launched. Its object was to capture key areas in preparation for a major offensive to come.

One account of the desert war, says: 'Operation Brevity began at dawn on May 15, and it soon became evident that neither Rommel nor his local commander . . . were either aware of or in agreement with the conclusions drawn by Paulus.'[13] The British attack captured one of its objectives, Halfaya Pass, but was otherwise a failure. Rommel's signals intelligence had given him good warning of what was coming, and even a weak and over-extended Afrika Korps was too much for the British as he staged a counter-attack that recovered the Halfaya Pass.

And when the British armour was unloaded from the convoy that had come through the Mediterranean at such risk it proved to be a mixed collection. Eight out of twenty tanks required a complete overhaul. Many of the others were already halfway through their effective life and some of the Matildas were in need of major repairs. All of them required 'tropicalization' and painting. Long before the armour was fit for battle, Rommel's 15 Panzer Division reinforcements had arrived.

On 15 June, in the terrible desert heat of summer, the promised British offensive, Operation Battleaxe, began. Repeatedly the Germans enticed the British tanks on to their well concealed guns. Only thirteen 8.8-cm guns were in action but their role was decisive. The British stuck to their 'naval battle' tactics, sending in tanks to fire broadsides at enemy tanks. Despite the consequences, some of the tank units – many of them smart cavalry regiments – preferred this dashing style and didn't want support from infantry and guns. There was no sign that the British, at any level, were learning lessons from their chronic losses. After only three days' fighting Wavell sent Churchill a cable: 'I regret to report the failure of Battleaxe.' Churchill sacked him.

The Germans were getting acclimatized to the desert. In the first few months they were given a monotonous diet of black bread, tinned sardines, tinned meat and grated cheese. This sort of diet led to medical problems, particularly jaundice. It also spurred them into action. British stores were coveted if only for the change of menu they provided. 'Our black bread in a carton was handy,' said a German war correspondent, 'but how we used to long to capture one of your field bakeries and eat fresh white bread! And your jam!'[14] When finally ovens came, fresh bread remained scarce; the German quartermaster supplied the Afrika Korps with the standard field bakeries fired by logs. In most of Europe logs were easy to find, but they are not common in the desert. Fresh bread remained scarce.

Though the desert war seemed to come to a stop, this was an illusion. In fact the whole war was changing. There were changes of men, of methods and of machines. On 22 June Germany invaded Russia. It would be months before this took full effect, but from now on the Eastern Front would always dwarf the North African fighting. Henceforth Rommel's calls for men, armour, transport and fuel would be subordinated to other more urgent needs.

Wavell was dispatched to India. The day-to-day demands upon him had been greater than anyone could have imagined. He had been fighting too many battles – hundreds of miles apart – with skimpy resources. Sir Claude Auchinleck came to Cairo as the new commander-in-chief for the Middle East. The appointment of a number of subsidiary commanders ensured that he would never have the power that Wavell had wielded. New aircraft arrived and Bostons, Marylands, Beaufighters, Tomahawks and tropical Hurricanes were to be seen flying over the desert. There were new Crusader tanks, new ideas and even a new name for the desert army: the Eighth Army.

The siege of Tobruk

Rommel tried to eliminate the Tobruk garrison which remained like a festering sore upon his rear. He needed the port. He was always desperately short of road transport and supplies landed at Tobruk would be much nearer his front line. Bombed by relays of Stukas, shelled by day and night, the British garrison of Tobruk stayed in place. So efficiently was it resupplied by the Royal Navy that troops manning the perimeter went on leave and came back to duty there again. Nimble destroyers were used for the supply run, as regular raids by the Luftwaffe made negotiating the wrecked ships in the harbour increasingly difficult. Yet nothing was permitted to delay the loading and unloading:

> One stick of bombs screams down on the south shore of the harbour; the next is closer – in the water five hundred yards away. The old hands continue working, unworried, but some of the new ones, like us, pause momentarily, shrinking down behind the destroyer's after-screen. From the man with the megaphone comes a sharp rebuke – 'What are you stopping for? Those bloody bombs are nothing to do with you.'[15]

Manned largely by Australians, Tobruk was, by October 1941, celebrating six months of siege. The curious life they led became the stuff of endless newspaper stories back home in England and Australia. It was General Blamey rather than General Rommel who eventually moved them. The Australian government felt their men had taken the brunt of the fighting long enough and insisted that they should be relieved. Most of the Aussies were replaced by British troops together with men of the Polish 1st Carpathian Brigade.

Supply and demand

By November 1941 the British had made ready a large number of tanks, and launched another offensive. Facing them was the newly named Panzergruppe Afrika: Germans and Italians under Rommel's command. Operation Crusader was designed to get around Rommel's inland flank, cut off his armoured units, and push on far enough to relieve Tobruk. It was a fast-moving battle that resulted in some of the fiercest and most confused fighting in the history of the North African campaign. Any doubt about the worth of the Italian soldiers was removed when the British 22nd Armoured Brigade was mauled at the hands of the Ariete Division. Everywhere the battle became a slogging match in which tanks were usually the decisive factor. Newly arrived Honey tanks with high profile, short base and smelling of fresh desert-coloured paint could travel at 30 or 40 miles an hour. The Honeys charged the German Mark IIIs and Mark IV tanks, passed them, turned round and charged them again. It was a desperate tactic invented by a commanding officer who knew that the little 2-pounder guns on his tanks would have to get within 800 yards to have any effect on the enemy steel. The 5-cm and 7.5-cm guns on German tanks could rip the Honey open at 1,500 yards. Some of the Honeys never got close enough to even fire a shot.

The 5-cm gun proved more valuable to the Germans than did their big 'eighty-eights'. These smaller guns were ballistically superior to any British tank armament. More than half of the German tanks had them, and there were plenty more used as anti-tank guns.

The British started with 748 tanks against Rommel's 395 tanks, of which half were very inferior Italian models, but the Germans were frugal. At night, British wounded, lying out on the battlefield, were surprised to hear foreign voices and spot so many people walking around in the darkness. They were the German tank salvage teams: recovery units bringing towing vehicles to drag their crippled steel monsters home for repair. For those even more badly damaged, huge tracked and wheeled transporters were brought up to the wrecks. The Germans worked hard, but here and there they managed to spare a blanket or a hot drink for British wounded suffering exposure in the chill November night. Anyone back in headquarters disbelieving these stories of the German recovery teams was in for a further surprise when they saw them moving around on the battlefield in daytime, salvaging German and British vehicles while the shooting continued.

Around an airfield at the top of the Sidi Rezegh valley, a notable battle went on for some days of separated and confused fighting. The Germans discovered that an attack very early in the morning could catch the British half-asleep, and that in the fury of battle some of the inexperienced British units became lost and confused. As the battle came to a climax, commanders on both sides were seen standing up in their small cars, amid the furious gunfire and burning tanks, shouting and waving their men into action. A Rhodesian survivor of the 2nd Black Watch, which was almost annihilated, recalled:

> The enemy held his fire until we were past the wire. And then his machine-guns let go. Such of us that survived fell flat to take

what cover we could; but our Adjutant, who had been wounded, crawled to where we were lying and got to his feet. 'Isn't this the Black Watch?' he cried. 'Then – charge!' He waved us on with his stick and was instantly killed.[16]

The Germans also sustained heavy losses of men and machines. The 23 November, marked on the German calendar as *Totensonntag*, when prayers are offered for the souls of the dead, not only saw the destruction of the 5th South African Brigade but also became a day of mourning for Panzer Group Africa. By the end of the battle the British tank force was reduced to less than 150 while the Germans could field 170. In the fighting further to the north, New Zealand infantry pushed forward and captured Afrika Korps headquarters.

Always an opportunist, Rommel used the confusion of the battle to press his Panzer divisions forward towards 'the wire', the Egyptian frontier. More Rommel legends were created as the tanks crashed through the British rear. Support personnel, clerks, dentists and men of mobile bath units saw Rommel's fighting men at close quarters, and related their stories of it ever after. Rommel thought victory was almost in his grasp, but in fact he was making a grave mistake. His fuel ran low, his men grew tired, the British lines through which he had come went back to work again, and most important of all the New Zealanders continued their advance along the coast road to Tobruk.

Demoralized by the destruction wreaked upon his force, the British Eighth Army's new commander, General Alan Cunningham, began to plan a dramatic withdrawal. When the new C-in-C Auchinleck arrived at his headquarters Cunningham explained that he was ordering the army to pull back out of Libya and form a screen that would prevent Rommel from getting to Cairo. Auchinleck sat down and wrote out a long careful analysis of the situation. The offensive would continue, and that was an order; a written order. Auchinleck's resolve saved the day but it marked the end for Cunningham. He was rested in hospital and sent back to command the Staff College while his replacement tried to sort out the confusion of the fluid fighting.

Rommel, enjoying the excitement of front-line action, could not be found to be told that forward elements of the New Zealanders had reached the Tobruk perimeter and made contact with the defenders. In his absence his subordinates took matters into their own hands. They pulled back from Egypt. When he surfaced Rommel greeted their insubordination with astonishment and rage, but when they showed him the maps he slowly recognized the dangers of leaving behind him substantial British forces that were already regrouping.

> 'He greeted nobody,' one of Rommel's personal staff recalled, 'but stalked silently into the operations bus and looked at the battle maps . . . Rommel suddenly announced that he was tired and was going to lie down.'[17]

Rommel had received no tanks since June. On 5 December, with Germany's Eastern Front in the grip of a Russian winter and the German high command looking again at its long-term supply position, he was told not to expect early replacements of his losses of tanks and men. Now he devoted all his efforts to the capture of Tobruk, but his understanding of the part played by his supplies had come too late. Tobruk resisted doggedly.

By mid-December, while Rommel was pulling all the way back to El Agheila, the Italian navy made an all-out effort on behalf of the African armies. Despite their chronic shortage of fuel oil, they sent four battleships, three light cruisers and twenty destroyers to escort a convoy to Libya. That represented 100,000 tons of warships to escort 20,000 tons of merchant shipping.

Signals concerning such sea movements were being intercepted by Bletchley Park, and it was known that Convoy No. 52 was taking tanks to Rommel. Such was the urgency of his needs that the convoy was split. Three ships went to Tripoli, while the *Ankara* – carrying 22 heavy tanks (Panzer III and Panzer IV) – docked at Benghasi, an inferior port but one much nearer to the fighting.

In Cairo, British military intelligence reckoned that, as Benghasi had no dockside cranes capable of offloading such heavy tanks, it was safe to disregard the warning. Subsequent sightings by the Long Range Desert Group of German Mark IIIs and IVs travelling along on the coastal road, and a corresponding report from 4th Indian Division, did nothing whatever to change the minds of the men in Cairo.

Two days after Christmas, 60 German tanks tore into the British spearhead and knocked out 37 British tanks for the loss of seven. With little but light armour left, the British 22nd Armoured Brigade was withdrawn from the fighting. The German ship *Ankara*, which had been built to carry railway locomotives to South America, did not need quayside cranes; its own derricks swung out the heavy tanks without trouble. On 30 December another tank action knocked out 23 more British tanks for a German loss of seven.

The British were always at a grave disadvantage. While all German tanks had a family resemblance, the British were coping with an amazing collection of different designs that crews had to learn afresh to operate. German tanks were delivered ready for use. When British tanks arrived, they needed overhauling and modifying for the desert, and this took a long time. 'Workshops worked at a leisurely pace with lots of breaks for tea,' said the Eighth Army's inspector of military equipment, J. K. Stanford, who investigated slackness, waste, mismanagement, misappropriation and theft of military equipment on a scale unequalled until the Vietnam war.[18]

Military paperwork was done in Cairo offices which all closed down from 1.15 pm to 5 pm. The whole British supply route from factory to desert workshops has to be blamed for any shortages of fighting equipment. In the rear areas Britain's army showed all of the bloody-mindedness and pernicious practices of prewar trade unions. Stanford said: 'officers, sent down to Suez for tanks spares needed urgently, had to wait a day because ten tons of beer was number one priority for unloading.' British ships were incompetently loaded. Armoured vehicles were known to be transported in ships' holds under five hundred tons of flour. American ships were packed beautifully but British ships, said Stanford, were 'haywire'.

The laxity of all concerned was revealed when a message from Egypt complained about two recently arrived samples of the new Churchill tanks.

> These vehicles were stowed on forward well-deck, unsheeted and unlocked. In consequence vehicles were exposed to sea-water, and when received both tanks had water on floors and showed rust markings nine inches up the walls.

The damage to electrical and wireless gear required fourteen days' expert attention before the tanks could run. The message added: 'All American tanks are dispatched with all crevices and doors pasted up with masking tape . . .'[19]

A follow-up report said that no one from the manufacturers saw the tanks loaded aboard. The Ordnance officer at the port did not inspect them. His staff sergeant entered one tank and noticed that it wasn't properly 'greased up' but reported the fact to nobody.

In addition to the wholesale thefts by local people, the troops in the rear areas stole all manner of equipment that was needed by the fighting men. Compasses and binoculars were coveted. Cigarettes, food and whisky from army stores were supplied by the truckload to local traders by army deserters in bandit gangs. Cars and trucks disappeared by the hundred. Stanford mentions 6,000 missing trucks in connection with one enquiry by his inspection team. The misuse of smaller items was equally damaging to the war effort:

> Anything up to thirteen blankets, stretcher pillows, or hospital sheets were purloined to soften beds. Blankets were used as curtains, carpets, or table-cloths, or nailed on walls to hang uniforms against. By the time 250,000 base details [soldiers] had equipped their beds, had borrowed ammunition boxes to hold their toilet sundries, or mess tins as soap dishes, a torch or a car inspection lamp for night use, a Tannoy set to listen in to a mess radio, and a W.D. padlock to secure their kit-bags, they had a great deal of stuff . . .[20]

Despite the inefficiency of supply services, and the suicidal tactics of the British commanders, there were still plenty of tanks left. The Eighth Army had started the Crusader battle with three times as many medium and heavy tanks as Rommel could field. Held in reserve (some in Egypt, some nearer the front) were 216 heavies, 129 mediums and 150 light tanks. It has been calculated that the British could lose medium and heavy tanks at the rate of four to every German tank lost *and still maintain a superiority of four to one over Rommel's armour.*[21]

There was no drastic change in the methods of British commanders. Always slow to respond to German moves, they failed to understand that, even with endless supplies of armour, cavalry-style charges made by tank formations would end in failure. Rommel had his army intact, and from his bases in Tripolitania he was prepared to continue the war in North Africa for a long time to come.

But while the army repeated its mistakes over and over again, the Desert Air Force was undergoing a remarkable transformation. The RAF had improved its maintenance services beyond recognition and was receiving more and more aircraft. The Luftwaffe's fortunes were waning, as lack of road transport allowed them to retrieve fewer and fewer of their damaged aircraft. By mid-December 1941 fuel shortage had reduced the Luftwaffe to one sortie per day,[22] and the Afrika Korps was getting occasional tastes of fighting an enemy with air superiority.

The threat to Cairo

Rommel threatened Egypt in a way that the Italians had never done. In 1941 this was the only land battle in which the British confronted the enemy with the determination to win. The British, in the words of one historian:

> still saw the Middle East as the epicentre of their struggle. The Suez Canal had become, if not in fact at least in theory, the fulcrum of their power in the world: their oil supplies, their links with India, their dominance of the Arab land mass – all seemed to depend upon their power in Egypt.[23]

Before the war Britain's only standing expeditionary force was one designed to go to Egypt, not France. Even in mid-1940, with an invasion army threatening across the Channel, Churchill sent an armoured brigade and 100 aircraft to Egypt and sent them via the Mediterranean at a time when the army and the navy brass advised him against doing so.

In 1940 and 1941 Cairo – as much as London – became the place from which Britain's war was waged. Technically Egypt was still neutral. Its plump young King Farouk had inherited the throne in 1936 and concerned himself with schemes of economic development and agrarian reform. Now he sat in his palace, surrounded by an entourage of Italians, and was bullied intermittently by a British agent, who confessed to his diary how much he enjoyed the baiting. In these exchanges between king and Foreign Office bureaucrat, British foreign policy was ill-informed and totally devoid of foresight or imagination. Present-day problems throughout the Middle East were created by such men of Whitehall, whose gunboat mentality was in the 1940s a century out of date.

Cairo in 1940 and 1941 provided the world's diplomats with a comfortable ringside seat for the heavyweight bout of the century. The world's Press could get cable facilities, whisky and hot baths in the city when they retired from the front line. In his map-room in Cairo the C-in-C listened to a stream of advice from Churchill and directed warriors in Libya, Greece, Yugoslavia, Crete, Italian East Africa, Persia, Syria, Iraq and on the high seas.

> Every kind of imperial uniform was to be spotted in Cairo, in the first years of the war. There were kilts and turbans and tarbooshes, slouch hats and jodhpurs. There were Kenyan pioneers, and Indian muleteers, and Australian tank crews, and

English gunners, and New Zealand fighter pilots, and South African engineers. There were scholarly staff officers straight from their Oxford colleges, and swaggering extroverts back from secret missions in the Balkans, and rumbustious troopers of the sheep station and the surfing beach.[24]

To lose Egypt would be for the British to lose the war. This is why such thoughts never surfaced in the military offices, bars, brothels, dance halls, nightclubs, open-air movie theatres, gambling salons, expensive restaurants and exclusive clubs of the amazing city of Cairo which, even before the war, had been the gossip capital of the world.

Casualties of the desert

Perhaps this desert war was not modern enough. Few of the gadgets and gimmicks that were necessities by war's end were to be seen in the desert in 1941. Even tank transporters were rarities, and without them tank tracks wore out quickly, causing further supply problems. Engines and all the other machinery of war suffered from the abrasive effect of the sand. The Germans showed the way with mobile workshops, and engineers and repairmen who worked on the battlefield to salvage tanks.

Preliminary bombardments caused a high proportion of the casualties. Neither side had penicillin or sulphonamides. The extensive minefields were a constant menace, and it was in the nature of fighting in this 'tactician's paradise' that men were constantly on the move. Thus their whole bodies were exposed to bullet, mortar and shell. This led to multiple wounds and medical complications. Tank crews, of course, suffered a high percentage of burns, and for wounded men the distances to succour were an added torment:

> An average medical chain at this time could involve successive journeys of 8–12 miles from the Regimental Aid Post [Battalion Aid Station] to the Advanced Dressing Station [Collecting Station]; 80–90 miles further to the Main Dressing Station; another 80 miles to the Casualty Clearing Station, and anything up to 250 miles more to a General Hospital. All these miles had to be covered in lorries with no suspension worth the name, in extremes of heat or cold, and in constant danger of air attack.[25]

Retreating armies have to leave injured men to die, and so retreating armies always show high casualty figures. In the fighting around Sidi Rezegh in November 1941 two New Zealand battalions lost 450 men, 120 of them killed, which was one of the highest casualty rates of any action in the war. Dominion units suffered higher casualty rates than did the British (or later, American) units because they consisted mainly of front-line fighting soldiers, with only a few men serving in the rear.

Submarines and the sea supply lines

In the Mediterranean campaign both sides depended upon supply convoys, and so submarines played an important part in the outcome. The 100 submarines of the Italian fleet were relatively ineffective, but in September 1941 six German U-boats entered the Mediterranean, and on 13 November one of them sank the carrier HMS *Ark Royal*. Less than two weeks later the *U-331* hit the battleship HMS *Barham* with three torpedoes. Still steaming ahead the great ship capsized and her magazines blew up in a titanic explosion that, captured on movie film, is one of the most horrifying sights in a terrible war.

The full-size Italian submarines scored fewer hits than did their tiny two-man electric 'chariots' ridden by frogmen in scuba gear. About 20 feet long, they had two propellers driven by an electric motor. The front section of the device the Italians called a *maiale* or pig was a warhead containing 550 lb of high explosive. The driver steered and dived by means of a control stick, and to guide him he had a compass and simple instruments. Behind him the other member of the team operated the diving-tanks to maintain trim. This daring, dramatic and individualistic form of naval war suited the Italian temperament. On the night of 18 December 1941 the Italian submarine *Sciré*, commanded by Prince Borghese, navigated through a minefield to launch three of them. They followed two Royal Navy destroyers through the anti-torpedo nets into Alexandria harbour. The frogmen teams, led by Tenente Luigi de la Penne, dismounted from their pigs and affixed warheads to the battleships *Queen Elizabeth* and *Valiant* and also to a naval tanker. Captured and held aboard one of the doomed ships, the Italians refused to talk and went down with their victim, but there was only six feet of water under the keels.[26] To keep the successes secret, the Royal Navy carried on as if nothing was wrong with its ships. On Christmas eve there was even a ball aboard *Queen Elizabeth*.

Many months later, when the Italians had changed sides, Admiral Morgan, who had been captain of the *Valiant* at the time of the attack, was present when de la Penne was awarded the Italian Gold Medal for Valour. In a sporting gesture, Morgan stepped forward and pinned the medal upon the man who had sunk his ship.

The Royal Navy submarines depended upon Malta as a base from which to attack the Italian supply lines to Africa. As well as being a submarine base, Malta was often described as an unsinkable air-craft-carrier, but after two weeks in which the inhabitants counted 115 air raids, they began to wonder whether the Axis bomber crews knew that.

The five islands of Malta, totalling 125 square miles of land, are 220 miles away from Tripoli in Libya and 60 miles south from Sicily. Ships approaching the island in wartime often spotted the rising smoke and dust of a bombing raid while still far out at sea. Back in history, chambers and galleries had been cut into the limestone beneath the capital Valetta, and these were enlarged to make shelters where many of the inhabitants spent every night. Some families moved in complete with clothes and furniture.

When Malta or the desert army needed supplies urgently, a convoy would be speeded through from Gibraltar under heavy escort. Seen from afar such convoys looked like a jam-jar at a picnic as the carrier-borne fighters battled against endless bombing and torpedo attacks. When they arrived, half the Maltese population seemed to be crowding the harbour for a glimpse of them, counting the ships, knowing that every packing case that came ashore was an assurance of next week's food ration.

The history of war provides many examples of the stubborn pride and determination that attack brings to a besieged population. In the manner of most garrison towns, Malta had learned to live with the Royal Navy but not to love it. As the bombardment continued for month after month, the Maltese showed no sign of wanting to give up the struggle. By war's end they calculated they had received 16,000 tons of bombs, and the harbour was filled with wrecks. Malta had the unenviable reputation for being the most bombed place in history. In a curious and unprecedented gesture of respect, the whole island was awarded the George Cross, Britain's highest award for valour.[27]

British air and sea operations from Malta and Egypt kept Rommel's supply lines under constant attack. In the autumn of 1941 Rommel blamed his failures on Italian sailors, persuading his masters in Berlin that the desert war was being lost at sea, but the figures do not support this excuse. Although there were desperate days like those in late October when his losses at sea were 75 per cent, such figures testify to the courage and determination of the Italian seamen. Take a broader view and we see that over the second half of 1941 Rommel's losses of fuel at sea were 16.4 per cent and of other supplies 26.8 per cent of the total dispatched. Severe losses, but not more than any prudent staff work would allow for supplies crossing seas where the Royal Navy was relentlessly active.

One can easily imagine how the army high command in Berlin reacted to such messages from Rommel, the Führer's impulsive protégé. The staff assessment from the meticulous Paulus had advised Rommel to be restrained and not over-extend himself. It had proved entirely correct. To prove Paulus wrong, Rommel would have had to husband his fuel, give great attention to his transport and supply line, then capture Tobruk to shorten that line. Rommel failed to do any of those things.

And if Berlin showed less than infinite faith in Rommel's decisions, doubt was also displayed by some of the men under his command. His immediate subordinates had had to pluck the Panzer troops out of Egypt where Rommel's ill-judged advance had landed them, while the rank and file had seen too many of those orderly but demoralizing retreats to think their commanders infallible. On New Year's Morning 1942, General von Vaerst, commander of 15th Panzer Division, went to check his outposts in person.

> From each slit trench the soldiers reported in the prescribed manner. Only one sentry had his field-glasses to his eyes and did not report. 'You must improve in the New Year,' said the general to encourage him. 'I hope Herr General will do the same,' was the reply. Old Vaerst laughed.[28]

If Rommel's crucial battles were being fought by Italian seamen on the supply routes, then the night of 8–9 November 1941 brought a notable defeat for him. Steaming out of Malta, two Royal Navy cruisers and two destroyers fought a night action against a convoy, sinking all seven merchantman and one escort. This, and an attack upon another convoy two weeks later, forced the temporary halting of the convoys.

By this time, Berlin had taken drastic action. Field Marshal Albrecht Kesselring had been sent to restore Rommel's sea supply line. 'Smiling Albert' was appointed Southern Commander (Oberbefehlshaber Süd) and given control of Luftwaffe units in Libya, Greece, Italy and Sicily. He was reinforced with an Air Corps from the Russian front, where winter had now lessened air activity. This experienced force included five bomber wings, Stukas, night fighters and long-range escorts. Kesselring's task was to gain total control of the air and sea lanes between Italy and Africa.

This would have been the moment for a German air assault and occupation of Malta, the key to Rommel's supply route. But it was already too late; the Luftwaffe's parachute army was decimated beyond recovery by the invasion of Crete. Germany's struggle with the Soviet Union was looking less like a blitzkrieg with every day that passed. Kesselring was bound to fail. To some extent his campaign would be lost in the shipyards (where for every ship the Axis build the Allies would build ten), but ships were of little use without trucks to carry supplies to the fighting men. Rommel's pleas for 8,000 trucks went unheeded in Berlin at a time when every German unit on the Eastern Front was crippled by a shortage of transport.

Once Rommel's November advance on Cairo was brought to a halt, it spelt the end of Hitler's ambitions in Africa and the Middle East. One distinguished military history concludes:

> Had Rommel, in November 1941, been fifty percent stronger than he actually was, the probabilities are that he would have taken Tobruk; that Auchinleck would never have dared to attack him; and that, after Tobruk had been eliminated, Rommel would have won Egypt.[29]

If! In fact the North African ports under Rommel's control did not have sufficient capacity to supply an army of the size he needed to take Cairo and hold it.[30] His road transport – which might have swung the balance – was inadequate in quality and quantity, and every reinforcement he received, every mouth, every gun and every tank, made his supply situation worse!

Rommel knew that history books bulge with the names of commanders who captured great cities, but he should have closed his ears to Cairo's siren song that repeatedly enticed him so far from his home and left him to languish. Rommel provides a perfect example of the 'Peter Principle' (that a person competent in certain tasks will be promoted to others he is less able to fulfil).[31] Rommel was a daring, and in every way exceptional, divisional commander, but he needed a superior who could keep him under control and make him understand the less glamorous realities of supply and maintenance.

Mussolini: no more triumphs

Every senior Italian commander knew that the appointment of Kesselring marked the end of Italy as an independent power. Mussolini went to war in June 1940 believing that the British were on the point of surrender. It was, he thought, simply a matter of dividing up the ships and overseas possessions of Britain and France. But after eighteen months, the real loser was Italy. There were grave shortages of cereals and oil and by the end of 1941 foreign exchange was so scarce that Italy's diplomatic corps had to be paid partly in lire. The fine Italian fleet – in which every Italian took such pride – had taken a battering and German U-boats roamed the Mediterranean. Italian East Africa had been conquered by the British and the Greek army had given the Italian army a bloody nose. Troops in Italian Libya were commanded by a German general, and Kesselring's appointment meant that the Germans had their army and air force based on the sacred soil of Italy. Count Ciano, Italy's foreign minister, wrote in his diary on 5 November 1941:

> Mussolini has swallowed the toad. He realizes the meaning of Kesselring's arrival in the general war situation, and within the country, but, like a good player, he takes the blow, and pretends that he doesn't feel it.[32]

By this time Mussolini had become so disillusioned that he engaged in regular anti-German outbursts to his followers, relishing the German setbacks in Russia, and telling them that if Germany could not be vanquished by arms, it would surely collapse in the end. At this time many Italians viewed the prospect of some sort of revolution in Germany as inevitable. The Germans thought the same about Italy, and also about Britain. The British thought that their bombing of German cities would soon precipitate revolution in Germany. It was a time of wishful thinking.

On 3 December 1941, the Japanese ambassador told Mussolini, who had been dragged into a war with Soviet Russia, that, under the terms of the Tripartite Pact, Italy would now have to declare war upon the United States. Mussolini accepted calmly the idea of war with America, but when he spoke from his balcony the crowd was 'not very enthusiastic'. It was three o'clock in the afternoon, Ciano reflected in his diary, the people were hungry and the day was quite cold. 'These are all elements which do not make for enthusiasm.'

The future

The 'unenthusiastic' crowd listening to Mussolini declare war on America were more perceptive than the Duce. Many Italians with relatives settled in the New World had a better knowledge of the United States and its resources than Mussolini, the King and Ciano would ever have. Soon they would all have a chance to meet and know Americans at first hand. Victorious Anglo-American armies would mass in North Africa and invade the Continent of Europe by sea from the south, and that meant Sicily, and then Italy. Italy would change sides and every mile of it would suffer. Its monuments and treasures and its people would not emerge intact. Mussolini was to be shot by Italian partisans and, with his mistress, to hang upside-down, like a carcass of meat, in a public square in Milan.

In mid-1942 Rommel's battlefield listening service, Fernmeldeaufklärung, was overrun and its chief killed. From captured papers the British saw how much intelligence material Rommel had received from their careless use of radio, and as a result radio discipline was tightened. Messages employed new codes and all sorts of false messages were inserted into the daily transmissions. It was also in the summer of 1942 that the US ambassador in Cairo was recalled and Rommel lost that incomparable source of intelligence too. From now onwards Rommel's genius is more severely tested.

The hardest fighting was yet to come. Germany's titanic assault upon Soviet Russia had shown, to those who wanted to see it, how puny were the forces Britain deployed. Until the end of 1942 Britain never faced more than four weak divisions out of Germany's total of 200. But the last words about events still to come should be those of the men fighting in the desert. The official British medical history gives an intimate glimpse into the minds of the soldiers in the Middle East in 1941:

> There was a general expectation amongst men in the M.E.F. that they would suffer much the same fate as their fathers, who had been glibly promised a 'country fit for heroes to live in' and had subsequently spent many years drawing unemployment benefits ... Men worried about their pay and the pay of their dependants; they had no confidence in the help dependants would receive in the event of their own death in the service of their country, and they frequently pointed to the vastly superior amenities enjoyed by soldiers from other parts of the British Empire and by American soldiers.

Part Four

THE WAR IN THE AIR

17 THE WARS BEFORE THE WAR

I always regarded instruction as a come-down,
a confession that the pilot was finished,
no use at the front, and condemned to flip young
aspirants round and round the aerodrome day after day on
obsolete types of machines.

Cecil Lewis, First World War fighter pilot[1]

MANY FEATURES of that earlier clash between the German and the British armies foreshadowed those of the Second World War. So it was with the air forces.[2] The British; spontaneous, ill-prepared, and resistant to modern methods and machines, depended upon their ability to muddle through. The Germans believed that improvisation must be based upon training and preparation, and the high esteem in which they held science and engineering made them receptive to new machines and new ideas.

Aerial combat was something in which Canadian pilots excelled. Canadians provided the backbone and the most effective elements of Britain's Royal Flying Corps, later to be renamed the Royal Air Force. Twenty-five British pilots were credited with 30 or more victories and ten of these were Canadians.[3] It was no coincidence that the Canadian government spent nearly $10,000 on the preliminary flying training of each of their pilots, while the British government spent £1,030 (about $4,000) on the entire training of each of theirs.[4]

With such drastic economy, crashes were common. One RFC flyer claimed that 'accidents in training were everyday occurrences and every training centre had its funeral fund, deducted from the weekly mess bills.'[5].

During the First World War, more British pilots were killed in training than were killed by the enemy, while German deaths in training were about a quarter of those killed in action. Asked about this chilling statistic in June 1918, Britain's secretary of state for Air blamed it on a lack of discipline among the trainees and gave a patronizing aside about the very high standards of the 'semi-trained Canadians'.

The British were determined to believe that the outstanding contribution to the war made by Canadian, Australian and New Zealand fighting men was due to the outdoor life they enjoyed in the colonies. Britain's chief aeromedicine researcher explained that these men from overseas had benefited from a 'lack of coddling, together with cold baths in the morning and cross-country tramping in all weathers'. It sounded comfortingly like the regime in Britain's most exclusive private schools. In fact, such rationalization was just the government's way of pretending that training and equipment were not important. Most of the successful Canadian pilots had grown up in towns.

Despite the emphasis the British army's high commanders laid upon air reconnaissance photography, the RFC provided no special training for observers. Long after it had become obvious that securing high-definition pictures was a demanding task, the British two-seaters were carrying in the back seat any volunteer who happened to be nearby at the time of take-off. The French were no better, and admitted that their air photos had failed to observe the Germans moving 23 divisions into place in five days in May 1918.

Reconnaissance failures occurred despite the obsession that the RFC showed with having their aircraft ceaselessly patrolling the German positions. 'Dawn Patrol' became a legendary necessity. Air force commanders explained that such patrolling gave a moral lift to British airmen and would lower German morale. In fact most Germans were out of sight in deep, comfortable dug-outs that only a direct hit by the heaviest missiles could penetrate.

German air commanders did not share this unsophisticated reasoning. They flew their reconnaissance missions when they needed them, and used their fighter force to shoot down enemy planes when they entered German airspace. The British assigned squadrons to their armies, so that aircraft were evenly distributed along the front. The Germans used aircraft where they were needed. Employing tents as hangars, a 'flying circus' could concentrate unexpectedly, achieve local air superiority, and then move on to another assignment. The British always delighted in the amateur approach, and this was especially true of the flying service. The eccentric commanding officer was revered. Violent horseplay in the mess, and improvised equipment, were regarded as being altogether essential to the British way of waging war.

The German air force, like the army, was run on strictly professional lines. Training was thorough, and to secure results observers were often given command of the aircraft. Fighter pilots were selected from men with two-seater experience. In a war in which superior altitude usually provided the victory, German flyers were equipped by early 1917 with electrically heated clothing, constantly improved instruments and parachutes.

The parachute was a device the British command resisted on the grounds that providing them would lower morale. The tacit implication was that with them British flyers would jump to safety rather than fight. Not until 1935 did the RAF seriously test parachutes.

Statistics of the First World War reveal the value of German thoroughness. According to the figures issued to the Press in February 1919 (and repeated in the Official History) the British suffered 6,166 dead airmen compared with the Germans' 5,853. Considering that the British air force shared the Western Front with the French air force, while the Germans fought both enemies and flew on their Eastern Front as well, these figures are deplorable. Even so, the British official air historian thought the true ratio far worse. Like other historians, he believed that the German archives in Potsdam were correct in recording that German fatalities amounted to less than a quarter of the British losses. (See Table 4. Each side of course had reliable figures for its own casualties but had to estimate the enemy's.)

Table 4   Airmen killed (Potsdam archives)

	German	British
1915	27	50
1916	67	357
1917	296	1,811
1918	662	2,508

Many who thought the British statistics had been doctored had new reasons to think so in 1922 when His Majesty's Stationery Office published statistics that, apart from other discrepancies, added up to the (clearly impossible) conclusion that 44 per cent of all British air casualties came in the final seven months of the war.

In the final months of the war changes of tactics and weaponry foreshadowed those of the Second World War. In time for the Kaiser's Battle – their major offensive in March 1918 – the German Air Service created Schlachtstaffeln. These squadrons of two-seaters were equipped with machine-guns and small bombs and trained to attack infantry flying extremely low 'to shatter the enemy's nerve'.

Such units were under the orders of the ground force commander and were used only at the decisive point of attack. They were not sent to scour the battlefront in the way that the British flyers were.

In the summer of 1918 the British improved on the German ideas, assigning aircraft to low-level attacks and sending them to support tanks. Their task was to knock out field artillery that was the worst threat to the armoured force. In these early days of armoured warfare there were no anti-tank guns. Air-to-ground wireless was still very primitive, and contact between air and ground units was maintained by flares and visual signals. By 1939, with better communications, these ideas would have been incorporated into German Blitzkrieg theory.

Zeppelins and strategic bombing

Load-carrying aircraft were slow to develop. The very first passenger-carrying airline started in January 1914. Wrapped in heavy flying kit, only one passenger per flight was taken from Tampa in Florida to nearby St Petersburg.

By this time Count Zeppelin's airships had flown 37,250 passengers over a 90,000-mile network of air routes without death or injury. Zeppelins started the era of scheduled passenger flights in 1900, long before the Wright brothers. The German army and navy were quick to form airship squadrons and, when war came, they were used for reconnaissance and bombing on both Eastern and Western fronts. In November 1914, Grand Admiral Alfred von Tirpitz wrote that if the Zeppelins could go and start thirty fires in London, 'what in a small way is odious would retire before something fine and powerful.'[6] In other words, the end justifies the means. By 1915 the German naval airship service was ready for its first raid on England.

At about 8 pm on the evening of 19 January, two airships reached the English coast near Ingham in Norfolk. Naval airship L.3 turned south and dropped seven bombs on Yarmouth, killing two people and injuring three. Meanwhile L.4 turned the other way and followed the coast round The Wash to drop seven 50-kg high-explosive bombs on King's Lynn. They killed a man and a woman and injured thirteen others.[7]

As the weather improved such raiders were to be sighted over London. The effect of the airship raids upon the government, and to a lesser extent upon the public, far outweighed the destruction they wrought. From now onwards a great deal of energy and time was devoted to the air-raid threat. Fighter planes were modified to climb as high as the airships and attack them with incendiary bullets that would ignite the hydrogen gas. New high-altitude Zeppelins were built. Soon Britain's air defence became a contest for altitude.

Airship losses persuaded the Germans to produce long-range heavy bombers, such as the Gothas and the Staakens. The word 'Gotha' (like 'Zeppelin' and 'U-boat') began to inspire horror and detestation in Britain. By war's end about 280 tons of bombs had been dropped on London, killing 1,413 people, most of them civilians.[8] While these deaths and the material losses played no part in deciding the outcome of the war, the moral and political effects of the German raids on London were grave and far-reaching.

As a direct result of bombing attacks in the summer of 1917, the British hurriedly created an Air Ministry. Its minister was instructed to amalgamate the Royal Naval Air Service and the army's Royal Flying Corps. The report[9] that advised this course of action added: 'Air power can be used as an independent means of war operations ... And the day may not be far off when aerial operations with their devastation of enemy lands and destruction of industrial and populous centres on a vast scale may become the principal operations of war, to which older forms of military operations may become secondary and subordinate.'

The British did not allow the raids on their towns to go unrevenged. By October 1917 there was a wing of Allied bombers dedicated to raiding Germany. In June 1918 this unit, which included French, Italian and American aircraft, was named the Independent Air Force. It was the brain-child of the commander-in-chief of the Royal Flying Corps in France, Brigadier-General Sir Hugh 'Boom' Trenchard, who became chief of air staff of the Royal Air Force when it was created on 1 April 1918. When the war ended the IAF disappeared from history, but from now onwards Trenchard's 'bomber barons' dominated the RAF's spending and its policies.

Hermann Göring

As a fighter pilot, Göring ended the First World War with Germany's highest award for valour, the Pour le Mérite, and command of the Richthofen squadron. He was proud of his association with the world's most successful fighter pilot, and later in his career he had for his personal use three identical all-red Junkers Ju 52 air-liners bearing the name Manfred von Richthofen.[10] A respectable middle-class hero, his membership of the Nazi party was valuable to Hitler. After being wounded in the unsuccessful Nazi putsch in Munich in November 1923, he was smuggled across the frontier to Austria. The delay in getting his wounds treated led to fevers and great pain, which were alleviated by morphine. For the rest of his life he was prey to the drug, although there were periods during which he was able to resist his addiction.[11] When Göring was taken into custody by the US army at war's end, the prison psychiatrist, Dr Douglas M. Kelley, estimated that Göring was taking one hundred paracodeine tablets a day. Keeping them in a large bottle on his desk he had fed himself a few periodically, in the way that a smoker uses cigarettes. The estimated daily intake was equal to three or four grains of morphine. It was not a large dose compared to other addicts, and the doctor cut his intake down until he took none at all.[12]

Göring was an exhibitionist, perhaps a transvestite, who delighted in dressing up in fancy uniforms and curious, often effem-inate, 'hunter's dress'. He made no secret of this habit, and many people remarked upon his heavily made-up face. Most of the Nazi leaders complained that he was lazy, a condition not helped by addiction and obesity. During the Second War he certainly devoted far more time to buying, exchanging and plundering paintings and works of art than he did to running the Luftwaffe.

Historians have preferred to categorize Göring as a buffoon, but this is not the impression he left upon people who had the chance to see him at close quarters. Sir Norman Birkett, a judge at the Nuremberg trials, said:

> it has been obvious that a personality of outstanding, though possibly evil qualities was seated there in the dock. Nobody seems to have been quite prepared for his immense ability and knowledge and his thorough mastery and understanding of the captured documents. Suave, shrewd, adroit, capable, resource-ful, he quickly saw the elements of the situation, and as his self-confidence grew, his mastery became more apparent. His self-control, too, was remarkable and to all the other qualities manifested in his evidence he added the resonant tones of his speaking voice, and the eloquent but restrained use of gesture.[13]

When Hitler gained power, he gave Göring control of Germany's civil and military aviation. Such concentration of authority caused little or no surprise in Europe, where aviation had remained under tight political control since the war. In 1919, led by the French, the signatories of the peace conference signed a Convention for the Regulation of Aerial Navigation. It showed how determined all governments were to control every aspect of aviation. The prospect of 'freedom of the skies' terrified Europe, which remained feudal in mentality. Using the excuse that foreign aviators might see their towns, docks and arsenals, every government formulated strait-jackets of licences and permits. This was the start of the subsidies, cartels and price-fixing that still today prevent competition between European airlines.

Yet Göring's power was not confined to the air. When the Nazis formed their first government in 1933, Göring – already Prussian minister of the interior – created the concentration camps into which political opponents were tossed without trial. He took under his ministerial control Prussia's political police office, which became known as the 'Gestapo'. No less important was Göring's creation of the Forschungsamt (FA), a wire-tapping organization that listened in to phone conversations. Berlin's foreign embassies provided choice secrets. Some of the FA reports influenced the course of history, as intercepts told Hitler that the British had decided not to come to the aid of Austria, and then that they had decided to abandon Czechoslovakia as well.

The FA used the Magnetofon, the world's first tape recorder, and a punchcard index that could be sorted by Hollerith machines, an early type of data processor. Bugged conversations were graded and cross-referenced. Typed copies of private conversations could be put into the hands of those who needed them within minutes. No one was exempt. Goebbels's phone calls to his mistress – Lida Baarova, a Czech actress – were carefully monitored, as were the 'intrigues' of the US ambassadors.

The listening service gave Göring immense power over his fellow Nazis, and made him important to Hitler in a way that none of the other leaders were. From FA intercepts Hitler became convinced that Ernst Röhm and his army of SA brownshirts were plotting against him. The plot was ended in the summer of 1934 when Röhm, and many other opponents of the regime, fell victim to Himmler's murder squads on 'the Night of the Long Knives'. Many said that Göring, and his ally Himmler (and on a secondary level Blomberg and Milch), had duped Hitler, using the murders to remove rivals and secure dominant positions in the Nazi hierarchy.

All Göring's early work for Hitler and the Nazis was rewarded in December 1934 when Hitler named him both deputy and successor. Soon, as well as controlling civil aviation and making preparations for a military air arm (forbidden under the terms of the peace treaty), he was given supervisory powers in respect of the production of gasoline and synthetic rubber. He assumed control of all foreign exchange reserves (from Hjalmar Schacht, the Reichsbank president) and also of iron, fertilizers and margarine. Before long permits to import such strategic materials as tungsten, chrome and nickel had to be secured from him.

By the end of 1936 Göring's creeping command over the German economy was ratified in a secret memorandum from Hitler. It gave Göring control of the 'Four Year Plan' and made him economic supremo of the whole nation. At the end of four years, said Hitler's written instructions, he wanted a nation and an army prepared for war. Meanwhile industrialists needing contracts, import licences or foreign exchange had to go to Göring for them. They were to discover that massive bribes usually made him adequately sympathetic to their cause.

But Göring's role as master of the economy did not mean a lessening of his interest in aviation. The massive new Air Ministry building he commissioned in Berlin was a showpiece containing 2,800 rooms, which soon filled with squabbling officers and ambitious bureaucrats.

The Spanish Civil War

The story of Spain's civil war starts in late July 1936. General Francisco Franco, a retired chief of staff who had been banished to the Canary Islands, rallied support amongst Spanish soldiers there and in Morocco. With the Spanish army everywhere declaring its opposition to the newly elected left-wing government, Franco borrowed some of Hitler's transport planes to ferry Moorish troops from Spanish Africa to the mainland so that they could fight and overturn the Republican government. Paul Fussell sardonically explained the Spanish Civil War with the words: 'The tradition in Hispanic countries . . . is that when democratic governments go too far with reforms, the army must step in to preserve Christianity, private property and order.'[14]

That certainly represented the view of the conflict that was to be found in the radio broadcasts and newspapers of Britain, France and the United States at the time. Nowadays history books provide a more complex story, less easy to judge. The Republican government, the Popular Front or Loyalists as they were sometimes called, was a loose and unhappy coalition of Communists, anarchists, 'radicalists' and Socialists whose programme included a drastic redistribution of wealth and property. As well as land reform and workers' rights, there was to be a reduction in the size and power of the army and a curbing of the role of the Catholic Church, particularly in education. With such a programme the new government did not have to look far for enemies, especially when it claimed a mandate from less than 50 per cent of votes cast. To add to the dismay reforming began within hours of the February 1936 election.

Gangs of left-wing militants burned churches and took over private and public property; the government – weak and divided – did little to stop the excesses. Instead the army was sent home on leave and the Civil Guard was restricted to barracks. Right-wing gangs responded violently, so that some regions drifted into anarchy. In Madrid 'every dawn found fresh bodies dumped into the gutter: victims of rival death squads.'[15]

Then on 17 July 1936 senior army officers staged a military coup. In the capital, Madrid, it failed but several important Spanish cities came under their control. During the night of 18–19 July the prime minister resigned and Martinez Barrio, a moderate known for his skills in political compromise, was asked to form a government. He phoned General Emilio Mola, the leader of the right-wing military factions, and offered him a seat in the government. Mola said:

> Everyone is ready for battle. If I tell these men now that I have made an arrangement with you, the first head to roll will be mine. The same would happen to you in Madrid. Neither of us can control our masses.[16]

On this same day, Sunday 19 July, with civil war breaking out, General Franco sent a message to Rome asking Mussolini for bombing planes. Three days later he asked the Germans for planes to transport soldiers from Tetuan in Spanish Morocco to mainland Spain. There was no other way to get them across the Strait of Gibraltar. The sailors of the Spanish navy had taken control of their ships on behalf of the Republican government, and two cruisers and two destroyers were on patrol to prevent Franco moving troops by sea.

While the navy supported the Republicans, the army, including the rank and file, was mostly opposed to them, so the Republicans formed an army of their own. They depended upon a mostly untrained collection of men with odds and ends of weapons, wearing armbands instead of uniforms. Local armies were formed by political parties and trade unions. So divided were the views of their supporters that in May 1937 the Republican army had to fight a Trotskyist force (POUM) and anarchists (FAI) to get to Barcelona.[17]

The world took sides. The Republicans were supported by the government of the Soviet Union. About 40,000 foreign volunteers comprising a broad spectrum of anti-Fascists and democrats came from all over the world to fight for them. Among them were 10,000 Frenchmen, 5,000 Germans and Austrians and 5,000 Poles. Smaller numbers came from Italy, Britain and the United States. About 10,000 medical staff also volunteered for service, and they were sorely needed, for a large proportion of the volunteers became casualties. Writers and intellectuals in the West were almost unanimous in their support of the Republicans. A questionnaire about the war, circulated to 145 such people in 1937, discovered only five supporting Franco.

Throughout his life Franco was noted for his good luck, and it did not fail him when he requested help from Germany. The Berlin War Office and Foreign Ministry refused to accept Franco's emissaries (two Germans with a Spanish officer). Showing commendable determination, these men went and sought out Hitler at the Wagner Festival in Bayreuth. They spotted him outside the Festspielhaus and, 'out of the euphoric mood of the moment, without consulting the ministers concerned, the decision was taken to lend active support to Franco.'[18]

Göring, who was also attending the Wagner festival, was ordered to give help to Franco and, all told, the Germans were unstinting with their aid. Twenty Junkers Ju 52/3m, three-engined transport aircraft, flew to Seville. Met there by a Luftwaffe officer,[19] the pilots were told: 'Maps don't exist; I have made a few calculations on a piece of paper about routes and flight times to Tetuan; apart from that follow me and land where I land!'

In Morocco men of the Spanish Foreign Legion were waiting. By squashing anything up to three dozen men into planes designed to carry a dozen, 3,000 soldiers were ferried to Spain in one day! Before long the SS *Usaramo* was steaming from Hamburg to Cadiz with spare parts for the Junkers, and with 85 Luftwaffe personnel and six Heinkel He 51 biplane fighters. At the end of November a far bigger German unit was on its way – a fighter group (three He 51 fighter squadrons), four squadrons of Junkers Ju 52/3m aircraft adapted for use as bombers, and a reconnaissance squadron with Heinkel He 70 aircraft. Seaplanes, anti-aircraft units and fully equipped maintenance staff went too. The existence of this Condor Legion was kept secret for as long as possible. On paper, the Luftwaffe personnel were designated as civilians who had personally volunteered for service in the war.

By August 1937 the first of the Casa Legionaria, a 'volunteer' group of the Italian Air Force, had arrived to help Franco. They were equipped with nine Savoia Marchetti SM.81 Pipistrello three-engined bombers, some Fiat biplane fighters and two-seat reconnaissance biplanes.

In mid-September help for the Republicans had started to arrive at Cartagena. It was an advance party of Russians awaiting Polikarov I-15 Chato biplane fighters and the Tupolev SB-2 high-speed bombers that Stalin was sending by ship. Soon after this, a complete squadron of the Red Air Force, with I-16 monoplane fighters, nick-named 'Rata' (rat), arrived at Bilbao. By November most of these aircraft were in action and large-scale air battles were becoming common. By the time the war ended, Russia had sent about 1,000 aircraft to Spain, compared to 600 supplied by Germany and 660 by Italy.

Lessons were learned very quickly. The large tight formations of the Republicans proved vulnerable to the aggressive tactics of Franco's flyers. The Germans, who pioneered loose formations of pairs, discovered that their Heinkel biplanes were inferior to the Rata, and that it was not easy to overtake the Russian SB-2 bombers. Eventually these Heinkel fighters were fitted with bomb racks and used in the fighter-bomber role.

Like Germany and Italy, the Soviet Union sent its very best equipment to Spain. The I-16 Rata, a low-wing monoplane with retractable landing gear and enclosed cockpit, was the world's first modern fighter. A British pilot who flew one said:

> The cockpit was narrow and uncomfortable despite the tubby fuselage. The instruments were basic – there was no fuel gauge or radio – and chaotically arranged. . . . The controls were all sensitive, and its featherlight ailerons gave a high rate of roll.

The Rata was agile and had an outstanding zoom-climb capability.
Top speed was 283 mph at 10,000 ft, but acceleration was surprisingly poor in the dive, when the nose showed a tendency to rise and
a rigidly mounted engine caused the airplane to shake and rattle
through the whole flight envelope. This made the Rata a poor gun
platform.[20]

Despite its limitations, the Rata – with engines and armament frequently updated – not only did well against the German and Italian
biplane fighters but proved more than a match for the Messerschmitt Bf 109B. Although the fighting fronts had varied fortunes,
during the spring of 1937 the Rata and the high-speed Tupolev
bombers gave the Republicans virtual control of the skies. Aces
emerged; the Americans, Albert G. Baumler and Frank G. Tinker,
were each credited with ten victories. Russian pilots were also
making names for themselves and many of the successful ones –
such as Ivan Serov – became famous aces in the Second World War.
So did Adolf Galland and Werner Mölders of the Condor Legion,
who went back to Germany to teach many of the tactics and formations that remain standard even today.

Foreign volunteers for the Republican cause were organized into
various battalions of the International Brigade. These formations
were largely composed of unmilitary idealists, but there was no lack
of political advice for them. Each unit was provided with a political
commissar and there were left-wing visitors too. The diary of one of
the British volunteers recorded:

> *Tuesday March 9th.* Reveille at 4. 30 am. Went up into the
> lines, marching in silence. Raining hard. All the same, everyone
> cheerful and tidy. Took up our positions in the reserve lines.
> Had a visit from the editor of 'New Masses' and four other
> American comrades.
> *Wednesday March 10th.* Pleasant morning. Not much firing, but
> shells falling very near us. Visit from the poet Stephen Spender.
> Had a surprise when reading Daily Worker of March 4th. It re-
> ports my death.
> *Saturday, March 13th.* It's very moving to hear the men, soaked
> to the skin, singing the Internationale.[21]

But the publicity sometimes backfired. The casualties suffered by
the foreign volunteers were awesome. One participant wrote:
'Where three weeks before on this same road there had been 900

1 Before Munich – Winston Churchill talks earnestly in Whitehall to Lord Halifax, Secretary of State for Foreign Affairs, after returning from the Continent in March 1938

2 General Wilhelm Keitel, Hitler's Army Chief of Staff, in conversation with the Führer on a flight to Munich in March 1938

3 Hitler receives Prime Minister Chamberlain at Obersalzberg in September 1938 – the prime move in 'appeasement'

4 Admirals Erich Raeder and Karl Dönitz planning the German U-boat campaign in the North Atlantic, October 1939

5 Six days after becoming prime minister, Churchill flew to France for talks on the imminent collapse with General Gamelin and General Lord Gort, commander of the British Expeditionary Force, May 1940

6 General Erwin Rommel, after sweeping through France in May 1940, became the notorious 'Desert Fox' of North Africa

7 Hitler meets the fascist Spanish dictator General Franco, October 1940

8 General Thomas Blamey, commander of Australian forces in the Middle East, talks to troops just returned from Crete to Palestine

9 General 'Dick' O'Connor with the Commander-in-Chief of British forces in the Middle East, General Sir Archibald Wavell, outside Bardia, Libya, January 1941

10 General Sir John Dill , Chief of the Imperial General Staff, with the Foreign
Secretary Anthony Eden in Cairo, March 1941

11 Prime Minister Churchill inspecting part of Britain's defences in 1940 with a Tommy gun under his arm

12 Hitler discussing progress of the war with the Italian fascist dictator Benito
Mussolini, August 1941

13 The German Luftwaffe chief, Field Marshal Hermann Göring, with his deputy Field Marshal Erhard Milch, March 1942

14 Joseph Stalin, the Soviet communist dictator

15 General Douglas MacArthur, Commander-in-Chief of all US forces in the
Far East, with President Roosevelt

16 General Arthur Percival, commander of Allied troops in Malaya – a clever and experienced leader who was utterly vanquished by a ferocious Japanese force employing 6,000 bicycles

17 Stalin's trusted General Georgi Zhukov began his career in the Tsar's dragoons and defeated first the Japanese and then the Germans

18, 19 General Tomoyuki Yamashita, the 'Tiger of Malaya', who was forbidden to return to Japan, and Admiral Isoruku Yamamoto, once a student of Harvard University, who master-minded the attack on Pearl Harbor

20 General Hideki Tojo, first Japan's war minister and then prime minister

Americans in two battalions, there were now 280. Wally Tapsall led the last of the 360 men of the British Battalion to join the Americans on the road – there were 37 of them, hardly enough for a section.'[22] The 15th International Brigade had in three weeks gone from close on 2,500 men to fewer than 600 survivors.

The most publicized air action of the war came soon afterwards, when, on 26 April 1937, German planes made a cruel and prolonged attack on Guernica, near Bilbao. Guernica was a town sacred to the Basques and was quite without defences. It was market day and many civilians were killed.[23] 'For more than an hour these eighteen planes, never more than a few hundred metres in altitude, dropped bomb after bomb on Guernica,' said a young Basque priest who was there at the time. 'The aeroplanes left around seven o'clock, and then there came another wave of them, this time flying at an immense altitude. They were dropping incendiary bombs on our martyred city. The new bombardment lasted thirty-five minutes, sufficient to transform the town into an enormous furnace.'[24]

Guernica was near the fighting front. Newspapermen were in the vicinity and the bombing received maximum publicity. Some said that the air attack was a cold-blooded military experiment by the German airmen. Even now feelings have not cooled, but the best research I can find[25] says that the Germans probably considered it a legitimate military target, a place where the Republican-Basque forces could regroup. The bombing of Guernica was perhaps the single most influential action of the war. Reports of the bombing played a major role in gaining the world's sympathy. Publications such as *Time*, *Life* and *Newsweek* gave their voice to the Republican cause.

In Berlin a secret report from a German navy staff officer said that such attacks on objects of little military importance seemed to strengthen the opponent's resistance rather than breaking it.[26] The report added: 'The memory of the air attack on Guernica by the Condor Legion still today [July 1938] affects the population and permits no friendly feelings for Germany in the population of the Basques, who earlier were thoroughly friendly to Germany and in no manner communistic.'

Luftwaffe professionals were critical of the attack on Guernica for another reason. Its planning and operation were an example of all too frequent Luftwaffe bungling. Most of the bomb-aimers simply dropped their loads into dust clouds and smoke they saw rising from the first explosions in the town centre. The targets they were sent to hit – a bridge and road junction east of the town – were not touched.[27]

In the final weeks of the war a few new Messerschmitt fighters arrived in Spain. This Emil version of the Bf 109 had been modified in the light of the excellent performance the Russian Ratas had shown over Spain. The Bf 109, in its many versions, remained in production until the end of the Second World War, by which time over 33,000 of them had been built. Eric Hartmann, the highest-scoring fighter pilot in history, used nothing but this machine.

Primarily an arena for the Luftwaffe, the Spanish Civil War was used as a laboratory by all the German armed forces. Their personnel rotated back to Germany in order to give active service to as many men as possible. At one time 10,000 Germans were serving in Spain. A wide range of weapons and methods were tested. During the Catalonia offensive, in the later stages of the war, the 8.8-cm Flak gun (which had emphatically proved its worth against aircraft) was towed behind tanks to serve as artillery against ground targets.

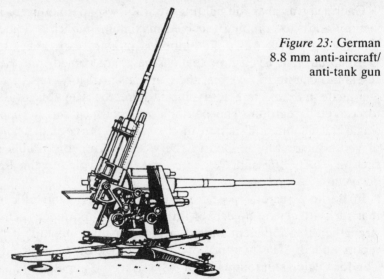

Figure 23: German 8.8 mm anti-aircraft/ anti-tank gun

Documents reveal that Hitler's primary aim at this time was not to help Franco end the war quickly.[28] Spain's civil war produced instability so that Western sympathies were sharply divided. Hitler enjoyed the benefits that came from politicians, and commentators, in discord.

As spring arrived in 1939, Spain's civil war ended in victory for Franco. Among the war's casualties were the hopes and idealism of the men who had gone to fight there. It had been a confrontation of totalitarian forces of left and right, with both sides committing abominable atrocities upon their enemies and innocents alike. People were slaughtered because of what they were rather than what they had done. Men who wanted bread for their families were killed for being Red agitators. Workers who owned books were killed as Communists. Men who cultivated their own tiny patches of land were killed for being capitalists. Republican prisoners were sentenced to death for armed rebellion.[29] Priests were slaughtered for being priests, and their servants were put to death for being the servants of priests. Both sides were ruled by men who saw no place on earth for their opponents.

For those who believe in the power of wealth the result was predictable. The Republicans had started out with many advantages, such as a stable currency and 700 tons of gold (worth $788m). Franco had no alternative but to fight a war on credit. One Texan oil company supplied him with $6m worth of oil and, upon being told they were breaking America's Neutrality Act, shipped still more via Italy.[30] Franco ended the war owing $225m to Germany and $273m to Italy. The Republicans, on the other hand, paid Stalin (mostly in gold) $600m for Russian armaments. Thus Germany and Italy had a vested interest in a Franco victory; it was the only way for them to recoup their money. Stalin, whose secret police, and teams of murderers,[31] unceasingly terrorized and manipulated the Spanish Republican leadership, could philosophically shrug at each Republican defeat. In November 1938 he finally decided to let Spain go.[32] The military and police advisers, and the hard-core Stalinists of the International Brigade, were withdrawn. Arms shipments ended.

By 30 March 1939 Franco's air forces were triumphant everywhere, and the leading ace of the war was Garcia Morato who, in more than 500 combat sorties, had scored 36 victories against the Republicans. On 4 April Morato was ordered to Griñon, south of Madrid, to take part in a film about the Condor Legion. Morato's mock dogfight ended as he stalled at the top of a steep climb and crashed. He was killed.

It was 22 May 1939 when the Condor Legion, in a formal ceremony at León, disbanded for return to Germany. A new war was only three months away and the men of the Condor Legion scarcely had time to change their badges before they were resuming their roles and fighting another enemy.

German flyers had returned to Germany with the exciting news that bombers could escape fighters and Flak by virtue of speed, something that both the He 111 and the SB-2 had done in Spain, although eventually the SB-2 had suffered heavy casualties. More far-reaching was their conviction that air power was at its most effective when used in close support of ground forces. In Spain there was no opportunity for anything in the nature of strategic bombing. The Spaniards were reluctant to batter to destruction the towns for which they fought. Wolfram von Richthofen, chief of staff to the Condor Legion and cousin to the First War ace, had had little alternative but to do what the army wanted. Working on his own initiative, and sometimes against strong opposition, he subordinated his air force to the requirements of army commanders. At first there had not been even rudimentary communications between ground and air units, but by war's end Luftwaffe officers serving with the front-line infantry were directing air strikes closely coordinated with the army's movements. All these techniques were studied closely in Berlin and written into training programmes.

In Britain the army minister, Leslie Hore-Belisha, suggested that the Spanish Civil War had shown the value of close air support. Britain's chief of air staff would have none of that. He immediately condemned it as a gross misuse of air power, and even after Germany's lightning campaign against Poland in 1939, Britain's air staff kept their heads pressed deeply into the sand. They issued a memorandum archly reiterating 'the Air Staff view – which is based on a close study of the subject over many years': aircraft must not be used to support armies on the battlefield. It was, said these high-ranking airmen, 'not only very costly in casualties but is normally uneconomical and ineffective'. The truth was that these entirely negative views, like their equally negative views about using aircraft for defence of the sea lanes, were simply the RAF brasshats showing fear that their authority might be eroded by cooperation with the army or the Royal Navy.

The most notable failure the German airforce suffered in Spain was discovering that even its most experienced bomber crews could not find their targets in bad weather or at night. An urgent request for some sort of radio navigation aid led to an immediate adaptation of the Lorenz airfield landing system to the task of target finding. It would be a long long time before the RAF admitted to any failing of that kind.

18 PREPARATIONS

I've seen the Reichsmarschall [Göring] nod off in
mid-conference – for instance, if the conferences went
on too long and the morphine wore off.
That was the commander in chief of our air force!

Luftwaffe General Helmut Forster

<hr>

BUILDING A FLEET of warships was an easy task compared to creating an air force. An air force had to start with the design and construction of training aircraft. Teachers and instructors had to be found and schooled. A construction industry had to be developed, and be complete with advanced research and design facilities. Airfields, with attendant technology, had to be built. Only then could an air force have ever-improving front-line machines, and a regular supply of skilled men to fly them.

Hitler and his Nazis came to power in 1933. He could not have taken Germany to war six years later without the resolute preparations put into effect by the Weimar Republic (as the democratic parliamentary governments of the period 1919–33 are conveniently known). It was during this pre-Hitler period that Germany signed the treaty of Rapallo, whereby the Soviet Red Army collaborated with the Germans to flout the terms of the Versailles peace treaty. Secret establishments in the Soviet Union were used for testing new weapons, and for secret training of German military flyers and tank crews. Here in the years from 1924 until Hitler withdrew from the arrangement in 1933, competent flyers added such military skills as gunnery and bombing to their repertoire. Hitler's Luftwaffe was born in Russia and its father was the Weimar Republic.

Göring's air commanders

When Hitler came to power the secrecy surrounding military preparations was abandoned. Göring was assigned to control all aviation, and in order to build a large Nazi air force quickly, he was permitted to head-hunt army officers. For his chief of staff he took

Colonel Walther Wever, Colonel Albert Kesselring was appointed as administration chief, and Colonel Hans-Jürgen Stumpff was given the vital job of personnel chief. None of these men had any experience of flying.

However the real creator of the new Nazi Luftwaffe was Erhard Milch. In the First World War he had been an observer with the Army Air Service. (Right up until the war in 1939 the Germans often appointed the observer, rather than the pilot, to command a two-seater aircraft.) Milch rose to become the deputy commander of his squadron and after a break, commanding an infantry company, he ended the First War commanding Fighter Squadron No. 6, without ever having learned to fly a plane. Although photographs suggest he was a pudgy little fellow, those who met him tell me he was handsome, attractive to women and imposing in real life.

In May 1922 Milch went to work for Junkers Airways, a subsidiary of the aircraft manufacturer, and soon showed himself to be a ruthless and unprincipled conniver. At the age of 36 he became the chief of Lufthansa, the German state airline created when the Weimar government forced small carriers into a nationalized conglomerate. Its routes stretched across Europe to China and to South America. As the Nazis became stronger Milch became involved in corrupt deals with them. It was Milch who arranged for Hitler to be flown from town to town during his political campaigns without being asked to pay fares. Hitler's arrivals by three-engined Junkers airliners were given great prominence by the Nazi propaganda experts, who exploited the ambiguous slogan 'Hitler Over Germany'.

When the Nazis gained power, Milch received his reward. He became second only to Göring in an empire that embraced all aspects of civil and military aviation, and which eventually included the anti-aircraft defences of the Reich, parachute troops and some infantry units too.

By living to a ripe old age, and talking to countless historians, Milch was able to bend many postwar historical accounts to his own advantage. A competent bureaucrat, with unusual administrative skills, his judgement was entirely inadequate. The Luftwaffe's subservience to the army, its neglect of production and research, the cancellation of plans for a strategic bombing force, the neglect of long-range fighter escorts, the disastrous failure of the Stalingrad airlift – these were all evidence of his shortcomings.

The same neglect of their duties was displayed by Göring and by his wartime comrade Generaloberst Ernst Udet, who took control of the Luftwaffe's technical department. Udet was only really happy in a cockpit, while Milch was largely concerned with his own grandiose ambitions, even trying to supplant Göring at one time. As the war progressed Milch's power declined, but by that time the damage he had done was beyond repair.[1] After the war, Milch was sentenced to 15 years' imprisonment for war crimes. Released in 1955, he was employed as an aviation consultant by Fiat and by Thyssen Steel.

The birth of the jet aircraft

Milch's most profound error of judgement dates from 27 August 1939, when Heinkel's He 178 – powered by Dr Pabst von Ohain's engine – made the world's first jet-powered flight. Milch saw it but was not impressed. Even when Heinkel developed his machine so that on 2 April 1941 he could offer the Luftwaffe the Heinkel He 280, the world's first jet fighter, Milch showed no interest in it.[2]

Figure 24: Heinkel He 280 – the world's first jet fighter

Like Udet, who was responsible for research, Milch saw no need for jet aircraft.

Britain was the only other country in which any work was being done on jet-propelled flight. Britain's Air Ministry showed much the same apathy as Milch and Udet had done. Frank Whittle, a young RAF officer, had published his jet-engine patents in 1930. Four years later the British official view was recorded in a letter written by the under-secretary of state for Air.

We follow with interest any work that is being done in other countries on jet propulsion, but scientific investigation into the possibilities has given no indication that this method can be a serious competitor to the airscrew-engine combination. We do not consider that we should be justified in spending any time or money on it ourselves.[3]

Despite the official attitude, Whittle got a practical engine running by 1937. In May 1941, installed in a Gloster E.28/39, this powered the first jet aircraft to take to the air outside Germany. America displayed no interest in jet planes until a Whittle engine was taken to the States in October 1941 and a number of copies were built. Developments came quickly. In effect, the United States jet industry grew directly from British engines.[4]

In the period from 1918 to 1939 the techniques and technology of the world's navies changed only minimally. Many of the warships engaged in the Second War had been at sea in the First. Such economies could not be effected in the air war. Aircraft designs had developed too radically. Biplane fighters made of wood and fabric were replaced by monoplanes with stressed metal skins.[5] Heavier and heavier planes with ever-increasing ranges were carrying bigger and more destructive bombloads. Theorists abounded and much was being written about the strategy of the warplane that could bombard capital cities into submission. No one, they said, would be immune from the 'war in the air'.

The strategic bomber: Britain

In 1917 Britain's flyers, hitherto the Royal Flying Corps, a part of the army, became an entirely separate service and were looked upon with envy by high-ranking airmen in foreign armies. When at war's end Winston Churchill was given both the War Office and the Air Ministry some thought he would dismantle the Royal Air Force and hand its parts back to the soldiers and the sailors. Instead he appointed Hugh 'Boom' Trenchard to be its chief of staff. Trenchard was a talented administrator who was still digesting the lessons he had learned while commanding the Independent Air Force, which had bombed Germany in 1918. He realized that advocating strategic bombing was the best, if not the only, way to make his RAF a service as important as the army and the navy.

And the prospect of bombing led to questions about the morale of the working class if bombed. Will *their* working class collapse before *ours* does? In the 1920s, with Germany in disarray, France had become the theoretical enemy. National pride always shines through British theories: 'the French in a bombing duel would probably squeal before we did,' said Trenchard in July 1923, and for good measure he added that aircrew losses would have a greater effect on French pilots than on British ones.[6]

By this time the fighter plane, which had proved such a decisive weapon in the 1914–18 war, was being prematurely relegated to history. An Air Staff memorandum of March 1924 said that 'as a principle the bombing squadrons should be as numerous as possible and the fighters as few as popular opinion and necessity for defending vital objectives will permit.'[7]

Trenchard made sure that the RAF put all its energies into plans for the bombing force, even though this was a time when the RAF was primarily engaged in colonial policing tasks. Cooperation with the army or the navy was rejected. Parachute infantry must not be formed, said the RAF chiefs of staff in 1938, for that would divert planes from bombing.

And yet, as war drew closer, the RAF had no big bombers and its medium bombers were mostly inadequate designs. Only the Wellington from Vickers, a geodetic airframe designed by Barnes Wallis, was good enough to face German defences and survive. Handley Page's Hampden and Avro Whitworth's Whitley were soon to be relegated to minelaying and training.

Britain's civil aircraft designs were equally disappointing. In 1918, the aircraft industry had been at peak production, and the Empire provided potential air routes across the world. But no British aircraft emerged to take advantage of this golden opportunity. In 1926, when other nations were flying excellent three-engined metal monoplane airliners, such as the Ford Tri-Motor, the Fokker F. VII/3m and Junkers G31, the British put into service the Armstrong Whitworth Argosy and De Havilland DH 66 Hercules. Both were cumbersome biplanes, with uncowled engines and a square-sectioned fabric-covered fuselage.

The 1930s are marked by the Air Ministry's vacillations and its failure to get a transatlantic flying boat.[8] Plans for long-range land-planes issued in 1938 went the same way. The British armed services were stretched across the world to a greater extent than those of any other nation, yet the RAF showed little interest in air transport. The new technique of moving infantry, and much other war material, by air was not encouraged. Even Franco's dramatic airlift of troops to mainland Spain did not prompt the RAF to offer such movements to the army.

When war began the RAF was forced to the humiliating measure of chartering 'almost every civil airline in Britain' to ferry equipment to France. In the words of the BBC's war correspondent Charles Gardner:

> Stately, if slightly coughing, Ensign air liners, and even the superannuated old Handley Page 42's, were filched from Imperial Airways. D.H. Albatrosses, Rapides, Dragons, and 86's were assembled from the smaller air-line concerns to reinforce the Royal Air Force's own small collection of troop-carriers . . . Food, field telephones, blankets, tents, cables, spare engines, maps, men, uniforms, guns, ammunition, aerodrome equipment – all these and a hundred more things, were flown out from England, without a single mishap.[9]

The absence of any modern long-range British designs made it necessary for the RAF to fly American transport aircraft in the war and after it. There are historians repeating the myth that America's prime position in the postwar air transport race was gained by an invidious arrangement whereby Britain produced the bombers and the United States produced transport aircraft. No such deal was ever made.[10]

Britain's progress with heavy bombers was little better than that of its commercial aircraft. When Britain went to war, the RAF was still flying the bizarre-looking Handley Page Heyfords: biplane bombers with huge spatted wheels that did not retract. One historian remarks: 'Considering that "strategic" bombing represented the raison d'être for the Royal Air Force, it is surprising that so little was done to prepare for this task.'[11] RAF target-finding was poor and bombing accuracy was, according to the assistant chief of air staff in 1938, 'very poor indeed'.

As war came closer, the RAF proposed the creation of a new fleet of heavy bombers. The Handley Page Halifax and the Avro Manchester were put forward as designs for an RAF strategic bombing force. Prime Minister Chamberlain intervened to postpone both. He said that building a Halifax bomber would provoke Germany into producing a super-Halifax bomber. Sensitive as always to cost, he added that a heavy bomber cost as much as four fighters.[12]

The most decisive technology was proving to be that of aircraft engines. A wonderful engine could make a second-rate plane into a winner, but a superb airframe powered by a poor engine could never be made a success. Britain had one superlative power-plant, the liquid-cooled Merlin, and it was in short supply. First priority for them must be the Spitfire and Hurricane fighters, but only after

Figure 25: British Avro Lancaster bomber

four Merlins were fitted into it did the accident-prone Manchester become the successful Lancaster.

The first four-engined bomber to see operational service was the Short Stirling, which had been ordered straight off the drawing-board, without waiting to see the prototype fly. It did not have Merlin engines and was the least successful of the RAF's heavy bombers. When becoming airborne it had a dangerous tendency to swing to starboard, and its tail and undercarriage provided enough wind resistance to make the tendency fatal in even a light cross-wind. The Air Ministry's specification foolishly limited the machine's wingspan to 100 feet, which produced a high wing-loading and a poor ceiling. The landing gear then had to be made higher to give the aircraft the angle of attack that would get it airborne in a normal take-off run. The result was an ungainly machine, with weak landing gear, that suffered high casualty rates because it could not climb high enough to avoid the Flak.

Trenchard's big bomber policy meant convincing everyone that bombing was decisive, so the bomber brasshats had to say that enemy bombing forces were similarly fearsome. It was such extravagant talk that led in December 1938 to official estimates that the first three weeks of war could see 465,000 houses totally destroyed and over 5 million damaged out of Britain's 14 million homes. The Committee for Imperial Defence in 1937, estimating compensation rates for casualties, began with a figure of 1,800,000 casualties in the initial eight weeks, of which one third would be fatal. Figures accepted by the cabinet in October 1938 estimated that 5 per cent of all property in Britain, valued at £550,000,000, would be destroyed in the first three weeks of war.[13] Such predictions as these lent weight to the spurious arguments of the appeasers and allowed Hitler to go so far unopposed.

The strategic bomber: Germany

Göring had contrived that his new Luftwaffe was also a separate service, and yet its role was narrow and firmly defined. The German air force was to be a form of long-range artillery, providing support to the army in short sharp wars that the sensitive German economy could endure.

One meticulous American historian, citing German sources, blames the German economy for the absence of a strategic bomber.[14] The worldwide depression that began in the United States in 1929 hit Germany severely. Even when it started to re-cover in the mid-Thirties there remained a shortage of foreign exchange. All imported raw materials were strictly allocated, and the army always had first priority. Thus there were never adequate resources to build a significant bombing fleet, and never the pros-pect of enough fuel to sustain one.

And yet before we accept this argument fully, it is well to remem-ber that Göring was second only to Hitler in his powers, and he had full authority over the economy. If Göring's influence and Milch's energy, cunning and organizational ability had been directed to creating a strategic bomber force, who can doubt that it could have been achieved whatever effect this had on the German economy? The fact is that the strategic bomber was abandoned because no one in the top ranks of the politico-military establishment wanted it.

It had not always been so. In 1933, when news came that Stalin was building factories deep in the interior of the USSR, the de-velopment of a 'Urals bomber' was begun by the German Air Ministry. The project director was Lt-Col. Wilhelm Wimmer, head of the Air Technical Office, and he had the support of Major General Walther Wever, the ex-army officer who was in effect the Luftwaffe's chief of staff. The two men agreed to have two four-engined designs developed, by Dornier and by Junkers. Within two years Wimmer was able to show the minister of war (General von Blomberg) a wooden mock-up of the Junkers, and was asked when it would be operational. 'In four or five years,' answered Wimmer. 'That will be soon enough,' said Blomberg.[15]

General Wever did not last that long. Like most of the other senior ex-army men, he went through pilot training, and took for his personal use a high-speed Heinkel He 70 Blitz. Impatience led to his undoing. Having waited too long for his engineer, Wever irritably hurried the man aboard the plane as soon as he arrived, and climbed in himself, forgetting that he hadn't done the routine pre-flight check. When the plane crashed with locked ailerons Wever died and was replaced in 1936 by Major-General 'Smiling Albert' Kesselring. At the same time, on Hitler's personal instructions Wimmer was moved to another job and Colonel Ernst Udet was given the Technical Office.

The strategic bomber had lost both its supporters. Udet had no qualifications for the post and no desire for it, but Hitler's word was law. To make things worse for him, the Air Ministry bureaucrats inflicted organizational changes that split the office into thirteen separate departments, and added nine procurement departments and all the complexities of the testing stations to it. Trying to deal with so many departmental heads, and with technical discussions that were beyond his understanding, Udet gave up.[16] He spent a great deal of his time at work reminiscing with old comrades. Subordinates sometimes waited months for his decisions, including those concerning the Urals bomber. On 29 April 1937, ten months after Wever's death, Göring ordered that the strategic bomber programme be cancelled. He had been persuaded by Kesselring and Milch that it was a waste of resources.

The RAF artfully helped to discourage the Luftwaffe from building a strategic bomber. On an official visit to the RAF at the end of 1937 Udet had a private conversation with Sir Victor Goddard, who was in charge of the RAF's European intelligence and a keen supporter of heavy bombers. Goddard was later to recall that Udet said 'he was being urged by the industry and by his colleagues in the GAF [German Air Force] to go for heavy bombers but he himself was strongly opposed to this . . . He then cited the disadvantages in manoeuvrability of large bulk; he cited the difficulties which would be involved by engine breakdowns and found various other reasons, all of which I endorsed . . .'[17]

As the cancellation was ordered the Urals bomber prototypes came rolling out of the hangars. Both of them were clumsy-looking machines and substantially underpowered. Dornier gave their prototype to the army, who used it to ferry troops, but Junkers persevered and modified theirs into a 40-seat transport plane, the Junkers Ju 90. Later in the war an improved version of this aircraft, the Junkers Ju 290, made regular flights between Odessa and Japanese airfields in China, taking radar sets and jet engines and returning with rubber latex and 'exotic metals'. An even bigger version was fitted with six BMW radial engines. Sent to Mont de

Marsan in France for trials, it flew to within 12 miles of New York and returned safely to base.[18]

Long-range aircraft were not unknown to German industry. Before the war a Focke-Wulf Condor airliner had created a world record by flying non-stop from Berlin to New York. (These were the aircraft that later proved useful for long-range reconnaissance over the Atlantic.) Curiously, the only four-engined bomber that the German Air Ministry persisted with was the Heinkel He 177. This had been ordered just a few days after the Urals bomber programme was cancelled. A complex design, the Heinkel had its engines mounted in pairs driving a common shaft. For this reason and others it gave endless technical problems, and its failure brought the final death of Germany's strategic bomber programme.[19]

The dive-bomber

Men like Göring and Udet, always nostalgic for the uncomplicated flying of their youth, accepted the Luftwaffe's role as a supporter for the army's battles. In this way they hoped to avoid the headaches associated with all-weather flying, long-range navigational aids, night fighters and the sort of bomb-sights needed for high-level precision bombing.

Dive-bombing was at the core of army cooperation flying, but it wasn't invented by the Luftwaffe. Lieutenant Harry Brown of No. 84 Squadron Royal Flying Corps is said to have invented it in 1917,[20] and after the war the Royal Air Force conducted trials before abandoning the technique. Its dedicated use dates from 1928, when the American Marine Corps pilots were dropping bombs from their Curtiss OC-1 (a modified F8C-1 two-seater fighter) in Nicaragua.[21] Curtiss called the second version of the plane 'Helldiver', and gave the name to many subsequent designs. The Japanese liked the dive-bombing technique, and in 1931 were flying their Nakajima N-35 Tokubaku dive-bomber, a two-seat biplane. Britain's Air Ministry strongly opposed the dive-bomber, and apart from a few Blackburn Skuas used by the navy, prevented their construction. Junkers' pioneering work on the cantilever monoplane led to the sort of massive main spars that could take the strain of pulling out of steep dives. So when the German Air Ministry wanted a machine built specifically for dive-bombing Junkers won the order.

Ernst Udet, always a showman, found dive-bombing very much

to his taste. He fitted a Focke-Wulf Fw 56 (Stösser) high-wing monoplane with improvised bomb-rack and concrete 'bombs', to give a show at Bremen airfield. One British aviator said:

> In 1936 I visited Berlin during the Olympic Games and made my first acquaintance with the new Luftwaffe in the person of Colonel Ernst Udet, enthusiastic proponent of dive-bombing and then head of the technical department in the German Air Ministry. In the early 1930s he had witnessed a demonstration by the US Navy Curtiss Helldivers at Cleveland, Ohio, and was so impressed that he influenced the placing of a contract for the design of such aircraft on 27 September 1933. The Junkers Ju 87 was the result; the prototype made its first flight in late Spring 1935 with a proud Udet as witness.[22]

The Junkers Ju 87 proved its worth in Spain. It could drop a 500-kg bomb with enough precision to hit a bridge or a head-quarters. Yet it was cheap and expendable: a small plane with only two men and a workaday engine. Its fixed landing gear and thick cranked wings made it immensely strong, and although it looked crude it was a delight to fly and brilliantly designed for the job it did.

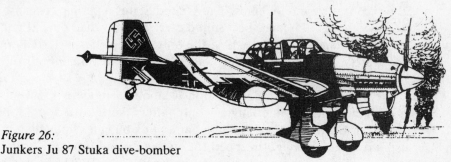

Figure 26:
Junkers Ju 87 Stuka dive-bomber

The monoplane fighter

Most pioneers of aviation, from Otto Lilienthal onwards, knew that the monoplane was the inevitable shape of aircraft to come. The earliest powered machines had been made with wings strung together like box kites only because that was cheap and strong. In 1912 the French and the British army authorities had done their best to impede progress by prohibiting the military use of monoplanes; this ensured that during the First War only the Germans made serious advances in applied aerodynamics. Although the most famous monoplane of that war – the wire-braced Fokker Eindecker – was little more than a German version of Blériot's monoplane, Fokker's D.VIII high-wing cantilever fighter of late 1918 showed what the future would bring.[23] So did a design team under Professor Hugo Junkers which, in making the world's first all-metal low-wing monoplane, created the configuration we still have in use today. First flown in December 1915, some 200 Junkers J-1s were built, and one of these machines was still flying in Spain in 1956.[24]

The Germans were 'air-minded'. Restricted by the terms of the Versailles peace treaty, they discovered that the glider provided lessons for both pilots and designers and more than 15,000 Germans earned certificates for gliding skill, far more than the rest of Europe combined. The aerodynamics of the gliders left no doubt of the monoplane's superior qualities. For powered flight too, Germany persevered with monoplanes. In 1922, when 60 per cent of German aircraft types were monoplanes, they comprised only 6 per cent of Britain's aircraft types, 9 per cent of French aircraft types and 27 per cent of American aircraft types.

By 1927, when 62 per cent of Germany's aircraft types were monoplanes, British policy had not changed much; 13 per cent of her aircraft types were monoplanes. France had seen the light, and 36 per cent were monoplanes. The United States – perhaps because the navy thought biplanes best suited carriers – now had only 21 per cent monoplanes.[25] Even by 1934 the only monoplanes in RAF service were a few special aircraft and 17 amphibian trainers; all the others were biplanes.[26]

The RAF started thinking seriously about a modern low-wing monoplane with in-line engine only after Fairey tried out an American Curtiss D-12 engine in a Fairey Fox biplane. Immediately inspired by the increase in speed the in-line engine brought, Rolls-Royce designed one exactly like it: the Kestrel. In 1933 Rolls put a Kestrel into a sleek Heinkel He 70 monoplane. To everyone's amazement the big six-seater was faster than the current RAF fighter, the Super Fury. 'Within a year the Air Ministry had issued its first specification for a retractable-gear monoplane fighter and the path to the Hurricane and Spitfire was open.'[27]

Of course this transformation of the He 70 attracted the attention of the Germans. Messerschmitt purchased a Kestrel to power his newly designed Bf 109 while he waited for a better engine.[28] Rolls-Royce, without government money, improved the Kestrel to make the Merlin engine. It was tried out in the Hurricane, a monoplane version of a long line of Hawker biplanes. When the more sophisticated Spitfire was ready, the Merlin powered that too. Perhaps it's not going too far to say that that Anglo-German hybrid, the Kestrel-powered Heinkel, inspired both the Messerschmitt 109 and the Merlin-powered Spitfire that confronted it.

The United States failed to produce the equivalent of a Spitfire or a Messerschmitt during the interwar years. America's aircraft industry was in a poor state after the years of Depression. In 1938 Pratt & Whitney was on the point of bankruptcy and only orders from the French government saved it. At this time the entire American aircraft industry employed only 36,000 workers, fewer than the number employed in the knit hosiery industry.[29]

The Spitfire and the Bf 109 marked a drastic change in fighter design. From being large, spacious and manoeuvrable biplanes with bracing wires, fixed landing gear and open cockpits, they became high-speed metal-clad monoplanes. Their wheels retracted into the wings and they were capable of climbing quickly to untold heights while their pilots, who had to get used to the cramped confines of the new configuration, communicated by means of short-wave radio-telephones.

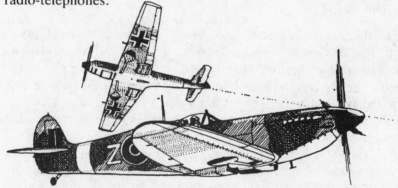

Figure 27: Supermarine Spitfire and Messerschmitt Bf 109

The cockpit – let's say it's a Spitfire – fits you like a glove. It just about touches your shoulders on either side. The perspex canopy almost touches your head above. You can move your booted feet a few inches in either direction; you can stretch your arms right forward or down, but need to bend your elbows if you pull them back or up. No matter; you can control a fighter with just a few inches' movement of hands and feet.[30]

By the summer of 1940 Messerschmitt's single-seat fighter was powered by a Daimler-Benz engine. The models that fought in Spain had given place to the Bf 109E or 'Emil'. It was directly comparable with the RAF's Vickers-Supermarine Spitfire II. The two rivals were remarkably alike. A postwar assessment put the Spitfire as the faster machine at lower altitudes, but slower than the 109 at high altitudes.[31] The Spitfire's rate of climb was slightly inferior too. 'The manoeuvrability of the two aircraft was considered nearly equal, the Spitfire having a slight edge, although pilot ability was often the deciding factor.'

Since few pilots flew their aircraft to the point of destruction, such vital matters as tight turning circles were more a matter of daring than of engineering. One pilot gives an example of flying to the very edge of performance:

> One had to enter the turn correctly, then open up the engine. It was a matter of feel. When one noticed the speed becoming critical – the aircraft vibrated – one had to ease up a bit, then pull back again, so that in plan the best turn would have looked like an egg or a horizontal ellipse rather than a circle. In this way one could out-turn the Spitfire – and I shot down six of them doing it.[32]

The theorist is likely to give too much importance to the ability to turn. The ace pilots found otherwise. Lt-General Adolf Galland complained that the Luftwaffe High Command were stuck on 'the idea that manoeuvrability in banking was primarily the determining factor in air combat . . . They could not or simply would not see that for modern fighter aircraft the tight turn as a form of aerial combat represented the exception.'[33]

Air Vice-Marshal J. E. Johnson, an RAF ace, agreed: 'Tight turns were more a defensive than an offensive tactic and did not win air battles.' The near parity of Spitfire and Bf 109 should take into account the fact that the Germans used 87 octane fuel while by the time of the Battle of Britain, the RAF had overcome the limitations of the Neutrality Act to secure from the United States supplies of incomparably superior 100 octane fuel. This vastly improved the performance of the Merlin engine, particularly the rate of climb. Speed was also improved. In the Luftwaffe only a few photo-reconnaissance machines enjoyed the benefits of such high-octane fuel before the Bf 109F came into service as the year was ending.

The Spitfires and Hurricanes were armed with eight machineguns, four in each wing. This was inferior to the armament of the

Emil, which had two machine-guns and two cannons.[34] Machine-guns could not inflict anything like the damage done by a cannon shell which had a longer range and exploded on impact. Unless it hit a crew member or vital piece of machinery, the machine-gun bullet simply punched a tiny hole in the metal. The RAF tried to get cannon-armed Spitfires ready for the summer battles, but failed.

British historians frequently depict the Emil as significantly inferior to the Spitfire. This does an injustice to the British pilots. One recent history said that the Messerschmitt's most significant weakness was its short endurance because it carried only 88 imperial gallons. The Spitfire II's tank held only 85 gallons.

German pilots liked their machines. One said: 'It seems to me that simply flying the Spitfire was a full-time job judging by the contents of the "Pilot's Notes". The Bf 109 was much simpler, technically speaking.'[35]

In 1940 Hawker Hurricane fighters outnumbered the Spitfires in RAF service. To speed its production the designers employed many components from Hawker's biplane fighters. Its design was simpler than that of Supermarine's Spitfire, and its performance was inferior to the Emil's, but the Hurricane was rugged. RAF fitters and mechanics were familiar with its components, and battle-damage could often be repaired at squadron workshops instead of having to be carried out by the manufacturers. Hurricanes could be manufactured more quickly than Spitfires. By the time war came, 299 Spitfires had been built using 24 million man-hours while 578 Hurricanes had been produced from only 20 million man-hours. The scarcity of Spitfires meant that very few could be spared for anything but front-line service in England. The RAF overseas were not given any, and even the British Expeditionary Force in France was without Spitfires to provide air cover.

Figure 28: Hawker Hurricane fighter

Rechlin – the eve of war

In the summer of 1939, with war more or less inevitable, Göring wanted to impress Hitler with his achievements and put on an air display for the Führer at Rechlin research station. The rocket-propelled Heinkel He 176 showed its phenomenal rate of climb. The Heinkel He 178, the world's first jet, was also put through its paces. Hitler was impressed but it was not made clear to him that these prototypes were a long way from going into production,[36] and the display played a big part in persuading him that the German armed forces were indomitable.

Ironically Hitler was more impressed than the Luftwaffe chiefs. None of them put any effort into supporting the new miracle aircraft. Milch failed to coordinate or encourage long-term research, and his Air Ministry was renowned for bureaucratic muddle and vacillation. Göring not only did nothing but had the audacity to complain about his own incompetence: 'What bunglers our finest magicians are in comparison [with the men who arranged the display]! We're still waiting for the things they conjured up there before my very eyes – and worse still, the Führer's.'

19 THE BULLETS ARE FLYING

Sing me a song of a lad that is gone;
Say, could that lad be I?

R. L. Stevenson, 'A Lad That is Gone'

B Y NOT BECOMING PRESIDENT in 1933 Hitler had avoided taking
the presidential oath to uphold the Constitution. Instead he invented for himself the title Führer while leaving the Reich president's
post unfilled. In 1939 he used this trick to flout the Constitution's
requirement that a declaration of war must be put before the
Reichstag.

Hjalmar Schacht (minister of economics and Reichsbank president) said he was going to army headquarters to remind General
Walter von Brauchitsch, the army C-in-C, and General Franz
Halder, the chief of staff, that this made no difference to the fact that
their oaths to the Constitution required Reichstag approval before a
war could be declared. Brauchitsch sent word that if Schacht showed
up at army HQ he would be arrested.[1]

On 1 September 1939 the German army invaded Poland. The invasion plan was largely the work of General Erich von Manstein, a
52-year-old divisional commander who many have agreed was the
best military mind on either side during the war. However his plan
was entirely conventional and depended upon the sort of very speedy
and efficient German mobilization that had won for Germany the
war of 1870. The German forces were brought up to the railheads, as
they had been in the previous war, and the attack was concentrated
in the south where the best railway systems were. The task of the invading armies was to cross the border and, in battles of encirclement,
overrun the Polish railheads and the other assembly areas, prevent-
ing the proper mobilization of Polish forces.

Although two German armoured corps were used to strike where
no railways existed, most armour was distributed in bits and pieces
along the front. In any case the German army was about 90 per cent

horse-drawn and the plan had to take this into account. Afterwards
more attention was given to a problem arising from German army
horse-shoes than from any other failure.

What gave the Germans the quick and easy victory in this traditional encirclement battle was the dimension added by the air
squadrons. It was the Luftwaffe that did most to hamper Polish
mobilization. Great numbers of aircraft were used, with Polish airfields their prime target. Bridges, railways and road junctions were
strafed to cut communications, with little concern for the deaths
among civilians. Some Polish air force units dispersed to continue the
war from smaller fields but the problems of maintenance and communications defeated them despite their ferocious courage.

When after three weeks the campaign was coming to a close the
Luftwaffe was directed to stage a massive attack upon Warsaw.
Although the German propaganda service claimed that only military
targets were being hit, one formation of thirty Ju 52 transports flew
over the city while men shovelled incendiary bombs out through the
cargo doors. Smoke from the resulting fires rose to 18,000 feet, and at
night the glow of the burning city was seen for many miles. The claim
that the Luftwaffe had obeyed the rules of war was not helped by the
Nazi documentary film *Baptism of Fire*, which showed the destruction from rooftop height. After the war General Kesselring, the
Luftwaffe commander, was charged with the war crime of deliberate
and unnecessary bombing.

When the German army's two vast pincers closed, meeting just
south of Brest-Litovsk, the Polish army was locked inside this ring.
Fighting continued but the outcome was inevitable. Poland collapsed
in such chaos that no Polish government survived to sign any sort of
peace treaty. Close behind the German combat troops came the SS
Einsatzgruppen (Special Task Forces). Their task was to systematically destroy the Polish middle class. Teachers, doctors, local
government officials and army officers were murdered in their thousands. The Soviet Red Army took over the eastern half of the
country and their secret policemen did the same sort of thing for
much the same reasons. Poland was buried alive.

The German army was satisfied and duly appreciative of the support the Luftwaffe had provided. It was aircraft more than tanks
which had transformed this campaign, and the quick defeat of the
Poles convinced German commanders that the strategic bomber was
not needed. The Luftwaffe was determined to become Hitler's loyal
and favoured 'Nazi' arm, and for a while it was.

The integration of state, armed forces and industry provided countless advantages. While fighting in Poland was still in progress, the Luftwaffe decided that quick and expert repair of machinery was cheaper and better than supplying new equipment. German aircraft manufacturers sent Werkstattszüge to front-line airfields. These 'trains' consisted of trucks equipped as mobile workshops with lathes, welding gear and so on, manned by experienced factory personnel.

Starting at the drawing-board stage, German designers were expected to pay great attention to the way in which repairs might be carried out and replacement parts fitted. Operational procedures, such as keeping the optimum ratio of pilots to fighter planes, enabled the armed services to make maximum use of the equipment that factories produced.

Heligoland: the first strike

By the time Britain entered the war, Berlin had already been targeted. On Friday 1 September 1939 Polish bombers were briefed to attack that city,[2] but according to a well-known Berlin resident's diary they achieved very little:

> We had our first air raid alarm at seven pm . . . the lights went out, and all the German employees grabbed their gas masks and, not a little frightened, rushed for the shelter . . . In the darkness and confusion I escaped outside . . . No planes came over.[3]

Britain's declaration of war came two days later, at 11 am on the Sunday morning. Within one hour the RAF sent a Bristol Blenheim to spot, and radio back, the position of German warships at Wilhelmshaven so that a bombing raid could immediately follow.

The Blenheim's radio failed and the attack was postponed until the following day, when 15 Blenheims were sent off on the first RAF bombing raid of the war. In the low cloud, some of the aircraft could not find the ships and jettisoned their bombs into the sea. The others attacked; one of them crashed upon the light cruiser *Emden*, another scored a hit on the pocket battleship *Admiral Scheer*, but the bomb – fused for an 11-second delay – bounced off the armour plate before exploding. Six Handley Page Hampden bombers were dispatched to follow up the Blenheims' attack but were recalled because of fears that they might bomb Heligoland and cause civilian casualties. Fourteen Vickers Wellington bombers pressed on, despite bad weather conditions at their target Brunsbüttel on the

Kiel Canal. Two Wellingtons were shot down. The problems of navigation, even in daylight, were illustrated by the fact that two bombs landed and killed two Danes in the neutral town of Esbjorg, 110 miles north of Brunsbüttel.

That day's operations had been costly and served no purpose except as a propaganda exercise. But daylight bombing was the RAF policy and similar attacks were mounted in the following weeks. The Germans retaliated with attacks on naval bases in Scotland. Both sides took extreme measures to avoid civilian casualties.

The 'Oslo Report' and radar

What few people in Britain knew, or even suspected, was that the RAF formations attacking German shipping had been detected by German radar stations. By November 1939 there was no longer any excuse for ignorance. Professor R. V. Jones of Scientific Intelligence recalled:

> Fred Winterbotham came into my room and dumped a small parcel on my desk and said, 'Here's a present for you!' I asked him what its background was and he said it had come from our Naval Attaché in Oslo. This was after the Attaché had received a letter, dropped privately through his letter box, saying that if the British would like to know about various German scientific and technical developments, would we alter the preamble to our news broadcasts in German so as to say, 'Hello, hier ist London . . .' instead of the normal preamble . . .[4]

This was the arrival of what is now acknowledged as the most amazing intelligence coup of the war: a list of secret German scientific developments that the British referred to as the 'Oslo Report'. It had come from an anti-Nazi German civilian scientist who ended the war in Sachsenhausen concentration camp but survived and died in 1980 with his identity still secret. In paragraph eight his report specifically said:

> In the attack by English airmen on Wilhelmshaven at the beginning of September, the English aircraft were already picked up at a distance of 120 kilometres from the coast. Along the entire German coast there are short-wave transmitters with an output of 20 kilowatts, these sending out very short pulses of a duration of 10 microseconds.

The report went on to describe a sophisticated system of radar but it did little good. In Whitehall, where few could understand the technical details, the whole thing was dismissed as a German plant. They found it difficult to believe that the Germans had developed radar apparatus as good as, if not better than the equipment the British had made. Thanks partly to Watson-Watt's genius for self-advertisement, most British people still do.[5]

After the battle of the River Plate in 1939, a British radar expert went to Montevideo in South America to examine a strange-looking antenna mounted on the German battleship *Admiral Graf Spee*. He climbed upon it while the wreck lay scuttled in the shallow water, and his report confirmed that it was radar, estimated to operate on a wavelength of 80 cm, but 'his report was shelved for 18 months, during which time Whitehall still continued to debate whether the Germans actually had radar.'[6]

In 1940 the RAF radio-monitoring service heard a German fighter pilot talking with the Freya ground radar unit that was helping him to find his prey, an RAF bomber. In January 1941 one of the German radar arrays was seen and photographed from the air. Yet on 24 February 1941 – after almost a year and a half of war – there was an Air Ministry meeting whose sole purpose was 'To discuss the existence of German radar'. By that time, Derrick Garrard, a 'boffin' impatiently waiting his security clearance to work with Professor Jones at Security Intelligence, had amused himself driving along England's south coast with a radio receiver. He was arrested for spying, but not before he succeeded in picking up transmissions from German Freya radar sets in France, and even taking rough bearings on where they might be. Plotted on a map the lines convinced Jones of the presence of gun-laying radar that was being used against British shipping in the Channel. One of Garrard's bearings went through a field where a large German antenna had been photographed from the air. Said Jones: 'So when the meeting started, I let it run on a little to let the doubters say that they did not believe that the Germans had any radar, and then I produced both the photographs and Garrard's bearings.' From that date German radar existed; and that was official. The task then was to discover how it worked, where it was and how to counter it.

Scandinavia

One of the surprises of the Norwegian fighting – and a foretaste of what was to come in the Pacific – was the sinking of a 6,000-ton cruiser after a brilliantly executed attack by 16 dive-bombers, 300 miles from their base and at the extreme edge of their range. Each aircraft carried one 500-lb bomb, and there were three direct hits. The cruiser – which had been damaged and was moored at a mole – rolled over and sank.

Perhaps even more surprising was that the cruiser was the *Königsberg* and the dive-bombers were the Royal Navy's Blackburn Skuas, flying from their base in the Orkney Islands. The Skua had been designed as the Fleet Air Arm's fighter and dive-bomber, but it proved to be inferior in the former role. The German cruiser was the first victim of such an air attack.

The Fleet Air Arm had other successes during the sombre Norwegian adventure. HMS *Ark Royal* flew Skuas in support of the Anglo-French land forces, and by the end of the campaign they had claimed nine Heinkel bombers and two of the Luftwaffe's new Junkers Ju 88s and produced the Royal Navy's first ace, Lieutenant W. P. Lucy, who was eventually killed in air combat.

The carriers HMS *Glorious* and HMS *Furious* were also in action off Norway, having transported RAF fighter planes to operate from Norwegian airfields. In the final hours of the British withdrawal it was decided to evacuate the squadrons by carrier. Gladiator biplanes were able to land on the carriers without too much danger, but Squadron Leader Kenneth 'Bing' Cross, commanding 46 Squadron, was told to destroy his Hurricane fighters. Instead the Hurricane pilots, who had no experience of carrier flying, took the desperate measure, despite their machines' high landing speed, of taking them down on to the carrier deck. These aircraft had no arrester hooks, but the impossible was achieved by means of a 40-knot wind over the carrier deck, a 14-lb sandbag in the tail of each machine, and partially deflated tires, which assisted in braking. Furthermore, it was done at night, the seventh and last Hurricane arriving at 0300 hours.

Resulting from radio interception and air reconnaissance, the Germans sent a flotilla – the battleships *Scharnhorst* and *Gneisenau*, the heavy cruiser *Admiral Hipper* and six support ships – searching for the convoys that were evacuating Allied troops from Norway. At Bletchley Park this flotilla's radio traffic had been noted. The Admiralty's Operational Intelligence Centre were told of the movement of 'certain enemy ships, class and type unknown, from the Baltic to the Skagerrak' any of which might take offensive action.

The notes were filed away without any warning being passed to British ships at sea.[7]

The *Glorious* was vulnerable to attack in every way. Her captain, a submarine specialist, had little knowledge or faith in air operations. Described as a very vain man who would not admit ignorance on air matters, he had, earlier in the Norway campaign, put his naval commander (Air) ashore to await a court-martial on a charge of cowardice.[8] The ship's crew, having returned from a long spell in the Mediterranean, was denied leave. The morale of the crew was very low; 'mutinous' said one eyewitness.[9] Despite the ship's lack of radar, there was no lookout posted in the crow's nest and a naval airman who had seen the *Ark Royal* sixteen hours earlier said: 'They could not fly patrols; their flight deck was solid with Hurricanes.'[10]

The German flotilla had already sunk a tanker and an empty troopship when HMS *Glorious* was spotted at 28 miles by a young midshipman in the foretop of *Scharnhorst*. At this time the German Seetakt radar provided more accurate range measurement than optical range-finders, and was of course unaffected by fog, smoke or darkness. The German ship opened fire at 28,000 yards and *Glorious* was hit. Set afire, she capsized and sank complete with most of her crew and two squadrons of battle-trained fighter pilots. Many of the ship's boats were holed by gunfire and others capsized in the heavy sea. In a letter home Squadron Leader 'Bing' Cross wrote: 'When we were in the raft the Germans came up, had a look and then went straight away. I have a real hatred for Germans now.'[11] On his raft were 29 men, of whom only seven were left when finally they were picked up after three nights and two days at sea, and of these two died later. Of the whole ship's complement of 1,400 men, only 39 survived.

At the time of the action two destroyers, *Acasta* and *Ardent*, which were the carrier's only escort, made smoke and retaliated with fearless torpedo attacks, but they too were sunk. One of *Acasta*'s torpedoes, fired while she was almost in her death throes, hit *Scharnhorst*, putting two of three engine rooms out of action, so that the flotilla had to limp back to Trondheim at 20 knots. Of the crews of the British destroyers only three men survived, but this gallant action no doubt saved the weakly escorted troop convoys to which the Germans had got so close.

The loss of the *Glorious* provoked the Admiralty into a retaliatory air strike upon the damaged *Scharnhorst* at anchor in

Trondheim. The carrier *Ark Royal* was chosen for the task. Instead of leaving the method of attack to the naval airmen, the navy's top brass ordered that Skua dive-bombers, rather than Swordfish torpedo planes, should be used, and this ensured failure.[12] The 500-lb bombs would not penetrate the deck armour of the battleship *Scharnhorst*, which in places was 105 mm thick. (The *Königsberg*, sunk by dive-bombing on the 10 April, was a light cruiser with deck armour no thicker than 20 mm.)

Trondheim lies in a deep fiord 50 miles from the coast. At midnight on 12–13 June *Ark Royal's* 15 Skuas began the long journey inland, but coast watchers sounded the alarm some 20 minutes before the aircraft reached their target. In these latitudes there was little or no darkness and the Germans always protected valuable targets with well-sited Flak. The sky was clear as the Skuas dived from 11,500 feet to find a screen of Messerschmitt fighters. Though they approached alternately from different directions, eight out of fifteen Skuas were lost, with little or no damage inflicted on the German ships.

It was another example of the failure of the men at the Admiralty to understand the role of aircraft, whether in reconnaissance, defence or attack. After the loss of the *Glorious*, Admiral Sir Charles Forbes, the C-in-C Home Fleet, remarked somewhat plaintively that although the Luftwaffe seemed to come over his fleet anchorage at Scapa regularly and often, 'we generally learn where his major forces are when they sink one or more of our ships.'[13]

There is no pilot braver or more skilled than the man who flies across the sea from a carrier, but Skuas and Gladiator biplanes were no match for modern fighters such as the Messerschmitt. Even when the Royal Navy's 'modern' eight-gun fighter, the Fairey Fulmar, began arriving in late 1940 it did not significantly improve matters. The Fairey Albacores were similarly ineffective. This biplane replacement for the Swordfish was such a disappointment that it was soon withdrawn from front-line duties and the old Swordfish biplanes put back into service.

A post-mortem was held on the sad fiasco in Norway. The RAF had sent Gloster Gladiator biplane fighters there to operate from a frozen lake which was under constant attack by enemy bombers. Their story is short but no less epic for that. On their return to London, the squadron commander of 263 Squadron and his flight commander Stuart Mills were summoned to the Air Ministry for debriefing. According to Mills:

When we pointed out the difficulties we had been confronted with – wrong aviation spirit, wrong oil, no serviceable starter batteries, unsuitable equipment, no maps, lack of ammunition – senior officers were unable to give any answers. We were simply told: 'You appreciate the squadron was sent to Norway as a token sacrifice.'[14]

Subsequently the pilots were asked to go to the House of Commons and tell their story to Sir Samuel Hoare, the secretary of state for Air, or not quite tell him:

We had been told by senior officers at the Air Ministry that on no account were we to relate to the Secretary of State any of the mistakes which had been made in Norway, but rather, to paint as favourable a picture as we could . . . I felt this whitewashing was all wrong.

The Luftwaffe emerged from the Norwegian campaign with prestige unchallenged. At Oslo it was the air force which was the deciding factor. German paratroopers took the airport and held it while waiting for airborne reinforcements. By keeping the Royal Navy at bay, supporting the advance of army units, and supplying isolated units from the air, the Luftwaffe had everywhere tipped the scales.

The attack westwards – May 1940

The air-policing duties that the RAF performed during the interwar years, in Iraq and at India's north-west frontier, had provided a cadre of aircrew skilled in working with ground units. But when in 1939 the British Expeditionary Force went to France, the RAF provided only four army cooperation squadrons. (In the First World War, when the Royal Flying Corps was a part of the army, the same mileage of front had been allotted 20 squadrons.) The Westland Lysander, specifically designed to support the army, proved so inadequate in front-line use that, when the German assault started, it was withdrawn from operations. 'I went to France with a squadron of Lysanders, an Army Cooperation squadron,' said Flying Officer Christopher Foxley-Norris.[15] 'We lost the lot – twelve out of twelve. Some of the men were killed and others baled out and were rescued. But we finished up with no aircraft.'

At the start of the war Bomber Command's Fairey Battle light bomber squadrons had been sent to France as a part of the 'Advanced Air Striking Force'. For a few quiet days the Battles flew along the frontier unescorted, and then they were bounced by German fighters and after that two squadrons of Hurricane escorts were added to their force.[16] As well as Hurricanes there were Gladiator biplane fighters in France, but no Spitfires, and the Spitfire was the only RAF fighter that could fight the Emil on equal terms.

During the phoney war the Gladiator pilots of Nos 607 (County of Durham) and 615 (County of Surrey) squadrons discovered that, apart from being totally outclassed by enemy fighters, their lack of speed prevented them from even catching up with German bombers. Like many other RAF squadrons, these were units of the Auxiliary Air Force which before the war was manned almost exclusively by civilians who gave up their evenings and weekends to learn how to fly warplanes.[17] The Gladiators survived little more than a week of the German offensive. Casualties caused the two squadrons to combine, and, when a bombing raid destroyed their last fuel supplies, the remaining five or six aircraft were set on fire by the squadron personnel and they returned to England by ship.[18]

There was no lack of valour shown by the RAF crews. When the Germans attacked westwards, the AASF went into action to bomb the advancing forces. On the early morning of 12 May nine Blenheim bombers flew to attack an armoured column near Tongeren. They encountered the constant air cover that the Germans provided to the advance, and only two Blenheims returned. With the two Blenheim squadrons decimated the more vulnerable Fairey Battles were sent into the fight. Only one aircraft returned after six volunteer crews bombed two bridges at Maastricht. Although one bridge was hit, engineers had a pontoon bridge in position within 30 minutes. A German officer told one of the few surviving flyers:

> You British are mad. We took the bridges early Friday morning. You gave us the whole of Friday and Saturday to build up our Flak entrenchments all around the bridge, and then on Sunday, when everything was ready, you came here with three planes and tried to blow the thing up.[19]

Two days later the striking force committed every available plane to stem the German tide. Battles and Blenheims were sent to bomb the German crossings of the River Meuse at Sedan. They destroyed two pontoon bridges, and damaged two more, but pontoon bridges can be replaced quickly. About 60 per cent of the attacking aircraft were shot down by fighters or by well positioned Flak. It was the worst percentage loss the RAF ever suffered in any comparable operation. There is little doubt that news of this disaster played a part in the war cabinet's reluctance to send more squadrons over to France.

Up until the start of the Battle of Britain, the Luftwaffe's role as a close-support weapon assisting the army to blitzkrieg victories seemed entirely vindicated. What point was there in having a strategic air force when nations could be totally defeated in short sharp tactical wars?

And yet this role called for sudden ruthless violence. In Guernica in Spain, the Luftwaffe showed no remorse for the civilian casualties that must result from bombing towns. In Warsaw and Rotterdam the German bombers left a great many dead and mangled people in the smouldering rubble.

The Rotterdam bombing provides a good example of that grey area in which war becomes terrorism. The Dutch defending army was moving to wipe out German paratroops at Overschie, north of the city. The advancing Germans were anxious to press on to relieve the paratroops, but that could not be achieved without getting into Rotterdam. When they received a surrender ultimatum, the Dutch defenders played for time by arguing about the message, which bore no name, rank or signature of the German commander. They asked for this to be rectified, which required an extension of the deadline. Negotiations were not made easier by the fact that Dutch time was 20 minutes ahead of Greenwich Mean Time. The outcome was that the land attack was halted but part of the air attack was not stopped in time. The centre of Rotterdam was razed. Some historians have called it a deliberate act of terror.

When I described the Rotterdam bombing in my book *Fighter* some Dutch readers told me I had let off the Luftwaffe far too lightly. One eyewitness wrote: 'I can categorically state that incendiaries were used, that the inner city was completely without any military strength, that a kilometre away from the river front, houses and entire streets were ablaze within minutes of the bombardment.'[20]

Yet it has to be added that the town was defended, however lightly, and at the Nuremberg Trials the bombing was judged to be militarily justified.[21] On the other hand, can anything done in pursuit of the brutal invasion of a friendly neutral country be justified? Such questions will not be settled easily.

Although the Luftwaffe had been designed for short sharp campaigns, these were following one after the other in quick succession, so that there was no respite in the air war. The soldiers could stop, rest and regroup, but they still needed air cover while they did it. The airmen were no longer finding things so easy, and they suffered heavy casualties during the campaign in France and the Low Countries. On 10 May, the first day of the attack, 47 bombers were lost as well as 25 fighters and a number of transport planes. It was as bad as any day of losses in the Battle of Britain. The following day another 22 bombers, 8 Stukas and 10 fighters were lost.[22]

During May and June 1,129 Luftwaffe aircraft were shot down on operations and another 216 became victims of accidents. Hundreds more were damaged beyond repair. The human casualties reflect these figures. And most of these flyers were experienced men very difficult to replace.

The spectacular conquest of France, Belgium and Holland and rout of the British Expeditionary Force had taken the Germans six weeks and cost them 27,074 dead.[23] Apologists for the French débâcle explained that the Germans had crushing superiority in tanks and aircraft. It was not true of tanks, but the value of the French air force is harder to assess.

The French aircraft industry during the 1930s was a chaos of muddle and corruption. In January 1938 an energetic new air minister, Guy La Chambre, found himself dealing with a collection of small factories spread across the whole country. Only one of them was equipped for mass-production. He bought American aircraft and called for a construction programme that would build 200 planes a month. It was slow in starting, but by June 1940 the Dewoitine D.520 – a fine fighter, equal to the Spitfire or the Messerschmitt Bf 109 – was coming off the production lines at one every hour.[24]

General Joseph Vuillemin, chief of the French air force, claimed that in the 1940 fighting he had been outnumbered five to one. Many of his planes were obsolete but in the matter of quantity the French were Germany's equal. The two German Air Fleets in action totalled 2,670 aircraft of which about 1,000 were fighters.[25] The French air force had 3,289 modern aircraft available. Of these 2,122 were fighters.[26] This does not take into account aircraft of the Royal Air Force or the air forces of Belgium or Holland.

Some French squadrons fought ferociously, but as the bombing started many French aircraft were flown out of the danger zone and parked at training fields and civil airports without any records being

kept. One eyewitness reported 200 aircraft on Tours airfield, most
of them fighters. When the fighting was over, 4,200 French military
aircraft were in the unoccupied zone. Some were old and useless
but 1,700 were judged suitable for front-line service. The Italian
Control Commission in North Africa discovered 2,648 modern
French aircraft there. Seven hundred of these were fighters, many
were new.[27] Whatever one makes of all these figures, the French
flyers were certainly not outnumbered five to one.

In Poland, in Scandinavia and in western Europe the Messerschmitt Bf 109 fighter plane, the Junkers Ju 87 dive-bomber and the
Ju 52 proved essential to the German victories. The Ju 52 three-
engined transport had shone particularly brightly. Most of them
were flown by Lufthansa crews who knew the civil routes. As reservists called to service they dropped paratroops and landed on
airfields, beaches and wide roads sometimes amid the battle.
Fighter squadrons used these aircraft to move their personnel and
equipment, leapfrogging forward from airfield to airfield. The army
used them too, and in the race across northern France the Ju 52s
had rushed 2,000 army technicians to Charleville to set up a tank
repair facility.

In Holland the Luftwaffe lost about a third of the 1,000 aircraft
deployed. Most of these fell prey to Dutch anti-aircraft guns. The
way in which paratroops were dropped from 400 feet made the
transport planes easy targets. Of the 430 'Tante Ju' used in the
Netherlands, some 220 were shot down and two transport formations were subsequently disbanded. However the Dutch did not set
fire to or otherwise destroy the wrecks. After the fighting ended 53
of the Junkers were repaired and another 47 were cannibalized for
spare parts.[28] Such figures show how difficult it can be to quantify
success and failure in battle.

Dunkirk: Operation 'Dynamo'

It was in the sky above the Dunkirk beaches that the Luftwaffe
began to prove inadequate. Göring had suggested that his Stukas be
let loose upon the besieged remnants of an army that was being
taken home by a motley collection of boats and ships. But to protect the Dunkirk evacuation the RAF sent Spitfires, previously
restricted to operations over Britain. At first the RAF pilots were
dismayed at the German tactics, but they learned quickly, as Spitfire ace Robert Stanford Tuck related:

We were flying over the beaches in formations which were much too tight . . . The Germans were flying much looser formations. They bounced us in our very first encounter over Dunkirk. We lost a pilot . . . He went down in flames. The next patrol that same day we lost our squadron leader, a flight commander and one or two others . . . I found myself squadron commander. I said to myself and all the boys, 'This is enough. Tomorrow we're flying open formation in pairs.'[29]

The Luftwaffe at this time had only one single-seat fighter, the Emil, which with its blunt rectangular wings was easy to recognize. To cover the evacuation there were Spitfires and Hurricanes, Defiants with their rotating turret behind the pilot, and Blackburn Skuas of the Fleet Air Arm. Misidentifications were not unknown. In the words of one naval flyer:

806 squadron with Skuas and Rocs was called in to assist in patrolling the Dunkirk beaches on 27th May during the evacuation. A section of three Skuas was attacked out of the sun at about 0700 hours by a Spitfire squadron. Two Skuas were shot down into the sea off Dover resulting in the loss of a friend of mine and injuries to two others. The remaining Skua, piloted by Sub-Lieutenant Hogg R. N. managed to get down into Manston with his aircraft riddled with bullets, and his air gunner badly injured. The sequel to this story was that Hogg retrieved his parachute, the only piece of his equipment which was still intact, and travelled back by train to our base airfield in his flying clothing complete with packed parachute. He was approached at Victoria Station by military police for being an enemy parachutist. Only eighteen at the time he had a pronounced stutter when he became excited. At his subsequent questioning at London Headquarters by an immaculately dressed Guards Officer, he managed to splutter out his indignant explanation to be greeted by the reply, 'After all, old boy, you must remember there is a war on!' Young Hogg who was quite fearless went on to gain great distinction in naval air combat operations in the Mediterranean, where he gained a D. S. C. and Bar before being killed sadly, and I believe unnecessarily, in a normal flying accident.[30]

Despite the captured forward fighter airfields, the Luftwaffe bombers were based in Germany and no closer to the Dunkirk beaches than were the RAF flying out of home bases across the Channel. German bombers – less mobile than their fighter squadrons – could not be moved as easily as the fighter units. The RAF fighters tried to get between the bombers and their targets. As one RAF fighter pilot explained:

> Our function was to get in the way of the German aircraft. It was no good patrolling over the evacuation beach if you were hoping to save the people underneath you. You had to be twenty miles further off to get in the way of the attackers before they reached the beaches.[31]

Such tactics meant that the soldiers on the beach saw little of the defensive fighting that the RAF provided, and a great many survivors came back from the beaches complaining that the RAF had done little for them. On 31 May Flight Lieutenant R. D. G. Wight, a Hurricane pilot of 213 squadron, who was later to be killed fighting in the Battle of Britain, wrote to his mother:

> If anyone says anything to you in the future about the inefficiency of the RAF – I believe the BEF troops were booing the RAF in Dover the other day – tell them from me we only wish we could do more. But without aircraft we can do no more than we have done – that is, our best, and that's fifty times better than the German best, though they are fighting under the most advantageous conditions. So don't worry, we are going to win this war even if we have only one aeroplane and one pilot left – the Boche could produce the whole Luftwaffe and you would see the one pilot and the one aeroplane go into combat.[32]

The fierce British air cover dismayed the Germans. Fliegerkorps II's war diary told of more aircraft lost on 27 May than in the previous ten days of fighting. The RAF flew 2,739 fighter sorties over Dunkirk, 651 bomber sorties directly concerned with the BEF's evacuation and 171 reconnaissance sorties.[33] On the whole front in the nine days from 26 May to 3 June the RAF lost 177 aircraft against the Luftwaffe's 240.

Sea Lion

The prospect of a seaborne invasion of England was not one cherished by any knowledgeable soldier. The German army's only experience with water had been river crossings and, despite the proficiency it had shown crossing the River Meuse, it didn't like them. Germany had no equivalent of the US Marine Corps or the Japanese Marines, units trained and equipped for amphibious operations. Apart from some Siebel ferries and a little LWS experimental amphibious truck, the Germans had no landing-craft and knew little or nothing about waterproofing tanks and trucks. Since the army was mostly horse-drawn, their prime headache was transporting thousands of horses across the Channel.

The difficulties of installing engines and screws into large craft forced them to the expedient of mounting aircraft engines, complete with airscrews, upon large raft-like vessels. But most of the German invasion fleet would be *Prähme*, river barges. The Germans began collecting them and bringing them up to the Channel ports. None of the barges had power enough to cross the open sea, and half of them had no engines at all. Tugs would be needed, each towing two barges. The top speed was estimated at 3 knots, but some elements of the invasion force would face 40 or 50 miles of water with some tidal currents of 5 knots. When they got to the English beaches the barges would be cut loose so that they could run ashore. The bows of each barge would have been converted so that a ramp allowed men, horses and vehicles to disembark on the beach. This was to have been the main assault force, preceded only by men in small assault boats and inflatable rafts.[34]

If the German army was ill-equipped for Sea Lion, as the invasion of England was codenamed, the navy seems to have given it no thought at all. After its casualties off Norway there were few seaworthy warships left. The Royal Navy, on the other hand, was at this time stripping its convoys bare to assemble four flotillas of destroyers (totalling 36) in the Channel. The Home Fleet battleships and cruisers would bring their guns to bear if the need arose.

All this by no means reduces the importance of the summer air battles of 1940 (from which Germans do not distinguish the period that we call the Battle of Britain). Had the Luftwaffe established control of the air, and been able to scour the skies unchallenged so that any moving object drew gunfire or bombs, then a seaborne landing would have been extremely difficult to counter.

It was indeed the damage suffered by the German navy in the Norwegian fighting that made it necessary for the Luftwaffe to gain *absolute control of the air* in the Battle of Britain. Only air supremacy over southern England and its coastal waters would make it possible to send an invasion force to sea with any hope of success.

The Battle of Britain

The Luftwaffe took a little time to discover that its task – to bring the British to submission by air power alone – was virtually impossible with the tools it possessed.[35] The Messerschmitt Bf 109 was limited by its range to only one section of England, and German bomber formations venturing further without them would be cut to pieces by RAF Spitfires and Hurricanes.

Thus the RAF might have to ask the extreme south-east of England country to endure heavy bombing but it could keep its own fighter and bomber bases safely out of range and commit its forces as it chose. And there was further comfort from the fact that by now British factories were producing 200 more fighter planes per month than were the Germans. With winter coming, rough seas precluding Sea Lion, and poor visibility making accurate bombing difficult, time was on Britain's side.

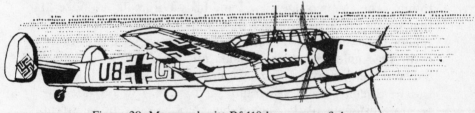

Figure 29: Messerschmitt Bf 110 long-range fighter

Before passing over these reasons for the German failure we should ask why the Messerschmitts were not equipped with long-range external fuel tanks. The Condor Legion's Heinkel biplanes were using these in the 1930s.[36] With such drop-tanks fighters could have escorted the bomber fleets to targets anywhere in Britain. No doubt this failure owes something to the unfounded faith the Germans (notably Göring himself) had in the performance of the twin-engined Messerschmitt Bf 110 as a long-range fighter escort.

Britain's radar defence network

In the first hours of the war a formation of RAF bombers, heading for the German coast, had been clearly seen on the German radar.

Pulses sent racing out across the flat surface of the ocean do not hit the hills and mountains and trees and buildings that cause the clutter and confusion on radar screens.

Britain's radar was simple, and necessarily so, for it was only just in place when war began. On the wall of Britain's experimental radar establishment a sign – 'Second best tomorrow' – reminded the scientists that there was nothing gained by having perfection if it arrived too late. In September 1939 Britain had Chain Home (CH) stations which could 'see' out to sea about 120 miles. In addition there were Chain Home Low (CHL) stations, which were specially designed to detect low-flying aircraft at a range of about 50 miles. A few mobile stations also existed to work while damaged stations were repaired.

But making good use of radar plots was just as important as obtaining them, and Air Chief Marshal Dowding's most remarkable creation was the air defence system. This network received all the available radar reports and set them out on constantly updated map tables and 'Tote Boards', so that enemy raids could be plotted, measured and met with adequate but minimal strength.

At this stage virtually no useful Enigma intelligence was available to him. The assets of Dowding, and his subordinate Air Vice-Marshal Keith Park, commander of Group 11 in south-east England, cannot be compared with those of generals who, later in the war, had remarkable scoops on German intentions. However Dowding did have the 'Y Service' which monitored the Luftwaffe's daily wireless test signals (both telegraphy and speech) to provide a very accurate estimate of the day-to-day German operational strength, and sometimes of intentions.

The British radar system had one incomparable advantage: the entire frontier of southern England faced out to sea. Placed along the coast, the radar operators reported by telephone to the plotting centres. The accuracy of electronic range detection could be improved if the angle of two radar 'sightings' of the same aircraft were drawn on a map and their intersection measured.

Once the enemy planes crossed the coast everything depended upon the 'Observer Corps': men armed with binoculars, a primitive 'sight' (that helped them estimate an aircraft's altitude), an aircraft recognition manual and a telephone. On cloudy days the Observer Corps could do nothing except report the sound of engines. At the plotting centres all the local sightings were compared and plotted on a map.

The coastal convoys

Luckily for the RAF, the Luftwaffe chose to make its initial attacks small-scale bombing runs against coastal convoys in the Channel, and this gave the RAF radar operators and plotters a chance to work with the fighter squadrons in laboratory conditions. Radar plots over the sea were relatively easy to read on the fuzzy cathode tubes. By the time the Luftwaffe began staging its larger raids on inland targets the radar system was operating at maximum efficiency.

Fighter Command had not yet faced the enemy's main offensive, but some of the pilots arriving at the squadrons were not properly trained. One of them said: 'I was given the usual training on biplanes before I was sent to join 1 Squadron in July. But I'd never flown a Hurricane before. They gave me forty minutes on a Miles Master trainer when I got to the squadron and then up in a Hurricane the next day.'[37] The unfortunate pilots who were shot down over sea during the Channel fighting had little chance of surviving. RAF pilots were not equipped with inflatable dinghies and the sea rescue organization was completely inadequate and was not expanded until the end of the year.[38]

As the attacks on Channel shipping ended in July, the Luftwaffe was reluctantly concluding that its twin-engined Messerschmitt Bf 110s could not survive one-to-one battles with Hurricanes or Spitfires. This meant a big reappraisal of the German strength. Bomber formations would have far fewer escorts to call upon, and from this time on, the Bf 109 pilots got little rest.

The main assault: Adlerangriff[39]

After July's Channel fighting (which the Germans called the Kanalkampf) there came the second phase of the battle. This was the major assault, and it lasted from 12 August (the eve of Adlertag, Eagle Day) until 24 August 1940.

It was the Nazi propaganda service that called it Adlerangriff, Eagle Attack, and it soon became a toe-to-toe slogging match in which the Luftwaffe tried to reduce Fighter Command by sheer force. Most of their vitally important Bf 109 squadrons had been crammed into the Pas de Calais region to provide maximum flying time over England.

One Spitfire pilot, shot down while chasing a Messerschmitt back to France, was taken prisoner and had drinks with the German flyers before watching them take off.

> It was impressive – several hundred aircraft going round and round, getting into their massive formations. I was then taken away and spent a day in the office of an adjutant. He was writing letters of condolence to families of Germans who were being shot down. He told me, 'Not only you. We lose a lot too.'[40]

This pilot's interrogators did not ask him anything about radar. 'They knew about it, but didn't realize how much it meant to us. One German asked me, "How is it you're always there when we come?" I said, "We have powerful binoculars and watch all the time." They didn't query that at all.'

This attitude seems to have been a general one, for few air attacks were made upon the British radar stations, despite the way in which the tall towers made them so conspicuous. The Germans were aware of radar, but failed to appreciate the use the British made of it. In that respect it was Dowding's system of fighter controlling that decided the battle.

On 15 August bombing raids were mounted from German bases in Scandinavia. The single-engined Bf 109s could not manage anything like this range, and the formations' fighter escorts were twin-engined Messerschmitt Bf 110s. It was hoped that the RAF would not have prepared defences of their central and northern coast with the same care and equipment they had deployed in the south-east. But Dowding was a careful man and the attackers suffered heavy casualties.

Although the raids from Scandinavia have usually been regarded as evidence of the Luftwaffe's foolishness, there was a method in their madness. From now onwards the RAF had to regard another attack upon that part of the country as a real possibility. Resources had to be assigned to that sector whatever the needs elsewhere.

The 'critical period': 24 August to 6 September 1940

Now the RAF fighter airfields in the south-east of England became the primary targets for the Luftwaffe's attacks. The pressure of the Adlerangriff was kept up but determined low-level bombing attacks hit the fighter squadrons on their own airfields and caused severe losses. Large and small groups of Bf 109s came prowling to find 'targets of opportunity' on the ground. Sometimes the British fighters were caught returning home, low on fuel and ammunition. Casualties among the ground personnel, damage to installations and delayed-action bombs frequently brought maintenance to a stop. Squadrons were sometimes sent into the air simply to avoid having them destroyed on the ground. This was just the opposite of Dowding's policy of conserving his forces, but there was no alternative but to fight the battle Göring's way.

Some squadrons were almost destroyed. Arriving from Scotland on 28 August, the 603 (City of Edinburgh) Squadron had by 6 September lost 16 Spitfires and 12 pilots. No. 253 at Kenley suffered the loss of 13 Hurricanes and 9 pilots in seven days, and No. 616 lost 12 pilots and 5 pilots in eight days.[41] As comparable losses came throughout Fighter Command, squadrons soon averaged 16 pilots, compared to a full complement of 26.

An additional limitation arose from the fact that the vitally important Spitfires were too advanced in design to be repaired as easily as the Hurricanes were. Surely one of the most surprising facts of the battle is that during July and August only eight airfields in the whole region covered by Groups 10, 11 and 12 were equipped to repair a damaged Spitfire.[42]

Fatigue took its toll of the flyers. Two weeks was usually enough to bring young fresh confident fighter pilots to a condition that

The Air Battlefield

required withdrawal and rest. Now Dowding was driven to the desperate measure of categorizing his squadrons into A, B and C quality, and deploying them accordingly. From now onwards C squadrons would be little more than training squadrons to give new pilots – among them Bomber Command, Coastal Command and Fleet Air Arm pilots – some sort of operational experience that would enable them to survive.

Though the supply of pilots was the worst worry, supply of aircraft was not unlimited. There was a time when RAF fighter plane losses exceeded the rate of production until, with aircraft enough for only three more weeks, the first Spitfire Mk II from the new factory at Castle Bromwich, Birmingham, was delivered to its squadron.[43] It had become a battle of attrition, and the depleted German squadrons began to study their opponents hoping to see signs that Fighter Command was cracking up. But Dowding and Park fed their sparse resources into the battle with consummate skill. The Germans saw no obvious signs of a shortage of fighter planes, and these were still being flown with determination and audacity.

Target London

It was not a quick and simple matter to train a fighter pilot. Some highly skilled and experienced pilots never became good fighter pilots. An aggressive confidence was needed, together with exceptional vision and a willingness to fly dangerously close to the enemy planes. But finding the enemy required some sort of sixth sense that told men where to look, and to recognize what they saw. The sky was immense, said one flyer:

> A lot of people were hit in their first flights and didn't know what hit them. If you look out the small window of a passenger aircraft today, you see there's a lot of space out there to look for an aeroplane. If you open up the whole area above and below you, there's an enormous amount of space for an aircraft to be in.[44]

In the months of July and August the Luftwaffe had lost 292 of their single-seater fighter pilots while the RAF lost 321 of theirs.[45] The Germans had at last recognized that their escorts were the key to the battle. For the British, although the work of Coastal Command and the night operations of Bomber Command continued, the outcome depended solely upon fighter pilots, and now the lack of them had become a crisis. Pilots from Bomber Command, Coastal Command and from Army Cooperation squadrons were put into the fighter planes, and operational training was cut from six weeks to three weeks to get trainees into combat.

This shortage of pilots was largely due to bad management by the Air Ministry. Churchill certainly inclined to that view. As early as 3 June 1940 he had sent a message to the secretary of state for Air expressing the cabinet's 'distress' upon hearing that the shortage of pilots was limiting operations:

> This is the first time that this particular admission of failure has been made by the Air Ministry. We know that immense masses of aircraft are devoted to the making of pilots, far beyond the proportion adopted by the Germans. We heard some months ago of many thousands of pilots for whom the Air Ministry declared they had no machines, and who consequently had to be 'remustered': as many as seven thousand were mentioned, all of whom had done many more hours of flying than those done by German pilots now frequently captured. How then therefore is this new shortage to be explained?[46]

Churchill's memory served him well. In 1939 the RAF's failure to organize its Service Flying Training Schools properly meant that many Civil Air Guard pilots, and RAF Volunteer Reserve pilots, all qualified and ready for operational training, were sent away and never used in the Battle of Britain.[47] RAF training was little more efficient than it had been in the First World War. In the year before the Battle of Britain, for instance, 4,000 training aircraft had been employed to produce 2,500 pilots.

Even at the worst of the pilot shortage, the RAF stuck to its policy of assigning more pilots to each squadron than there were planes to fly. In peacetime this provided for the men on leave or away from their squadrons on special assignments. When a crucial battle was waging it was a most inefficient deployment technique. Other pilots were available. It had always been the policy of the RAF that career officers should be trained to fly, and in 1940 there were countless pilots on administrative duties. Many of these men had recent and extensive flying experience, but during the Battle of Britain only 30 pilots were transferred from desk jobs to flying duties.

Air Vice-Marshal Keith Park, who commanded 11 Group during the Battle, had this to say about the chronic shortage:

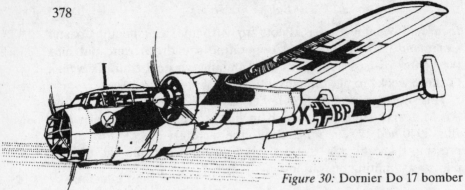

Figure 30: Dornier Do 17 bomber

it was not until the battle was nearly lost that Air Staff at the Air Ministry assisted by borrowing pilots from Bomber Command and the Royal Navy. Incidentally, [after the Battle of Britain] when I was posted to Flying Training Command, I found that the flying schools were working at only two-thirds capacity and were following peacetime routines, being quite unaware of the grave shortage of pilots in Fighter Command.[48]

Had the RAF used its pilots in a more efficient way it would have transformed the battle into a resounding British triumph. As it was, August 1940 ended with Fighter Command depleted and exhausted. But such was the energy and determination shown by the squadrons that the Germans still detected no weakening of the defences, and Göring made a fundamental change of tactics.

On Saturday 7 September, Göring arrived in the Pas de Calais in his pale blue uniform, gold braid and medals, to assume personal command of the battle. The Luftwaffe's target was now to be London: specifically, the London docks.

Just before 4 o'clock in the afternoon, when it seemed that the Germans had stood down that day, the calls started to come in from the RAF radar operators. The coloured counters were shunted across the plotting tables to display the largest raid to date: 348 bombers with 617 fighters. By half-past four that afternoon, every fighter in Park's Group was either at take-off orders or in the air. The defenders failed to see that this was to be an attack against London, and prepared for another onslaught against the air bases.[49] It was this that enabled the Germans to bomb before the interception started. One of the battle's most careful historians sets the scene:

At this moment the first British pilots were experiencing a sight which would haunt the survivors for the rest of their lives.

Breaking out of a layer of haze east of Sheppey, they found themselves on the edge of a tidal wave of aircraft, towering above them rank upon rank, more than a mile and a half high and covering 800 square miles, blotting out the sky like some vast, irresistible migration.[50]

The German bombing was accurate. The Thames Estuary coast-line was easily recognized, and for those bombs that went astray, the river was jammed with shipping. By 6 pm the Germans were heading home. As night came, the fires reached high into the sky and burned all night. Many ships, and their vital cargoes, were lost. Warehouses full of paint, rubber, whisky, sugar and spice added to the flames. Hundreds of fire pumps were in action, and no one who was there ever forgot that night.

From that time until 13 November an average of 160 aircraft raided the capital every night, except once when operations were cancelled due to bad weather. Yet despite the destruction, switch-ing from military targets to the principally civilian one of London was a fatal error that marked the end of German hopes for air supremacy over England.

On 15 September, after a relatively uneventful week of probing attacks and night raids, the pilots of 11 Group were called upon to counter another very big daylight attack. Somewhat rested, and with their aircraft in better repair than they had known for weeks, the RAF men 'put up a good show'.

This Sunday was a day of melodrama, and Churchill responded to it. He went to Park's HQ and watched the day's fighting on the plot-ting boards. History records Churchill asking what other reserves Park had, and of him 'looking grave' when Park replied: 'None.' But the controllers had never put all the Group's aircraft into the air together, and a more likely explanation is that the squadrons just landed were not yet shown as 'available' on the indicator.[51]

In any case the answer depended upon what you called 'reserves'. There were adequate numbers of fighter planes, and the ambitious Air Vice-Marshal T. L. Leigh-Mallory, who so coveted command of

Figure 31:
Junkers 88 bomber

Park's Group, was sitting in his HQ to the north of London, itching to put more squadrons into the fight. British factories were now manufacturing three planes to every two that the Germans made. Repaired aircraft further increased RAF resources now that repair had been taken away from the Air Ministry and put under the direction of an energetic and unorthodox newspaper proprietor, Max Beaverbrook. Spurred no doubt by the battles in the sky above them, the British repair staff got 4,196 damaged aircraft back into service in the second half of 1940. Between July and October 35 per cent of fighters reaching the squadrons were repaired machines.[52]

More drama followed next morning when the RAF claimed no fewer than 183 enemy aircraft shot down. The true figure was a fraction of this, but such figures came from the Air Ministry policy of generously allowing the fighter pilot's extravagant claims, while avoiding criticism by adding primly that no claims were official. The fighting was almost all taking place over British soil, and the wrecks were sitting there to be counted. Every crashed plane, home-based or enemy, was reported to the police and an armed sentry immediately posted to guard it. The correct figures were all recorded and available to the authorities, but in the period between 16 August and 6 September the BBC consistently announced substantially incorrect figures, reducing RAF losses by 15 per cent and increasing German losses by 62 per cent.

Some experienced American reporters were not taken in by the figures. They asked if they could visit the fighter squadrons and see other hard evidence. Churchill stepped in to prevent them getting such facilities. He wrote to the secretary of state for Air, Sir Archibald Sinclair: 'I must say I am a little impatient about the American scepticism. The event is what will decide all.'[53]

Churchill was right. The event did decide all. The battle was won by the unflinching bravery of exhausted young men, most of them from the peacetime RAF, but many of them 'part-time' airmen of the Auxiliary Air Force and the Volunteer Reserve. About one out of every six RAF fighter pilots was from outside the United Kingdom. As in the First World War, men from the Commonwealth made a notable contribution. There were many New Zealanders, and of 22 Australians, 14 were killed. Irishmen, Frenchmen, South Africans and Canadians were all represented. The Poles, numerically second only to men from Britain, gained a reputation for ferocious bravery, and the most successful ace was a Czech. It is also interesting to note that in the list of ten top aces of the battle the Hurricane plays as prominent a part as the Spitfire.

Some flyers had journeyed at their own expense from the far side of the world. One pilot recalled:

> We had three Americans in our squadron – Red Tobin, Andy Mamedoff and Shorty Keogh. Shorty Keogh was an ex-professional parachute jumper and barnstormer. These three had volunteered for the Finnish air force when Finland was fighting the Russians in 1939, but Finland packed in. They had then volunteered for the French air force, but the French packed in. They had got to Bordeaux, I think, where they were taken pity on by the skipper of an English freighter and brought back to England ... They went to drown their sorrows in a pub in London, where they met an air commodore one night. They explained their sad predicament to him and he said, 'Get in touch with me tomorrow.' They got in touch with him the following morning. By noon, they had been commissioned in the Royal Air Force and sent off with some money to buy uniforms and that kind of thing ... They were a grand lot, very picturesque characters. Red Tobin, a long, gangly chap, used to dash out to his aircraft with his long legs, shouting, 'Saddle her up boys. I'm riding!'[54]

The 15th of September is said to be the climax of the Battle, but the 7 September raid on London was the real turning-point. In any case it was *time*, rather than matériel, that was defeating the Germans. Even Hitler saw this, and issued an order officially postponing the invasion plans. He had left the decision until the last possible moment, hoping all the while that the British would want to discuss terms, and that no invasion would be necessary. There can be no doubt that the Germans would have been hard-pressed to muster anything like an invasion force. Barges of shapes and sizes that could be adapted to the task had proved hard to find. It was a laborious voyage to the northern ports, and once there, RAF Bomber Command had diligently bombed them night after night. 'We won the Battle of Britain,' said one of these airmen who felt their contribution had gone unrecognized in all the history books.

The Germans could scrap the leaflets[55] they had prepared to guide their occupation force through the complexities of British social life:

Some said that Churchill had deliberately provoked the Germans into switching their attack to London.[56] It was pointed out that on the night of 24–25 August a Luftwaffe navigator's error caused some bombs to be dropped on London. Churchill, disregarding his advisers, ordered a bombing raid on Berlin the following night, and

Guidelines for the behaviour of troops in England.

1. The Englishman suffers from a certain lack of imagination when faced with new situations. Therefore he reacts more slowly to given instructions or inquiries than do most European peoples. His slowness in reaction is not necessarily malevolent.

2. The greatest strength of the Englishman is to appear ignorant (stupid). He is a master at questioning others while not giving away anything of himself. When he disagrees he almost always has a hidden purpose. Mostly by disagreeing he wants to get others to speak.

3. The Englishman doesn't like to say yes or no, he doesn't like to commit himself and is a master at the art of evasion. Instead of yes he likes to say: 'It's possible'; instead of no: 'That might be difficult.' The Englishman will not tell others, even when they ask, that they have done something wrong, he doesn't correct.

4. The Englishman is very reserved. Pushiness is considered in bad taste in England. It is considered extremely tactless to intrude in another's domain, or to push oneself upon someone. That explains the cool attitude to strangers. Compared to the Englishman the Scotsman is avowedly taciturn, the Welshman is much more open-minded and temperamental. With him one has to watch his cunning.

5. The Englishman is used to having even orders and instructions preceded with the word 'Please', whereas the word 'verboten' will automatically arouse resistance in him.

6. Extreme friendliness and humour especially pay off with members of the public (lower class). With a joke one achieves more than with an order when dealing with a workman.

7. The working-class man, when handled with reserve and friendliness, is easily trusted (won over). He is then reliable up to a certain level and will be grateful for being treated decently.

8. The English woman of all classes is used to an unusual amount of consideration and courtesy from the opposite sex.

more such raids to follow it. The conclusion is that this cunning gambit of Churchill's caused the Germans to shift their attacks to London, and that it was one of his most brilliant moves.

That may well be what Churchill intended, but a closer look at these events does not support the idea that they were connected so neatly. A map showing where in London, and at what time, those first bombs were dropped on the night of August 24–25 contradicts the idea that it was an isolated accident, or due to navigational error, or even that only one plane was engaged. Bombs fell on widely different parts of the capital at times ranging from 11 pm to 3.40 the following morning.

As for the RAF's retaliatory attack on Berlin, as early as 19 July Churchill had asked Sinclair about mounting a raid on the German capital at 24 hours' notice. Sinclair did not, as it happens, advise against it. He promised that by 2 August the RAF would be ready to employ the whole bombing force and drop 65–70 tons of bombs on Berlin and continue the bombing for a week.

The subsequent RAF Bomber Command raid of 25–26 August was delivered through cloud. Most of the bombs went down on the open countryside south of Berlin. The only casualties were two people slightly injured in a northern suburb. The raid was so perfunctory that leading Nazis were in considerable doubt about whether it was anything but an accident of navigation and a few jettisoned bombloads.

Göring had ordered that London should not be bombed, and was angry to be disobeyed. On the morning after the raid he demanded that the crews responsible be punished. He even threatened to post the aircraft captains to infantry regiments. Perhaps that is why the Luftwaffe document – a map – that would identify the crews concerned is missing from the official records.[57]

Everything suggests that the Luftwaffe's raid on London by several bombers was some sort of bungle – the Luftwaffe was not renowned for its organizational efficiency – that was hastily covered up by all concerned. Churchill responded promptly with a raid on Berlin but one that had been widely discussed and approved. The RAF retaliation on Berlin played no part in the Luftwaffe's decision to concentrate its attacks on London. It was only after a few more visits to Berlin by the RAF that Hitler became convinced that these were deliberate raids on the capital.

And the Luftwaffe Air Fleet commanders' decision to switch the attacks from Fighter Command airfields to assaults on London was

not a thoughtless whim. Field Marshal Sperrle wanted to continue
the airfield attacks, but Field Marshal Kesselring argued that the
RAF always had the option of pulling back north, in the same way
as the Royal Navy had kept its ships out of range. These discussions
and decisions were based upon inaccurate figures from their intelligence service. On 30 August the commanders were told that the
RAF was down to 420 fighters plus 100 in reserve. At this time
Fighter Command had about 750 fighters operational with about
200 in reserve. The German intelligence report added that the RAF
was receiving from British and American factories fewer than 650
planes per month. In fact British factories alone were manufacturing about 500 fighters as well as 1,000 bombers and other aircraft
per month.[58]

Misled by their optimistic figures, the Germans believed that the
time had come to destroy these remaining RAF fighters by attacking a target they must defend: London. But the attacks on London
restored to Fighter Command – in effect to Park – the chance to
commit his group to battle in the way, and the quantity, he chose.

The Luftwaffe scaled down and then abandoned its daylight
bombing campaign. The plans for Sea Lion were set aside. It would
be a winter of night bombing. No matter that today many German
historians deny it: the Germans had suffered a major defeat. And it
was a defeat that the world's Press watched at first hand, with correspondents and photographers clicking their cameras and typing
their stories about both the bombed and the bombers. The message
that emerged was that 'Britain could take it'; the conclusion was
that war materials sent to Britain would be going to a worthy cause.
Whether they would be paid for was another question entirely.

The most far-reaching event of September 1940 was Hitler's order
to cut back on aircraft production. By February 1941 it would have
fallen by as much as 40 per cent. It seems an inexplicable decision,
coming at a time when the Luftwaffe could be seen to have lost the
Battle of Britain, and in a month when the number of Luftwaffe
aircraft lost in combat exceeded new production.[59] But the
shortcomings of the Luftwaffe, from the dazed and dozy Göring to
the myopia of Milch and the muddle of Udet's Technical Office,
were shown in the failure of the Luftwaffe to formulate an aircraft
construction programme, or rather the way in which no less than 16
such programmes had been started and abandoned during the first
two years of war. But this is how dictatorships were run, and no one
questioned the Führer's order.

Dowding, Park and Leigh-Mallory

Air Chief Marshal Sir Hugh Dowding is rightly given credit as the man who won the Battle of Britain. Dowding, on the Air Council as Air Member for Supply and Research, had made most of the decisions about the machinery with which the battle was fought. As chief of Fighter Command, he set limits to the number of fighters sent to France during the battles in May 1940, and he commanded the home-based fighter forces that summer. Dowding and his staff decided how many squadrons would be provided to each of the Groups and he supplied the replacements and made all the longer-term decisions.

The day-to-day tactics of the battle were those of a tough New Zealander who fought at Gallipoli and on the Western Front before becoming a pilot in the First War. Air Vice-Marshal Keith Park commanded 11 Group, which extended over south-east England where most of the air battles took place. He and his staff decided which German attacks were real and which were feints. They also decided which squadrons should be scrambled and to what heights they should go. Decisions about which industrial areas should be defended and when to take risks with his limited forces were entirely in the hands of Park.

The region to the north of Park's was commanded by Air Vice-Marshal Trafford Leigh-Mallory. His constant criticisms of the way in which Park was fighting the battle, and the faults he found in Dowding too, added an extra dimension of drama to the summer's thrills. Leigh-Mallory refused to allow his squadrons to be used as replacements for Park's battle-worn units. He repeatedly contended that bigger and bigger formations of RAF fighters must be sent against the Germans. One of his squadron commanders, Douglas Bader, was particularly vociferous in support of this 'big wing' theory.[60] When such formations did get into the fighting, they seemed to score well, but in air warfare duplicated claims always arose in proportion to the number of aircraft engaged. Exercises later proved this 'big wing' theory wrong; the time the fighters took in forming up gave the Germans time to reach their targets unchallenged. In the words of Squadron Leader Tom Gleave:

> Douglas Bader was completely wrong on tactics at the time. He was very brave. But he'd been out of the air force for ten years. He lagged completely behind in modern concepts. All he could think of, as far as I could see, was the old First World War

flying circuses, which had nothing to do with what we were up against in the Battle of Britain.[61]

A Byzantine touch was added to the controversy when the adjutant of one of Leigh-Mallory's squadrons, in his spare time a member of Parliament, took his version of the 'big wing' controversy straight to the under-secretary of state for Air and to the prime minister. As a result Park and Dowding were called to give an account of themselves, and their tactics, to a board which included Leigh-Mallory and was chaired by Air Vice-Marshal W. Sholto Douglas.

The written record of this inquisition omitted Park's stated views about the shortcomings of the big wing in both theory and practice. Park objected, but the Air Staff secretariat kept their own version of history intact. They refused to correct the minutes, curtly saying they were, 'intended more as an aide-mémoire than as a detailed report of the discussion'.[62]

The secretary of state for Air and the Air Staff were unanimous in their determination to remove Dowding from his job. Leigh-Mallory's disloyalty did not go unrewarded. When the battle was over he was given Park's command. Sholto Douglas, who had been in league with Leigh-Mallory, took over Dowding's (by now) coveted job of C-in-C Fighter Command.[63] Park was sent to Training Command and Dowding to the United States. The Air Ministry wanted the two men eradicated from history. When the official booklet about the Battle of Britain was published Dowding was not mentioned in it, although both Göring and Goebbels were named. Of the booklet Churchill told Sinclair: 'It grieves me very much that you should associate yourself with such behaviour . . .', and added:

> The jealousies and cliquism which have led to the committing of this offence are a discredit to the Air Ministry, and I do not think any other Service Department would have been guilty of such a piece of work. What would have been said if the War Office had produced the story of the Battle of Libya and had managed to exclude General Wavell's name, or if the Admiralty had told the tale of Trafalgar and left Lord Nelson out of it?[64]

About 3,000 flyers defended Britain in the summer of 1940. Many bled and burned and some 500 died while life went on almost normally on the land below them. Pilots would be drinking beer in a village pub only a few minutes before engaging in a life-and-death battle in the sky above it. Such intimacy proved a two-edged sword. Let the last words on the Battle be those of Squadron Leader Peter Devitt:

> As squadron leader, it was my job to write letters of bereavement to the parents of the pilots in my squadron who were killed. And you got parents coming down to see you when you'd been fighting all day and were dead tired. The officer of the watch would ring through and say, 'We've got Mr so-and-so here and he'd like to see you.' You had to go down and go through the whole thing with them, and tell them how it had happened. That was the worst part, though on the whole the parents took it well.[65]

20 HOURS OF DARKNESS

Sing a song of Pilots from the Pilots Pool,
Were it not for this war they would be at school.

RAF 55 Squadron song circa 1918[1]

FIGHTER COMMAND had won the Battle of Britain, but it did not come through unscathed. About 500 fighter pilots had been killed, together with many lost before the battle commenced. Many of these men were experienced professional flyers who were needed as leaders and teachers. The Luftwaffe had lost about the same number of fighter pilots, but when the crews of the larger aircraft were added in the total came to no less than 2,662 flyers.[2]

But in technology the race went to Germany. Britain had declared war without possessing the financial or industrial resources that a major war demanded. There was a crippling shortage of engineers and of skilled workers. Design and research had been chronically neglected. Even more far-reaching was Britain's inability to make machine-tools, the machines needed for manufacturing. This was especially true of precision machinery. In the period 1933–37 Germany had 48.3 per cent of the world trade in machine-tools, the United States 35.3 per cent, while Britain languished far behind with 7.1 per cent. Correlli Barnett comes to a severe and justifiable judgement in his book *The Audit of War*:

> The bleak historical truth is that those great symbols of British myth, the Battle of Britain Spitfire and Hurricane and their Merlin engine, were largely fabricated on foreign machine tools; more, their armaments and much of their instrumentation too were foreign in design, and, in the case of earlier production batches, foreign in manufacture as well.[3]

It is in the nature of combat aircraft that putting a model into action six months ahead of the enemy's equivalent development brings untold advantage. The German failures were mostly organizational. Muddles by the civil servants, and their counterparts in the armed services, were compounded by personal vendettas and the corrupt influence of the Nazi party, but the factories usually overcame the problems. Delays and difficulties in British factories – and the great importance German design teams gave to ease of manufacture and repair – meant the RAF was continuously pitting outmoded aircraft against more sophisticated German ones. Barnett adds that it was a burden made heavier by the way in which, during the period 1934–36, the Air Ministry had ordered 'large quantities of obsolescent or obsolete types . . . in pursuit of the government's then faith that sheer numbers of aircraft and squadrons would serve to cool Hitler's fevered ambitions.'[4]

The first American aircraft arrive

The Lockheed Hudson had been used by the RAF since before the war started. It was a small airliner, incongruously fitted with a large gun turret, but it had proved successful as a reconnaissance machine that could carry a bombload. The Douglas DB-7 Boston Mark I, a twin-engined light bomber, reached Britain in late 1940, and some were immediately converted into night fighters. Those who doubted that Americans were capable of producing aircraft suited to the rigours of war could be reassured at the performance of Jack Northrop's design. Used extensively in Europe and North Africa by many different air forces, it put to shame the mediocre Bristol Blenheims. And the Boston's engines – whether Pratt & Whitney or the later Wright Cyclones – did not suffer the chronic problems that plagued the Taurus radials fitted to the brand-new Bristol Beauforts.

The Royal Navy's Fleet Air Arm had always been a neglected service, going to war with antiquated biplanes such as the Walrus, the Fairey IIIF and the Swordfish. Navy flyers were glad to get even marginally better aircraft, and their first American plane, the Brewster Buffalo (an F2A-2 without arrester gear or catapult spools), was not an encouraging start.[5] But the Grumman F4F 'Wildcat' (designed as the US navy's first monoplane fighter) was something of a revelation. For the first time the Royal Navy's pilots had a fighter designed to fly from carriers. In late 1940 they fitted a flat deck on to a 5,000-ton captured German ship, and proved their new planes could fly off it and get back again: the tiny escort carrier was born.

On Christmas Day 1940 two of these Grumman Wildcats, flown by RN pilots, shot down a Junkers Ju 88 over Scapa Flow naval base.[6] It was the first such victory by an American-built plane.

But the first six months of 1941 was the time of Britain's greatest peril. In January the Luftwaffe showed that it could also dive-bomb ships. On 10 January an air attack upon the carrier HMS *Illustrious* in the Mediterranean did enough damage to put her out of action for ten months. The next day Stukas sank the cruiser *Southampton*.

Winter 1940–41: the German night raids

The Luftwaffe's operational plans for the summer air battles of 1940 had been detailed and specific. They would strike against Fighter Command in the air and on the ground, its airfields and 'ground control system'. They would strike against the whole structure of Bomber Command, against the British aircraft industry, particularly its engine factories, against ports both civilian and naval, against supplies and against imports. They would also bomb the cities to intimidate the civilians who lived there. A more limited campaign might have been within the Luftwaffe's capabilities, but to have attempted such an onslaught was a reflection of the megalomania of the men at the top.

As 1940 ended, and the days shortened, the method changed to night bombing, but this ambitious programme was not trimmed. In theory they were still trying to bomb a list of targets much like the ones they had failed to hit in daylight. In practice they did as RAF Bomber Command was doing: they tried to find a big city centre and set light to it.

The Luftwaffe had neglected such technical devices as radio-navigational aids until the Condor Legion in Spain found them necessary. In haste the technicians turned to the excellent blind landing system that Telefunken, the German electronics company, had built for airliners, and converted it to long-distance use. Two Lorenz blind-landing beams were transmitted from different places in Germany to cross at a selected place in England. Trained 'pathfinder' crews flew along one radio beam; when they heard the intersecting Lorenz transmission they were over the target. This Knickebein system worked on the same frequencies as the Lorenz receivers carried in all the German bombers, so there was no new equipment to be fitted. Its straight-line characteristics meant that an aircraft could receive the signals when 270 miles away from the transmitter (provided it flew as high as 20,000 feet).[7] The beams widened the further the aircraft went, so that at 180 miles the bomber could be brought to within a mile of an unseen target.[8] A bomb landing a mile from where you wanted it to go was good enough to find the right town but could not pinpoint a factory.

But pinpointing a factory was exactly what the far better X-Gerät could do. Again it used intersecting beams with the bomber flying along one of them, but there were now three cross-beams to give greater precision. In each bomber there was a simple clock, very much like a clockwork kitchen-timer. The first cross beam alerted the navigator. Immediately after this he heard the second cross-beam and started the clock ticking. As the third cross-beam was heard, he pressed a button that stopped one hand of the clock. The other hand kept moving towards the stationary one. When the hands met, the electrical contact was made, and that released the bombs.

This remarkable little device did away with calculations for discovering that most elusive of secrets: an aircraft's ground speed. The clock timed a sector of their flight between cross-beams. With their actual ground speed known (without errors due to navigation or inaccurate wind forecasts) the clock ticked on and released bombs or markers exactly over the chosen target. The main bomber force followed behind, and bombed the fires or coloured flares. With X-Gerät a well trained crew flying at 20,000 feet and 180 miles from the transmitter could be brought to within 60 feet of a chosen target.

As early as 13–14 August, at the height of the summer battles, the pathfinder force Kampfgruppe (KGr) 100 was testing its skills against the British aircraft industry. That night nine Heinkel He 111s went to Birmingham and hit the Castle Bromwich factory which was tooling up for Spitfire production. Only four crews found the target and the eleven 250-kg bombs they dropped did only minor damage. On that same night fifteen Heinkels of the same pathfinder group hit the Short Brothers factory in Belfast and destroyed five of the RAF's new Stirling four-engined bombers.[9]

It wasn't easy. Flying at night, with winter worsening all the time, meant that accidents became more and more common. Crews lost their way home: some even landed on British airfields. Details of the direction and wavelengths of each mission's beams were intercepted by the Bletchley Park analysts and radio counter-measures teams used jammers to distort the signals and hamper the task of bomber crews. But night after night the bombers came.

Londoners were the first inhabitants of a large modern city to be subjected to systematic night-bombing over long periods. They were forbidden to stay in the underground railway stations overnight, but had sense enough to defy this order. They bought their train tickets and tottered through the barriers and down to the platforms loaded with blankets, sandwiches, vacuum flasks of tea, cushions and eventually with beds too. The authorities had no alternative but to change their attitude. Money was given to local authorities to provide chemical toilets, bunks and canteen facilities, and eventually these facilities appeared to make this subterranean world into a substitute home and social club where families cheerfully gathered, guarding each other's bed spaces and going home only for a bath and change of clothes.

From the beginning it was perfectly clear that there was no effective weapon against the night attacks. Perhaps this accounts for the way in which the morale of many Londoners was shaken in the first weeks of the night raids.[10] The government prepared for the worst. In October 1940, members of the 4th Battalion of the Grenadier Guards at Wanstead, outside London, were ordered 'to hold themselves in readiness to help the police in the event of rioting or severe bombing in the East End of London.'[11] They stayed on call for eleven months.

But Londoners – like the residents of other towns – soon adapted to what they called 'The Blitz'. The pattern of bombing, like the evolution of London itself, followed the line of the Thames. Although it is difficult to measure bombing in terms of suffering, the more fortunate districts of central London – Westminster, the City and Southwark – took 20–30 bombs per hundred square acres during the first two months of the night attacks. The unfortunate districts – the Surrey & London docks, Shoreditch, Holborn and Chelsea – received 31–52 bombs.[12]

The bombing came as a curiously exciting and unifying experience to many Londoners. Everyone had their own bomb story. One young woman described the sounds:

> Another bomb, nearer this time – and then, suddenly, the weirdest sort of scratching sound just above the roofs – the sound was as if someone was scratching the sky with a broken finger nail. It lasted a second, no more, and then there was the most God awful crash – it seemed only a couple of gardens away (actually it was in Upper Park Road), I felt the earth juddering under me as I sat.[13]

I remember the fall of bombs sounding more like paper-wrapped parcels sliding down a metal chute, but the fingernail is more vivid. The Luftwaffe employed a very wide variety of explosives in containers of different shape, size and construction. At the outbreak of war, the Luftwaffe's high-explosive bombs ranged from 50-kg up to 500-kg, but before long there came the plump-looking 1,000-kg (2200-lb), which contained 600 kg of explosive and was nicknamed Hermann by the British Bomb Disposal teams. The heaviest bomb dropped during the Blitz was the SC 2500, the Max, which was nearly four metres long and weighed almost two and a half tons. Only two crews (both of III Gruppe Kampfgeschwader 26) were authorized to drop it over Britain. Its first recorded use was on 20–21 November 1940.[14]

Incendiary bombs were the most destructive of air weapons. Fire distorted even heavy engineering machinery that high-explosive failed to damage permanently. Incendiary bombs came as Flammenbombe that exploded to spread flaming oil and as Phosphorbrandbombe using a benzine-phosphorus mixture.

The most common bomb – the one that almost everyone in London coped with at close quarters at some time during the war – was the 1-kilogram incendiary bomb using magnesium and thermite. If tackled in time they were easy to douse with a bag of sand, but some were fitted with high-explosive charges. Thousands of incendiary bombs were dropped, and the resulting fires probably caused three-quarters of the air-raid damage done to British and German towns during the war.

Until the bombs began to fall, the official Home Office attitude to unexploded devices was the same as its regulations about stray dogs: they would be collected by the police and put in a compound somewhere. It took the Home Office several months of war – and some unexploded bombs dropped on the Shetland Islands – before it was admitted that no one had any idea of how to deal with them. On 2 February 1940 the War Office sent the Royal Engineers to take over the task. Before long the soldiers with red-painted mudguards on their vehicles and curious beetle-shaped yellow badges on their sleeves became special heroes to Londoners. At first it was an unsophisticated trade. One of the bomb disposal men explained that until the end of June:

> They uncovered a bomb by cautious excavation; they removed, or tried to remove, the fuse-locking ring, often using a cold

chisel and hammer; then, if they were still alive after that, they extracted the fuse and gaine, or 'initiating charge'. This last delicate operation was done either by hand or by tying a piece of string to the fuse and then retiring some way off and pulling until it came clear of the bomb. In spite of the losses inevitable with such methods, prospects did gradually improve.[15]

As the bombing continued the teams found their task overwhelming. By August 1940 there were about 2,500 unexploded bombs waiting to be dealt with. By the following month the number had grown to 3,759. By this time the navy and the RAF were helping to tackle the problem. There were civilian volunteers too – the Voluntary Auxiliary Bomb Disposal Service – and by March 1941 these had been joined by 250 conscientious objectors from the Non Combatant Corps.

Delayed-charge bombs frequently brought the capital to a standstill. Those dropped on railway yards were particularly disruptive. The bomb that caused the most consternation was the 'Hermann' which made a hole alongside the steps of St Paul's Cathedral. Closer inspection revealed that the bomb had penetrated the ground in a curving path that had taken it to a position fifteen feet down and almost underneath the clock tower. This Wren cathedral, its distinctive dome a feature of the skyline, has always been regarded with special esteem by Londoners. The prospect of its façade being ripped apart caused great distress to Londoners everywhere.

The job of disposal was given to 16/17 section of No. 5 Bomb Disposal Company, commanded by Lieutenant Robert Davies. Soon after work started, 'Hermann' shifted and dropped another twelve feet. Digging revealed that this one was fitted with a Type 17 series long-delay fuse which was usually protected by a ZusZ 40 anti-withdrawal device. This was disheartening news. No way of tackling this device had yet been discovered, and orders laid it down that all bombs with Type 17 fuses had to be exploded without moving them.

The disposal team did not obey orders. A truck was brought as close as possible to the lifting tackle and the 1,000-kg bomb was hoisted up on to it. Lt Davies took the wheel and, with the police holding up traffic at the intersections, he drove to the Hackney Marshes, an open space where retrieved bombs were regularly exploded.

For a brief time Lt Davies and his team were the most famous men in Britain, cherished and admired in the way that sports stars are today. They received congratulatory messages from far parts of the world. Davies and Sapper George Wylie were the first service-men to be awarded the newly instituted George Cross. Two years later Davies ran afoul of the army. He was found guilty of fraud, and cashiered.[16] Sapper George Wylie's story also had a sad ending. In the 1980s, disillusioned he said by finding himself living in a land where women and pensioners were mugged, he offered his George Medal for sale. The buyer – a nearby bank – donated it to St Paul's.

Bomb disposal teams were sometimes asked to deal with other strange objects. One officer, having disarmed a bomb, was standing sipping tea when he was approached by an old lady who said that part of an aeroplane had fallen into her backyard. When asked what it looked like, she said it resembled a large boiler.

> 'I think perhaps I'll come along with you and see what can be done,' the officer said, and they set off for her house a few streets away.
>
> From the scullery four steep flagged steps led down into the little yard enclosed by a high brick wall. Close at the foot of the steps lay a parachute mine, most of it concealed by an elaborate wooden staging and steps!
>
> 'I built that so we could get to the coal and the dustbin.'[17]

The old lady's husband had hammered together a wooden frame and steps in the close vicinity to one of the sea mines that the Ger-mans were parachuting on to land targets. Called land mines by Londoners, they were triggered by barometric pressure, exploding above ground to cause widespread horizontal devastation.

Fire over England

For three months the Luftwaffe's navigational beams had locked into an intersection high in the air over the Royal Docks, but now they had been realigned to cross above the very centre of London. At about 7 o'clock on the dark evening of 29 December 1940 the Luftwaffe bombers arrived over the 'City', the banking area where much of London's finest architecture was to be found. The first wave were men of KGr 100, the Luftwaffe's pathfinder experts. On the airmen's maps it was target area 'Otto'. The pathfinders dropped 10,470 incendiary bombs, and as they banked and turned away the area was well ablaze. It is generally remembered as the grimmest night of the whole Blitz. The 136 aircraft employed were operating at short range which, by lessening fuel loads, permitted maximum bombloads. A high percentage of incendiaries caused fires worse than anything London had suffered since the Great Fire of 1666. For many it remains the night when London died. On that December night, eight Wren churches were destroyed.[18] So was London's lovely fifteenth-century Guildhall.

The Luftwaffe had chosen a Sunday night for every big raid since the night the Blitz had begun in November. The City's square mile of offices was virtually empty, as it always was at weekends. The Thames was at its lowest. Firemen went wading through cold deep mud trying to connect the pumps to the water. The authorities had yet to set up any compulsory system of fire-watchers. Fires burned undetected, and the reporting of others was made difficult by the destruction of the telephone exchange. An incendiary bomb can be extinguished in half a minute by anyone with half a bucket of sand. Herbert Mason, whose photograph of St Paul's Cathedral amid the flames has become one of the great icons of the war, wrote:

> Single-handed I could have prevented thousands of pounds worth of damage being done, but the buildings were locked, there was nobody present to force an entry. There were so few people. It was pathetic.[19]

So threatening were the heat and flames that – as in 1666 – engineers demolished buildings to make fire-breaks across which the sparks and flames could not jump.

After three hours of bombing, the raid ended. By a miracle, dense cloud over northern France, and poor visibility below it, cancelled the remainder of what had been planned as a nine-hour operation. The next day the weather grew worse until finally snow closed down the Luftwaffe's bomber bases. It gave Britain a respite.

Night bombing continued, but those who were there said that no raid was ever quite such a nightmare as that one had been. Too late the authorities instituted fire-watching and began organizing civil defence services. Government – both local and central – had been proved particularly inept by the air raids.[20]

The king and queen went to Windsor each night and many other city dwellers found ways for their families to sleep somewhere away from the target towns. Those unable to escape found a widespread official reluctance to provide comfortable air-raid shelters, in case people remained in them day and night. Neither would they provide anything but the barest quarters for bombed-out families, lest they remained in their new accommodation too long. But the failures of local government did not go unremarked, and some public officials inspecting bomb damage found themselves the targets of vocal protests.

From now onwards there would be very slow, but steady, improvement in night fighter radar that would eventually enable the RAF to fight the night bombers. Night 'intruder' missions were sent to linger over Luftwaffe airfields and attack the bombers as they came in to land, on fully lit runways, with landing lights on.

Air Marshal Sholto Douglas, who had become C-in-C of Fighter Command, promoted the use of twin-engined American-made Douglas Havoc aircraft against the German night bombers:

> A more promising idea upon which there was spent a great deal of money and time and effort was an extension of the use of airborne radar. Known as Turbinlite it called for the combined use of radar and an airborne searchlight ... The object aimed at with Turbinlite was to place the two aircraft behind the enemy raider. The Havoc would detect it with its radar and illuminate it with its searchlight in such a way that the Hurricane could then close in for the kill.[21]

Getting a 2,700-million candlepower searchlight to function inside a plane was difficult. Flying a Hurricane in formation with a Douglas Havoc weighted in this way, and doing it in darkness, was virtually impossible. What a pity that before Sholto Douglas 'spent a great deal of money and time and effort' on this idea it didn't occur to him that if the Havoc pilot had the enemy on his radar, and in front of him, he didn't need a friend in a nearby Hurricane. He could blow the raider out of the sky with a gun.

As more was known about the German beam guidance equipment, British counter-measures grew more effective. Shrill signals jammed the German guidance system, but these counter-measures were not infallible. The British knew in advance about the attack upon Coventry on 14 November 1940, but the note the radio jammers put out was not properly tuned to the German one. 'The difference – it was the difference between a whistle and a shriek – was just perceptible to the human ear; but the filter circuits in the German receivers were sensitive enough to pick the beam signals out of the jamming with ease.'[22] It was this that enabled the German pathfinder crews to find Coventry, and the successive waves to deal it a devastating blow. The centre of the town was destroyed, the ancient cathedral demolished, and many civilians killed and injured, but an employee of the City Engineer's department wrote: 'It was said that the bombing was indiscriminate but our survey showed that the Germans had attacked targets with the object of doing damage to industrial installations.'[23]

The navigational beams appeared to be working, but as early as January 1941, German losses, and British interference with the radio guidance signals, persuaded the Luftwaffe chiefs to change their targets from inland industrial centres to coastal towns which were easier to find without radio aids. For seven successive nights in May the Luftwaffe made heavy attacks on Liverpool and Merseyside. The centre of the city was gutted. A ship loaded with 1,000 tons of munitions for the Middle East exploded, causing extensive damage to the docks and other shipping. As many as 160 people were killed in one school shelter, and another 60 in a hospital. Troops were called in to help clear the streets of wreckage. More than 70,000 people were made homeless.

An improved pathfinder device, called Y-Gerät, was put into use. Counter-measures followed. There is no doubt that the Germans could have further improved their radio navigation equipment, instead of changing their targets, but in the spring of 1941 the Luftwaffe's bombing campaign lost momentum. This was not so evident at the time, and by the light of a full moon on 10 May, London suffered one of its worst bombing raids. The House of Commons, the roof of Westminster Hall and the Victoria Tower were hit. The Tower of London and the Mint were also set alight. Some 2,000 fires were started, of which nine were classified as 'conflagrations' requiring 100 pumps. London's services were stretched to their limit. It was the Luftwaffe's adieu. The combined effects of the shorter nights and preparations for the invasion of the Balkans and the titanic assault upon the Soviet Union saw the German bomber squadrons packing their bags and moving south. They had other work to do.

High-altitude air combat

In November 1940, while the German night raids continued, the RAF day fighters began to encounter an improved opponent: the Messerschmitt Bf 109F. They were picking off Spitfires by bouncing them from above. Spitfires could not equal the high-altitude performance of the newcomers, and the Hurricane was completely outclassed by it.

By the end of 1940 no one could doubt that fighter aircraft were among the war's most important weapons, and both sides regarded them as the measure of their technology. Before the war the prospect of air fighting at great altitude was not considered by the RAF, but now it could be seen as the trump card of fighter combat. Height gave any pilot a great advantage over an opponent. Only speed was more important, and height could always be exchanged for high speed.

At Fighter Command HQ[24] the top brass heard that it was not an easy task to modify the Spitfires to meet the high-altitude threat posed by the Germans. They needed longer wings, but this could not be done without strengthening them. High-altitude flying would also impose engine modifications, and at greater heights the de Havilland constant-speed propeller units would ice up. In other respects the Spitfire lagged behind the Messerschmitt. It still had fabric-covered ailerons and its engine was fitted with float carburettors, while the German engines had fuel-injection. All these marginal deficiencies in fighter performance affected the RAF flyers more than they might have done due to the obsession that the top brass had developed about invading enemy air space.

Daylight 'sweeps'

In the spring of 1941 the new RAF Fighter Command brass, who had used their 'big wing' theories to dispose of Dowding and Park, were eager to demonstrate that the theories were correct. They adapted the idea and sent fighter wings on sweeps across northern France (codenamed 'Rhubarbs'). These missions were not popular with the pilots, who were told that, if no German fighters were in evidence, they must attack targets of opportunity on the ground.[25] The Air Ministry Press Department on the other hand made the most of this 'lean forward into France' and the newspapers, always eager for news of British successes, obliged with headlines.

The RAF fighter sweeps did little towards winning the war, and soon a new tactic was evolved. The fighters would be accompanied by bombers. A new codename was chosen: 'circuses'. The RAF said: 'The object of these attacks is to force the enemy to give battle under conditions tactically favourable to our fighters.' What this really meant was that RAF fighters were at a disadvantage at heights where the Messerschmitt Bf 109F operated so well. The RAF would therefore tempt the Germans down to fight at low level. When the Germans proved reluctant to participate in this game, the RAF sent along some bombers as bait. The Short Stirling – the RAF's only four-engined bomber designed as such – was apt to be chosen for this unenviable role. It had a poor ceiling, and in daylight the German Flak could shoot it down without the Spitfires getting a chance to fight. The history of 74 Squadron records that 'casualties were severe and the losses far greater in experienced pilots than gains in new ones trained.'[26] Between the beginning of the year and the middle of June 1941 the RAF flew 104 rhubarb missions and 11 circuses. It lost 33 pilots while shooting down 26 German aircraft.[27]

The ineffectiveness of the RAF sweeps can be measured by the way in which the Germans withdrew their fighter units from France while the sweeps continued. By May only two – Jagdgeschwader (JG) 2 (Richthofen) and Jagdgeschwader 26 (Schlageter) under Adolf Galland – remained in the West.

Messerschmitt's fighter was a fine machine and the 109F was perhaps its best model. But Mitchell's Spitfire was a masterpiece which lent itself to endless modifications and improvisations right up till war's end. And while the Messerschmitt wings were too frail to incorporate weightier armament, the Spitfire, having started with four Browning guns in each wing, could swallow almost anything. Half a dozen or more different versions of the Spitfire were hurriedly produced, mostly from old machines. These Mark V variants had bigger Merlin engines, better propellers, cannons in the wings or metal ailerons: some had all of those improvements. While the performance of the Messerschmitt 109F was still marginally superior the Spitfires could now stand up to them,[28] and there were many of the older Emils still in service.

But the Luftwaffe had long seen the limitations of Messerschmitt's design and, while the 109s were kept in full production, an entirely new fighter was being tested. The Focke-Wulf Fw 190 was a lightweight machine with a powerful BMW engine. In the summer of 1941 one of them was sent to JG 26 at Abbeville/St Omer for combat evaluation.

In September RAF combat reports began to mention the new fighter, although it had been flying there since July. Alan Deere, one of the war's best fighter pilots, remembered an early encounter:

'The North Weald Wing was to fly above the Hornchurch Wing, thus forming a mass formation which would sweep into enemy territory with the object of "seeking and destroying the enemy" as the order, detailing the operation, put it.' But the Fw 190 proved a formidable opponent and Deere saw it in action against a fellow pilot:

> For a brief second the Spitfire seemed to stop in mid-air, and the next instant it folded inwards and broke in two, the two pieces plummeting earthwards; a terrifying demonstration of the punch of the FW 190's four cannons and two machine guns.
>
> [Deere returned to base and] As I taxied towards the dispersal after landing I noticed nothing unusual at first, but when I got close I was amazed, and somewhat taken aback, to see how very few Spitfires there were in the parking area. I could see 'Brad' Walker waiting to greet me, and from the look on his face I knew something dreadful had happened.
>
> 'Relieved to see you back, sir, we thought you had bought it too,' was his depressing greeting.

Deere's squadron had lost two-thirds of its Spitfires.[29] For the intelligence staff the shape of this new German fighter came as a surprise. The liquid-cooled, in-line engine seemed to have established its superiority for all modern fighter planes,[30] yet here was a radial-engined fighter proving that it could move faster than a Spitfire VB. The engine in question was a 42-litre 14-cylinder BMW 801, its cylinders arranged in two rows. There were improved Merlins, and other engines for the Fw 190, but the BMW 801 was perhaps the ultimate piston engine. Jet propulsion was just around the corner.

Bomber Command operations 1939–41

RAF Bomber Command began the war ill-prepared for the task it had so persistently proclaimed was going to be the sole way to victory. Its heaviest aircraft were twin-engined Armstrong Whitworth Whitleys, Handley Page Hampdens and Vickers Wellingtons, and in March 1939 these types together totalled less than fifty. The rest of the bomber force were Fairey Battles and Bristol Blenheims which could carry only 1,000 lb of bombs and had such short ranges that using them against Germany from bases in Britain was impractical.

There were no four-engined bombers, and no heavy bombs. In 1918 the RAF's largest bombs weighed 1,650 lb; in 1939 the heaviest were 500 lb.[31] Despite the prewar plans for bombers to fly in day-light, little thought had been given to defending the bombers, and the possible use of fighter escorts had been rejected out of hand.[32] Much publicity had been given to the powered gun turrets, but the small-calibre machine-guns inside them were no better than those used in the previous war, and certainly not an effective weapon against a fast-moving enemy plane of metal construction. Neither did Bomber Command have a reliable bomb-sight. The Course Set-ting Bomb-sight was little better than a calibrated metal rod.

Lacking any navigational guidance systems, apart from a radio with a loop aerial, Bomber Command expected its aircrew to navi-gate by means of the triangle of velocities. Such 'dead reckoning' gave a pilot his heading by drawing to scale a triangle depicting how far the forecast winds would send him off course. For local flights in daylight, such methods suffice for flying club pilots, but an estimate made by Bomber Command said it would bring an aircraft only to within about 50 miles of its target.[33] So the RAF gave its navigators a four-week course in logging astral sightings by using the Mark IX bubble sextant. As anyone who has tried it knows, measuring the angle of a star, and consulting tables to estimate one's position on earth, is difficult. Doing so in a cramped fast-moving bomber is a remarkable feat. On cloudy nights of course it was impossible to navigate by this method; on clear nights the bombers were vul-nerable targets for fighters and in full view of anti-aircraft gunners on the ground.

On the first night of the war – before the RAF's daylight attacks on German shipping – ten Whitleys were sent to drop 13 tons of propaganda leaflets over Germany. The RAF did not relish this task but it became a regular part of Bomber Command's operations. The actual text of the leaflets was classified secret. Air Vice-Marshal Arthur Harris, commanding Bomber Command's 5 Group, said that the leaflets: 'had to be handled under all the complicated secret document procedure on our bomber stations and, in spite of repeated applications, we could never get these instructions with-drawn . . . Many of these pamphlets were patently so idiotic and childish that it was perhaps just as well to keep them from the knowledge of the British public, even if we did risk and waste crews and aircraft in dropping them on the enemy.'[34]

In the first three months of these futile missions Whitley bombers, which carried out most of them, suffered 6 per cent casualties. It was not insignificant, considering that the raids were not strenuously opposed, but compared to the terrible losses its air-craft suffered in daylight, it convinced the RAF brass that night operations were the only future for Bomber Command.

Until May 1940, on the government's instructions, the RAF had avoided the bombing of German targets other than military installa-tions. The German attack westwards and Churchill's appointment as prime minister changed all that. On 15 May 99 aircraft were sent to bomb railway and oil targets in the Ruhr. This was the start of the strategic bombing offensive which did not end until 1945.

During the summer of 1940 the shipping and concentrations of barges being prepared for the Sea Lion invasion provided vital tar-gets for air attacks by night, yet the bomber barons could not be brought to see the logic of this. They maintained that such tactical targets were much less important than strategic targets. Their con-cession to the immediate peril went no further than listing aluminium plants and other targets in some remote way concerned with equipping the threatened German onslaught. Considering that these raids would only be attempted in moonlight, and that the bombers would be unlikely to find these distant targets, such a con-tribution would be less than decisive. Of course the fact was that the air force chiefs were still frightened that tactical bombing would bring them under the orders of the army or the navy and challenge their hard-won independence. A compromise was reached as heavy bombers which had failed to find distant targets at night were in-structed to bomb airfields in occupied territory on the way home. Blenheims of No. 2 Group suffered such heavy losses in daylight that they were told only to press home their attacks when there was ample cloud cover over the target. In July this resulted in 90 per cent of the sorties being aborted. It was not until 13 September that the whole of the bomber force was sent to attack invasion targets. This account comes from the pilot of a Blenheim attacking Ostend:

> The whole of the 'Blackpool Front' as we call the invasion coastline stretching west from Dunkirk, was now in near view. It was an amazing spectacle. Calais docks were on fire. So was the waterfront of Boulogne, and glares extended for miles. The whole French coast seemed to be a barrier of flame broken only by intense white flashes of exploding bombs and varicoloured incendiary tracers soaring and circling skywards.[35]

By 23 September photographic cover revealed that the number of barges in the ports between Flushing and Boulogne had decreased by nearly a third. The immediate threat of naval invasion seemed to have passed.

The Battle of Britain was over, but there was no indication that any of the world's bomber commanders had learned anything from it. The Luftwaffe high command showed no sign of changing its tactics, and when the Germans attacked the vast spaces of the Soviet Union, their air force was no bigger than it had been in 1939! Its quality had fallen.

The US army air force chiefs saw no reason to change their theories about daylight bomber operations. They believed the Luftwaffe's failure over Britain was due to poor formation-keeping, low altitudes, inadequate defensive armament, inadequate speed and airframes that were too frail and small. In other words all that prevented the Heinkel He 111 bombers from operating unescorted was that they were not Boeing B-17s. No lessons were learned about the meagre range of the escorting Bf 109s, the need for external fuel tanks, nor about the devastating losses the bombers suffered when no escorts were present.

RAF Bomber Command learned nothing from the Battle of Britain, nor from the night 'Blitz' that followed it. The fact that Londoners had not lost morale through the night bombing raids did not change the attitude of the RAF's C-in-C, Sir Charles Portal, towards strategic bombing plans. The Germans, he said, would not be able to take bombing in the way the British could.

Even with pathfinder forces and electronic guidance systems (which the RAF did not possess), the German bombing of England had been too scattered and too haphazard to be effective. With this fact in mind the target reports and 633 photos taken on one hundred different RAF raids during June and July 1941 were subjected to very careful analysis under the direction of D.M. Butt of the cabinet secretariat:

> He reported that [of the two-thirds of crews who claimed to have hit the targets] only one-third had come within five miles of the aiming point. Against the Ruhr this proportion fell to one-tenth ... Mr Butt found that moonlight was indispensable to the crews of Bomber Command: two crews in five came within five miles of their targets on full moon nights; this ratio fell to one in fifteen on the moonless ones.[36]

The frightening inference was that attacking the heavily defended Ruhr in anything other than the light of the full moon would be a waste of resources. But it was then that the defences were at their most ferocious. In addition to this startling disclosure there came the depressing news that British explosive was of poor quality, and that many RAF bombs did not explode at all.

The four-engined bombers

Before the winter of 1940-41 was over, Bomber Command was receiving the first of its heavy four-engined bombers. Supplies of these were slow and teething troubles considerable. The Short Stirling arrived first, making its first operational sortie in February 1941.

Poor speed and low ceiling were not the Stirling's only hazards. With the development of better RAF heavy bombers, danger increased. It was 'not much fun making your bombing run at 10,000 feet or so knowing that the Lancasters and Halifaxes were at 18,000–20,000 plus feet above you and that their bombs and incendiaries had to pass you on the way to the target – and sad to say many went through or struck aircraft with dire results.'[37]

The results were dire indeed, because most of the bombs from above were incendiaries, and the wings they hit contained the Stirling's fuel. These shortcomings kept the losses in Stirling-equipped squadrons well above average. Eventually Stirlings were withdrawn from mainforce operations and given such tasks as towing gliders and dropping parachute mines into the sea.[38]

The year of 1941 began with grand plans. Reasoning from entirely wrong facts, the Air Ministry, the chiefs of staff and the war cabinet Defence Committee all endorsed 'The Oil Plan'. The planners said that, since the Germans were desperately short of fuel, bombing raids could deprive them of about 1.5 million tons of it and 'place the enemy in a most critical position'. On 15 January the directive went to Bomber Command saying: 'The sole primary aim of your bomber offensive, until further orders, should be the destruction of the German synthetic oil plants.'

The Germans were not desperately short of fuel. They were receiving the complete output of Romanian oilfields, beside a great deal more from the Soviet Union. These were not closely guarded secrets; they were what William Shirer, an American newspaperman in Berlin, had seen as self-evident, and written into his diary.

Sir Richard Peirse, who had become chief of Bomber Command, declared himself confident that this new strategic bombing plan could be carried out. But he was well aware that nothing achieved by the previous year's offensive supported such a rosy view.[39]

To what extent did any of the people who so enthusiastically paid lip-service to this ambitious plan believe in it? Churchill certainly had doubts. Pinpoint bombing would be needed to hit the compressor house of the atmospheric distillation units used to make synthetic fuel. As winter turned to spring it was quite clear that this degree of accuracy was not within the capabilities of Bomber Command's night operations.

Any last belief that Bomber Command's attacks had brought the Germany economy to the sort of low point that the Ministry of Economic Warfare liked to describe disappeared in June 1941. The offensive that Hitler launched against the USSR in June displayed the awesome might of the Third Reich for all to see. German morale was clearly unshaken, and the RAF bombing raids had been no more than pinpricks. Perhaps the men in the Air Ministry realized this, for on 9 July the deputy chief of Air Staff quietly directed 'the main effort of the bomber force, until further instructions, towards dislocating the German transportation system and to destroying the morale of the civil population as a whole and of the industrial workers in particular.'[40] In case anyone missed the point an appendix added that specific targets needed moonlight so: 'For approximately three quarters of each month it is only possible to obtain satisfactory results by heavy, concentrated and continuous attacks on large working-class and industrial areas in carefully selected towns.'

Out with the Oil Plan; in with the Transport Plan. The men in the Air Ministry backed up their new ideas with specific rosy forecasts. Assuming, for instance, that 90 aircraft reach the target and that there is an average aiming error of 600 yards, then 112 bombs will fall into the target area, along with nearly 2,000 incendiaries. Thus 15 tons of explosive (50–100 bombs) should put a railway centre completely out of action for a week and perhaps cause widespread delay and dislocation for months. Where had the RAF found such fantasists?

About six weeks after the Transportation Plan started, the Butt Report brought a chilling wind of reality into the hot air of Whitehall. But it did nothing to cool the enthusiasm of Sir Richard Peirse. Upon his copy of the report he scribbled a note of his disbelief. His senior air staff officer shared Sir Richard's scepticism. The only real problem, as they saw it, was that Bomber Command was not yet a heavy bomber force. By November 1941 the RAF had 66 heavy bombers, of which 18 were Stirlings. Raids, by day or night, were made by twenty or thirty bombers.

In September 1941, an experimental four-engined bomber had gone to be evaluated by No. 44 Squadron. It had been cobbled together by extending the wings of an Avro Manchester to make space enough for four Rolls-Royce Merlin engines. Without waiting for the results of the evaluation, the RAF forwarded a report to Churchill saying that bombing raids could strike a decisive blow against Germany in only six months. But to do it they would need 4,000 such heavy bombers.

Churchill replied curtly that, since only a quarter of the RAF bombs were hitting their targets, an improvement in accuracy could raise the bomber force to four times its present effective strength.

No matter how outdated the RAF methods and equipment might be, Air Ministry propaganda was expert, modern and unrelenting. In August 1941 an excellent 50-minute film, *Target for Tonight*, was shown as the main feature in many cinemas. Shot on a Bomber Command airfield, as well as in the studios, it had the strength of all good documentary film, with real RAF men playing themselves: men diffident, attractive and unassuming. Its story was serialized in the *Daily Express* and a fully illustrated booklet of the film was published. A few weeks later came a 130-page book, *Bomber Command*, illustrated with photos and diagrams, which put the case for the Command with warmth and vigour. The response to this publicity left no doubt that whatever battles the Air Ministry had lost, it had won the most important battle, that for public support. But not everyone was fooled. In April 1942 the US air attaché in London reported to Washington: 'The British public have an erroneous belief which has been fostered by effective RAF publicity, that the German war machine can be destroyed and the nation defeated by intensive bombing.'[41]

Criticism of Bomber Command's policies, and its operations, were cogent and varied; objections were both moral and practical. They came from the army and the navy and the Church. But from this time onwards these critics would tread carefully. The bomber crews appeared to be the only men in Britain able to hit back at the Germans and, in pub and club, the British people showed them warm appreciation. They little suspected that in 1940 and 1941 Bomber Command suffered more fatal casualties than did the Germans at the receiving end, nor that the bombing did little to reduce German production of war material. In 1945, after the British and

American bombers had pounded Germany for years, they succeeded in reducing German production by less than 10 per cent (some accounts say about 4 per cent).[42]

Kammhuber Line

As RAF Bomber Command night raids continued the Germans became more expert at intercepting them. The German night fighters had originally operated over German cities, spotting the bombers with the aid of the searchlights. Changes took place after General Joseph Kammhuber was given command of the German air defences. Flak, searchlights and radar were positioned along the northern coast, each 'box' working in conjunction with its own night fighter. By 1943 this 'Kammhuber Line' would stretch along the Rhine to continue along the Dutch and German coast all the way to Denmark. More defences were concentrated round the major German industrial centres.

The RAF's most practical response to this was to push the bombers through the Line in a tight, fast-moving stream that would overwhelm the defences at that one spot. But without electronic aids, RAF navigation was not good enough to get the stream tightly together. On 7 November 1941 the RAF lost 37 aircraft, almost 10 per cent of the raiding force. Such attacks could not continue. Not only were they too damaging to morale, but Bomber Command would soon have had no more bombers left.

Centimetric radar

And yet the year of 1941 ended with a significant development in British radar. The aim of getting interception radar sets small enough to fit inside night fighters had long been the dream of British scientists. A Blenheim from the Fighter Interception Unit at Tangmere had shown that it was possible as early as 23 July 1940. Helped into position by a radar station on the ground, the Blenheim's radar operator had got a blip on his experimental set and found a Dornier Do 17 in the dark. The Dornier was shot down into the Channel. This was the world's first radar-directed night interception,[43] but the scientists were after something better. Since the beginning of the war, J. T. Randall and A. H. Boot of Birmingham University had been working on centimetric radar. Quite different from the simple 'floodlight' devices used along the British coastline, centimetric radar produced a pulsed narrow beam of short wavelength that was less susceptible to jamming and opened the way to miniaturization.

Now Randall and Boot made a major breakthrough that gave the British a considerable lead. The heart of it was the cavity magnetron valve and the way the cavities were cut through it. Manufacture demanded accurate machining of a block of copper, water for cooling and a powerful electro-magnet. To design it, called for a blend of industrial experience and advanced theory, plus a big measure of luck. Working on a shoestring budget, the two men got their machine working on 21 February 1940.

Small and very accurate, the new sets could be put inside night fighters and used to detect enemy aircraft through cloud or darkness. During the various flight trials it was noticed that the cathode tubes showed sketchy 'pictures' of the landscape below. Water, buildings and countryside were different tones. Modified and fitted to bombers, such sets could depict target towns as recognizable shapes upon a cathode screen.

The valve was a solid chunk of metal and would certainly survive a crash landing. Immediately there came new worries about what might result if the Germans salvaged the secret device from a shotdown RAF bomber. The Germans would find no great difficulty in copying it. The Royal Navy had the answer: this was just what was desperately needed for detecting U-boats on the surface. Over the ocean there would be no worries about the Germans retrieving the secret devices. Furthermore centimetric radar had arrived at a time when Britain's sea routes were in grave peril. Yet Bomber Command won the political battle for the centimetric radar set, and after the second raid in which it was used, the Germans salvaged one of the new devices from the wreckage. Nine days later it was being discussed at a top-level conference of German staff officers and technicians.

The weight of strategic bombing

Over Christmas 1941 Air Marshal Arthur Harris, then head of the RAF delegation in the United States, was appointed to take over Bomber Command. Few Americans who had met Harris had failed to hear of his belief in strategic bombing, and with him in charge the RAF's bombing war would surely be intensified. Until now Bomber Command had lost 7,448 aircrew (killed in action or in accidents or made prisoners of war). By war's end the Command would possess 1,600 heavy bombers and the losses would have reached 72,350.[44] German suffering would continue on an ever-increasing scale. In the final eight months of the war, the USAAF would drop 350,000 tons of bombs, and the RAF 400,000 tons, ten times the weight the Germans dropped on Britain during the entire war, including V1 and V2 missiles.[45]

After the war area bombing was severely criticized and Sir Arthur Harris became the focus of this criticism. In June 1992, a statue of 'Bomber' Harris was unveiled by the Queen Mother, who had been Queen during the war, while a Lancaster bomber flew overhead. The service was attended by Margaret Thatcher, the ex-prime minister, and by Bomber Command veterans including Leonard Cheshire VC, but neither the defence minister nor any member of the British cabinet attended for fear of offending the Germans. A small crowd of demonstrators booed and jeered the ceremony.

21 THE BEGINNING OF THE END

*Air Force Captain Glenn Miller adapted jazz to parade
ground tempi in such classics as the 'St Louis Blues
March'. 'Our men marched to regular marches in the last
war,' said his commander. 'They didn't need any of that
jazzy music, and they did pretty well too, didn't they?'
Miller replied: 'Let me ask you one question, Major. Are
you still flying the same planes you flew in the last war?'[1]*

As with most other war material, the Allies produced aircraft in overwhelming numbers. As shown in Table 5, even before the United States came into the war in December 1941, British aircraft production was significantly greater than that of the Germans. In the second half of 1941, when Hitler's armies attacked the USSR and brought the Red Air Force into the fight, the Germans were hopelessly outmatched in the quantity of material.

Table 5   Aircraft production 1939–44

	1939	1940	1941	1942	1943	1944
Germany	8,295	10,826	11,424	15,288	25,094	39,275
UK	7,940	15,049	20,094	23,672	26,263	26,461
USSR	10,382	10,565	15,735	25,436	34,845	40,246
USA	5,856	12,804	26,277	47,836	85,898	96,318
Japan	4,467	4,768	5,088	8,861	16,393	28,180

The figures in the table[2] show that the 'narrow margin' by which the Battle of Britain was supposedly won was wider than anyone thought at the time. Although many RAF aircraft were poor in design and quality, some – such as the Spitfire – were first-class. Clearly it was never necessary to commit British troops to battle without air cover of any sort – in the Western Desert, in Crete or in Malaya.

The workforces: Britain and Germany

The war's decisive battle was won in the factories. Workforces are a vital part of its history. Yet the overwhelming might that the Allies used against Germany has made it easy to overlook the chronic shortcomings of the British contribution to the production war.

Less than a century before, Germany had been a collection of 38 small principalities and fiefdoms, tiny states centred upon a town with a market, a palace, a city square and a cathedral. Each had an opera house; most had two.[3] Strong regional cultures developed, each with a competitive spirit and a distinctive dialect. Citizens were obedient and law-abiding, for in such communities rebellion was quickly seen and punished. The police were given wide powers.

The industrial revolution brought workers from the countryside to work in factories. New urban districts were added to such towns as Dresden, Leipzig, Düsseldorf, Berlin and Cologne. These flourishing cities fed upon the culture that had nourished the small towns. Prussia had led the world in the provision of technical schools. Over most of Germany there survived a strong tradition of dedicated workers and craftsmen. In 1937, while four out of five of Britain's 14-year-olds went off to work as unskilled labour, German factories were obliged by law to provide their young employees with a general education, as well as technical training, until they reached the age of 18.

Higher education provided some social mobility within Germany's local communities. But German workers, like workers everywhere, were most concerned with security and stability. Huge firms, such as Krupp, pioneered social welfare schemes that included medical care, schools and housing. Other factories in other lands provided such amenities, but in Germany workers' welfare was backed by the state. Bismarck was determined to raise the physical fitness of army draftees, and counter the lure of Socialism. 'The State is not only an institution of necessity but also one of welfare,' he said as his parliament passed acts insuring workers against sickness, accident and old age.[4] Planning regulations for homes and factories remedied some of the worst excesses of earlier urban squalor. By the time war came in 1939 Germany was unified and German-speakers were happy to be so. Under Hitler, despite rationing and financial controls, the standard of living climbed steeply to become the highest in Europe. Craftsmanship brought both prestige and good wages. Germany was so plentifully provided with machine-tools and precision machinery that they were freely exported.

In the second half of the nineteenth century Britain had been overtaken as an industrial power largely because of social attitudes. The components of manufactured goods such as guns were hand-made by men working in their homes or tiny workshops. Master gunmakers collected the pieces and employed more men to fit them together in a lengthy process that called for detailed hand-work and filing. The result was an example of craftsmanship that the Englishman cherished in the way he did his custom-made suits.

Even in large factories the spirit of cottage industry was preserved. Men were classified according to their tasks and bound in a complicated system of internal contracts and subcontracts from one man to another. To conceal the profit made by each, some were paid by the piece and some by the hour. From this system grew the craft unions, strictly ruling which task each man was permitted to perform and how much he would be paid to do it. Soon the social system was so rigid and interdependent that no factory owner dared to change it.

The result was an inflexible workforce of which in 1857 a man with experience in England and America (where machinery was welcomed as something that would bring prosperity) said:

> In America they might set to work to invent a machine, and all the workmen in the establishment would, if possible, lend a helping hand. If they saw any error they would mention it, and in every possible way they would aid in carrying out the idea. But in England it was quite the reverse. If the workmen could do anything to make the machine go wrong, they would do it.[5]

The industrial revolution had come earlier to Britain, and water power and coal and iron were mostly to be found in northern England, south Wales and the Scottish lowlands. Britain's industrial towns were created in bare impoverished regions, and there were not many opera houses to be found there. Here were the primitive little dwellings in which workers spent their brief periods of rest between shifts. In Middlesbrough in 1939 one house in three was over 70 years old, and 90 per cent of the houses had no baths. In many places sewerage and running water remained luxuries.

There was a wide gulf between the haves and the have-nots. It was a difference in health, in education and expectation. Even stature was different: an official British health survey in 1941 found boys in private schools to be four inches taller than their working-class contemporaries, solely because of their better diet. The traditional British system of exclusive boarding schools, to which the rich sent their sons, lessened the chances of good schools being created in the industrial areas. The trap into which the poor had fallen was compounded by the way in which universities – primarily concerned with their own power and privileges – usually found places for academic failures from wealthy or influential families while offering little to the talented poor. One half of 1 per cent of children at elementary schools went to a university.[6] Such education was not considered vitally important even for those to whom the doors were open. Winston Churchill never went to a university.

Even more far-reaching was the antipathy the British ruling class showed to science and engineering, and even such subjects as mathematics and foreign languages. The Church had always been steadfastly opposed to scientific progress. Isaac Newton's refusal to accept the doctrine of the Trinity was enough to prevent his becoming the Master of any Oxbridge college – that is why he accepted his job with the Mint. During the same period when amazing individuals such as Fox Talbot, George Stephenson, Isambard Kingdom Brunel and Michael Faraday were dazzling the world, Dr Thomas Arnold – headmaster of the English public school of Rugby from 1828 until his death in 1842 – was loudly and widely proclaiming his opposition to science. Other such private schools accepted Arnold's views that their essential function was to produce good Christian gentlemen.

In 1859 Darwin published his theories of evolution. They were logical, and easily understood by educated and uneducated alike, and they were supported by work already done on fossils, the discoveries in chemistry and by the classification of flora and fauna. Darwin's work frightened the religious-educational establishment which controlled the nation's schools (private and public) and its universities. His theories confirmed them in their view that all science was heresy.

It was a closed shop. The private school system fed upon itself. The influence that the private schools had upon the British nation was noted in a secret handbook – Informationsheft GB – issued in 1940 by the Reich Security Head Office:

> Of all school age children in England today, scarcely 1 per cent goes to Public Schools; and about 80 per cent of all political and

socially important jobs go to the 1 per cent. These are the schools of the English governing upper class.[7]

The entrance exams for the British civil service reflected Arnold's view that government, like every other important task in Britain, was best done by such 'Christian gentlemen', rather than by men or women trained to deal with the ever more complex and ever more competitive world that Britain faced. In his book *Audit of War*, Correlli Barnett wrote:

> Thus in the early 1850s was born the Whitehall mandarin, able at a touch to transmute life into paper and turn action to stone. Henceforward the British governing elite was to be composed of essay-writers rather than problem solvers – minds judicious, balanced and cautious rather than operational and engaged; the temperament of the academic rather than the man of action . . . And where would such mandarins be recruited other than from Oxford and Cambridge, their original breeding grounds? The cosiest of symbiotic relationships had thus been established.[8]

Such costly muddles as the campaign in Norway brought a vivid demonstration of the shortcomings of the Whitehall bureaucracy. The army, navy and air force were strangled in red tape by men who saw no reason to change their ways. In November 1940 the Foreign Office was still not starting work until 11 am. At the newly created Ministry of Economic Warfare even the minister found it difficult to collect his staff together for a meeting at 10.30 am.[9]

As the nineteenth century ended it was investment rather than manufacturing that was the basis of Britain's wealth. The families who had grown rich from the marvels of the industrial revolution did not want their sons to wield tools and have oil on their hands. They wanted to become like the landed gentry. Men who ran the factories saw no need for training for themselves, their children or their employees. It was assumed that 14-year-olds would pick up enough skills from those who worked alongside them. Very bright youngsters, who were exceptionally lucky, might eventually find a job in the design or research department, where the manager or chief designer was also likely to have had no technical education. And if Christian gentlemen found science and engineering of little importance, they also found art, and design, suspect. (It is not without significance that Germany and Japan, countries where design and engineering are highly regarded, today enjoy strong economies.)

In 1939 many of Britain's factories were antiquated and inefficient. Machine-tools were in short supply and inadequate for any modern war, especially for a long war which would demand more and more precision engineering (for example, ever smaller and more complex radar sets and high-technology fuses). While in January 1940 1,300,000 people remained unemployed, there was an irremediable lack of skilled workers, and those who were skilled were often not skilled enough. There was a grievous shortage of every sort of expert, from cost accountants to physicists. The lack of specialized designers with engineering backgrounds resulted in trucks, tanks, engines and aircraft being difficult to maintain and repair. Delivery dates were frequently missed. 'Don't you know there's a war on?' was a response that usefully answered any complaint. Often fighting machines were completely outdated and outclassed on the battlefield by the time they arrived there. Mechanisms of only moderate complexity, such as aircraft instruments, had to be ordered from American factories because British factories could not make them.[10]

The way in which Britain had always been two separated communities was evident in the political divisions. Unofficial strikes, go-slows and sheer bloody-minded attitudes, fomented by trade and craft unions, were a constant part of life on Britain's home front. By 1944 lost working days were three times what they had been in 1938. Sailors who'd just endured gruelling convoy duty on a corvette in the North Atlantic were unprepared for life ashore. Nicholas Monsarrat, author of the bestselling novel of wartime life on a corvette, *The Cruel Sea*, wrote in his memoirs:

> Most of these people 'concerned with our refit' were hardly concerned at all. They were not working very hard. Some of them, as far as I could judge, were not working at all. The first time I came on a school of card-players snugged down in the captain's sea-cabin at ten o'clock in the morning, I was furious, and showed it. I remained furious on all later occasions, but I was officially told not to be, and above all not to 'interfere'. There might be a strike . . . In July, a member of the Boilermakers' & Iron and Steel Shipbuilders' Society (there must have been a whole gang of them on board at that very moment) had been fined £3 by his union's board of discipline for working too hard.[11]

The entry of the Soviet Union into the war, and the worldwide activities of Communist parties under Moscow's malign directions, added more confusion to the task of being a patriot.

Patriotism was also a complex matter for the 74,000 enemy aliens in Britain, most of whom had escaped from Nazi persecution. In a foolish and tragic reaction to baseless stories about the contribution that spies and saboteurs had made to the German victories, they were locked up in the most squalid of improvised accommodation. At one rat-infested disused factory (Wharf Mills) 2,000 internees shared 18 water taps. Sixty buckets in the yard served as toilets and there were straw mattresses only for the chronically sick. At another such British internment centre, two men who'd already experienced a Nazi concentration camp committed suicide: 'this camp has broken their spirit,' said an investigator. When the war cabinet read the report on the camps they would not allow it to be published. But neither would they release the internees, thinking that it would reveal the muddle and injustice.

There were Draconian punishments for British subjects too. On 17 July 1940 a man was sent to prison for a month after saying that Britain had no chance to win the war. A man who advised two New Zealanders 'You don't want to get killed in this bloody war,' got three months. A woman who said 'Hitler was a good ruler; a better man than Mr Churchill,' was sentenced to five years in prison. The British newspapers were also warned against thoughtless utterances. Editors were told quite unequivocally that 'irresponsible' criticism would not be tolerated and the government would decide what was responsible and what was not.[12]

A propaganda poster that promised that *your* resolution will bring *us* victory was greeted with such derision that it was hurriedly withdrawn. Perhaps such clear identification of who were the rulers and who were to be ruled was not different to the bitter divisions that had done so much to cause France to collapse in 1940, and triggered Spain's long and bloody civil war. In Britain the division had not gone so deep, but it was to last far longer, and remains today to account for many of Britain's ills.

Hitler – the most popular leader Germany had ever had, as A.J.P. Taylor emphasized – brought German living standards higher than any in Europe, believing that his regime would be secure only as long as it remained popular with the German public.

The German economy never geared up for total war in the way that Britain's did. Taxes remained low and rations high. Generous amounts of such items as steel were set aside for civilian use, and in

1943 even such luxury items as wallpaper (13,000 tonnes of it) were still being produced. Women were not subject to direction of employment and there was a plentiful supply of domestic servants for the middle classes. The extensive conquests brought back to Germany all kinds of luxuries from fur coats to caviar.

Occupied Europe saw the other side of Germany's bounty. Every conquered nation had its people robbed by fixed exchange rates, and subjected to repressive military occupation. Jews, and anyone else the Nazis categorized as enemies, were hounded, harassed, and sent to camps to be systematically murdered.

In the Thirties and the Forties Germany's education system had brought notable achievements. While German industry remained closely integrated with German education and with the government, the same did not apply to science in general. The Nazi regime did nothing to harness science to the national effort or to the war machine. The persecution of the Jews ensured that a steady stream of the most valuable and educated citizens left the country, causing setbacks to German science from which it has still not recovered.

The Nazi regime, and the military establishment which threw in its lot with them, had a fundamental distrust of science. During the war research was discouraged at virtually all levels of Germany's high command. There was no system of preserving scientists from the draft; conscripted in the normal way, they were given lowly tasks in the armed services. But despite the neglect of the higher reaches of science, dedicated technicians and scientists at factory level produced some remarkable steps forward, particularly in the advancement of aviation.

For instance, the Flettner Fl 282 Kolibri (Humming Bird) was a helicopter built for the German navy. Using side-by-side intermeshing rotors this small machine flew in May 1939 and was the first helicopter to go into production and into operational service.[13]

The unique rocket-powered Messerschmitt Me 163 Komet was the fastest aircraft used in the war. In September of 1941 a famous glider pilot, Heini Dittmar, made the first powered flight in this design and soon broke the world speed record.

Germany's primary role in the development of jet aircraft is beyond question, Heinkel developing not only the airframes but jet engines too. The only jet aircraft to have an operationally significant role in the war was Germany's Messerschmitt Me 262.

There were other German jets such as the Arado 234 'Blitz' bomber which incorporated such advanced features as a pressurized

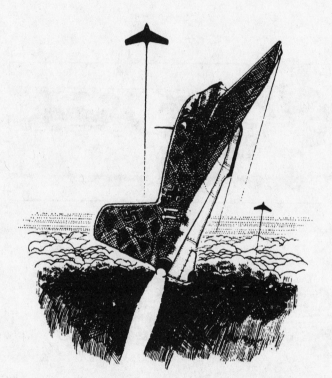

Figure 32: Messerschmitt Me 163 Komet

cabin, ejection seat and rocket-assisted take-off. The more austere Heinkel He 162 'Volksjäger' flew ten weeks after Heinkel received the order to make it.

After the war ended, the US Bombing Survey, which made its investigations as far-ranging as possible, appraised the German air force's accomplishments. It concluded that Germany led the world in aircraft armament, jet propulsion, advanced aerodynamics and guided missiles.

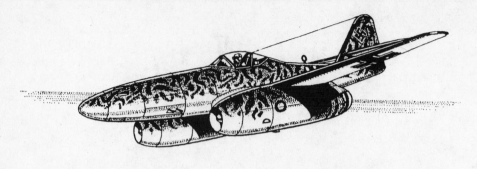

Figures 33, 34 and 35:
Jets – Me 262, Arado 234 'Blitz'
and the Heinkel 162 'Volksjäger'

'What else is there in an air force?', asked Colonel John Driscoll
(the chief of the Air Weapons and Tactics Branch of this exhaustive
survey). On Driscoll's office wall a visitor might have noticed a
plaque: 'Without armament there is no air force.' They were the
words spoken by Sir Hugh 'Boom' Trenchard.

Flying the Pacific

The United States armed forces have always been a part of the civilian economy. They still are so today, and that is their strength. It is easy to look back at American air power in the interwar years and dismiss it as improvised and ineffectual, but a closer inspection shows its potential.

The Boeing B-17 'Flying Fortress' prototype took to the air in the summer of 1935, many years before any other nation built a comparable long-range bomber. Designed for anti-shipping duties, its poor payload has to be weighed against its second pilot, its ten-man crew, and the massive armament that enabled it to survive daylight formation bombing. Its Norden bomb-sight was a technical advance far ahead of its time. Its turbocharged engines provided it with a speed of 232 mph and its service ceiling was a phenomenal 35,000 feet. Coming years later, Britain's Avro Lancaster had a ceiling of 24,000 feet and the Short Stirling 17,000 feet. The Boeing company went to considerable financial risk in building the B-17, but it can now be seen as one of the most successful planes of the war years. In January 1940, almost two years before the USA entered the war, General 'Hap' Arnold was already writing a specification that led to the remarkable B-29 that was a part of the postwar world.

The immensity of the Pacific Ocean called for different aircraft and different pilots to those used in the war in Europe. The ability to return to a carrier in mid-ocean demanded navigational skills as well as an iron nerve. The naval pilots of America and Japan were recruited from men of the highest calibre.

The Japanese pilots of the air flotillas, Koku Sentai, were initially selected at the age of 14, from boys of the very top physical and academic standards. Their five-year training course, which included advanced study of the theory of flight and aircraft design, was more demanding than that given to pilots in other air forces. By the time a Japanese naval pilot joined his squadron he would have logged about 100 flying hours. Officers were given more training and had anything up to double the number of flying hours. Consequently, in the 1930s the Japanese navy produced only about 100 pilots a year. When the losses sustained in the opening months of the war devastated this elite force, the navy showed little or no inclination to cut the length of its course, or increase the numbers of graduates. Neither did it take much trouble about rescuing pilots or helping them to preserve their lives. On the contrary, the idea of sacrificing one's life for the Emperor was in every way applauded. Pilot short-ages crippled the Japanese war effort. Within a year it was not unusual for carriers to suffer delays in departing to sea duties while a full complement of pilots was found.

With a high standard of living, and a high percentage of its youth going to college, America had no shortage of men physically and intellectually suited to pilot training. The US navy's prewar flying training was done in the fine weather at Pensacola, Florida. To cope with the wartime influx other schools at Jacksonville in Florida and Corpus Christi in Texas were opened, but the programme was not much changed from the peacetime one.

Three months of 'elementary' flying were followed by three months of theory and then on to 'Primary' flying and Intermediate Flight Training. At this stage a pilot was selected for fighters or multi-engine training. Those destined for carriers went to Glenview, Illinois, to practise landings on two 'baby flat-tops' that had been converted from old Great Lakes steamers. A pilot joining his squad-ron was likely to have logged as many as 400 hours, sometimes more. That pilot would probably have six months with a land-based squadron before going with it to sea. America never suffered a shortage of well trained pilots.

The primary flying schools

In September 1938 Major-General Henry H. Arnold was appointed chief of the Air Corps,[14] since 1926 a part of the US army. The other nations had already discovered that the training of pilots was the most time-consuming element in the building of modern armed forces. The Germans had started training aircrews long before the Luftwaffe was officially created. When he took over his new job 'Hap' Arnold found that the United States had only 700 candidates deemed suited to flying training, and only two places – Randolph Field and Kelly Field, both in Texas – at which to train them.

Arnold was a remarkable man. It may not be going too far to say that any other man in the same job would not have solved the prob-lem of training the army's pilots with the reckless grace that he employed. He knew many of the men who had pioneered civil and military aviation in the Twenties and Thirties. Now he asked some of those who owned flying schools if they would take part in his military programme. The schools would be responsible for 'primary' (elementary) flight instruction, the student's first step in learning to fly. The course would last three months and include 65 hours of flying and 225 hours of technical instruction. In May 1939 Arnold told a gathering of eight flying school owners that he wanted to start training his men in forty days!

Many military men were appalled at the thought of civil schools teaching soldiers to fly. But the immediate problem that faced those eight men who all said 'yes' was that Arnold had no money, and his programme had not been ratified by the politicians. Despite this risk, the flying school operators borrowed money and set to work. Huts were built, instructors and ground personnel engaged. In June 1939, Congress authorized the programme by just two votes! By July, Arnold had delivered the training aircraft – mostly PT-13 biplanes – and a few military personnel to the schools. Pilot training commenced. On 31 July 1939 Flight Cadet Russell M. Church created a record by being the first student pilot of the civil scheme to crash a plane. His PT-13 took the top off a tree when landing at Parks Air College Inc., East St Louis, Illinois. He was allowed to continue training.

Randolph and Kelly Fields would be expanded in time to take the graduates for further training ('Basic' at Randolph, and then 'Advanced' at Kelly). Arnold's original goal was 2,400 pilots per year, but eventually the US army's Flying Training Command would be producing 100,000 pilots a year. (This figure is even more impressive when one remembers that a 30 per cent washout rate was not unusual.)

Of those first days one officer said:

> The flying instruction was comparable to any Army school, but it was the hardest thing to get the instructors to realize they had to eliminate some of the cadets. Not a single student was put up for elimination by the instructors at our school in the first class. The Army had to step in and jerk men.[15]

That Arnold's bold plan came just in time was best illustrated a few days after Pearl Harbor. On 16 December 1941 the aforementioned Lieutenant Church, accompanied by another graduate of the very first class at the civil schools, was shot down while attacking a Japanese airfield at Vigan in the Philippines. He was awarded the DSC, and the Japanese were impressed enough by his bravery to give him a military funeral.

Part Five

BARBAROSSA:
THE ATTACK ON RUSSIA

22 FIGHTING IN PEACETIME

In the West the armies were too big for the country. In the East the country was too big for the armies.

Winston Churchill, *The Eastern Front*, 1931

RUSSIA HAD BEEN soundly defeated by Japan on land and sea in the early years of the century. Subsequent treaties and agreements had left Japan in control of Korea and with powerful armies occupying Manchuria on the Chinese mainland.

The 1917 Bolshevik revolution provided to Lenin and then to his successor Stalin a completely renewed and reinforced army which had fought interventionist armies sent by the Western powers, and beaten them. Elements of this confident Red Army found itself along Soviet Russia's eastern border facing Japan's battle-trained Kwantung Army, commanded by brutal and belligerent commanders who cared little about orders from Tokyo. Fighting was sure to follow.

In the summer of 1938, without war being declared, Soviet frontier forces found themselves drawn into fierce battle against the Japanese army in the Chankufeng Hills, at the extreme eastern coast, where Manchuria, Siberia and Korea meet. The fighting started when the Red Army dug trenches in a buffer zone and shot Japanese secret police who tried to photograph the works.[1] The Japanese now used infantry, cavalry and tanks in a push forward that seemed to threaten the nearby Soviet naval base of Vladivostok. Armed with reports from Richard Sorge, a spy in Tokyo, that the Japanese government were determined to prevent the fighting growing into a full-scale war, Stalin responded with a fierce offensive that dislodged the Japanese and drove them back to their starting points. Hurriedly Tokyo dispatched politicians to Moscow to salvage this military failure with explanations that put the blame entirely upon the Kwantung Army commanders. To lend credence to this device the vice war minister General Tojo was moved to another job. There had been about 10,000 casualties on each side, and although the fighting ended with a

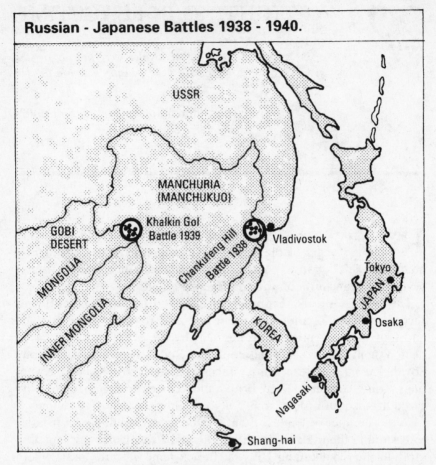

Russian - Japanese Battles 1938 - 1940.

USSR

MANCHURIA
(MANCHUKUO)

Khalkin Gol
Battle 1939

GOBI
DESERT

MONGOLIA

INNER MONGOLIA

Chankufeng Hill
Battle 1938

Vladivostok

KOREA

JAPAN

Tokyo

Osaka

Nagasaki

Shang-hai

truce and a return to the earlier positions, it was generally regarded as a defeat for the Japanese.

At Khalkin Gol on the border of the Mongolian People's Republic in May 1939 fighting started again. The previous year's encounter had been a loss of face for the Japanese army, and so when frontier units with Mongolian horsemen on both sides skirmished, the Japanese responded with an air attack and the Russians guessed that this would escalate into a fierce battle.[2] In mid-June Lieutenant-General Georgi Zhukov, a mobile warfare expert, was sent to take command of the Red Army in this region.

Zhukov had been born the son of a cobbler in 1896 in a one-room cabin that stood in the middle of the village of Strelkovka in Kaluga Province. His father had been adopted from an orphanage by a childless widow, and had inherited the cabin from her. As a youngster,

Georgi was drafted into the Tsar's dragoons. He had already learned to read, and this distinguished him in an army which was largely illiterate. Decorated for bravery while fighting in the Ukraine and Bessarabia, Zhukov was rapidly promoted. Because Stalin decided that officers of the Red Army cavalry were his most trustworthy soldiers, most of the high-ranking commanders came from the cavalry arm. By 1931, Zhukov was commanding a division and then, by 1937, a corps. Now, at Khalkin Gol, he was given the most crucial opportunity of his life.

Zhukov arrived to discover that his corps commanders had never been to look at the fighting front. They were directing operations from 120 kilometres in the rear. He immediately made a detailed survey of the frontier zone and prepared for a large battle. Facing him there was a Japanese force of about 75,000 men, 500 aircraft, 500 artillery pieces and 200 tanks.[3]

From Richard Sorge, its Communist agent in Tokyo, Moscow learned that a Russian defector, General Lyushkov, an intelligence officer concerned with the security of the frontier region, had betrayed the full details of the defences.[4] Unless something was done to reinforce Zhukov's force, the Japanese would annihilate it. Moscow had little alternative but to reinforce Zhukov, and soon he deployed 100,000 men, 500 aircraft, 1,000 artillery pieces and about 700 tanks. Among the tanks there were some brand-new BT-7Ms which had been unveiled at the May Day Parade in Moscow on 1 May 1938. They had good engines and 7.6-cm high-velocity guns, and were in fact test-beds for the T-34 that was to become one of the most effective tanks of the war.

It was August. The weather was steamy hot, rising to 130 degrees F, and the bare and almost uninhabited terrain a nightmare of sand-dunes, quicksands and deep ravines. The whole region was infested with ravenous mosquitoes and other insects, whose bites made even the sturdy Japanese and Russian infantry fall sick. Zhukov's first priority was to gain command of the air. For this he had a dedicated group of pilots which included 21 'Heroes of the Soviet Union'. In preparation for his main assault, he used camouflage and elaborate deceptions to convince the enemy that he intended to do no more than build, and man, new defences. Then, carefully keeping the element of surprise, Zhukov used probing attacks, supported by artillery fire and aerial bombardment to soften up the foe. Used to fighting the Chinese, this was the first time the Japanese encountered a modern mechanized force.

The main attack began at 5.45 am on a Sunday morning, a day Zhukov chose knowing that many Japanese commanders were likely to be on recreation trips away from their units.[5] As daylight appeared the Japanese front-line units were hit by a coordinated bombardment by artillery and aircraft. Flamethrower tanks led the Russian frontal attack that broke the Japanese line. At the same time, the Russians committed an independent tank force to strike into the enemy's rear and block any retreat. Delivering fierce successive blows, this force bypassed pockets of Japanese resistance and left them to the Red Army infantry to subdue later.

From out of the sky came a fleet of TB-3 four-engined all-metal monoplane bombers, each carrying 5,800 kg (12,790 lb) of bombs.[6] While the Red Army demonstrated its newest ideas, the Japanese stuck to the old-fashioned tactics that had worked when fighting Chinese peasants. Their tanks plodded along with their infantry; while many more tanks were held in reserve and not sent into battle.

Although Zhukov's encirclement battle inflicted calamitous casualties upon the Japanese, he had not won by outstanding generalship so much as by brute force. His clever use of tanks was largely due to his having so many of them, and his deployment of infantry displayed a callous indifference to casualties. But Zhukov won a durable victory and the Russian propaganda machine made the most of it. Tokyo admitted losses of 18,000 men but some historians believe that the true figure was probably twice that number.

Using their experiences in this encounter, the Russians modified their tank designs. The BT tanks, using petrol engines, Zhukov found 'too fire-hazardous', and top priority was given to building the new T-34. This battle with the Japanese had a far greater effect upon the Red Army's planning than anything that happened in the Spanish Civil War. More importantly, it singled out Zhukov as a ruthless winner of battles. He personally reported to Stalin that the Japanese were:

> well disciplined, diligent, dogged in combat, especially in defence. Junior commanding officers are well trained and fanatically persistent in battle. As a rule they do not surrender and do not stop short of hara-kiri. Officers, especially senior officers, are not adequately trained, lack initiative, and are apt to act according to the crammed rulebook.[7]

Later Zhukov was to boast: 'The Japanese are not good against armour. It took about ten days to beat them.'[8] But not much about this significant battle was ever heard in the West. Still today details of the battle are hard to find.

Nearer to hand in November 1939 were events that Europe's statesmen found more encouraging, and the Press made into head-lines. From Finland Stalin demanded territory along the border – and some island bases – that would make the defence of Leningrad more secure. By Stalin's standards the demands were reasonable but the Finns, seeing that yielding to blackmail would bring more demands, flatly refused.

Stalin's response came at the very end of November. He bombed the Finnish capital Helsinki, and the port of Viipuri, without any declaration of war. Russian armies totalling a million men attacked Finland from the east and south-east while an amphibious force crossed the Gulf of Finland to land on the southern coast. They were repulsed.

In what is generally known as the Winter War, the Finns put into the field about 300,000 men and of these 80 per cent were reservists. They were motivated and well led, and Stalin had chosen the wrong moment to start his war. In Karelia in November and December heavy cloud and mist made the days short and visibility poor. The hard winter had not yet come and the terrain was still muddy. The rivers and lakes, that form a treacherous lacework through this region, were not yet frozen to a depth that would support mechan-ized vehicles and tanks. The Finns had equipment that suited war in this latitude. Their troops wore white and used short-range machine-pistols that were the perfect weapon for hit-and-run tactics by infantry on skis. There were many Russian-speakers among the Finns. One such went breezily to a Red Army field kitchen for hot food, and continued to do so for fourteen days of continuing battle, before being taken prisoner.[9] One Soviet officer described how:

> In one case in one of our rear sectors a group of Finnish soldiers, disguised in Red Army uniforms, wearing arm-bands and with flags in their hands – thus impersonating traffic controllers – quietly directed a large Soviet supply column towards their own lines.

The Russians' greatest weakness, said Marshal Mannerheim, the Finnish commander, was their lack of familiarity with skis. Hardy peasants, the Red Army infantry displayed a fatalism that was astonishing to the Finns. 'In the initial fighting in December the Russians would advance in close formation, singing, and even hand in hand, against the Finnish minefields, apparently indifferent to the explosions and the accurate fire of the defenders.'[10]

After some initial Red Army successes, the attack stalled due largely to the way that the weather and terrain restricted movements. Red Army units failed to coordinate their elements; tanks were separated from infantry and both destroyed. But while the Finns showed unexpected individuality and vitality the Russians displayed unexpected courage and determination and an ability to learn from their errors. As winter bit harder, and became particularly severe, the Red Army brought in better and heavier tanks and artillery and made sure they worked closely with aircraft and infantry. The Finns found themselves fighting a Red Army which was totally different in equipment and generalship from the one they had brought to a halt in the earlier fighting.[11]

In recognition that they could never win a war against the might of the Soviet Union, the Finns opened secret negotiations at the end of January while the war continued. By mid-March they were almost totally beaten, and had to endure harsher terms than were originally demanded. To rub salt into the wounds, the Red Army ended the war by a cruel bombardment that in the final minutes of the fighting caught the Finns in the open and quite unprepared. Bitterly the Finnish president ratified the peace treaty saying: 'Let the hand wither that is forced to sign such a treaty.' A few months later a stroke paralysed his right side.[12]

Stalin's war was ill-judged as well as ill-timed. He had made his Finnish neighbours into implacable enemies of the Soviet Union. The Red Army would need to garrison the frontier constantly in case the Finns tried to get their revenge, as eventually they did.

In keeping with the spirit of his agreement with Stalin, Hitler had made sure that no aid was given to the Finns and took steps to prevent arms shipments to Finland being routed through Germany. The German General Staff evaluation of the Red Army's performance in Finland said it had inferior equipment and inferior leadership, with equally poor transportation and communications.[13] Likewise, the Western powers judged the Red Army to be a ponderous and ineffective fighting force. But at least one German officer had quite a different view of the war:

> unprejudiced observers also noticed some very positive characteristics of the Soviet soldier: his incredibly tough conduct in defence, his imperviousness to fear and despair, and his almost

unlimited capacity to suffer. Above all, the Soviet command had shown that it was willing to learn from experience and able to communicate what it had learnt to the subordinate formations, coupled with the resolve to enforce such instructions.[14]

The Red Army's high command immediately started a drastic reorganization. Abandoning Trotsky's revolutionary and impractical reforms, they reintroduced officer ranks and grades with orthodox rank insignia, and saluting too. The army's political commissars would no longer have any say in military operations or tactics. About 4,000 officers who had been sent to labour camps and prisons on trumped-up charges were suddenly released and reinstated. A 'front of reserve armies' was formed, which meant changes all along the Soviet frontier and temporarily rendered the defences vulnerable. It is unlikely that the German military planners took this fact into account, or even knew of it, but in June 1941 it played a big part in helping the German invaders to unbalance the Soviet defences.

For Stalin, a pact of non-aggression with Hitler must have seemed like a guarantee of military security for the foreseeable future. Until this time, all Russian military contingency planning had been based upon the supposition that any invasion force coming from the west would consist of the combined German and Polish armies. To these the armies of the Baltic States – Lithuania, Latvia and Estonia – would probably be added. In 1936 the Polish army was a formidable 50 divisions and Hitler said the German army had 36 divisions. Mobilization would probably have increased the German army to 100 divisions.

Hitler's offer to split Poland down the middle, and give the Soviets a free hand to deal with the Baltic States, seemed to solve all Stalin's problems. A Russo-German friendship pact would also deter the Japanese who were at that very moment fighting on Stalin's eastern border. In return, Hitler wanted only friendship and trade. It was an irresistible proposition. Nothing that France and Britain were offering in the way of alliances could come near to matching it. Stalin signed.

The destruction of Poland went as planned. Stalin waited two weeks, leaving the German invaders to crush Poland's initial resistance, and then took over the eastern half of the country. Many of its inhabitants were White Russians and Ukrainians living under the Polish flag. The occupation was not without incident. The Red Army suffered 700 dead, and Stalin sent his NKVD secret police to

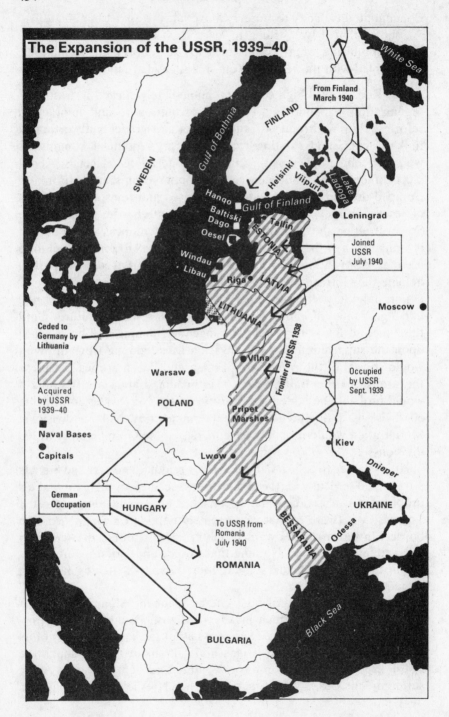

The Expansion of the USSR, 1939–40

From Finland
March 1940

Joined
USSR
July 1940

Occupied
by USSR
Sept. 1939

Ceded to
Germany by
Lithuania

Acquired
by USSR
1939–40

■ Naval Bases

● Capitals

German
Occupation

To USSR from
Romania
July 1940

White Sea

FINLAND

Gulf of Bothnia

SWEDEN

Helsinki   Viipuri

Hango   Gulf of Finland

Baltiski   Tallin
Dago
Oesel   ESTONIA

Windau
Libau   Riga   LATVIA

LITHUANIA

Lake
Ladoga

● Leningrad

Moscow ●

Frontier of USSR 1938

Vilna ●

Warsaw ●

POLAND

Pripet
Marshes

Lwow ●

HUNGARY

● Kiev

Dnieper

UKRAINE

BESSARABIA

● Odessa

ROMANIA

BULGARIA

Black Sea

eliminate the middle-class leadership around which any political opposition might form. Systematically, thousands of officers of the Polish army were murdered in order to extinguish it as a fighting force.

Russo-German trade

After Britain and France had declared war upon Germany, Stalin kept his side of the bargain by supplying Hitler with grain and other raw materials. These supplies became more vital as the Allies set up a naval blockade to cut Germany's sea trade. In 1940 the Russians sent to Germany 900,000 metric tons of crude oil, 500,000 metric tons of manganese ore, 100,000 tons of chrome ore and a million tons of fodder to feed Germany's horse-drawn army.

The Germans were hoping to return the trade by means of long-term projects such as industrial installations, which would put little or no extra strain on the German economy. The Russians however demanded armaments and armament technology. It was agreed eventually that the Russians could have the complete plans and drawings of the *Bismarck* (the world's most powerful and modern battleship), and samples of operational aircraft and experimental ones, including a helicopter. They were also to receive a plant to manufacture titanium. The Germans haggled about prices, and created a mountain of time-wasting paperwork, so that the trade was very much in Germany's favour by the time Hitler invaded the Soviet Union.[15]

The bargain had not worked entirely in Hitler's favour. He was pleased with the coup, and the political surprises, but he had hoped that the dramatic announcement of his pact with the Soviets would deter France and Britain from declaring war upon him. It was a major miscalculation. And although he had agreed to allow Stalin to enlarge his empire unhindered he didn't enjoy watching it happen.

During 1940, while German armies invaded Scandinavia and western Europe, Stalin was active. As well as taking over Finland, he had annexed the Baltic states and made them into republics of the USSR.[16] From Romania he had demanded and got the province of Bessarabia, once a part of Tsarist Russia, bringing Red Army garrisons very close to the Romanian oilfields – a presence which made Hitler uneasy. For him, the real failure of his bargain with Stalin was in the effect that it had upon his self-respect. This friend-

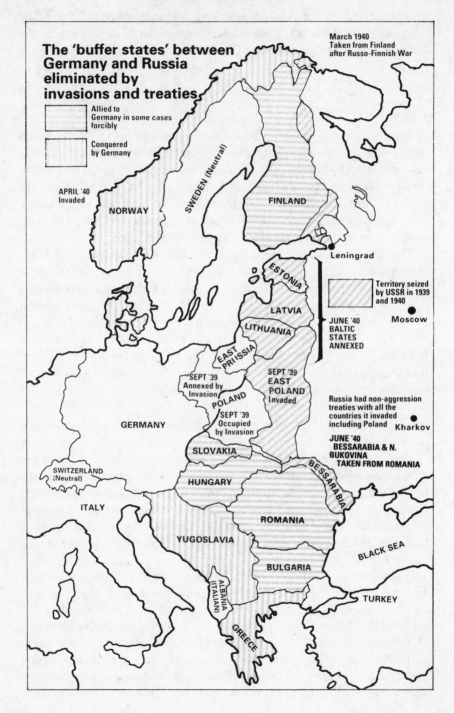

The 'buffer states' between Germany and Russia eliminated by invasions and treaties

Allied to Germany in some cases forcibly

Conquered by Germany

March 1940
Taken from Finland after Russo-Finnish War

APRIL '40 Invaded

NORWAY

SWEDEN (Neutral)

FINLAND

Leningrad

ESTONIA

LATVIA

LITHUANIA

EAST PRUSSIA

Territory seized by USSR in 1939 and 1940

Moscow

JUNE '40 BALTIC STATES ANNEXED

SEPT '39 Annexed by Invasion

POLAND

SEPT '39 EAST POLAND Invaded

GERMANY

SEPT '39 Occupied by Invasion

Russia had non-aggression treaties with all the countries it invaded including Poland

Kharkov

SLOVAKIA

JUNE '40 BESSARABIA & N. BUKOVINA TAKEN FROM ROMANIA

SWITZERLAND (Neutral)

HUNGARY

BESSARABIA

ITALY

ROMANIA

YUGOSLAVIA

BLACK SEA

BULGARIA

ALBANIA (ITALIAN)

TURKEY

GREECE

ship with Moscow, the heart of that Bolshevism which Hitler had spent all his life denouncing, ate into his soul. He felt ridiculous and, like most men, he found ridicule an unendurable burden. Hitler detested Marxists and was determined that they should again be his enemy.

Even while facing a defiant Britain in July 1940, Hitler told Colonel-General Alfred Jodl, chief of operations staff of the OKW, that he had decided to invade the Soviet Union. Of all the Führer's generals Jodl, the Bavarian, was the closest to Hitler, briefing him every day and sitting next to him at meals, though in no way a lackey. Intelligent and independent, Jodl was forced to become a go-between for Hitler and the other generals, and this was his task on 29 July when he took his private train to Bad Reichenhall railway station for a briefing.

Aboard the train came Colonel Walter Warlimont, Jodl's planning chief, and three of his senior officers. Warlimont was a Rhinelander, clever, handsome and sophisticated; the army often used his social talents to persuade foreign diplomats and others to accept its point of view. He had limited regard for Hitler's ideas. With him on this day was one of his best military planners, Colonel Bernhard von Lossberg.

The four men thought that this secret and unprecedented summons might be the occasion for awards or promotions. They were somewhat mystified to see Jodl go round the train compartment, checking that all the doors and windows were firmly closed. Then quietly he confided to them that Hitler had decided to rid the world of Bolshevism 'once and for all'.

Warlimont nervously grasped at his chair. 'The effect of Jodl's words was electric,' he said later. Lossberg said: 'That's impossible!' Britain was still fighting, and all four men began to point out the dangers of a two-front war. Jodl responded: 'The Führer is afraid that the mood of the people after a victory over England would hardly permit him to embark on a new war against Russia.' When arguments continued, Jodl stilled them by simply saying: 'Gentlemen, it is not a question for discussion but a decision of the Führer.'[17]

Each of the three Army Groups then in existence was told to submit a plan.[18] It seems as though all the planners took into account such self-evident facts as the impassable nature of the vast Pripet Marsh region in central Russia. This, said General Marcks, chief of staff of the 18th Army, would divide the frontier zone into two separate operational areas. It was his belief that the invasion would not fail, as Napoleon's had failed, because 'the Russians cannot avoid a decision as they did in 1812. Modern armed forces of 100 divisions cannot abandon their sources of supply. It is expected that the Russian army will stand to do battle . . . '[19] When the assault, codenamed Fritz but later dignified with the name Barbarossa, came, such convenient assumptions were among the very early casualties.

Inexplicably, Hitler did not confide his intentions to his Japanese friends, so while his soldiers were preparing to march upon Russia, the Japanese were abandoning their ideas of attacking the Soviet Union in favour of the 'strike southwards' into the Pacific. What if the Germans and Japanese had coordinated their attacks upon Stalin's vast empire, rich with oil and the raw materials they both wanted? It is an interesting academic question, though Hitler was convinced that he needed no help to crush Russia. The OKW planners said it would be done in eight weeks, ten at most.[20] Hitler preferred to allow the Japanese to get into a fight with the Americans. In this way, the Japanese would be occupied while he plundered the USSR, and the Americans would no longer have resources to spare to help the British.[21]

The way the Germans saw it

It was of course Hitler's stupendous victories in 1940 that persuaded him he could conquer the Soviet Union. In the West, his Panzer forces had pierced Allied defences and spread panic through the rear areas to strike at the 'brain' of command. In total disarray the French, British, Dutch and Belgian armies had all collapsed, one after another. Hitler considered Stalin's empire more ramshackle than the Western democracies, and the Red Army even less efficient. All that was required, Hitler thought, was a slightly larger army to do the same thing on a big scale in the East. Then the USSR would disintegrate in the same way.

There was much to support this belief. When news of Barbarossa broke, virtually every military expert in the world predicted Russia's rapid collapse. American military experts estimated that the Soviet Union could last no more than three months.[22] Churchill was assailed by wrong forecasts: Field Marshal Sir John Dill, Britain's Chief of the Imperial General Staff, gave the Red Army as little as six weeks. Britain's ambassador in Moscow, Stafford

Cripps, thought it would last a month. Most inaccurate of all, British intelligence thought the Russians would last about ten days.

Any pundit could scribble on the back of an envelope the figures to prove that the Wehrmacht would have an easy victory: it had conquered Poland in 27 days, Denmark in 24 hours, Norway in 23 days, Holland in 5, Belgium in 18, France in 39, Yugoslavia in 12, Greece in 21 and Crete in 11 days. On the other hand the Red Army had taken over three months to subdue the Finns. Wasn't that enough to prove that Hitler would be in Moscow long before Christmas?

The Soviet Union had been in political turmoil for years. Show trials, staged at Stalin's order, had done away with high-ranking Communists for treason without bothering too much about evidence. Yet there were countless influential, educated people in the West who believed – and vociferously told those who would listen – that the Soviet Union was a workers' paradise which soon the whole world would imitate. Such people included esteemed writers, artists, reporters and politicians, many of whom had enjoyed conducted tours of this utopia. H. G. Wells, whose first-rate science fiction novels included *The Shape of Things to Come*, *The War of the Worlds* and *The Time Machine*, met Stalin and announced: 'I have never met a man more candid, fair and honest . . . He owes his position to the fact that no one is afraid of him and everybody trusts him.'[23]

But those who pursued facts, rather than wishful fantasies, were more inclined to believe that Stalin was a mentally deranged tyrant whose paranoia had him murdering his own people by the million.[24] He had set up 'punishment camps' where men and women prisoners were quickly worked to death. There were special work camps for the widows of men executed, and prison orphanages for their children. Stalin personally signed death warrants for thousands at a time. To eliminate opposition of even the mildest kind, he had many highly placed Soviet officials killed. The Soviet Marxist historian, Roy Medvedev, estimated that about a million died each year in the camps.[25]

The Red Army was not exempted from these 'purges'. Since 1937 three out of five marshals had gone. So had thirteen (of fifteen) army commanders and over half of all the division and brigade commanders. Stalin's vindictive persecution mania had left the Red Army's morale in a state of shock, and deprived it of many of its most experienced and expert soldiers.

Rumours of war

Members of Communist parties all over the world were told that their primary loyalty was to Moscow. When Stalin made his pact with Hitler, Communists everywhere obediently denounced the war as 'imperialist'. The Communist party's membership in Britain was small, but in France the party was strong and active, and in some units subversion played a part in the collapse of the French armies in the summer of 1940.[26] Communists working in crucial jobs in industry and government endowed Stalin's tyranny with the finest espionage system the world has ever known. In addition, there were two worldwide spy networks, one run by the secret police and the other by the armed forces. Many of these professionals provided the postwar world with countless wartime true-life adventures. Dr Richard Sorge, Press assistant at the German Embassy in Tokyo, gave Moscow a wealth of accurate intelligence about Japanese military intentions. The astonishing Leopold Trepper, 'Grand Chef' of the spy-ring called 'die Rote Kapelle', the Red Orchestra, was a dedicated Communist who ran a successful business as a cover while he passed information through the Soviet Embassy in Berlin. In Brussels Viktor Sokolov, a major in the Soviet intelligence network, ran another section of the 'Rote Kapelle'. Some of the best intelligence of all came from the Lucy Ring in Switzerland. Rudolf Rössler, working with an Englishman who eventually found employment with the ministry of agriculture and fisheries in London, sent detailed dispositions of the German army on the Eastern Front. Whether the Lucy messages were selected items from Bletchley Park's Ultra intercepts that Churchill wanted passed to the Russians without revealing their source is a question still argued.

Stalin ran a police state in which millions of people spied upon their friends, neighbours and colleagues. Every foreign embassy was riddled with planted microphones and spies. Foreigners were under constant surveillance. Yet none of this espionage apparatus was needed to learn that a German attack was imminent. In the months immediately before Barbarossa, any observant traveller on the Moscow-Berlin express would have noticed German preparations in the frontier area. For months foreign residents in Moscow had been whispering about the possibility of an invasion. On 25 April the German naval attaché in Moscow sent a telegram to Berlin:

Rumours about impending German-Russian war greatly increasing in scope. British Ambassador gives 22nd. June as date of beginning of war.[27]

Communists all over the world sent to Moscow evidence of an impending German invasion, but Stalin's paranoia was impregnable. He decided that there was a capitalist plot to provoke him into war with Hitler, and the more messages he received, the more convinced of that he became. His generals and intelligence chiefs soon learned that to bring him news of German activities along the frontier was a dangerous errand. Stalin gave strict orders that no preparations must be made to defend the nation against the Germans. Even reconnaissance planes flouting Russian air space could not be fired upon.

With only nine days to go, Stalin was still denouncing rumours of German troop concentrations along the frontier. Such was his mesmeric power that even soldiers who had firm evidence of the German preparations believed that 'Stalin knows best'.

Air reconnaissance

The blitzkrieg theories decreed that the Luftwaffe air attacks must knock out the Russian armour and air force at the earliest moment. But where to start? The prospect of planning an attack on the Soviet Union found Colonel-General Franz Halder, the army's chief of General Staff, starved of information:

> Information concerning Russia was comparatively scanty. We had in our possession the captured archives of Holland, Belgium, Greece, Yugoslavia and even of the French General Staff, but none of these countries was any better informed about the Russians than we were.[28]

Another way had to be found. Persisting with their old and unexceptional Ju 86 model, Junkers had fitted some of them with longer wingtips, special engines, and pressurized crew compartments to make them capable of operating at high altitude. In 1940, the Luftwaffe's Aufklärungsgruppe Rowehl was given the first of the new machines to pioneer high-altitude photo-reconnaissance. Flying out of Beauvais in occupied France, these unarmed aircraft had mapped England from above 40,000 feet, far beyond the reach of guns or RAF fighters.[29] In October 1940 Lt-Col. Rowehl was given a personal instruction from Hitler to photograph the Russian defences in this same way.[30] The 'Rowehl Geschwader' produced photo-coverage that pinpointed targets along the entire front and up to 200 miles behind it. Gradually the mosaics of air photos were pieced together and a complete picture of the enemy emerged.

Meanwhile German generals were comparing plans for invading. There were few alternatives. As with the invasion of Poland, Barbarossa required the German army to go to its jumping-off points by railway, and depend upon railheads for supplies to its depots. There were not many railway lines running to the frontier, and once across it the journey onwards would be a rough one. Russia's railway tracks were of a different width to German ones, but using the foundations of a railway line or road was a far easier prospect than surveying and building a new one from scratch. On that basis three vital objectives were singled out.

In the north lay Leningrad, the birthplace of the Soviet revolution and home of the Tsars. Leningrad was an industrial and commercial centre, important for sea trade and for the Russian navy. It would be needed by the German Baltic fleet. Latterly Leningrad had become something of a showplace for the Communist regime, and if the Finns could be persuaded to ally themselves with Germany, a common front could be formed with them. In this northern region the advancing troops would use the relatively better roads and resources of the Baltic states of Lithuania and Latvia. It could be safely assumed that local people, so recently annexed to Stalin's empire, would assist the German invaders.

On the central front was Moscow, the capital of the most centralized dictatorship the world had ever seen. General Marcks's plan was concerned about bad roads that would be encountered in the Russian interior. Noting that the roads were better to the north of the Pripet Marshes, he was inclined to give top priority to a drive for Moscow. It would take the direct route and go through Minsk and Smolensk. The army generals believed the Russians would put their armies in front of Moscow, which would give the Germans a chance to fight and crush them. Hitler did not contest this, but his priority was men, not towns. In his first directive concerning Barbarossa he ordered that: 'The bulk of the Russian army stationed in Western Russia will be destroyed by daring operations led by deeply penetrating armoured spearheads. Russian forces still capable of giving battle will be prevented from withdrawing into the depths of Russia.' The main weight of the attack would be north of the Marshes and its object was to destroy the enemy forces. 'Only after the fulfilment of this first essential task, which must include the occupation of Leningrad and Kronstadt, will the attack be continued with the intention of occupying Moscow.'[31]

The third alternative was an attack south of the Pripet Marshes, through Lwow and Vinnitsa. General Marcks said that this terrain, although lacking good roads, was well suited to tank operations. In the Ukraine there was wheat and oil, together with the industry of the lower Dnieper; all were needed by the German wartime economy. Hitler was to become particularly keen on this target, and would be heard complaining that his generals did not understand the importance of such vital contributions to the war, but his directive said it was something to capture after the main battles were won.

Having looked at the alternatives the whole front offered, Colonel von Lossberg decided that the decision must be based upon the existing communications. He saw no alternative but an attack along the Warsaw-Moscow line where the railway was best and a main highway ran alongside it. But Lossberg was cautious, and predicted difficulties after the initial lunge forward.

So desirable was each of these objectives that the German high command decided they must take all three with a plan to strike simultaneously with three army groups. Each would be commanded by a field marshal, Field Marshal Wilhelm von Leeb commanding Army Group North, Field Marshal Fedor von Bock leading Army Group Centre, and Field Marshal von Rundstedt taking Army Group South. Each Army Group would be provided with an Air Fleet and an Armoured Group. Bock, aiming for Moscow, where the bulk of the Red Army was expected to concentrate, was given two Panzer Groups.

The front line would be stretched to about 2,000 miles by Finland declaring war and attacking along the northern boundary, while Romania, a close German ally, was expected to help by striking east to regain the lost territory of Bessarabia, and manning a section of the southern front.

Hitler told his generals that the Russians 'will think a hurricane has hit them'. It was necessary to believe this, for otherwise the calculations of the planning staff became sobering. There were insufficient trains, trucks, fuel and ammunition for the five-month campaign that would be needed to destroy the Red Army. In a remarkable feat of self-deception the general staff simply changed their estimates to persuade themselves that they could win in four months, perhaps even one month.[32] Field Marshal von Rundstedt, who had experienced some of the problems of fighting on the Eastern Front in the First World War, nodded the estimates through, despite thinking that 'a war with Russia might last for years'.[33] Neither did any strenuous objections come from the two soldiers closest to Hitler: Field Marshal von Brauchitsch, commander-in-chief of the army, and Halder, his chief of staff, although they had access to all the planning and intelligence. The German general staff of this period proved irresolute and less than competent, and these two men must share particular responsibility for the disaster.

It was not difficult to see why Generalfeldmarschall Walter von Brauchitsch hesitated before contradicting his Führer. Born into an old Prussian military family, Brauchitsch was not a Nazi but was deeply obliged to Hitler for helping him to get his divorce. Hitler, strongly disapproving of Brauchitsch's prolonged adultery, had persuaded his first wife to give him the divorce and had even paid the 80,000 Reichsmarks settlement out of his own pocket.[34] By accepting this gift, Brauchitsch delivered himself to Hitler, and the second 'Frau Generalfeldmarschall' von Brauchitsch, a dedicated Nazi, kept the sixty-year-old C-in-C under her influence and regularly reminded him how much they owed to Hitler. Although known to complain about the way in which a fellow general was treated,[35] Brauchitsch was certainly not a man who would readily confront Hitler on any major issue.

Generaloberst Franz Halder had been chief of the army's general staff since 1938. A tight-lipped scowling figure, he is easily distinguished from the generals around him. With small pince-nez clipped to his nose, in mufti he might have been mistaken for a bad-tempered schoolteacher of some long bygone time. He was not a Nazi either. As a thoughtful Roman Catholic, he had, before the war, opposed Hitler's policies. But the blitzkrieg successes undermined Halder's opposition, and by the time of Barbarossa he made no real attempts to oppose Hitler's ideas. It is a curious irony that Halder, regarded as a man who never took risks, was chief of staff when the German army mounted the most foolhardy operation that it ever embarked upon.

Almost all the generals regarded the Barbarossa plans with the same reckless optimism that their Führer showed. General Guderian said: 'All the men of the OKW and the OKH with whom I spoke evinced an unshakeable optimism and were quite impervious to criticism or objections.' As part of this self-delusion the number of Panzer divisions was doubled, but only by depriving the existing ones of half of their tanks and pressing into use tanks and guns taken from the French and Czech armies. The tactical advantages claimed for this arrangement were problematic, it was a waste of headquarters staff and specialists, and the new divisions required almost as many trucks as the old ones had.[36] But doubling the number of armoured divisions looked good on paper, and Hitler liked magic tricks that he thought would dismay his enemies.

But modern battles are not won by tricks, or by good luck either. In the main they are won by supply officers who, thoroughly understanding the operational plan, contrive to have the right ammunition, fuel and food in the right place at the right time. The supply services could not depend upon motor transport. Quite apart from the primitive nature of the roads, the German army had too few trucks, even after stripping the conquered countries for them. The mixture of over 2,000 different types of motor vehicles, many of them inferior models coming from occupied countries, was already a storekeeper's nightmare, with over a million different spare parts in stock. To entirely replace rail with road movements would have required ten times the number of vehicles the army possessed in 1941.

There was no alternative to using Russia's inadequate railway network. Locomotives with boilers that would keep going in sub-zero temperatures would have to be manufactured and, because Russia's lines were of a different gauge to German ones and of a different construction, new track would have to be laid as they advanced. The speed of the advance would be limited to the speed at which a new railway could be built. The wishful dream, of capturing Russian railways intact and running them with German crews, was not only doubtful but would still require lengthy and laborious unloading from German trains and into the Russian ones.

A plan that acknowledged some of these problems was cobbled together. It cut back on the estimates for fuel and ammunition and demanded unreal performance from the German army's railway operating troops. It also included a demanding schedule for the motorized forces which were to leap forward in a series of pincer movements for 500 kilometres (300 miles), bringing them to Smolensk, where a halt would be called while new railways were built and supply depots formed for the final assault.[37]

The German generals blithely decided that their armies would reach a line Volga-Archangel within three or four months. After

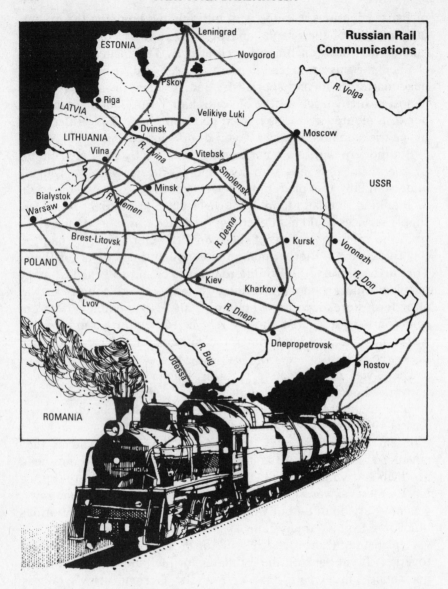

Russian Rail Communications

this, a force of 50 to 60 divisions would remain in place as an occupying army. Hitler's despotism and the army's subservience ensured that no contingency plans were drawn up for use should the invading armies fail to secure these objectives. No winter clothing was manufactured beyond that for an occupying force,[38] thus ensuring the deaths of countless thousands of German soldiers who

fought through snowstorms in their summer uniforms. The Luftwaffe and the Waffen SS high commanders, always contemptuous
of the army, were not taken in by these ambitious estimates, and
made sure that their men were adequately equipped with cold-
weather clothing.[39]

Tanks were Hitler's obsession, yet the 'hurricane' he fielded looks
less than adequate for a country as vast as the Soviet Union. If only
the powerful Panzer III and Panzer IV models are counted, there
were 1,404 of them stretched out along a front of more than 2,000
miles. Even the better tanks were not superlative. Many of them
were equipped with the L42 gun which, having proved inadequate
in France, was slowly being replaced by the higher-velocity L60
gun. Leaving aside the size and condition of the Red Army's
armour, the inadequacy of Hitler's tank forces remains obvious.
Theory says an attacking force must be three times as strong as that
of the defenders, and the German tanks would have to subdue
strongpoints, attack fortresses and overcome tank obstacles.

23

THE LONGEST DAY OF THE YEAR

There is no doubt that millions of people will be starved to death if we take from the country the things we need.

German General Staff economic directive on Barbarossa[1]

T HE GERMAN GENERALS liked to explain the way in which Barbarossa was delayed. General Günther Blumentritt (chief of staff of Fourth Army) said that 'several important Panzer units required thorough overhaul and partial re-equipment after their long march across the Greek mountains . . . The Balkan incident postponed the opening of the campaign by five and a half weeks.'[2] The army's chief of mobile forces, General von Thoma, later estimated that about 800 of the 2,434 tanks available for Barbarossa had been used in the Balkans. General Guderian said that the weather was the principal culprit: 'There was a definite delay in the opening of our Russian campaign. Furthermore we had a very wet spring; the Bug and its tributaries were at flood level until well into May, and the nearby ground was swampy and almost impassable. I was in a position to observe this during my tours of inspection in Poland.'[3]

General Siegfried Westphal blamed the campaign in the Balkans: 'The troops needed for the conquest of the Balkans had of necessity been drawn from our eastern armies. This led to a most unwelcome postponement of the date fixed for the invasion of Russia, which cost us a good six weeks of the limited campaigning season provided by the brief East European summer.'[4] Field Marshal Keitel agreed, bitterly blaming 'Italy for her senseless Balkan war'.[5]

Hitler said that his bid for Moscow failed by exactly five weeks. Liddell Hart, a military writer who interviewed the defeated commanders after the war, did a lot to support their claims that the Balkan campaign was responsible for their failure to take Moscow. But other historians disagree and believe that mid-June had always been the date chosen by the Germans. It was the longest day of the year, and offered the best field conditions. John Keegan, for in-

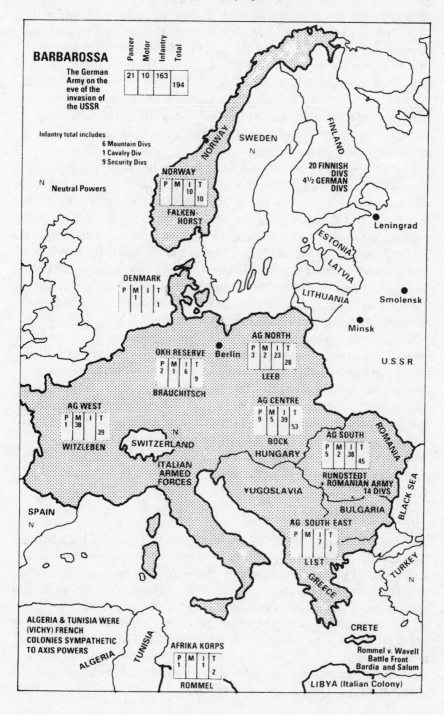

BARBAROSSA

The German Army on the eve of the invasion of the USSR

Panzer	Motor	Infantry	Total
21	10	163	194

Infantry total includes:
- 6 Mountain Divs
- 1 Cavalry Div
- 9 Security Divs

N Neutral Powers

NORWAY

P	M	I	T
		10	10

FALKEN-HORST

NORWAY

SWEDEN N

FINLAND

20 FINNISH DIVS
4½ GERMAN DIVS

Leningrad

ESTONIA

LATVIA

LITHUANIA

Smolensk

Minsk

DENMARK

P	M	I	T
		1	1

OKH RESERVE

P	M	I	T
2	1	6	9

BRAUCHITSCH

Berlin

AG NORTH

P	M	I	T
3	2	23	28

LEEB

U.S.S.R.

AG WEST

P	M	I	T
1	38		39

WITZLEBEN

SWITZERLAND N

ITALIAN ARMED FORCES

AG CENTRE

P	M	I	T
9	5	39	53

BOCK

HUNGARY

AG SOUTH

P	M	I	T
5	2	38	45

RUNDSTEDT
+ ROMANIAN ARMY
14 DIVS

ROMANIA

YUGOSLAVIA

BLACK SEA

BULGARIA

SPAIN N

AG SOUTH EAST

P	M	I	T
		7	7

LIST

GREECE

TURKEY N

CRETE

ALGERIA & TUNISIA WERE (VICHY) FRENCH COLONIES SYMPATHETIC TO AXIS POWERS

ALGERIA

TUNISIA

AFRIKA KORPS

P	M	I	T
1		1	2

ROMMEL

Rommel v. Wavell
Battle Front
Bardia and Salum

LIBYA (Italian Colony)

stance, points out that the date for Barbarossa depended upon the weather and other factors.[6] In his view, the difficulties the army encountered in positioning its units, and the lateness of the spring thaw that year, meant that Hitler could not have invaded earlier than he did. That doyen of historians, A.J.P. Taylor, is scornful of the 'legend invented by German generals to excuse their defeat by the Russians'. He says that the 15 divisions sent to the Balkans were only one-tenth of the total force and their absence would not have been a real impediment to launching the attack.

The 'delay theory' is not easy to sustain in the light of other German activity. For a timetable that scheduled a quick and easy victory, mid-June was a sensible starting date. Besides, once the attack was launched, the leisurely way in which decisions were taken does nothing to suggest men fretting at the loss of a month of fighting.

Some said Hitler chose 22 June because it was the first anniversary of the armistice the French had signed in the Compiègne forest. Nor did it go unremarked that Napoleon had chosen 23 June for his invasion of Russia in 1812. German schoolchildren were taught that half of Napoleon's Grande Armée were Germans.[7]

Delayed or not, on 22 June 1941 the bombardment began and about 3,200,000 men moved forward. The mechanized forces led the attack and news bulletins echoed the names of Russian towns and rivers that were strangely familiar to those who had studied Napoleon's campaign. When the staff of 4 Panzer Group arrived in Borisov, on the bank of the Beresina River, General Blumentritt walked down to the river and noticed, through the clear water, ancient wooden structures. They were supports for a bridge built by Napoleon's engineers when the Grand Army was in retreat in 1812.[8]

The air attacks begin

The Luftwaffe used many of the techniques pioneered by Rowehl Geschwader to bring high-altitude bombers over their targets at dawn so that the bombing exactly coincided with the opening of the artillery barrage. The initial targets were aircraft and air force installations. The Red Air Force was the world's largest, and some of its aircraft designs were excellent, but the bombers found them lined up wingtip to wingtip, for Stalin had forbidden precautions against surprise attack lest it provoke a war. Within 48 hours the Red Air Force had suffered devastating losses and its commander, General Kopels, had committed suicide.

All the same this was not the complete victory that it may sound. The Red Air Force started off four times the size of the Luftwaffe: to eliminate it was a big task. Although devastation had come to the airfields in the western part of the Soviet Union, many more aircraft were available in the rear, and some of these were notably good.[9]

Figure 36: Ilyushin 2 Shturmovik

They were being produced at three or four times the rate of German production. The cut in aircraft production that Hitler ordered in September 1940 resulted by February 1941 in a fall of 40 per cent.[10] Despite their good training, experience and equipment, the Germans had a formidable task to maintain air superiority.

The Luftwaffe's true failure became apparent in those early days of the assault on the Soviet Union. Such a vast country might have been fatally crippled by strategic bombing, but Göring, Milch and Udet had made sure that Germany had no long-range bombers, and no men trained in its demanding techniques.

Stalin the war-lord

At 3.40 am Zhukov, now Soviet chief of staff, phoned Stalin at his large villa at Kuntsevo. Here in one room, the dining-room, Stalin worked, ate and slept on a sofa. When Zhukov told him of the German invasion there was no reply for a long time, just the sound of heavy breathing. At last Stalin called a meeting of the Politburo for 4.30 am.

Far from providing leadership, Stalin seemed to give way to despair. For eleven days he locked himself away, taking time to come to the realization that he had been totally wrong about Hitler's intentions, that the warnings he had angrily spurned were true. It was 3 July when he emerged from hiding to address the nation on radio. His coarse accent came as a surprise to most listeners; so did the pleading note in his voice, calling the people he had mercilessly enslaved 'Brothers and sisters . . . my friends!' In a totally unexpected change of disposition Stalin made little reference to Socialism or its heroes; instead he invoked Russian heroes hitherto condemned as class enemies by Soviet history books. Winston Churchill received greater praise than Lenin.

This reinstatement of Russia's Imperial and Orthodox past continued as Guards regiments were revived and the orders of Lenin and the Red Banner were replaced by those of (Prince) Suvorov, (Prince) Kutuzov and (Grand Duke) Alexander Nevski.[11] The churches were reopened and its dignitaries, such as the Metropolitan Sergei, rallied the faithful to resist the Germans. In a more immediate decree Stalin called up no less than 15 million men by his mobilization order of 22 June. He named this struggle 'The Great Patriotic War', the designation still given it in the countries of the former Soviet empire.

Stalin, the supreme commander-in-chief of the armed forces, took over the war in much the same autocratic way that Hitler did. Like Hitler, he was a psychopath, and his skill as a military commander was about the equal of Hitler's. There were other resemblances between the two dictators; Stalin had a good memory and sometimes came up with the sort of sensible ideas with which laymen often outwit the experts. But his foremost contribution to this war came from his obsessional secrecy.

Stalin's unending fear of rebellion had always caused him to keep a tight hold upon the army, and from it he now separated a High Command Reserve consisting of divisions, corps and whole armies, together with tanks, artillery and air forces. The state of these reserves was marked by means of tally boards at his desk. The front commanders were kept totally ignorant of what reserves were available in order to frustrate their pleas for reinforcements. One specialist historian of this period says that: 'Neither tactical threat nor tactical defeat could force him to disgorge his precious reserves and he held on to them tightly until he could be reasonably sure that the enemy had committed all his forces.'[12]

While Hitler took control of his armed forces by taking over the high command of the army (OKH), and that of the armed forces (OKW) too, Stalin exercised his iron grip through the Communist party. The party apparatus was everywhere: from factory bench to front-line positions. The slightest divergence from its wishes, or indeed failure or bad luck, meant being worked to death in a slave-labour camp or summary execution. When Stalin added 'or you'll answer with your head' to his commands it was not a joke. By the time war ended 238 generals and admirals had been executed, or had died in penal battalions, simply because they had failed to win.[13] This horrifying dimension of terror played an important part in saving Moscow in 1941, and indeed in winning the war.

At Stalin's elbow during that first year there was Marshal Shaposhnikov, the chief of general staff, who was quite unlike the one-time NCOs, rough-voiced commissars and other sycophants who made up most of Stalin's staff. Shaposhnikov was a genial, avuncular gentleman who had been a colonel in the Tsar's army. In the postwar period, German and American historians were inclined to guess that Shaposhnikov was the brains behind the Red Army's successes. Modern appraisals are more inclined to see him as a technical adviser, serving the same function that Jodl did for Hitler.

It was Zhukov who emerged from the war with the soundest military reputation. His success against the Japanese had impressed Stalin as well as Zhukov's fellow soldiers. In 1941 the defence of Moscow was put into his hands. Stalin frequently consulted Zhukov, but during these first months of the war Zhukov's influence extended only to his own battle front. Even then his decisions were constantly supervised and questioned by Moscow.

The Russian secret

Within days of the German attack, a Council for Evacuation was formed. Its task was to arrange for the movement of industry and national treasures to safer regions, and Stalin's centralized authority ensured that any decision it made became law. With news of German advances pouring in, the Council sometimes over-reacted. For instance, on 2 July the armoured plate mill at Mariupol, in the southern Ukraine hundreds of miles from the front line and not in danger, was ordered to move to Magnitogorsk. Yet it was moves of this sort that saved the Soviet Union. In the five months from July to November 1,523 industrial enterprises, including 1,360 large armaments plants, were moved east – to the Urals (667), to Siberia (322), to Kazakhstan and Central Asia (308).

The Russian movements of heavy industry also seemed to reinvigorate it. Workers who had proved so inefficient under the centralized industrial planning of the Communists thrived when permitted to improvise. A foundry that originally took two years to build had its replacement ready in 28 days. The planners found that a factory could be moved and production resumed within six weeks. The Chkalov aircraft plant, moved from Moscow to Tashkent, had aircraft ready in forty days. Sometimes factories, assembled in the open in bad weather, had production lines moving even before walls and roof were finished. One worker arriving at such an improvised factory said she was astounded to discover that almost everyone at work was either a young child or an old woman. The Russians were preparing for a long hard war.

Two plants – from Leningrad and Kharkov – were moved to Chelyabinsk, east of the Urals, to be combined with the Chelyabinsk tractor factory. This vast enterprise, renamed Tankograd, was the largest tank factory in the Soviet Union – perhaps in the world – and the greater part of the T-34 production took place here. The hardiness of the T-34 had been demonstrated by one of the first prototypes. It came out of the Kharkov factory at the end of 1939 and was sent on a trip to Moscow and back, via Smolensk, Minsk and Kiev, a distance of 1,800 miles. February and March were chosen for the trip, so that it would encounter the sort of bad weather that later was to defeat German tanks.

It had a good cross-country performance and top speed of 32 mph, but the most evident aspect of this radical new tank was its sloping armour, which gave it a distinctive profile as well as deflecting hits that might otherwise have penetrated it. It was armed with a high-velocity gun that could tear through German armour at long ranges while its own armour remained impervious to the current German 3.7-cm anti-tank guns.[14]

The technology of tank design was challenging to any country's industrial capability. Because the precision machining of large surfaces is so demanding, a reliable measure of a tank's sophistication is the diameter of its turret ring. The T-34's turret was small, providing scarcely enough room for two men. Since loading was a full-time task this meant the tank's commander was also its gunner. Having such calls upon the tank commander during battle was the tank's most serious disadvantage.

Most Second World War tanks ran on petrol, but the T-34 had a diesel engine. This was a breakthrough in tank technology that even the Germans, with their great experience of diesels, failed to make. The engine was probably based upon a Fiat design (some say it copied a Hispano-Suiza) but the transformation was extraordinary. Lightened by the use of many alloy components, this 38-litre engine produced about 500 bhp and could go about 280 miles at 25 mph before refuelling. Economy – for purposes of range rather than expense – had been a prime consideration in pursuing the diesel format, but such engines were desirable for their lessened fire risk too. Their worst feature was – as anyone who has driven behind a truck will verify – that diesel engines emit black smoke, and exhaust could be fatal when it revealed a tank's position.

Had the Russians used these tanks in forces large enough to punch through the enemy lines, the Germans might have been repulsed in the early weeks of the war. But the Red Army's T-34s were committed in twos and threes, and mixed with inferior models. With radios only fitted to the tanks of company commanders, orders had to be passed by flags or hand signals. Everything was made especially difficult when the tank was closed down because Russian optical glass was of very poor quality.

The T-34 Christie-style suspension, invented by an American engineer whose ideas were copied by every other nation, was efficient over rough ground but a gunner stood little or no chance of hitting a target while on the move. All the same the Russian high command ordered their men to keep firing during any encounter, reasoning, rightly perhaps, that the sight of oncoming tanks, firing as they went, was demoralizing. When all the rounds were spent, the tank drivers were ordered to crush the enemy by rolling right over them. Opposing tanks had to be rammed.

Figure 37:
Russian T-34 tank

Like most other economies the Soviet Union suffered a shortage of the high-quality steel needed for guns, tanks, ships and shells. In the early days of the war some tanks were improvised from boiler plate which gave little protection against anything but small-arms fire. When fighting the Japanese and the Finns the Red Army had used armour-piercing shells based upon designs produced for the imperial navy in the previous century. It was only after German armour-piercing shot was captured that it was copied. But making steel is not an art that can be mastered overnight. The failure to control perfectly the tempering of the steel had a great effect upon the quality of ammunition for the tank guns. So the Red Army tank crews had to get used to the way that the tungsten carbide cores of their armour-piercing shells often broke up on impact, and hope that they would not fall victim to one of the premature explosions in the breach that were not unusual in Soviet gunnery.

'Wolfsschanze' Rastenburg

As part of the preparations for Barbarossa, Hitler had a military headquarters built from which he would supervise the battle. The site chosen by Dr Todt and Hitler's army adjutant was eight kilometres east of Rastenburg in East Prussia. It was constructed in conditions of great secrecy, under the guise of a bomb-proof war production plant, and was ready for Hitler to start using only a few days before the attack was launched. He moved in on 24 June and named it 'Wolfsschanze', wolf's lair: the wolf was an animal with which he constantly identified.

The site was poorly chosen. Up to the time of the attack, the daily Aeroflot airliner passed over it on its schedule between Berlin and Moscow. The region was an airless, fetid swamp with stagnant lakes. Even shallow diggings were subject to flooding, and, despite strenuous efforts, mosquitoes plagued everyone for much of the time. Hitler said: 'No doubt some government department found the land was cheapest here.'

Hitler was in Wolfsschanze for most of the time, so everyone who wanted to keep in touch with the Führer had to go there too. It was a complex of makeshift and uncomfortable offices for people and organizations that functioned more efficiently in the premises from which they had been brought. The OKH was established here, as was Hitler's high command of the armed forces, the OKW. Hitler said: 'this whole headquarters will one day become a historic monument, because here is where we founded a New World order.' Jodl thought the place better suited to a military detention camp.

Despite elaborate security measures, more than one person wandered into the Wolfsschanze by accident. A colonel got off the train at the wrong station when looking for Mauerwald close by. He walked right into the compound to take breakfast at the officers' mess. When challenged by the Führer's naval aide, Admiral von Puttkamer, the intruder refused to believe he was in the Wolfsschanze until Puttkamer pointed to Hitler exercising his dog 'Blondi'.[15]

Nor did Hitler's prediction come true. Rastenburg is now Ketrzyn in Poland. All that remains of the Wolf's Lair are massive chunks of concrete overgrown by the forest.

Bock's first objective: Minsk or Smolensk?

Field Marshal Fedor von Bock had been given command of Army Group Centre, where the maximum effort was made. Sixty years old, Bock was a tall thin man described by General Blumentritt as a Prussian of the old school. 'He was vivacious, often sarcastic, and expressed his thoughts clearly and well. He did not look his age and might have passed for a man of forty. However his health was not perfect, for he suffered from frequent stomach pains.' His physical courage in the First World War had earned him the Pour le Mérite, the highest German award for valour.

Bock resented the way in which von Brauchitsch, an officer junior to him, had been promoted to become army C-in-C and so his boss. This resentment was fanned in 1940 when Brauchitsch changed the plans for the attack on France and the Low Countries. The weight of the attack was switched away from Bock's Army Group so that his rival Rundstedt's Army Group made the breakthrough and got all the glory. That change still festered in Bock's mind, as did a bitter argument with Guderian about mechanical breakdowns during the occupation of Austria. Bock was a patrician, a capable but difficult man with a long memory for slights, real or imagined.

Bock's cynical attitude to Hitler was rather like his pragmatic relationship with Hermann Hoth and Heinz Guderian, his Panzer Group commanders. As long as these plebeians assisted his career he would use them. Hitler was in control so Bock obeyed him, but when he noticed signs of anti-Hitler conspiracies in his own headquarters he turned a blind eye to them.

In Russia Bock commanded 50 divisions, including Panzer Group Hoth and Panzer Group Guderian, placed on the outer flanks of his central front. The initial idea had been a drive for Smolensk, but three days after the assault was started Hitler interfered, giving a direct order that Bock's force was to encircle and converge on Minsk. At the same time, the infantry forces were to make an inner pincer that closed behind Bialystok. Such encirclements had not been the key to victory in France. There the armour had simply struck forward, overrun headquarters, and watched the enemy command collapse at ever higher levels. But Napoleon's invasion of Russia had failed because the Russian army withdrew and avoided battle. Hitler demanded a Kesselschlacht, a 'kettle' or cauldron battle, that would encircle and then annihilate the enemy armies and not just push them back. Many of his generals, notably Guderian, believed it better to strike at the enemy's brain – for example Moscow – and then victory was bound to come. These two opposing points of view had never been resolved and agreed, although Hitler's initial Directive had given emphasis to the destruction of the enemy army:

> General Intention.
> The bulk of the Russian army stationed in Western Russia will be destroyed by daring operations led by deeply penetrating armoured spearheads. Russian forces still capable of giving battle will be prevented from withdrawing into the depths of Russia.[16]

The Panzer divisions raced ahead as they had in France. One of the first clashes came as the Germans encountered the well-equipped 4th Armoured Division. This Russian division had 355 tanks, while Guderian's whole Panzer Group of five divisions and three and a half motorized divisions had only 850. But Red Army leadership was poor and the Soviet elements were separated, out-manoeuvred and completely smashed. Its commander, 43-year-old Major-General Potaturchev, with hair and moustache groomed like Stalin's, was rounded up while trudging back to Minsk dressed as a civilian. He became the first Soviet general to go into captivity.[17]

Bock's Army Group Centre moved forward as fast as it could, but inevitably the armour and motorized divisions became separated from the infantry, who plodded along far behind, fighting all the way and cursing at the lack of armour support. Great encircling movements, on a scale never seen before, demanded both initiative and organization. Army Group Centre's first attempt ended in failure. The German formations were not sufficiently concentrated and the greater part of the trapped Russians fought their way clear. A second attempt closed near Minsk. Although many escaped some 300,000 were captured. Such numbers of men are difficult to imagine. One witness said:

We suddenly saw a broad, earth-brown crocodile slowly shuffling down the road towards us. From it came a subdued hum, like that from a beehive. Prisoners of war. Russians, six deep. We couldn't see the end of the column. As they drew near the terrible stench which met us made us quite sick; it was like the biting stench of the lion house and the filthy odour of the monkey house at the same time. But these were not animals, they were men. We made haste out of the way of the foul cloud which surrounded them . . . All the misery in the world seemed to be concentrated here.[18]

Of course the figures coming from the fighting front were not accurate. They were the establishment figures (or at best ration-strength figures) from files captured in various unit headquarters the Germans had overrun. All the same, such numbers made heady reading in Berlin. So did the news that some of 'Hurrying Heinz' Guderian's foremost troops had reached the Dnieper, about half-way to Moscow. On 3 July General Halder wrote in his diary: 'It is probably not an exaggeration when I contend that the campaign in Russia has been won in fourteen days.'

However, the Germans were suffering casualties too. The Panzer force encountered 52-ton KV tanks that were like nothing they had ever seen before. To stop them was difficult: 'The general himself stood thoughtfully in front of a KV, counting the tank shells lodged in its plating – 11 hits and not a single penetration.'[19]

In these early actions the tank was the decisive weapon. It was Lt-General Andrey Ivanovich Yeremenko who is given credit for creating the most frightening of anti-tank weapons – although simpler petrol bombs had been used in Spain, and in Finland too. Yeremenko had been brought from the First Far Eastern Army as part of Stalin's 'central front'. Facing General Heinz Guderian's Panzer Group, he ordered that a depot in Gomel should fill 10,000 glass bottles with KS (a petrol and phosphorus mixture used for flamethrowers) so that his men could use them against enemy tanks. The weight and the shape made them easy to grip and to throw. The contents were sufficient in quantity, and fierce in effect. They were cheap and quick to make. The Germans who saw them explode to spill the blazing mixture through the slots and ventilators of their tanks called them 'Molotov Cocktails'.[20] The name stuck.

The Germans had never properly grasped what numbers of men they would need to surround half a million Russians and then fight

them to a standstill. There were not enough combat soldiers to en-
close these vast areas, and not enough support troops to keep them
supplied. Adding to these demands on German manpower were
what now proved to be mistaken notions about the Pripet Marshes.

The Pripet Marshes

Sometimes called the Rokitno Marshes, this area is a huge blot
upon the map of European Russia. It is 300 miles broad and

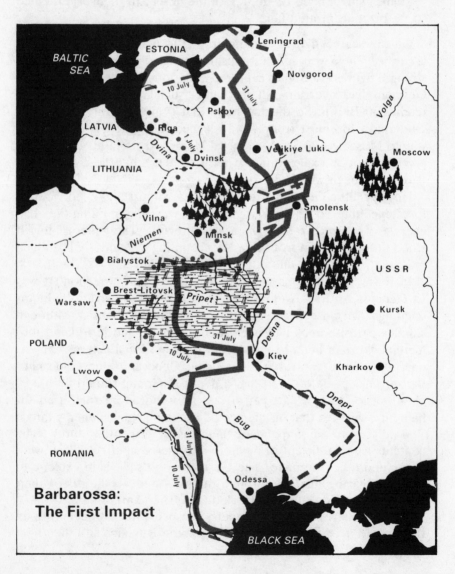

**Barbarossa:
The First Impact**

roughly as large as Bavaria. General Blumentritt told how in the German army: 'It was regarded as an almost inaccessible area, covered with woods and swamps, which eliminated it from plans of operation.'[21] Army Group South used this inaccessible region to rest its flank, as had Army Group Centre. But 'for Russian troops it is no particular obstacle, for they cross it everywhere with whole army corps ... it even offered our eastern adversaries a very good defence area from which they could, on any side, fall on the flank of troops advancing east.'

The Pripet Marshes had probably acquired the plural form of name because the region was not all marshland and large areas of it had been drained and improved over the years. There was firm open ground amongst the marshes and forests and its rivers had ancient wooden bridges suited to local traffic in this primitive region. In short it was totally unsuited for the rapid deployment of German armour but excellent ground for Russian cavalry and units guided by locals. So the German Barbarossa plan was flawed. There was no excuse for this planning oversight, for German staff officers had heard lectures about the marshes in connection with studies of the Russo-Polish War of 1920.[22] Yet the mistake remained, and now there was a 300-mile-wide hole in the German front. Men would be needed to close this gap.

Everywhere behind the German advance, Communist party workers were organizing partisan units to continue the fight. On 18 July 1941 the central committee of the Communist party adopted a resolution defining the aims and tasks of the underground struggle. Quite unlike the resistance organized in the West, these partisans lived in extremely primitive conditions in the countryside and swore 'to take revenge on the enemy cruelly, tirelessly and without mercy.' Their oath required them to die rather than surrender.[23]

The Germans found it impossible to prevent escapes when tens of thousands of prisoners were herded in the open countryside. The terrain – mostly forest and swamp with poor roads – exactly suited fugitives, and it suited guerrilla warfare too. Escaping Red Army soldiers joined the partisans and added a dimension of military skills to the partisan struggle. A special section of the Red Army's Chief Political Administration was devoted to directing partisan warfare.

As one example of this guerrilla warfare, partisans in the Pskov region in the autumn of 1941 killed more than a thousand German soldiers, destroyed 30 bridges and derailed five military trains. By February 1942 Army Group Centre had assigned four field divisions to fight partisans in the Smolensk and Bryansk area. It was not enough, and soon another three German divisions were withdrawn from the fighting front to combat the partisans.

By mid-July 1941 great changes were made to the Red Army. To speed orders through the military bureaucracy corps headquarters would be eliminated. Mechanized corps were disbanded, to release desperately needed trucks, and men of the motorized divisions became infantry. 'Small armies' of about six divisions were formed. There was no shortage of infantry, but experienced leadership was so scarce that the Soviet Union's many slave-labour camps were scoured to find senior officers who could be released and sent back to the army.

Army Group Centre: Hitler intervenes

Smolensk was seen to be 'the key to Moscow'. Army Group Centre planned another encirclement like that at Minsk, though by now the Red Army was learning how to punch a way out of encirclements. The Soviets were becoming more formidable opponents in every way. Their counter-attacks were becoming better organized and more frequent. Sometimes such attacks prised into the gap that the Germans left between their fast armoured columns and the slower infantry.

Guderian dismissed suggestions of waiting for the infantry to catch up with him. He pressed on to demonstrate his theories until, on 19 July, Hitler intervened in the battle with an audacious plan that would split the central thrust. While the infantry of Army Group Centre continued their advance on Moscow, its twin armoured forces (Panzergruppe Hoth and Panzergruppe Guderian) were to diverge. Hoth would wheel northwards, to become an outer pincer for Army Group North's drive on Leningrad. Guderian would wheel southwards to form an outer pincer for Army Group South's drive into the Ukraine.

Hitler's idea was inconceivable. So inconceivable that Brauchitsch the C-in-C filed it away and tried to forget it. Hitler persisted, and it is at this moment that the campaign, and perhaps Hitler's war, was lost, for instead of saying no, Brauchitsch temporized. He told Hitler that the armoured forces must stop for overhauls, repairs and replacements. Hitler agreed. It would appear at this stage that Brauchitsch had no intention of obeying Hitler's order. Halder had already approved (on 30 June) an OKH oper-

The German advance towards Moscow

GERMAN ADVANCE WITH ROMANIAN AND PANZER GROUPS UNTIL OCT/DEC 41

☆ MAJOR RUSSIAN ENCIRCLEMENTS

▬ MAJOR RUSSIAN DEFENSIVE ACTION

MAJOR RUSSIAN COUNTER-ATTACK

•••••• FRONT LINE 4 DECEMBER 1941

GERMAN ARMY GROUP BOUNDARIES

BALTIC SEA

LENINGRAD • Tikhvin

Novgorod

Riga

KALININ

Velikiye Luki

Volga

Army Group North

Vilna

Dvina

MOSCOW

Army Group Centre

Minsk

Niemen

Smolensk

Bialystok

WARSAW

Brest Litovsk

Pripet

Desna

Don

Lvov

Army Group South

KIEV

Lochvitsa

KHARKOV

Uman

Dnieper

Donets

Dniester

Pruth

Odessa

Bug

BUCHAREST

Danube

BLACK SEA

ational draft ordering the advance on Moscow to be resumed about 12 August. But this was easier said than done. Bottlenecks and confusion had caused the snarling-up of roads and railways, creating a supply crisis that made it impossible for Army Group Centre to mount an attack in August, except one using less than a quarter of its combat strength.

An extra dimension was given to the strategic disagreement between Hitler and his generals when, for the first time since the last war, Hitler became sick.[24] The stress of the campaign, his visits to distant Army Group headquarters and the unhealthy conditions at the Wolfsschanze had given him a fever together with dysentery, stomach cramps, nausea and accompanying aches and pains. Those around him were alarmed by an evident deterioration in his health. An electro-cardiogram, sent to a heart institute with a false name on its label, was diagnosed as rapidly progressive coronary sclerosis, hardening of the arteries. Hitler's personal physician neglected to tell his patient the true facts, embarking on a programme of doubtful treatment that kept his patient going on heart stimulants, vitamins and glucose.

In his weakened physical condition, Hitler did not waver in his orders to split the attack. When Guderian heard of the plan to switch his Panzergruppe southwards, he was so strongly opposed to it that he flew to the Wolfsschanze to make his plea to Hitler in person. Artfully, neither Brauchitsch nor Halder accompanied him to this meeting. Guderian recalled:

> I reported at once to the C-in-C of the Army, Field Marshal von Brauchitsch, who greeted me with the following words: 'I forbid you to mention the question of Moscow to the Führer. The operation to the south has been ordered . . . Discussion is pointless.' I therefore asked permission to fly back to my Panzer Group.[25]

Brauchitsch was not the sort of man who would confront Hitler, but Guderian was just such a man. He stayed to plead his case. He told Hitler that Moscow was the crucial target: a road, rail and communications centre, industrial centre and political centre, whose capture would have a psychological effect upon the whole world. With Moscow in German hands, the Russians would be unable to move their forces between the north and the south. Guderian said that much time would be wasted in diverting his Panzer Group south to attack Kiev. The round trip of 500 miles, cross-country on terrible Russian roads, would cause great wear on his tanks.

Hitler let Guderian speak without interruption but was unmoved by his arguments. He wanted the raw materials and agriculture of the Ukraine. He said they must deprive the Russian air force of bases in the Crimea, lest they bombed the Romanian oilfields upon which Germany depended for most of its fuel. 'I here saw for the first time a spectacle with which I was later to become very familiar,' Guderian said. 'All those present nodded in agreement with every sentence that Hitler uttered, while I was left alone with my point of view.' According to Guderian's account the nodding men included Field Marshal Keitel and General Jodl. These two men, closely supervised by Hitler, ran the office of the OKW, Armed Forces High Command, and without their support Guderian's cause was lost. 'Hurrying Heinz' went back to his headquarters but his Group didn't move in any direction.

Bock supported Guderian. Losing Hoth's Panzer force to Field Marshal Leeb in the north was endurable, but to reinforce his rival Rundstedt with precious Panzer divisions for a dash into the Ukraine sounded too much like what had happened in France in 1940. So Bock, fully engaged with the enemy all along his front, did nothing to hurry things along, hoping that Hitler would have a change of mind. The delay continued long after the Panzer forces were refitted and made ready to go again.[26] Guderian deliberately engaged his armoured force in battles that would make disengagement and the big movement south difficult. General Blumentritt had no illusions about what happened: 'Army Group Centre remained inactive on the Desna during the best months of July to September,' he said. Göring took Hitler's side in the argument. He was convinced that had Bock, and the other commanders, promptly obeyed Hitler's orders, the war would have been won by early 1942. He told his interrogators so during his imprisonment after the war.

But Bock's Army Group Centre – like the other Army Groups – was wrestling with ever worse supply problems. The railway operating troops (*Eisenbahntruppe*) were undermanned and inefficient. German civilian railway workers were brought to assist them but the difficulties were deep-seated and could not be corrected overnight. Having suffered losses of men and machines in the battles around Smolensk, the whole Army Group was trying to refit and regroup, but it also had to cope with square mile upon square mile of captives. Even when the encircled Red Army units stopped fighting they had to be tightly guarded and defended to prevent

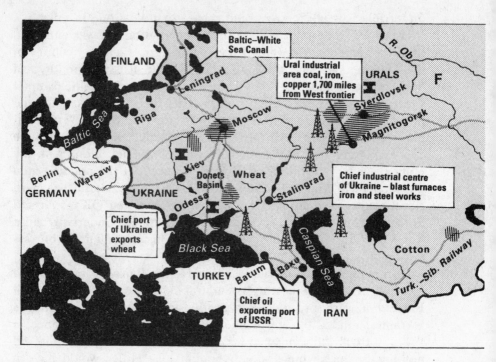

Russian counter-attacks from trying to break in and release them.

Perhaps Hitler had recognized this weakening condition of Bock's Army Group Centre before anyone else did. Perhaps that was what influenced him into diverting the armour and switching the centre of gravity to the southern fighting. In any case, the discussions about switching the Panzer forces to other Army Groups was evidence enough that the German army was numerically incapable of fighting the campaign that its generals had planned. It showed that they did not have enough Panzer divisions to attack simultaneously with all three Army Groups. Barbarossa had opened with 150 German divisions, only fifteen more than were used for the attack westwards in May 1940 and with only about 30 per cent more tanks than they had used at that time. Yet the area in which the armies were to be deployed in the Barbarossa plan – about a million square miles – was twenty times the size of the ground involved between 10 May and 25 June 1940.[27] To add to this worrying overall picture was the way in which the front got broader and broader as the Germans fought their way further eastwards!

Although the Red Army were losing men by the hundreds of thousands they always seemed to find more. In mid-August

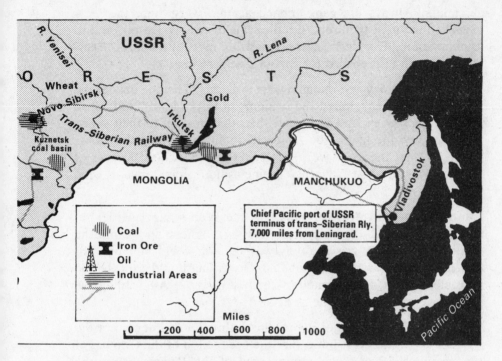

Halder's optimism changed to a mood of concern:

> we have underestimated the Russian Colossus . . . This conclusion applies as much to its organization as to its economic resources and its system of communication, but above all to its purely military efficiency. At the beginning we reckoned with some 200 enemy divisions and we have already identified 360. These divisions are admittedly not armed or equipped according to our standards and in many respects the tactical leadership is inadequate. But there they are, and when a dozen of them are destroyed the Russians throw in another dozen. Time is with them. Their resources lie close by. Our forces are stretched along an immensely broad front, without any depth, and are subjected again and again to enemy attacks. These are successful partly because we have too many gaps in our line owing to the stupendous space.

The war in the East never did form a continuous line from north to south. Everywhere attackers tried to find space between units, with gaps closing and reappearing between them. Sometimes siege conditions evolved around the great cities, and around pockets of defenders. Always big gaps opened again. Everywhere the Germans had to adapt themselves to the scale of eastern Europe and to its climate too. The Berliners who made up most of 3 Panzer 'Bear' Division were unprepared for Russia's August weather.

> It was a hot day and the men were sweating. The fine dust of the rough roads enveloped the columns in thick clouds, settled on the men's faces, and got under their uniforms on to their skins. It covered the tanks, the armoured infantry carriers, the motor cycles, and the jeeps [*Kubelwagens*] with an inch-thick layer of dirt. The dust was frightful – as fine as flour, impossible to keep out.[28]

In the unhealthy August climate of the Wolfsschanze Hitler remained convinced that trapping Russian soldiers and capturing economic resources was the only way the war could be won. For this reason he was determined that Guderian should execute the movement south. Exasperated by the delays, on 21 August he gave the army direct orders to do as he said:

> Of primary importance before the outbreak of winter is not the capture of Moscow, but rather the occupation of the Crimea, of the industrial and coal-mining area of the Donets basin, the cutting of the Russian supply routes from the Caucasian oilfields.

The generals bristled. Halder urged Brauchitsch to send in their joint resignation but was told that Hitler would simply refuse to accept it. Halder had already confided in his diary that Brauchitsch was 'at the end of his tether and hides behind an iron mask of manliness so as not to betray his complete helplessness.' Jodl, the general closest to Hitler, said the Führer 'has an instinctive aversion from treading the same path as Napoleon; Moscow gives him a sinister feeling.'[29] In any case, Hitler had promised that, once the encirclement at Kiev was completed, Guderian's armour could rejoin Army Group Centre and resume the drive on Moscow.

Reluctantly the army did as Hitler ordered: Guderian turned south and Southern Army Group's panzer group came north to meet them. The Führer's Kiev encirclement worked perfectly. After terrible fighting, on a front measured in hundreds of miles, the Panzer forces closed 150 miles east of Kiev. The resulting encirclement trapped 665,000 men.

On 26 September 1941, as the Kiev battle ended, von Manstein's army in the south broke through the narrow isthmus that led into the Crimea. It was a dramatic victory on the map, but the Crimea was another great land area that would soak up men by the tens and scores of thousands.

Meanwhile the drive by Field Marshal von Leeb's Army Group North was building to a climax. Successive attempts to take Leningrad had failed but German forward elements were fighting in the suburbs, and the defenders had been worn down to a point of near collapse. In one action women of the Red Army medical corps defended their position with pistols and hand-grenades until they were all killed.[30] So desperate was the position that Zhukov was sent there to command a last-ditch stand. His appointment was a political sign that Leningrad was to be defended to the very end. Then, under continuous bombardment, with hospitals reporting 4,000 casualties per day and their soldiers yielding to the pressures of heavy fighting, the Red Army's intelligence began receiving reports of German tanks outside Leningrad being loaded on to railway flatcars.[31] These were elements of Hoth's Panzer Group which had been on loan and were now being returned to Bock for the coming assault on Moscow. Leningrad had been reprieved, and the pressure from both the Finnish and German armies noticeably slackened. The Finns had decided that after regaining the land they had lost in the Winter War they would advance no farther. Everywhere on Leeb's Northern Sector the tactics of assault had been abandoned in favour of siege. The go-ahead was now given to Bock's drive to Moscow.

Hitler's permission for Army Group Centre to strike at Moscow had come too late. A wiser man would have wanted to fight the Moscow battle first. As Table 6 shows, Moscow temperatures take a sudden dive in December. The southern front had two months more campaigning weather than Moscow; Leningrad had one month more than Moscow.

Table 6   *Average monthly Fahrenheit temperatures in four Soviet cities*

	J	F	M	A	M	J	J	A	S	O	N	D
Leningrad	18	18	25	37	49	58	63	60	51	41	30	22
Moscow	12	15	24	38	53	62	66	63	52	40	28	17
Kiev	21	23	31	45	57	64	67	65	57	46	34	24
Astrakhan	19	23	33	48	64	73	77	74	63	49	36	27

From now on it would be a race against time as the dusty Russian climate turned cooler. The German high command was drastically changing all its estimates of a blitzkrieg against the Soviet Union. The discovery that the Red Army had first-class tanks startled the whole German army. In October 1941 Guderian's reaction was made plain in a report he sent to his Army Group:

> I described in plain terms the marked superiority of the T-34 to our Panzer IV and drew the relevant conclusions as they must affect our future tank production . . . The officers at the front were of the opinion that the T-34 should simply be copied, since this would be the quickest way of putting to rights the most un-happy situation of the German Panzer troops.[32]

Guderian was not alone in his view. Field Marshal von Kleist called it the finest tank in the world; Major-General von Mellenthin said that in 1941 the Germans had nothing comparable; General Blumentritt thought it adversely affected the morale of the German infantry.

Only the incompetence of Russian generals saved the Germans. Despite the studies they had made of the German victories in France, the Red Army commanders were still spreading their tanks into a thin ineffective screen, instead of using them like battering rams. The Germans claimed that 17,000 Russian tanks were des-troyed in the first five months of fighting, while only 2,700 of their own tanks were lost. But as Soviet production went into top gear these terrible losses were being replaced at a greater rate than those of the Germans. In 1942, when the Germans manufactured 5,056 tanks (a figure that includes self-propelled artillery), the Soviet Union produced 24,500 tanks, of which some 5,000 were the T-34.[33]

The Germans had put every tank they could find into the Barba-rossa invasion force in the belief that the campaign would be a short one. Now, many of the smaller German tanks, some of the Czech designs and most of the French ones were succumbing to the rigours of climate and terrain.

It was not only tanks that found the going difficult. Any sort of mechanical vehicle suffered. Dust got through air filters to kill engines. Mud swallowed vehicles whole. Temperatures dropped until crankcases and radiators cracked. The Russian roads proved far worse than the planners had allowed for, and the Germans were using far too many civilian trucks, not designed for the wear and tear of even normal military duties.

Mud and horses

The dark spot on the horizon was a raincloud. By the time the Kiev battle ended, the weather had changed enough to slow the final stages of the encirclement. The primitive quality of Russian roads, many of them no more than tracks that became deep mud when the rain started, saved Moscow that year. Or as one military theorist said, it was the German dependence upon wheels, rather than having tracked mobility for all arms, that cost them victory.[34] However, tracked mobility for all arms would have meant thousands more thirsty vehicles for an army that could not find fuel for those it already had.

The men who endured that mud said that it was a soft sticky morass that prevented all movement. Many such descriptions, like those of choking Russian dust, are no doubt exaggerated, but the virtual absence of paved roads meant that mud was an obstacle on a scale never encountered in western Europe. Wheels immediately succumbed to deep mud but, while power-driven wheels sank deeper and deeper, a horse-drawn cart could sometimes clamber away. A German front-line surgeon said:

> There was keen rivalry between the two medical companies in the division. As far as mobility and speed were concerned, the motorized company naturally had the advantage over us at first. But as soon as there was any mud about, our horses would still be going strong long after their vehicles had got bogged down.[35]

The German army depended mostly upon heavy draft horses, but these breeds proved unsuited to cold conditions. Without shelter they collapsed and died at temperatures below minus 4 degrees Fahrenheit. When fit they consumed excessive amounts of forage. Yet only these powerful horses could pull the heavy wagons the army used, and in a major example of German army incompetence there was a grave shortage of winter horseshoes, without which the horses not only had lessened draft power but sometimes could not even negotiate the distance from railway depot to stables.[36] Major Vogt, the commander of 18 Panzer Division support units, asked himself how the Russians endured the winter conditions year after year. Paul Carell describes the solution he hit upon:

> He got hold of the small tough horses he had seen the local peasants use, as well as their light farm-carts, and used them for sending his divisions' supplies forward, a few hundredweight on

each cart. It worked. The motorized convoys were stuck in the mud, but the small peasant carts got through.[37]

And so the proudest and most successful war machine the world had ever seen, in the most ambitious campaign in history, was reduced to the use of small farm-carts. It had to be admitted that the horse was more effective in this sort of war and the Red Army showed discernment in its use. In 1941 its force of 30 divisions of cavalry was increased to 41 divisions. Some were Cossacks and Kalmuks, fierce tribesmen who had lived with horses all their lives. The cavalrymen fought as infantry, using the horses to drag mortars and light artillery across impossible country. With shaggy-coated Siberian Kirghil ponies, that could endure temperatures as low as minus 58 degrees Fahrenheit, such units could cover 100 kilometres in one night, caring nothing for lines of supply and communications.[38]

24 'A WAR OF ANNIHILATION'

*He that observeth the wind shall not sow; and he that
regardeth the clouds shall not reap.*

Ecclesiastes xi. 4

As early as 30 March 1941, Hitler had told 250 senior German officers, summoned from all parts of his newly won territories, that while the war against France had been conventional, in Russia 'We have a war of annihilation on our hands.' Perched on their delicate gold-painted chairs in the panelled splendour of the New Chancellory, his generals and admirals, seated in order of seniority, did not seem to comprehend the full import of this definition but they were soon to learn.

In time for the occupation of the Sudetenland Himmler's SS had organized Special Task Forces (Einsatzgruppen) to work in the areas conquered by the advancing German army. Their task was the systematic murder of people for whom there was no place in the Nazi state. These would include the commissars (political officers attached to Red Army units), guerrillas, saboteurs, Jews and Bolshevik agitators. In practice, the Einsatzgruppen sought out and killed not only Jews but all educated people, especially those who were socially influential, such as doctors, teachers, writers, priests and rabbis. Their families were not exempt. During the remaining months of 1941 about 500,000 European Russian Jews were slaughtered by these teams, and perhaps as many non-Jewish Russians as well. The commander of one such group, Otto Ohlendorf, admitted after the war that his men murdered 90,000 men women and children during 1941.

Nor were the front-line units squeamish about their methods of cold-blooded killing. One young Waffen-SS soldier remembered an incident during the fighting around the town of Uman in the encirclement of Kiev:

an order was received by Division to the effect that all prisoners captured during the last three days were to be shot as a reprisal for the inhuman atrocities which the Red Army had committed in our sector. It so happened that we had taken very many prisoners during those fatal days and so the lives of four thousand men fell forfeit.

They lined up eight at a time, by the side of a large anti-tank ditch. As the first volley crashed, eight men were hurled forward into the depths of the ditch, as if hit by a giant fist. Already the next file was lining up. It was strange and incomprehensible to us how these men used their last minutes in this world . . . One took off his overcoat and folded it neatly before laying it sadly on the ground . . . Others greedily smoked a last cigarette, which they had rolled clumsily from a filthy scrap of newspaper; nobody wrote a last message home; there were no tears.

Then suddenly one of them, a tall Georgian or Ossete, seized a spade lying beside him, and brought it down like lightning on the skull – not of the German guard who was standing next to him – but of a red commissar.[1]

Red Army soldiers had no alternative but to fight or die. Officers and men were executed for the slightest suspicion of cowardice or treachery. Lesser offences meant being sent to a penal battalion where life expectancy was very short indeed.[2] Even such luminaries as the Army Group commander in the West, D.G. Pavlov, a noted tank expert, were executed on Stalin's orders. A special field security force named Smersh was set up to deal mercilessly with lesser ranks. Lenin had long since decreed that becoming a prisoner was a crime, and all soldiers knew that if they were captured by the Germans their family would be sent to a slave-labour camp.

Some of the best-fed and best-equipped battalions to be found in the Soviet Union were not sent to face the Germans. These NKVD units were directly responsible to Lavrenti Beria, the man who controlled the secret police, the frontier guards and the labour camps. Assigned to follow the fighting forces, their job was to shoot men who tried to retreat and provide 'blocking detachments' which sent soldiers forward at gunpoint over minefields or into enemy gunfire.[3] Combat troops who fought their way out of German encirclements were not treated as heroes. On the contrary, such men were rounded up and executed. Stalin's daughter Svetlana recalled how Beria's men 'carried out the abominable liquidation of whole army units, at times very large ones, who, during the swift German advance into the

Ukraine and Byelorussia, had found themselves cut off from their
own lines, and who later, against frightful odds, had found their
way back.'[4]

Behind the lines of both armies, the slaughter was even more grim
than at the front. While the Soviet execution squads roamed behind
their front lines, the German Einsatzgruppen did the same, killing
unarmed and unprepared men, women and children for no other
reason than that they were perhaps born Jewish. On 28 August the
SS in Lithuania carefully recorded that the unit had killed 710 Jewish
men, 767 Jewish women and 599 Jewish children. The next day, at
Kamenets Podolsk, about 200 miles behind Rundstedt's headquarters, SS General Franz Jaeckeln dutifully reported that he had
disposed of some deported Hungarian Jews which the Hungarian
government refused to have back. His men made them undress
before opening fire on them with machine-guns. In all his men
murdered 23,600 people in three days. Behind Bock's Army Group
Centre, von dem Bach Zelewski claimed that to early August, his
men had killed 30,000, while the SS Cavalry Brigade put the number
'executed' in the Minsk region at 7,819.[5]

These reports from the murder squads were encoded by Enigma
machines and transmitted to Berlin by radio. At Bletchley Park in
England they were intercepted and deciphered and included with
other Enigma traffic regularly read by the prime minister. Churchill
was so moved by the evidence of this insane and savage bloodbath
that, on 25 August, he broadcast to the world news of 'scores of
thousands of executions in cold blood' taking place in occupied
Russia and Poland. Yet his disclosures were circumscribed by the
need to protect the secret of Enigma.

The Nazis did not tolerate criticism of Hitler's war of annihilation.
Being a German officer gave little protection against the secret police
who could be found everywhere. One German army surgeon who
witnessed the SS wholesale killing of Jews at the prison in Sevastopol
said:

> If anyone had protested or undertaken some positive action
> against the murder squad he would have been arrested twenty-
> four hours later and disappeared. It was one of the most inge-
> nious stratagems of the totalitarian systems of our century that
> they gave their opponents no opportunity to die a martyr's death
> for their convictions.[6]

After witnessing an execution, at which he was spattered with brains and blood, Himmler ordered that a new means of mass killing be found. At Auschwitz concentration camp in August 1941 a commercial pesticide called Zyklon-B was used in the experimental killing of Russian prisoners of war.[7] The manufacturers, I. G. Farben, were asked to manufacture the gas without the special irritant that warned commercial users of danger. They obliged. The Nazi death machine was about to go into mass-production.

The assault on Moscow resumed

By the time Guderian's Panzer Group had completed its vast detour to Kiev, rejoined Army Group Centre, and resumed the drive towards Moscow, it was October and winter was approaching. Bock's Army Group Centre comprised 70 divisions including 14 Panzer and 8 motorized divisions. The offensive was codenamed Typhoon, and an order of the day sent from the Wolfsschanze promised: 'The last great decisive battle of this year will mean the annihilation of the enemy.'

Now wearing the coveted oak leaves on his Knight's Cross, General Heinz Guderian that day noted two changes that were to become significant:

> This was the first occasion on which the vast superiority of the Russian T-34 to our tanks became plainly apparent ... During the night of October 6–7 the first snow of the winter fell. It did not lie for long and, as usual, the roads rapidly became nothing but canals of bottomless mud, along which our vehicles could only advance at a snail's pace and with great wear to the engines. We asked for winter clothing – we had already done this once before – but were informed that we would receive it in due course and were instructed not to make further unnecessary requests of this type.[8]

It was already late if the campaign was to be won by Christmas. Professional soldiers the world over realized the significance of what was happening. In October, a reporter[9] visiting General Douglas MacArthur at his headquarters in the Philippines asked what he thought of the German campaign. The American general went striding across the floor saying:

> The German offensive against Russia is a magnificent achievement. Never before has an offensive of such magnitude been

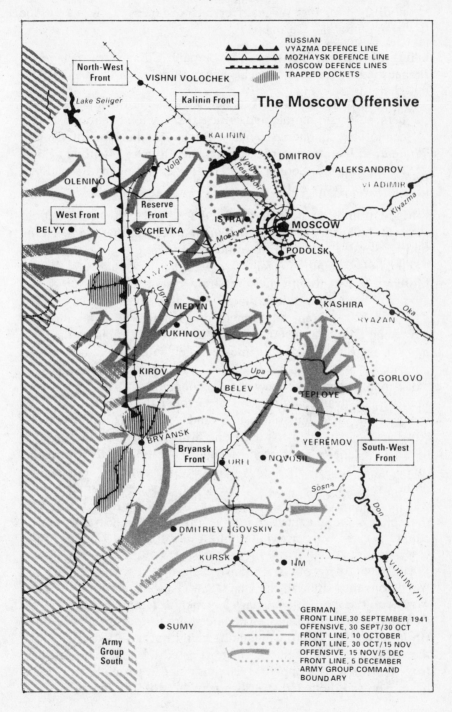

The Moscow Offensive

RUSSIAN
VYAZMA DEFENCE LINE
MOZHAYSK DEFENCE LINE
MOSCOW DEFENCE LINES
TRAPPED POCKETS

North-West Front
VISHNI VOLOCHEK
Kalinin Front
Lake Seliger
KALININ
DMITROV
ALEKSANDROV
VLADIMIR
OLENINO
Volga
Volga Reservoir
Klyazma
West Front
Reserve Front
ISTRA
MOSCOW
BELYY
SYCHEVKA
Moskva
PODOLSK
VYAZMA
Ugra
MEDYN
KASHIRA
Oka
RYAZAN
YUKHNOV
KIROV
Upa
BELEV
TEPLOYE
GORLOVO
BRYANSK
Bryansk Front
OREL
NOVOSIL
YEFREMOV
South-West Front
DMITRIEV-LGOVSKIY
Sosna
Don
KURSK
LIM
VORONEZH

GERMAN
FRONT LINE, 30 SEPTEMBER 1941
OFFENSIVE, 30 SEPT/30 OCT
FRONT LINE, 10 OCTOBER
FRONT LINE, 30 OCT/15 NOV
OFFENSIVE, 15 NOV/5 DEC
FRONT LINE, 5 DECEMBER
ARMY GROUP COMMAND BOUNDARY

SUMY

Army Group South

nourished for such a time over such distances . . . It is a logistic triumph for the Germans.

But MacArthur went on to compare China's war against a Japanese army 'superior in nearly everything'.

China's defense has proved that a people with sufficient numbers, sufficient morale and sufficient space to retreat into simply cannot be conquered by any Blitz. On the base of China's defense I venture to predict that the German offensive against Russia will fail. Sooner or later, at this spot or that, it will bog down and peter out.

MacArthur is to be congratulated for this faultless prediction. And yet the history of both China and Russia was there to teach the same lessons to anyone who would learn them.

Zhukov was shifted again. He was now in command before Moscow, provided with divisions from distant parts of the Soviet empire. There were units from Siberia, the Volga region, the Far East and Kazakhstan, all formed into a defensive line which the advancing Germans encountered on 10 October. In places the Germans broke through, but the line decisively interrupted the German advance.

German soldiers were nevertheless undaunted; they soon forced their way eastwards. By the end of October the pincers of another vast German encirclement closed round Vyazma. This time 600,000 Russians were trapped. At least one historian believes that if Bock had been properly reinforced he could have taken Moscow in this offensive.[10] But Bock's supply services were already at breaking-point. His basic need for 30 trains a day was never fulfilled. Fuel was in desperately short supply. Food had such a low priority that the soldiers were expected to live off the demonstrably barren country. Tyres were arriving at the rate of one per month for 16 vehicles.

The Red Army was strenuously fighting everywhere along the front from the Arctic to the Black Sea. This ensured that the Germans would not be able to spare any men to reinforce Army Group Centre from another sector. They need not have worried: even had Bock been given reinforcements he could not have fed or supplied them. Some say Bock should have resisted the temptation to destroy the Russians trapped at Bryansk and Vyazma.[11] He should have bypassed them and struck directly at Moscow, for by the time

Bock had extricated his armies from the Bryansk-Vyazma fighting, winter had taken a grip upon the Germans. The men at OKH gave Bock the option of attacking or simply holding on to his gains. Inevitably – and despite any reservations his supply staff may have expressed – he chose to attack.

By now the cold weather was restricting the movements of the armour and motorized units. Zhukov reasoned that the Germans were committed to an attack along the direct route to Moscow, and across this line of advance he built anti-tank defences in depth.

Then, on Saturday morning, 18 October, the Soviet Union suffered a setback in faraway Tokyo where their agent, Richard Sorge, was arrested. He had been a professional Communist activist since his days at college. With a doctorate of political science from Hamburg University, he became the special Tokyo correspondent for the *Frankfurter Zeitung*, as well as a close personal friend of the German ambassador.[12] He had been providing his masters in Moscow with both the German and Japanese viewpoints of current events, and many secret decisions. The Japanese officer who arrested him described Sorge as a man who knew everything. His interrogator said: 'I have never met anyone as great as he was.'

Sorge admitted to his spying, but at first tried to pretend it was done for the Germans. Then he cast pretences aside and told the preliminary hearing that he had completed his task. 'I had confirmed that Japan would not enter the war against the Soviet Union.' It was a notable contribution to the war. Secure against Japanese aggression the Red Army could move army units from its eastern frontiers to fight the Germans. Sorge was hanged at the age of 49 on 7 November 1944, the 27th anniversary of Lenin's Revolution. It was a futile anti-Russian gesture, difficult to reconcile with the Japanese spirit. After the war his Japanese wife found his decomposed body abandoned in a burial plot for vagrants. It was not until 1964 that the Russian public was allowed to hear of him and his services to Moscow. Stalin did not want the world to know that he had ignored Sorge's warning about Barbarossa. Eventually a Moscow street was named after Sorge.

The winter dimension

The frost came early that winter. A sudden drop in temperature on 15 November turned the mud and extensive swampland into hard going that allowed German tanks and personnel carriers to move more easily. In mixed rain and snow, Bock launched another attempt to take Moscow.

The next day, along most of Bock's front, the temperature dropped again, and so did German morale as Russian ski troops went into action for the first time. A confidential German message told of panic when the Russians appeared suddenly in their white suits. The British intercepted an Enigma message from a Luftwaffe liaison officer on the Kursk front which spoke of no German fighter planes being seen in the air for two weeks. The next day Ernst Udet, the Luftwaffe's director-general of equipment, and after Richthofen the greatest fighter ace of the First World War, committed suicide. Returning from the funeral, Germany's most famous fighter pilot of the Second War, Werner Mölders, flew into a factory chimney and died.

Both Hitler and Stalin liked to interfere with the day-to-day conduct of battles and to give specific orders about tiny details in the belief that such omnipresence would show them to be super-humanly knowledgeable. Once more at the end of November Stalin displayed this megalomania to Zhukov:

> 'Do you know that Dedovsk has been captured?'
> 'No, comrade Stalin, I don't.'
> The Supreme Commander lost no time in giving me a piece of his mind. 'A commanding general should know what's happening on his front,' he said irritably, and ordered that I should go to the spot at once so as to 'organize a counter-attack personally and recapture Dedovsk'.[13]

When Zhukov telephoned to tell Stalin that Dedovsk had not fallen to the enemy, and that the place had been confused with 'a few houses across the gully in the village of Dedovo', Stalin became even more furious. He was not a man ever to admit to being mistaken. He told Zhukov to take the commander of the 5th Army with him to Dedovo and stage a personal counter-attack. Eventually the two men went to the Divisional headquarters and instructed a rifle company and two tanks to recapture the houses. Dryly, in his heavily censored memoirs, Zhukov said that 'the divisional commander was hardly glad to see us. His hands were full as it was.'

Russian infantry

In the early weeks of their attack German military reports remarked upon the excellent physical fitness of the Russian private soldiers. They were hardy and able to endure the minus 40 degrees that arrived well before Christmas. In this sort of cold, when the Germans were digging in and expecting static warfare, the Russians continued to be active and aggressive. One German report spoke of the Russian soldier having a 'kinship with nature'. This meant the natural ability of Red Army soldiers in using ground, in employing camouflage and in remaining still and unseen for many hours. As part of this same kinship with nature, the Russians continued the battle after darkness had fallen. There was very little choice in winter, when dusk followed soon after lunch. Night attacks were something of a Red Army speciality in small-scale combats, and sometimes in large ones too.[14]

Germans were astounded at the pitiless way Red Army infantry were sent to overwhelm opposition by sheer weight of numbers. Large formations charged into machine-gun fire, and if that failed, a second attack using identical formations, timing and tactics would follow, then another, and another, and another.[15] Russian commanders would be prepared to let units suffer 80 per cent casualties in order to gain a piece of ground and would fight to the death for a slightly elevated position even when it had little tactical value.[16] After getting a few men into place, they showed great agility and skill in reinforcing them, and securing the new position. Tightly closed formations of men from penal battalions, or unarmed Russian civilians from local towns and villages, were driven shoulder to shoulder in front of an advance, or across a minefield as a way of clearing it for an attack.[17] (Such desperate methods of clearing mines were freely admitted by the Soviet generals after the war in conversations with their Allied counterparts. Most people in the West simply refused to believe such things had happened.)

The mass surrenders of Red Army units that had marked the early days of Barbarossa became a much more rare event once the word spread of the fate that awaited captives in German hands. Some were shot out of hand, others left to starve or die of exposure. Fiercer resistance forced the Germans to rethink their tactics and procedures. Whenever possible, older men were taken from front-line units and replaced with younger, fitter soldiers better able to endure the terrible hardship. Many of the Soviet soldiers – but by no means all of them – were used to the hard winter. Frostbite was a harshly punished offence in the Red Army and men took every precaution to avoid it, surviving in conditions that would have killed most German troops. But even for the Soviets the winter battles were hard, and opposing forces would sometimes fight for the broken walls of a ruined village knowing that the ones who failed to get into its shelter would be frozen by morning.[18] A wound froze if left uncovered for fifteen minutes, and crippled men who remained in the open soon froze to death. Red Army medical facilities were primitive. Most of the wounded could expect nothing more than a shot of vodka spiked with morphine, the standard Red Army treatment for any kind of shock or injury.

The Red Army had been quick to adopt the machine-pistol as a standard infantry weapon. The Federov Avtomat was used against the White Russians in 1919, and the PPD 1934/38 against the Finns in 1939. In the Second World War it made wider use of this weapon than any other army. Over 10 million of these rapid-fire weapons were manufactured.[19] A full-size rifle round would have been bigger, heavier, more expensive, and given the gun a violent kick, so such guns used a pistol cartridge instead. These came in big drum magazines. They were not intended for hitting a distant target but for spraying the enemy at close range, and this remains the standard infantry tactic for most of the world's armies at the time of writing.

Figure 38: Russian machine-pistol PPSh 41

Machine-pistols suited the half-trained men who went into combat in 1941. Neither did their manufacture require the extensive machining work that most small-arms required. Instead they were assembled mostly from pressings and stampings; just 83 parts in all. Some were even constructed by cutting rifle barrels in two.[20] As the snow arrived, in a replay of the tactics the Finns had used so successfully against them, warmly clad Russians in white camouflage smocks came whizzing out of the mist on skis, spraying bullets in prodigious amounts at astonished Germans.

In addition the Russians set great store by the use of snipers. These were recruited from hunters and members of factory rifle clubs. Women were recruited to the sniper's task, as they were to flying combat planes and almost every other combat role. Sharp-shooters became Russian heroes. Newspapers liked to print their pictures, and their scores were published like those of footballers. Medals were devised and distributed widely. 'If you saw a Russian soldier without a decoration of some kind on his left breast,' said American war correspondent Walter Kerr, 'you could be sure that he had not seen much action.' The 'guards' title was revived for regiments that distinguished themselves in battle. In a ceremony that required everyone to kneel bare-headed, these units were awarded a new flag bearing a portrait of Lenin. Their pay was doubled, and sometimes such units would be equipped with new weapons.

The Russians took great pride in their artillery, and even formed artillery divisions and artillery brigades for mass deployment. Their efficiency, however, was limited by the schooling of the available re-cruits. In Tsarist times the people had been largely illiterate. By 1941 literacy rates had improved dramatically but education was patchy and, in the rural areas, poor. Red Army artillery was about as good as Western Front artillery in 1918 – which is not to say bad. In the battles to come about 50 per cent of German East Front casualties were to be caused by artillery fire, compared to 90 per cent from Anglo-American artillery.[21]

At the end of November, General Franz Halder noted in his diary that the Germans had lost 743,112 men killed, wounded and captured. This figure (which did not include sick) was 23.12 per cent of the total strength. It reduced the fighting strength very consider-ably, because most battle casualties are suffered by the men who do the actual fighting, rather than by the clerks and grooms and cooks and drivers. Halder estimated that he had lost no less than 50 per cent of the fighting strength of his infantry. German replacements for this same period were fewer than 100,000 men.

For some time Brauchitsch had been suffering the strain that came from interpreting Hitler's sudden notions. In his sleep he was regularly heard having with Hitler the arguments that he failed to have when awake. So when a heart attack struck him down it was hardly unexpected. It was on this same day, 10 November, that Field Marshal Bock received from Brauchitsch a secret report pro-posing to organize some of the 3,500,000 Russian prisoners into 'special units'. These would fight alongside the German army and be led by high-ranking Russian officers. Bock – a conservative officer of the old school – was shocked. Such desperate notions were a measure of the German predicament.

The crisis in the availability of combat-ready tanks was still more alarming, but these figures were shamelessly juggled by commanders who wanted to do something other than what was ordered. Thus a unit with only a quarter of its tank complement ready for action on a given day miraculously has three-quarters of them ready for action tomorrow. For that reason armoured force statistics have to be read with considerable caution. Even so, the Germans were losing tanks at a rate that convinced the Panzer generals that this was no blitzkrieg.

The air control staff at Orsha on 12 November saw the personal transport aircraft of one of the Army Group chiefs of staff come in to land. After that another arrived and then another. Soon all three of the Army Groups were represented. Halder was there too. A top-secret conference was to decide what must be done. Should the armies dig in for the duration of the winter, or should there be another assault on Moscow?

Around this conference has raged one of the great arguments about the German failure. Who precisely influenced the decision to try once more to take Moscow? After the war, a Soviet general staff officer, Kyrill Kalinov, gave the controversy new impetus by suggesting that it was a device of Stalin![22] Kalinov maintains that the Russians provoked the final German attack, and goes so far as to say that Zhukov, at a postwar military lecture, revealed that the Russians leaked a story greatly exaggerating Red Army losses through a diplomat in Moscow. At the same time the Russians manned their front line with a workers' militia. These civilian defenders were deliberately sacrificed to persuade the Germans that Moscow's defences were all but exhausted.

Whatever the truth of Kalinov's story, and whether the presence of the workers' militia played a part in the German decision, the generals decided to try again.

Red Army communications

Barbarossa planners had reckoned on the Red Army being as totally dependent on lines of supply and communication as the Germans were. Günther von Kluge, commander of Bock's 4th Army, stopped his advance every time there was a difficulty in the rear. Disapprovingly, one military historian said that, 'like a jockey, a bold tank general should have his eyes fixed on the winning post, and not, like a cautious transport leader, on the tail of his convoy.'[23]

The Red Army was not like this at all, as General von Manteuffel has testified:

> The advance of a Russian Army is something that Westerners can't imagine. Behind the tank spearheads rolls on a vast horde, largely mounted on horses. The soldier carries a sack on his back, with dry crusts of bread and raw vegetables collected on the march from fields and villages. The horses eat the straw from the house-tops – they get very little else. The Russians are accustomed to carry on for as long as three weeks in this primitive way, when advancing. You can't stop them, like an ordinary army, by cutting their communications, for you rarely find any supply columns to strike.[24]

Hungry and short of everything, the advancing Germans were not plundering dumps of food, fuel or supplies. There were no dumps. The Red Army supplied its units directly from the trains at the railheads. No matter what decisions were made at distant conferences, as Christmas approached, the snow, the appalling casualties and the fatigue to be seen in the faces of their soldiers convinced many German generals that it was time to dig in for winter.

No provision had been made for delayed blitzkrieg. By now the German supply lines were 1,000 kilometres long. Over 70 per cent of German locomotives lay idle with boilers burst by low temperatures. The transhipment depots, where German tracks met Russian-gauge ones, were a chaos. Along much of the railway network and the roads Russian guerrilla forces were creating havoc. As the German advance slowed, the balance of the fighting changed. An advancing army leaves its casualties and its damaged equipment to be salvaged by rear area units, while taking possession of enemy wounded and damaged equipment. An advancing army suffers minimally from artillery bombardments, for the enemy's guns are constantly being moved back. It was time for the Germans to adapt to the painful consequences of position warfare. The Russians excelled in harrying attacks, and for the first time the Germans were presented as static targets for Russian artillery.

Wanting to see the situation for himself, on 20 November Bock travelled in his special train to Istra, about 30 miles west of Moscow. From there he went in a tank to an artillery command post about ten miles from the city centre. Through field-glasses he stared through falling snow to glimpse the spires of Moscow. On returning to his headquarters, he found a telegram from Hitler instructing him to cease all frontal attacks and instead take Moscow by encirclement from north and south. The Orsha conference had ended in grudging agreement that the attack on Moscow should be resumed, but now Bock was having second thoughts. He was critically short of combat troops, and those he had lacked food and supplies and were without winter clothing and equipment.

Ten days later, with the temperature 45 degrees below zero, Bock was again in a forward observation post. A phone call from Berlin provided him with a chance to talk to Brauchitsch, the C-in-C, who was recovering from the heart attack he had suffered in the early days of November. Bock told Brauchitsch that his Army Group was at the end of its strength, but this had no effect.

Bock set the scene by telling Brauchitsch that: 'I have last night relieved a divisional commander who reported that the Russians had repulsed his men with hammers and shovels.'[25]

Brauchitsch: The Führer is convinced that the Russians are on the verge of complete collapse. He desires a definite commitment from you, Field Marshal von Bock, as to when this collapse will become a reality.

Bock: Army High Command has falsely estimated the situation here. I have reported dozens of times during the past days that the Army Group no longer commands the strength to force a decision. Unless we obtain ample reserve forces immediately I cannot be responsible for the outcome.

Brauchitsch: The outcome of the operation is your responsibility.

Bock: And I have discharged this responsibility by informing you of the critical situation that has developed. For many weeks now we have been begging for winter clothing and supplies. At this moment the temperature is forty-five degrees below zero. German soldiers, dressed only in field coats, are fighting against an amply supplied enemy.

Brauchitsch: But the winter supplies have been delivered.

Bock: I wish to assure you, Field Marshal Brauchitsch, that they have not been delivered. The supply situation has been very precarious since early October. We have considered ourselves extremely fortunate if we could obtain the bare necessities for the conduct of the operation – munitions, fuel, rations. The fact that winter supplies have not arrived is to me the best indication that higher headquarters are not aware of the true situation here.

Brauchitsch: The winter supplies for Army Group Centre have been under way since early October. I do not have the statistics at hand, but Wagner has taken care of that.

Bock: Statistics will show, I believe, that the necessary winter supplies for my Army Group are safely ensconced in storage areas and warehouses far behind the front. That is, if they exist at all. I repeat, Field Marshal Brauchitsch, a gross miscalculation has been made. Army High Command, and the Führer as well, have unfortunately overestimated the situation . . . Brauchitsch, are you still there? Hello! has the connection been cut? Brauchitsch, are you listening?'

Brauchitsch: What were you saying, Bock?

Bock: I said that higher headquarters has miscalculated. Please inform the Führer that Army Group Centre is no longer in the position to achieve its objective. We do not have the strength any more. Are you listening, Brauchitsch?

Brauchitsch: Yes, I am listening. The Führer wishes to know when Moscow will fall.

That same afternoon Bock was told that two air corps were being withdrawn from his command. They were going to North Africa together with Field Marshal Kesselring. The German and Italian forces there needed reinforcement.

The next day Bock sent a telegram telling Brauchitsch at OKH:

Any concept at higher headquarters that the enemy is collapsing is, as the events of the last days will show, only a wild dream. The enemy now has numerical superiority before the gates of Moscow . . . Even if the improbable takes place, and my troops enter the city, it is doubtful if they can hold it.

25 THE LAST CHANCE

Despotism tempered by assassination – that is our
Magna Charta.

Russian aphorism

FIELD MARSHAL Fedor von Bock could not summon up the courage to say no to the daydreams of Hitler and his nodding men, and on 2 December he launched a futile attack upon the capital. Units of Hoth's Panzer Group, accompanied by infantry, got as far as Moscow's suburbs. So did one highly decorated German army doctor[1] who visited the infantry of 106 Division, when they were positioned across the main road from Klin to Moscow:

> We walked silently down the road to the stone shed. There was not a movement around us as we stopped and stared at the wooden seats on which thousands of Muscovites had sat and waited for the tram to clang down the road from Moscow.
>
> There was an old wooden bin attached to one wall. I felt inside and dragged out a handful of old tram tickets. We picked out the Cyrillic letters, which by now we knew spelled 'Moskva'. Slowly we trudged back to the car . . . The snow was falling a little more heavily now.

The doctor had come as close to Red Square as any German ever did. After the last assault slowed and failed, never again did the Germans attempt a concerted attack all along the front. The Germans were bled white, Zhukov told Stalin, but they must be dislodged from their positions or else there would be the danger of them bringing up other troop reinforcements. Already the Germans had been seen placing siege guns in positions from which they could start bombarding the capital.

On 5 December a massive Russian counter-attack began. The 1st Shock Army and 10th Army were added to Zhukov's command. Another army was contrived from odd and ends. Called the 20th

Army, it was commanded by General A.A. Vlasov,[2] who was captured the following summer. Vlasov eventually commanded an anti-Soviet force organized by the Germans and for this his name, and the Russian forces he led, were erased from history by Soviet historians.

Zhukov asked Stalin for two armies and 200 tanks, and was told he could have the armies but not the tanks. On the eve of the offensive, Zhukov repeated his request for tanks and Stalin answered tersely '*Tankov nyet*'. The attack was massive but it was not the force that legend would make it afterwards. For instance, the newly arrived 10th Army comprised only 80,000 men. It had no artillery and no tanks. It was short of everything, from infantry weapons to trucks.[3] In deep snow that made even their movement to jump-off positions laborious, the great force went into battle.[4]

Although no fresh armour was made available to him, Zhukov was supported by air attacks, ski troops, cavalry and airborne troops. There were men from the Caucasus, the Iranian border and from Siberia.[5] Some of the troops had been trained in winter warfare – Kalinin was recaptured by ski troops moving guns and equipment on sleighs. The assault was timed in accordance with Stalin's dictum that the enemy should be brought to a point of complete exhaustion before a full counter-attack began. Accordingly partisans in the German rear stepped up their activities.

Russian preparations had been made with consummate skill. The Germans monitoring battlefield radio traffic discovered nothing of the intended attack. Prisoners interrogated by the Germans only confirmed the idea that Moscow's defenders were at their last gasp and had fought to their very last battalion. On 2 December Halder wrote in his diary that the Soviet defence had reached its climax and had no fresh forces available. His intelligence service (Fremde Heere Ost) agreed. Luftwaffe pilots who contradicted this comfortable conclusion with reports of extensive Red Army movements were ignored.

At 0300 hours on Friday 5 December the offensive opened south of Kalinin. The snow was a metre deep, and Red Army ski troops crossed the Volga on the ice. From one German headquarters after another there came calls for help. Tanks were abandoned as engines failed to run in temperatures that had now dropped to 50 degrees below zero. Light and heavy guns, their recoil mechanisms frozen solid, would not fire. Fingers that touched cold metal adhered to it. Mines did not function and only the wooden-handled stick-grenade could be relied upon. On the following day Zhukov's forces joined in a coordinated assault on the huge Klin salient where Germans threatened to outflank the defences north of the city. Communications between German units failed, and once-invincible Panzer Groups found themselves fighting for their lives. Many feared that Bock's whole Army Group was about to disintegrate. At noon on Sunday 7 December, Red Army forces appeared out of nowhere and overran 56 Panzer Corps headquarters. Now it was the Soviets who had stuck a knife deep into the brain of command.

A special Red Army unit of tanks, motorized riflemen, ski troops and cavalry was sent to cut the German escape route westwards. They found a German Panzer division on the only road back through Klin. The road was solid ice, crowded with freezing German wounded and jammed with heavy equipment.

Soon even the mighty Fourth Panzer Group (now called a Panzer Army) was in retreat. The Russians brought their Katyusha multiple rocket batteries into action. The Germans called them 'Stalin Organs', and never forgot the whooshing sound they made in the air or the earthquake they made of the target. It was during this chaos that the first winter clothing arrived. A doctor remembered it: 'There was just enough for each company to be issued with four heavy fur-lined greatcoats and four pairs of felt-lined boots . . . Sixteen greatcoats and sixteen pairs of winter boots to be shared among a battalion of eight hundred men!'[6] On 10 December Guderian recorded a temperature of minus 63 degrees. Soldiers lucky enough to find a soup kitchen discovered that boiling hot soup froze solid before they could finish it, while those who dropped their trousers to excrete in the open, died as their bowels froze solid.[7]

'Stand fast'

Hitler sent frantic orders that the whole army must stand and fight, but after only eight days Army Group Centre had reeled back 50 miles or so. It would have been pushed back further but for blizzard conditions that slowed even the Red Army.

The supremely diplomatic Bock had a long telephone conversation with Hitler's adjutant on 16 December.[8] He described his health as precarious – 'my health hangs on a silken thread',[9] ulcers were giving him great pain. In reply, a cryptic message from the Führer said: 'I would like Bock to be assured that he will be given a chance to recover.'[10] The commander of Bock's Fourth Army, von

Kluge, took over his commander's duties and Bock departed, still not sure whether he was being fired, replaced or rested. General Blumentritt, Kluge's chief of staff, described conditions at that time:

> Only for a few hours each day was there limited visibility at the front. Until nine o'clock in the morning the wintry landscape was shrouded in a thick fog. Gradually a red ball, the sun, became visible in the eastern sky and by about eleven it was possible to see a little. At three o'clock in the afternoon dusk set in, and an hour later it was almost completely dark again.[11]

Hitler's 'stand fast' order was minimizing the German retreat, and its consequent losses, but all chance of capturing the Russian capital had gone. His diversion of Guderian's armoured forces to Army Group South had not proved decisive there either. The Germans managed to reach the Crimea, and the Donets basin, but they failed to take the Caucasian oilfields. The forces that took Rostov on Don were pushed out by a determined Russian attack.

After its encouraging early successes, Army Group North had come to a halt too. Blows that would have knocked out other nations had not even stunned Russia. Leningrad, like Moscow, had become a fortress. Despite chronic hardship and starvation rations, there was no sign of surrender. Colonel von Lossberg's pre-Barbarossa assessment could now be seen as remarkably accurate. The Germans had proved capable of a lunge to Smolensk, to the Dnieper in the south and Luga in the north. Then they had run out of steam.

It took the Red Army about six months to train a division to the state where it could be committed to battle. Such divisions were at this time comprised of about 12,000 men, most of them equipped with a rifle (or sub-machine-gun) and not much more. By December 1941 the first of such hastily assembled divisions were becoming available from men drafted at the time of the German attack. Creating soldiers had now become a continuous process. Millions more would come – the Soviet Union had about 35 million men available for military service!

With no one immune to the drop in temperature, and its cost evident everywhere, most of the German commanders wanted to prepare a proper winter defence line and retreat to it. Preparing such a line would not have been easy. 'There could be no question of digging in,' said Blumentritt. 'The ground was frozen to the consistency of iron.' And in those days leading up to Christmas, it was not just the men of Army Group Centre who were suffering from the harsh cold. By now the entire front was frozen solid. The doctor recalled:

> In this unearthly cold, in which the breath froze and icicles hung from nostrils and eyelashes all day long, where thinking became an effort, the German soldiers fought . . . Habit and discipline kept them going; that and the flicker of an instinct to stay alive. And when the soldier's mind had become numb, when his strength, his discipline and his will had been used up, he sank into the snow. If he was noticed, he was kicked and slapped into a vague awareness that his business in the world was not finished and he staggered to his feet and groped on. But if he lay where he had collapsed until it was too late, as if forgotten he was left lying at the side of the road and the wind blew over him and everything was levelled indistinguishably.[12]

Hitler prohibited any retreat. Mockingly he asked his ill-clad soldiers if they thought it would be less cold 50 miles to the rear. Field Marshal von Bock was not the only one to lose his job: all the Group commanders were fired, and so was Field Marshal von Brauchitsch, the army's commander-in-chief. Grey-faced and noticeably disturbed as he came from a meeting with the Führer, Brauchitsch said: 'I am going home. He has sacked me. I can't go on any longer.'

Field Marshal Keitel, who spent his days truckling to Hitler's ill-considered ideas, said: 'What is going to happen now then?'

'I don't know; ask him yourself.'[13]

Hitler in command

Keitel didn't have to ask. Hitler summoned him and read out an Order of the Day appointing himself to command the army. The date was 19 December 1941. From now on, Hitler would not have to argue with OKH, the army high command. As the Führer's military adjutant, Schmundt, dryly remarked to the now inactive Bock, Hitler became busy acquainting himself with the tactical aspects of the German army's commitments in Russia, North Africa, the Balkans, Western Europe and Scandinavia.

Like most good jokes, Schmundt's remark was not far from the truth. Germany's military commitments were not limited to the fighting fronts. Occupation armies in Scandinavia, France and the Low Countries, as well as those in Greece, Yugoslavia and Poland, absorbed a large proportion of manpower, and ensured a climate of terror for anyone Hitler's regime frowned upon. In Poland ghettos had been created by walling off, and guarding, sections of the cities, and keeping Jewish families imprisoned in them. In Lodz, which the Germans renamed Litzmannstadt, over 300,000 Jews were kept on starvation rations[14] and in conditions of squalor:

> Re: use of fire-arms.
> On 1 December 1941, I was on duty between 1400 and 1600 hours at Sentry Post No. 4 in Holstein Street. At 1500 hours, I saw a Jewess climb on to the fence of the ghetto, stick her head through the fence and attempt to steal turnips from a passing cart. I made use of my fire-arm. The Jewess received two fatal shots. Type of fire-arm: Carbine 98. Ammunition used: two cartridges.
>
> Report of Wachtmeister Naumann,
> Litzmannstadt, 1st December 1941.[15]

Bock's retirement did not last long. In mid-January 1942, Field Marshal von Reichenau, who had assumed command of Army Group South, died of a heart attack. Bock was sent to take over.

But Army Group South was not a welcoming spot for a man coming out of retirement. When Bock landed at the airfield at Poltava the temperature was 30 degrees below zero. He was amazed at the sight of his soldiers clad in multicoloured sweaters, Persian lamb coats and red earmuffs. These were clothes collected by desperate appeals to the German public.

The Nazi will falters

In December 1941 the threat from the T-34 had been to some extent reduced by a new German anti-tank gun. This 7.5-cm Pak 40, made by Rheinmettal-Borsig, was a bigger and superior version of the same company's 5-cm gun, which had proved inadequate against the better Russian tanks.

In fact Krupp had made a far better 7.5-cm Pak 41 which utilized an amazing new technology. Its tapered bore squeezed the missile's light alloy sheath so that it emerged from a muzzle measuring only 55 mm! But the missile required tungsten, a metal the German economy could not spare, so Krupp's rival furnished Germany's standard anti-tank gun for the rest of the war.[16] The Soviet Union didn't have the problems posed by this sort of gun technology. It didn't have advanced metallurgy. It didn't even have anti-tank guns. The Red Army used its 7.6-cm field guns against tanks.

In the summer of 1941, with reports of German advances coming in to the Wolfsschanze, and generals telling each other that the Soviet Union was as good as conquered, Hitler had ordered cutbacks in artillery pieces, heavy infantry weapons, light infantry weapons and Flak. Only tanks escaped this axe. By December, production had fallen dramatically.[17]

Tank production had not been cut back but the wear and tear of Russian conditions was taking a toll, and the Soviet workers were determined to produce tanks in numbers that would overwhelm the invaders. In 1941, while the Germans manufactured 2,875 of the best tanks, Soviet factories turned out 4,135 of theirs.[18]

In Army Group Centre alone, no fewer than 21 generals were sent home before the end of 1941, including the acclaimed Guderian. From now onwards, Hitler used the army high command, OKH, to control the war on the Eastern Front. (All the other fronts were controlled by OKW, which Hitler also ran.) He said he wanted 'to train the army in a National Socialist way'. When taking over the job he told Halder that he 'knew no general who could do that as I want it done.' Only a politician such as Hitler could have remained concerned with indoctrination while on the verge of a military calamity.

Some said that only Hitler's fanatical determination that the army should stand and fight saved it from total destruction that winter. 'If they had once begun a retreat it might have turned into a panic flight,' said one German general.[19] Many historians also feel that Hitler's stand-fast order was the best thing he could have done under the circumstances.[20] It is a favourite situation for war game replays but, so great is the human element, it will always remain speculation.

Many veterans of the fighting in the Ukraine and the Baltic republics said that a saner political attitude to the conquered regions would have produced independent governments pleased to collaborate with the Germans. In the 1990s we can see that this might well have been the case. But, despite all the Nazi talk of 'living space' in the East, the German armies invaded the Soviet Union only because Hitler and his SS men wanted to murder the Jews and the 'Bolsheviks'. Remove the atrocities and you remove the motivation for invading Russia in the first place. The Germans were getting all the supplies they needed from Russia before June 1941. When all their plunder is added up, it never equalled what they had been getting from the Soviet Union without fighting.

The future

Until December 1941 Germany had functioned on the unchanged peacetime economy for which Göring was largely responsible. Blitzkrieg was a triumph of technique and technology, and Hitler valued it because it could bring victory before its cost affected Germany's economy. In fact Hitler's plunder improved Germany's living standard, providing his people with luxuries from far parts of Europe and foreign workers to slave for them. Then, in December 1941, came the failure at the gates of Moscow. Germans found their country locked in a war of attrition and faced the need to change to a war economy of the sort that Britain already had, and which the United States would experience very soon.

On 7 December the Japanese attacked Pearl Harbor and Malaya. No doubt there were many German soldiers freezing on the Eastern Front and saying, as Field Marshal von Bock noted mournfully in his diary: 'How different would things be if the Japanese had attacked the Russians.'

To add to the dismay of such men, four days later Hitler declared war upon the United States. We now know that the leading Nazis – Hitler, Göring and Goebbels – had not the slightest idea of the potential strength of the USA. When they read the accurate economic projections that the American themselves published, they laughed them to scorn.

Once Hitler was in full control of the German war machine the major decisions were seldom good ones. But the German army cannot escape blame for its excesses or its failures. While Hitler's foolish ideas may have contributed to the disaster of Barbarossa, the seeds of failure had been sown long before, when the entire planning staff of the German army wrongly assessed their enemy, and formulated a plan that could never have conquered him.

It is right to note the contributions of money and material that came to the Soviet Union from Britain and the United States. At the war's end four out of six vehicles in use by the Red Army were from the West. America also sent 2,000 locomotives, 540,000 tons of rails and 13 million pairs of boots.[21]

However the bulk of the German army was defeated by the Red Army, using equipment made in their own factories. It was a gargantuan struggle. A calculation based upon the deployment of German divisions in combat per month shows that seven-eighths of all the fighting in which the Germans engaged in 1939–45 took place on the Eastern Front.[22] In other words, only one-eighth of the entire German war effort was put into their campaigns in North Africa, Italy and on the Western Front.

The failure in December 1941 decided the outcome of the war. The Germans had tried to decapitate a sleeping bear, and by Christmas 1941 – with their army exhausted – had only succeeded in tormenting it. Once aroused, it would devour them. Mighty battles would be fought at Stalingrad, in the Caucasus and at Kursk, but the Germans could hope for nothing better than to slow the Russian advance and delay the inevitable defeat.

The scale of this immense conflict is difficult to comprehend. A maximum of 35 million men were available to the Soviet armed forces in 1941. About 25 million of them served and of these 13.7 million were killed. Another 7 million civilians died. The Germans lost about 2 million soldiers on the Eastern Front, and another 2 million German civilians disappeared in the flight of refugees before the westward advance of the Red Army at the end of the war.

On 22 June 1941, Hitler, the compulsive gambler, made his greatest wager. Like many such men he was perhaps seeking his end.

26 THE WAR FOR OIL

See that the Enemy gets no Petrol.

'If the Invader Comes', Government leaflet 1940

THE COUNTRIES that fought the First World War had grown strong from the coal and iron-ore dug from their own soil. But the development of oil-fired ships and the internal combustion engine shuffled the cards and dealt them afresh. The oil age was slow to start. For many years oil was something that came from whales or was made from coal to fill oil lamps in mansions and peasant huts.

As kerosene became a better and cheaper lamp oil, the mining and production of it became an extremely profitable industry. The wide availability of paraffin, kerosene, oil and petroleum encouraged experiment with internal-combustion engines which had started with coal dust as fuel. Unlike the cumbersome steam engines which needed heavy boilers, these new power plants could be made small and lightweight to power cars, trucks and even aircraft. Oil could do everything coal could do, including generate electrical power. As the twentieth century got under way, advanced nations needed oil, and without it they would revert to unthinkable hardship.

It is tempting to depict the Second World War as nothing but a struggle for oil.[1] The war in the Pacific was clearly motivated by Japan's need for oil. The United States, self-sufficient in oil at the time, hoped that a threat of embargo would force Japan to cease its aggressive moves into Asia. It didn't. Instead, Japan, a nation without sources of oil or other energy, embarked upon its war in the Pacific in order to seize the rich wells of the Dutch East Indies and Burma. The Dutch oil technicians demolished the drilling machinery, and when the Japanese got the oil flowing again, the United States navy's submarines struck at the Japanese tankers sent to collect it.

Britain had no oil sources, and when war in Europe began, 90 per cent of her oil was coming across the Atlantic from the United States,

Venezuela and Trinidad. The other 10 per cent was obtained from
the Middle East, but the Mediterranean became too dangerous for
such traffic and the route around the Cape too long, so by 1940 virtually all Britain's oil was coming across the Atlantic.[2] To save tanker
space, most of it was refined before being shipped, and refining in
Britain dwindled to almost nothing. Britain's wartime oil supplies
depended upon the Royal Navy defeating the U-boats in the Battle
of the Atlantic.

For many centuries petroleum has been used by those fortunate
enough to find natural bitumens on the earth's surface. Such substances are mentioned in the Bible. But it was the use of kerosene in
lamps that first made oil a household necessity. In 1900 Russian and
the USA were producing most of it, but in 1908 oil was discovered in
the Middle East. At first gasoline was an unwanted side-product, but
the coming of the motor car and the First World War together
changed oil mining from a profitable industry to one of strategic
importance.

The British pioneered oil exploration in the Middle East and the

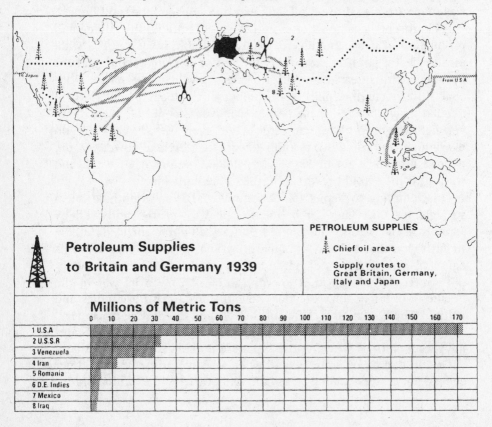

PETROLEUM SUPPLIES

**Petroleum Supplies
to Britain and Germany 1939**

PETROLEUM SUPPLIES

⚒ Chief oil areas

Supply routes to
Great Britain, Germany,
Italy and Japan

Millions of Metric Tons

	0	10	20	30	40	50	60	70	80	90	100	110	120	130	140	150	160	170
1 U.S.A																		
2 U.S.S.R																		
3 Venezuela																		
4 Iran																		
5 Romania																		
6 D.E. Indies																		
7 Mexico																		
8 Iraq																		

industry was stimulated when the 1917 revolution in Russia reduced supplies from eastern Europe. The Twenties and Thirties saw motor cars being mass-produced, and farm tractors replacing horses. Gas pumps were to be seen in the most remote towns and villages in America and Europe.

By 1939 the sources in Iran, Iraq and Bahrain were all to a greater or lesser extent under British control and they were crucial to her war effort. A pipeline brought fuel from Iraq to Haifa so that the Royal Navy's ships could fight in the Mediterranean. The same pipeline supplied British forces in Palestine and North Africa, supplemented by some crude oil from Egyptian wells that went to a refinery at Suez. In 1940, Iran produced approximately 10 million barrels of oil per day, Iraq 4 million, and Bahrain 1 million.

Iran's output was sent to North Africa, as well as to South Africa, India and West Australia. Aviation spirit from Iran and Bahrain was used by the RAF in the Middle East, and some was supplied to the Soviet Union, which could not make high-quality fuels.

Hitler's Germany never successfully completed the switch from coal to oil. Bereft of its colonies, and always short of foreign exchange, Germany turned to its scientists for a solution to the energy problem. (Table 7, p. 501, indicates how well they performed.) Using techniques which no other country ever mastered, coal was transformed into synthetic oil so that in 1940 the Germans made about 4.25 million tons of it, of which a great deal was refined into aviation spirit. To the total there was added a little oil from Austria and other small sources. Germany's bountiful supply of high-quality coal and lignite (brown coal) was used whenever possible; for instance Germany's electricity supply came from coal.

Hitler's long-term oil supplier was Romania, and he guarded this source with anxiety all through the war. When, in July 1940, Hungary and Romania argued and came close to blows, he quickly settled their differences. Later, when Russia and Bulgaria quarrelled with Romania, again he played peacemaker to secure his flow of oil.

Hitler's friendship pact with Stalin in the summer of 1939 gave him access to oil from the Soviet Union. When the French and British governments realized just what effect this would have in strategic terms, they panicked. At a meeting of the Anglo-French Supreme War Council late in 1939 it was decided simply to bomb (neutral) Russia's oil wells without the formality of declaring war.

France's Armée de l'Air assigned five squadrons of Martin Maryland bombers, flying from north-eastern Syria, to bomb Batum and Groznyy. A light Gallic touch was added by the use of the code-names Berlioz, César Franck and Debussy for the targets. The RAF were to use four squadrons of Bristol Blenheims and a squadron of antiquated single-engine Vickers Wellesley bombers flying out of Mosul in Iraq.

To prepare for this night bombing mission, the target area was photographed. On 30 March 1940 a civilian Lockheed 14 Super Electra took off from the RAF airfield at Habbaniyah in Iraq with British commercial markings and registration. Its crew wore civilian clothes, and carried false identity papers. They were members of RAF 224 Squadron which was equipped with the Lockheed Hudson, the military version of the Electra. They took photographs of Baku without any difficulty, but when, on 5 April, the photographic mission went to Batum oilfields the Soviet anti-aircraft gunners were ready for them. The Electra returned with only three-quarters of the target on negatives. All the pictures obtained went to GHQ Middle East in Cairo to be made into 'mosaics' and for target maps to be drawn up from them. The Lockheed Electra returned to England and landed at RAF Heston on 9 May 1940, the eve of the great German assault.

The German assault on France and the ensuring armistice and confusion put an end to all ideas of a bombing attack on the Soviet Union. In the aftermath of the defeat, on 16 June a signal-man of 9 Panzer Division was searching through the contents of a captured French army train when he found the plans for the attack. Here were all the documents, carelessly typed, annotated and scrawled through: 'ATTAQUE AERIENNE DU PETROLE DU CAUCASE. Liaison effectuée au G.Q.C. Aérien le avril 1940.'

The big rubber stamps saying 'TRES SECRET' made it even more tantalizing. So did the absence of a date. Gleefully the Germans published the documents together with all the exchanges about the Anglo-French plan to invade Norway on the pretence of helping the Finns. It made good propaganda, and looking at these documents now makes one question the sanity of the Western leaders who sanctioned such mad ventures.[3]

The trump card that supplies of Soviet oil provided to Hitler was recognized by just about everyone but the Führer himself. He became convinced that the Soviets were stirring up these frequent quarrels involving Romania and suspected that it was all part of a cunning strategy that would provide the Russians with an excuse to

Table 7   Sources of German oil supplies in 1940 (approx. barrels per day)

Germany	750,000	
Austria	850,000	
Poland & Czechoslovakia	550,000	
Romania	2,500,000	
Hungary	900,000	
		5,550,000
Synthetic Oils	4,250,000	
Misc. (benzol, alcohol, tar, etc.)	1,000,000	
		5,250,000
		10,800,000

annex the Romanian oilfields. These suspicions were given new encouragement when, in June 1940, Russia annexed Bessarabia, a part of Romania. Not only did Stalin have the excuse that this had been Russian territory until the Bolshevik Revolution of 1917, but this annexation was in accord with the Stalin-Hitler agreement,[4] and yet still it rankled with Hitler.

Romania and its oilfields were never far from his thoughts, and when, in 1941, the British occupied the Mediterranean islands of Lemnos and Crete he immediately saw these places as bases from which the RAF could strike at Romanian oilfields. Urgent plans were laid for dislodging the British. Hitler's anxieties were not allayed until Greece and Crete were occupied by German forces.

The German bid for Iran and Iraq in early 1941 was frustrated, and provoked the British into securing Vichy-held Syria and Lebanon, countries close to the oilfields. That it meant fighting against ex-Allies did not deter the British. Where sources of oil were involved both sides were driven to desperate measures.

Once Barbarossa began, the map changed. The almost unlimited supplies from the Soviet Union, which could produce 31 million tons every year, were denied to the Germans. Hitler now depended upon Romanian oil, which was far from unlimited. Even in the years 1943 and 1944, when they were pumping at their maximum capacity, the Romanian fields could provide only about 5.5 million tons to Germany – plus another million tons to Italy – each year.

Although the Romanian fields were a long flight away from RAF bombers, they were close to the Soviet Union. When Hitler became obsessed about turning Barbarossa south, away from Moscow, one of the reasons he gave was that unless he occupied the Crimea the Red air fleets would use bases there to bomb the Romanian oil-fields.

Oil from different sources varies a great deal in quality. Germany's synthetic oil provided the Luftwaffe with aviation spirit, but this was not the equal of the aviation fuels that the American oil company scientists could produce. During the 1930s they had solved some very complex problems of chemistry and were starting off with the incomparable refined natural oils of Aruba and Curaçao in the Dutch Antilles. The decision to supply the British with such superb 100-octane aviation fuel was a major advantage to the RAF, helping them to improve speed, altitude and range.

While the Germans, the Italians and the Japanese spent the entire war fretting about their oil supplies, the British, the Americans and the Russians had fuel in abundance. The movements of oil by the Axis powers were increasingly subject to attack. The Japanese tankers in the Pacific, like the Italian tankers in the Mediterranean, could not prevail. The difficulties and dangers the German army faced when trying to move fuel long distances on land made decisive contributions to their defeats in the Soviet Union and in North Africa. In Europe the German army lurched to a halt for lack of fuel, and the Luftwaffe's ability to defend German skies dwindled as more and more of its aircraft were grounded for the same reason. Not long afterwards the Japanese military machine, desperately short of fuel, could not even defend the skies over the Emperor in Tokyo.

Although there were times when Germany's U-boats scored notable successes against Atlantic tanker convoys, the Allies were never short of high-quality fuel, and it was always delivered to where it was needed. This was a tribute to the supply services and a major factor in ultimate victory.

Part Six

JAPAN GOES
TO WAR

27

BUSHIDO: THE SOLDIER'S CODE

Cowboy and samurai – sense their faults and their virtues and you have practically and comparatively psychoanalysed two nations.

Walt Sheldon, *Enjoy Japan*[1]

EVER SINCE THE SHOGUNATE, the military dictatorship established in the late twelfth century, and probably for some centuries before, Japan had been controlled by feudal nobility who, being the only ones permitted to bear arms, believed that a soldier's career is mankind's highest aspiration. The behaviour of this samurai class was codified in the seventeenth and eighteenth centuries; Bushido, the way of the warrior, exalted loyalty and self-sacrifice for one's superior and for the sake of honour. A Westerner born in Tokyo said Bushido was 'the traditional samurai mystique of killing with honour, of magnanimity towards the chastened and defeated, of utter ruthlessness towards the base and the mercantile, of appreciation mainly for the contrived artistic beauty of poems and paintings in life, and for the moonlight reality of the spirit world in death.'[2]

The second half of the nineteenth century saw dramatic improvements in the war technology of Western powers: breech-loading guns, rifled barrels, warships with ironclad hulls and screw propulsion brought new methods and tactics on land and sea. These developments gave the colonists of Europe and America overwhelming power, and the Japanese were becoming more and more vulnerable to it.

In this same period China was seen to be growing weaker, and Japan's ruling class became determined to take over her dominant role in the Far East. But it could not be done without modern technology and a mass army. Having decided that reforms should start at the top, provincial war-lords overthrew the Shogun – a hereditary commander-in-chief who ruled in the name of the Emperor – and in 1868 established the Emperor Mutsuhito on the throne. This 'Meiji restoration' led to a constitution based on Prussia's, while more liberal Western models were rejected as unsuited to Japan. A period of such radical change has never been equalled anywhere in the world's history. Local war-lords disbanded their private armies, although not without some blood being spilled, and a national army was created by conscription. Railways, factories, hospitals and schools were built, and compulsory education changed a nation virtually illiterate in 1860 to one with 95 per cent literacy before the end of the century.[3] Schoolchildren bowed towards the Imperial Palace every morning, and each day answered the call: 'What is your dearest ambition?' with the chorused answer: 'To die for the Emperor.' Such teaching fitted well with the modernization of Japan's armed forces and conscription, but older people felt that the samurai code was incompatible with arming conscripts. So a distorted form of Bushido was revived as a way of reconciling traditional Japanese values of honour, humility and unassertiveness with a newly formed army that would be obedient in training, savage in battle and pitiless in victory.

To get Japan's industries moving, the emperor's officials simply gave factories to high-ranking men they favoured. Vast commercial conglomerates came into being. Although Japan's economy derived the most benefit from the production of textiles, heavy industry proved equally efficient. In appreciation of the gifts, owners of these great concerns, the financial clique – zaibatsu – unwaveringly supported whatever was government policy. Soon Japan's whole economy was run by giant corporations. Entrepreneurs, especially foreign ones, were excluded.

The Japanese saw the Prussian victory over France in 1870 as confirming the wisdom of their drastic changes. Inspired by this well planned campaign, the Japanese conscript army – trained by French and German instructors – prepared to attack China, a medieval nation plagued by war-lords who knew only primitive ways of fighting.

At noon on a sweltering hot September day in 1894, at the mouth of the Yalu River where Korea meets China, Japanese warships inflicted a naval victory upon the Chinese that surprised the whole world. It was followed by equally impressive victories on land. Until now the Western powers had regarded the Japanese as a quaint race who made fine porcelain, carved ivory and stamped out cheap toys. It was difficult to reconcile a polite and picturesque people with these soldiers, dressed and armed like Westerners, colonizing Asia in the same lordly way that the European powers had acquired their vast overseas empires. The defeated Chinese ceded the right to 'protect' Korea and occupy that part of Manchuria called the Kwantung Peninsula. But before the treaty could be put into effect, Russia, backed by France and Germany, stepped in and forcibly arbitrated the settlement to deprive Japan of her plunder.

Europeans, like the Americans, were not sure how to react to the new balance of power in the Pacific. Overnight the Japanese had gone from being jolly little tenors in Gilbert & Sullivan's *Mikado* to what the German Kaiser called 'the Yellow Peril'. Britain declined to take part in the pressure that was applied to the victorious Japanese, but with the support that Russia was getting, the Japanese were left in no doubt that if they persisted in their delusion of being a Western power, they would find themselves crushed.

The Japanese bowed to these threats, but in doing so the nation suffered an unbearable humiliation. The Emperor told them to 'bear the unbearable'. Although they were permitted to keep some of their gains, the disgrace was never to be forgotten, and made more painful when, a year or two later, the Russians forced the Chinese to concede to them the right to build railways across Manchuria and to lease Port Arthur, exactly the sort of concessions the Japanese wanted. This period marked a turning-point in Japanese history, and at all levels of society there was recognition that the only way to redeem the Emperor's honour was at the point of a gun. The first-line strength of the army was doubled, and in 1896 a naval programme was started to build 43 new warships from destroyers to battleships.

Suddenly, as the century was drawing to a close, the United States reached out and grabbed the Hawaiian Islands and Guam, and then conquered the Philippines in a fiercely fought campaign that cost the lives of 20,000 Filipinos and 4,000 Americans. Uncle Sam's well chosen stepping stones had brought him all the way to the shores of Asia, and many applauded this claim to the Pacific Ocean. Rudyard Kipling urged America to colonize her conquests while making the task sound like a sacrifice:

> Take up the White Man's burden –
>   Send forth the best ye breed –
> Go, bind your sons to exile
>   To serve your captives' need . . .

But there was no applause from the Japanese, who saw it as the savage colonization of territory that was in their own sphere of influence. Japan continued to build her armed services while acquiring new territories such as the island of Formosa off the Chinese mainland. By 1904 Japan was ready to avenge itself upon the Russians and astound the world. For a small Asian nation to make war upon the gigantic power of Russia was audacious. Almost within living memory the most formidable army the world had ever seen, with Napoleon at its head, had been decimated and humbled at the Tsar's hands.

The Japanese move focused upon the holdings Russia had gained from China, holdings which the Japanese considered rightfully theirs. In the darkness of a February night in 1904 Japanese torpedo-boats attacked the Russian Asiatic fleet at anchor off Port Arthur. Two Russian battleships and a cruiser were damaged at no cost to the attacking force, and the Russian ships took refuge in Port Arthur harbour. Only then did Japan declare war and, with the ocean secure, dispatch a Japanese expeditionary force to besiege Port Arthur. Months of struggle provided, for those who wanted to see it, a glimpse of what the First World War would be like. In massed advances Japanese infantry were slaughtered by Russian machine-gun fire. Here were the trenches, the barbed-wire and machine-guns that tied up the Western Front in Europe for so long. Sappers detonated mines under the fortifications, and to aid the Japanese assault, three Russian officers were promised a $65 million bribe to supply details of the minefields and defences.[4] In early December the Japanese commander, who had watched his own two sons slaughtered in previous charges, saw the third assault reach the summit and raise the Japanese flag there. On New Year's Day 1905 the Russian commander surrendered the town of Port Arthur to which he had withdrawn.

Thousands of miles away in St Petersburg, the Tsar would not admit defeat. Demonstrating their tenacity and human endurance, the Russians took seven months to sail their Baltic fleet all the way round Europe, Africa and India to engage the might of the Japanese navy in the Pacific.

The opposing fleets sailed into action with Admiral Togo's fleet 'crossing the T' so that all his ships could fire upon the leading Russian ones. Togo, who had been trained in Britain, adapted Nelson's famous signal to order his men: 'The fate of the Empire depends upon this battle. Let every man do his utmost.' Within little more than an hour the turret of the Russian flagship was smashed and superior Japanese gunnery had decided the battle. By the end of the day the Russians were virtually wiped out, and the battle of the Tsushima Strait was recorded as one of the most decisive fleet actions in history. The place of interception, between Korea and the Japanese mainland, had been chosen by Togo because it was believed that the souls of those who had died there seven centuries before, defending Japan against Kublai Khan, would come to his aid.

For the first time in modern history an Asian nation had beaten a major European power. The president of the United States of America summoned negotiators from Russia and Japan to Portsmouth, New Hampshire, and hammered out a peace that gave Korea, Port Arthur, the Kwantung Peninsula and the Russian railways in southern Manchuria to the Japanese. Public opinion in both Japan and Russia violently objected to what were considered unsatisfactory terms. Riots in Japan resulted in martial law and the resignation of the cabinet, while in Russia the dissatisfaction helped to touch off Trotsky's premature and unsuccessful revolution.

In territorial terms Japan's negotiators had gained a great deal. Japanese garrisons protecting the railways in Manchuria gave her a foothold on the mainland. With the elimination of Russia as a seapower, and the blessing of Great Britain her ally, Japan now dominated the Pacific Ocean. This was a time when the major nations regarded battleships as the prime measure of their power, and the influence of Royal Navy officers serving with the Japanese fleet did much to confirm the British decision to start building a new class of super battleships: the Dreadnoughts. Japan would not be left out of the race.

'The Japanese do not have deep religious feelings but they do have a profound belief in themselves,' said the manager of a Tokyo pachinko arcade. Such self-confidence had to be firm to enable the Japanese so readily to accept the role of conquerors of the vast territory of China and the whole Pacific and eventually far beyond. It seemed to be ordained.

With Korea under their control the Japanese could look back over the period since the 'Meiji restoration' and consider how they had flourished on a judicious mixture of combat and negotiation. The First World War offered them a chance to exploit this combination, as well as avenging past German insults. Japan's declaration of war upon the Central Powers was a chance to grab the German concession at Tsingtao and establish rights of its own in China, and, from the postwar negotiations, obtain strategically

important islands – the Marshalls, the Carolines and the Marianas –
in the Pacific. No other Allied power gained so much for so little
effort. Australia and New Zealand protested about the presence of
these new Japanese outposts so close to their shores, and blamed
Britain for endangering them with concessions that they viewed as
diplomatic folly. Their fears eventually proved well founded.

The First World War had done nothing but enrich Japan. Its
armaments industry flourished, and no fewer than 236 ships were
built for Britain, so that by war's end the country could boast 57
major shipyards. From now onwards Japan could build its own warships. The only cautionary note was sounded by the Royal Navy's
Queen Elizabeth class battleships, which had proved beyond doubt
that oil was the required fuel for modern navies. Japan had no oil.
Japan's army had no such limitation. By 1930, its leaders could look
back on 60 years of successes, with the army – significantly a career
for sons of the nobility – an unchallengeable force in Japan's social
system.

The Japanese class system is far more rigid and deep-seated than
that of any European country. Rank and breeding is everything in
Japan; class and colour are restrictive barriers. The Japanese admit
to their wish to conform and their liking for group activities – but
this is not to be confused with a desire for equality. Company
employees take vacations together and there is no craving for
solitude or 'getting away from it all'. Emphasis of any sort is not
admired in Japan. The Japanese language gives equal stress to each
syllable: none are accented. This, said one teacher of Japanese, is
the rule that foreigners find most difficult. A Japanese musician who
became famous in America found that his friends in Japan disap-
proved of his success. 'When a nail stands out, it must be hammered
down,' says an old Japanese proverb approvingly. This conformity
without equality today helps Japan to muster an unsurpassed workforce. In the past it enabled Japan to field a formidable army, hampered only by the lack of vital minerals, the absence of indigenous
energy sources apart from a little coal, and, as the population grew,
a scarcity of arable land.

The Fifteen Years War

The 1920s in Japan were marked by calamitous droughts, earth-
quakes, bank failures and unemployment. As in Germany,
democratic politicians were blamed for the slump while demagogues

and extremists flourished. A Communist party was formed and then brutally suppressed by *tokko* – the specially trained secret police. By equally drastic economic measures, Japan made a quick recovery from the world depression. Abandoning the gold standard it devalued the yen, suppressed home consumption and brought living standards down. At the same time the government was doubling steel production and investing in heavy industry.

But the world depression had sharpened Japan's need for raw materials and cheap labour. Adding Manchuria to the Japanese empire would provide both. Its Kwantung Army was already stationed throughout the region to guard the railways and other interests acquired by the Russo-Japanese peace treaty in 1905. In September 1931, it attacked local Chinese army units without bothering to get orders from Tokyo. Ruthless tactics and dedicated professionalism soon brought this territory completely under Japanese control. Factories were built and forced labour used to man them. The trucks and planes made in Manchuria were a vital contribution to the growing Japanese war machine, and helped to establish an industrial structure upon which Japan's present-day prosperity was built. Manchuria was renamed Manchukuo and provided with a puppet government. The otherwise unemployed ex-emperor of China was named as its ruler – a calculated insult to the Chinese republic that had deposed him.

This huge territorial gain did not satisfy the generals, and soon the Kwantung Army was pushing southwards into mainland China. Throughout the 1930s Japanese troops were kept constantly fighting. They bombed Chinese cities and killed civilians by the thousands. The battles were cruel and bloody, and usually accompanied by torture, rape and massacre. Newsreels and Press photographs brought such chilling scenes to the entire world, and Japan found itself isolated and exposed as a ruthless exploiter of its newly acquired armed forces.

China had been a republic since the revolution of 1912 forced the Emperor to abdicate. But war-lords constantly fought the government armies, and it was not until 1927 that Chiang Kai-shek emerged as the leader of the first United Front alliance. This curious mixture of conservatives and radicals was united only by expediency, and their belief in the diluted Marxist teachings of Dr Sun Yat Sen, to whom Chiang was distantly related.

Chiang established himself as generalissimo by expelling from his alliance the Communists, who, under their leader and founder Mao

Tse-tung, went to the mountains of Kiangsi province. There they resisted Chiang's attacks until 1934, when a determined assault on the 'Kiangsi Soviet' dislodged them. About 100,000 survivors made the 'Long March' to north-west Shensi but only one in four of them survived the ordeal.

While Chiang Kai-shek's nationalists devoted great efforts to pressing foreign governments for aid, the Communists sought more lasting power by recruiting the peasants to their cause and pledging to expel the Japanese. An American intelligence report stated:

> Wherever the Eighth Route [Communist] Army penetrated, its retinue of propagandists, social and economic workers, school teachers, etc., immediately started organizing and training the peasant masses for resistance through guerrilla warfare. Their central idea in all these efforts was that the social and economic level of the peasants had to be improved in order to maintain morale and to instil among the people a will to resist Japan and support their own armies.[5]

Chiang's nationalists depended upon the support of the landlord class, and did not dare to organize the peasants to fight the Japanese lest they went off to fight Chinese 'class enemies' instead. Chiang's army was largely made up of men seized in the fields and pressed into military service. His military commanders were little more than war-lords paid per capita. It was not the best way in which to mould an effective fighting force.

By December 1936 the Japanese successes forced Chiang to come to terms with his Communist enemies, and to form a united anti-Japanese front. Agreement did not come easily – Chiang was imprisoned by a war-lord during a journey to the north and threatened with execution – but eventually an agreement and a modus vivendi were established, and this weird and uncertain alliance, little more than an armed truce, continued until 1945.

The Communists were forced into the 'alliance' with Chiang because they received no support or encouragement from Moscow. Stalin's ambitions in China were limited to the Manchurian ports and railways, and the Japanese retained their hold on those. A turbulent China suited Stalin, who was not eager to see a strong united China whether it was Communist or not.

Chiang's network of government was based upon family cliques and corruption; as long as his military commanders were paid cash they remained loyal. Cash was more vital to him than armaments, and to get it Chiang was prepared to be whatever his benefactors wanted him to be. To the Russians, he presented himself as an ally against Japan, and between 1937 and 1939 he received from them $500 million in military credits, as well as such extras as a fighter squadron loaned complete with Russian pilots. While in receipt of this Russian aid, he frightened Washington with stories that the Chinese Communists were being armed by Moscow, and in this way added American backing to the aid from Russia. (In fact the Soviets gave virtually nothing to the Chinese Communists until 1945.)

All things to all men, Chiang made sure that the American envoys, ambassadors and special representatives saw his antipathy to the Japanese and his opposition to the Communists in the proportions they would most welcome. Dismissing the Japanese as 'a disease of the skin',[6] he said the Communists were 'a disease of the heart'. But he tempered his warnings with optimism, claiming that the Communists would be effortlessly crushed as soon as the time was right. For those who wanted to hear it, he said that the United Front – his nationalists and Mao's Communists – would together defeat the Japanese.

In fact Chiang's forces had neither the will nor the means to expel the Japanese, nor even to vanquish Mao's Communists. But luckily for him, the Japanese did not have enough men with which to conquer China, and certainly not enough to occupy it. Over the following years of what the Japanese call 'The Fifteen Years War' fighting was spasmodic but unending. Chiang had made the war into a lucrative career, while the Japanese generals were locked into a conflict that they could neither win nor negotiate. The Kwantung Army had become obsessed with China: they insisted upon giving it priority over all other battlefronts, and this vast theatre of war drained national resources until the war's final end in 1945.

Tokyo never secured control of its Kwantung Army. While the generals remained single-minded, Japan's government was chronically lacking in stability, its many different factions fought for power, and political assassinations were commonplace. Between 1912 and 1941 six prime ministers were murdered, along with other politicians who fell into disfavour. The assassins were often respectable middle-class officers who invoked the spirit of *gekokujo*. Like so many other aspects of Japanese life, gekokujo is untranslatable. Japanese translators are inclined to make it 'rule from below' while Westerners prefer 'insubordination'. Either way it is a form of disobedience practised from patriotic motives. (One naval historian[7] compares it to Nelson turning his blind eye to the signal to break off action at Copenhagen.) But the Japanese disapprove of individualism – the nail that stands out – and so gekokujo is the action of a group of young men, usually young officers, who in the violent days of the 1930s were manipulated by the top brass. Indeed senior officers used gekokujo as an excuse for letting certain violent acts go unpunished.

The government, unable to get its own affairs in order, tightened and tightened the controls upon its population. A *hijoji*, a state of emergency, was declared and the tokko were reinforced by a brutal force of military police – *kenpeitai* – and 'thought-control police' too. No one was exempt from their powers of arrest and detention. Written and spoken words came under the censor's scrutiny and anything 'un-Japanese' was removed, which meant that only extreme nationalism was tolerated. The army used the climate of political repression to increase its own power, until one day in 1936 the 1st Infantry Division staged a coup. It occupied government buildings including the War Ministry, police headquarters and the prime minister's residence. Selected politicians were sought out and killed. So were some senior officers, including the army's inspector-general. For four days Tokyo held its breath as the army's top ranks and important politicians were deciding whether to join the revolution. When at last the emperor intervened with a few words of disapproval the putsch collapsed.

Some 1,483 conspirators were identified and implicated. The courts-martial of the mutineers lasted one hour. The ringleaders were shot and others were banished to distant commands while the army protected its favoured men. One such, Tomoyuki Yamashita, a 51-year-old staff officer, will appear again in our story. He was sent to Korea and promoted to command a brigade. It was a typically Japanese anomaly that while some officers were promoted and others punished the army steadily gained power. Subsequent reforms gave the army and the navy the right to appoint service ministers, which meant that the war minister and the navy minister were under the direct orders of their senior officers. From now on the military could force a cabinet to resign by withdrawing a minister, or prevent the formation of a cabinet by refusing to appoint a minister to it.

In July 1937 the Kwantung Army's resumption of full-scale war in China made headlines the world over. Shore-based, and carrier-based, bombers of the imperial Japanese navy blasted Nanking.

The United States navy's gunboat *Panay* was sunk in what many eyewitnesses said was a deliberate attack. The city was occupied in a mad frenzy of wanton killing, rape, arson and looting. A middle-range estimate of deaths – from shelling and subsequent atrocities – is 200,000.[8] The commander, General Iwane Matsui, condoned his troops' behaviour, but many Japanese were appalled. The *Osaka Daily* said of the Japanese soldiers: 'their cruelty is beyond description.'

Half a century afterwards, in 1991, a musical show about the last Emperor of China was staged in Tokyo. On the first night there was the line: 'I hear nasty rumours about a massacre at Nanking.' By the second night the word 'massacre' had been deleted. The musical's director, Shinji Ueda, said the word made some older people in the audience 'feel uneasy'.[9]

Uneasy too were the Chinese rural population in 1937, to whom it was evident that systematic terror and murder was the method by which the Japanese army ruled.

The Flying Tigers

While the Chinese had virtually no navy and few aircraft, the exploits of Claire Chennault's Flying Tigers were eventually to capture the world's imagination. Chennault had been leader of the US Army Air Corps aerobatic team when he was spotted by a Chinese general and offered the task of organizing an air force.

> Claire Chennault was nearing forty-seven as a captain with little hope of future promotion. He had chronic bronchitis, low blood pressure, partial deafness (an occupational hazard of open cockpits), general physical exhaustion, and a thorough exasperation with the Air Corps bureaucratic establishment. If Chennault was fed up with the air force the feeling was mutual . . . so when retirement was offered on medical grounds, Chennault accepted. He left the U.S. Army on 30 April 1937 and the next day left his home in Waterproof, Louisiana, for China. Arriving in China in June he hardly had time to get his feet on the ground before war broke out in July.[10]

Chennault's Chinese aviators were no match for Japan's excellent and professional air forces. But despite the terrible losses suffered by his collection of antiquated flying machines the Japanese did not always have the air to themselves. Chennault flew a Curtiss Hawk

75, and some say he became the most successful American ace of the war, with 40 or more victories. He had made himself unpopular in the American army by insisting that bombers needed fighter escort. Now he proved his theory correct by shooting down so many Japanese bombers that they were forced to include fighter escorts on their bombing missions. (Had the United States Air Corps generals noted this persistent fact of air warfare, many lives might have been saved over Europe in the years to come.) Then on 19 August 1940, a new Japanese navy fighter, the Zero, made its first combat sortie, escorting bombers on a mission to Chungking. A month later the Zero was tested in air combat when a formation of 13 pounced upon 27 Polikarpov I-15 and I-16 fighters. All the Chinese aircraft were shot down without loss to the Japanese. The Zero's two cannons proved a new and devastating weapon. One Japanese ace reported:

> I pulled out at low altitude, coming up behind one I-16 fighter as it rolled down the field. It was a perfect target, and a short cannon burst exploded the fighter in flames. I flashed across the field and spiralled sharply to the right, climbing steeply to come around for another run. Tracers and flak were to left and right of me, but the Zero's unexpected speed threw the enemy gunners off . . . I pulled out of a dive to catch another plane in my sights. A second short cannon burst and there was a mushrooming ball of fire. There was nothing left to strafe.[11]

For years to come the Zero was to rule the skies over China.

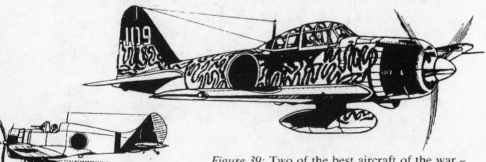

Figure 39: Two of the best aircraft of the war – the Mitsubishi 'Claude' and 'Zero' fighters

The Zero fighter plane

The Mitsubishi A6M Reisen – classified 0, to denote the Japanese year 2600 (1940) – was one of the finest aircraft of the war. The official American codename was Zeke, but most Americans called it the Zero, and so did the Japanese, its nickname being Reisen, a shortened form of Rei Sentoki or zero fighter. The twelve Zeros over Chungking were from a pre-production batch of 15 assigned to the 12th Combined Naval Air Corps (12th Rengo Kokutai), accompanied by engineers and factory technicians, to evaluate the plane in combat conditions. The Zero was replacing the Mitsubishi 'Claude', an open-cockpit low-wing monoplane with fixed undercarriage. One Japanese flyer said that 'the Zero had almost twice the speed and range of the Claude, and it was a dream to fly.'

Even so this Type 96 A5M1 'Claude', which the Japanese were dumping, was well ahead of its time. It had been designed by Jiro Horikoshi, designer of the Zero, and had come into service in early 1937, at a time when both the British and American navies were flying such biplanes as the F3F-1 and the even more outdated Hawker Nimrod.

The Zero was a breakthrough. Its wings were made in one piece and were integral with the centre section of the fuselage – the wing's top actually forming the cockpit's floor – thus eliminating the need for any wing-joining structure and giving the airframe immense strength. The wingtips folded back to conform with the 11-metre width of the regular Japanese carrier deck elevators. (In later models the wingtips were left off.) An amazing innovation was the way that the back and the front halves of the fuselage were bolted together, so the planes could be stored in halves, or unbolted to give maintenance men access to the interior.

An entirely new alloy,[12] ahead of anything known to the American aircraft industry, was used in the wing spar, and the flush-riveted metal skin was very thin. As a result, when a Zero came out of its hangar into the hot sunshine the metal could be heard popping for 15 minutes or so.

With its good visibility and a wide undercarriage, which made landings safer on decks that were rolling in heavy seas, most Americans who flew the Zero found its performance excellent[13] but, in keeping with Japanese military thinking, the pilot's well-being was virtually ignored. The exhaust stacks made it very noisy and there was no armour protection, no bulletproof windscreen and no self-sealing fuel tanks.

As with most Japanese aircraft design, light weight was the top priority of the Zero, and determined its very long range. Its engine was an NK 1C Sakae-12, a 14-cylinder radial manufactured by the rival Nakajima company. It played a vital part in the configuration, giving at full power 1,360 hp. The delicate Zero handled like a little high-powered sports car. Its opponents at the time of Pearl Harbor, the rugged Grumman F4F-4 Wildcat, the Curtiss P-36 and P-40, were heavier like big four-door cars,[14] and had engines with less power.

The most notable feature of the Zero's engine was its ability to run for a long time on a very lean mixture. This gave the Zero its amazing range of 1,000 miles compared to the Grumman F4F-4 Wildcat's range of 770 statute miles. Range was a dramatic and precious asset in carrier tactics; enabling the vulnerable carriers to keep far away from the enemy. And the Japanese pilots found ways of increasing this range:

> I personally established the record low consumption of less than seventeen gallons an hour; on average our pilots reduced their consumption from thirty-five gallons per hour to only eighteen . . . On our long-range flights we lowered propeller revolutions to only 1,700 to 1,850 rpm and throttled the air control valve to its leanest mixture.[15]

Chennault took a little time in realizing that he had the power, brains, influence and money to create an air force of his own. His position as China's air force supremo brought him into personal contact with top Chinese leaders, and through them he could influence President Roosevelt. He also found out how to cultivate American newspaper men and radio reporters.

With money from Chiang's coffers, Chennault went to America in the spring of 1941 and bought 100 Curtiss P-40B Tomahawks that had been built for the RAF. With a little string-pulling he persuaded the British to relinquish their rights to them. His skills as a publicist were demonstrated when, upon seeing a photo of RAF fighter aircraft in North Africa, he copied the shark's-teeth livery and established 'the Flying Tigers' as his own brain child.

The extent of Chennault's influence was demonstrated on 15 April 1941 when President Roosevelt authorized reserve officers and enlisted men from the US armed services to join the American Volunteer Group. Even more surprising was the way in which Chennault's civilian recruiters were permitted to travel round military bases to sign up volunteers, offering the pilots $600 per month, with a bounty of $500 for each downed Japanese plane. In another unprecedented concession, the flyers would not lose US citizenship and would be reinducted into the military when their twelve-month contracts ended. One of the American volunteers – Gregory 'Pappy' Boyington, who later became a Marine Corps ace – was told by his recruiter: 'The Japs will be flying antiquated junk over China. Many of your kills will be unarmed transports. I suppose you know that the Japanese are renowned for their inability to fly. And they all wear corrective glasses.'[16]

Chennault made sure that the American Press followed the fortunes of these AVG mercenaries, who were depicted as exciting freebooting heroes and became the subject of a popular strip cartoon adventure. In the event, the preparation and organization of airfields took so long that none of the volunteers saw combat until after the attack on Pearl Harbor in December, but Chennault's story did not end there. The man who retired as a sick and unwanted Air Corps captain ended up taking charge of the United States Army Air Force in China.

The Japanese navy

Unlike the army, the imperial navy was always concerned with technology, and managed to attract the finance to develop any ships and aircraft it needed. The fleet ranged from a two-man submarine that went to sea on the deck of a larger one, to the *Yamato*, the biggest warship ever built, with almost double the displacement of HMS *Hood*. Such spending encouraged the naval flyers to press for more money for naval aviation. As well as its aircraft-carriers the navy developed land-based bomber squadrons, and built submarines that could carry aircraft – some of the I-400 Class had a hangar 120 feet long and came complete with catapult. Aircraft from submarines flew reconnaissance missions over Wellington, Auckland, Sydney and Melbourne, as well as over Pearl Harbor both before and after the December 1941 attack.[17]

The Japanese navy developed torpedoes which outclassed those of all other nations. Their 'Long Lance' 34 Type 93 was a 24-inch oxygen-driven torpedo. Its speed, range and explosive power were so awesome and unexpected that it ranks with the Zero fighter as a crucial weapon of the opening months of the war.

During its experience in Chinese waters, the imperial navy had abandoned the scrubbed decks, gleaming awnings, polished brass and white-painted rails that were deemed essential to British and American peacetime routines. One Royal Navy officer, remember-

ing his service with the British China fleet, said: 'whereas we went
in for . . . very smart ships in appearance, the Japanese were entirely utilitarian. There was very little spit and polish; everything
was painted over . . . At first one saw these very drab-looking craft
and one thought that they were not well looked after . . . but what
we soon realized was that that was the whole Japanese philosophy;
the ships were after all much nearer to war.'

But the need for fuel oil influenced everything the imperial navy
did. Contempt for the Kwantung Army's costly and indecisive
struggle on mainland China was mingled with the fear that it would
one day provoke the Soviets into the war as China's ally. The only
sort of war that made sense to the admirals was one fought southwards to the oil-rich Dutch colonies. The admirals kept their own
strategic objective in mind while they aided the army in amphibious
operations on the coast of China, using the world's first amphibious
transport, which floated landing-craft through its stern well, and
their 'Naval Special Landing Forces', which soon became the only
experienced amphibious fighting force in the world.[18]

Foreign travel had made the Japanese navy's men more sophisticated than the narrow-minded despots who commanded the army.
While the curriculum at the Shikan Gakko – Japan's West Point –
was limited to such military skills as tactics, drilling, fencing, shooting and riding, naval officers studied engineering, economics and
political science. Many naval officers, trained in American or
British naval academies and speaking fluent English, knew that
America was an enemy they could not match.

Yet it was the navy's planners who eventually urged the strike
southwards. The point of decision came in July 1940 when Roosevelt approved a 'Two-Ocean Naval Expansion Act' promising
Americans a fleet that would dwarf the imperial navy's. The
Japanese admirals saw that time was running out for them. If they
were to strike they would have to do it before America's vast new
fleet was ready.[19] Or they would be number two forever.

Russia fights

The traditional antagonism that Japan had for Russia, had been
strengthened by fears of Communism. In the 1930s the Red Army
faced Japan's battle-trained Kwantung Army. Inevitably there were
continual shooting incidents along the frontier and eventually full-
scale battle in 1938, and again in 1939.

One incident in the 1939 fighting made a deep impression on the men who were present. During the early Red Army attacks on 24 July, a Japanese lieutenant of artillery, Higashikuni Morihiro, the 23-year-old son of a prince and intended husband of one of the Emperor's daughters, decamped from the field of battle without orders. This royal scandal was suppressed by the censors, but the divisional commander saw it as an ill-omen and his fears proved rational when a Japanese divisional assault, led by company officers waving samurai swords, ran into well prepared Red Army tank forces. Pinned down, and without water, the Japanese suffered under the punishing heat of day, and from freezing cold nights. They asked for massive air support but Tokyo had neither the resources nor the will to escalate the battle.

On 20 August Zhukov counter-attacked with air, armour and artillery. The Japanese had never encountered a modern force like this before, and Zhukov no doubt enjoyed the thought of avenging the humiliating surrender of Port Arthur. His four-engined bombers hammered the Japanese positions before the heavy tanks, many of them equipped with fearsome flamethrowers, cut through them. Outflanked and outnumbered in heavy equipment, the Japanese suffered devastating losses. Two regimental commanders burned their battle flags. One committed ritual suicide – seppuku – and the other deliberately exposed himself to enemy fire.

Once more the time had come for Japan's soldiers to give place to her equally resolute negotiators. This engagement had shown Russian skills in the use of tanks, heavy artillery and aircraft. Had Western intelligence services been other than comatose, or Western newspaper reporters more open-minded, it might have been re-marked that Japan's experienced and capable army had been soundly thrashed by a superior one. Instead, wishful thinkers said that even the Red Army could beat the Japanese, and offered it as yet more evidence of Asian inferiority.

The Red Army's Khalkin-Gol victory in 1939 should have pro-vided a note of caution to the German army planners who soon would be assessing their chances of taking Moscow, but the only one who never forgot the fierce Mongolian fighting was Marshal Zhukov, who was to say in 1945 that the Germans lacked the fanaticism that he had encountered in his Japanese enemies.

28 THE WAY TO WAR

*I have no hesitation in saying that military training is the
most unpopular feature of Japanese school life. Every student
I knew loathed it and would seize eagerly upon the slightest opportunity
to avoid attendance . . . Among the students personally known to me,
two committed suicide by throwing themselves in front of trains on
the eve of their being called to the army.*

John Morris, Winter 1942[1]

THE SHOCKING NEWS that Hitler had concluded a friendship pact
with the Russians was proclaimed in August 1939, while the
Japanese were being soundly beaten at Khalkin-Gol. What Hitler
contrived as a threat to France and Britain served also as Stalin's
caution to Tokyo. The events of that summer gave weight to the imperial navy's warnings that only disaster could come from the army's
reckless adventures on the Chinese mainland.

Perhaps all plans of conquest would have been shelved had the war
in Europe not suddenly flared in the summer of 1940. While Germany
conquered and occupied France, Belgium and Holland, and seemed
poised to add Britain to Hitler's New Europe, the men in Tokyo took
a close look at the vulnerable European colonies in the Far East.

Shortly before Christmas a Japanese military mission travelled by
way of the trans-Siberian railway to Germany to study German
weaponry and blitzkrieg methods. Its leader, Tomoyuki Yamashita,
had learned German while he was assistant military attaché in Berne
where, according to his biographer, he had a love affair with a German girl.[2] Once back in Tokyo Yamashita's final report to his
masters advised caution about getting into conflict with the British or
the Americans. However he was soon to demonstrate in Malaya
some blitzkrieg techniques of his own devising.

A Japanese government formed around a team of men who saw
Nazi Germany as Japan's guiding star. With France, Holland and
Britain virtually helpless, Japan's foreign minister, Yosuke Mat-
suoka, described as 'a notorious firebrand', began to cast a covetous
eye over their unprotected possessions in the Far East. Lieutenant-
General Hideki Tojo, the hardline hawk who had been chief of staff
of the Kwantung Army, became war minister.

Remembering perhaps Japan's almost effortless gains after attaching itself to the winning side in the First World War, these men now started to put pressure on the administrators of European colonies such as French Indo-China. At the same time they sought Hitler's agreement to their adventures: expansions to Burma in the west, and New Caledonia in the south. India, Australia and New Zealand were not excluded from Japanese aspirations!

Although Hitler had little sympathy for the Japanese, these ideas dovetailed well into his global strategy. The Japanese in the Pacific would occupy the attentions of the United States and the British Empire. The imperial navy's activities would send American warships hurrying to the Pacific, away from assisting the Atlantic convoys to Britain. In the same way some of the Royal Navy's ships, already thinly spread, would have to be sent to the Pacific. And when Hitler's still secret plan to invade the Soviet Union was implemented, the Japanese army would be threatening its Far Eastern frontiers, while Hitler struck towards Moscow.

In Berlin on 27 September 1940, five days after it began to take over French army, navy and air force bases in Indo-China, Japan joined Germany and Italy in the Tripartite Pact. Because Emperor Hirohito retained his throne after the war, and was received by the heads of state of the Allied powers, it became convenient for historians and politicians to pretend that the emperor had been a pacifist opposed to all the events that led to the war. However there is much to suggest that Hirohito was deeply concerned in the very earliest preparations for war, including the opening attack on Pearl Harbor. A memorandum from the army's chief of staff records: 'In January 1941, in answer to Commander of Great Fleet Yamamoto, Emperor orders Rear-Admiral Onishi to research Hawaii attack.'[3]

Admiral Isoruku Yamamoto, commander-in-chief of the Japanese Combined Fleet,[4] was a small, slight man who seemed to be able to scramble out of a submarine, or the cockpit of a bomber, looking neat and well-groomed. He had been wounded in the great naval battle of the Tsushima Strait in 1905, and his scarred hand and missing fingers were regarded with awe because of the place that naval battle held in the Japanese history books. After a year at Harvard he had become Japan's naval attaché in Washington in 1926. He read English well, and firmly believed that newspapers, and other published material, provided the best source of intelligence, so he would scan anything up to 40 newspapers and magazines before starting work. At least one acquaintance remembers him as being a non-drinker, but his boisterous, extrovert behaviour at parties – mad dancing and acrobatics – make this difficult to believe. More plausible is his reputation for playing five games of chess every day. He loved games, especially if a wager was involved. He regularly played bridge, mah-jong, shogi, go, billiards and roulette. He would organize poker games that went on for 30 or even 40 hours non-stop. In London for a conference, Yamamoto won £20 from Lord Chatfield – Britain's chief of naval staff – in a game of bridge.

Yamamoto's dedication to air-power was longstanding. In the 1920s he had commanded the Naval Pilots' School at Kasumigaura and in the 1930s he was the chief of the Technical Bureau of Naval Aviation. In this role he had decided that, with international treaties limiting Japan's construction of carriers, the navy should design and develop long-range medium bombers that would operate only from land bases. This led to the twin-engined Mitsubishi 'Nell' and the 'Betty', and to the long-range capability of the navy's Zero fighter.

Many historians see Japan's signing of the Tripartite Pact as a major step towards war. It shocked the Americans. They interpreted Japan's blatant alliance with Nazi Germany as a hostile act, and it moved many Americans into accepting China's Chiang Kai-shek as their close ally.

The months leading up to the Tripartite Pact had seen Japan's leaders becoming more and more bellicose on every side. In mainland China, Japanese forces came to the Kowloon border to peer through the wire at the British in Hong Kong. The men in Tokyo demanded that the British close the Burma Road along which war material was travelling to Chiang's nationalist army. Britain, then isolated in what looked like a forlorn last stand against German invasion forces in Europe, appealed to the United States for help, and ways to counter the Japanese threats. One suggestion was that the Americans should cut off exports to Japan, and another that part of the US Pacific fleet should move to make its base in Singapore.

The Americans rejected all the British suggestions. They would not put a general embargo on exports to Japan. They had already moved the Pacific Fleet from the West Coast to Pearl Harbor in Hawaii, and moving it further west might be criticized as dangerously exposing America's West Coast. The time was approaching for a new presidential election. Any cosy arrangements to aid the British would be politically unacceptable to many American voters. This was particularly true of anything that might be seen as supporting Britain's colonial Empire, of which America had once been an unhappy part.

Dismayed, the British offered the Japanese a compromise: they would close the Burma Road for three months during the monsoon when there was little traffic.

In July 1940, in an action calculated not to look like a response to the British, President Roosevelt stopped the export to Japan of aviation fuel, lubricants and certain scrap iron and steel. In September he tightened the regulations. In November, after he had been re-elected, copper, zinc, brass, oil-drilling equipment and other strategic exports could no longer go to Japan. By this time Britain's successful conclusion of the Battle of Britain had won her a breathing space. Even the worst pessimists in Washington began to think that Britain might survive.

Breaking Purple

American work on breaking Japanese government codes and reading their secret messages began in 1922, but six years of remarkable success were undone when the leader of the team, Herbert O. Yardley, turned traitor and sold all the work to the Japanese for $7,000. Consequently the Japanese turned to coding machines which produced messages far more difficult to read. But 'with the help of mathematical analysis, call girls, fake power failures, and outright safecracking, US Naval Intelligence finally built its own replicas of these first-generation Japanese coding machine in 1935, when they had been in use for four years.'[5]

Unaware that their mechanical instruments had been duplicated, the Japanese designed the Alphabetical Typewriter 97, the world's first electronic coding device, which completely baffled the American cryptanalysts who called it 'Purple'.

While the work on Purple, in which diplomatic messages were encoded, was at a standstill the codebreakers were reading the most secret of the imperial navy's codes, and then suddenly in November 1940 that was greatly modified and the bonanza ended.[6] To discover the location of Japanese warships the Americans were forced to depend upon their direction-finding network across the Pacific and plot ships' movements by means of traffic analysis.

The difficulties of transmitting written messages in Japanese script persuaded the Japanese to use Roman letters for their machine-encoded texts, and they preferred ciphers, the substitution of one letter for another, to codes using groups of letters or numbers. Ciphers, being closer to the original text, were easier to break and more vulnerable to mechanical decryption. But this does not mean that calculating the maze of circuits that were used in the Purple machine was easy; one of the foremost experts says that breaking Purple was 'the greatest feat of cryptanalysis the world had yet known.'[7]

Using largely the work of William Friedman, the Signal Corps' chief cryptanalyst, who had laboured without respite, the Americans assembled their own version of a Japanese Alphabetical Typewriter. It was apt to vomit sparks and make loud noises, but from it in August 1940 there came for the first time the deciphered text of a message in 'Purple', Japan's most secret diplomatic code.

Reliable Americans who could translate Japanese were even more scarce than good cryptanalysts. There was official reluctance to use Americans of Japanese race, and yet, without the ideograph as a guide, only those with a thorough knowledge of both languages could translate the messages. In the words of one intelligence specialist: 'Any two sounds grouped together to make a word may mean a variety of things. For instance, "ba" may mean horses or fields, old women, or my hand, all depending on the ideographs with which it is written.'[8] In the light of this, it is a wonder than any messages at all were accurately translated.

In December Friedman collapsed with a breakdown from which he never did fully recover, but by that time, as part of a wider operation codenamed 'Magic', the Americans had several machines that, once the daily key was broken, would read Japanese diplomatic secrets including what Tokyo told its Japanese ambassador in Washington and what he reported back.

1941: Britain is bleeding

U-boat victories in the Atlantic threatened to starve the British and, on 10 February 1941, President Roosevelt reacted to this crisis. He instructed the National Maritime Commission to tell shipowners (many of them using foreign flags) that, unless they voluntarily diverted more ships from the safe Pacific routes to the hazards of the Atlantic, they would see strong controls established. By the end of March, 200 ships were under orders to switch routes. This device was also a subtle method of depriving the Japanese of oil, for Japan had insufficient tonnage to ship its own fuel imports.

By now, well informed American leaders began to believe that war with Germany was inevitable but most of them hoped that war with Japan could be avoided. In April 1941 there were staff conferences between American, British and Dutch officers to discuss what response their armed forces would make to Japanese aggression.

Starved of strategic materials by the American restrictions, the Japanese were putting ever heavier pressure on the Dutch administration to supply oil, rubber, tin and bauxite from the East Indies. When the Netherlands fell to German invasion, and the government moved to London, they did not weaken but permitted only small amounts of such strategic materials to go to Japan. The Japanese negotiators pressed their demands and, on 10 June 1941, talks between the Japanese and the Dutch in Batavia (today known as the Indonesian capital Djakarta) in the Dutch East Indies ended in deadlock. The frustration felt by the Japanese at this moment could well have tipped the scales for war.[9]

When, a few days later, Hitler invaded the Soviet Union and removed their fears of Russian aggression, even Japanese generals began supporting the admirals' theory that only a military occupation of the vital Dutch oil installations in the Far East would give them what they wanted. In Tokyo an Imperial Conference on 2 July laid down that their newly gained bases in Indo-China must be made ready as springboards for such an attack. The decree added that the possibility of war with Great Britain or the United States was not to stand in the way. Meanwhile the policy was to woo the Americans, in the hope that supplies would be resumed and no military action would be needed.

When the bellicose and highly secret conclusions of the Imperial Conference were sent by radio, American codebreakers intercepted and decoded the messages. Richard Sorge, the Communist spy in Tokyo, also got wind of these high-level Japanese secret decisions and informed his masters in Moscow.

Sorge's message was read with interest in Moscow. With the Red Army in full retreat before the relentless Germans, Stalin knew he would soon desperately need reinforcements. As summer, and the chances of Japanese military action on his extreme eastern frontier, came to an end, and assured by Sorge that the Japanese were preparing a strike southwards, Stalin ordered 200,000 men, plus tanks and planes, from his eastern provinces and started them on the long journey westwards. In the weekend of Pearl Harbor they would be flung into the battle and shock the Germans.

America reacted to the secret decisions of the Imperial Conference by freezing Japanese assets in the United States. The British, who were being provided with the secrets of the 'Magic' traffic in exchange for the German Enigma secrets, also froze Japan's assets and cancelled all their commercial agreements. Soon afterwards the Dutch did so too. This new action of the Americans, the British and the Dutch had a more immediate effect than the ever-lengthening list of banned exports. About three-quarters of Japanese foreign trade stopped dead, and her oil imports were cut by 90 per cent.

It did not deter the Japanese from their war plan. By the end of July, having taken over the French naval bases at Saigon and Camranh Bay in Indo-China, they disembarked 50,000 Japanese soldiers. America and Japan were now on a collision course.

Dean Acheson's private embargo

Until recently that was the official record of events in the history books. But Jonathan Utley at the University of Tennessee dug into official papers and came up with an altogether new account based on a careful study of official papers, as well as diaries and the revelations of people now prepared to speak more openly. He showed in his book *Going to War with Japan* that Cordell Hull, the US secretary of state, and the president were not, after all, responsible for bringing America into the war. In his view, the president was defeated by a small group of highly placed Washington bureaucrats who 'ultimately acted on pragmatic views rooted in deeply held economic beliefs.'[10]

The revised story reveals that, in his move of 26 July, President Roosevelt did not completely cut off Japan's oil supplies, nor did he totally freeze its assets. The scheme was more complex than that. Frozen Japanese funds could be unfrozen by means of US government licences that would permit the Japanese to buy non-aviation petroleum products to equal those of 1935–36.

It was the assistant secretary of state, Dean Acheson, who decided on his own authority not to release any funds for oil purchases. Aided by like-minded subordinates, he arranged to entangle all Japanese applications in bureaucratic red tape from which no permits would emerge. According to one official, 'the Japanese tried every conceivable way of getting the precious crude oil, but to each proposal the Division of Foreign Funds Control had an evasive answer ready to camouflage its flat refusal.'

It was not until 4 September that Cordell Hull discovered Acheson flouting government orders and sent for him. Hull found himself facing a dilemma. Suddenly to put things right, and release the oil, would look like an encouraging signal to the Tokyo hard-liners. The Japanese hawks had been predicting that the Americans would give way.

But the Americans were determined not to give way. Hull decided to let Acheson's unofficial embargo continue. The Japanese – always obsessed with loss of face – found unendurable the prospect of bowing to US pressure. They watched their stockpiles of oil dwindle, knowing that when the storage tanks ran dry the Japanese economy would wither and die. Acheson's action had started a countdown to war.

Without Acheson's reckless unilateral action there might have been a chance for compromise. But any agreement would take time. Talks with the Japanese mission sent to Washington showed how far apart the two sides remained. Japan even offered to withdraw the garrisons from China, but wanted 25 years in which to do it, while America must stop supporting the Chinese Nationalist army and persuade it to stop hostilities against the Japanese.

At home Japanese responses to the serious new situation varied. Some simply wanted to go to war immediately, before the oil reserves ran out. The hawks tried to allay fears of a fighting war. They promised that the destruction of the American Pacific fleet, and landings in Burma, Malaya, Dutch East Indies and the Philippines, would bring all concerned – the United States, Britain and Holland – to the negotiating table. In that way Japan would obtain a permanent and honourable settlement. Japan's Supreme War Council on 6 September 1941 approved plans for simultaneous attacks on Pearl Harbor and other targets in South-East Asia. War games off the Japanese coast were under way before the month was over.

There were other more cautious voices which urged War Minister Tojo to endure the unendurable and withdraw Japanese forces from China. It was over this issue that, on 16 October, the cabinet resigned. The army's hawkish Tojo became premier, retaining for himself his post as war minister and that of home affairs minister too. At the same time Tojo kept his active service commitment to the army. Civilian influence in the government had declined to almost nothing, and while there were those who feared the army's control of the country, there were many who thought that having a general in the seat of power would tell the Americans that government and army were in accord.

At 57, Tojo was a confusing mixture of harsh disciplinarian and

Western-style politician. His plain military jacket, bald head, glasses and moustache made him easy to recognize wherever he went. Never before had the Japanese seen one of their leaders chatting with workers and checking for himself the prices in the markets. Tojo's authority was not exercised through the cabinet, which had no power, but through a 'liaison group' which consisted of the prime minister, the army and navy chiefs of staff, the army and navy ministers (who were always serving officers) and the foreign minister. Decisions of this group were rubber-stamped by the emperor, sitting in silence at an Imperial Conference.

The Japanese regarded the Americans and the British as people who would compromise. The British desperately needed tin and rubber for the war in Europe; surely they would not jeopardize these supplies simply to restrain Japanese territorial ambitions? Surely the Americans, having thrown off the colonial yoke, and always voluble about freedom and justice, would not fight to maintain British and Dutch colonial possessions? Aware that these were questions they might face from the American Press reporters, the British declined to take any part in the Japanese-US negotiations in Washington.

The Americans, by now active participants against German U-boats in the Battle of the Atlantic, said that Japan would have to renounce the Tripartite Pact before the relationship could be improved. American public opinion could not tolerate a deal with 'Hitler's partner'. The Japanese claimed also to have a problem with public opinion. They could not renounce the pact, they said, but they might let it fade away.

The final exchanges

On 20 November 1941 the Japanese proposed a 'modus vivendi': a three-month suspension of the 'cold war'. They would withdraw from southern Indo-China but not from the north; they would continue to fight the Chinese but not 'make armed advancement' southwards. In return they wanted the Americans to resume exports to Japan, including oil, and stop sending war material to Chiang's forces in China.

Cordell Hull called it 'preposterous'. While he was drafting a reply, an intercepted Japanese signal was put before him. It was a secret message from Tokyo advising their envoys in Washington that the deadline for a satisfactory reply from the Americans had been extended to 29 November. A sinister confidential footnote confided to the Japanese envoys that: 'This time we mean it, that the deadline absolutely cannot be changed. After that things are automatically going to happen.'

Aware that time was running out, Hull slaved over the draft of a response. He then showed his proposed reply to the envoys of Britain, China, Holland and Australia, and asked them to consult their governments about it. In the drafted reply Hull kept to the idea of a modus vivendi, proposing a three-month cooling-off period, with concessions by both sides. He wanted some Japanese withdrawals, troop reductions in Indo-China; in return he offered some resumption of oil for civilian use, and some other supplies.

Hull was pleased with what he'd written and hoped it would bring a breakthrough. And if all his efforts failed, at least the US army and navy would have three months in which to become better prepared for war. Anxiously he waited for responses from the four consulted governments, but his enthusiasm was not shared. At the next meeting Lord Halifax, on behalf of Britain, and the Australian envoy were both noncommittal; only the Dutch envoy had been conscientious enough to seek instructions from his government. The Chinese envoy objected to 25,000 Japanese troops remaining in Indo-China. The Chinese were afraid that the Americans were about to stage a 'Munich' that would dump them as Chamberlain had dumped the Czechs. Their fears were quite unfounded. Many Americans were far too concerned about what might happen if a permanent peace in China released a million Japanese troops for service elsewhere.

The American secretary of state was deeply disappointed and bitter that – apart from the Dutch – the governments had not given him unqualified and unanimous approval. Later he wrote:

> 'Each of your governments,' I said bluntly, 'has a more direct interest in the defense of that area of the world than this country; yet at the same time they expect this country, in case of a Japanese outbreak, to be ready to move in a military way and take the lead in defending the entire area. But your governments, through some preoccupation in other directions, do not seem to know anything about this matter under discussion. I am definitely disappointed at this unexpected development, at their lack of interest and lack of disposition to cooperate.'[11]

Hull said that, lacking the views of the other governments, he was

not at all sure he would present this reply to the Japanese. More
response was not long in coming. The vociferous Chiang Kai-shek
cabled protests to various members of the American government
and to Churchill. Lord Halifax handed in a memorandum that Hull
said provided 'half-hearted support'. The British, clearly influenced
by Chiang, wanted no oil to go to Japan and considerably fewer
soldiers in Indo-China. Hull regarded this as impracticable if they
were to get any sort of agreement from the Japanese.

Churchill repeated the British reservations to Roosevelt, asking if
Chiang Kai-shek wasn't getting 'rather meagre rations'. It was the
last straw. In a sudden reverse of opinion, Hull dropped his plan.
After working sixteen hours a day, he was physically and mentally
exhausted. He had always felt that temporary agreements were only
a step away from appeasement, and feared widespread American
public opposition to resuming the oil supplies.

The modus vivendi proposal was never sent. A breathing space
might well have meant that war was avoided, for by the spring of
1942 German victory did not seem quite so inevitable, and strengthened American forces might indeed have deterred Japanese
expansion.

For themselves, the Japanese were expecting America's counter-
proposals with which in turn they would bargain. Instead they received what was tantamount to an ultimatum. Hull disregarded the
old axiom 'for your enemy build a golden bridge', and instead of
tailoring his reply to make it something the Japanese could swallow,
he went back to his previous stance of trying to impose permanent
and fundamental changes. Japan must withdraw its troops from all
of China and Indo-China and recognize the Chiang nationalist
government there. (By an oversight, no one told the Japanese that
Manchuria could remain theirs.)

The terms horrified the Japanese. Extricating their army from
China after so many years would present enormous technical problems: to do so in response to American demands would have been
unthinkably humiliating. It seemed to them that the United States
was threatening their 'national existence'. The military chiefs submitted their reactions to a council of former prime ministers who
decided that Japan would have to go to war. Tojo instructed his envoy in Washington to keep trying to obtain acceptable terms, but a
pugnacious speech by Tojo, and the reports of more Japanese troop
movements, made Roosevelt and Hull adamant in their resolve.
The unending atrocities in China, the bombing of the USS *Panay*,

the close relationship between Japan and Nazi Germany, and the way in which the army had taken political control of the nation – all these played a part in forming the West's image of Japan. Like Nazi Germany, Tojo's was perceived as an evil regime.

The fault was neither Hull's nor Acheson's. Americans and Japanese had a heartfelt distrust of each other. And while Japan treated China with contempt and brutality, America had a romantic attachment to that nation. War arose from a complex combination of events and hardened attitudes. An opinion poll published on Friday 5 December 1941 found that 69 per cent of Americans wanted steps to be taken to prevent Japan growing more powerful.

European warships from Britain, Holland, France, Germany and Italy were busy fighting each other. The fast-moving events in Europe had taken a great deal of Roosevelt's attention, and American military resources, which might have deterred Japan, were put into the Atlantic battle. The whole Pacific area was cleared of challengers while conquered France left Indo-China available as a jumping-off place for the 'armed advancement' southwards. All of these things fitted together and played a part in Japan's resolve – as did Japanese belief that Germany would very soon win the war in Europe.

On the afternoon of Monday 1 December 1941, at the Imperial Palace in Tokyo, the fatal decision was taken before the emperor, who was seated at a small table, before a golden folding screen. At each hand, there was an incense burner and before him two long tables covered with large-patterned brocade. At one table sat four naval officers with stiffened backs and close-cropped heads. They were dressed in formal uniforms, complete with medals and swords, their caps aligned on the table like dinner plates, their white-gloved hands resting upon their thighs, eyes directed straight ahead. Facing them, like the image in a mirror, were their four army counterparts. Using the archaic language of the court, Tojo informed the meeting that the United States had conspired against Japan and that 'in the circumstances our Empire has no alternative but to go to war'. The director of the Cabinet Planning Board gave his consent. By tradition, the emperor did not speak at the gathering, but when the meeting ended he remarked quietly that regrettable though the decision was, it was the lesser evil. According to one account, he showed no sign of uneasiness and seemed to be in excellent spirits.[12]

The huge Japanese striking force was already at sea, on its way to

Hawaii. That night the Japanese navy changed its codes and ciphers. Messages to fleet commanders, confirming the plan for the attacks, were in 'Admirals Code', which could not be deciphered by the Americans. A cryptic and momentous message – 'Climb Mount Niitaka 1208' – went out to the commander of the Combined Fleet. Niitaka was the Empire's highest mountain and the number signified that X-Day was to fall on 8 December. Japanese leaders were confident that it was just a matter of time before they would be sitting at the table with American, British and Dutch negotiators, all of whom would be totally demoralized by German and Japanese successes.

By Thursday 4 December Japan's intention to strike south was anticipated by top officials and experts on both sides. When Walter Foote, US ambassador in the Dutch East Indies, went into his yard to burn his codebooks he found his next-door neighbour, the Japanese ambassador, doing the same thing on the other side of the garden fence.

On Saturday 6 December Tokyo sent to their envoys in Washington thirteen parts of a fourteen-part message that was to be delivered to the Americans next day. To be sure that no misunderstanding arose in translation, it was sent in English. As in embassies the world over, the Japanese diplomatic staff were not noted for their strenuous weekends. Long before Japanese embassy clerks had finished their deciphering, the American codebreakers, working round the clock, had the message on Roosevelt's desk.

Roosevelt, who had a full appointment book that day, heard that both the American and British navies had been reporting Japanese troop convoys creeping along the coast of Cambodia.[13] Having been host at a dinner party for 34 people, Roosevelt left his guests immediately after the main course and returned to his desk in the Oval Office where White House resident Harry Hopkins, his closest adviser, was waiting. At 9.30 pm the thirteen parts of the intercept were delivered by an officer of naval intelligence. In the presence of the messenger Roosevelt read and reread the document for ten minutes or so. 'This means war,' he resignedly told Hopkins, the only other official in the room.[14] It was Saturday night, and the document was not shown to General George Marshall, the army chief of staff, nor to Admiral 'Betty' Stark, the chief of naval operations, who was enjoying a performance of *The Student Prince* at the National Theater. By the time Stark got home from the show and telephoned the White House, Roosevelt seems to have become less agitated. Stark was later to recall that Roosevelt gave him the impression that the Japanese dispatch was no more than a rehash of previously stated views.[15]

At 9.15 am that Sunday morning the fourteenth and final part of the Japanese message was being read by Admiral Stark, and his senior intelligence officers. It was not a declaration of war. It ended: 'The Japanese government regrets . . . it cannot but consider that it is impossible to reach an agreement through further negotiations.' There was no ultimatum or threat of conflict. Despite Roosevelt's interpretation, others who read the message hoped that the Japanese were preparing new proposals.

An hour later the American naval officers were reading a more significant supplementary instruction telling the Japanese in Washington to 'please destroy at once the remaining cipher machine and all machine codes. Dispose in like manner also secret documents.' They were to deliver the whole fourteen-part text to Cordell Hull at 1 o'clock.

Lunchtime on Sunday being an unusual time for such diplomatic exchanges in Washington, the navy men studied their maps for clues to the significance of the timing. Someone noticed that 1 pm in Washington would be two or three hours before dawn in the British colony of Malaya – a suitable time to start an amphibious landing – and this fitted perfectly with reports of two Japanese convoys moving down the coast of French Indo-China. It was only then that someone added that it would be about 7.30 am on Sunday morning in Pearl Harbor and 'probably the quietest time of the week aboard ship'.

Admiral Stark was urged to warn the C-in-C Pacific fleet, but Stark replied that defence of the Hawaiian islands was the army's duty. By the time the army's General Marshall had returned from his habitual morning horse ride and read the message it was 11.15 am in Washington. Marshall thought that such commands as Panama and Hawaii should be alerted, but urged 'give the Philippines first priority.' Declining an offer to send his warning over the US navy signals network, he asked his own army signals men to use 'the fastest safe means'. Marshall was told by his signals officer that his warning would be received by his various Pacific commanders within 30 or 40 minutes. This was a somewhat optimistic calculation, for it allowed no time for deciphering, decoding and delivery.

There is no evidence to suggest that either Stark or Marshall anticipated an attack upon any US base. Like most other high-ranking officers, they saw only an imminent Japanese move south. And if escorted Japanese convoys were gathering near Malaya, why would anyone suspect that the bulk of their best warships would be 6,000 miles away, heading for Hawaii?

The maps on the wall showed circles radiating from Japanese bomber bases on land. The destructive power of a carrier-borne bombing raid, using an unprecedented force of six carriers at sea, was not taken into account. No one was expecting bombers to appear in the skies over Hawaii.

In the event atmospherics causing static had forced the army to lose connection with Honolulu, and so Marshall's warning was sent not by army radio but by the far more powerful commercial transmitter. Sent at noon it took about an hour to reach Honolulu where, at 7.30 am local time, it was picked up by a motor-cycle messenger for delivery to the army administrative headquarters. It was not marked priority, and there was no reason to believe it to be anything other than an everyday message. In fact it was not much more than a routine message, for it simply repeated previous instructions to be on the alert.

While the messenger, who happened to be Japanese, was on his way the air attack began. With great difficulty he passed through a police roadblock by showing them the envelope addressed to the commanding general and finally reached his destination at 11.45 am.

The air attack on Pearl Harbor and Oahu began punctually at 7.55 am local time, which was 1.25 pm in Washington. The Japanese diplomatic note should have already been delivered to Cordell Hull but it was not delivered for another hour, by which time the Pearl Harbor attack was almost over. In Malaya, Japanese troops were already ashore. The move against Hong Kong, and the air attacks on the Philippines, all took place between noon and 9 pm Washington time. They would have been more closely concentrated, but fog obscuring the Japanese air bases in Formosa (Taiwan) delayed for three hours the bombing raid on the Philippines.

In any case a warning received in Pearl Harbor would have made only marginal difference to the outcome of the attack. The Japanese had overwhelming force, said a US naval intelligence officer, W.J. Holmes: even a week's warning would not have prevented disaster. Had the whole Pacific fleet put to sea against the Japanese carrier force 'the most probable outcome would have been the sinking of the [American] battleships in deep water beyond hope of salvage and much greater loss of life.'

*'The "Advertiser" didn't come,' [my 11-year-old son, Eric]
exclaimed. 'Mr Herndon says to get up, the Japs are taking the
island and you have no coffee.' His mother opened her sleepy eyes and
replied, 'Call up the "Advertiser". There is a fresh can of coffee in the
lower closet.' 'The Japs aren't taking the island,' I reassured him. 'They
are thousands of miles away, taking an island in the Dutch East Indies.'*

W.J. Holmes, US Navy Intelligence, Honolulu, Hawaii[1]

IT IS EVIDENT from the spectacular postwar rise in Japan's fortunes
that its people are cultured, hard-working, disciplined and intelligent. Yet its economy is precarious, lacking indigenous raw materials
and sources of energy. Japan's war of conquest was a bid to obtain
markets by forming a 'Co-Prosperity Sphere', but the main reason
for going to war was to seize control of the Dutch East Indies, with
its oilfields and wealth of minerals. In 1941, most of Japan's planning
and military resources were directed to this thrust southwards.

The Japanese troop convoys were spotted and tracked. Most of the
Western intelligence officers knew that the Japanese would strike.
But, like a herd of gazelle transfixed by prowling lions, no one
wanted to believe that he would be the victim.

In Washington on the morning of 6 December, US Navy Secretary
Frank Knox asked: 'Gentlemen, are they going to hit us?'

Admiral Turner, head of the Navy's War Plans Division,
answered: 'No, Mr Secretary. They are going to hit the British. They
are not ready for us yet.'[2]

His complacency was understandable. Eliminating America's
Pacific fleet by means of an attack on Pearl Harbor was not an essential part of Japan's seizure of oil and minerals, and seen against the
whole Japanese war plan, this bombing raid was a side-show.

So why did they not leave the United States out of the war? Why
did the Japanese not simply attack Dutch or British possessions and
leave the Americans alone? After all, the United States had not
interfered when Japan invaded China and then bullied the French
into letting them create military bases in French Indo-China.

The answer lies in a self-destructive delusion of grandeur. Fundamental to all Japanese thinking was the belief that they were a chosen

race, with a divine emperor, destined to rule Asia. Emotionally they saw Washington, with its oil embargo, as a wayward obstructor of divine right who had to be punished. The Japanese reasoned that the Americans would be sure to fight if Dutch or British possessions were attacked. American bases in the Philippine Islands dominated the routes south that a Japanese attacking force must take. To safeguard its lines of communication, Japan would have to secure the Philippines, even if that meant bringing the Americans into the war. For added security Borneo and Malaya had to be occupied too. Only then would the link, and the invasion route, to the oil-rich Dutch East Indies be safeguarded.

The date of the attack was decided by the weather. The sea battles must be fought before the winter storms came to the north Pacific. The Philippines, Borneo and Malaya must be occupied before the north-east monsoon arrived in the South China Sea. During the first weeks of war, the southern sea lanes would be vital to the Japanese army as it occupied and fortified the new possessions, and so the US Pacific fleet had to be kept out of those southern waters. The Pearl Harbor attack would eliminate that fleet and so deny American naval protection to the Philippines, the East Indies, Malaya, and Borneo. Such a vast amphibious operation was unprecedented in the whole of recorded military history. Only a nation convinced of its divine purpose would have embarked on it.

It is difficult to envisage the immense size of the Pacific Ocean from an armchair. Sit in Hawaii and it is 5,400 miles to Panama and nearly 4,000 miles to Yokohama in Japan, while Auckland, New Zealand, is no less than 7,500 miles away. Include its adjacent seas and the Pacific Ocean is larger than all the land surface in the world. This was the battlefield, and such were the distances that men and material must travel in order to fight. Japan's sea supply problems were comparable to Britain's, but more demanding. Yet at the end of 1941 Japan's merchant fleet was less than one-third of the tonnage Britain had registered in 1939. This lack was to prove decisive.

The Americans had a large Pacific fleet but, for reasons of treaty, cost and international relations, they had no practical naval base west of Pearl Harbor. (Their base at Manila Bay in the Philippines was not suitable for a fleet of big ships.) The British, on the other hand, had a superb naval base at Singapore but no Pacific fleet! It is interesting to consider what might have happened if Roosevelt had disregarded political objections and put his ships and planes into Singapore.

Since her great victory against the Russians in 1905, Japan's prevailing naval theory was that the enemy fleet must be lured into Japanese home waters for a carefully planned set-piece battle. Admiral Yamamoto in 1941 rejected these old ideas. He didn't want a battle on Japan's doorstep, he needed his naval forces spread out to protect the far-flung supply routes. Any naval action should take place in distant waters and as early as possible.

The decision to seek out America's Pacific fleet and destroy it was first taken in December 1940. Yamamoto speculated that a gunnery battle between surface ships could be replaced by a one-way assault, or *katamichi kogeki*, employing carrier-borne torpedo planes that would ditch in the sea, where small ships would rescue the aircrews. He outlined this plan to his superiors in a paper called 'Views on Preparation for War', dated 7 January 1941.

Yamamoto had been a student at Harvard University and an attaché in Washington. A voracious reader, he certainly would have known that, in the US navy's spring exercises of 1932, Admiral Harry Yarnell had invented the 'carrier task force'. At a time when fleets moved only en masse, Yarnell left his main force behind and used only two carriers and a destroyer escort, sailing in poor weather, without lights and in complete radio silence. From these two ships his planes made their mock attack upon Hawaii at dawn on a Sunday. The exercise was a success.

Despite Yamamoto's experience of America and Americans, he was convinced that the sinking of their big battleships would demoralize the American public and have them clamouring for peace. This misconception shows the gulf of understanding that existed at all levels between Americans and Japanese. In other circumstances such illusions might have been corrected by intelligence experts or diplomats, but the Japanese were as ill-informed about America as the Americans were about them. One expert remarks:

> Prior to 1940, the Imperial Army virtually ignored the United States and Great Britain altogether in its intelligence gathering, being more focused on China and the Soviet Union; English was not even taught in the Army schools. Neither the Imperial Navy nor any other key government organs made a major investigation of United States productive capacity before initiating the war.[3]

Commander Minoru Genda

The idea of an air attack on the Pacific fleet was put to 36-year-old

Commander Minoru 'madman' Genda, one-time leader of his navy's aerobatic team. Genda, who was well known for his willingness to take risks, thought the air attack plan should be changed to an invasion that occupied the Hawaiian Islands, so depriving the Americans of their only Pacific naval base. This suggestion was rejected by the high command, which was too deeply committed to the thrust southwards.

Genda was a torpedo expert, nicknamed for his 'mad' claims about the way in which aircraft could sink battleships. While he was in London serving as the assistant naval attaché, an attack by Italian torpedo planes on the Royal Navy at Alexandria had failed when the torpedoes hit the muddy bottom. Since then the Royal Navy had shown how it should be done. They had dropped torpedoes in the shallow waters of the Italian anchorage at Taranto, disabling half the Italian fleet for a loss of two Swordfish aircraft.

Genda noted that Taranto was 42 feet deep; Pearl Harbor 45 feet. When finally he endorsed the Yamamoto plan and was appointed to work out the details, he began at once to modify torpedoes for use in shallow water. He guessed that the Royal Navy had changed the fins so that a torpedo dropped from a plane would not end up stuck deep in the mud at the bottom of the harbour.

Japanese airborne torpedoes contained almost 50 per cent more explosive than their US equivalents and travelled almost twice as fast. Driven by compressed oxygen and kerosene, they were dangerous to handle, but one hit could tear a large hole in thick armour plate and sink even a big ship.

One carrier would not be enough. Genda knew that when he first looked at the proposal. The attackers would need a fleet of carriers. A fleet of aircraft-carriers? It was an idea unheard of at that time. Even today it would be considered extremely audacious. Until now the world's battleship admirals had seen the carrier as an adjunct to the fleet, used to give air protection to the other ships and send a few aircraft off to observe the opposing armada. Sometimes carrier aircraft might be permitted to attack enemy ships but this was not something the battleship admirals encouraged. In a postwar paper, Genda said that the idea of using a carrier fleet came to him while watching a newsreel of four US carriers sailing in column.[4] He dismissed the idea of katamichi kogeki and insisted that the carrier force should go close to Hawaii, so that there could be more than one attack. As well as attacks with aerial torpedoes there must be horizontal bombing and dive-bombing.

Genda also stressed the importance of the fighter plane. At this time theorists saw the fighter's role as no more than a defensive umbrella above the home carrier. Genda wanted them to go all the way to the target, giving the bombers protection, as well as securing the air above enemy ships and bases.

Carrier aviation

Despite Britain's reputation as the mightiest of naval powers, its close relationship with Japan and the way in which it pioneered almost every aspect of naval aviation, Japan's early influences and aircraft came from France and the United States. When the First World War began, Japan made history by sending four Maurice Farman float planes, flying from a seaplane tender, to attack the German concession at Tsingtao in China. They even sank a German minelaying ship.[5]

Yet it was not until the visit of a British aviation mission in 1921 that Japanese eyes opened to the way that naval aviation suited her ambitions in the Pacific. In 1923, shortly before Britain's HMS *Hermes* was ready, their own *Hosho* was commissioned, giving Japan the distinction of producing the world's first purpose-built aircraft-carrier.[6] From this, and from two larger carriers based on cruiser hulls, they could fly the experimental monoplane Mitsubishi 1MF 10, the world's first aircraft designed specifically for carrier operations. Sopwith's former chief designer, Herbert Smith, was employed by Mitsubishi and worked on the Type 10, and a British pilot, Captain Jordan, made the first take-off in February 1923, but by this time the Japanese were making significant contributions to both designing and operations.

By the end of the 1920s the imperial navy, like the United States navy, had three carriers; the French navy had one, and the British six. But the RAF had gained control of British naval aviation and it was in serious decline, and continued to be neglected until well after the Royal Navy regained control of its aircraft in 1937.

What the Japanese government called 'incidents' in China provided the armed services with continuous military action, including strikes from carriers off the China coast. In 1937 the fighting in China flared into a full-scale war. The rapid advance of Japan's aviation industry was largely due to the way in which two vast industrial conglomerates, Mitsubishi and Nakajima, between them controlled about two-thirds of the entire industry. During the 1937 battles, the results of concentrated research, hard work and expenditure could be seen, as the Japanese air forces took control of the skies over the fighting, putting into service many of the aircraft they would eventually use in their war against America.

It was relatively simple to produce a serviceable aircraft-carrier. A flight deck was built upon any suitable hull, a couple of large elevators were fitted to bring aircraft down to the hangar deck, and after that the main problem lay in diverting the smoke from the flight deck. Designing and producing aircraft suited to carrier use was far more difficult. Such aircraft had to be reliable and rugged to endure rough handling and seawater corrosion. Air-cooled radial engines were preferred because they were simpler than liquid-cooled types. Landing-gear had to be wide and rugged to withstand the shocks of repeated landings on a heaving deck. When arrester-wire landings were used, an aircraft's internal strength had to be re-inforced to withstand the immense and sudden shocks these gave to the whole fuselage structure. Slow landing speeds and short take-off capability were also priorities. Biplanes, with wires and struts, could easily be made to fold back for compact stowage. For this reason, the biplane, with its low wing loading, and the radial engine were still naval configurations after monoplanes were favoured for land-based operations.

When eventually monoplanes came into service their slow landing speed necessitated large stubby wings and excellent flaps. Folding-wing monoplanes required complex engineering, especially if the wheels were set wide apart, something the hazards of deck landings made important. Folded wings had to fit under low-roofed between-deck hangars. This sometimes entailed folding wingtips too. Retractable undercarriages brought additional problems to designers of wings and landing-gear.

These manifold problems caused the Germans, the Italians and the French to fall behind, so that by 1941 only Britain, America and Japan had an effective naval air arm. But the demands of the Pacific Ocean made Japanese and American carriers substantially different to British ones in design and purpose. The Americans and Japanese demanded big carriers holding large numbers of long-range aircraft designed solely as bombers, fighters or torpedo-carriers. Britain's Fleet Air Arm was equipped with multi-task aircraft, a requirement which often marred their design. Of the carriers with which Britain entered the war, only *Ark Royal* was purpose-built, and although her designers said she could carry 72 aircraft, in fact she never carried more than 54. Due partly to the hull structures, partly to Royal Navy prohibition on parking aircraft on deck, most British carriers held from 33 to 48 aircraft, according to aircraft size.[7]

The United States navy demanded capacious carriers with large long-range aircraft. The Essex class, with vulnerable wooden decks, were lighter than their British counterparts, but carried 109 aircraft. The 'strength deck' was under the hangars, which, with planes parked on the flight deck, were devoted mostly to repair and maintenance. The Japanese had a variety of carrier types, from the *Shoho* carrying only 20 aircraft to the *Akagi* carrying 91. The force of six carriers sent to Pearl Harbor together launched almost 400 aircraft.

Table 8 shows displacements in tons, launch dates, and speeds in knots of those Japanese carriers that delivered the attacking force at Pearl Harbor. Because specifications about aircraft space on carriers are notoriously incompatible with the number of planes actually carried, I have shown below the aircraft numbers known to have been carried operationally at some time or other. For the Pearl Harbor attack the Japanese crammed additional planes into the hangar spaces. The newest carriers, *Shokaku* and *Zuikaku* ('heaven-bound crane' and 'lucky crane'), were not ready for sea

Table 8   Japan's Pearl Harbor carrier attack force, 7 December 1941

		Displt. tonnage	Launch date	Speed (knots)	Planes
1st Carrier Div.	*Akagi*	26,900	1925	31	91
	Kaga	26,900	1921	28	63
2nd Carrier Div.	*Soryu*	10,050	1935	34	56
	Hiryu	10,050	1937	34	54
3rd Carrier Div.	*Zuikaku*	29,800	1939	34	63
	Shokaku	29,800	1939	34	63
For comparison	HMS *Ark Royal*	22,000	1938	31	72 (54)
	USS *Yorktown*	19,900	1938	29.5	100

duties until August and October 1941, so their aircraft attacked the Oahu airfields, while the more practised crews of the other carriers attacked the anchored American fleet.[8]

The Japanese carrier was, like so much of their weaponry, crude but effective. There were no deck officers, wielding bats, to help the pilots to land. They had to manage with a wisp of smoke to show the wind direction, and two rows of lights to show the deck. There were no catapults; the planes were light enough to become airborne as the ship steamed into wind. They had no radios with which to communicate from plane to plane, so when, over Pearl Harbor, Commander Mitsuo Fuchida, the leader of the first wave, saw one of his planes drop a bomb prematurely he closed formation and asked what had happened by writing the question on a board and holding it up for the other pilot to read. The bomber pilot wrote 'Fuselage hit' on the small board he carried and held that up for Fuchida to read. This was the standard way of communicating from plane to plane.[9]

The British techniques of carrier aviation had never taken the prospect of a Pacific war into account. In Europe Britain faced no enemy carriers; its attackers would all be land-based aircraft. The Royal Navy wanted aircraft as recce planes, anti-submarine forces and spotters for naval battleships. The attack on Taranto was flown by a small force at night, and assisted by radar. Such missions could be dispatched efficiently without rush. The daylight war in the Pacific was different. To fly fighter squadrons as air patrols, as well as flying off bombers quickly enough for them to get into formation, required very rapid work on the flight deck and many more aircraft. When war began the Japanese had the largest carrier-borne air force in the world. Additionally the Japanese navy had many squadrons trained and equipped solely to fly from shore-based airfields. These were used on inland targets in China while navy dive-bombers supported the army's front line. The Japanese army air force played only a minor role in the operations against China. Considered inferior, the army squadrons were for years used on transport duties and confined to the region along the Soviet border. Only when the strike southwards demanded more air power than the navy could supply was the army air service given an opportunity to fight on a larger scale. It provided air cover to the Malaya landings and sent into action its new monoplane fighter, the Nakajima Ki-43 'Oscar', which looked very like the navy's Zero and was almost as good.[10]

During its carrier operations in the summer of 1937 the imperial navy consistently operated 200 carrier-borne aircraft against Chinese coastal targets. The Chinese had fewer than half this number of planes, and the fast Japanese carriers were able to evade retaliation. But in the early fighting there were reverses. In fierce air battles over Nanking the navy's Nakajima A2N fighters proved so inferior that 50 were lost and the carrier *Kaga* was sent back to Japan to get the Mitsubishi A5M2 Type 96-2 'Claude' fighters as replacements.[11] As the fighting progressed the Japanese navy continued to improve and modify its equipment. It also made more and more use of land-based naval squadrons.

Carriers were regarded with special respect by the Japanese, and this is reflected in their names. While Japanese cruisers took the names of mountains and rivers, and battleships were named after ancient provinces (as the Americans named theirs after states), the carriers took their names from mythology.

As Yamamoto's plan to remove the US Pacific fleet from the chessboard gathered momentum, concern about whether the American battleships would be at anchor or at sea revealed a failure of strategic understanding. The destruction of the storage depots, replacement stores and repair shops at Pearl Harbor would deal a more crippling blow to America than the destruction of its battle-wagons. But all admirals are battleship admirals at heart, and Yamamoto was so determined upon sinking the American ships at anchor that a Japanese harbour at Kagoshima, chosen for its re-semblance to Pearl, was the site of repeated practice torpedo drops by the naval aviators.

In October, while torpedo-dropping experiments were proceeding, Lt-Com. Takeshi Naito arrived to lecture Genda's staff. He had been Japan's assistant air attaché in Berlin and had been to inspect the damage done at Taranto. Having made a close inspection of the damaged ships, and the depth of the water, Naito told his audience of naval officers that their problems were no greater than those the British crews had overcome at Taranto.

Shipborne radar

One wonders if Naito appreciated that the British naval aircrews had found their target by means of airborne radar. This had enabled them to strike under cover of darkness. The imperial fleet had no radar in operation or they too might have attacked by night.

In the early months of the war, good optical equipment and first-rate training enabled the imperial navy to equal the fighting performance of radar-equipped Allied ships. By the end of 1942 radar was being fitted to Japanese ships, but as time went on, improved radar and better training gave the US navy a marked advantage, especially through smoke or by night. Radar had a profound effect on the US navy's fast carrier task forces, enabling them to keep formation in any weather and in darkness. The Japanese needed combat air patrols constantly aloft to protect their ships, while American fighters were launched only when attackers approached. American naval forces were commanded from a 'combat information centre' into which everything was fed, while the Japanese failed to coordinate their elements with great precision. Under attack, American ships remained in close formation, concentrating their firepower, while the Japanese reaction was to scatter.

Although the United States armed forces suffered a good deal from rivalry and a lack of inter-service cooperation, this was as nothing compared to the deep hatred with which many senior officers of the Japanese army and navy regarded their counterparts. Completely separate attempts by the imperial army and navy to develop their own radar resulted in delays and failures for both services. It is an extraordinary fact that each service built its own merchant ships, and when the army even went to the extent of constructing its own submarine fleet, it rejected navy advice. The army's submarines were inferior, and such perversity resulted in duplication of effort, wasted materials and wasted manpower. With the Japanese army in control of conscription, not only was little done to keep skilled workers at the benches, the army took a perverse delight in drafting workers from plants devoted to navy contracts. In that spirit, 4,500 workers from the Kyushu Aircraft Company were taken into the army. There was a shortage of scientists and no central policy governing the distribution of vital materials. Oil from newly conquered territories was assigned to the army or the navy according to which service had contributed most to the conquest.

The prevailing spirit of the imperial navy was 'attack'. Thus the Pearl Harbor raid; thus the neglect of anti-submarine warfare and of radar. This attitude led to a chronic lack of oilers for the fleet and a shortage of small escorts to defend convoys. Tankers and freighters remained in short supply. No adequate construction programme had been started, despite the fact that 60 per cent of Japan's peacetime trade had been carried in foreign merchant ships. Shortage of materials hampered shipbuilding and so the situation became steadily worse. All of this eventually added up to a crisis of supply and reinforcement that cost Japan the war.

Admiral Yamamoto chose as his task force commander Admiral Chuichi Nagumo. It was not one of his best decisions. First and foremost, Nagumo was known as a torpedo expert, and involved with the use of that weapon from ships, not aircraft. He had no experience of commanding carrier forces and was far too concerned about their vulnerability compared to the strength of heavily armoured battleships. He departed for Pearl Harbor believing that his primary duty was to preserve his fleet. When, after the amazing success of the first strike against Pearl Harbor, his strike leader Commander Mitsuo Fuchida pleaded for a follow-up attack, Nagumo refused.

Nagumo was a deeply committed battleship admiral, and like others of his kind he did not abandon his dreams of another battle of the Tsushima Strait. They would still be pursuing the set-piece battle at Midway the following June when they lost Japan their carrier force, and even two years later at Leyte Gulf.

In November 1941 the Japanese armed forces committed their invasion forces and began the long-awaited thrust southwards. A conspicuous task force of 21 transports was sighted in the South China Sea; Singapore reported battleships and cruisers steaming past the southern tip of Indo-China. The Japanese did little to conceal this large amphibious force.

At the same time, in strict secrecy and keeping radio silence, battleships, carriers, cruisers, tankers and supply ships weighed anchor and slipped in twos and threes out of Japan's Inland Sea. Soon a great fleet was assembled at Hitokkapu Bay, standing off a desolate volcanic shore in the Kurile Islands, which string out like beads from northern Japan. The local fishing fleet was confined to port and the mail service suspended. On 26 November, Nagumo's Kido Butai or carrier striking force formed into columns and set sail eastwards, heading out, by a circuitous northern route, to Pearl Harbor.

Orders were laid down that if the force was observed it must turn back. With a fleet speed of 27 knots it had nothing to fear from the old American battlewagons of the Pacific fleet, which would have had difficulty maintaining a fleet speed of 19 knots. On 2 December the 'Climb Mount Niitaka' message meant that there would be no recall.

The world had plenty of evidence that some sort of Japanese offensive was imminent. For the first time, Zero fighters were seen landing at Saigon in French Indo-China. The number of Japanese aircraft based in South-East Asia rose suddenly from 74 to 245. Most significant of all, photo-reconnaissance planes were seen lazily ploughing the skies of Burma, Malaya and the Philippines. But no intelligence agency existed to co-ordinate such reports, which were lost amid the abundance of conflicting stories.

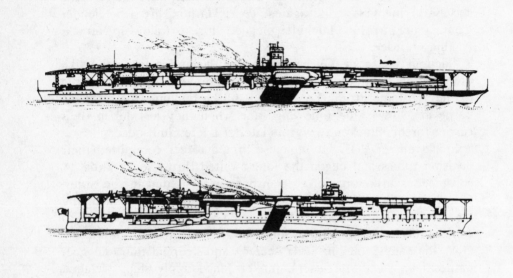

Figure 40: The Japanese aircraft carriers *Akagi* and *Kaga*

The imperial navy's carriers were not so easy to find. The American radio listening stations had heard nothing from them, but this was not unusual. In February, and again in July, the Japanese carriers had remained in home waters while other warships went to escort troop convoys to Indo-China. On those previous two occasions the anchored carriers had communicated with the shore stations by means of low-powered transmissions that had not been picked up by American monitoring stations anywhere. Both the Pacific fleet intelligence officer, Lieutenant-Commander Edwin Layton, and Commander John Rochefort, a Japanese-speaking cryptologist who was in charge of the monitoring and direction-finding units across the whole of the Pacific, believed the Japanese carriers were again anchored in home waters. But when Admiral

Kimmel asked exactly where the carriers were, Layton had to admit that he couldn't be sure.

'Do you mean to say that they could be rounding Diamond Head and you wouldn't know it?' Kimmel demanded.

Layton had to admit that it was true, but later that day a message from Naval Intelligence reassured him by providing what the Washington experts said were the carriers' exact locations: *Akagi* and *Kaga* were in southern Kyushu, while the rest were at the naval base at Kure.[12]

The Japanese army

Japan's army was hard and primitive. Its fighting quality arose almost entirely from tough individual soldiers who showed little reaction to pain, persecution and death, whether suffered by friends or enemies. The Japanese had no specialist divisions; no armoured, airborne or even cavalry divisions. Their tanks were second-rate and poorly deployed, but the artillery was good and well distributed. All the supporting arms, from supply to medical services, were minimal. Only the engineering services were the equal of a Western army.

Japanese skills were those of the infantry: infiltration, improvisation, camouflage and rapid movements on foot. Their jungle craft was learned in a training school on the island of Formosa which had been going since 1934. With horrifying logic the army school gave its trainees practical experience by systematically killing the people of primitive tribes in the interior. Ferocity and obedience made the Japanese formidable, said Field Marshal Slim, who had fought them in Burma.

The way in which Japanese soldiers in combat made do with little more than a handful of rice each day led to legends that the whole army was primitive, ill-fed and neglected. This was not true. In addition to such locally obtained foodstuffs as fish, chicken and vegetables, Japanese garrisons were supplied with tinned food, such as crabmeat, sliced beef and various vegetables. To accompany this there was canned seaweed and abundant rice together with Japanese beer and sake.[13]

The Japanese did not see their grandiose plan as an aggressive war to take over and subjugate the colonies of the European powers. They were going to establish a 'Co-Prosperity Sphere' and liberate the Asian peoples. This point of view appeared in official publications such as *The Way of the Subject* (*Shinmin no Michi*), distributed in August 1941 by the Education Ministry, which claimed that it was the European powers which for centuries had aimed at world domination, brutally suppressing the peoples in their colonies and imposing the evils of their materialistic values and their exploitation of the weak.

The Japanese military believed in indoctrination. Every officer and man embarking for the southern campaigns was given a 70-page booklet with a snappy title that one might have associated with Madison Avenue: *Read This and the War Is Won* (*Kore dake Yomeba Ware wa Kateru*). Its editor was a colonel who commanded an intelligence unit at the jungle warfare school in Formosa. Colonel Masanobu Tsuji was a rude and irritable man who supplied the army's secret police with reports on his superiors. As chief of operations to the commanding general, he was largely responsible for the excellent planning behind the invasion of Malaya. Tsuji said his booklet was designed to be read by men lying on their backs on hot, crowded ships. As well as practical advice about life in the tropics, the soldiers were told that the 6 million people of Malaya were ruled by a few thousand British, 60 million natives in the East Indies were ruled by 200,000 Dutchmen, and 350 million people in India were ruled by about half a million British. The Asians were squeezed to give the whites a life of luxury. White men – always with many personal slaves – lived in splendid houses on mountainsides from which they looked down on the thatched huts of the natives. The Japanese, linked by ties of blood and colour to the oppressed peoples of Asia, would lead these emasculated wretches to liberation. It was a holy task, worth dying for, and the reader was advised to write his last will and testament without delay.

It was stirring stuff, and not without a basis of truth. But how did it seem to those Japanese readers who for a decade had fought in China and seen their Chinese 'brothers' murdered, tortured and enslaved in ways that no European colony would ever tolerate? Indeed how did it sound to its editor, who saw his Formosan brothers murdered as part of the jungle school's infantry training programme?

30 ATTACK ON PEARL HARBOR

*I fired him because he wouldn't respect the authority of
the President. That's the answer to that. I didn't fire him because he
was a dumb son of a bitch, although he was, but that's not against the
law for generals. If it was, half to three-quarters of them would be in jail.*

Harry S. Truman on removing MacArthur from Korea[1]

THE DATE OF the attack on Pearl Harbor was not mere chance. In
a report to his Emperor, Admiral Nagano (chief of Naval
General Staff) explained: 'it will be to our advantage to choose Sunday, their day of rest, when a relatively large number of ships of the
US Fleet are in port in Pearl Harbor.'[2]

Nagano also told the Emperor: 'we consider that the most suitable
time will be about the twentieth day in the lunar cycle, at which time
there will be a moon from midnight till about dawn.' Looking
through the lunar calendar the Japanese planners found that Sunday
7 December 1941 was the nineteenth day of the lunar cycle and
decided that was near enough.

With the unprecedented six carriers of Admiral Nagumo's task
force there were two fast battleships, three cruisers, nine destroyers,
three submarines and eight tankers for refuelling en route. Daring
winter's rough seas and winter storms, they chose a northerly track
well clear of regularly used sea routes, circuiting areas known to be
patrolled by aircraft. Considering the season and the latitudes, the
weather was kind. Refuelling, which might have proved extremely
difficult in heavy seas and storms, was carried out in smooth waters
under fog banks that hid the fleet from sight. Even in the final
moments the weather aided them. When the first strike reached Pearl
Harbor, clouds divided at exactly the right moment, so that all concerned were convinced the gods had favoured the strike.

The Japanese expected that their ships would be found and
attacked. Yamamoto had briefed his men that they would probably
have to fight their way to the fleet's launch position. They were
amazed to find that the Americans were totally unprepared and their
attack unopposed.

Unlike the Western powers, Japan recognized the importance of intelligence. Their secret agents had provided them with excellent plans of the Pearl Harbor anchorages and a record of the coming and going of the battleships. The fact that the American fleet was usually in port over the weekends was a vital consideration in the planning. But nothing contributed to the Japanese success more than the lack of American long-range air reconnaissance. The excuse given at the subsequent investigations was that there were only 36 suitable planes, and so 360-degree searches would have been thin on the outer circumference. The US navy could have asked for army planes to help, but childish inter-service rivalry made this unlikely. In any case, it was generally agreed that an attack, if it came at all, would come from the north, and the prevailing wind supported this view, so the planes could have concentrated in that sector.

On 3 December the codebreakers read Tokyo's message to its Washington embassy instructing the code clerks to destroy all but one code machine and a set of codes. Under-Secretary of State Sumner Welles saw this intercept and said 'the chances had diminished from one in a thousand to one in a million that war could be avoided.' Roosevelt felt the same way. 'When do you think it will happen?' he asked the naval aide showing him the intercept. But Admiral Husband E. Kimmel, commander of the US Pacific fleet, did not interpret it as meaning war was imminent. The navy continued with its peacetime routines. Despite the torpedo-plane attack on Taranto, American admirals clung to the idea that all aerial torpedoes needed at least 100 feet depth of water in which to operate. Kimmel refused to permit the installation of anti-torpedo nets in the harbour, saying they would restrict boat movements.

The generals and the admirals seemed to be agreed on one thing only: no concession was to be made to the threat of war. On the day before the Japanese attack, Rear-Admiral Leary, inspecting the light cruiser *Phoenix*, wore white gloves in order to check for dust. Only after the inspection was complete were the crew permitted to go ashore for liberty, but so little practical preparation had been made that, when the attack began next morning, the locks had to be hacked off the ammunition lockers, and the awnings above the anti-aircraft guns torn down to provide a clear field of fire. Even then many of the anti-aircraft fuses proved defective and unexploded shells 'rained down on shore'.[3]

Officers who replaced peacetime routines with preparations for war were not popular. The executive officer, or second in command, of the *Indianapolis*, who went to 'modified conditions two' with guns ready and ammunition available at all times, heard complaints from his wife. She said: 'All the wives have been calling me, asking: "What's *Indianapolis* trying to do? Fight the war by itself?" Their husbands aren't coming home and they're upset.' When the attack came, and the executive officer was proved right, the captain said: 'In another week the crew would have thrown us overboard.'

Long ago in 1921 Army Air Corps General 'Billy' Mitchell had sent his bombers to attack some old warships in a series of demonstrations that proved that the bombing plane could sink a battleship. This did not please the powerful companies which made steel and constructed these mighty fleets, nor any of the battleship admirals who commanded the world's navies.[4] The sunken leviathans were explained away by those who argued that Mitchell had not kept to the restrictions placed upon him by those who were determined that his demonstration should fail. Despite some lessons taught in the first year of Europe's war, the destructive power of bombing aircraft was conveniently forgotten. Even in Japan, Yamamoto himself faced opposition to his plans to sink big battleships from the air.

The conspiracy theories

The misunderstandings and confusion leading up to the attack have attracted hundreds of fallacious theories. Roosevelt's domestic policies had produced bitter enemies who were ready to believe anything of him. Books and articles, some by high-ranking American eyewitnesses, abound. Many allege that President Roosevelt deliberately provoked and permitted the Pearl Harbor débâcle. Some have misrepresented and distorted accounts of the Japanese negotiations in support of their view that Roosevelt anticipated the Pearl Harbor attack.

Gordon W. Prange's 3,500-page result of 37 years' research into the Pearl Harbor attack, and its consequences, is the most complete account of the period.[5] It rightly dismisses all such allegations. How can anyone contend that the president would sacrifice his Pacific fleet – the most vital weapon in a coming war – to justify a declaration of war?

Some of the most bizarre theories implicate Churchill for conspiring to bring the United States into the war by permitting an attack at Pearl Harbor. One recent book declared that the British were reading the signals traffic from Nagumo's attack force and that

Churchill kept these intercepts from the Americans. In fact the Americans were adept at reading Japanese signals but Nagumo's task force was so determined upon maintaining radio silence that the operator's keys were physically removed from the radio shacks.

No one knew better than Winston Churchill how vulnerable were Britain's colonial possessions. For over two years Britain had been draining its Far Eastern defences to maintain the struggle against the German war machine. Only with the unstinting help of Roosevelt, and the support of the US navy in the Atlantic, had Britain survived 1941. Of all the things that Churchill wanted to avoid, a Japanese assault on Malaya and Burma (and the inevitable diversion of American resources to the Pacific) must have been at the top of his list.

Errors and short-sighted foolishness abound. Prange's history rejects the idea that specific blame should be attached to anyone.

> The stain of error permeates the entire American fabric of Pearl Harbor from the President down to the Fourteenth Naval District and the Hawaiian Department. There are no Pearl Harbor scapegoats.[6]

On the morning of the attack, Commander Mitsuo Fuchida, the officer Genda had selected to command the air strike, got up at 5 and was told at breakfast 'Honolulu sleeps'. Asked how he knew that, the officer told Fuchida that the Honolulu radio was playing soft music.

Having completed the final refuelling, Nagumo signalled Yamamoto's message to the men of his task force. Just as Admiral Togo in 1905 had modelled his signal closely upon Nelson's message to his fleet before Trafalgar, so Yamamoto now declared: 'The rise and fall of the Empire depends upon this battle. Every man will do his duty.'

The armada reached its attack position, 235 miles north of its target, at 6 o'clock on the morning of 7 December 1941. Vice-Admiral Nagumo was aboard the carrier *Akagi*. Flapping in the wind at its mast-head was the historic Z pennant that Admiral Togo had flown when inflicting his crushing defeat on the Russian fleet in 1905.

Two of Nagumo's carriers, *Shokaku* and *Zuikaku*, were very new, and their flying personnel were inexperienced. They were there in support only. The first to take off were the float planes Aichi E13A (Jakes). They flew ahead to make sure that the planned track of the strike force was clear of ships. Then all the carriers turned east, into the wind, and increased speed to 24 knots. Their decks were tilting to an angle of ten degrees. Fuchida said afterwards that in normal circumstances 'no plane would be permitted to take off in such weather . . . There were loud cheers as each plane took off into the air.'[7] The flagship and *Kaga*, *Soryu* and *Hiryu* launched their planes. Most of the flyers refused to wear parachutes, having decided that they would 'self-bomb' – make a suicide crash – if their planes were severely damaged.[8]

This first wave consisted of 183 planes. The first away from the decks were 43 of the A6M2 Zeros which climbed to form top cover for the launch. Then came 51 Aichi D3A4 (Val) dive-bombers, followed by 49 Nakajima B5N2 (Kate) bombers and lastly 40 of the same type fitted with the vitally important torpedoes. Two aircraft failed to get to Pearl that day. The engine of a Kate failed and a Zero crashed on take-off. All 181 planes were airborne in 15 minutes: in practice they had never done it in less than 20 minutes.

The plan dictated that if total surprise was achieved, the Kates would go in first, but if the strike went in against opposition, the dive-bombers would lead the attack. Commander Fuchida would make the appropriate signal at the time.

As he flew above the dense cloud, Fuchida could hear the American 'soft music' for himself, and used the commercial radio station KGMB Honolulu to home on his target. It was unusual for this station to be broadcasting at such an early hour, but the US Army Air Force[9] had paid the station to keep playing music all night so that some B-17 bombers, heading for Hawaii, could tune in their direction-finders and home on its transmission.[10] Some said this was poor security, for it told everyone that aircraft from the mainland were on the way to Hawaii.

At six-thirty that morning a US navy PBY flying boat spotted a Japanese midget submarine nearing the harbour defences, dropped depth charges and sank it. At 0645 hours US army radar operators picked up a blip from one of the Japanese seaplanes that had been sent to recce the track. The soldiers were in an SCR-270 Long-range Aircraft Detection Radar Unit at Opana, facing out across the water in the direction of the Japanese fleet. This contact was not considered significant, but a few minutes later the screen showed a large group of aircraft approaching.

On weekdays the radar crews normally worked all day, but on Sundays the crews finished at 7 in the morning and the radar was shut down. On this particular day the truck had not arrived

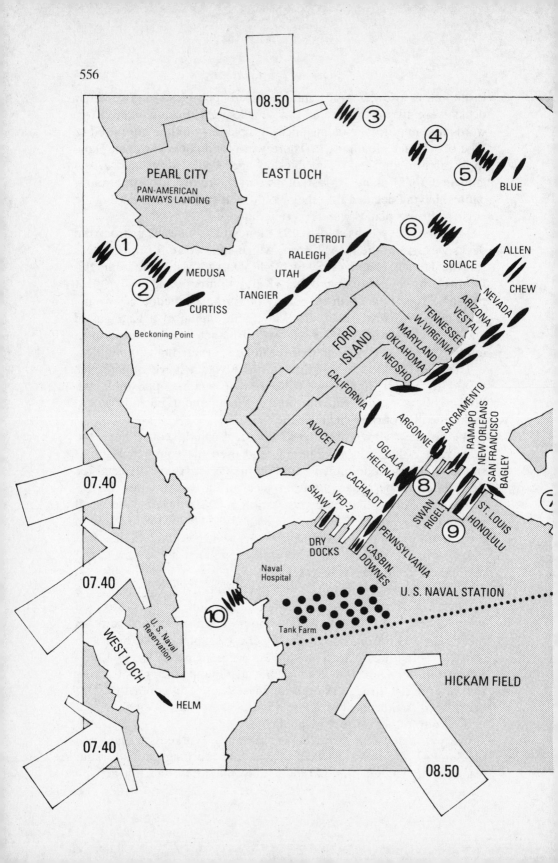

556

PEARL CITY
PAN-AMERICAN
AIRWAYS LANDING

EAST LOCH

08.50

③

④

⑤

BLUE

①

②

MEDUSA

CURTISS

DETROIT
RALEIGH
UTAH
TANGIER

⑥

ALLEN

SOLACE

CHEW

NEVADA

ARIZONA
VESTAL
TENNESSEE
W. VIRGINIA
MARYLAND
OKLAHOMA
NEOSHO

Beckoning Point

FORD
ISLAND

CALIFORNIA

AVOCET

ARGONNE

SACRAMENTO

RAMAPO
NEW ORLEANS
SAN FRANCISCO
BAGLEY

OGLALA
HELENA

CACHALOT

⑧

07.40

SHAW
VFD-2

DRY
DOCKS

CASBIN
DOWNES

PENNSYLVANIA

SWAN
RIGEL

ST. LOUIS
HONOLULU

⑨

⑦

07.40

Naval
Hospital

U. S. NAVAL STATION

07.40

⑩

U. S. Naval Reservation

WEST LOCH

Tank Farm

HICKAM FIELD

HELM

08.50

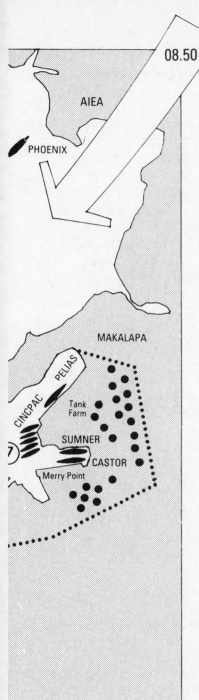

The Japanese Assault on Pearl Harbor

07.40 Attack   30 mins duration
   40 Torpedo Bombers
   49 High Level Bombers
   51 Dive Bombers
   43 Fighters
    9 Shot down

08.50 Attack   65 mins duration
   54 High Level Bombers
   78 Dive Bombers
   35 Fighters
   20 Shot down

1-10 KEY TO MAP OF PEARL HARBOR
(Reading NW to SE in nests of ships)

1 Destroyer-minecraft RAMSAY, GAMBLE, MONTGOMERY
2 Destroyer-minecraft TREVER, BREESE, ZANE, PERRY, WASMUTH
3 Destroyers MONAGHAN, FARRAGUT, DALE, AYLWIN
4 Destroyers HENLEY, PATTERSON, RALPH TALBOT
5 Destroyers SELFRIDGE, CASE, TUCKER, REID, CONYNGHAM tender WHITNEY
6 Destroyers PHELPS, MACDONOUGH, WORDEN, DEWEY, HULL; tender DOBBIN
7 Submarines NARWHAL, DOLPHIN, TAUTOG; SEAPLANE tenders THORNTON, HULBERT
8 Destroyers JARVIS, MUGFORD, (inside ARGONNE and SACRAMENTO)
9 Destoyers CUMMINGS; destroyer-minelayers PREBLE, TRACY, PRUITT, SICARD; destroyer SCHLEY; minesweeper GREBE
10 Minesweepers BOBOLINK, VIREO, TURKEY, RAIL, TERN

Other ships not shown, were moored up West Loch. There were also several tugs and utility craft, not shown, in the area of the map.

to take them to breakfast. The operator, Joseph Lockard, said:

> At 7:02, Elliot had just sat down at the screen and said, 'What's this?' I said, 'Well, let me see.' There was this thing on the screen. It was the largest blip I'd ever seen!
>
> When we first picked them up, they were about 155 miles away, I believe. I'm not sure of these numbers anymore but I know they were directly north of us ... At first we thought something was wrong with the equipment, so we ran through a series of tests ... There was nothing electronically wrong that we could see, so we started plotting the blip. We did that for a while, then decided we'd call to see if there was anybody down there on the phone. [The telephone operator went to find someone to talk to them and brought Lt Kermit Tyler to the phone.] He came back and said, 'It's okay, it's okay.' They were expecting a flight of B-17s from the States, but if the B-17s were that far off course they'd never make it.
>
> We continued to track it, and called them back again. This time we got Lt Tyler on the phone with us. He still said, 'Don't worry about it.'
>
> We tracked it within 20 some miles of the island and the reason we stopped then was that we lost it on the screen because of the mountain range behind us. The reflection wiped out the signal as they got closer to us.[11]

At 0740 hours Fuchida, flying along the coast of Oahu, fired a flare. This told the bombers to peel off for their bombing runs on Haleiwa Field, Schofield Barracks and Wheeler Field. However, the fighter element did not see the flare, so Fuchida was forced to fire a second. Two flares were the signal that showed the defences had not been taken by surprise.[12] So the alternative plan was put into operation. Instead of the torpedo-bombers going in first, the attack became a free-for-all.

At Hickham Field a 550-lb bomb hit the barracks, exploded in the dining-room, and killed men at breakfast. Unopposed, the Japanese pilots flew in very low. Some of the planes with fixed landing gear ripped away the telegraph and utility wires. Afterwards men on the ground had vivid memories of the faces of the pilots peering down at them, so low were the planes flying. The Japanese attack on Hickham Field coincided with the arrival of the B-17 bombers, and some were shot up as they landed. Others diverted to Bellows Field only to meet more Japanese fighters. The bombers could not fight back: their machine-guns were packed in grease and stored away. Aircraft parked on the airfield made easy targets. By order of the army commander the American planes had been positioned very close together – to prevent sabotage, he explained.

Through a pair of binoculars, Fuchida inspected the harbour below and saw the battleships packed closely together at Ford Island. At 0749 hours he sent the prearranged signal to notify the fleet that the raid had started. History records this as being a battle-cry of Tora! Tora! Tora! (Tiger! Tiger! Tiger!)

In fact the aircraft radios were crude. Signalling was carried out not by speaking over a radio-telephone but by tapping a Morse key. Lt-Comdr Tadakazu Yoshioka of the *Akagi* had arranged all the signals procedure, and he chose two Morse signals that were completely different, and so easy to distinguish. He told Fuchida to order the attack by sending dot dot dash dot dot (to), and to follow this with dot dot dot (ra) if the enemy was surprised. To ensure clarity each signal would be sent three times. Yoshioka said it was never his intention that to-ra would be made into Tora, which is tiger in Japanese. In any case, it was Fuchida's radio operator who tapped out the signals.

Pearl Harbor, on the southern coast of Oahu, is an intricately shaped inlet that forms a perfect closed harbour. In the middle of the open water stands Ford Island, and around it there were arranged many anchorages, including a line of double-banked big ships known as 'Battleship Row'.

At 8 o'clock each morning the colours were hoisted on the moored battleships. On the *Nevada*, the band was playing 'The Stars and Stripes' as the Japanese bombers came in to attack. So deeply engrained was the 'it can't happen here' feeling that most of the American sailors wouldn't believe their eyes and ears. Many of the men could hear nothing but the music. A coxswain aboard *Arizona* said:

> But then the bombs were dropping and you could hear them ex-ploding and bang! – one of them hit the bow of the ship. I told somebody with me, 'Boy, somebody's going to catch hell now. They hit the ship.' I still thought it was practice, but it was awful heavy for practice because it jarred that battleship.[13]

Another of the *Arizona's* crew, Don Stratton, seaman first class, gave his account in a special edition of *Life* magazine 50 years after the event:

We took a hit on the starboard side, and it went right into the magazines and aviation gasoline. There was a terrific explosion, and a fireball went into the air 400 feet or more. Of the 50 or 60 men manning the station where I was, I think only about six of us survived. I was burned over sixty per cent of my body. The *Vestal*, a repair ship that was tied up alongside us, threw us a line and we went across hand over hand, 45 feet in the air.[14]

To breach the heavy steel battleships the Japanese used 16-inch shells which had been converted into (1,760-lb) armour-piercing bombs. One of these hit the deck of the *Arizona* near No. 2 turret and penetrated to the magazine where over a million pounds of explosive was stored. It caused a gigantic explosion which lifted the whole ship about 20 feet out of the water and broke it in two. She sank quickly in 40 feet of water.

Admiral Kimmel was still pulling on his white uniform as he rushed out on to the lawn of his house, from which he could see battleship row. His next-door neighbour (the wife of Captain John Earle, his chief of staff) said Kimmel's face was as white as his jacket. Kimmel recalled: 'The sky was full of the enemy.' He saw the *Arizona* 'lift out of the water, then sink back down – way down.'

Mrs Earle said: 'Looks like they've got the *Oklahoma*.'

'Yes, I can see they have,' said Kimmel.

Providing that attacking aircraft approached very low to make the drop, the wooden stabilizers fitted to the Japanese torpedoes ensured that they would descend only 35 feet, and come quickly to running depth without sticking into the muddy bottom. (In May 1991 dredging brought one of these torpedoes to the surface. The tail section with its modified stabilizers is on display at the *Arizona* Memorial.)

A sailor on the quarterdeck of the *West Virginia* saw the dive-bombers coming. He was so sure that it was an army exercise that he went to the other side to watch the torpedoes drop.

We saw three planes come in, about fifteen feet off the water. They dropped torpedoes. My friend tapped me on the shoulder and said, 'Now all you're going to hear is a little thud when it hits the ship.' The next thing I remember was a hellacious loud noise, and a wall of water that looked like a 50-foot wave came across the deck and washed us both to the other side of the ship. Six more torpedoes hit us. A bomb came down and hit the *Tennessee*. A large piece of shrapnel took out most of the captain's stomach. We started carrying him down, and he was still giving orders until he died.[15]

Oklahoma was struck by seven torpedoes. The first hit on her was scored by Lt (junior grade) Jinichi Goto, who says he flew about 60 feet above the water. 'The anti-aircraft fire was heavy,' he remembered on the fiftieth anniversary of the attack. As he saw the waterspout rise from the explosion, he had shouted 'Atarimashita! – It struck!'

Oil from *California's* tanks caught fire and sent black smoke billowing across the harbour. *Oklahoma* rolled over and sank. One of the sailors aboard her, George DeLong, was in the after-steering compartment, three levels below the main deck, a tomb-like place avoided even in normal conditions by those likely to suffer from claustrophobia. DeLong was woken by a call to action stations and then heard 'Set water-tight conditions!' and the compartment was closed from the other side and dogged tight, sealing DeLong and his seven fellow sailors inside.

Almost immediately the torpedoes struck and the huge battleship started to turn over. 'Furniture and equipment in the compartment began crashing around the deck.' The lights went out and the ship kept rolling. 'I realized my head was where my feet had been. By the time the ship settled down and we let go of the things we were holding on to, we knew that the ship had turned over.'

Now water began pouring through the ventilation system. They used everything they could find to stuff into the vents, but still the compartment kept filling with water. When it was up to their waists, they started striking the bulkhead with a wrench, tapping out SOS in Morse code. Eventually DeLong was rescued when a hole was cut through the hull with pneumatic drills. He was 19 years old, and would live to remember it 50 years later.[16] Most of his shipmates were killed.

By 8.25 six of the battleships were sunk, sinking or very badly damaged. The first air assault had lasted about 30 minutes. The second major attack consisted of 167 aircraft and arrived at 8.40. It began with level bombers, continued with dive-bombers, and then came the fighters. By now more American guns were in action and they shot down three of them as they came in.

One young Naval Reserve ensign taking messages to the Cincpac (Commander-in-Chief Pacific) that morning remembered it vividly:

That fateful morning I was in and out of Admiral Husband Kim-

mel's office many times. He was a lean middle-aged man with a
fiery temper. He wasn't at all like the actors playing his part in
later movies. Far from being very cool and collected, the real
Admiral Kimmel was cursing and ranting and raving whenever
he read all the dreadful messages I brought him about battleships blowing up and sinking, the planes and hangars at Ford
Island being demolished, and the Army's Schofield Barracks
being bombed and strafed. He was red-faced and flustered. I
didn't blame him and I didn't resent his anger at my many
appearances with nothing but bad news.[17]

Kimmel had every reason for his bad temper. He had been promoted over the heads of other contenders for his post after the
previous C-in-C had protested at the fleet's move from San Diego to
Pearl Harbor. Now Kimmel guessed that anger would focus upon
him – along with the local US army commander – and that he would
be relieved of his command.

The Japanese action at Pearl Harbor had taken place while the
US carriers were away. The *Saratoga* had been assigned to California for routine repairs and upkeep. *Enterprise*, which had been
transporting aircraft to the Marine base at Wake Island, was due to
anchor 30 minutes before the attack, but was delayed by refuelling
procedures. Flying ahead of their carrier to Ford Island, her SBD-2
Dauntless planes encountered the first wave of Japanese attackers.
The navy flyers thought the aircraft they saw over Ewa Field – a US
Marine Corps base – were army planes, but then they encountered
anti-aircraft fire and came under attack by Japanese fighters. Still
they didn't believe that war had started. Over the radio Ensign
Manuel Gonzalez was heard to say: 'Please don't shoot. This is six
baker three. This is an American plane,' before being shot down by
a Zero. Five of the sixteen Dauntless planes were lost. Some were
shot down by Japanese fighters, some by American anti-aircraft
fire. *Enterprise* turned west and did not come back until nightfall.
Even then the sky was not safe for any flyers. Said a pharmacist
mate at the Naval Hospital:

At about dusk we saw four planes flying low, coming up the
channel toward the harbor. Almost every anti-aircraft gun in
the Navy Yard started firing at them. The sad part is, they
turned out to be US Navy planes from the carrier *Enterprise*.
Three were shot down, and the fourth pilot was brought into the
hospital wounded. We had a bed capacity of about 300 people.

At midnight that night we had 960 patients. And we had 313 dead, stacked outside like cordwood.[18]

It was vital to Japanese plans that no American aircraft survived to follow the attackers back to their carriers and locate the Japanese fleet. So airfields were a priority target and, of the first wave, more aircraft were assigned to strike at airfields than to attack ships. At 9 o'clock that morning another wave of Japanese aircraft arrived. They were assigned to specific targets with particular emphasis on airfields.

The last of the Japanese aircraft had departed by about 9.45 am. On the airfields 188 American planes were destroyed and 159 damaged. Fuchida lingered over the target as long as possible to observe the effects of the strikes. On his way back he found two lost Zeros which followed him home. During the attack the Japanese fleet had sailed 40 miles nearer to Pearl Harbor in order to help any Japanese pilots low on fuel.

As Fuchida landed he could see planes on the deck armed and fuelled ready for take-off. While the task force remained in the same area, to provide a chance for more damaged planes to find them, an exchange of views took place on the bridge of the *Akagi*. Fuchida was not the only advocate of a third strike. The men of the carriers *Hiryu* and *Soryu* were eager to go back. The captain of the *Kaga* specifically asked for an attack on the installations which his pilots told him were so far undamaged. On the other hand, the deck crews could not help noticing how much more battle-damage had been inflicted upon the later strike. The American gunners were awake and the guns were ready. Another strike would not escape retribution.

There was also the possibility that the American carriers would suddenly pounce upon them. This alone seemed reason enough for moving away, although in fact the remaining American warships would have been in grave danger from such a mighty Japanese fleet. The ever-cautious Nagumo decided that enough had been done. As he sailed away his ships kept radio silence. Two Japanese bombers, calling up for directions, went unanswered.

The Japanese airmen did not get away completely unchallenged in the air. With poor scores at gunnery, the Army's 47th Pursuit Squadron (5th Fighter Group) had been exiled to Haleiwa on the north-west coast of Oahu for extra practice. Two of these army pilots managed to get their P-40B fighters into the air. They had been to the Saturday night dance at Schofield Barracks and then to a poker game that went on very late. The best story goes that they took off attired in their tuxedos but, alas, recent research says they had gone to bed and were asleep when the attack began.[19] Without permission or even pre-flight checks, the two lieutenants took to the air and headed towards the Marine airfield at Ewa where the air activity was most evident. Between them, Kenneth Taylor and George Welch shot down four Kates. Welch later added a Val and a Zero to his kills. No one can be sure which of the two men scored America's first air victory. Taylor said: 'George and I agreed we would never know which one got the first – so we agreed that the survivor could claim that honor.' Both flyers survived and both received medals, but a request for a Medal of Honor for Welch was refused because he had taken off without orders!

One of the Dauntless pilots from the *Enterprise* looked down while descending beneath his parachute. He could see the *Nevada*, which had got up steam and started moving slowly away from 'battleship row'. 'Anywhere you looked her guns were going,' he said. Even after another bomb hit the deck with a 'tremendous ear-splitting explosion' the gunners kept up their barrage. 'Some were killed, more were hurt; but only one gun had stopped firing.'[20]

The American gunners put up a spirited defence. Lt (senior grade) Zenji Abe, one of the Japanese flyers:

> When I reached the air over Kaneohe Bay, I watched the anti-aircraft fire over the clouds. I was surprised at how quick American anti-aircraft had responded. So quick, so prompt. The electricity danced on my back. Over Pearl Harbor there was black smoke. And big fires. I concentrated my mind. I tried to find my target. I chose a big ship. That was the *Arizona*, I found out later.[21]

The American army radar at Opana had been switched on again at 9 o'clock. This was in time for the operators to watch the Japanese aircraft flying back to their carriers. But no one asked the radar men what they knew, so the six B-17s that took off at 11.40 in search of the Japanese fleet headed southwards and found nothing.

Now that only twenty-five PBYs and a dozen B-17s remained intact, the commanders found it *was* possible to fly reconnaissance patrols. Soon the flying boats were ranging out 700 miles in every direction. The Flying Fortress bombers were put on 30-minute readiness.

Meanwhile a desperate fight was being waged to rescue men trapped inside the great steel hulls. One 16-year-old apprentice shipyard worker said:

> 'The following morning, I went with my tools to the *West Virginia*. It had turned turtle, totally upside down. We found a number of men inside . . . We spent about a month cutting the superstructure of the *West Virginia*, tilting it back on its hull. About three hundred men we cut out of there were still alive by the eighteenth day.' Asked how the men survived, Garcia replied, 'I don't know. We were too busy to ask.'[22]

In a superb demonstration of naval engineering skill the battleships were salvaged. Before the war ended all but three of them were restored and back in service. But with torches cutting into the steel of the shattered warships the US government did not feel that the American public was ready to hear the whole truth about what had happened at Pearl Harbor.

The secretary of the navy, Colonel Frank Knox, returned to New York from Hawaii with cheering news. At a Press conference he told correspondents that one battleship, *Arizona*, had been lost and another, *Oklahoma*, had capsized but would be righted. He assured them that the entire balance of the American Pacific fleet 'with its aircraft-carriers, heavy cruisers, light cruisers, destroyers and submarines is uninjured and is all at sea seeking contact with the enemy.'

Noticing the absence of battleships in this list of units seeking contact with the enemy, one correspondent asked if battleships were with it. Knox said they were. In London the *Times* newspaper reported the Knox statement and remarked that: 'The full disclosure of losses made by the Secretary of the Navy has had a wholly steadying effect. Americans are no more afraid of truth than Britons . . . It is only tyrants who must keep their people in the dark.'

Extraordinary luck had been with the Japanese in every aspect of their assault. Until then few people had realized that the aircraft-carrier was the navy's decisive weapon. The ultimate irony of Pearl Harbor was that in proving the carrier so important, the Japanese proved that their attack had failed. The American carriers had escaped at the beginning of a war in which the carrier would play the star role. The ancient battleships that settled into the shallow waters of the anchorage were expendable. In fact their loss helped the American admirals to accept the dominant role of fast carrier task forces.

And fortunately for the Allies the American carriers were fine ships, the newest of them as good as anything afloat. The sister ships *Yorktown* and *Enterprise* were built with great attention to detail and of the finest materials. They were, said one expert, 'the Cadillacs of aircraft carriers . . . Fast, 33 knots, manoeuvrable, stable, and capable of carrying and operating a large air group, the carriers of the *Yorktown* class had good internal subdivision to control flooding and good armour protection at the hangar deck level and above machinery spaces.'[23]

At Pearl Harbor there remained 4.5 million tons of fuel oil in the storage tanks, untouched by the attack. Intact too were the dry docks, stores containing every kind of spare part the fleet needed, and the machine shops where precision parts could be made. This was not a matter of luck: none of these were on the Japanese target list. Neither was the US submarine base at Quarry Point.

The submarines

In 1930 the imperial navy's general staff planners recorded their opinion that Americans were too soft to endure the physical rigours and mental stress of long-range submarine operations. As a result they neglected anti-submarine warfare, an error that was to prove fatal. Always short of shipping space, the Japanese were to have the life strangled out of them by the US submarine force, just as the British almost succumbed to the U-boats in the Atlantic. Later in the war, one of the most noted American submariners, a Medal of Honor winner, said:

> we learned we were going to join one of the first wolf packs in the Pacific. We were adopting the successful procedures of the German wolf packs in the Atlantic . . . More and more attacks were made on the surface at night.[24]

The vastness of the Pacific, and the way in which the Japanese fought to the death, produced a comparably ruthless attitude to men drowning in the ocean. He added:

> There was nothing more we could do there, so we continued on our way. Actually we had no place for them on board. If we had to try and keep them under surveillance in a submarine during

the patrol, it would have been a difficult problem.

Although the Japanese navy underrated the American submarine threat they regarded their own submarine service very highly. Time and money was spent on such amazing submarines as the 6,500-ton STo class. Submarines which carried aircraft were also widely used. Many Japanese admirals believed that it would be their submarine service, rather than the naval air arm, that would distinguish itself in the Pearl Harbor attack. In all 28 submarines and five midgets took part, but achieved no success whatever.

Wrongly classified as a part of the fleet, and continually sent against enemy warships, the Japanese submarine service suffered from the same 'attack' obsession that marred so much of Japanese planning. Submariners consistently found themselves opposed to the strongest elements of the US navy. The submarine's war-winning capability came from its use against the weak: torpedoing freighters and tankers.

31 THE CO-PROSPERITY SPHERE

Great Britain provided time; the United States provided money and Soviet Russia provided blood.

Josef Stalin[1]

M ORE THAN 60 per cent of the injuries sustained during the Pearl Harbor attack were burns. Gun crews had rushed into action in shorts or in pyjamas instead of donning protective gear. A great number of these burns would have proved fatal except for one lucky fact. In June 1940 a New York doctor[2] organized a voluntary blood transfusion programme to aid Britain and France. Money was donated to start the campaign and none of the doctors, nurses, workers or the eighteen thousand regular donors were paid salaries or fees. Out of this campaign came new methods of separating, freezing, drying and storing blood plasma. As a result 750 flasks of plasma powder had arrived in Hawaii just six weeks before the attack and were ready for immediate use with the casualties. To keep the supply going, the mayor of Honolulu announced next day that traffic fines could be paid in donated blood.

Many Pearl Harbor casualties were treated with the US army's new Standard Dry Plasma package, an ingenious contraption comprising two sealed bottles, one of dry plasma and the other of 300 cc of sterile water. By means of pull-top devices the two were mixed and made ready, and the transfusions were calculated on a simple chart compiled by a London doctor who had used it when treating air-raid victims.[3]

The Philippines

With fog over their airfields in Formosa, the twin-engined Japanese naval bombers and their escorts of Zeros were late in setting course for the Philippine Islands. These land-based Mitsubishi G4 'Bettys' and their earlier version, G3 'Nells', had been a part of the plan that

Yamamoto had contrived back in the 1930s to offset the limitations on Japanese carrier construction brought about by international naval treaty.

One formation of 54 Nells with 50 Zeros as escort was heading for the American planes at Iba air base, and a similar formation was destined for Clark Field. It was 9.30 in the morning on 8 December 1941 local time, and over six hours since the devastating attack on Pearl Harbor.

The Philippines was an American colony in everything but name. Its chief military adviser, and de facto military commander, was Douglas MacArthur. He had been the US army chief of staff until, in 1935, it was discovered that he kept a Eurasian mistress, whereupon he had been asked to resign by President Roosevelt.[4] MacArthur left the army and went to the Philippines, where he had lived when his father was its military governor. He concerned himself with the training of the Philippines army, of which he was made a field marshal, and then in January 1941, with Japan becoming more and more belligerent, his US army commission had been restored to him. Made a major-general, he was appointed commander of US forces in the Far East.

A Press conference in Washington as recently as 15 November had told Americans they had at the ready 'the greatest concentration of heavy bomber strength anywhere in the world'. It could set Japan's 'paper cities' afire, promised the army's chief of staff, and make the Philippines independent of sea power. If this boast was intended as bluff it did not work.

This morning, in the full knowledge of the Pearl Harbor attack, MacArthur abandoned the dynamic image portrayed in his memoirs and froze. The weather delay suffered by the attacking Japanese air formations had provided an opportunity for his Flying Fortress bombers to attack Japanese air bases in Formosa and Indo-China. His planes were fuelled and ready, but he refused to order them into the air. Despite the warnings from the European war, that aircraft parked on the ground would be destroyed if not camouflaged and dispersed, on 8 December MacArthur's planes were still lined up wingtip to wingtip as the Japanese formations came to bomb them. The historian S.E. Morison[5] said:

> If surprise at Pearl Harbor is hard to understand, surprise at Manila is completely incomprehensible. Some eight or nine hours after General MacArthur was informed of the attack on

Pearl Harbor, his planes were caught grounded, and his air force as badly destroyed as that of the army at Pearl Harbor.

The attacking planes had come from Formosa, a round-trip of 1,125 miles, and fighter planes were included in the attacking force. With their drop-tanks, the Zeros had a range of 1,930 miles. The Americans remained convinced that a carrier force was nearby. This ruse was repeated time and time again, and whenever Zeros were identified in the attacking force the Americans began searching for a Japanese fleet.

America's 'Asiatic fleet' at Manila – a relatively light naval force previously based in Shanghai – was also effectively hit. The Americans seemed dazed by this assault. Within a couple of days, bombers, reconnaissance planes and large warships were withdrawn from the Philippines and neighbouring waters.

The Japanese invasion of the Philippines was not long in coming. On 8 December the first of the carefully planned Japanese landings began with the capture of Batan,[6] one of the offshore islands. From here the Japanese soon had fighter aircraft operating.

MacArthur, who persisted in believing that many of the Japanese planes were manned by 'white' pilots, was somewhat premature in his messages to Washington, and to the world in general.[7] When his headquarters said that the Japanese had landed at Lingayen Gulf and been repulsed, their landing ships sunk and the beaches there strewn with Japanese corpses, Carl Mydans, a photographer from *Life* magazine, went to take pictures. He discovered that so far no invasion had taken place.

Despite his loss of the air force, MacArthur's handling of the defence of the Philippines has been described as 'one of the greatest in military history', although his timing is widely seen as faulty. Administration was not MacArthur's strong card. During the Japanese advance, while his men were on half-rations and ill-supplied, he lost to the enemy 4,500 tons of rice, 500,000 rounds of artillery ammunition and 3,400,000 gallons of oil and gasoline plus food, clothing and drugs. This hastened their inevitable surrender.

Not that surrender came so very quickly. MacArthur withdrew and, uniting what forces he could muster, he took them into tropical jungle of the most hostile sort. On the peninsula of Bataan his men laced the rivers and the deep green gorges with barbed-wire and mines to form a bastion the Japanese found challenging. Plagued by dysentery, beri-beri, malaria, hookworm and countless other local hazards, this motley force of 65,000 Filipinos and 15,000 Americans held on with a tenacity that put to shame those who had too readily bowed to the first assaults of the emperor's soldiers.

MacArthur remained in a deep shelter on Bataan's offshore island, Corregidor. His supporters claimed he needed to be in this communications centre to stay in contact with Washington. His detractors were unconvinced, and he was widely called 'Dug-out Doug'. It might have been better if MacArthur had been out of touch with Washington, for he was told nothing but extravagant stories about the help that was on its way, and he repeated these assurances loudly and with melodramatic measure: 'I give to the people of the Philippines my solemn pledge that their freedom will be retained.'

Despite such unfulfilled promises, MacArthur did not go unrewarded. On 17 December he was given his fourth star and the Medal of Honor, normally awarded only for bravery under fire. On 28 December he phoned Jorge Vargas – who had been left to deal with the Japanese invaders – to inquire about his expense account and ask that the $35,000 he was owed should be invested in blue-chip stock. Vargas later calculated that this phone call made Mac-Arthur a millionaire by war's end. On 3 January President Quezon of the Philippines gave MacArthur half a million US dollars from the national treasury together with payments totalling $140,000 US dollars for other American advisers to the Philippines army.[8]

MacArthur's solemn pledges of reinforcement made the final tragedy all the harder to bear. Yet, by the time of the surrender in April 1942, the defenders had shown that the Japanese were not supermen. 'The battling bastards of Bataan' became a legend. The story of the 'death march' they were forced to make to camps in northern Luzon, costing thousands of lives, was amongst the first accounts to reach America of the violent and inhuman treatment meted out by the Japanese to their captives. It appalled the world and united Americans in fury. The writer William Manchester, a Marine veteran who returned to the Pacific in the 1980s, wrote:

> They fought on with a devotion which would puzzle the generation of the 1980s. More surprising, in many instances it would have baffled the men they themselves were before Pearl Harbor. Among MacArthur's ardent infantrymen were cooks, mechanics, pilots whose planes had been shot down, seamen whose ships had been sunk, and some civilian volunteers. One

civilian was a saddle-shoed American youth, a typical Joe College of that era who had been in the Philippines researching an anthropology paper. A few months earlier he had been an isolationist whose only musical interest was Swing. He had used an accordion to render tunes like 'Deep Purple' and 'Moonlight Cocktail'. Captured and sentenced to be shot, he made a last request. He wanted to die holding his accordion. This was granted, and he went to the wall playing 'God Bless America.' It was that kind of time.[9]

Before Bataan fell MacArthur had been flown out to Australia. A heartfelt poem written in a Japanese prison camp spoke for many:

Let him go, let him go, we are the braver,
Stain his hands with our blood, dye them forever.
Recall, oh ye kinsmen, how he left us to die,
Starved and insulted by his infamous lie;
How he seduced us with boasts of defense;
How he traduced us with plans of offense.[10]

But at this traumatic time, America's need was for a hero. The Press and radio, aided by MacArthur's truly astonishing publicity department, answered the call. Of 142 communiqués issued at this time, 109 identified only one person by name: General Douglas MacArthur. Fighting units were identified simply as 'MacArthur's men'. His enemies called him a megalomaniac, while some military experts such as B. H. Liddell Hart said he was the most brilliant Allied general of the war. When asked about his old boss, the mild-mannered General Eisenhower was moved to say: 'Oh, yes, I studied dramatics under him for twelve years.'

As he left the Philippines, MacArthur said 'I shall return' and along with other memorable lines of the Pearl Harbor attack, such as 'Praise the Lord and pass the ammunition', it became a national catchphrase.[11] Some grammarians asked why not: 'I will return'[12] pointing out that used after I, 'will' provides 'determination, intention, a promise, an assurance' while 'shall' indicates only future time. Many of MacArthur's fighting men would have preferred 'We will return', remembering that Churchill in June 1940 had said 'We shall fight on the beaches, we shall fight on the landing grounds . . .' Perhaps the Marine Corps spoke for many when later they sang: 'By the grace of God, and a few Marines, MacArthur returned to the Philippines.'

The armada sailing southwards

Malaya was the first to be attacked. The British had been expecting it ever since the troop convoys were first spotted off Indo-China. It is by no means certain that the imperial navy's planners assembled their troop convoys in Cam Ranh Bay in order to divert the world's attention away from Admiral Nagumo's Kido Butai as it ploughed its way towards what the Japanese always called the 'Hawaiian Operation'. In fact the commander of the troop convoys went to a great deal of trouble to remain unseen, even sailing by a circuitous route in order to suggest that his true destination was the coast of Thailand.

It was Admiral Thomas C. Hart, C-in-C of the Asiatic fleet and now the senior United States naval officer in the Philippines, who first tried to discover the facts. On his own initiative, he sent a PBY Catalina[13] flying boat to see what they were doing off the Indo-China coast. He briefed the aircrews personally. 'Try to do it without being seen, and don't bring on a war,' he told them.

It was not so easy to see what was happening without starting a war. On 2 December one of the flying boat crews saw 20 transports and warships in the bay. The next day 30 ships were assembled there, and on 4 December the bay was empty. The search was hampered by the weather, which was stormy and overcast, so that the airmen could find no sign of the convoy anywhere until, on the afternoon of 6 December, a Lockheed Hudson of the Royal Australian Air Force, flying out of Kota Bharu in Malaya, spotted the Japanese ships. Another British plane, a PBY Catalina of 205 Squadron RAF, ventured too close and was shot down by a Nakajima Ki-27, a monoplane with fixed landing gear, from one of the army fighter squadrons that were supporting the invasion fleet. It was the first aerial victory of the Pacific war, although the British knew only that their flying boat failed to return to base.

By this time Japanese intentions were becoming obvious even to those who didn't have reconnaissance aircraft at their disposal. On 6 December the *Malaya Tribune* was running a headline: '27 Japanese Transports Sighted Off Cambodia Point'. The British continued to exchange sighting reports with the American command centre in Manila in the Philippines.

The Royal Navy's Vice-Admiral Sir Tom Phillips had arrived in Singapore on 3 December with his ships, the *Prince of Wales* and HMS *Repulse*. He was 53 years old, five feet two inches tall, and seemed remarkably confident. From Singapore, he flew to Manila to talk to MacArthur about the overall situation. As more sightings came in Admiral Hart told Phillips about them and asked him when he was going back to Singapore.

'I'm taking off tomorrow morning,' said Phillips.

'If you want to be there when the war starts, I suggest you take off right now,' Hart told him.

The Japanese convoy sailed onwards, joined by ships from other ports of embarkation. In London, at about 5 in the afternoon on 6 December, General Sir Alan Brooke was about to leave his office when he was told that two Japanese convoys, escorted by cruisers and destroyers, had been sighted heading westwards towards Malaya. An emergency meeting of service chiefs was convened, with Sir Alexander Cadogan present on behalf of the Foreign Office. According to Brooke's account:

> We examined the situation carefully but from the position of the transports it was not possible to tell whether they were going to Bangkok, to the Kra Isthmus, or whether they were just cruising round as a bluff ... Second message came in while we were there, but it did not clear up situation in the least and it only said that convoy had been lost and could not be picked up again.[14]

Cruising round as a bluff? The Americans in Washington were also watching the progress of the Japanese troop transports. They were not so baffled. At 7.30 pm, as he went home after a day of sighting reports and speculation, Captain Charles Wellborn remarked to the aide of Admiral Stark: 'Well, the British are sure going to catch it tomorrow at Singapore.'[15]

The Japanese convoys divided into five separate task forces. In due time they would invade at seven different places. Six landings were made on the Thailand coast while the largest task force was heading for Kota Bharu in Malaya. One of the Australian Hudson aircraft spotted it 65 miles offshore and heading south. An observer in the Hudson said it was a T-shape, with warships at the front, and transports behind: 'like a giant scorpion in the water.'

The Japanese attacks ranged right across the Pacific from Malaya in the west to Pearl Harbor on the easternmost side. In Tokyo it was 2.20 am and in Washington twenty minutes past noon. The sun was coming up at Hawaii, and the clocks there said 6.50 am but it was midnight local time in Kota Bharu when the Japanese warships stood off the Malayan beaches and waited while their naval gunners bombarded the defence positions there.

Malaya

The defence of the Philippines was controversial, but the British army's defence of Malaya was universally condemned. Malaya produced 38 per cent of the world's rubber and over 60 per cent of its tin and was an obvious target for a nation desperate for raw materials. Yet little was done to prepare the peninsula for attack. Even when the British army's chief engineer made a number of specific recommendations about defence works, the army's commander decided that defence works were bad for morale, and so very few were built.

There was little doubt about the basic tactics the Japanese would use. Malaya is a peninsula 600 miles long, with dense jungle, deep rivers, marsh, and a mountain range that runs almost its entire length. The only practical way to conquer it was to drive down the west coast, following a narrow cultivated strip, and then attack the 'fortress' of Singapore island.

Air Chief Marshal Sir Robert Brooke-Popham commanded British land and air forces in Malaya, as well as the amazingly widespread territories of British Borneo, Burma and Hong Kong. He had seen Japanese soldiers in December 1940 while in Hong Kong and didn't think much of them: 'I had a good close-up, across the barbed wire, of various sub-human specimens dressed in dirty grey uniform, which I was informed were Japanese soldiers,' he told his masters in London and added: 'I cannot believe they would form an intelligent fighting force'.

Such low opinions of the Japanese were prevalent in the British Far Eastern forces. More realistic estimations were not welcomed. In April 1941, the British military attaché in Tokyo told officers of the Singapore garrison that he regarded the Japanese army as a first-class fighting force, well trained, well officered, and possessing high esprit de corps. As the talk ended, Lt-Gen. Lionel Bond, head of Malaya Command, rose to declare that such talk was 'far from the truth'. He added: 'You can take it from me that we have nothing to fear from them.'

Brooke-Popham had bolstered British complacency in September 1941, by saying that even if Germany forced Russia to seek peace before winter came, the Japanese would not be able to move their northern forces quickly enough to threaten Malaya 'for some months'. Furthermore, said the air chief marshal, the bad weather in the South China Sea between November and January made it improbable that Japan was contemplating an imminent attack. This belief was firmly shared by Lt-Gen. Arthur Percival, the army commander in Malaya. Yet there was no reason to believe that the north-eastern monsoon period would bring immunity. In China the Japanese had regularly fought through monsoons. Now, in December, they were using the bad weather to hide their reconnaissance aircraft and their fleets.

Perhaps the British commanders would have revised their opinions about the inferiority of the Japanese had they looked into the sky above. Ever since October 1941 the Japanese army had been flying reconnaissance missions over Malaya's coastal areas, using one of the most outstanding aircraft of this period, the twin-engined Mitsubishi Ki-46 'Dinah'. Its outstanding cruising speed, range and ceiling enabled it to fly from bases in French Indo-China and work undetected, while its top speed ensured that it could escape just about anything sent after it.[16]

It was a predictable part of the Japanese plan that some elements of the force invading Malaya would force their way through Thailand. With the Japanese moving into Thailand, from their bases in neighbouring Indo-China, Brooke-Popham could get no definite answer from London as to whether he should be sending his forces across the border for the pre-emptive strike that was the contingency plan. Even when the Japanese ships were offshore at Kota Bharu and preparing to land their marines, he was ordered not to cross his northern border until the outlook became clearer. He waited for the men in London to make up their minds. 'The outcome was a delay which not only served no useful purpose but proved disastrous.'[17]

Plans had been made to provide Malaya with a substantial air force. The RAF had rashly promised to defend Malaya against air attacks and seaborne landings.[18] To this end the RAF had built airfields in northern Malaya, but no modern aircraft had ever arrived. Facing the Japanese there were No. 36 Squadron and No. 100 Squadron at Singapore with 158 aircraft including Vickers Wildebeest torpedo bombers. These obsolete biplanes, with uncowled engines which gave them a top speed of about 150 mph, were the only torpedo planes the RAF possessed. The first day of fighting cost the RAF more than half of the 110 aircraft they had available.[19]

The fighters, American Brewster Buffaloes, were indifferent air-craft that had been sent from Britain because it was felt that while they were not good enough to face the Germans they would certainly be able to counter anything the Japanese might send against them. In other places, in other hands, the tubby little American fighters did well enough, but everything militated against them at this time. British, Australian and New Zealand squadrons flew them but there were not many Allied pilots with the level of skill, pugnacity and combat experience that the Japanese had gained in years of war in China. Perhaps the climate played a part in the disaster, for there were constant failures of the retracting landing-gear and difficulties with the engine valve gear and the gun-firing mechanisms, so that large numbers of planes could not fly. Those that did fly were soon being lightened by jettisoning every piece of equipment not absolutely needed, but even then they couldn't catch up with Ki-21 'Sally' bombers.

Against them there was the Japanese army's very newest fighter, the Ki-43. The Nakajima company, in a bid to rival the Zero that Mitsubishi had built for the navy, had produced the 'Oscar', a look-alike army fighter. Like most Japanese aircraft, it was light and nimble and, although it was armed with only two machine-guns, in the hands of Japanese veterans it far outclassed the opposition. In one encounter on 22 December five Australian Brewster Buffaloes were lost while the Japanese (of 2nd Chutai, 64th Sentai) lost only one aircraft.[20] Within a short time the Japanese were boasting of having forty 'Oscar' pilots with ten or more victories.

Many British aircraft had been used and lost in the campaign in Greece, and others were being supplied to the Soviet Union, which had no urgent need of them. British factories were devoting a great deal of their output to providing RAF Bomber Command with its heavy machines, and Fighter Command was using good modern fighters in profitless 'sweeps' across northern France. According to one account: 'Greece and Russia between them cost Britain 600 first line aircraft; these would have been beyond price in Malaya.'[21] Meanwhile the airfields became a liability as, to save them falling into Japanese hands, British infantry which otherwise might have been repelling the invaders were tied down guarding them.

The seasonal weather pattern that in Formosa was delaying the Philippine mission sent heavy rain that grounded the aircraft waiting at Phnom Penh in Indo-China. Only support units from Saigon got their Ki-21 'Sally' bombers into the air and bombed the airfields in northern Malaya, destroying a number of Buffalo fighters that were on the ground.

Four and a half hours after the first men of the Japanese invasion force waded ashore at Kota Bharu, Singapore island was bombed by 27 Mitsubishi G3 'Nells'[22] which had also come from airfields in the Saigon region, flying through very bad weather and keeping to wave-top height. They were picked up by British radar when they were about 75 miles from the coast, but still broke through to their targets, the RAF airfields at Seletar and Tengah.

Like the Americans, the British commanders completely and fatally underestimated the ruthless fury and professional dedication of their Japanese foes. Lieutenant-General Arthur Percival had seen what the Germans could do in France in 1940, and he knew Malaya, having served there during the 1930s, but he was clever, cautious and conciliatory when determined single-minded leadership was needed. Percival's two subordinate commanders, in charge of the Indian Corps and the Australian Division, were difficult personalities. So were the civilians with whom he had dealings. When General Percival awakened the governor of Singapore to tell him the Japanese were landing at Kota Bharu, the response he received was: 'Well, I suppose you'll shove the little men off!'

The leader of the 'little men' was Lt-General Tomoyuki Yamashita. In the sort of decision that is rare among military commanders, he had reduced his attacking force from five divisions to three, believing this to be the largest force he could control while keeping the momentum of the advance. Among his soldiers were many with long experience of fighting in China, and also members of the Imperial Guard. They were equipped with 6,000 bicycles, which would play an important part in the campaign. So would his 600 or more aircraft, for Yamashita knew a great deal about air power, having previously served as inspector-general of the army air force.

The Japanese bullied the government of Thailand into giving their armies transit rights. It was this main force which went by rail to Malaya and fought its way down the west coast as every tactician had predicted. The Japanese 56th Infantry Division landing at Kota Bharu met stiff initial resistance both from the British army, most particularly the 3rd/17th Dogras of the 8th Indian Brigade, and the air force. The Lockheed Hudsons, little different to the airliner from which they were developed, had been fitted with bomb-racks for four 250-lb bombs. They did well. The Japanese admitted to the loss of three ships of the landing force, and to suffering 320 dead and 538 wounded.[23] But the Japanese were not delayed for very long. The infantry were pushed back, and within two days the air squadrons in northern Malaya were virtually wiped out. Air cover would decide the outcome of the fighting on the ground, and with no carriers assigned to this attack the Japanese were determined to capture them. By late afternoon on 8 December the airfield at Kota Bharu was in Japanese hands. It was at about this same time that Brooke-Popham asked MacArthur to bomb the Japanese air bases in Indo-China. It was too late. General MacArthur no longer had an air force.

The Japanese plan was simple. They would grasp the neck of the Malayan peninsula, then push south as fast as possible, using their bicycles and their well trained engineers. The invading force was constantly reinforced by small landings made behind the British fighting line. Some years later Yamashita was to explain the board game Go to an interviewer as 'very Japanese indeed. The idea of so many counters is so you can take as much territory as you can from your opponent in the shortest time.'

Along the Malayan coast, two of the Royal Navy's most formidable warships – dispatched from Europe in the hope of deterring Japanese aggression – were sailing without air cover. The new carrier *Indomitable* should have been with them, but it ran aground during trials in the West Indies and was being repaired. So the two big ships and their destroyer escorts, having conspicuously failed to deter Japanese aggression, sailed north hoping to surprise the landing. But there was little chance that a force sent to deter the enemy by its presence could also keep its position secret. A search and destroy force of Nells and Bettys had failed to spot it but it was sighted by a Japanese submarine, *I-65*, and by a reconnaissance plane from the heavy cruiser *Kumano*.

The commander of Force Z was Vice-Admiral Sir Thomas Phillips, a desk man who had little experience of the sea. He had never before commanded such a force, nor even a battleship, and was contemptuous of air power. The contempt was infectious. A CBS radio reporter aboard HMS *Repulse* noted that an officer laughed when told that a Japanese battleship, three heavy cruisers and some destroyers were close at hand. '. . . they are Japanese. There's nothing to worry about.'

The contempt that Phillips displayed for air power was widespread in the Royal Navy and must have played a part in the Naval Ordnance Department's choice of its anti-aircraft gunnery control system. Captain Stephen Roskill, a naval historian who was also a gunnery expert, said that 'enemy aircraft movements were in effect guessed instead of being actually measured'. This 'High Angle Control System' was so ineffective that in 1937 the Home Fleet had failed to score one hit on a radio-controlled target aircraft that circled the warships for two and a half hours.[24]

The British navy's rejection of the more effective tachymetric system (fitted to both German and American vessels) had made its ships vulnerable to Luftwaffe bombers, notably in the Mediterranean. It was now to have disastrous consequences in the Pacific, where the Royal Navy's Force Z was about to be attacked by shore-based Nells and Bettys flown by navy crews trained for long-range strikes against shipping. This unit had been specially reinforced as soon as the news came that the Royal Navy's ships were nearing Singapore. Interviewed 40 years after the event, one of the flyers, Furusawa Keiichi,[25] said:

> We'd been looking for the ships for two days – we had no real idea where they were. Each of our torpedo bombers was armed with a single torpedo; it weighed one ton, and had 800 kilos of explosive. There was a seven-man crew in each plane, I was observer in mine. When we spotted the ships on the 10th we'd already flown over the limit of safety, we'd used more than half our fuel and were returning to base when there they were! Two thousand metres below us, and about 20 kilometres away. They looked so small, especially the destroyers – like toys. We dived, and approached at about 160 miles an hour; we dropped our torpedoes about a kilometre from them, flying at 20 metres above the waves. . . . we were so close I could see sailors on deck – and I think some of them were firing rifles, or even hand-guns, at us, as well as the anti-aircraft barrage, which was very thick.

At 11.30 in the morning of 10 December HMS *Repulse* was straddled by a stick of bombs, one of which hit and caused a small fire. Ten minutes later the torpedo planes arrived, coming in two or three abreast and (according to survivors) 'in no way perturbed by our gunfire'. The Japanese were using 24-inch torpedoes with 1,760 lb of explosive, compared with the 18-inch Mk XII torpedoes with 388 lb of explosive that the Fleet Air Arm had used against *Bismarck* and in the Taranto attack. One tore a large hole in the hull of the *Prince of Wales* and bent one of the prop shafts.[26] The shaft revolving at full power ripped out oil and fuel lines and cracked

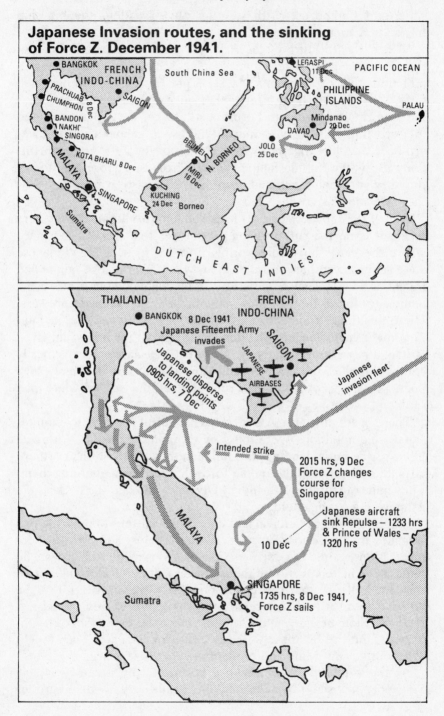

Japanese Invasion routes, and the sinking of Force Z. December 1941.

BANGKOK
FRENCH INDO-CHINA
South China Sea
PACIFIC OCEAN
LEGASPI 11 Dec
PRACHUAB 8 Dec
CHUMPHON
SAIGON
PHILIPPINE ISLANDS
PALAU
BANDON
NAKHC
SINGORA
Mindanao 20 Dec
DAVAO
MALAYA
KOTA BHARU 8 Dec
BRUNEI
N. BORNEO
JOLO 25 Dec
SINGAPORE
MIRI 16 Dec
KUCHING 24 Dec   Borneo
Sumatra
DUTCH EAST INDIES

THAILAND
FRENCH INDO-CHINA
BANGKOK   8 Dec 1941
Japanese Fifteenth Army invades
SAIGON
JAPANESE
Japanese disperse to landing points 0905 hrs, 7 Dec
AIRBASES
Japanese invasion fleet
Intended strike
2015 hrs, 9 Dec
Force Z changes course for Singapore
MALAYA
Japanese aircraft sink Repulse – 1233 hrs & Prince of Wales – 1320 hrs
10 Dec
SINGAPORE
1735 hrs, 8 Dec 1941, Force Z sails
Sumatra

watertight bulkheads. With steering out of action, the big ship turned in a circle.

Next it was the turn of the *Repulse* to feel the terrible shock of the big torpedoes. The Japanese planes came in from different directions to score four hits. At 12.33 pm *Repulse* turned over and sank. Less than an hour after that, *Prince of Wales* capsized. With the long return journey to Formosa still to go, the Japanese spared the escorting destroyers. Admiral Phillips, commander of the Eastern fleet, was lost together with 839 men of the 2,921 complement. Some Brewster Buffalo fighters arrived from Singapore only to see the survivors being rescued from the debris-strewn water. Now there was no Eastern fleet left.

One of the Japanese aircraft returned and two floral tributes were dropped upon the still gurgling oil patches that marked the place where the battleships were settling into the seabed. The Japanese were generous in their praise of the way in which British sailors had fought and died. They could afford to be magnanimous after such a demonstration of the big ships' vulnerability and Japanese prowess. Up to this time Britain's prestige in the East was awesome, its military might unchallenged. The lone stand against the Nazis had given Britain a new moral leadership. Now, with the Japanese so expertly conquering the Malayan peninsula, and sinking so effortlessly such peerless symbols of Britannia's rule, the authority of the white man sank and was gone.

There were now no Allied ships powerful enough to counter Japanese amphibious operations anywhere in the Pacific. Within 72 hours of the initial landings the Japanese had captured the northern airfields and battered the Indian force that had been guarding them. They had overrun the 11th Indian Division, and had the neck of the isthmus in a stranglehold.

If at this moment Percival had taken from eastern Malaya the two brigades that were there to protect the airfields, and thrown them into action against the Japanese pushing down the west coast, he might have halted or slowed the advance. But Percival would not do this. He believed that it was still possible to regain control of the air, and to do it he 'was prepared to make almost any sacrifice.'[27] Percival thought he could slow the advance by orthodox withdrawals, but the Japanese were not orthodox enemies. They fought ferociously, infiltrating and outflanking at every chance.

At the southern tip of Malaya, connected by a causeway, lay Singapore, an island 26 miles long by 15 miles wide, with a harbour in the centre of its southern coast, and a naval base in the north-east corner. For this final assault upon it the Japanese held back a reserve force of 30,000 fresh troops.[28]

The assault on Singapore began on 7 February 1942. In motor boats and launches the Japanese advanced across the narrow Johore Strait, with Australians of the 22nd Brigade fiercely resisting them. From the tall tower of the Sultan of Johore's Palace Yamashita had a grandstand view of the landing and the battle. Outnumbered, the defenders fell back. Soon the first of the water reservoirs was captured and by 13 February Singapore's entire water supply was in Japanese hands. The outcome had never been in doubt. The British high command had made no serious preparations for war and gave no sign of knowing what modern war was like, or of listening to those who did. In 1940 Lt-Col. John Dalley, of the Federated Malay States Police Force, had been refused permission to create an auxiliary military defence force of Chinese civilians. But after the Japanese invaders landed, the British decided it was a good idea after all. Training began four weeks before the surrender.

The same curious apathy permeated through all ranks. Fifty years after the event E. W. Swanton, an artillery officer who was defending the island, wrote in *The Spectator*:

> Churchill notes . . . that there were no permanent fortifications on the landward side and, what was 'even more astounding', no field defences had been attempted after the war in the East had begun. This is the exact truth. Not a coil of wire did we find, and when we sent to the RAOC depot on the afternoon of Saturday the 31st to get some, we found they had closed down for the weekend.[29]

Singapore – much-vaunted fortress and symbol of Britain's power – soon succumbed. Built at untold expense, it had been of more value as a symbol than as a fortress. It had proved unable to provide major repairs to warships damaged in the Mediterranean in 1941, and only for a day or so did it serve any unit of the British fleet. Arguments about whether some of Singapore's big fortress guns should have been placed to cover the approach from the north were to little purpose when General Yamashita was sitting in the boardroom of the Ford factory, watching Percival put his signature to a surrender document, having won his battle a month ahead of his stringent timetable. On 17 February he ordered: 'The Army will not hold a celebration. Instead of a triumphal entry ceremony, a ceremonial commemoration service for the dead will be solemnized.'[30]

Outnumbered three to one, Yamashita had inflicted upon the British what Churchill described as the largest capitulation and the worst military disaster in their whole history. Looked at another way, a lecturer at the Royal Military Academy, Sandhurst, called it 'one of the most impressive and well-conducted campaigns in this or any other war',[31] and it had been carried out in 70 days, by men in baggy uniforms who had failed to impress generals who measured armies by their polished buttons and precise footdrill. The really painful aspect of the British defeat was the improvisation shown by the Japanese and the stolid inflexibility of the defenders. One Japanese officer thought that the conquest of Malaya was made easy by expensive British roads and cheap Japanese bicycles.[32] Yamashita said that, although some of the British and Australian troops fought like brave men, many of the Indian troops 'disappeared into the jungle when they saw us', adding:

> What beat the British troops, I think, was our tactic of landing behind them in little ships and cutting them into small sections.[33]

Figure 41:
Japanese infantry cyclist

In Japan the fall of Singapore was celebrated by an extra ration of sugar and an order that every house should display the national flag.[34] Yamashita was hailed as 'the Tiger of Malaya' and made a national hero. There was talk of him being made war minister, a post that Prime Minister Tojo was keeping for himself. Tojo, who strongly disliked the general, was jealous of the publicity he was getting and had him immediately posted to a field command in Manchuria. Moreover Yamashita was forbidden to go to Japan, and was not permitted even to spend leave in Tokyo, thus depriving him of the customary meeting with the emperor. All news of Yamashita was censored. Tojo was able to deflect any criticism of this arrangement by saying that Japan's most successful general was now in Japan's most vital post: facing the ever-present threat of the Soviet Union.

Yamashita was upset by this treatment. His adjutant said he asked Imperial Headquarters several times for permission to visit Tokyo but this was always refused. In Formosa, en route to his new post, the local headquarters sent to him the three most beautiful geisha they could find. Yamashita paid them, sent them away and ate supper alone in his room. He lived with his wife in Manchuria, 60 miles from the Russian border, until Tojo fell from power.

The Japanese army was different to any force that Europeans or Americans had encountered. A US military intelligence publication dated 1944 said that the average infantry soldier was 5 feet 3 inches tall and weighed about 118 pounds.[35] As such publications go, it was useful, neither encouraging racist stereotypes nor persistently underestimating the enemy. However it went on: 'Despite the reputation of the Japanese for quickness and agility, the average soldier even after rigorous training is apt to be awkward. His posture is faulty, and his normal gait shuffling.'

The Japanese were no more militaristic than any other nation. One Englishman living in Japan during the war has testified to the unpopularity of military training and service. But there were no options available. Military training began in Japanese schools, so that by the time men went into the army they were semi-trained. Enlisted men and NCOs were encouraged to apply for commissions, and successful graduates from officer training served a four-month probation as sergeant-majors before getting their officer rank. Training was hard and realistic, with great emphasis placed upon harmonious relations in the unit, on comradeship and honesty, and on resistance to enemy propaganda and rumours.

Contrary to what has been published about the Japanese having
no awards for valour, the Orders of the Golden Kite, the Sacred
Treasury and the Rising Sun were awarded for bravery, sometimes
carrying with the medal a lifetime annuity. There were also campaign medals and good conduct awards.

Uniforms, like most things in the Japanese army, varied greatly
from unit to unit. A typical infantryman fighting in the jungle
dressed in lightweight cotton uniform, and puttees and tabi – rub-
ber-soled boots with separate big toe. Often a division designed its
own insignia. Some units wore a breast-patch, or arm badge, displaying name, rank and regiment, and even the unit commander's
name was also incorporated in some of the insignia.

Obsolete leather accessories were abandoned in favour of well
designed equipment made from rubberized fabric. This was used for
packs, belts, holsters, and so on. The standard pack was 13 inches
square and five inches deep. It was secured by tapes, with more
tapes to tie extras to the outside. The Japanese equipment was, like
their aircraft, lightweight and practical. Their philosophy stressed
lightness and adaptability even at the expense of durability.

The British infantry were anything but lightly attired. Weighed
down by heavy boots and a steel helmet, they wore a webbing pack
on the back, another dangling at the side, and a gas-mask bag
strapped to the chest. The equipment was held together by countless straps of canvas webbing each fitted with a brass buckle at one
end and a brass tab at the other. Failure to keep each tiny piece of
brass polished was punished far more severely than shortcomings of
shooting or fieldcraft. The Lee-Enfield rifle and its bayonet added
another ten pounds of weight. The whole outfit was virtually the
same as that British soldiers had worn in the First World War, and
it had proved impractical then.

Burdened under this load, men were not able to go quickly from
place to place. Units tended to depend upon trucks for movement,
and keep to the roads. To rationalize these limitations, the British
commanders told their men that an enemy would limit their movements in the same way. The Japanese did not comply. Said one
British officer:

> Before the war we would be working from a map to conduct our
> manoeuvres. Our colonel or the brigadier would say, 'Now this
> is thick jungle here and this is mangrove swamp. We can rule
> this out. In this sector all we have to concern ourselves with is
> the main road.'

Thus we based our strategy on that type of operation. We kept to the roads everywhere. Why, I went through a mangrove swamp the other day and nowhere did I go down in the mud over my ankles.[36]

The No. 1 Lee-Enfield rifle, used by the British in 1940, has now become a respected collectors' item. With an optimum range of about 400 yards, it was designed for First World War battlefields and was quite unsuited to the close-quarters snap-shooting of a jungle war. Allied veterans of the Malayan campaign spoke of the effect of the Japanese infantry's 8-mm sub-machine-gun that sprayed pistol-sized rounds, and of and the two-man 50-mm mortar which threw a 10-lb bomb a hundred yards or more. They also remembered the use made of the small cylindrical hand-grenades which Japanese infantry used with great effect. Although these Japanese weapons were later replaced with heavier models they were exactly right to dismay and defeat ill-led and ill-equipped British forces.[37] Especially when the Japanese infantry was suddenly appearing on flanks and rear as they pressed forward with their infiltration tactics.

While attacking Malaya Japanese troops also moved on 8 December into Britain's Chinese colony of Hong Kong. Soon the Parliament in London would hear how 50 British officers and men were bound and bayoneted to death. This was not an isolated incident; neither were such things only done in hot blood. The staff and 150 patients in the Alexandra Hospital in Singapore were crammed all night into a space that permitted them room only to stand before being taken out and murdered. In a rare example of Japanese contrition for the sort of atrocity that was widespread, on 15 February 1942 Lt-Gen. Yamashita visited the Alexandra Hospital and apologized for the massacre on the previous day.[38]

Wherever they went the Japanese forces pursued a bizarre and inhuman obsession with killing. Bayoneting, being quick and cheap, was the most common method but many of their victims were machine-gunned and some were burned or buried alive. Women and children, nuns, babies, priests, doctors and nurses: no one was immune to the terror the Japanese wrought. As their Chinese victims had discovered years before, terror was a policy. Neglect was another dimension of the policy of torture and terror. By the end of the war 27 per cent of their British and American prisoners were to have died in captivity, compared to 4 per cent who died in German and Italian camps.

After the war Yamashita was hanged as a war criminal. 'What I am really being charged with,' he told a visitor to his prison near Manila, 'is losing the war.' He might have said he was being charged with overthrowing Asia's illusions about white man's power in a manner that was little short of traumatic. Just how traumatic can be judged from the postwar writings of General Percival, the man Yamashita vanquished at Singapore.[39] The British general could not believe that his force, which he gives as well over 100,000 men, had surrendered to a Japanese force of 30,000. He wrote: 'It is safer to say they [the Japanese] employed 150,000 men in Malaya, although some Japanese reports suggest a much higher figure.'

Safer?

Deaths and suffering did not end when the fighting stopped. Life in prison camps was utterly horrific, and death was an everyday occurrence.

At Kranji memorial cemetery 4,500 are buried and the names of 24,000 Allied dead are inscribed on the marble columns. At sunrise exactly 50 years after the fall of Singapore an official service of remembrance was held there. Survivors and relatives of the dead came from as far as Britain and Holland. The Australian government sent an honour guard and ministerial representation. No government official from Britain attended the ceremony.[40]

Wake Island

The only glimmer of heartening news came from the defenders of Wake, a small atoll 2,000 miles from Hawaii. When the Japanese began to fortify the Bonin, Marianas, Caroline and Marshall island groups, possessions they had gained from Germany after the First World War, Wake Island was set up by Pan American Airways as a station for their Pacific routes. It was in fact an American military field built in defiance of international agreement, and in 1939 it was officially declared to be a base for US naval aviation.

The heavy air attack on Wake failed to soften the defences to the extent expected by the Japanese invasion force. US Marine Corps gunners, waiting until the last moment, damaged two transport ships with artillery fire. Three Japanese destroyers, moving in to draw fire away from the transports, were hit and damaged. One sank with all hands. Another destroyer, *Kisaragi*, was attacked by some of Wake's few surviving F4F Wildcat fighters, so recently delivered by the US carrier *Lexington*. A chance hit caused the depth charges aboard *Kisaragi* to explode, blowing the vessel to pieces. At this, with not one man yet ashore, the Japanese invasion force withdrew.

Admiral Kimmel, commander of the US Pacific fleet, immediately ordered all three of his carriers to Wake to fly strikes in support of the garrison. With the Japanese invaders in disarray, air attacks on the invasion force could perhaps turn withdrawal into disaster. But Kimmel was relieved of his command, and while his replacement was on the way, Kimmel's deputy, Admiral Pye, decided that such a mission was too dangerous for the precious carriers. The location of Nagumo's massive fleet was unknown, and the stand-off at Wake might be a cunning trap. Perhaps sharing Pushkin's view – that one should never risk the necessary in search of the superfluous – Pye decided that, when the new commander arrived, he would rather face him with news of the loss of Wake, than with news of the loss of the carriers. He ordered them to safer waters.

Hindsight tells us that gambling the carriers in the waters off Wake would probably have brought an American victory, but it wasn't to be. Soon the Japanese returned and the plucky defenders of Wake were overwhelmed.

Burma

On 23 December the Japanese attacked Burma, also an important oil producer. Limited at first to devastating air attacks on Rangoon, the invasion force crossed the border late in January 1942.

Burma provided an example of Anglo-American differences. The British wanted the country defended because it belonged to them. The Americans were determined not to fight to preserve imperialism but needed the Burma Road for the transport of supplies to Chiang's forces in China. The British had little faith in Chiang but, in need of American assistance, they did not argue.

General Wavell, recently appointed to be Commander-in-Chief India, and hastily assigned to supreme command of the south-west Pacific (ABDA – American, British, Dutch and Australian forces), was in charge of a vast region stretching from northern Burma to northern Australia. Having presided over military disasters in Africa and Greece, Wavell, given average luck, might have had a chance to recuperate in India. Now he was plunged into the even greater calamity of the Japanese offensives. Before long General

MacArthur took over, to command all the Allied forces in the south-west Pacific.

Australia

Japan's initial successes brought bitter recriminations from the Australian leadership. They saw men being appointed to defend the region and make decisions about Australian army units without consulting them. Perhaps it could have been smoothed over but the differences between Winston Churchill and John Curtin, Australia's Socialist prime minister, were long-standing ones.

Australians were widely regarded as the most effective combat infantry on either side in the war, and Curtin was one among many who believed that they were doing more than their fair share of the hard fighting in the Middle East. Curtin was not a man to mince his words. Churchill wryly recalled: 'Our discussions about the relief of the Australian troops in Tobruk had not been agreeable.'[41] To add to Australian discontent, the Australian General Blamey felt he had been tricked into giving approval to the costly campaign in Greece, which had proved as fruitless as the one in Crete. Now Curtin expressed fears that the Pacific fighting would 'be a repetition of Greece and Crete'. Curtin resented the way in which Malaya had been kept short of air, land and sea forces, while Australian divisions had been taken away and used to fight in the Middle East. If Churchill's decision to send the battleships *Repulse* and *Prince of Wales* to Singapore was intended to placate Curtin, it failed to do so. On 27 December 1941 a signed newspaper article by the Australian prime minister published in the *Melbourne Herald* was a cry of pain: 'We refuse to accept the dictum that the Pacific struggle must be treated as a subordinate segment of the general conflict.' He added, somewhat bitterly, that Australia must look to America rather than to Britain for salvation.

Churchill complained that this article 'was flaunted round the world by our enemies.'[42] As Churchill saw it, the Australian Socialists had not been aware of dangers in the past and were not facing up to present realities.

> It will always be deemed remarkable that in this deadly crisis, when as it seemed to them and their professional advisers, destruction was at the very throat of the Australian Commonwealth, they did not all join together in the common effort. But such was their party phlegm and rigidity that local politics ruled

unshaken. The Labour Government, with its majority of two, monopolised the whole executive power, and conscription even for home defence was banned.[43]

In a telegram he sent on 14 January 1942 Churchill's resentment flared:

> I do not accept any censure about Crete and Greece. We are doing our utmost in the Mother Country to meet living perils and onslaughts. We have sunk all party differences and have imposed universal compulsory service, not only upon men, but women.[44]

Yet Curtin's fears about Malaya being overrun soon came true. By 17 December Japanese forces were landed on the northern coast of Borneo. With astonishing dispatch, Prime Minister Tojo was telling the Diet that an inspection had been made of the 150 oil wells there. They would be getting oil from 70 wells within a month – a daily production of 1,700 tons. For the first time in history, Japan had a source of oil. It had taken them two weeks to secure it.

Within six weeks Wavell was back in his job in India and MacArthur became C-in-C Allied Forces in the Far East. He faced a jubilant enemy. In 100 days virtually the whole of South-East Asia had fallen into Japanese hands, and it had been achieved by an army with little or no experience of the tropics, or of jungle warfare. The victories were due mainly to skill and planning, their land forces seldom, if at any time, enjoying numerical superiority over their enemies.

Japan's war plans had estimated that the initial objectives would be taken in one year, at a cost of one-third of her naval strength. Most of those objectives had been gained in four months with naval losses of four destroyers and six submarines. In fact the imperial navy had grown stronger rather than weaker, for, since the opening of hostilities a light cruiser had been built and added to the Japanese fleet. The fleet had also gained the battleship *Yamato*, a gigantic vessel displacing 75,000 tons, with nine 18.1-inch guns, an armour belt 16 inches thick and a speed of 27 knots, the most powerful warship ever built. Japan was now stronger than ever.

This strength however was not replenished. Japan would fight a war constantly short of machines and raw materials and depleted of skilled manpower. Every sailor, soldier and airman lost from this time onwards was to be one more nail in Japan's coffin. Eventually the Japanese would resort to suicide attacks by kamikaze bombers, simply because they did not have enough trained aviators to make conventional air attacks.

Meanwhile the proficiency of their men and the advanced and original design of their machines shocked the West. British and American politicians and commentators had constantly assured everyone who would listen that the Japanese were inferior people, both physically and mentally. These strange oriental people were said to copy the West slavishly and to make cheap tin toys. Such people would never dare attack the Western powers. Suddenly in a rapid about-face, the message changed: the Japanese were supermen, with miracle weapons, death-defying fighters completely at home in the jungle.

Co-Prosperity

The idea of an Asian brotherhood, liberated by Japanese conquest, was the basis of all Japanese propaganda. At first many were deceived into helping them. The Thai government gave the Japanese rights of transit to attack British Malaya. The natives of Guam, and other small islands in the South Pacific, welcomed the Japanese. In French Indo-China, Governor Vice-Admiral Jean Decoux promised to cooperate with the Japanese in their war against the Anglo-Saxons. Not all such declarations were made under pressure: in faraway Argentina the Japanese victories were reported with unalloyed pleasure.[45]

Talk of Co-Prosperity proved to be no more than high-minded flim-flam. The Japanese used nationalist aspirations to assist them in their war against the European colonists, but when victory was theirs they quickly assumed the role of the colonist. Everywhere the Japanese language became paramount. Native people were expected to bow low to uniformed Japanese, and often the same tribal leaders and bosses who had served the European masters were retained in the service of the Japanese.

Terror was the favoured way of controlling the local population. In Manila, Filipinos who failed to bow three times to Japanese soldiers were to be found hanging in public places. For striking a Japanese soldier, you could be chained to a section of galvanized iron and left in the sun to scorch to death.

Here and there however a few Japanese took the 'spirit of Asian brotherhood' seriously. Such men showed what a more imaginative policy might have achieved. A certain Major Fujiwara Iwaichi helped organize the Indian National Army under Mohan Singh to fight the British. In Burma, Colonel Suzuki Keiji organized the Burmese Independence Army for the same purpose. In the Dutch East Indies, too, some genuine efforts to help the local population bore fruit, but good will vanished as the Japanese drafted an estimated million Indonesian workers into forced labour. Many were sent to construct the infamous Burma-Siam railway. No one knows how many died. A United Nations calculation puts the figure at more than 300,000, plus many more who subsequently succumbed to hunger, wounds or disease.

A racial war?

The way in which the Pearl Harbor attack came without warning, the humiliating loss of the fleet, the treatment of American and British prisoners of war, and racial differences, brought deep hatred to the surface, conspiring to make the Pacific war one long series of atrocities. Both sides tortured and killed prisoners and massacred men attempting to surrender. American newspapers and magazines spoke of the Japanese with a racial contempt and distaste quite unlike anything applied to other enemy nationals.

Japanese families which had come to America seeking a new start in life were hard hit by the war. While Americans of Italian or German ancestry continued with their normal life, Americans of Japanese origin (many of them native-born American citizens) were given 48 hours to sell their houses, farms and businesses. They were sent to ten primitive detention camps, mostly in desolate regions with extremes of climate. Most of the vacated properties they left behind were vandalized, others became derelict. In the detention camps, each family was assigned a room 20 by 25 feet and many were kept there for years. Detained on security grounds, young men growing up in these camps were, somewhat illogically, called for military service as they reached draft age. Eight thousand such men served in the American armed forces. There is no recorded example of espionage, sabotage or disloyalty of any kind from any one of these Japanese Americans. In 1988 Congress approved a Bill expressing apology for a 'fundamental injustice' and granted a $20,000 tax-free payment to each surviving internee.

In Berlin, feelings about the Japanese entry into the war were mixed. In his diary on 30 January 1942, Joseph Goebbels wrote:

'The Führer profoundly regrets the heavy losses sustained by the white race in East Asia, but that isn't our fault.' In Japan the war was not depicted as a racial struggle. Their alliance with the Germans and Italians prevented such stereotyping. Instead they concentrated upon showing up the Americans as racists and regularly used items from US papers as evidence of the ill-treatment of black Americans. American battlefield behaviour was constantly criticized. A photo in *Life* magazine, showing a young woman and a Japanese soldier's skull she had received as a gift from her fiancé at the front, was widely reproduced in Japan.

One propaganda stereotype upon which both sides agreed was that Americans were old and the Japanese were young. Youthful-looking Japanese faces encouraged Americans to write of Japan's foolishness and inexperience. Here were violent children who must be chastised and punished. The Japanese depicted Americans as senile cripples, plutocratic colonists in decline being pushed aside by a vigorous young nation.

Racial stereotypes were invoked, and the resulting bitterness played a part in the Pacific war. Most important, it persuaded the Allied governments – as well as fighting men in the field – that the Japanese were a nation of robots who could not be reasoned with. Consequently the war would have to be decided by massive and unrelenting firepower on land, sea and air. And so it was.

Conclusion: 'Went the Day Well?'

When you go home,
Tell them of us, and say,
For your tomorrow
We gave our today.

Inscription, British War Memorial, Kohima, India[1]

A S THE INHABITANTS of Washington sat down to Sunday lunch on that chilly December day, a land war that had already reached from Finland to Dakar and across the north and south Atlantic exploded into a conflict that encompassed almost the whole globe.

While aircraft of the Kido Butai were attacking Pearl Harbor other Japanese forces were bringing war to the whole of Asia with attacks that were coordinated through six time-zones and across the International Date Line. The Malayan coast had been the first to suffer, a bombardment of the landing areas taking place almost two hours before Pearl Harbor was raided. Long-range naval bombers went to Singapore. Hong Kong was also bombed, so were Guam and Wake. In Shanghai, Japanese troops moved in to the International Settlement and the US gunboat *Wake* was boarded and taken over in darkness. The crew of the British gunboat *Peterel* defied a Japanese ultimatum, fought back and their ship was sunk.

The imperial navy's 3rd Fleet escorted the 14th Army – 43,000 men on 60 or more troop ships[2] – to Luzon in the Philippines, while naval bombers from Formosa bombed the American bases there. The 15th Army invaded Thailand en route to Malaya, while the 2nd Fleet stood off the Pescadores Islands in support of the 25th Army's landings on the Malayan coast.

Colonies were run by so few Europeans that it required only small bodies of Japanese troops to seize them. The whole of South-East Asia was captured by eleven Japanese divisions.[3] The Japanese 55th Regimental Group – 'The South Seas Detachment' – was assigned to take Wake Island and Guam, the Gilberts, the Bismarcks and New Guinea. The 38th Infantry Division that occupied Hong Kong was

soon redeployed so that these same men could participate in the
assault on the real prize: the Dutch East Indies. In China a 'Christmas offensive' was launched in the Kiangsi and Hunan provinces.

In the USSR the German armies outside Moscow fighting a slogging match against the Russians and against the terrible climate were
suddenly sent reeling as Stalin launched his counter-offensive on Friday 5 December. Red Army forces north and south of the city began
the assault, and on the following day the 'South-West Front' also
went into action until fifteen armies were attacking the Germans.

Despite the pitiless winter climate, fighting continued all along
Germany's Eastern Front. A deep salient driven into the Russian line
by Army Group North at Tikhvin was pummelled by the Red Army
all over the weekend. When on Monday its defenders gave ground a
Directive from the Führer decreed that the whole front should abandon offensives and go over to the defensive. Aided by the weather,
Russian defenders of the more northerly city of Leningrad continued
the frantic struggle that had brought the Germans to a halt there.
When nearby Lake Ladoga froze, convoys of trucks drove across it to
bring supplies to the besieged city.

In North Africa that weekend, Rommel's Afrika Korps and the
Italian Motorized Corps were disengaging to withdraw from Cyrenaica. After two weeks of heavy fighting, short of fuel and under air
attacks by the RAF, Rommel was forced back across an extended
battlefield where Indians, Italians, Australians, New Zealanders,
South Africans, Germans and British were milling about in a confusion fomented by the captured vehicles used by both sides. On the
afternoon of 7 December the adjutant of one of Rommel's reconnaissance battalions spotted the unique profile of a German 8-wheel
armoured car, and drove alongside the column shouting in German
and then in Italian.

> There followed a moment's conversational hiatus, broken
> eventually when the driver, dust-covered and naked to the waist,
> looked down and shouted irritably: 'Oh, piss off, mate . . . for
> Christ's sake!' And he did.[4]

In Europe there were seldom to be heard any complaints about the
bad weather, for ice and cloud protected the city-dwellers far better
than guns or fighter planes. In London the RAF was suffering a loss
of confidence, with some of its personnel believing that unless some
miracle navigational aid could be brought into use 'the future of
Bomber Command would certainly be bleak and possibly even non-

existent.'[5] A night operation, a month before, had proceeded despite forecasts of storms, hail and icing. The heavy losses it suffered were largely due to the weather, and raids on Berlin were stopped. As December began, a bombing attack against Hamburg lost 13 aircraft of the 129 dispatched. Now there was little air activity anywhere and Air Marshal Sir Richard Peirse was moved to another post.

In America the first news that the nation was at war came at 2.25 on the Sunday afternoon when the wire service teleprinters clattered out seven words: 'White House says Japs attack Pearl Harbor.' By 3 o'clock all the radio networks had interrupted their programmes with dramatic announcements that were not universally appreciated. WOR, broadcasting a Sunday afternoon football game, received many complaints about the interruption to the commentary. In Denver the cancellation of a religious hour brought KFEL a call from a listener who asked if the station thought war news more important than the gospel.[6]

It was a bulletin on an American radio station that first alerted occupants of the Wolfsschanze. On Sunday at about midnight a Press officer took the news to Hitler, who was chatting with some guests and his female secretaries in a sitting-room of the grim bunker building. Hitler slapped his thigh and said, 'The turning-point!' and then ran outside through the ice and darkness to tell everyone what had happened. General Jodl was later to describe his astonishment when in the middle of the night Hitler came barging into his map room to tell the news to him and Field Marshal Keitel.[7]

In Poland, on Monday 8 December, 700 Jews taken from the small Polish town of Kolo were gassed in five special closed trucks that had been driven into the woods at nearby Chelmno. In batches of eighty – fit and infirm, men and women – they were killed by fumes from an exhaust pipe connected to the trucks' interior. Their bodies were thrown into pits. On the following days the same procedure was used to kill people from neighbouring villages. This was the start of the Nazi programme of systematic genocide.[8]

On Thursday 4 December 1941 – in one of the potentially most damaging scoops of the century – the isolationist *Chicago Tribune* and the *Washington Times-Herald* published details of a secret document called 'Rainbow Five' which had been stolen from the US army's War Plans Division. It was a contingency plan, of the sort that all armies and navies prepare in peacetime, outlining the strategy should the United States go to war with both Germany and Japan. The newspapers angrily offered it as proof that President Roosevelt was secretly planning to expand the army and navy and send them to fight overseas. The timing seemed calculated: Congress was debating an $8 billion supplementary defence bill. It was no doubt hoped, by those involved, that publication of America's war plans would deter Roosevelt and Congress from giving the armed forces more money. Three days later the Japanese attacked Pearl Harbor.

The Japanese attack ensured that the sensationalized revelations had little effect in Washington. But, in one of those curious twists of history, Hitler was provided with translations of the newspaper accounts, and it was these that persuaded him that Germany too must go to war against the United States. Hitler referred to the *Chicago Tribune* in the speech he made to the Reichstag on Wednesday 11 December, the day on which Ribbentrop summoned the American chargé, Leland Morris, and shouted at him: 'Your president wanted this war, now he has it.' In fact it is most unlikely that Congress would have agreed to go to war against Germany. Hitler's reckless declaration of war upon the Americans made his defeat certain. However, the short-term effect was a shock to America. U-boats sought targets along the American coast from the St Lawrence to the Gulf of Mexico. In the following six months, over two million tons of shipping were lost.

America's response to the Pearl Harbor attack was immediate and overwhelming. In the first six months of 1942 the government placed orders worth $100 billion, more than the economy had ever produced in a single year! Manpower, oil, rubber and strategic materials were assigned for military and civil purposes by 'tsars' with all-embracing powers. Donald M. Nelson was appointed head of the War Production Board. Told to write his own directive, Nelson was granted powers over the economy second only to those of the president. Nelson was an imaginative choice. As merchandising vice-president of Sears Roebuck, he knew where to buy what at the best price.

On 14 December 1941 a brigadier-general who had been chief of staff in the Philippines was summoned to the office of the US army chief of staff, General George C. Marshall, and asked his views on the Pacific war. He gave a realistic assessment. The Philippines would have to be sacrificed and American forces must reform in northern Australia. This was also Marshall's view, and that of the president. The brigadier was immediately appointed head of the Pacific Section of the War Plans Department. His name was Dwight D. Eisenhower. Soon he would be appointed to supreme command of the Allied forces in Europe.

Winston Churchill was with American guests at Chequers, his country residence, when he heard of the Pearl Harbor attack. He was not given the news by his intelligence or monitoring service. Like Hitler, he had to depend upon the accuracy of a radio news bulletin, but not having heard it clearly enough, he consulted his butler, Sawyers, who had heard the same BBC 9 pm broadcast in the servants' room.

Churchill picked up the telephone and was connected to Roosevelt in two or three minutes. 'Mr President, what's this about Japan?'[9]

'It's true. They have attacked us at Pearl Harbor.'

Accompanied by some high-ranking service chiefs and his personal physician Churchill went to America on the battleship *Duke of York*. The voyage took eight days, but within two weeks of the attack on Pearl Harbor Churchill was in Washington talking to Roosevelt. At this 'Arcadia conference' General George Marshall emerged as one of the truly great leaders of this period. Having already worked miracles in reorganizing the American army, he proposed a 'Combined Chiefs of Staff' to coordinate Allied strategy in global terms, a concept quite beyond the imagination or the abilities of the Axis powers. The decision that Germany must be defeated before Japan was reaffirmed by both Churchill and Roosevelt, but Marshall went further and insisted – despite British reluctance – that an amphibious assault upon the coast of France and an advance into Germany was the way this should be done. Churchill, fearful that this would entail millions of casualties, argued for strategic bombing, psychological warfare and military attacks upon the periphery of German-held Europe. A compromise was reached. Anglo-American armies would land in Algeria and Morocco to link with British armies advancing out of Egypt. General Eisenhower was appointed to command this invasion force.

A committee that met in Washington on the Saturday morning of that eventful weekend had come into being because of a letter that President Roosevelt received in August 1939 from the world's most famous scientist, Albert Einstein:

it may be possible to set up a nuclear chain reaction in a large mass of uranium, by which vast amounts of power and large quantities of new radium-like elements would be generated . . . a single bomb of this type, carried by boat and exploded in a port, might very well destroy the whole port together with some of the surrounding territory . . .

The letter had pointed out that the Germans had confiscated the uranium mines of Czechoslovakia and that in Berlin scientists were examining these same ideas. The sub-committee decided that the A-bomb could be built. Only 24 hours later the motive for building such a device was given fresh impetus as news of Japan's 'Hawaiian Operation' came over the radio bulletins. President Truman said the programme eventually cost 2 billion dollars.

The two atomic bombs dropped on Japanese cities did not bring the war to an end. The Japanese continued to execute captured American flyers, a policy they adopted when the heavy raids on Japan's towns began. It was 800 heavy bombers striking Tokyo a week after the dropping of the second atomic bomb that enabled the Japanese to overcome their pride and call for a cease-fire. By that time the American bombing raids were virtually unopposed. Japan had no fuel to train pilots, aircraft engine production was down by 75 per cent, airframe production by 60 per cent and refined oil by 83 per cent.

The oil that Japan gained from its advance southwards was of little help. The US navy's submarines sank Japanese transports so that of the oil extracted in 1942 only 42 per cent got to the homeland; in 1943 15 per cent; in 1944 5 per cent; in 1945 none. The way in which subsequent history overlooked the submariners' contribution to victory was not an accident. It was due to a wartime Navy Department directive. The US navy prohibited all Press references to the submarines, whether or not there was any security aspect to the story. The navy didn't want their story told that way. Several correspondents filed reports but all were stopped.[10] It was probably feared that the true story would bring an end to the big ships and reduce the navy's influence.

In 1941 Japan decided to grab oil sources rather than accede to international demands to stop the pointless campaign in China. A long and costly war brought Japan to an even worse position. In that same year, Hitler followed an even more futile course of action. Instead of continuing to trade with Stalin, who was supplying him with ample oil and raw materials, he sent his tanks and bombers to conquer the Soviet Union, and never again had sufficient supplies. For nations of energetic, highly intelligent and well educated people, where engineering, art and product design were more highly esteemed than they were anywhere else in the world, trading could be cheaper and far more beneficial than making war. The history of the second half of the twentieth century clearly indicates that both Japan and West Germany learned that simple lesson.

But of course Hitler didn't fight a war to improve his adopted country's living standards. His invasions, like his totalitarian regime, were fundamentally a result of a pathological hatred of foreigners, especially those ill-defined foreigners that he liked to classify as Jews.

Hitler's oppressive intolerance and his racial policies played an important part in mobilizing Americans to Britain's cause. Since that time America's racial balance has changed dramatically, so that soon Americans of European descent will be a minority in the United States. Asian, Black and Hispanic Americans are increasingly influential minorities. Europe has also changed so that most of the countries engaged in the war have become multi-racial societies. The clear-cut issues for which America fought in those times may never come again.

Only Japan has kept its racial integrity. At the time of writing the world is witnessing a power struggle between the world's most closed and racially exclusive society, and the world's most open and dynamic one. The success of the United States of America in this economic clash will show all countries that open, integrated societies prosper. The success of Japan's closed, class-conscious, racially exclusive society will convince them otherwise.

For the French, Dutch, Belgians, Norwegians, Greeks, Danes and everyone else suffering under German occupation, the Pearl Harbor attack brought a ray of hope. Soldiers, sailors and airmen already fighting the Axis were given a new purpose. Until now the casualties had cried:

> Went the day well?
> We died and never knew.
> But, well or ill,
> Freedom, we died for you.[11]

After Pearl Harbor, men and women drowning in the Atlantic, crews in stricken planes, tank men bleeding into the desert sand and the soldiers and civilians alike expiring in horrifying prison camps, knew that eventually the incomparable resources of the Allies would bring victory.

Notes and References

In book references, publishers are British unless otherwise stated. Full publication details are given with first reference to a work and in short thereafter.

INTRODUCTION

1 Harry E. Figgie Jr, with Gerald Swanson, *Bankruptcy 1995* (Boston, Mass., Little, Brown, 1992).
2 Japan's non-defence R&D is at time of writing 2.8% of gross national product compared with about 1.8% in the USA. This and other comparisons from *US News & World Report*, 12 April 1993.
3 Hans A. Schmitt, *Lucky Victim* (USA, Louisiana State University Press, 1989).

1 BRITANNIA RULES THE WAVES

1 Jacques Mordal, *Twenty-Five Centuries of Sea Warfare* (New York, Bramhall House, 1959).
2 *Proletariat, Culture and Lifestyle in the 19th Century*, edited by Dietrich Mühlberg (Leipzig, GDR Edition, 1988).
3 Including those building there were 62 Royal Navy battleships compared with the rest of the world's 96. See Paul Kennedy, *The Rise and Fall of British Naval Mastery* (HarperCollins, 1976).
4 In 1890 the populations of some key countries were: Britain 37.4 million; Germany 49.2; USA 62.6; Austria-Hungary 42.6; Japan 39.9; France 38.3; Russia 116.8. Only Italy, with 30 million,

had a smaller population. See Paul Kennedy, *The Rise and Fall of the Great Powers* (New York, Vintage Books, 1989).
5 Robert K. Massie, *Dreadnought: Britain, Germany and the Coming of the Great War* (Jonathan Cape, 1992).
6 Admiral Sir Reginald Bacon, *The Life of Lord Fisher of Kilverstone* (Hodder and Stoughton, 1929).
7 Richard Hough's excellent book *Dreadnought* (Michael Joseph, 1965).
8 *The Economist* in its 'Survey Britain', 24 October 1992, said, 'The irony is that Britain just missed having one of the best education systems around. In 1868 the government dithered then squashed a Royal Commission's recommendations for a twin-track school system broadly similar to the German Realschulen and Gymnasien. The government of the day found it too Prussian for English tastes. The Scots sensibly thought otherwise and have fared better ever since.' On the other hand, Scottish children were still leaving school at the age of 14 even until the Second World War.

2 DAYS OF WINE AND ROSES

1 James Morris in *Farewell the Trumpets*, vol. 3 of the superb *Pax Britannica* trilogy (Faber, 1968).
2 The first lord was Eyre-Monsell. The initial impulse for the agreement came from the foreign minister, Sir Samuel

Hoare. See Richard Lamb, *The Drift to War* (W. H. Allen, 1989).

3 By 1954 the Admiralty staff had grown to 33,788. See C. N. Parkinson, *Parkinson's Law* (Penguin Books, 1970).

4 Five million is the overall number. Only 1,300,000 served overseas. In the case of India 3,698,000 served in the army, of which 398,613 served overseas. These figures from John Ellis, author of *Brute Force* (André Deutsch, 1990) etc.

5 The two main types of U-boat – the Type VII and the Type IX – were usually referred to in Allied documents as the 500-tonner and the 700-tonner.

6 Lothar-Günther Buckheim, *The Boat* (New York, Knopf, 1975).

7 As above.

8 As above.

9 David Kahn, *Seizing the Enigma* (Boston, Mass., Houghton Mifflin, 1991).

3 EXCHANGES OF SECRETS

1 The number almost invariably given is 57, because this was the number that had been commissioned, but *U-18* sank after a collision in 1936 and, after salvage, was commissioned a second time. See J. P. Mallmann Showell, *U-Boats under the Swastika: an Introduction to German submarines 1935–1945* (Ian Allan, 1973). The official history, *British Intelligence in the Second World War*, says that documents secured from *U-49* 'proved that Germany had entered the war with 57 U-boats completed', which is wrong, but in a footnote on the same page calls it the number of U-boats commissioned, which is of course correct.

2 The US navy had similar problems: its torpedoes ran too deep and the magnetic pistols failed. The Royal Navy had more success with its magnetic pistols but was apt to switch to contact pistols when the outcome was vital.

3 Mrs Elizabeth Turner of Toronto, quoted in *The Battle of the Atlantic* by Terry Hughes and John Costello (Collins, 1977). These authors give the figure of 118 deaths after the *Athenia* sinking.

4 After the war – at the Nuremberg War Crimes Tribunal – Dönitz testified on oath that Lemp's attack on the *Athenia* was the only instance of falsifying a war diary. In fact, we know that the captain of the *U-123* was also ordered to fake his war diary after sinking the neutral ship *Ganda* on 20 June 1941 off the coast of Morocco. *Ganda*, a Portuguese freighter, had taken two torpedo hits and then been shelled with the 10.5-cm gun. With two lifeboats smashed, fuel poured out of the broken hull and ignited on the sea. The U-boat reversed engines to get away.

When *U-123* returned to Lorient, Dönitz personally ordered the captain to fake his diary to show no action of any kind on that date, and he was ordered to tell no one of the sinking. Five doctored copies of the diary were filed in the normal way, but no one remembered to falsify the Schussmeldungen – shooting report – which went to Torpedo command. See Michael Gannon, *Operation Drumbeat* (New York, HarperCollins, 1990). Gannon interviewed the captain at length for his book about the *U-123*'s operations off Florida.

5 Germany's highest awards for valour were based upon the Iron Cross. As well as being awarded for individual acts of heroism – or in one case to a female test pilot – the Eisernes Kreuz 1 Klasse could be awarded en masse, as happened to the 1,300 crewmen of the *Admiral Scheer* in April 1941. By war's end about 300,000 EK1s had been awarded together with 2.5 million of the EK2 or Iron Cross Second Class. Winners of the EK2 usually wore only the ribbon.

The Knight's Cross, Ritterkreuz, was a much higher award. It was worn at the collar, and 6,973 were awarded during the Second World War. It could be earned over a period by a points system: adding up the tonnage sunk by U-boat captains or the aircraft shot down by fighter pilots. It could also be awarded to high-ranking officers for military leadership.

Small metal additions distinguished higher awards. In ascending order the Knight's Cross could be won with oak leaves (853 awarded), swords (150), and with diamonds (27). The highest category was the Knight's Cross with golden oak leaves, swords and diamonds. This was awarded to only one man – Col. Hans Rudel – who made 2,530 sorties as a Stuka pilot and was credited with the destruction of 532 Red Army tanks and two Russian warships.

6 Churchill, *The World Crisis* (Sandhurst edition, Thornton Butterworth, 1933).

7 Merlin Minshall, *Guilt Edged* (Bachman & Turner, 1975).

8 The only time, according to the specialist naval historian Antony Preston in *Navies of World War II* (Bison/Hamlyn, 1976). Preston, author of several naval histories, was a research assistant in charge of Admiralty records at the National Maritime Museum, Greenwich.

9 Correlli Barnett, *Engage the Enemy More Closely* (Hodder & Stoughton, 1991).

10 More strictly speaking (although still a rough rule) codes are in letters; ciphers in numbers.

11 The first lord of the Admiralty was a politician, in effect the navy minister. The first sea lord was the senior naval officer at the Admiralty.

12 Conversations with Merlin Minshall.

13 An award somewhat like a medal usually given for gallantry.

14 To complete the story: Hans-Thilo Schmidt's treachery was revealed to the Germans by the man who recruited him – Rodolphe Lemoine – in March 1943. In German-occupied Paris, Lemoine, by now 73 years old, was plied with kindness by his German interrogators, first the Abwehr, then the SD and Gestapo. He admitted to being an intelligence officer and told the Germans that he had received information from Schmidt, but the Enigma machine was never mentioned by his interrogators. Lemoine's superior, Bertrand, was captured and interrogated in January 1944 but he too avoided any mention of the Enigma machine. By the time he was arrested in May 1943 Hans-Thilo Schmidt had taken to carrying cyanide tablets, concealed in his hernia belt. He died – probably by suicide – at Lehrterstrasse 61, Berlin, on 16 September 1943 while in SS custody.

In April 1943 Colonel General Rudolf Schmidt – who had secured his brother's engagement in the top-secret Cipher Office in Berlin but had no notions of his work as a spy – was now commanding the Second Panzer Army on the Eastern Front. It was obvious that much of Hans-Thilo's military information had come from confidences the general shared with his brother. He was relieved of his command. He survived the war, to be imprisoned in Russia until he was released after the intervention of Chancellor Konrad Adenauer. Rudolf Schmidt died in 1957.

15 By David Kahn, *Seizing the Enigma* (Boston, Houghton Mifflin, 1991).

16 The most interesting and reliable material about the French and Poles comes from Hugh Skillen's three books, *Spies of the Airways* (1989), *Knowledge Strengthens the Arm* (1990), and *Enigma and Its Achilles Heel* (1992). All published by Hugh Skillen, 56 St Thomas Drive, Pinner, England HA5 4SS. The quote is from General G. Bertrand's book *Enigma ou la plus grande Enigme de la Guerre 1939–1945*. See also Kahn, *Seizing the Enigma*.

17 Kahn, *Seizing the Enigma*.

18 Gordon Welchman, *The Hut Six Story – Breaking the Enigma Codes* (New York, McGraw-Hill, 1982). This is a good description of the Bletchley Park work, and highly recommended to anyone interested in detail.

19 Brian Johnson, *The Secret War* (BBC Publications, 1978). BBC TV built a 'bombe' based on descriptions of those who had seen them. Kenneth Macksey, in *Technology in War* (Arms and Armour Press, 1986), says the bombes used 'punched-hole sheets of paper' of the sort used in calculating machines. Welchman gives a better description of the sheets. So far the British government has refused to release details of the bombes, or of the breaking of the even more secret Siemens Geheimschreiber encoding machine. Welchman suggests that postwar British silence on the subject was due to the British selling coding machines like Enigma and not wanting their overseas customers to know they were vulnerable.

20 Ralph Bennett, writing in the periodical *World War II Investigator*, September 1988.

21 Welchman, *The Hut Six Story*.
22 Some accounts talk of 'fingerprints' as the identification of a 'fist' or sending style of a Morse key operator. German ships could, and often did, leave their radio operators ashore in order to fool enemies who could recognize the 'fist'. The unique value of Minshall's innovation was that it identified the transmitter itself.
23 I took this irresistible description from David Kahn's *Seizing The Enigma*.
24 Gannon, *Operation Drumbeat*.
25 Kahn, *Seizing the Enigma*.
26 This story, and some details of the Tracking Room, from Donald McLachlan, *Room 39* (Weidenfeld & Nicolson, 1968).
27 Gannon, *Operation Drumbeat*.
28 McLachlan, *Room 39*.
29 Minshall, *Guilt Edged*.

4 SCIENCE GOES TO SEA

1 J. G. Crowther & R. Whiddington, *Science at War* (HMSO, 1947).
2 Captain Kenneth Langmaid, *The Approaches are Mined!* (Jarrolds, 1965).
3 Ronald W. Clark, *The Rise of the Boffins* (Phoenix, 1962).
4 Langmaid, *Approaches*.
5 Sir Charles Goodeve in conversation with Guy Hartcup. See Hartcup's *The Challenge of War* (David & Charles, 1970).
6 Crowther & Whiddington, *Science at War*.
7 Wolfgang Frank, *The Sea Wolves* (New York, Rinehart & Co, 1955).
8 I am indebted to Michael Gannon's wonderfully researched *Operation Drumbeat* for some details of day-to-day naval activity.
9 Admiral Dönitz, *Memoirs* (Weidenfeld & Nicolson, 1959).
10 J. P. Mallmann Showell, *U-Boat Command and the Battle of the Atlantic* (Conway Maritime Press, 1989).
11 This instructor was a US navy ensign: Leonard Smith, of Missouri. He was forever after called 'Bismarck' Smith.
12 *Coastal Command* (HMSO, 1942).
13 Although, using a VLF (Very Low Frequency) receiver, a submarine could receive messages if not submerged deeper than 65 feet.

14 Chambers Dictionary defines a boffin as a 'research scientist, esp. one employed by armed forces or government', but offers no source for the name. *A Dictionary of Forces Slang 1939–45* edited by Eric Partridge (Secker & Warburg, 1948) suggests that it derives from a series of books for children called Boffin Books. Certainly the term does not appear before the Second World War.
15 The contraflow of warm water and cold water through the Strait prevented the U-boats diving deep.
16 Hartcup, *The Challenge of War*.
17 Donald MacIntyre, *The Battle of the Atlantic 1939–1945* (Lutterworth, 1970).
18 These figures from Gannon, *Operation Drumbeat*.
19 Commander D. A. Rayner, *Escort* (Kimber, 1955).
20 A for Ausland – or foreign country – because the U-boat had originally been built for Turkey in 1938 and designed as a mine-layer.

5 WAR ON THE CATHODE TUBE

1 *Tirpitz*, 42,900 tons, and *Bismarck*, 41,700 tons, together with *Gneisenau* and *Scharnhorst*, 31,800 tons, were classified as battleships. *Admiral Graf Spee* and *Admiral Scheer*, 12,100 tons, and *Deutschland* (renamed *Lützow*), 11,700 tons, were at first called Panzerschiffe and then reclassified as heavy cruisers. The Western press called these three ships 'pocket battleships'. *Prinz Eugen*, 14,800 tons, *Blücher* and *Admiral Hipper*, 13,900 tons, were heavy cruisers. *Nürnberg, Leipzig, Köln, Karlsruhe, Königsberg* and *Emden* were light cruisers of less than 7,000 tons. This list (it is not a complete one) is based upon *Die Schiffe der Deutschen Kriegsmarine und Luftwaffe 1939–45* by Erch Gröner (Munich, J. F. Lehmanns Verlag, 1954).
2 HMS *Norfolk* had Type 286 radar, a development of the ASV Mark II, an old fixed-antenna set.
3 Lt-Commander T. J. Cain RN on HMS *Electra*. From *HMS Electra* (Muller, 1959). Quoted by John Winton in *The War at Sea* (Hutchinson, 1967).

4 Ian Cameron, quoted in *In the Cockpit*, ed. Anthony Robinson (Secaucus, New Jersey, Chartwell Books, 1991).
5 According to the inspection of the wreck in June 1981.
6 Dr Douglas H. Robinson, 'Normandy and After', unpublished MS.
7 William L. Shirer, *The Sinking of the Bismarck* (NY, Random House, 1962).
8 G. Bennett, *Naval Battles of World War II* (Batsford, 1975).
9 Details of this inspection done by Dr Robert Ballard in June 1981, supplemented by drawings, photographs of the wreck, and other research aided by German and British survivors of the encounter, were published in what must surely be the final word on the subject in the US Navy's *Proceedings*, June 1991, 'Who Sank the Bismarck?' by William H. Garzke Jr, and Robert O. Dulin Jr. It concluded that the *Bismarck* was sinking because of uncontrolled progressive flooding, exacerbated by the flooding of magazines. German use of scuttling charges rapidly diminished the reserve buoyancy and caused the ship to begin to sink at 10.40.
10 A. and G. Franklin, *One Year of Life: Prince of Wales* (Blackwoods, 1944). Quoted in Winton, *War at Sea*.
11 Gannon, *Operation Drumbeat*.
12 It is often written that Britain's wartime oil came from Persia (Iran) and Iraq. Such oil was used by forces in the Middle East, including the Royal Navy in the Mediterranean, but almost all Britain's fuels came across the North Atlantic.
13 Capt. Gwilym D. Williams, letter to author.
14 A. J. P. Taylor, *The Second World War* (Hamish Hamilton, 1975).
15 Harris was not the only person to do all he could to prevent the Atlantic sailors getting the air cover they so desperately needed. America's Admiral King (who inexplicably in 1942 allowed the U-boats to massacre US coastal shipping for six months before agreeing to start a convoy system) also stubbornly denied air cover to the sea lanes. At a time when Coastal Command had only 23 of the very long-range Liberator aircraft in use, King controlled 112 of them. Seventy of these

were flying in non-combat areas, but King would not spare the handful needed to fly out of Newfoundland and close the 'Atlantic gap'.
16 John Ellis points out in *Brute Force* that the US navy's submarines in the period 1942-45 sank 8,616,000 tons of Japanese shipping, which cut the Japanese merchant fleet by 75 per cent. The Allies during the same period lost 12,590,000 tons, while their merchant fleet increased in size from 32 to 54 million tons.
17 J. P. Mallmann Showell, one of the most reliable historians of the U-boat war, in *U-Boats under the Swastika*.
18 It is not easy to find reliable figures. Dönitz in his memoirs says of 1,170 U-boats 863 became operational, 603 were lost at sea through enemy action, 20 at sea causes unknown, and 7 at sea by accidents. In port 81 were lost by air attack and mines and 42 by all other causes. Another 215 were destroyed by crews at war's end (some were refitted and used). During the war 38 were scrapped either because they were badly damaged or obsolete. Eleven boats were handed over to foreign navies or interned in neutral ports after sustaining damage. At war's end 153 were handed over in Allied ports.

6 GERMANY: UNRECOGNIZED POWER

1 See Frank S. Pepper, *Dictionary of Biographical Quotations* (Sphere, 1985).
2 The Napoleonic Wars were no exception. The Peninsular campaigns were launched on the mistaken idea that there were powerful Spanish armies with which the British could unite. Wellington went to the Low Countries to fight alongside Prussians, Austrians and Russians. In earlier times, the victories at Crécy and Agincourt were won during extensive raids rather than wars.
3 Wellington's army consisted of 24,000 British, plus 43,500 Dutch, Belgians and Germans from the Duchy of Nassau (present-day Hesse). The Prussian army under Field Marshal Blücher reduced the proportion of the British still more.
4 John Ellis, *Armies in Revolution* (Croom

Helm, 1973).

5 *Proletariat, Culture and Lifestyle in the 19th Century*, ed. Dietrich Mühlberg.

6 'We Don't Want to Fight' was written in 1878 by G. W. Hunt, advocating British intervention against Russia in the Russo-Turkish war. People disposed to fight the Russians were called Jingoes, and so eventually were any super-patriots. See *Stevenson's Book of Quotations*, by Burton Stevenson, 9th edition (Cassell, 1958).

7 Morris, *Farewell the Trumpets*.

8 This theory is explored by John Ellis in *The Social History of the Machine Gun* (Croom Helm, 1975).

9 Barbara Tuchman, *The Proud Tower. A Portrait of the World Before the War 1890–1914* (Hamish Hamilton, 1966).

10 For this graphic description, and for many other stimulating ideas and facts, I am indebted to vol. 3 of Major-General J. F. C. Fuller's classic work, *The Decisive Battles of the Western World* (Eyre & Spottiswoode, 1956), as well as to his other writings.

11 There was a treaty of 1839, but it did not define Britain's exact obligations and certainly didn't make it necessary for Britain to send her troops overseas to defend Belgium's frontiers.

12 This quote from Eduard David is taken from *Rites of Spring* by Modris Eksteins (Bantam Press, 1989).

13 This was a development of the convoluted but simplistic ideas of General Langlois, who said: 'A battle lost is a battle one thinks one has lost; for a battle cannot be lost physically.'

14 Victor Wallace Germains, *The Kitchener Armies* (Peter Davies, 1930).

15 Colonel Clay was the chief recruiting officer for the London District. He said one doctor was examining 400 hundred men per day. See A. Babington, *For the Sake of Example – Capital Courts Martial 1914–18, the Truth* (Leo Cooper, 1983).

16 Churchill's words, see *The World Crisis* (Sandhurst Edition, Thornton Butterworth, 1933).

17 Of 2.4 million men examined in the 1917–18 period, over 1 million were either unfit for military service or suited only to non-combat duties. See J. M. Winter, *The*

Experience of World War I (Macmillan, 1988).

18 John Keegan, *The Face of Battle* (Jonathan Cape, 1976).

19 Michael Howard, 'Haig-bashing', *London Review of Books*, 25 April 1991.

20 Musketier Karl Blenk, 169th Regiment, quoted by Martin Middlebrook in his remarkable account, *The First Day of the Somme* (Allen Lane, Penguin, 1971).

21 Ellis, *Social History of the Machine Gun*. The statement about the positioning of German machine-guns is quoted by Ellis and taken from Lt-Col. G. S. Hutchison's *Machine Guns: their History and Tactical Employment* (Macmillan, 1938).

22 A. J. P. Taylor, *The First World War* (Penguin, 1970). Some sources give a figure of 620,000. Taylor gives German casualties as 450,000 and says that many years later the British official history 'performed a conjuring trick on the German figures, and blew them up to 650,000' to make it seem that the Germans had suffered a defeat.

7 PASSCHENDAELE AND AFTER

1 B. H. Liddell Hart, *A History of the World War 1914–1918* (Faber & Faber, 1936). Liddell Hart called it 'the last scene in the gloomiest drama in British military history'.

2 E. W. A. Hobart, *Pictorial History of the Sub-Machine Gun* (Ian Allan, 1973).

3 Martin Middlebrook, *The Kaiser's Battle* (Allen Lane, Penguin, 1978).

4 Trooper C. H. Somerset, 9th Machine Gun Squadron, quoted in Middlebrook, *The Kaiser's Battle*.

5 Col. H. C. B. Rogers, *Tanks in Battle* (Seeley Service, 1965).

6 Michael Howard, 'Haig-bashing'.

7 Denis Winter, *Haig's Command* (Viking, 1991).

8 Winter, *Haig's Command*.

9 My father was one of them.

10 Figures from Clive Ponting, *1940: Myth and Reality* (Hamish Hamilton, 1990).

11 These figures from Samuel Hynes, *A War Imagined – the First World War and English Culture* (Bodley Head, 1990). Hynes says that the Germans executed 48 soldiers, the French executed about the same number as the British, while the Italians executed twice as many as the British. Anthony Babington, *For the Sake of Example*, quotes the Service Historique at Vincennes as saying that up to the end of January 1918 the French executed 133 soldiers. The German archives at Freiburg im Breisgau say there are no figures available and blame a British air raid, a response I have had to many other queries. Babington says the Canadians executed 25 soldiers but only one of these was sentenced for cowardice.

The German armed forces in the Second World War had a quite different policy. Between 26 September 1939 and 31 January 1945 German courts martial pronounced death sentences upon 12,545 men. Of these about 6,000 were carried out.

12 Australians were exempted from the death penalty by the Australian Defence Act for all crimes except mutiny and desertion to the enemy. The Australian government resisted very strong pressure by Haig and kept it their way. No Australians were executed. See Hugh McManners, *Scars of War* (HarperCollins 1993). The American Expeditionary Force executed 11 of its soldiers. The Judge Advocate said that all of them were found guilty of murder or rape.

13 McManners gives a different total for the First World War British executions: 3,080 death sentences with 312 actually carried out. Of these he says 277 were British, of whom 3 were officers. Babington, *For the Sake of Example*, says 346 executions and gives details of soldiers subjected to brutal punishments such as the wearing of leg-irons. Babington gives details of the way questions were answered in Parliament.

14 Winter, *Haig's Command*.

15 Mussolini became dictator despite the monarchy being retained, but in the long term this ensured continuity as Italy changed sides and Mussolini was assassinated.

16 One of the few reliable histories of the Freikorps is *Vanguard of Nazism – the Free Corps Movement in Postwar Germany*

1918–23, by Robert G. L. Waite (Cambridge, Mass., Harvard University Press, 1952).

17 Paul Johnson, *A History of the Jews* (Weidenfeld & Nicolson, 1987).

18 Dreyfus was an Alsatian Jew. Falsely accused of spying, he was sentenced to life imprisonment by court martial. Subsequent developments revealed corruption and prejudice in the French army and deep-seated anti-Semitism throughout French society.

19 Albert Speer, *Spandau, the Secret Diaries*, translated R. & C. Winston (Collins, 1976).

20 Liddell Hart, *History of the World War 1914–1918*.

21 Antony Kemp, *The Maginot Line – Myth & Reality* (New York, Military Heritage Press and Stein & Day, 1988).

22 Kemp, *Maginot Line*.

23 Kemp's book is a clear and concise account that also provides a good bibliography and details of which parts of the Line can still be visited.

8 FRANCE IN THE PREWAR YEARS

1 Cabinet Papers. See Ian Colvin, *The Chamberlain Cabinet: how the meetings in 10 Downing Street, 1937–1939, led to the Second World War* (Gollancz, 1965).

2 Figures (except France aircraft) are taken from R. A. C. Parker, *Struggle for Survival* (OUP, 1989). The figure for French aircraft production – which was still in chaotic disorder – is hard to find. In September 1939 only 60 aircraft were manufactured. On the other hand, some American Curtiss planes were bought. To give a more realistic idea of French capability in other fields, I have calculated this total from the number of aircraft delivered in August 1939 according to evidence given at the Riom trial, a post-mortem on the French defeat instituted by Marshal Pétain in 1942. This public relations exercise was devised so that the politicians ruling defeated France could lay all the blame for their country's disaster upon their predecessors. Nevertheless, the trial does yield some useful insights into what took place, although the aircraft figure remains unreliable.

3 Colvin, *Chamberlain Cabinet*. Colvin used cabinet documents released by Act of 1967. See also *The Eden Memoirs: Facing the Dictators* (Cassell, 1962).

4 He told Sir Horace Wilson this. See Colvin, *Chamberlain Cabinet*.

5 Sumner Welles, *The Time for Decision* (Hamish Hamilton, 1944).

6 Lord Ironside, *The Ironside Diaries 1937–40* (Constable, 1962).

7 A. J. P. Taylor, *The First World War*.

8 At the time of writing 1991 the Czech government is once again desperate for hard currency and finding it hard to abandon the armaments market.

9 Richard Overy and A. Wheatcroft, *The Road to War* (Macmillan/BBC, 1989). They refer to H. Aulach, 'Britain and the Sudeten Issue 1938', *Journal of Contemporary History*, 18 (1983).

10 Lord Swinton to Colvin. See Colvin, *Chamberlain Cabinet*.

11 Quoted in Leonard Mosley, *On Borrowed Time* (NY, Random House, 1969). Mosley was a respected foreign correspondent and his book is a carefully researched account of the years leading up to the outbreak of war in 1939.

12 William L. Shirer, *The Nightmare Years* (Boston, Mass., Little, Brown, 1984). The Sir Lewis B. Namier quote comes from Shirer's *In the Nazi Era* (1952).

13 This opinion from a Treasury statement classified Most Secret, attached to Cabinet Minutes and uncirculated. See Colvin, *Chamberlain Cabinet*.

9 AN ANTI-HITLER COALITION?

1 Donald Cameron Watt – in his *How War Came* (Mandarin, 1990) – suggests it was Halder and gives German sources and circumstantial reasoning.

2 Colvin, who knew his way around Whitehall, took his story to Sir Alexander Cadogan who, as permanent under-secretary, was immediately in charge of Britain's Secret Intelligence Service.

3 General Sir Frederick Pile, G. O. C. Anti-Aircraft Command 1939–45, in his book *Ack-Ack* (Panther, 1956).

4 Pile, *Ack-Ack*.

5 The Secretary of State for War was the war minister. Chief of the Imperial General Staff (CIGS) was a title given to the 'first military member' of Britain's Army Council. He commanded the entire British army in its outposts throughout the world, although orders were given in the name of the Council. Local British army forces had their own commanders including the commander-in-chief Home Forces, who had direct control of the army in the United Kingdom. A British infantry division of this period had 17,500 men, an infantry brigade about 3,000 men. An infantry battalion – more usually called a rifle battalion – had about 800 men. A rifle company had about 120 men of which five would be officers.

6 In 1928 Germany took over 28 per cent of Soviet exports and sent them a similar percentage of their imports. In 1933 Germany supplied 46.5 per cent of Soviet imports. After that trade reduced and dried up.

7 There is considerable disparity about what this agreement should be called. I have followed the Stationery Office and Churchill in calling it a German-Soviet Pact.

8 Anthony Read & David Fisher, *The Deadly Embrace – Hitler, Stalin and the Nazi-Soviet Pact 1939–1941* (Michael Joseph, 1988).

9 These were the words of Gustav Hilger, a Russian expert with the German diplomatic corps. See Read & Fisher, *Deadly Embrace*.

10 W. S. Churchill, *The Second World War*, vol. 1, *The Gathering Storm* (Cassell, 1948).

11 Various dates have been given for this meeting. Donald Cameron Watt says 26 July. Read & Fisher give June, which may be a printer's error. Also some accounts give the restaurant's name as Ernest, but Ewest at 26a Behrenstrasse was a famous restaurant listed in *Grieben's Berlin Guide* (Berlin, 1936).

12 Donald Cameron Watt provides the Foreign Office references.

13 *Documents concerning German Polish Relations and the outbreak of hostilities*

*between GB and Germany on September 3,
1939* (HMSO, 1939).

14 For Hitler and Goebbels' opinion noted
in Goebbels diary entry for 23 August, see
diary extracts, *Sunday Times*, 12 July 1992.
15 Halder's position in the army command
can be seen from this chart. The
Wehrmacht meant the Armed Forces of
Germany's Third Reich. In 1935 a small
office – Oberkommando der Wehrmacht
(OKW) – had been formed on the clear
understanding that it was a bureau to
coordinate matters of interest to all three
services, and not to subordinate them. But
Hitler used this OKW to control the High
Command of the Army (OKH) and the
other armed services.

Führer & Chancellor: Adolf Hitler

OBERKOMMANDO DER WEHRMACHT – OKW Chief: Wilhelm Keitel Chief of Operations Staff: Alfred Jodl Deputy: Walther Warlimont

OBERKOMMANDO DES HEERES – OKH Commander-in-Chief: Walter von Brauchitsch Chief of Staff: Franz Halder

16 Donald C. Watt, 'Before the
Blitzkrieg', in *History of the Second World
War* (Purnell, 1966).
17 Mr J. McLoughlin, the telephone
operator, said: 'This human touch at the
beginning of the world's greatest conflict
will always remain vividly with me.' See
The Last Day of the Old World, by Adrian
Ball (New York, Doubleday, 1963).
18 E. S. Turner, *The Phoney War* (Michael
Joseph, 1961). Turner takes his story from
Vic Oliver's memoirs, *Mr Showbusiness*.
19 Flak (Flugabwehrkanone) is a gun used
against aircraft. Some German guns were
dual-purpose weapons designed for use
against aircraft and against ground targets.
　Panzerkampfwagen, abbreviated PzKw,
is an armoured fighting vehicle.
　Panzerabwehrkanone, Pak, is an anti-
tank gun.

20 More exactly there were six armoured
and four 'light' divisions fighting in Poland.
(Guderian is in error in his memoirs when
he includes only three light divisions in the
units that fought there.) There were
additional army and SS motorized units as
part of 'Panzer Verband Kempf'. Light
divisions were Panzer divisions with fewer
tanks. See Len Deighton, *Blitzkrieg –
From the Rise of Hitler to the Fall of
Dunkirk* (Jonathan Cape, 1979).
21 Louis Ducloux, *From Blackmail to
Treason – Political Crime and Corruption
in France 1920–40* (André Deutsch, 1958).
Ducloux was director of the Criminal
Investigation Department of the Sûreté
Nationale.
22 Guy Chapman, *Why France Collapsed*
(Cassell, 1969).
23 General André Beaufre, *1940 The Fall
of France*, translated by Desmond Flower,
with preface by Basil Liddell Hart
(Cassell, 1967).
24 Martin Alexander, *The Republic in
Danger: General Maurice Gamelin and the
Politics of French Defence 1933–1940*
(OUP, 1993).
25 Chapman, *Why France Collapsed*.
26 Ponting, *1940: Myth and Reality*.
Reference CAB 66/1 WP (39) 15 (8.9.39).
27 Major Robert M. Kennedy, *The
German Campaign in Poland*, Pamphlet
20-255 published by the US Department of
the Army in April 1956 and based upon
information from German commanders,
says that a total of 55 divisions were
arrayed against Poland on 31 August 1939.
Major-General F. W. von Mellenthin in
Panzer Battles (Cassell, 1945) says 44
divisions.
28 George Forty & John Duncan, *The Fall
of France – Disaster in the West 1939–40*
(Nutshell Publishing, Tunbridge Wells,
1990). A most interesting contribution to
the writings on this subject.
29 Gamelin sent the orders through
General A. L. Georges, although it would
have been more logical to have sent them
through his local commander.
30 Brigadier Sir John Smyth, *Before the
Dawn* (Cassell, 1957). Quoted in *The War
on Land*, edited by Ronald Lewin (Arrow,
1972).

31 Ralph Arnold, *A Very Quiet War* (Rupert Hart-Davis, 1962). Quoted in Lewin (ed.), *The War on Land*.

32 John Keegan, *The Second World War* (Hutchinson, 1989). Keegan's credentials as senior lecturer at Sandhurst for 26 years endorse these descriptions of the BEF.

33 Quoted in M. Hamilton, *Monty*, vol. 1 (Coronet, 1985).

34 R. A. C. Parker, *Struggle for Survival* (OUP, 1989).

35 Ponting, *1940: Myth and Reality*.

36 A. J. P. Taylor writing in *The Observer* newspaper in October 1978. Also Taylor in conversations with me.

37 Albert Speer, *Inside the Third Reich* (Macmillan, 1970).

38 Churchill, *The Gathering Storm*.

39 On 13 April 1940 Hitler personally instructed General Dietl, defending Narvik, to 'If necessary destroy ore railway through mountains beyond repair.' This showed how little importance he gave to ore supplies. Within a few weeks of the Norwegian fighting the Germans were in possession of France's ore fields in Lorraine. In the later stages of the war, technical improvements in weapons (e.g. high-quality armour) meant that the Germans did need Swedish low-phosphorus ore.

40 Notably Alfred Rosenberg, who in December 1939 brought the Norwegian Fascist Vidkun Quisling to Berlin to discuss a possible German takeover of Norway. See David Irving, *Hitler's War* (Papermac, 1983), and Sir John Wheeler-Bennett, *The Nemesis of Power – the German Army in Politics 1918–1945* (Macmillan, 1967).

41 Hugh Skillen, *Enigma and Its Achilles Heel* (H. Skillen, 56 St Thomas Drive, Pinner, Middlesex, England, 1992). One battery-operated model was used by a war correspondent dropped by parachute in Crete.

42 The tappers intercepted a telephone conversation by the French ambassador in Paris. He repeated a remark made by the French prime minister.

43 Actually there were a handful of 143-ton Siebel ferries and a few 13-ton LWS amphibious vehicles that would hold 20 men. They were not suited to this operation and not used in the campaign as far as I know.

44 Hans Bertram. The film was made primarily for domestic release but was shown widely abroad. See David Welch, *Propaganda and the German Cinema 1933–1945* (OUP, 1987).

45 Kahn, *Seizing the Enigma*.

10 GERMAN ARMS OUTSTRETCHED

1 Letter to author from John Peet, who added: 'A senior Danish Communist told me how on May 1941 he stood on the Press stand as representative of "Land og Volk" the Party paper which was still appearing quite legally every day, at a Nazi military parade in honour of May Day. The paper was naturally under censorship, but the censors did not interfere with news of the trade union movement, inner-Danish political squabbles and similar. All this changed of course in June 1941 and my Danish friend was soon in a concentration camp.'

2 Sir Adrian Carton de Wiart, *Happy Odyssey* (Jonathan Cape, 1950).

3 A. J. P. Taylor, *English History 1914–1945* (OUP, 1965).

4 Channon diary, see Martin Gilbert, *Finest Hour, Winston S. Churchill 1939–1941* (Minerva, 1989).

5 John Peck, 'Bull & Benediction', unpublished MS; see Gilbert, *Finest Hour*.

6 For instance, the Chief Whip David Margesson and Sir Alexander Cadogan, permanent under-secretary for foreign affairs Jan. 1938–Feb. 1946, both commented on it. Gilbert, *Finest Hour*.

7 *The Holy Fox*, a recent biography of Halifax by Andrew Roberts (Weidenfeld & Nicolson, 1991), says that Halifax stood aside when the post of PM stood open to him. Roberts also says that Halifax stopped being an appeaser on 25 September 1938 (during the Czechoslovakia crisis) and became gung-ho for rearming while temporizing and vacillating so that ships and planes could be built. This is what he was doing by means of his contacts with the Nazis during the summer of 1940, says Roberts. I am not persuaded.

8 John Costello, *Ten Days That Shook the West* (Bantam Press, 1991).
9 The younger Churchill was named John Strange Churchill after Colonel John Strange Jocelyn. For the number of lovers she took, Ted Morgan gives the Irish novelist George Moore as the source of his allegation. See Ted Morgan, *Churchill, the Rise to Failure* (Triad Granada, 1984).
10 Randolph S. Churchill Companion volume 1, part 1 (1967), to vol. 1 of the official biography, *Youth, 1874-1900* (Heinemann, 1967).
11 *Newcastle Leader* on 7 December 1895. See Morgan, *Churchill*.
12 Martin Gilbert, 'Churchill: Voice in the Wilderness', in *History of the 20th Century* (Purnell, 1969).
13 This Churchill anecdote from Jonathon Green, *Says Who? A Guide to the Quotations of the Century* (Longman, 1988). Green suggests that Churchill (who said 'It is a good thing for an uneducated man to read books of quotations') may have been inspired by Garibaldi's words: 'I offer only hunger, thirst, forced marches and death.' A. J. P. Taylor in *English History 1914–1945* points out the similarity to Clemenceau: 'Finally you ask what are my war aims? Gentlemen they are very simple: Victory.'
14 Ponting, *1940: Myth and Reality*.
15 See Telford Taylor, *The March of Conquest* (Edward Hulton, 1959), for comments about Alan Brooke and this quote from Westphal, *The German Army in the West* (1951).
16 *The Rommel Papers*, edited by B. H. Liddell Hart (Collins, 1953).
17 Later, in the East, with primitive tracks often transformed by mud or snow, the Germans would advance cross-country and resort to the orthodox pincer movements that they used in Poland.
18 Beaufre, *1940 The Fall of France*.
19 Col. J. C. Kemp, *The History of the Royal Scots Fusiliers 1919–1959* (privately printed by Robert Maclehose & Co., for The University Press Glasgow, 1964).
20 David Fletcher, *The Great Tank Scandal – British Armour in the Second World War* (HMSO, 1989). Fletcher is the librarian for the Tank Museum,

Bovington, Dorset, England.
21 Fletcher, *Great Tank Scandal*.
22 Patrick Forbes, *The Grenadier Guards in the War of 1939–1945*, vol. 1 (Gale & Polden, 1949).
23 Although such figures can be very misleading the rough approximation is that the Belgians suffered about 1,400 killed and wounded each day, the Dutch nearly 2,000 and the BEF 1,700 (from an army diminishing in size as the evacuation continued). This calculation depends on the BEF fighting 40 days (when Nantes and St Nazaire were cleared). Actually men were still being evacuated from the Mediterranean ports in August.

11 RETREAT

1 Helmuth James von Moltke, *Letters to Freya 1939–1945* (Collins Harvill, 1991). Count von Moltke, whose mother was English, worked in the Abwehr until he was arrested and executed by the Nazis in 1945.
2 Lt-Col. the Viscount Bridgeman started the contingency planning. Lt-Col. Hewer of the Quartermaster's staff went to London. See Nicholas Harman, *Dunkirk: the necessary myth* (Hodder & Stoughton, 1980).
3 'Blanchard is pretty wet. He is no commander at all,' wrote Gort's chief of staff in his diary entry of 23 May. *Chief of Staff – the Diaries of Sir Henry Pownall* edited by Brian Bond, vol. 1, *1933–1940* (Leo Cooper, 1972).
4 Gort's orders came from Gamelin via Georges. Alistair Horne, *To Lose a Battle* (Macmillan, 1969).
5 Technically Dill did not become CIGS until 27 May, but he had been assigned to the CIGS since April and was taking over from his predecessor in easy stages.
6 Diary entry 25 May 1940. *Chief of Staff – the Diaries of Sir Henry Pownall*, vol. 1.
7 As above.
8 Kemp, *Royal Scots Fusiliers*.
9 The special liaison officer from the cabinet was Admiral of the Fleet Lord Keyes, who was horrified by Churchill's failure to rectify matters and sued the *Daily Mirror* for libel in respect of its

reporting of the matter. The cabinet ordered Keyes to drop his case but he received damages and apologies. Keyes' son edited all his father's papers and on the death of Leopold wrote a letter to the *Daily Telegraph*, 30 September 1983.
10 'Gun Buster', *Retreat via Dunkirk* (Hodder & Stoughton, 1940). Written under a pseudonym, it was one of the very first accounts of this summertime débâcle to be published. Several passages were included by Desmond Flower in *The War 1939–1945* (Cassell, 1960), probably the biggest and best war anthology.
11 Nicholas Harman's harshly realistic *Dunkirk* is essential reading.
12 I have written of the halt order and other aspects of this campaign in more detail in *Blitzkrieg*.
13 For details of the signal and Churchill's response see *The Eternal Summer* by Ralph Barker (Collins, 1990).
14 L. W. Salmons, quoted by A. J. Barker in *Dunkirk the Great Escape* (Dent & Sons, 1977). My editor says it's badly written but I see no harm in that.
15 Churchill's speech 4 June 1940: *Hansard*, columns 787–96.
16 Helmuth von Moltke was an administrative officer with equivalent rank of Major. Working for the Abwehr, he was attached to the OKW as a legal adviser. See his *Letters to Freya 1939–1945*.
17 Telford Taylor, *The March of Conquest*.
18 As above.
19 The actual railway car was destroyed in Berlin by an air raid. After the war, the French produced a replica to recreate their 'armistice museum' as it had been in the 1930s. Nowhere in any of the signs and notices displayed is there any mention of the French humiliation of 1940.
20 For these responses, see John Lukacs, *The Duel* (Boston, Mass., Houghton Mifflin, 1990).
21 Swedish Foreign Ministry telegram 723 received in Stockholm 2220 local time and now in the Riksarkivet (archives) where Costello found it. Despite British interventions to prevent it in 1946 and again in 1964 it was published in 1965. For more details about the peace overtures see

John Costello, *Ten Days that Saved the West* (Bantam Press, 1991).
22 Writing in *The Spectator* 6 July 1991, Richard Lamb says of the reasons for R. A. B. Butler never becoming PM: 'Another reason was that many Conservatives never forgave him for wanting to negotiate with Germany after France fell in 1940. This is well documented and Randolph Churchill with glee maliciously peddled the story whenever there was a chance of Butler becoming Prime Minister.'
23 Ponting, *1940: Myth and Reality*.
24 As Cecil King told in his somewhat mistitled book, *With Malice Towards None* (Sidgwick & Johnson, 1970). Chamberlain wrote to his sister on 18 June saying that Lloyd George 'was ready to form another government & make peace for the terms which he would be able to blame on the maladministration of his predecessors'. It was Chamberlain, talking to Churchill, who likened Lloyd George to Pétain. (Chamberlain's diary of 18 June 1940.)
25 Broadcast 17 June 1940. *BBC Written Archives*. See Gilbert, *Finest Hour*.
26 Speech 18 June 1940: *Hansard*, columns 51–61.
27 John Martin, quoted in Gilbert, *Finest Hour*.
28 Although it was Churchill's 'finest hour' broadcast on 18 June 1940 which sounded odd to some listeners, David Irving claims in his book *Churchill's War* (Avon Books, New York, 1991) that Norman Shelley mimicked the great man's voice on the radio when he refused to broadcast the stirring words ('We shall fight on the beaches . . .') he delivered in the Commons on 4 June. But Irving's account is confused and inaccurate. He says the broadcast followed the news that night but, unlike those on the 17th and 18th, which preceded the news, no prime ministerial broadcast is listed for the evening of the 4th. Vita Sackville-West said that an announcer reading some of Churchill's words 'sent shivers' down her spine. Irving also mistakes Shelley's BBC Children's Hour role – he played Winnie the Pooh, Denis the Dachshund and even Toad, but never Larry the Lamb – and

attributes his story to an interview he had with the actor in December 1981. In fact Shelley died in the summer of 1980, and obituaries in the *Times*, the *Guardian* and other papers drew attention to the recordings of Churchill's speeches that Shelley had made at the request of the British Council for American audiences.

There is a recording in the BBC Sound Archives of an interview by drama producer Raymond Raikes on the occasion of Shelley's 75th birthday in which Shelley gives his own account. The recordings went to Churchill for his approval and word came back through the PM's private secretary that he had said with a chuckle: 'He's even got my teeth.' A recent voice test conducted by *New Scientist* magazine on commercial Churchill recordings that purport to date from the late 1940s claimed that three were not by Churchill. It is a pity the BBC cannot come up with more conclusive proof that Shelley was not passed off on BBC radio as Churchill in June 1940, but the weight of evidence seems to be against any such secret ruse.

29 Michael Ginns, 'Operation Green Arrow and the 216 Infantry Division in the Channel Islands', *Channel Islands Occupation Review* (Guernsey, Channel Islands Occupation Society, 1991).

30 There were differences in the two guns. The old wooden butt was gone and the MP 38 was the first gun of its type entirely made from metal and plastic.

31 In fact it was very slightly changed – by Czech designers – from the First World War design. Technically a carbine, it could fire only five rounds before reloading while the British army's rifle could fire ten rounds without reloading. Some front-line German units in the Polish fighting were still using the even more old-fashioned Mauser Gewehr 98, later relegated to second-line troops.

32 I have been taken to task for – in *Blitzkrieg*, an earlier book – dismissing so lightly the role of the lighter German tanks. Even a lightweight tank, equipped with no more than a machine-gun, can effectively deter unlimited numbers of infantry and soft-skinned supply vehicles. And this is what happened again and again

and again in 1940. 'There is no such thing as a puny and primitive tank,' said one correspondent, Mick Taylor, Leicester.

33 Terry Gander, 'Machine Guns Used in the Channel Islands', *Channel Islands Occupation Review* (Jersey, Channel Islands Occupation Society, 1977).

34 Evidence of this is the survival of military equipment in the collectors market. While today British and German vehicles are rare, American vehicles are still widely available and in everyday use 50 years after the war.

35 In 1991 the British army evaluated four different tanks and rated the British design the worst. The politicians compelled the army to reorder the British tank.

36 There were always stories about tanks that readily burst into flame. German tanks seemed to be less flammable. Experiments in the desert indicated that such 'brew-ups' were mostly due to internal stowage of ammunition and personal kit rather than to tank design.

37 The French air minister, Guy la Chambre. Gamelin said there were 2,000 modern fighters on hand in May but fewer than 500 were used on the north-east front. For more figures see *Blitzkrieg*.

38 McManners, *Scars of War*. The leaderless group tests were later used by many other armies. In 1948 the British army decided to stop using psychologists on their selection boards and smart regiments 'slipped back into old ways' says McManners.

39 Nigel West, *MI6: British Secret Intelligence Service Operations 1909–1945* (Weidenfeld & Nicolson, 1983).

40 Walter Schellenberg, *The Schellenberg Memoirs* (André Deutsch, 1956).

41 A. C. Brown, *The Secret Servant: The Life of Sir Stewart Menzies* (Sphere, 1989). See also West, *MI6*; Schellenberg, *Memoirs*; and F. H. Hinsley and others, *British Intelligence in the Second World War* (5 vols, HMSO, 1979–90), vol. 1.

42 Brown, *Secret Servant*.

43 Hinsley, *British Intelligence in the Second World War*, vol. 1. See also Brown, *Secret Servant*, and *The Diaries of Sir Alexander Cadogan O. M. 1938–1945*, edited by D. N. Dilks (Cassell, 1971).

44 See Brown, *Secret Servant*, and Hinsley, vol. 2.

45 M. R. D. Foot, *SOE in France* (HMSO, 1966).

46 Speech 18 June 1940: *Hansard*, columns 51–61.

47 Harry Hopkins, *The White House Papers of Harry Hopkins*, vol. 1, edited by Robert Sherwood (Eyre & Spottiswoode, 1948).

48 And of course the most famous soldier of the Second World War – MacArthur – was by far the most dedicated and accompished self-publicist.

49 David Brinkley, *Washington Goes to War* (NY, Knopf, 1988).

50 David Irving says in *Churchill's War* that Belgium's prime minister agreed to lend $300 million in gold.

51 Iceland had a close political association with Denmark, which had been occupied by the Germans. The US secretary of state and the Danish minister signed an agreement about the bases.

52 Dates and comparisons from R. A. C. Parker, *Struggle for Survival* (OUP, 1989).

53 Otto Frisch and Rudolf Peierls were helped by another refugee named Simon.

54 A Sub-committee on Uranium held two meetings early in 1940 before it was formally constituted by its parent committee, the Committee for the Scientific Survey of Air Warfare (CSSAW). A less revealing name was provided by a telegram sent by Niels Bohr to Otto Frisch when the Germans overran Denmark, asking him to 'tell Cockerman and Maud Ray Kent' – a phrase interpreted as a garbled message about radium or uranium disintegration. In June, when the CSSAW ceased to exist, the MAUD Committee became independent, answerable to the Ministry of Air Production. Only after the war did it turn out that a lady called Maud Ray, the governess of the Bohr children, had lived in Kent. See Margaret Gowing, *Britain and Atomic Energy* (Macmillan, 1964).

55 Postwar sensations about Hitler almost getting the atomic bomb are the fantasies of Germany's wartime scientists.

56 Vannevar Bush, physicist and engineer, was president of the Carnegie Institution and director of the Office of Scientific Research and Development.

12 THE WAR MOVES SOUTH

1 Introduction to *The Ciano Diaries, 1939–43*, edited by Hugh Gibson (Heinemann, 1947).

2 Sumner Welles, *The Time for Decision*.

3 Paul Johnson, *A History of the Modern World* (Weidenfeld & Nicolson, 1983).

4 John Lukacs, *The Last European War* (NY, Anchor – Doubleday, 1976).

5 *Ciano Diaries*.

6 *Ciano Diaries*.

7 Admiral Sir Dudley Pound's words according to Correlli Barnett in *Engage the Enemy More Closely*. Pound was Britain's senior admiral.

8 Artemis Cooper, *Cairo in the War 1939–1945* (Hamish Hamilton, 1989).

9 Richard Ollard, *Fisher and Cunningham: a Study of the Personalities of the Churchill Era* (Constable, 1992).

10 Richard Ollard thinks Churchill even resented the bloodless success at Alexandria because it put the fighting at Oran 'in a different light from which he wanted it to be viewed.' Richard Lamb reviewing the book in the *Spectator* (11 Jan. 1992) said that he'd read the minutes of a meeting of the Cabinet Office's Historical Committee in 1952 at which the official historian – General Playfair – said no account of the Mers-el-Kébir decision which contradicted Churchill's must be published. Cunningham, who was on the committee, objected and said that a true account might remove some of the bitterness felt by the French.

11 See *Evelyn Waugh – a Biography* by Christopher Sykes (Penguin, 1977). Waugh's *Put Out More Flags* was published by Chapman and Hall in 1942. A brief account of the Dakar operation is to be found in his *Men At Arms* (Penguin, 1964).

13 A TACTICIAN'S PARADISE

1 Paolo Caccia-Dominioni, *Alamein 1933–1962. An Italian Story* (Allen & Unwin, 1966).

2 This claim is made by Ian G. Stott, *Fairey Swordfish Mks I-V* (Profile Publications, no date). While I cannot say it is wrong, I feel that if all tonnage is included there must have been an aircraft type in the Pacific which sank more.

3 Colin Jones, 'Fairey Swordfish' (*War Monthly*, Marshall Cavendish, 1977).

4 Samuel Eliot Morison, *The Rising Sun in the Pacific*, vol. 2 of *The History of United States Naval Operations in World War II* (Boston, Mass., Atlantic Little, Brown 1951).

5 Heinz Hegenreiner, *The Operations of Marshall Graziani Prior to the Arrival of German Troops* (Washington DC, Office Chief Military History, MS.0-216). See also *Afrika Korps* by R. J. Bender and R. Law (Mountain View, Calif., Bender Publishing, 1973).

6 R. A. Bagnold, *Early Days of the Long Range Desert Group*, Lecture to Royal Geographical Society, 15 Jan. 1945.

7 According to oil exploration teams with whom I spoke. Only soft sand moves and covers tracks; some marks from heavy vehicles are still to be seen.

8 The surface areas of Nimitz's command in the Pacific and Wavell's later ABDA command in the East were larger in extent but neither compares in diversity and complexity.

9 Bernard Fergusson was the junior officer and relates the story in *Wavell, Portrait of a Soldier* (Collins, 1961).

10 Alan Moorhead, *African Trilogy* (Four Square, 1959). This passage is also selected by J. F. C. Fuller to illustrate his own theories of irregular warfare.

11 Michael Mason, *Life in the Desert* (Purnell & Sons, 1966).

12 Barrie Pitt, *The Crucible of War*, vol. 1, *Western Desert 1941* (Cape, 1980).

13 The 4th Indian Division at this time consisted of three brigades plus attached units. Two of these brigades had the usual configuration (2 Indian battalions with one British battalion). As a temporary measure, the third brigade was made of three British battalions.

14 This memo was sent by Wavell to Lt-Gen. H. Maitland Wilson on 28 November 1940. 'Jumbo' Wilson was senior officer

commanding 'British Troops in Egypt', of which the Western Desert Force was a part. See also John Connell, *Wavell, Scholar and Soldier* (Collins, 1964). Also see Pitt, *Crucible of War*, vol. 1.

15 Alexander Clifford, *Three Against Rommel* (Harrap, 1943)

16 Pitt, *Crucible of War*, vol. 1.

17 See von Thoma's post-war conversation with B. H. Liddell Hart, *The Other Side of the Hill* (Panther, 1956).

18 Blamey had just become a commander of the Australian Imperial Force when he wrote this letter to Menzies. See *Blamey – Controversial Soldier* by John Hetherington (Canberra, Australian Government Publishing Service, 1973).

14 DOUBLE DEFEAT: GREECE AND CYRENAICA

1 The historian A. J. P. Taylor (in a letter to me dated 13 November 1980) wrote: 'over Greece Churchill has been for once unjustly blamed. The impetus came from Eden and surprisingly from Wavell as John Terraine shows in his recent biography. The main motive was honourable obligation, mixed in with a hope that it would cause the Germans trouble. When you add Crete to Greece the reputation of Wavell as a great commander seems less impressive.'

2 Fergusson, *Wavell*. The only staff officer to oppose the idea of intervention in Greece was Francis de Guingand, then GSO I in Joint Plans and afterwards chief of staff to Montgomery.

3 Major-General Sir Francis de Guingand, *Operation Victory* (Hodder, 1947).

4 Hetherington, *Blamey*.

5 As above.

6 As above.

7 Major-General Sir Francis de Guingand, *Generals at War* (Hodder & Stoughton, 1964). His later recollections are far more pointed than the somewhat more restrained account in *Operation Victory*.

8 De Guingand, *Operation Victory*.

9 Correlli Barnett, *The Desert Generals* (Kimber, 1960).

10 By February they were limiting use to about 75,000 tons per month.

11 H. P. Willmott, *The Great Crusade* (NY Free Press, Macmillan, 1991). Willmott is a lecturer at Sandhurst.

12 Samuel W. Mitcham Jr, *Men of the Luftwaffe* (Novato, Calif., Presidio Press, 1988). He gives US Dept of the Army Pamphlet 20-260 as his source for the higher figure.

13 Willmott, *Great Crusade*.

14 This is a conservative estimate. Mitcham, *Men of the Luftwaffe*, says that Col. Gen. Alexander Loehr's 4th Air Fleet, the Luftwaffe force assigned to supporting the invasion of Greece, was reinforced with 576 aircraft from Sicily, France and Germany to make up about 1,000 aircraft by 5 April 1941. To this Italian aircraft must be added.

15 Philip Guedalla, *Middle East 1940–1942. A Study in Air Power* (Hodder & Stoughton, 1944).

16 Basil Collier, *Hidden Weapons* (Hamish Hamilton, 1982).

17 Kenneth Macksey, *Panzer Division, The Mailed Fist* (Macdonald, 1969).

18 Lt.-Col. R. P. Waller, 'With the 1st Armoured Brigade in Greece', *Journal of the Royal Artillery*, July 1945. And quoted by I. McD. G. Stewart, *The Struggle for Crete* (Oxford University Press, 1966).

19 Many accounts say Student had only the 10,000 parachute soldiers of the Air Division. This figure from Samuel W. Mitcham Jr for the reinforced division seems more accurate.

20 Anthony Beevor, *Crete. The Battle and the Resistance* (Penguin, 1992).

21 Martin Gilbert, *Second World War* (Weidenfeld & Nicolson, 1989).

22 Keegan, *Second World War*.

23 Stewart, *Struggle for Crete*.

24 Beevor, *Crete*.

25 Barrie & Frances Pitt, *The Chronological Atlas of World War II* (Macmillan, 1989).

26 Paul Freyberg, *Bernard Freyberg VC: Soldier of Two Nations* (Hodder, 1990).

27 Stewart, *Struggle for Crete*.

15 TWO SIDE-SHOWS

1 *The Abyssinian Campaigns* (HMSO booklet, 1942).

2 Winston Churchill, *The Second World War*, vol. 3, *The Grand Alliance* (Cassell, 1949).

3 W. E. D. Allen, *Guerrilla War in Abyssinia* (Penguin, 1943).

4 Willmott, *Great Crusade*.

5 Giulio Douhet, *The Command of the Air*, translated from Italian by Dino Ferrari (Faber & Faber, 1943).

6 Basil Collier, *Leader of the Few* (Jarrolds, 1957).

7 Guedalla, *Middle East 1940–42*.

8 Most histories say the bullet was fired by excited Arabs into the air, but John Connell's biography, *Wavell, Scholar and Soldier*, gives this more authoritative account.

9 Heinz J. Nowarra says that ten Junkers Ju 52s and three four-engined Junkers Ju 90s were 'sent to Iraq' and that six Heinkel He 111s of KG 4 'General Wever' were assigned to the attack on Habbaniyah. 'The operation was broken off on 31 May,' says Nowarra, who was with the Junkers company in Leipzig during the war and later worked for the Luftfahrt-Bild-und-informationsarchiv (the State aviation archive). See his *Ju 52 Aircraft & Legend* (Yeovil, Somerset UK, Haynes, 1987).

10 The 'Levant States' was the mandated territory, but this roughly corresponded to Syria and Lebanon.

11 Chiefs of staff to General Wavell and others concerned, 6 May 1941. Churchill, *Grand Alliance*.

12 Prime Minister to General Ismay for COS Committee, 6 May 1941. Churchill, *Grand Alliance*.

13 Telegraph, Prime Minister to General Wavell, 9 May 1941. Churchill, *Grand Alliance*.

14 Letter to the author from John Peet. Peet's experiences with the CID in Palestine are also mentioned in his memoirs *The Long Engagement* (Fourth Estate, 1989).

16 QUARTERMASTER'S NIGHTMARE

1 I am indebted to R. W. Thompson, *Generalissimo Churchill* (Hodder & Stoughton, 1974), for this quote from

Liddell Hart's *Why Don't We Learn from History?* (Allen & Unwin, 1944). Also for pointing out the use of Cicero's quote by the official history (see pp. 280-1).

2 *The Rommel Papers*, edited by B. H. Liddell Hart (Collins, 1953).

3 The mistaken estimate was based upon the strength of other German divisions, but 'plug-in capability' made it possible to change and adapt German divisions to specific tasks.

4 D. J. Payton-Smith, *Oil: a Study of Wartime Policy and Administration* (HMSO, 1971).

5 Driver quoted in *Desert Rats at War* by George Forty (Ottenheimer, 1980).

6 I am guided by Barrie Pitt's fine *The Crucible of War*, vol 1 (Cape, 1980), in using the words relinquished and disintegrated, and the O'Connor quote.

7 Pitt, *Crucible of War*, vol. 1.

8 Von Mellenthin, *Panzer Battles*.

9 For Battleaxe, Beresford-Peirse had his HQ 60 miles from the battle, and even the divisional HQ of 7th Armoured was 30 miles back. Cunningham, during the Crusader battles, was at Fort Maddalena, 80 miles from Sidi Rezegh. At Gazala Ritchie's HQ was near Gambut, 60 miles from the front. I am indebted to Ronald Lewin's *Rommel as Military Commander* (Batsford, 1968) for this notation from Liddell Hart's *Positioning of Commanders*.

10 John Ellis, the master of statistical analysis, in *Brute Force*.

11 Albert A. Nolfi, 'Campaign Analysis North Africa 1940-1942', *Strategy & Tactics* No. 23 Sept.-Oct. (NY, Simulations Publications, 1970).

12 David Kahn, *The Codebreakers* (Weidenfeld & Nicolson, 1966).

13 B. & F. Pitt, *Chronological Atlas of World War II*.

14 Hans von Esebeck, cousin of the general, talking to Desmond Young, who served in the desert and was captured. He quoted Esebeck in his biography *Rommel* (Collins, 1950).

15 Chester Wilmot, *Tobruk 1941* (Angus & Robertson, 1945).

16 J. A. I. Agar-Hamilton, quoted by John Ellis, *World War II: The Sharp End* (Windrow & Greene, 1990).

17 David Irving, *The Trail of the Fox* (Futura, 1978).

18 J. K. Stanford, *Tail of an Army* (Phoenix House, 1966).

19 Telegram from General Auchinleck to Churchill dated 25 December 1941. See Churchill, *Grand Alliance*, Appendix L, 'Tanks for the Middle East'.

20 Stanford, *Tail of an Army*.

21 Ellis, *Brute Force*.

22 Martin van Creveld, *Supplying War – Logistics from Wallenstein to Patton* (Cambridge University Press, 1977).

23 J. Morris, *Farewell the Trumpets*.

24 As above.

25 John Ellis, *The Sharp End of War* (David & Charles, 1980).

26 Willy Brou, *The War Beneath the Sea* (Frederick Muller, 1958).

27 The Victoria Cross was the British forces' highest award for valour. It could be forfeited, and over the years at least 8 of them were, including one confiscated from a misguided warrior who was sent to prison for bigamy. During the Second World War 182 were awarded. The George Cross, of which 105 were awarded, was equally prestigious and civilians were eligible for it, as were soldiers showing unmilitary bravery such as defusing unexploded bombs. The award of the George Cross to Malta was unique; other awards were to named persons.

28 Paul Carell, *The Foxes of the Desert* (Bantam, 1962).

29 J. F. C. Fuller, *The Second World War. A Strategical and Tactical History* (Eyre & Spottiswoode, 1948).

30 Creveld, *Supplying War*.

31 As originally expounded in *The Economist* and later by L. Peter and R. Hull in *The Peter Principle* in 1969.

32 *Ciano Diaries*.

33 F. A. E. Crew (ed.) *Official History of Second World War Medical Services*, vol. 2 (HMSO, 1953-56).

17 THE YEARS BEFORE THE WAR

1 Cecil Lewis, *Sagittarius Rising* (Corgi, 1969).

2 In my book, *Fighter – the True Story of the Battle of Britain* (Cape, 1977), I dealt in detail with the creation of the Luftwaffe and the men who were its leaders. It described aircraft design – Luftwaffe and British – and radar development and provided a detailed account of the Battle of Britain. In *Blood, Tears & Folly*, I have dealt with the air fighting as it affected the whole war 1939–41. As far as is possible I have not gone over the same ground as *Fighter*, to which the reader is referred.

3 Canadian aces include Bishop (72), Collishaw (60), Barker (59), Maclaren (54), McElroy (46), Claxton (39), McCall (37), Quigley (34), Carter (31), McKeever (30).

4 Denis Winter, *The First of the Few: Fighter Pilots of the First World War* (USA, University of Georgia Press, 1983).

5 Charles Illingworth, *The Airmen's War – 1914–1918*, quoted by Jeffrey Ethell in *Smithsonian Air & Space* vol. 6, no. 4 Oct./Nov. 1991.

6 This quote from the second volume of the Tirpitz memoirs. See also Williamson Murray, *Luftwaffe* (Grafton Books, 1988).

7 Captain Joseph Morris, *The German Air Raids on Great Britain 1914–1918* (Pordes, 1969: facsimile reprint of original publication).

8 There are many different figures given for the First World War bombing raids. I have used these quotes by John Sweetman in *The World Atlas of Warfare* (Mitchell Beazley, 1988). Dr Sweetman is a specialist on military aviation, and head of Defence and International Affairs at Sandhurst.

9 The report came from General Jan Christiaan Smuts to Lloyd George the prime minister on 17 August 1917. I use the word hurriedly because the report said that a ministry should be 'instituted as soon as possible'.

10 Nowarra, *Ju 52*.

11 There are so many myths and legends about Göring's life – his drug addiction and so on – that I have been cautious about repeating them. The most recent biography is David Irving's *Göring* (Macmillan, 1989).

12 Ben E. Swearingen, *The Mystery of Goering's Suicide* (Robert Hale, 1990).

13 Leonard Mosley, *The Reich Marshal: a biography of Hermann Goering* (Weidenfeld & Nicolson, 1974).

14 Paul Fussell, *The Norton Book of Modern War* (NY, Norton, 1991).

15 C. Bishop & Ian C. Drury, *Battles of the Twentieth Century* (Hamlyn, 1989).

16 David Mitchell, *The Spanish Civil War* (Granada Publishing, 1982).

17 Luis Buñuel, *My Last Sigh* (1983). The Buñuel memoir is quoted by Fussell.

18 Joachim C. Fest, *Hitler* (NY, Harcourt Brace Jovanovich, 1974). Albert Speer told me that he found the Fest biography to be the most reliable account of Hitler's life.

19 The officer was Oberleutnant Rudolf Freiherr von Moreau according to Nowarra, *Ju 52*.

20 Captain Eric M. Brown, *Duels in the Sky* (Annapolis, Maryland, United States Naval Institute, 1988; Airlife, 1989).

21 The diary of Jock Cunningham as recounted in *The Battle of Jarama 1937*, published by Frank Graham, Newcastle upon Tyne NE2 2PC, UK, 1987. Subtitled 'The story of the British battalion of the International Brigade's baptism of fire in the Spanish War,' this booklet is based upon one section of *Nos Combats Contre le Fascisme* published in May 1937 with the author's own eyewitness account added.

22 Arthur H. Landis, *The Abraham Lincoln Brigade* (NY, Citadel Press, 1967). Landis served in the International Brigade.

23 Fussell says 1,654 civilians were killed. Karl Ries, a careful historian, says the true figure was just over 300. Other accounts say between 1,000 and 2,000.

24 Father Alberto de Onaindia quoted in *The Civil War in Spain*, by Robert Payne (Secker & Warburg, 1963).

25 Phillip Knightley, *The First Casualty: the war correspondent as hero, propagandist and myth maker from the Crimea to Vietnam* (Deutsch, 1975). Knightley provides a brief but excellent comparison of the evidence and supplemented it by going back to some of the writers.

26 The staff officer was Captain Heye of the OKM. His report, dated 14 July 1938, is quoted by Murray in *Luftwaffe*.

27 Karl Ries, *The Luftwaffe – a Photographic Record* (Stuttgart Motobuch Verlag, 1983; Batsford, 1987).

28 Fest, *Hitler*.

29 For shooting of prisoners, see Arthur Koestler, *Dialogue With Death* (Hamish Hamilton & Collins, 1960). See also Payne, *Civil War in Spain*.

30 Texaco was the supplier according to A. Craig Copetas in *Metal Men* (NY, Harper & Row, 1986).

31 See Paul Johnson, *A History of the Modern World*, for a summary of the wide-ranging murders.

32 Watt, *How War Came*.

18 PREPARATIONS

1 In 1944 he was given Udet's old post, but it was a way of severely limiting his power.

2 William Green, *Warplanes of the Third Reich* (NY, Doubleday, 1973).

3 Charles H. Gibbs-Smith, *Aviation – An Historical Survey from its Origins to the end of World War II* (HMSO, Science Museum, 1970).

4 Two American-built Whittle W.2B engines powered the Bell XP-59A Airacomet, the first American jet, flown in October 1942. In 1943 a De Havilland centrifugal flow engine powered the prototype Lockheed XP-80 which became the Shooting Star.

5 A stressed metal skin implies that the bending, end-loads, torsion and direct shear are all taken by the strength of the metal skin.

6 Compare Hitler's words on 4 September 1940: 'The hour will come when one of us will break, and it will not be National Socialist Germany.' Hitler too was talking about retaliatory air raids on cities in Germany and Britain.

7 Murray, *Luftwaffe*. This excellent work by a professor at Ohio State University provides many valuable facts, figures, ideas and opinions.

8 The Air Ministry cancelled the Vickers-Supermarine 179 in 1932 and then found the range of the Short Empire flying boats could not be stretched. When land planes were tried the Miles X.2 went nowhere and the Short S.32 and Fairey F.C.1. were scrapped.

9 Charles Gardner, *A. A. S. F.*

(Hutchinson, 1940).

10 Peter Brooks, *The World's Airliners* (Putnam, 1962). See also Dr Richard K. Smith, 'Fifty years of Trans-atlantic Flight' (part II), *American Aviation Historical Society Journal*, vol. 35, no. 3, Fall 1990.

11 Murray, *Luftwaffe*.

12 Ian Colvin, *Chamberlain Cabinet* (Gollancz, 1965), for this and other references to cabinet material released by Act of Parliament in 1967.

13 Tom Harrisson, *Living Through the Blitz* (Collins, 1976), published for the Mass-Observation archive.

14 Murray, *Luftwaffe*.

15 Herbert Malloy Mason, *The Rise of the Luftwaffe 1918–1940* (Cassell, 1973).

16 As Above. Mason quotes General Freiherr von Hammerstein, the Luftwaffe's top legal officer.

17 Letter to author from Sir Victor Goddard.

18 Frank Mason, *Luftwaffe Aircraft*, with illustrations by Michael Turner (Newnes, 1986).

19 The nearest that the Germans came to a strategic bomber was the FZG 76 (V-1) flying bomb, which was a primitive pulse-jet engine in a pilotless plane with an explosive warhead. It fell to earth when its fuel ran out. Derided by Allied propaganda, this design impressed the Americans so much that it was copied to become the Republic JB-2 Loon. Two thousand were ready for use against the Japanese mainland when the war ended.

Even more dramatic was Germany's V-2 rocket, which was copied by the US as the A-4 and became the first step in the US space programme. But these developments came later than the events in this book.

20 Peter C. Smith, *Stuka Squadron* (Patrick Stephens, 1990).

21 Louis S. Casey, Curator of Aircraft at the Smithsonian, a historian specializing in Curtiss aircraft. See *Naval Aircraft 1914–1939* (Phoebus BPC, 1977).

22 Captain Eric M. Brown, *Duels in the Sky* (Annapolis, Maryland, United States Naval Institute, 1988). Brown was a Royal Navy pilot who became chief naval test pilot at Farnborough. He is a highly regarded authority on aeronautics.

23 In 1917 Dornier pioneered a metal-skinned seaplane, the Dornier Cs1, and the following year built the D.1, a stressed-skin metal fighter with cantilever wings. The Silver Streak of 1919 built by the British pioneer Oswald Short also had a claim to original work in the matter of metal-skinned aircraft.

24 Philip S. Meilinger, 'The Impact of Technology and Design Choice on the Development of US Fighter Aircraft', *American Aviation Historical Society Journal*, vol. 36, no. 1 (Spring 1991).

25 These figures – taken from *Jane's* – are of aircraft types (not totals) and include military, civil and seaplanes. If totals are considered the biplanes would be even more predominant.

26 Derek Wood & Derek Dempster, *The Narrow Margin* (Arrow, 1969). The specials were the Supermarine Schneider Trophy contenders and the Fairey long-range monoplane. The 17 amphibians were Sara Clouds.

27 Taken from the excellent book *Aircraft Piston Engines* by Herschell Smith (McGraw-Hill, 1981).

28 The Kestrel also powered Messerschmitt's rivals, the Ar 80 and the He 112, when the three fighter prototypes were evaluated by the Luftwaffe.

29 Meilinger, 'Impact of Technology and Design Choice . . .'

30 J. E. Johnson, *Wing Leader* (Chatto & Windus, 1956).

31 *US Strategic Bombing Survey confidential report on the relative performance of Allied and German fighters*. Made available to the author by Colonel John Driscoll, chief of the air weapons and tactics branch of the survey.

32 Erwin Leykauf, 'Fighting the Spitfire', in *Messerschmitt Bf 109 at War* by Armand van Ishoven (Ian Allan, 1977).

33 Quoted by Robert L. Shaw in *Fighter Combat – the Art & Science of Air to Air Combat* (United States Naval Institute, Annapolis, Maryland, 1988), a technical book about the theory and mechanics of air combat.

34 A potent myth perpetuated in many books about the Battle, and continuing even now, is that the Bf 109E-3 mounted a cannon in the spinner. R. Hough and D. Richards, *The Battle of Britain* (Hodder & Stoughton, 1989), say: 'the most recently delivered 109s in the Battle of Britain were armed with a single cannon firing through the airscrew hub supported by four heavy machine guns.' The only Bf 109s with a cannon in the engine were a few old Bf 109E-2s flown by II./JG 27, and these cannons were causing endless trouble. Few Bf 109E-2s were made. Messerschmitt had abandoned the engine-mounted cannon until the BF 109F was ready. Even then the F-0, the F-1 and F-2 all experimented with different versions of the cannon, then the F-4 was changed again. See the catalogue of all such variations: *Messerschmitt 'O-Nine' Gallery* by Thomas Hitchcock (Boylston, Mass., Monogram, 1973).

35 Leykauf, 'Fighting the Spitfire'.

36 This is how Göring remembered it, according to his biographer. See David Irving, *Göring*. The He 176 was not a success but was linked to the programme that produced the Me 163B Komet. The Heinkel jet plane had just made its first flight. Just what Hitler saw at Rechlin that summer may be open to question, but the influence it had upon him was important.

19 THE BULLETS ARE FLYING

1 Wheeler-Bennett, *The Nemesis of Power*.

2 Willmott, *Great Crusade*.

3 William L. Shirer, *Berlin Diary* (NY, Knopf, 1941), entry for 1 September. In his memoirs *The Nightmare Years* Shirer adds that the Polish planes did not come that night or any other night to Berlin.

4 Professor R. V. Jones, *Most Secret War* (Hamish Hamilton, 1978). For more see also Jones' later book, *Reflections on Intelligence* (Heinemann, 1989).

5 Few history books acknowledge German radar development. But see David Pritchard, *The Radar War: German Pioneering Achievement 1904–45* (Patrick Stephens, 1989).

6 Pritchard, as above.

7 Kahn, *Seizing Enigma*.

8 Correlli Barnett, *Engage the Enemy*

More Closely (Hodder & Stoughton, 1991). In his fine book Barnett describes the captain of the *Glorious* as 'a throwback to the worst kind of arrogant, authoritarian and choleric Edwardian naval officer'.

9 See Laddie Lucas, *Wings of War* (Grafton, 1985).

10 The state of the flight deck of HMS *Glorious* has been the subject of controversy. I am indebted to Dr T. C. Carter for providing this eyewitness account from R. S. Rolph, an airman aboard HMS *Ark Royal*, which had been with *Glorious* until shortly before the sinking. Dr Carter suggests that a Hurricane, which didn't have folding wings, would possibly not have fitted on the lift to be struck into the hangar below. Correlli Barnett however says the hangar deck was congested with Hurricanes and Gladiators.

11 (Later Air Chief Marshal Sir) Kenneth Cross in a letter dated 26 June 1940. See Lucas, *Wings of War*.

12 The order came through Pound and his Deputy Chief of Naval Staff. The final decision was that of the C-in-C Home Fleet, who was offered the chance of changing the order to use the Skuas. He didn't. See Correlli Barnett, *Engage the Enemy More Closely*.

13 S. W. Roskill, *The War at Sea*, vol. 1 (HMSO, 1954). Quoted by Barnett.

14 See Lucas, *Wings of War*.

15 See Norman Gelb's *Scramble – a Narrative History of the Battle of Britain* (Michael Joseph, 1986). He survived to become Air Chief Marshal Sir Christopher Foxley-Norris KCB, DSO, OBE, MA. Gelb's book is mostly composed of interviews with eyewitnesses of the Battle.

16 Michael Shaw, *Twice Vertical – the History of No. 1 (Fighter) Squadron R. A. F.* (Macdonald, 1971).

17 Leslie Hunt, *Twenty-One Squadrons – the History of the Royal Auxiliary Air Force 1925–1957* (Garnstone, 1972).

18 Robert Jackson, *Air War Over France 1939–1940* (Ian Allan, 1974). More detail is provided in the superb series of special issues of *ICARE: revue de l'aviation française* from issue no. 53 to issue no. 94.

19 Janusz Piekalkiewicz, *The Air War:*

1939–1945 (Poole, Dorset, Blandford Press, 1985). This is a translation (by Jan van Heurck) of *Luftkrieg 1939–1945* (Munich, Sudwest Verlag, 1978). Although this quote has been used a great deal elsewhere it is so apt that I have included this accurate translation.

20 H. Bernards in a letter to the author.

21 *Nazi Conspiracy & Aggression. Opinion and Judgment* (Washington, State Department, 1948).

22 Murray, *Luftwaffe*.

23 27,074 dead, 111,034 wounded and 18,384 missing.

24 Jackson, *Air War Over France*.

25 Said Kesselring.

26 Said the French air minister Guy La Chambre.

27 Jackson, *Air War Over France*, gives the figures of French aircraft surviving the armistice as 1,705 fighters and 1,136 bomber and reconnaissance types. He points out that this includes unserviceable aircraft and new aircraft still in their packing cases. He says there were 1,705 combat aircraft in first-line service at home and overseas.

28 Jean Paul Pallud, *Blitzkrieg in the West – Then and Now* (After the Battle Publications, 1991).

29 Gelb, *Scramble*.

30 I am greatly indebted to Captain Desmond Vincent-Jones RN for this story contained in a letter to the author.

31 Pilot Officer Steve Stephen, quoted in Gelb, *Scramble*.

32 See *Dunkirk – the Great Escape* by A. J. Barker (Dent, 1977). Flt Lt Wight DFC, a Hurricane pilot, was killed in August at the height of the Battle of Britain.

33 A sortie is one mission by one aircraft.

34 Telford Taylor, *The Breaking Wave* (Weidenfeld & Nicolson, 1967).

35 See also Murray, *Luftwaffe*. Mr Murray's view of the air war through German eyes is provocative reading and provides many fresh ideas.

36 When researching *Fighter – the True Story of the Battle of Britain* I tracked down a German training manual that had been used by the Condor Legion units in Spain. It contained diagrams showing the way in which drop-tanks were fitted to the

Heinkel He 51 biplane fighters. Long-range tanks required shackles and fuel connections. These were incorporated in the Bf 109E-7 model. For more on this and comments by Milch see *Fighter*.

37 Pilot Officer Tim Elkington in Norman Gelb's *Scramble*.

38 Wood & Dempster, *Narrow Margin*.

39 I have divided the phases of the battle in the same way that I did in my book *Fighter*, but these are not precise divisions: the tactics and targets varied and overlapped.

40 Sergeant Philip Wareing, quoted in Gelb, *Scramble*.

41 Frank Ziegler, *The Story of 609 Squadron – Under the White Rose* (Macdonald, 1971).

42 Edward Shacklady, 'Hurricane Wind of Change'. *Twentyfirst Profile* magazine, vol. 1, no. 2 (21st Profile Ltd, New Milton, Hants, 1992). A most interesting sidelight on the battle.

43 Edward Shacklady, 'Nuffield's Spitfire', *Twentyfirst Profile*, vol. 1, no. 3 (1992).

44 Pilot Officer Peter Brown, quoted in Gelb, *Scramble*.

45 These figures are taken from Francis K. Mason in *Battle Over Britain* (McWhirter Twins, 1969). The single-seat pilot losses listed for September are 264 RAF and 229 Luftwaffe. Such figures are useful as a guide but treacherous as a crutch. The difficulties of assessing the battle in numerical terms are described in my book *Fighter*.

46 Winston S. Churchill, Prime Minister to Secretary of State for Air, 3 June 1940. See Winston Churchill, *The Second World War*, vol. 2, *Their Finest Hour* (Cassell, 1949), Appendix A.

47 Derek Wood, *The Battle of Britain* (Bracken Books, 1990).

48 Gelb, *Scramble*.

49 Derek Wood and Derek Dempster in their detailed *The Narrow Margin* say the Germans bombed Hawkinge airfield at 11.15 am, which fooled the RAF plotters into thinking that airfields were to be the target. Francis K. Mason in *Battle Over Britain* records only a photo flight over Liverpool before the London raid developed. Thus the two most detailed

histories differ on this point. Winston G. Ramsey in *The Battle of Britain – Then and Now* (1980) and in *The Blitz Then and Now* (3 vols, 1987) (all edited by Ramsey and published by Battle of Britain Prints International, London) doesn't comment on this.

50 Mason, *Battle Over Britain*.

51 Basil Collier, *The Battle of Britain* (Fontana, 1971), for the Churchill and Park exchange and also for the probable explanation.

52 Wood, *Battle of Britain*.

53 Gilbert, *Finest Hour*.

54 Flying Officer John Bisdee, quoted in Gelb, *Scramble*.

55 One copy that was not scrapped is in my collection.

56 For instance Frank H. Ziegler in his *The Story of 609 Squadron* (Macdonald, 1971), who says 'It is now generally conceded' that this was a deliberate act by Churchill in defiance of his air advisers.

57 Ramsey (ed.), *The Blitz Then and Now*, vol. 1.

58 Telford Taylor, *Breaking Wave*. In *Brute Force* John Ellis provides a comparison of annual military production showing British production trebling while German production went up less than 50 per cent. Ellis adds that in August 1940 Britain had placed orders in the USA for 25,000 aircraft and 25,000 aero-engines.

59 See Ellis, *Brute Force*. Also B. H. Klein, *Germany's Economic Preparation for War* (Cambridge, Mass., Harvard University Press, 1959).

60 See Hough & Richards, *Battle of Britain*. The authors believe that virtually everything the Air Ministry did in 1940 was right and proper. They feel that removal of Dowding and Park was justifiable. But even they do not claim that Leigh-Mallory's 'big-wing' ideas were sound.

61 Quoted in Gelb, *Scramble*.

62 Hough & Richards, *Battle of Britain*.

63 Derek Wood says the two men were in league.

64 Churchill to Sinclair. Prime Minister's Personal Minute, M.432/1, 12 April 1941: Churchill Papers 20/36. Quoted in Gilbert, *Finest Hour*. Gilbert wrote to *The Times* to refute the suggestion that Churchill

wanted to get rid of Dowding. He quoted from a Churchill letter dated July 1940 urging that Dowding's appointment should be indefinitely prolonged while the war lasted.
65 Quoted in Gelb, *Scramble*.

20 HOURS OF DARKNESS

1 C. H. Ward-Jackson & Leighton Lucas, *Airman's Song Book* (Blackwood, 1967).
2 I have taken the figures from Winston G Ramsey's *The Battle of Britain – Then and Now*.
3 Correlli Barnett, *The Audit of War* (Macmillan, 1986). Barnett also provides the machine-tool figures.
4 Barnett, *Audit of War*.
5 According to Eric Brown, who flew it and many different Allied and Axis Second World War aircraft.
6 The early Wildcats were called Martlets by the RN.
7 The range limit applied because the straight line didn't bend round the curvature of the earth.
8 A. Price, *Instruments of Darkness* (Kimber, 1967).
9 Shorts 'Airport Factory' at Rochester, a second factory building Stirling heavy bombers, was also bombed at this time, so that by early September it was totally wrecked and the workforce was paid off. Letter to author from Edgar Harrison, a fitter at the factory.
10 Harrisson, *Living Through the Blitz*. Professor Harrisson was co-founder of the social research organization Mass-Observation during the war. In the preface to his book he remarks soberly on the 'massive, largely unconscious cover-up of the more disagreeable facts of 1940–41'.
11 Patrick Forbes, *The Grenadier Guards in the War of 1939–1945*, vol. 1 (Gale & Polden, Aldershot, 1949).
12 Cartographic Division of the National Geographic Society. See *National Geographic Magazine*, July 1991.
13 Harrisson, *Living Through the Blitz*.
14 Ramsey (ed.), *The Blitz Then and Now*. Ramsey's three-volume work is amazingly detailed and the section on bombs by my old friend Peter

Chamberlain (copyright 1986) is exemplary.
15 Major Bill Hartley MBE, GM. See *Highly Explosive* by John Frayn Turner (Harrap, 1961).
16 According to Ramsey, *The Blitz Then and Now*, vol. 2.
17 Major Bill Hartley, previously mentioned.
18 According to the expert John Betjeman in *The City of London Churches* (Pitkin Pictorials, Andover, Hants, 1974), nineteen of the City's lovely Wren churches had already been destroyed by successive bishops of London. These were sold mostly to raise money (from the ever-increasing City land values) to build churches in the new suburbs.
19 The Mason quote is from Ramsey (ed.), *The Blitz Then and Now*, vol. 2.
20 See Ponting, *1940: Myth and Reality*, for detailed criticism.
21 Sir Sholto Douglas (Lord Douglas of Kirtleside), *Years of Command*, written with the aid of Robert Wright (Collins, 1967).
22 Price, *Instruments of Darkness*.
23 From the account of his experiences as a part-time worker with the air-raid rescue teams written in 1986 by Reginald King and published in Ramsey (ed.), *The Blitz*.
24 A meeting on 15 November 1940 discussed the general problem of high-altitude combat. See *Twentyfirst Profile*, vol. 1, no. 6 (1992).
25 Douglas Tidy, *I Fear No Man – the History of No. 74 Squadron RAF* (Macdonald, 1972).
26 Tidy, *I Fear No Man*.
27 Piekalkiewicz, *The Air War: 1939–1945*.
28 On 15 July the wing commander at Hornchurch listed the tactics needed if the Spitfires were to cope with the Messerschmitts.
29 Deere's encounter is described in his book *Nine Lives* (Hodder & Stoughton, 1969).
30 Radial engines were preferred for bombers because they could take more damage without stopping. In November 1941 officials at Wright Field, the US Army Air Force test facility, rejected the P-51 partly because its (Allison) engine, being

liquid-cooled, was too vulnerable to enemy bullets. See *HAP*, the biography of General H. 'Hap' Arnold, by Thomas M. Coffee (NY, Viking Press, 1982).

31 Apart from some bombs specifically set aside for use against battleships. See Sir Charles Webster & Noble Frankland, *The Strategic Air Offensive against Germany 1939–1945* (HMSO, 1961).

32 A suggestion about fighter escorts had been made by the C-in-C in a letter of 30 August 1938 but the Air Ministry paid no attention to it. See Webster & Frankland, mentioned above.

33 The estimate was made by the Air Officer Commanding 3 Group on 17 May 1939. See Webster & Frankland, mentioned above.

34 Norman Longmate, *The Bombers* (Hutchinson, 1983).

35 Flying Officer R. S. Gilmour, quoted in Denis Richards, *Royal Air Force 1939–1945*, vol. 1 (HMSO, 1954).

36 Max Hastings, *Bomber Command* (Michael Joseph, 1979).

37 Stirling Flight Engineer Charles Potten's article, 'Warts and All', in *Flypast Bomber Special* (Key, 1991).

38 Ken Delve, 'The First Heavy', in *Flypast Bomber Special* (Key, 1991). The mines weighed 1,500 lb and seven of them could be carried.

39 See Norman Longmate's *The Bombers*.

40 Quoted in Longmate, as above.

41 Hastings, *Bomber Command*.

42 Speer, *Inside the Third Reich*. Speaking about the bombing that came later in the war, he estimated that a 9 per cent production loss came from it but said that the loss was made up for by increased effort that the bombing raids produced in the workers. Speer said that the cost to Germany of the bombing was to be measured in the German defences. Thus 10,000 high-velocity Flak guns could have been used against Red Army tanks. This, Speer maintained, would have doubled German defences. Again the Flak 'tied down hundreds of thousands of young soldiers'. One-third of the optical industry and half the electronic industry was engaged in the sights, radar and communications needed for air defence.

43 Wood, *Battle of Britain*.

44 Hastings, *Bomber Command*.

45 R. A. C. Parker, *Struggle for Survival* (OUP, 1989).

21 THE BEGINNING OF THE END

1 George T. Simon, record sleeve notes for *This is Glenn Miller and the Army Air Force Band* (RCA London, 1973).

2 Figures are taken from Parker, *Struggle for Survival*.

3 Paul Johnson, *The Birth of the Modern: World Society 1815–1830* (NYC, HarperCollins, 1991).

4 Sickness insurance 1883; accident insurance 1884; old age insurance 1889. See S. C. Burchell, *Age of Progress* (Time-Life, Nederland, 1976).

5 Alfred Hobbs. See Martin Daunton, 'Toil & Technology in Britain and America', *History Today*, April 1983.

6 This, and some other statistics in this section, come from Clive Ponting, *1940: Myth and Reality*.

7 Wood, *Battle of Britain*.

8 Barnett, *Audit of War*.

9 Ponting, *1940: Myth and Reality*.

10 Barnett, *Audit of War*.

11 Nicholas Monsarrat, *Breaking Out*, volume 2 of his autobiography, *Life Is a Four-Letter Word* (Cassell, 1970).

12 The stories of the internees, the report and the jail sentences are from Ponting.

13 The VS-300 flown by Igor Sikorsky at Stratford Connecticut on 14 September 1939 was the first fully controlled single-rotor helicopter.

14 In 20 June 1941 the Air Corps became the Army Air Forces with Arnold as their first chief. This was a part of the fundamental reorganization of the US army undertaken by General George Marshall, chief of staff.

15 This quote and other facts from Robert F. Schirmer, Col. USAF (Retd), 'AAC & AAF Civil Primary Flying Schools', *American Aviation Historical Society Journal* vol. 36 no. 1 (Spring 1991).

22 FIGHTING IN PEACETIME

1 David Bergamini, *Japan's Imperial*

Conspiracy (Heinemann, 1971).

2 Watt, *How War Came*, provides a good account and includes a useful map.

3 Robert J. Icks, *Famous Tank Battles* (NY Doubleday, 1972), contains a short but detailed account of this battle.

4 *The Case of Richard Sorge* by F. W. Deakin & G. R. Storry (Chatto & Windus, 1966).

5 *The Memoirs of Marshal Zhukov* (Cape, 1971).

6 The Tupolev TB-3, which made its first flight in December 1930, was the world's first modern long-range bomber. The design, cantilever wing, corrugated metal construction and the four BMW VI engines of the initial production version left little doubt that Andrei N. Tupolev's design team had been helped by German aircraft designers. In particular the engineering skills of General Fuchs, a veteran of the First World War, made a major contribution to it and to much of the Red Air Force of this period.

7 *Zhukov Memoirs.*

8 Zhukov said this to Bedell Smith, Eisenhower's chief of staff. See Bergamini *Japan's Imperial Conspiracy.*

9 Colonel G. I. Antonov, 'The Red Army in the Finnish War', a section in *The Soviet Army*, edited by B. H. Liddell Hart (Weidenfeld & Nicolson, 1956).

10 Marshal Mannerheim, *Memoirs of Marshal Mannerheim* (Cassell, 1953). Quoted by Desmond Flower & James Reeves in *The War 1939–1945* (Cassell, 1960).

11 Willmott, *Great Crusade.*

12 Read & Fisher, *The Deadly Embrace.*

13 Read & Fisher, as above.

14 Lt.-General Dittmar, 'The Red Army in the Finnish War', a contribution to Liddell Hart (ed.), *The Soviet Army.*

15 A. S. Milward, *War Economy and Society 1939–1945.*

16 It is often said that Stalin broke the terms of the agreement by annexing Lithuania because that was to be in the German sphere of influence. Actually the pact was modified; Germany got an enlarged share of Poland in exchange.

17 John Toland, *Hitler* (NY, Doubleday, 1976).

18 In addition on 29 July, Generaloberst Franz Halder, chief of the army's general staff, told General Erich Marcks, chief of staff of the 18th Army, to prepare a plan.

19 Matthew Cooper, *The German Army 1933–1945* (Macdonald & Janes, 1978).

20 *The German Campaign in Russia. Planning and Operations 1940–1942*, D A pamphlet 20-261a (Washington, 1955). See also Earl F. Ziemke, *Stalingrad to Berlin: the German Defeat in the East* (Washington, US Army, 1968).

21 Hitler at the Berghof conference on 31 July 1940. See, amongst other accounts, Telford Taylor, *The Breaking Wave.*

22 A. J. P. Taylor, *The Second World War*, for these figures and many other ideas and insights.

23 Michael Coren, *The Invisible Man: The Life and Liberties of H. G. Wells* (Bloomsbury, 1993).

24 Paul Johnson's *A History of the Modern World* provides references to countless sources.

25 Johnson, as above.

26 My conversations with French veterans of the 1940 fighting during my research for *Blitzkrieg.*

27 Paul Carell, *Hitler's War On Russia* (Harrap, 1964).

28 Milton Shulman, *Defeat in the West* (Secker & Warburg, 1947).

29 In 1990 a BBC producer used these air photos, now in a US government archive, to make a programme about the changes in the English landscape. See 'Country File', transmitted by BBC 1 on 7 October 1990. For other reference see the incomparable *The Warplanes of the Third Reich* by William Green (NY, Doubleday, 1973).

30 Carell, *Hitler's War On Russia.*

31 See Hitler's directive No. 21 of 18 December 1940. *Hitler's War Directives 1939–1945*, edited by H. R. Trevor-Roper (Sidgwick & Jackson, 1964).

32 Creveld, *Supplying War.*

33 According to his biographer. See Günther Blumentritt, *Von Rundstedt – the Soldier and the Man* (Odhams, 1952).

34 *Hitler and His Generals – the Hidden Crisis January–June 1938*, by Harold C. Deutsch (USA, University of Minnesota

Press, 1974).

35 According to his fellow general, F. W. von Mellenthin, in *German Generals of World War II* (University of Oklahoma Press, 1974).

36 Kenneth Macksey, *Panzer Division. The Mailed Fist* (Macdonald, 1968).

37 Creveld, *Supplying War*. He is quoting Windisch, *Die deutsche Nachschubtruppe im Zweiten Weltkrieg* (Munich, 1953), and I have used Creveld/Windisch in other details of the Barbarossa logistics story.

38 Walter Görlitz, *The German General Staff* (NY, Praeger, 1967).

39 Heinz Guderian, *Panzer Leader* (NY, Ballantine, 1952).

23 THE LONGEST DAY OF THE YEAR

1 See A. J. P. Taylor, *The Second World War*.

2 Blumentritt's contribution to *The Fatal Decisions*, edited by S. Freidin & W. Richardson (NY, Sloane, 1956). This collection of accounts by German commanders about the battles of the Second World War is based on staff studies that the US army made with the aid and co-operation of the German commanders detained at Oberursel and other camps in the postwar period. S. L. A. Marshall, Chief Historian European Theater, was in charge of this project and wrote the foreword for the book. It seems that he accepted this reason for the Barbarossa delay.

3 Guderian, *Panzer Leader*. In his three-volume *Decisive Battles of the Western World*, J. F. C. Fuller uses Guderian's remark to support his belief that the invasion was not delayed by six weeks if at all.

4 Siegfried Westphal's contribution to *The Fatal Decisions*, ed. Freidin & Richardson.

5 *The Memoirs of Field Marshal Keitel, Chief of the German High Command 1938–1945* (William Kimber, 1965).

6 Keegan, *Second World War*.

7 Although this has become the accepted figure in Germany, David Chandler's *The Campaigns of Napoleon* (NY, Macmillan, 1966) says that of a total of 614,000 first-

and second-line troops of Napoleon's Grande Armée de la Russie, 302,000 were French, a further 190,000 were Germans, Austrians, Prussians and Swiss, with a further 90,000 made up of Poles and Lithuanians.

8 Leonard Cooper, *Many Roads to Moscow* (Hamish Hamilton, 1968).

9 Among the best were the MiG-3, LaGG-3, Yak-1 and Il-2.

10 Klein, *Germany's Economic Preparations for War*. See Ellis in *Brute Force*. He adds that this cutback was made in a month when Luftwaffe losses in the Battle of Britain exceeded production.

11 Nikolai Tolstoy, *Stalin's Secret War* (Jonathan Cape, 1981).

12 Albert Seaton, *The Battle for Moscow 1941–1942* (Rupert Hart-Davis, 1971).

13 Willmott, *The Great Crusade*.

14 The T-34's 7.6-cm high-velocity gun could penetrate 48-mm armour at 2,000 metres, or 61-mm armour at 1,000 metres.

15 Peter Hoffmann, *Hitler's Personal Security* (Macmillan, 1979).

16 Hitler's Directive No. 21 dated 18 December 1940. See *Hitler's War Directives 1939–1945*, ed. H. R. Trevor-Roper.

17 Carell, *Hitler's War on Russia*.

18 Benno Zieser, *In Their Shallow Graves* (Elek, 1956).

19 Carell, *Hitler's War on Russia*.

20 Carell, *Hitler's War on Russia*. It seems that the content of the petrol bombs used in Spain and in Finland was different to the mixture used in Red Army bombs. Although some say that the petrol bombs got their name during the Soviet-Finnish war of 1939–40, I have not been able to find uses of the name Molotov Cocktail earlier than 1941.

21 Blumentritt, *Von Rundstedt*. Blumentritt was Rundstedt's chief of staff from the end of 1942. At the time of Barbarossa he was Kluge's chief of staff with Fourth Army under Bock.

22 Blumentritt delivered the lectures. See *The Fatal Decisions*, ed. Freidin & Richardson.

23 A. V. Karasev, *The People's War*, in the 7-volume *History of the 20th Century* (BPC, 1969).

24 *Adolf Hitler: The Medical Diaries.* The private diaries of Dr Theo Morell, edited by David Irving (Sidgwick & Jackson, 1983).
25 Guderian, *Panzer Leader.* The account of the meeting with Hitler is from the same source.
26 B. H. Liddell Hart (ed.), *The Soviet Army* (Weidenfeld & Nicolson, 1956).
27 Matthew Cooper, *The German Army 1933–1945* (Macdonald & Janes, 1978). Cooper says that although the number of armoured divisions had more than doubled – 15 to 32 – the tanks had increased by less than a third.
28 Carell, *Hitler's War on Russia.*
29 Jodl to Col. Adolf Heusinger, the OKW Operations officer. See Keegan, *Second World War.*
30 *Russian Combat Methods* by an unnamed German army group commander, and his officers, at the interrogation enclosure, Neustadt, Germany. *German Report Series –* Pamphlet No. 20-230 (US Army, Washington DC, June 1953).
31 John Erickson, *The Road to Stalingrad* (Weidenfeld & Nicolson, 1975).
32 Quoted by J. M. Bereton and Major Michael Norman, *Russian T-34/76* (Profile Publications, 1971). See also *Russian B-T Series* by John F. Milsom in the same Profile AFV Weapons series.
33 Bereton quotes Senger und Etterlin's estimate in *Kampfpanzer von 1916 bis 1966.* He also says 115 T-34 tanks were manufactured in 1940; 2,810 in 1941. The 1941 figure compares nicely with Erickson's figure of 2,996 – see *The Russian Recovery* (Purnell, 1966).
34 Liddell Hart (ed.), *The Soviet Army.*
35 Peter Bamm, *The Invisible Flag* (USA, John Day, 1956).
36 *Effects of Climate on Combat in European Russia,* by an unnamed Germany army group commander, and his officers, at the interrogation enclosure, Neustadt, Germany. *German Report Series – Pamphlet No. 20-291* (US Army, Washington DC, Feb. 1952).
37 Carell, *Hitler's War on Russia.*
38 Alan Clark, *Barbarossa* (Hutchinson, 1965).

24 'A WAR OF ANNIHILATION'

1 Erich Kern of Waffen-SS Division Leibstandarte Adolf Hitler. See his memoirs, *Dance of Death* (Collins, 1951).
2 Nikolai Tolstoy in *Stalin's Secret War* says one such penal battalion lost 500 men of its full complement of 1,500 in a typical attack.
3 Tolstoy, as above. He gives more than one reference to such activities.
4 Tolstoy quotes this passage from Svetlana Alliluyeva's book, *Only One Year.*
5 Gilbert, *Second World War* (revised edition, Fontana, 1990).
6 Bamm, *The Invisible Flag.*
7 A type of prussic acid disinfectant, Zyklon-B was an I. G. Farben patent. It was formed from decomposing chemicals in almonds and other vegetables. Rights to manufacture were acquired by Tesch und Stabenow of Hamburg and Degesch of Frankfurt am Main. They supplied tons of it to the SS camps. See Louis L. Snyder, *Encyclopaedia of the Third Reich* (Hale, 1976).
8 Guderian, *Panzer Leader.*
9 Edgar Ansel Mowrer. He quotes this in *Global War – An Atlas of World Strategy* (Faber & Faber, 1942), which he co-authored with cartographer Marthe Rajchman.
10 John Strawson, *Hitler as Military Commander* (Batsford, 1971).
11 Alfred Turney, *Disaster at Moscow – Von Bock's Campaigns 1941–42* (Cassell, 1971).
12 Deakin & Storry, *The Case of Richard Sorge.*
13 *Zhukov Memoirs.*
14 *Night Combat,* by General Alfred Toppe (Germany Army). *German Report Series – Pamphlet No. 20-236* (US Army, Washington DC, June 1953).
15 *Russian Combat Methods,* as cited in chapter 23, n. 30.
16 As above.
17 Tolstoy, *Stalin's Secret War.* See also *Russian Combat Methods,* as above.
18 *Effects of Climate on Combat in European Russia,* as cited in chapter 23, n. 36.

19 Major F. W. A. Hobart, *Pictorial History of the Sub Machine Gun* (Ian Allan, 1973).

20 Walter Kerr, 'The Russian Army', article in *The Infantry Journal*, Washington 1944, said sub-machine-guns were made by cutting old rifle barrels in half.

21 James Dunnigan, 'Organization of Soviet Ground Forces', *Strategy & Tactics*, no. 23, September–October 1970 (NY, Simulations Publications Corp.). Dunnigan provides a list of excellent sources for this analysis.

22 Carell, *Hitler's War on Russia*.

23 General J. F. C. Fuller in vol. 3 of *The Decisive Battles of the Western World*.

24 Quoted in B. H. Liddell Hart, *The Other Side of the Hill* (1951).

25 Bock's unpublished diaries were purchased from his daughter. Alfred Turney in his *Disaster at Moscow* (Cassell, 1970) makes great use of the diaries and quotes this remarkable telephone conversation.

25 THE LAST CHANCE

1 Dr Heinrich Haape, who won the German Cross in Gold, Iron Cross first and second class and many other awards, including one for personally destroying two Russian tanks in combat. *Moscow Tram Stop* (Collins, 1957).

2 Georgi K. Zhukov, *Marshal Zhukov's Greatest Battles*, edited by Harrison Salisbury (Macdonald, 1969).

3 Erickson, *The Road to Stalingrad*.

4 The attacking force was 17 armies. Each one of them was about the size of a German corps.

5 There were no Red Army regional forces. In theory at least, all units were composed of men from all over the USSR. Thus a Latvian might serve alongside Armenians and Cossacks. In fact some units were predominantly regional. The cavalry units were sometimes tribal in their constitution, as with the Cossacks.

6 Haape, *Moscow Tram Stop*.

7 Clark, *Barbarossa*.

8 Samuel W. Mitcham, *Hitler's Field Marshals and their Battles* (Grafton Books,

1989). Mitcham, a graduate of the US Army Command and General Staff College, makes a special study of German commanders. His *Men of the Luftwaffe* is similarly useful.

9 Turney, *Disaster at Moscow*.

10 Turney, as above.

11 Günther Blumentritt in *The Fatal Decisions*, ed. Freidin & Richardson.

12 Haape, *Moscow Tram Stop*.

13 John Toland, *Adolf Hitler* (New York, Doubleday, 1976).

14 Gerhard Schoenberner, *The Yellow Star*, translated from the German (*Der gelbe Stern*) by Susan Sweet (Transworld Corgi, 1969). This author provides a report from the Ghetto administration to the Gestapo complaining of rations in detail and saying: 'The clearest demonstration of the food situation is the rapidly rising mortality rate.'

15 Schoenberner, as above.

16 Ian V. Hogg, *The Guns: 1939/45* (Purnell, 1969).

17 Light infantry arms, which had reached peak production in April, had fallen to 62 per cent of that. Artillery production had fallen to 33 per cent of its April peak. Heavy infantry arms production had fallen to 51 per cent of its August peak and Flak guns had come down to 71 per cent of November's peak production.

18 Of the better German armour (Panzer IIIs, Panzer IVs, and tracked assault guns) 2,875 were made in 1941. Of their comparable tanks (T-34s and KV-1s) the Soviet factories manufactured 4,135.

19 General Kurt von Tippelskirch quoted by Clark as under.

20 Alan Clark, 'Hitler's Purge of the Eastern Marshals: Russian Winter 1941–2', in *History of the Second World War* (Purnell, 1966).

21 Of 665,000 vehicles used by the Red Army at war's end 427,000 were from the West (mostly from Detroit). Keegan, *Second World War*.

22 John Ellis, Interview in *Military Illustrated* (journal) October 1990. See also same author's *Brute Force*. The East Front used 7,800 division-months and the rest of the war fronts totalled 1,100 division-months.

26 THE WAR FOR OIL

1 For much of this material I am indebted to the Hon. Sir Maurice Bridgeman (ex-chairman of British Petroleum) and to the immortal Geoffrey Keating, one of the most remarkable characters of the Second World War.

2 A minute from Churchill to the Secretary for Petroleum dated 21 February 1941 – Churchill, *Grand Alliance*, Appendix C – asks that as much oil as possible should be brought across the Atlantic to avoid the journey around the Cape. I am assured that this was being done long before this date.

3 See the widely distributed *Die Geheimakten des französischen Generalstabes* (Berlin Zentral-Verlag der NSDAP, 1941). My copy shows no date, but the documents might have been changed before publication. See aso article by Wayne R. Austerman, 'Allied fears over Soviet oil almost resulted in an airstrike against the USSR's oil facilities', in periodical *World War II* dated March 1992 (Leesburg, Virginia, Empire Press, 1992). Many other references to this episode have been published.

4 John Lukacs, *The Last European War* (NY, Anchor Press Doubleday, 1976), for more on this point.

27 BUSHIDO: THE SOLDIER'S CODE

1 Walt Sheldon, *Enjoy Japan* (Tokyo, Tuttle, 1968).

2 Bergamini, *Japan's Imperial Conspiracy*.

3 Several people I spoke with contested this figure, saying that literacy was widespread before the reforms and that literacy is hard to define in a nation using three alphabets and up to 30,000 combinations of characters.

4 When the three Russians tried to collect their bribe after the war they met death in mysterious circumstances. See Bergamini, *Japan's Imperial Conspiracy*. It seems uncertain whether the attacking force benefited from the betrayed defence plans.

5 Far Eastern Section G2 Regional File dated 27 December 1941, quoted by

Michael Schaller, *The US Crusade in China 1938–1945* (NY, Columbia University Press, 1979).

6 Chiang's choice of words is interesting in the light of the fact that Madame Chiang suffered from a chronic skin ailment which T. V. Soong, Chiang's brother-in-law, blamed upon the stress caused by her husband's bad temper.

7 Stephen Howarth, *The Fighting Ships of the Rising Sun* (NY, Atheneum, 1983).

8 John W. Dower, *War Without Mercy: Race & Power in the Pacific War* (NY, Pantheon, 1986), provides more details of this estimate.

9 Robert Whymant, writing in *The Daily Telegraph*, 7 December 1991.

10 Roy M. Stanley, *Prelude to Pearl Harbor* (NY, Charles Scribner's Sons, 1982).

11 Saburo Sakai, quoted in *In the Cockpit*, ed. Anthony Robinson.

12 Called ESD by the Japanese, it resembled the alloy 75S used in America some years later.

13 Edward T. Maloney and Donald V. Lykins, *Zero Fighter Flies over Japan* (Planes of Fame, Box 278, Corona del Mar, Calif., 1978). This is an illustrated technical account of the restoration of a Japanese navy Mitsubishi A6M5 built by Nakajima in May 1943. It is the only airworthy Zero in the world. Also see *Eagles of Mitsubishi* by Jiro Horikoshi (Orbis, 1970), which is the classic account of the design and development written by the Zero's chief designer.

14 The weight of the Zero empty was 3,704 lb (1,680 kg) while the weight of the Wildcat was 5,238 lb with an engine that produced a little over 1,000 hp. The P-40 was even heavier with no better power. See Gordon Swanborough & Peter M. Bowers, *United States Military Aircraft since 1908* (Putnam, 1971); *United States Navy Aircraft since 1911* (Putnam, 1968).

15 Saburo Sakai, quoted in *In the Cockpit*.

16 Gregory Boyington, quoted in *In the Cockpit*.

17 Terry C. Treadwell, *Submarines with Wings – the Past, Present and Future of Aircraft-Carrying Submarines* (Conway Maritime Press, 1985).

18 The US Marine Corps were also experienced, but not on the same scale.
19 In mid-1941 the imperial navy's projections showed that even with Dutch oil, a war delayed only a couple of years more would bring certain defeat. The navy urged that war must come soon. The projections proved seriously in error. In the first year of fighting, the Japanese navy used 60 per cent more oil than any assessment had allowed. For a detailed account of Japanese assessments and the consumption see H. P. Willmott, *Empires in the Balance – Japanese and Allied Pacific Strategies to April 1942* (Annapolis, Md, Naval Institute Press, 1982).

28 THE WAY TO WAR

1 John Morris was a lecturer at Tokyo University in wartime Japan and on being repatriated wrote his account of this time in *Traveller From Tokyo* (Penguin, 1946).
2 John Deane Potter, *A Soldier Must Hang* (Frederick Muller, 1963).
3 The army's chief of staff was General Sugiyama and this memo is to be found in David Bergamini's *Japan's Imperial Conspiracy*.
4 The Combined Fleet was the whole imperial navy apart from some ships on the China Station.
5 Bergamini, *Japan's Imperial Conspiracy*.
6 The imperial navy's 'flag officer' code's new version was a four-character one with a transposition encipherment. See David Kahn, *The Code-Breakers* (Weidenfeld & Nicolson, 1973).
7 Kahn, as above.
8 The officer was Capt. Arthur H. McCollum, head of the Far Eastern Section of the Office of Naval Intelligence. See Kahn, as above.
9 The historian H. P. Willmott feels that this failure doomed later Washington talks, and set Japan on a course for war. See Willmott, *Empires in the Balance*.
10 Jonathan G. Utley. In 1985 his work was published by the University of Tennessee as *Going to War with Japan 1937–1941*.
11 *The Memoirs of Cordell Hull*, vol. 2 (NY, Macmillan, 1948).

12 From a record kept by Chief of Staff Sugiyama and quoted by David Bergamini in *Japan's Imperial Conspiracy*.
13 One report was from Admiral Hart USN in Manila and the other came via the American ambassador in London. See A. A. Hoehling, *The Week before Pearl Harbor* (Robert Hale, 1964). This book also gives the complete text of the 14-part Japanese message.
14 Hoehling interviewed the 'messenger', Lt Lester Schulz, US Marine Corps, who said the president spoke in matter-of-fact, almost resigned tones.
15 Hoehling interviewed Admiral Stark to this effect.

29 IMPERIAL FORCES

1 W. J. Holmes, *Double Edged Secrets: US Naval Intelligence Operations in the Pacific during World War II* (Annapolis, Maryland, Naval Institute Press, 1979).
2 Stanley Weintraub, *Long Day's Journey Into War* (NY, Dutton, 1991). Weintraub's book is a detailed study of worldwide events in the few hours leading up to the Pearl Harbor attack.
3 John W. Dower, professor of Japanese studies at the University of California, San Diego. I am indebted to his book *War Without Mercy* for this and other observations about the Japanese character and its influence on the war.
4 'Tactical Planning in the Imperial Japanese Navy' (*Naval War College Review*, October 1969). Genda gave many lectures, became chief of staff of the postwar Japanese 'Air Self-Defence Force', and was awarded the US Legion of Merit by President John Kennedy in 1962. Although a great deal of the Pearl Harbor planning is credited to Genda it must be remembered that of his contemporaries he was one of the few to survive the war and make his version of events available to historians.
5 R. J. Francillon, *Japanese Aircraft of the Pacific War* (Putnam & Co, 1970).
6 Many British histories claim the purpose-built carrier as a British first, but the Japanese shipyards worked faster. HMS *Hermes* was designed and laid down

in January 1918 and commissioned (10,850 tons) in February 1924. The *Hosho* was laid down in late 1919 but completed (7,470 tons) in late 1922 with flying trials commencing in February 1923. *Hermes*, although a larger vessel, carried 15 aircraft to *Hosho*'s 21. The first US purpose-built carrier was *Ranger* (14,500 tons)in 1934. It carried 86 aircraft. The world's first carrier, HMS *Furious* (1917), was built on a cruiser hull. The USS *Langley* (1922) was a converted collier.

7 The new Illustrious class carriers were similarly restricted in hangar space due to their armoured flight decks.

8 Some accounts say the two newest carriers did not participate in the attack on the Hawaii targets. This misunderstanding arose because Japanese accounts simply said they did not participate in the attack on the US Pacific fleet.

9 Weintraub, *Long Day's Journey*.

10 Basil Collier, *Japanese Aircraft of World War II* (Sidgwick & Jackson, 1979). Also Francillon, *Japanese Aircraft of the Pacific War*.

11 The rather cryptic system of Japanese aircraft designations uses a first letter to describe the aircraft category: A was a carrier-borne fighter. The second letter showed the manufacturer – M for Mitsubishi, N for Nakajima. The other numbers indicate modifications from the original and so on. Claude is the codename given to it by the Americans.

12 Kahn, *The Code-breakers*.

13 Such stores were captured by the US Marines on Guadalcanal in 1942. One account – *Goodbye Darkness*, William Manchester (Boston, Mass., Little, Brown, 1980) – says the Marines enthusiastically digested it all.

30 ATTACK ON PEARL HARBOR

1 Merle Miller, *Plain Speaking: an Oral Biography of Harry S. Truman* (USA, 1974).

2 Masami Tabata, 'Japan: The Triumphant Overture', in *History of the 20th Century* (BPC, 1969). Masami Tabata was a correspondent with Mainichi Newspapers, Tokyo.

3 Ronald Lewin, *The American Magic: Codes, Ciphers and the Defeat of Japan* (NY, Farrar Straus Giroux, 1982).

4 Conversations with Ruth Mitchell, sister and biographer of William Mitchell.

5 Gordon W. Prange, *At Dawn We Slept; the Untold Story of Pearl Harbor*, in collaboration with D. M. Goldstein and K. V. Dillon (NY, McGraw Hill, 1981). See the same authors' *Miracle at Midway* (NY, McGraw Hill, 1982).

6 Prange, *At Dawn We Slept*.

7 *Time* Magazine, 2 December 1991, article by Otto Friedrich.

8 According to Thomas B. Allen, 'Return to Pearl Harbor', *National Geographic Magazine*, December 1991.

9 The Army Air Corps became the Army Air Force in the summer of 1941.

10 Allen, 'Return to Pearl Harbor'.

11 This interesting interview was conducted by Blaine Taylor in 1988. It was published in *Pearl Harbor 50th Anniversary Collectors Edition*, edited by Blaine Taylor (NY, Starlog Telecommunications, 1988).

12 I have taken this and some other details from 'Rising Sun', an article by François Prins in the journal *Fly Past*, Stamford, Lincs, England, dated December 1991.

13 James Leamon Forbis in *The Pacific War Remembered – an Oral History Collection* by John T. Mason Jr (Annapolis, Maryland, Naval Institute Press, 1986).

14 *Life* Magazine, Special Pearl Harbor Issue, Fall 1991.

15 Dick Fiske, quoted in Thomas B. Allen, 'Return to Pearl Harbor'.

16 George DeLong's story from Allen, as above.

17 Thomas J. Larson, 'Remember Pearl Harbor', *World War II* magazine (Leesburg, Virginia, Empire Press, November 1991).

18 Burt Amgwert, *Time* Magazine, 2 December 1991.

19 Dr William Wolf, 'Aerial Action . . . Pearl Harbor Attack', *American Aviation Historical Society Journal*, Spring 1989, is the most detailed source of this day's flying. Stanley Weintraub's excellent book says they put their tuxedo pants back on, because they were not sleeping in their own quarters. So we may be able to keep this great story at least half intact.

20 Stephen W. Sears, *Carrier War in the Pacific* (NY, American Heritage, 1966).

21 *Life* Magazine, Special Pearl Harbor Report Issue, Fall 1991.

22 John Garcia, a pipe-fitter apprentice aged 16, interview by Studs Terkel in *The Good War* (Ballantine Books, 1985).

23 Dr Steve Ewing, 'Development of the US Navy's Aircraft Carriers to 1961', published Spring 1990 in *Foundations – Journal of the Naval Aviation Museum Foundation*, Pensacola, Florida.

24 Commander 'Red' Ramage of the US submarine *Parche* was awarded the Medal of Honor for his action against a Japanese convoy. He is quoted in *The Pacific War Remembered*.

31 THE CO-PROSPERITY SPHERE

1 A. J. P. Taylor, *Essays in English History* (Pelican, 1976).

2 John Scudder of New York's Presbyterian Hospital, who worked with John Bush, president of the Blood Tranfusion Association.

3 D. A. K. Black, according to *Miracles of Military Medicine* (NY, Garden City, 1944).

4 William A. Renzi & Mark D. Roehrs, *Never Look Back* (NY, Armonk, Shape, 1991).

5 Author of *History of US Naval Operations in World War II*, 15 vols (Boston, Mass., Little, Brown, 1947–62).

6 Not to be confused with the Bataan Peninsula on Luzon.

7 Weintraub, *Long Day's Journey*.

8 As above.

9 William Manchester, *Goodbye Darkness – A Memoir of the Pacific War* (Boston, Mass., Little, Brown, 1979).

10 'The Lost Leader', written in June 1943 and quoted in *The Dictionary of War Quotations*, edited by J. Wintle (NY, Macmillan, 1989).

11 'Praise the Lord and pass the ammunition' was a line used during the Pearl Harbor attack and credited to the American chaplain Howell Forgy.

12 The grammar reference book is *The Right Word at the Right Time: a Guide to the English Language and How to Use It* (Reader's Digest, 1985). Churchill in June 1940 said: 'We shall fight on the beaches, we shall fight on the landing grounds etc.' but in February 1941 he said: 'Give us the tools and we will finish the job.'

13 Although the RAF called them Catalinas, the US did not give these flying boats that name until 1942.

14 Arthur Bryant, *The Turn of the Tide*, based on the diaries of Field Marshal Viscount Alanbrooke (Collins, 1958).

15 Weintraub, *Long Day's Journey*.

16 Bill Gunston, *Weapons & Warfare* (NY, Columbia House, 1971/77/78). Bill Gunston says the Mitsubishi Ki-46-Model 2 could maintain a speed of 400 kph (248 mph) for six hours at an altitude band between 4,000 and 6,000 metres (13,000 to 19,700 feet). Its top speed was 600 kph (373 mph). This twin-engined army machine was not only 'stolen' by the Japanese navy but at one time was going to be built under licence by the Germans.

17 Basil Collier, *The War in the Far East*.

18 Keith Simpson, 'Percival', *Churchill's Generals*, edited by John Keegan (Weidenfeld & Nicolson, 1991). Simpson is a senior lecturer at Sandhurst.

19 H. P. Willmott, *Empires in the Balance*.

20 Bill Gunston, *Weapons & Warfare*.

21 Willmott, *Empires in the Balance*.

22 From Mihoru Kokutai. One element of the Japanese bombing force – Air Group Genzan – had been turned back by the bad weather. Kokutai is translated Navy Air Corps, Koku Sentai is carrier division or air flotilla, Koku Kantai is Air Fleet.

23 Weintraub, *Long Day's Journey*.

24 Barnett, *Engage the Enemy More Closely*. Barnett also provides the quote from Roskill's *Naval Policy Between the Wars*.

25 He was interviewed on 9 December 1981 – one day before the twentieth anniversary of the action. Quoted by Stephen Howarth, *The Fighting Ships of the Rising Sun*.

26 Barnett, *Engage the Enemy More Closely*. A RN diving team inspected the wreck in 1966. Barnett gives great detail of the results of the air attack.

27 Keith Simpson. The quote is from A.
E. Percival, *The War in Malaya* (Eyre &
Spottiswoode, 1949).

28 Capt. S. G. Chaphekar, *A Brief Study
of the Malayan Campaign 1941–42* (Poona,
S. V. Damle, Maharashtra Militarisation
Board, Tilak Road, 1948). This publication
was endorsed by such luminaries as Capt.
B. H. Liddell Hart and Lt-Gen. A. E.
Percival, who declared himself in
agreement with the author's conclusions.

29 E. W. Swanton, who after the war
became cricket correspondent for the
Daily Telegraph. This memoir from *The
Spectator* of 15 February 1992. He refers to
Churchill's *The Second World War*, vol. 4,
The Hinge of Fate.

30 Anthony Livesey, *Great Commanders
and Their Battles* (NY, Macmillan, 1987).

31 Willmott, *Empires in the Balance*.

32 Colonel Masanobu Tsuji of the 25th
Army's planning staff. Quoted by Basil
Collier.

33 Interview with John Deane Potter
quoted in Potter's biography of
Yamashita, *A Soldier Must Hang*
(Frederick Muller, 1963).

34 John Morris, *Traveller from Tokyo*.
Morris was living in Tokyo at the time of
the fall of Singapore.

35 *Soldier's Guide to the Japanese Army*,
Military Intelligence Service Publication,
Special Series no. 27, 15 November 1944
(War Dept, Washington DC).

36 Cecil Brown, *Suez to Singapore* (NY,
Random House, 1942).

37 Chaphekar, *Malayan Campaign*.

38 Livesey, *Great Commanders*.

39 Percival, *The War in Malaya*.

40 See *Sunday Times* Magazine, London,
8 November 1992.

41 See W. S. Churchill, *Second World
War*, vol. 4, *The Hinge of Fate* (Cassell,

1951).

42 As above.

43 As above.

44 As above.

45 Edwin P. Hoyt, *Japan's War* (McGraw
Hill, 1986).

CONCLUSION: 'WENT THE DAY
WELL?'

1 John Maxwell Edmonds (1875–1958).
The epitaph appeared in *The Times
Literary Supplement* (London) of 4 July
1918. As well as being inscribed on the 2nd
British Division's memorial at Kohima
War Cemetery, Assam (now Nagaland,
India), it appears on many graves
throughout the world. For this research I
am indebted to *The Quote Unquote
Newsletter* by Nigel Rees, 24 Horbury
Crescent, London W11 3NF, England.

2 Weintraub says 85 transports with an
equal number of escorting warships.

3 While in the small but difficult country
of Yugoslavia the Germans used many
more divisions than this and still failed to
suppress the partisans.

4 Pitt, *Crucible of War*, vol. 1.

5 The official history uses these words.
See Sir Charles Webster & Noble
Frankland, *Strategic Air Offensive Against
Germany 1939–1945*, vol. 1.

6 *Time* Magazine dated 15 December 1941.
See also *Time Capsule 1941*, by Maitland
A. Edey (NY, Time, 1967).

7 It came into the evidence in Jodl's trial
at the end of the war.

8 Martin Gilbert, *The Holocaust*
(Fontana-Collins 1987).

9 Churchill, *The Grand Alliance*.

10 Knightley, *The First Casualty*.

11 This epitaph by John Maxwell Edmonds
appeared in *The Times* of London, 6
February 1918.

Index